IN SPITE OF MYSELF

IN SPITE OF MYSELF

A MEMOIR

Christopher Plummer

ALFRED A. KNOPF   *New York* • *Toronto* 2008

This Is a Borzoi Book Published by Alfred A. Knopf and Alfred A. Knopf Canada
Copyright © 2008 by Christopher Plummer

All rights reserved. Published in the United States by Alfred A. Knopf,
a division of Random House, Inc., New York, and in Canada by Alfred A. Knopf Canada,
a division of Random House of Canada Limited, Toronto.

www.aaknopf.com
www.randomhouse.ca

Permission to reprint previously published material may be found at the end of the book.

Library of Congress Cataloging-in-Publication Data
Plummer, Christopher.
In spite of myself : a memoir / by Christopher Plummer. — 1st ed.
p. cm.
ISBN 978-0-679-42162-7
1. Plummer, Christopher. 2. Actors — Canada — Biography. I. Title.
PN2308.P49A3 2009
791.4302'8092 — dc22
{B}   2008031229

Library and Archives Canada Cataloguing in Publication
Plummer, Christopher, 1929–
In spite of myself : a memoir / Christopher Plummer.
ISBN 978-0-307-39679-2
1. Plummer, Christopher, 1929– . 2. Actors — Canada — Biography. I. Title.
PN2308.P497A3 2008   792.02'8092   C2007-905094-8

Designed by Iris Weinstein

Manufactured in the United States of America

First Edition

FOR FUFF, BRIGGIE, RAGS, TOADIE AND PADDY,
WITH GRATITUDE AND LOVE

BOOK ONE

I was brought up by an Airedale. I won't deny it, 'tis the truth and nothing but, Your Honour—a bumbling, over-sized shaggy great Airedale. The earliest memory I have of anything resembling a pater familia, bouncer, male-nurse or God is that dear slobbering old Airedale. My sword, my lance, my shield, he never failed to stand at the ready to rescue me from all my early Moriarties! Wherever I happened to be—on the floor, in my bath

Me and Byng

or on the potty, there—looming above me, panting heavily, one large, drooling Airedale reporting for duty, sir! If I went for a ride in my little cart, I would look away and pretend there was no one there at all and then when I did look back, of course he was there. He was always there padding along beside me—how could I miss him? He was my only horizon—he filled the sky. Like Romulus or Remus, I was his cub and he was my Wolf of Rome. His name was Byng.

He was christened after another shaggy old Airedale, Field Marshal Lord Byng of Vimy, whom my grandparents had known when he was governor general; and also for the very good reason that if any of our household showed guts enough to sit down to tea or play a hand at bridge, the day's calm would invariably become a stormy séance as tables, taking on a life of their own, began to shake violently and with one quick loud explosion, Bing! they would catapult themselves ceiling-ward as teapots, cups, toast, crumpets, cards and markers flew madly across the room! My canine patron had, quite simply, decided to rise.

> *But I like Byng, my dog, because*
> *He doesn't know how to behave*
> *So Byng's the same as the First Friend was*
> *And I am the Man in the Cave*
> (Apologies to Kipling)

Nothing ever came between us—Your Honour—nothing—he was my world; I knew no other. Until one day, one sobering day, the spell was broken when a meddling family friend pointed out to me that the nice tall lady pushing my pram was my mother.

Mummies and dogs! You can beat 'em, kick 'em, treat 'em as shabbily as you like—they will eternally forgive you and still come back for more. Such degree of devotion is as hard to grasp as it is unshakable. Being a child, I had no comprehension of it. It embarrassed me. I regularly ran away from it; in fact, I still do.

> *I didn't throw myself into the struggle for life—*
> *I threw my mother into it.*
>
> —G. B. SHAW

I came into the world that monster of infant monsters, who can clear a room more swiftly than a Sherman tank; that very monster which causes fear, dread, revulsion to seal the lips of those that dare to speak its name—The Only Child! And being an only child I was more than frequently left on my own. Can you blame 'em?! A little boy's mind can play some pretty macabre tricks on itself. I was so damned terrified of the dark that Mother had to sing me to sleep, snatches of old French songs she particularly loved.

> *Chante, rossignol, chante,*
> *Toi qui as le coeur gai*
> *Il y a longtemps que je t'aime,*
> *Jamais, je ne t'oublierai.*

But the terror never left. It stayed through all the early years. Because of books, which Mother insisted I read, my imagination began to take over, and the long winters gave one so much time to dream up horrors. My grandparents' tall, forbidding house in the city could be pretty ominous, full of dark corners to jump out of and scare yourself to death. Every time I tried to rob my grandfather's overcoat pocket of change so I could sneak downtown to Ben's delicatessen for a smoked-meat sandwich and a Coke, some sudden sound would force me to drop everything and run like hell. My room was on the very top floor and in the middle of the night I would steal from my bed and sit shivering on the uppermost step, clinging tight to old Byng, staring down into the center of the long circular staircase, down into that

black hole, that bottomless pit, and wait—
wait for "them," whoever "they" were, to
climb up and get us.

Every spring we moved to the country.
Lingering in the city after school, I generally took one of the late-night trains. As
they never knew when I'd arrive, there
was no family car to meet me and I was
obliged to walk the long way home.
When finally I reached our gate, I was
tired and hungry but there was still some
distance to go. Our driveway from the
gate to the house was at least a half-mile
long—it was always dark—no street-
lamps lit the way. The first portion of the
drive was long and straight but suddenly
it dipped precipitously and turned a
sharp corner. It was next to impossible to
see. I could only feel my way and would
invariably slip and fall on the loose gravel.

Mother and me in our driveway

The drive resumed, snaking along by a deep swamp to my left near
the edge of the lake. The dense woods which made the darkness even
more impenetrable gave out a dank fenlike smell. I kept glancing
behind as I hurried along but there was never anyone following me. To
gain confidence I tried singing, but the sound of my voice was more
sinister than the darkness itself, so I quickly gave up. A faint light
glowed from the fields to my right and more than once I was sure that I
saw, lit by a young moon, a still, solitary figure standing there. I bolted
the rest of the way up the hill and it wasn't till I reached the top and
could see, through the eight tall poplars the lights from the house
beyond, that my heart stopped pounding.

> *Very softly down the glade runs a waiting, watching shade,*
> *And the whisper spreads and widens far and near;*
> *And the sweat is on thy brow, for he passes even now —*
> *He is Fear, O Little Hunter, he is Fear.*
>
> —RUDYARD KIPLING

More than once in the mountains north of the city, snowshoeing in
the woods, I would lose my way. Night fell and I'd stop and stand dead

still listening to the wind. The ice-bound trees cracked and rattled like the bones of skeletons. I was sure I would freeze to death. I started to cry and the tears froze against my face—little icicles hanging from my eyelids. The wind was stronger now and began to moan and howl through the tops of the pines, a sad and terrifying sound. I was certain at any moment I would be snatched up by that Spirit that hovers high above the trees the half-breeds talk of—that carries you away into the sky at such frightening speed that you burn alive. And so the energy that imagination generates warmed me, and at last, I could concentrate and find my bearings.

In the snow-covered city, I would ski from the top of Mount Royal down its winding trails past the great stone wall surrounding an estate called Raven'scrag and onto our street, Pine Avenue. Often Mother would join me on her skis, but she also loved taking walks up those same trails. Frequently alone, as her selfish wayward son had less and less time for Mummy, she very seldom wore an overcoat even on the most frigid day, just a heavy tweed suit, thick brogues and flowing scarf. Very thirties, very smart, very brave! One late afternoon as I whirled down the hill full speed along by Raven'scrag's wall, I saw her coming up toward me on foot. I waved at her as I whisked past and out of the corner of my eye I saw her wave back. When I reached the bottom I looked around, but to my astonishment there was no one there, just an empty hill. I climbed up the trail again on my skis; how could she have disappeared so quickly? Was she behind the wall? But there was no door, hole or space into which she could have vanished. Had my eyes deceived me? Had I seen her at all? I kept still and listened for footsteps on the hard crust—there was nothing but silence. The sun dipped behind the mountain and a chill set my teeth chattering. I turned and skied the rest of the way home faster than I had ever made it before.

AS A FAMILY we were knee-deep in dogs—Canines Unlimited. That was all right by me. I adored them all. But to one in particular, a long-suffering cocker spaniel called Scampy, I am ashamed to say I was rather cruel. We played "power games" together, instigated by me, of course, and I caused him to suffer a bit, I'm afraid—just the sort of tricks a lonely, spoiled-brat child with too much time on his hands might play. Until one day I saw something that made me swear that I would never *ever* hurt an animal of any kind again.

It was dead winter in Montreal, an uncomfortable cold, the roads treacherous, icy—almost impassable—no traffic to speak of. I was staring out of our living room bay window onto the streets below. The familiar little horse-drawn cart carrying coal came clattering with difficulty up the steep hill. The same horse, the same old man that had made this trip together winter after winter since time began. The ancient horse, now almost all bones, was faithfully struggling to reach the summit—the old man urging him on with his whip. But the hooves could not get a grip on the ice. The horse bravely kept up the struggle, slipping backwards as he went. The old man, beside himself, gave the poor nag a severe lashing—but in vain—the horse stopped. He could move no longer. One last lash of the whip proved too much. His heart cracked as he sagged to the ground between the halters. It began to snow. Something heaved inside me—I ran from the window to hide and when I returned I looked down and the old man, his livelihood gone forever, was sitting in the middle of the road cradling the horse's head in his arms—rocking back and forth in silent grief as the big gentle flakes began to cover everything beneath them in a warm soft blessing.

> There's an island deep down in my sleep
> A lost land I long to find
> But I wake 'ere I reach the island
> So it must only live in my mind.
>
> It could be the dream we yearn for
> That on earth we may never attain
> But I know there was love on that island
> For it chased away all of my pain.

If you looked through the oaks and the balm of Gilead across the bay from our country house on the shore, you could just see the island. You couldn't always quite make it out, not all at once, and sometimes it simply decided in its mischievous way to hide behind a fog—but from my earliest infancy, I knew it was there. It seemed to float on its own, just a little above the water, not too permanent a thing as if, free of its moorings, it would drift away at any moment. I just hoped it wouldn't forget me but beg me to follow.

It had a habit of disappearing and reappearing through the mist and beckoning . . . always beckoning. When I grew older I was allowed to go there with my mother. It was like playing truant; it was the most wonderful escape. It didn't take me long to realize it was an escape for Mother too.

It belonged to her greatest friend—a lady of similar age with the warmest, most sympathetic of hearts and the deepest, darkest, most beautiful eyes I had ever seen. Her name was Pauline but everyone called her "Polly" and the island was "Polly's Island." She was Canadien Français, spoke a little of all sorts of languages and her English was unique. Her voice was coated with a husky timbre which was not unmusical and in an extraordinary way enhanced her attractiveness; its Creole-like drawl made you want to smile. It gave her conversation an unusual extravagance—an almost theatrical cadence—she elongated her "ma chères," affectionately stretching them out to infinity. When she spoke, the world was an easy place to be in. She made me feel as grown-up and as wise as she, and she listened as if I were her only friend.

The island on weekends overflowed with guests from all over the globe, it seemed, considering the variety of tongues, and Polly, with breathtaking ease, practiced her phenomenal talent for making every-one feel that this was perhaps the only home they'd ever had. No one wanted to leave. Whenever there was a crowd, Mother and I knew just where to hide. On the way up to the house there was a bridge where we could stare down at the giant lily pads that carpeted the black waters below. There were lots of mysterious paths through the woods with surprise openings where we could both get splashed from the waves crashing against the shore; the swimming hole, with a raft you could swim out to, the stables which housed the ponies, and the inlets through which we would paddle our canoe and watch the bitterns stand on one leg or listen to the long sad chorale of the frogs.

Polly had the most exquisite eye, and there was always the heady fra-grance of fresh-cut flowers that penetrated every room. The great screened-in porch with its burnt-sienna tiles where cool drinks were served was the place to while away many an hour looking out across the lawn to the far point at the island's tip and watch the sun go down. This enchanted isle would remain for me throughout my life, a hidden world . . . a place lodged firmly in the heart. It also became for me all the islands I never knew, perhaps too far at times to reach, and almost always, a little too wondrous to be true.

Lord Ronald said nothing; he flung himself from the room,
flung himself upon his horse and rode madly off in all directions.
— STEPHEN LEACOCK

I couldn't stay on and I couldn't fall off! I clung for dear life to the coarse tufts as the monster bucked and reared. I had perched myself on a high stone wall eagerly waiting for one of them to meander my way, at least near enough that I could slide on without having to mount, which at my size was not possible. I was only nine or ten years old. It was my first time—it looked easy—it was. I slipped onto its bare back, no saddle, no reins—just a quiet, docile farm horse. Suddenly a piercing cry sounded directly behind me and something crashed into us with the force of a freight train. Limbs and hooves slashed the air high above my head—my steed bolted, almost throwing me to the ground, then abruptly jerked to a jolting stop. This was repeated over and over. Miraculously, I stayed on. The creature would ram into us as before, madly pawing the sky. Dear God, it was trying to climb on! I'd been too dumb and naive to realize it was a mare I'd picked for my first ride—and a mare in heat, to boot! Now the furious hot stallion was alongside banging against my legs with its flank determined to remove me from the object of its affection—I was clearly in its way. I dared not let go for fear of falling and being trampled to death. How long this endured I cannot say. My legs were black and blue, searing with pain. Finally I fell to the ground exhausted. I managed somehow to avoid those pounding hooves, and limping away as fast as I could into a nearby barn, I threw myself onto a stack of hay where I remained till at last I regained my breath. For a good part of my life I've been riding these dinosaurs both professionally and socially, but ever since that mad, unbalanced morning a keen wariness and a sharp tremour of apprehension has stayed with me always. Consequently, to use the silliest of expressions, I have never found my seat.

Of course I dared not relate this episode to anyone. Too many "cry wolf" stories had fallen on deaf ears; my grandmother would simply have boxed mine. In fact, very few paid heed to a would-be Eulenspiegel, whose merry pranks had the consistent habit of backfiring, so to gain the attention of my elders I began to imagine I was someone else, someone far superior, who like Kipling's Kangaroo cried with frivolous impudence, "Make me different from all other animals! Make me also wonderfully popular by five this afternoon." I blush to admit I quickly became a rather ruthless fabricator of facts who under the tender care of some blind and senile god had so far remained impervious to discovery. I also confess that from the very outset, my timing in life has been a trifle askew, slightly off season. Whenever an auspicious occasion has arisen, I have arrived just when the moment has decided to move on—a split second after the climax, if you'll forgive the phrase. As I have never been at one with a horse, so have I never felt quite at ease in the present. The French have two little words for it— "sans epoch"! If there is to be any blame attached to this somewhat hapless state, let it point to the time warp in which I found myself growing up.

UNLIKE MOST theatrical "gypsies" on this continent, life began for me on a tiny atoll of privilege in a late-blooming fin de siècle. Looking back, none of it seems quite real. There was always present a whimsical sense of the intangible, as if it were all a mirage—a Narnia among the tomahawks. It came and went in the time it takes a boy to become a youth, but it left behind its ghost—a lingering, not unsmiling ghost to remind me of its secret. In a land which many still believe is inhabited only by the Bear, the Beaver and the Mountie, it was a secret to be cherished, a jewel in the tundra. I was caught in an eddy which whirled about this little princedom by the lake; it made me drunk and it made me dizzy—I may be caught there still.

CHAPTER TWO

A COLONIAL PARADISE

My great-great-great-grandfather, John Bethune, is the first known member of the Canadian branch on my mother, "Belle" Abbott's side of the family. Boswell mentions him in his *Journal of a Tour to the Hebrides with Samuel Johnson* in 1785. According to genealogy, Bethune claims descendence from a man named Bethan or Beaton who came to the Isle of Iona with Saint Columba around AD 563. For a great many years the Beatons were ministers in the pre-Reformation Church. At the time of Boswell's interview with my ancestor, Bethune was on his way to North Carolina. When the American Revolution broke out, he opted for the British side and was captured at the Battle of Widow Moores Creek Bridge in the winter of 1776. Being a padre he was released in exchange for prisoners and made his way north across the border where he founded many a Presbyterian congregation all over what is now eastern Ontario, including St. Gabriel's in Montreal, considered the mother church of Presbyterianism in British North America.

Norman Bethune, the eccentric and rebellious doctor of the nineteen twenties and thirties, famous for throwing instruments away in disgust during operations, then going home and inventing new ones, is a descendant. In direct contrast to his patrician forebears, he was one of Canada's earliest Communists. While serving a prison term he contracted TB, which he cured by operating on himself in his cell. Norman Bethune joined the freedom fighters in the Spanish Civil War. He had invented a method for transporting blood plasma and the mobile blood unit, which he used to great effect operating on the battlefield. He brought his units with him to China, where he formed a bond with Chairman Mao Tse-tung and served at his side against the Nationalists in the famous Long March where he saved a staggering amount of lives during the height of battle. He had to work so fast in the midst of gunfire that he became cocky and threw away his rubber gloves, complaining they were a waste of precious time. Ironically, he eventually was infected and died of blood poisoning. Bethune was just about the only white man Mao ever trusted, and to this day, he is considered somewhat of a saint in China. Whenever Chinese delegations, including their Ping-Pong team, come to Canada, the first thing they do is to go straight to Norman's home in Gravenhurst, Ontario, to pay him homage.

Back in the early nineteenth century the elder Bethune's son, Rev. John (John, Jr.), having converted to the Church of England, became rector of Christ Church Cathedral and Dean of Montreal. He was also a founding member of McGill University and its acting principal for eleven years until 1846, thus fortifying the foundations of our family's long history with that great college. Settled comfortably in Montreal, the good reverend married and had a daughter, Mary, who became the wife of my direct great-grandfather, the Right Honourable Sir John Joseph Caldwell Abbott, one of Canada's earliest successful corporation lawyers and its first native-born prime minister.

Great-grandfather reading on his yacht, ignoring everyone about him

Having amassed a considerable fortune and fascinated by the need for railroads to link our vast country, he bought his own, the Montreal and Bytown Railway. He also became president of the Canada Central Railway, which he amalgamated with the Brockville and Ottawa Line, and tracks like tentacles slowly began to extend westward. It is of little surprise, therefore, that he further encouraged Prime Minister John A. Macdonald's own private vision for the construction of a trans-Canadian railroad and that he, with his client and friend Sir Hugh Allan, then the country's wealthiest man (Allan Steamship Lines, Merchants Bank, etc.) would begin to set the wheels turning.

Sir Hugh saw the railroad as a means to gain total control of the sea on both coasts, and he and Abbott were convinced that to achieve this link successfully and efficiently, the job could not be done without financial aid from the United States.

With Premier John A. Macdonald's full knowledge, they secretly enlisted backing principally from American railway tycoon Jay Cooke, clearly aware that if this was uncovered, it would be extremely unpopular and highly embarrassing.

Unfortunately, the documents concerning the negotiations were stolen, and bribery, not so frowned upon then as it is now, became a necessary evil. A royal commission was formed to "investigate," and this bold, daring and delicate exercise came to be known as the Pacific Scandal.

Macdonald resigned, Allan and Abbott went to England for backing there and were successful to a point, but Sir Hugh, fed up to the teeth, withdrew from the project and went back to his family business and his large estate, the Raven'scrag I have already mentioned, atop Mount Royal, whose stone walls I climbed many a time as a young boy. Although immersed in the scandal up to his sideburns, it failed to sink my great-grandfather. He survived and prospered and never once gave up on the Canadian Pacific dream. With Macdonald's party back in power, he spent the major part of his time arranging financing for this massive undertaking. So, when his two clients, Lord Strathcona and Lord Mount Stephen who, with R. B. Angus and Sir William Van Horne, formed the big foursome that finally made the Canadian Pacific Railway a reality, it was the sole author of its charter, John Abbott, whose historic contract with the government had paved the way.

In the rather infamous St. Albans case of 1864, Great-Grandfather acted for the leaders of escaped Confederate soldiers who, after seeking asylum in Canada during the American Civil War, raided (in plain-clothes) the town of St. Albans over the border in Vermont. There they seized its principal officials, rifled several banks, tried to set the town on fire and finally withdrew back over the frontier. This breach of Canadian neutrality could not be overlooked and the leaders were arrested, but a writ of habeas corpus was requested. There ensued a certain amount of correspondence between my great-grandfather and President Lincoln, but the White House insisted the offenders were not Confederates, just ordinary criminals masquerading as army. Abbott proved in the court proceedings that followed the raiders to be indeed Confederate soldiers committing an act of war and not criminals and his clients were discharged. Two years before when Canada was threatened with invasion from the south during the Civil War, Sir John raised and commanded as its lieutenant colonel his own regiment, the Eleventh Argenteuil Raiders, and twice led them on active service "to repel brigands within our neighbor's territory."

It was, however, in advising big business on both sides of the border that he excelled. His comrades jokingly nicknamed him the "Great Pooh-Bah" or "Lord High Everything Else" because he headed so many different organizations—government leader of the Senate for many years, Montreal's chief justice and its mayor, a director of the Bank of Montreal and, keeping up the family relationship with McGill University, member for some considerable time of its Board of Governors. He had even found time to teach law there—one of his prize students, the future prime minister Sir Wilfrid Laurier. Later on, his niece, Dr. Maude Abbott (my grandaunt), would also become a fixture of McGill and one of the world's authorities on congenital heart problems.

The ruins of Fort Senneville on our property

When I was a child, I loved this jolly, bustling, rotund, generous lady because every time she visited us she would bring me presents and make me laugh.

She had become the partner and friend of Dr. Paul Dudley White, the famous heart surgeon from Boston, and would travel with him and his family, lecturing throughout Europe. She was recognized and admired by the leading pioneer of heart disease, her teacher and mentor Sir William Osler. She was known and respected in Vienna and Rome, at Edinburgh University and Harvard, and in Mexico, where Diego Rivera painted her in his famous mural for Mexico City's National Institute of Cardiology. But McGill, in spite of her incredible ground-breaking work for that college, refused to accept her on its faculty. This was not just because she was a woman in a man's world—it was sadly due to the consistent failure of our country to recognize its own talent. Only at the end of her selfless and uncomplaining life was she finally accepted and came to be known affectionately as "Maudie of McGill."

Her uncle, my great-grandfather, had himself paid homage to medicine as incorporator of the country's then foremost hospital the Royal Victoria, selecting the architect, supervising its building and serving as its president and chairman of the Board of Governors till he died in 1893.

The Golden Square Mile on the southern slopes of Mount Royal had since 1850 been the most influential and affluent neighborhood in the country. Three-quarters of Canada's wealthiest families lived there. One luxurious mansion after another exhibited a diversity of architectural styles—Gothic Revival, Romanesque, Scottish Baronial and the favorite of all, French Second Empire.

Very early on, my great-grandfather built his mansion on the Sherbrooke Street side of the "Mile," swiftly followed by his railway compatriot the "Brasspounder from Illinois," Sir William Van Horne, who erected his own on the adjacent corner of Stanley Street. He also took particular delight in the salmon river he owned on the north bank of the Gulf of St. Lawrence. It was called the Great Wacheeshoo and boasted rushing falls where the salmon jumped, and for most of his free days, he fished there regularly.

On one occasion, while sailing by the Wacheeshoo on his steam yacht towards the mouth of the St. Lawrence, he was passing Anticosti Island when the vessel came to ground on some rocks and was wrecked. He and his surviving party somehow made it to shore, where they were rescued by a group of men who took them straight to a large castle on the island. They were warmly greeted by its owner, who, it turned out, not only owned the castle but the vast island as well. Monsieur Henri Menier was a descendant of the famous founder and maker of France's Menier Chocolates, known the world over as the "Chocolate King." He insisted that his marooned guests stay as long as it took to repair the boat. Menier was so tickled and amused that the country's prime minister had been discovered wading onto his shores that he never forgot the incident and for the next half century, our family received carton after

Boisbriant, my great-grandfather's old pile, of which I knew every cranny

Bois de la Roche, Polly's family home, which I haunted as a boy

carton of miniature wooden trunks furnished with golden keys filled with delectable Menier bonbons! More shipwrecks, s'il vous plaît!

Great-grandfather's happiest leisure hours were spent at Bois-briant. In the mid-nineteenth century, he had acquired an ancient seignory, at the tip of the island of Montreal, which not only satisfied his sense of history's continuity but endeared him the more to the local French Canadians whose language he spoke so accurately and fluently. It had been created a fief noble in favour of the Seigneur de Boisbriant as far back as 1672 by the original de Casson family who were the ancient seigneurs of Montreal's island. It included a large, ruined fort, Fort Senneville, down by the water (still standing today), which had been built as protection against the Iroquois in 1679.

Great-grandfather at once transformed the seignory into a beautiful estate, upon which he built an imposing country house overlooking the Lac des Deux Montagnes and the Oka Mountains. He had also purchased a considerable portion of the surrounding countryside, which was called Senneville, and another large Abbott house was built nearby for his brother Christopher (for whom I was named) called Bally-Bawn. Sir John began to cultivate his estate with extensive gardens, a model farm and spacious conservatories, where he developed a great variety of rare orchids; here were fine orchards slanting towards the lake, and in his fields grazed Guernsey cattle, which he was among the first to import for the improvement of the Canadian strain.

While all this landscaping and development was in progress, others followed suit, tycoons and railway barons, both French and English, each trying to outdo the other, and between them they literally turned Senneville and neighboring Cartierville into the Newport of Canada. Apart from Boisbriant, two of the large houses I would play in so many years later as a little boy were Pine Bluff, which had belonged to the railway magnate R. B. Angus, and Bois de la Roche, Senator Louis-Joseph Forget's house, Polly's family home. They had both been modeled on French chateâux and were bountifully supplied with mysterious rooms and secret passages. I never dreamed that one day I would be making films at Bois de la Roche when it was an empty shell and being rented out to motion picture companies. I made two there, one opposite Bette Davis in *Little Gloria Happy at Last,* about the Vanderbilts, and one with Nicholas Cage called *The Boy in Blue.* For a good long time I had become as much a part of the wainscoting in that old house as any bold, inquisitive termite.

A few years before the century's close, as my great-grandad's clock began to slowly wind down through a lingering, undiagnosed illness, Fortune's smile vanished, and gradually the grand Victorian days dwindled until very little of them were left. Whether there were simply too many Abbotts to care for amongst his huge and widespread brood, or whether he had sunk too much of his personal wealth into the various causes and schemes which drove his life—no one has yet come up with the answers.

Some say he went quite mad and this conjecture could have been entirely conceivable—for though his career both in law and in business was past any doubt a brilliant one, a lofty achievement, the journey there had been intense and quite ruthless, and being in private a gentle, retiring and rather religious soul, his assumed guilt according to his enemies could have pierced deep enough to have made him turn the corner. But not so—for it was cancer that claimed him in the end.

AS THE ELDER statesman crumbled, so did the farm, the stone walls, the fort, the boats and Boisbriant itself, the ceilings flaking, the colours fading from the rooms, the aviaries empty of birds. The once impeccable gardens were now wildly overgrown, but that sad and sorry state was not prolonged, for to the rescue with a welcome reprieve hot in their hands came the Cloustons—may their tribe increase!

The Cloustons were connections of ours by marriage only, but at least we could say that Boisbriant was to be kept as nearly in the family as we could wish, so to speak.

Sir Edward Clouston

The tribe's chief, Sir Edward Clouston, had been quick to snap it up and, like some conquering potentate, began with a vengeance to reface, rebuild, reshape the old pile, furiously magnifying its already considerable proportions—building bridges, adding bakeries, laundries, ice houses, extra stables and dredging the lake for his yachts. Sir Edward had made his millions in banking—he was a director of the Hudson's Bay Company, where he had begun as a boy, and was a founder of the Royal Trust. All this had helped make him one of the country's richest men. The young Max Aitken of New Brunswick, later the powerful press baron and Churchill's air minister, had as a boy mightily impressed Sir Edward, who had hired him over a great many aspirants—"Send me back the little man with the big head." Clouston gave the young man the boost he needed to embark on the sensational career he had cut out for himself.

To the end of his days, Max, Lord Beaverbrook never ceased to show his gratitude to the Clouston tribe. I use the word "tribe" not in the least frivolously, for they were indeed legitimately blessed with Indian blood. Several generations back, one of their ancestors had married a Cree Indian squaw with the magical name of Nahovway, which had brought their blood to a rich, boiling red.

Many generations had now passed. I was awakened one late night by the smell of smoke and snuck down to the lakeshore in my bare feet. There they were, the Cloustons, sitting around a fire which they had lit on the grounds of the old fort. I could see them through the cracks of the crumbling turrets and hear their soft laughter as they enjoyed a late picnic supper under the stars. They looked pale and ghostlike in the light of the dying embers; but there were others with them, I was sure of that, paler even than they, and to this day, I am firmly convinced that they had been joined for a peace pipe and a powwow by the phantoms of the lost Iroquois braves who had perished under those battlements.

Ah, Cloustons! Usurping Cloustons! They had saved our kingdom and they'd stolen our kingdom and yet the sharp twinge of pique that tweaked our sides told us no one had more right to be there than they. For Hiawatha was their kin—they held the ancient rite to send smoke signals to their gods, the right to worship with the long-dead souls, worship that planet of the night—the mother of earth. They could come here at will, to sit on the grass and watch the moonbeams creep through the gun holes in the ruined walls and feel the force of that bond which held them fast and forever to their cousins under the earth.

CHAPTER THREE

THE CRUMBLING PAST

I had come upon that scene simply covered in weather and Edwardian colonialism. The background score, had there been one, would have sounded like a bizarre mix of Elgar and "Gentille Alouette," the fife and drum of Kipling's Empire and "En roulant ma boule!"

My gran and grandad had long since moved into a more modest house on the old property. Because Mother's old-fashioned divorce had left us with nowhere to go, she and I moved in with them. It was close by the fort where I could dig for Indians and their skulls. A charming house dating back to the sixteen hundreds and of quite good size, which we called "The Cottage," would never be big enough for four formidable ladies plus Granddad, a Nanny, a maid and a cook!

> *In the room the women come and go*
> *Talking of Michelangelo.*

It took me some time to realize this was my family—this stoic, forthright little regiment of women, all exceptionally well read, well spoken, each one a skilled athlete—all staunch and devout members of the Audubon Society. Most weekends became, from dawn to dusk, one long bird-watching expedition as, armed to the teeth with picnic baskets, cameras and field glasses, they made their reverent way into the deep woods, treading as softly as Indians with me in tow. Not too much

*My granddad, who had the most
explosive laugh*

fun for yours truly. In spite of what the poets say, youth is not always the happiest of seasons. None of my aunts ever bothered to conceal their displeasure at my ignorance on the subject of ornithology and remained for the most part coolly disapproving. Until one day when I petulantly ran from an unfinished lunch to seek relief in the great outdoors—there, on top of a spruce which was bent over from the weight of it, sat an enormous bird with strange claws the likes of which I'd never seen. Forgetting all unsettled scores, I ran back inside and announced my discovery. They all came out onto the lawn and stared so hard at the poor creature, I thought it would fall off. The experts identified it immediately, in hushed tones, as an Arctic three-toed woodpecker—probably the first ever to be seen in our part of the world. Thank God and Mister Audubon! For a little while at least, I was to be treated with a certain deference and a courteous if grudging respect.

The younger of my two maiden aunts and the most athletic of the three sisters was Phyllis, and I am quite positive she had lived her almost forty years a virgin. Suddenly one day, she fell in love, perhaps for the very first time deeply, deeply in love. He was tall and swarthy and was the most gentle of men. His name was William Beatty and he lived across the lake at Como. He worshipped the ground she walked on, and she worshipped him. He proposed. It was, in those days, for someone of Phyllis's age more than a little late for such a thing as marriage, but here it was—it had come at last like a gift at sunset.

Early on the morning of the event, for the umpteenth time, she tried on her wedding dress. Willie was expected much later. She was so excited her fingers were all thumbs as she struggled with the countless buttons and hooks, but my mother took pity and came to her aid and at last it was on. There stood Phyllis, in her wedding dress, straight and tall, confident and radiant, waiting for her man. Willie never did make it that day, for on the way his car apparently spun out of all control, and he was killed instantly. My poor mother had to break the news. For the longest time, there was only silence except for the sound the corsage made as it slipped from Phyllis's hand to the floor.

Mother told me afterwards that a strange, faraway look had come into Phyllis's eyes, and her mouth closed in a thin, tight, angry line as she whispered so softly she could hardly be heard, "I knew it was too good to be true." Slowly, mechanically, she began to unbutton her dress. For a whole week, I remember, Phyllis remained in her room; she never came out. Then one day she finally emerged, head held high as if nothing had happened and life went on.

She spent most of it looking after her mother and the entire family, and she always seemed quite happy and content with her lot. But on that fateful day her heart had snapped and, convinced that she brought nothing but bad luck, never once did Phyllis date another man.

Whenever there was a household drama or any sort of domestic problem, the women would form a silent phalanx and close ranks — a combined force that was, to say the least, intimidating.

All the older family members were bilingual by necessity and choice. So I was made to read La Fontaine as well as Aesop, Ronsard as well as Keats, Balzac and Gabrielle Roy on the one hand, Robert Service and William Henry Drummond on the other. And then there was Stephen. For giggles there was always Stephen — good old Professor Stephen Leacock, that illustrious progenitor of utter nonsense. Several nights a week we would indulge in that quaint but delightful Victorian diversion — we read aloud to each other after dinner. On my own I rattled my chains with Marley's ghost, snuggled up with Peter and the Lost Boys in Barrie's Never-Never Land and whiled away the time by the river with Tom Sawyer and Huck Finn. Even further back, when I identified with "Yeller Dog Dingo" or "Lobo the Wolf" from the animal world of Ernest Thompson Seton, Mr. Toad in *The Wind and the Willows* or Lancelot in *Le Mort d'Artur,* I already knew some Shakespeare, the Lake poets and Robert Louis Stevenson. The ladies had seen to that. The ladies saw to everything! In fact Grandpa and I seemed to be the last two males on earth.

> *Let's go up to the pigsties and sit on the farmyard rails!*
> *Let's say things to the bunnies, and watch 'em skitter their tails!*
> *Let's — oh, anything, Grandpa, so long as it's you and me,*
> *And going truly exploring, and not being in till tea!*
> (Apologies to Kipling)

Teatime, daily at five, was a splendid affair—the women bustling, the food plentiful. Hot buttered crumpets by the fire, scones, tomato and cucumber sandwiches, two cakes, one with icing, one without, and always gingerbread. This ritual was by no means an indication of the day's close, for there were huge suppers to follow. And the breakfasts were just as piggish: two kinds of porridge, various choices under silver covers; finnan haddie or eggs, bacon and sausages, kippers, kedgeree or veal kidneys on toast. Astoundingly, no one ever had a weight problem. Granddad and I had become Peer Gynt, Sr., and Peer, Jr., surrounded as we were by female trolls, and like the Gynt family of those northern fjords, so the purse strings of the Abbott family had been severely cut, but we still managed to hang on in a world of country mansions, regattas and croquet on the lawn.

There was always a scattering of flappers about and numerous lounge lizards doing very little of anything and, of course, the usual "piranha fish" and attendant eccentrics. One such was a very posh-looking colonel, who paid the occasional abortive visit to my grandmother's house—I don't know quite why as he never uttered. One day, he arrived in immaculate blazer and white flannels; he was only in his late forties but already boasted a "companion," who took him by the hand and literally pulled him toward the house where we were all waiting to greet him. It took almost five minutes to get him from the car to the front door (a distance of several feet only) as my grandmother advanced and held out her hand for him to shake. The colonel extended *his* very slowly and then suddenly with a great deal of warmth and vigor shook the doorknob instead! An explosion erupted inside me and got strangled somewhere in my throat as my grandmother wheeled on me and hissed, "Behave yourself at once! Don't you realize that Uncle Fred is blind?!" "Blind? Blind drunk, you mean!" I thought as a waft of dragon breath from Uncle Fred hit my mother and me at one and the same time, which sent us reeling into the next room, where, collapsing on separate sofas, we buried our faces in the cushions to silence our uncontrollable hysteria!

Several years later, I had a mad crush on Uncle Fred's eighteen-year-old daughter. It happened at her "coming out" dance. The average age that evening was from sixteen to nineteen. Suddenly the doors were flung open and Uncle Fred, this time in white tie and tails, was being pulled in by yet another "companion," who led him to the center of the dance floor, where she promptly deserted him. Very red in the face, he rocked back and forth on his pins and gazed lustfully at the fair young maidens around him with a leer that would have made Humbert Humbert look like a choirboy and then, without warning, plunged forward onto the dance floor flat on his face! That was the last I ever saw of Uncle Fred. To this day, I don't believe he ever got up!

Peering through an upstairs window at Gran's house, I would watch visitors arrive in a variety of spectacular automobiles—old Pierce-Arrows, Lincolns, McLaughlin-Buicks, Dusenbergs, the great Packard limousines with the wooden spokes, and on one gloriously special day, an ancient Hispano-Suiza. I would sneak down the stairs and make friends with the waiting chauffeurs, who allowed me to sit inside and marvel at the plush interiors and smell the seductive scent of polished leather. My affair with the motorcar had begun.

Me as a repulsive youth of indeterminate age

To keep up with my sports-conscious family, I knew I must compete. There was always sailing, riding, golf, squash and tennis. Tennis parties galore! Tennis till the cows came home. Everyone in the surrounding countryside had their own courts—gravel, cement, en-tout-cas—à vôtre choix. Ours was grass, one of the only private grass courts in Quebec—rather ambitious in a climate known for its eight months of winter and four of mosquitoes, but it attracted enthusiasts from all over, so consequently it had to be kept in mint condition. If there was an overflow at Montreal's exclusive Mount Royal Tennis Club (where before the war, Mother had partnered with the Nazi bigwig vön Ribbentrop in mixed doubles), the visiting Davis Cup teams would use ours to warm up before their tournaments.

I remember feeling proud as Punch as I watched, awestruck, the great Fred Perry play on it. My entire family were all good club players (my uncle a potential Davis Cupper himself), and especially my grandparents—she, still in skirts down to the ankles, he in long white flannels, both of them gracefully moving about the courts showing off their tricky "between the leg" shots and dazzling us with their quicker-than-the-eye half volleys. Grandad was the country's racquets champion five years running and that mode of play had crept into his tennis.

Tradition demanded that teas, ices and cold drinks such as ginger beer in stone bottles be served at courtside under colourful umbrellas or in the tennis pavilions. These parties were always carefully organized as proper matches, "very professional," and treated as an occasion. No matter whose court it was, my granny used to silence anyone who dared talk during a rally. Guests would bring their own guests—you never knew who would turn up—one day, our gov. gen., the old Earl of Bessborough, appeared, incongruously attired in white flannels and winter overshoes!

The tennis parties I loved most were those given by a stylish lady everyone called "Aunt Mary" (Mrs. Forbes Angus)—her grub was the best! She was always moving at great speed across the grounds, swathed in long flowing chiffon scarves attached to her bracelets billowing out behind her, as peacocks in her path scurried away squawking. Her red-clay court was superbly situated on a promontory overlooking the lake with a gigantic aviary stretching the whole length of one side of it. The air was filled with the screeching of exotic birds of paradise, an assortment of parrots and some startlingly colourful macaws. The noise was so overwhelming, you could never hear the score.

With Machiavellian intent, unbeknownst to Aunt Mary, her gardeners had been secretly giving the macaws elocution lessons—with great success, I shudder to say. Their vocabulary was bilingual and fairly

Grandpa (second from the left). Canadian "Racquets" champion

extensive but certainly not dulcet. At one particularly sedate tennis gathering I remember hiding under the bushes trying unsuccessfully to stifle my giggling as one of the macaws, who had managed to get worked up over something, decided to shatter the afternoon's serenity by shrieking, at regular intervals, a volley of ear-piercing "Mange la merde!" and "Cocksuckers!" Incredibly, no one reacted and like some old forgotten quadrille, the tennis continued in stately fashion without missing a single beat.

WHEN THE WINDS ceased and all was still, the look of that time might have been described as pre-

Grannie: that proud and warlike Campbell

Raphaelite. Everything seemed slightly posed, waiting to be painted. Even mundane daily tasks were executed with extra care and style. In summer, fresh bread (pain chinois and galette au beurre) would be delivered in gaily painted calèches drawn by four horses; and in winter, the same, only this time in colourful sleds and the same horses had bells on their harnesses.

You could also be certain there was always some graceful sailing vessel caught in the rays of the moon rippling on the water. Grandad sketched hundreds of them. Every so often in the late evening on the Oka Mountains across the lake, you could see through the pines the flames of many torches held by invisible Trappist monks, zigzagging their way up the hill for the Seven Steps of the Seven Crosses. It was these very Trappists who made the now famous Oka cheese. "They pound it with their bare feet; that's why it smells so bad" was a familiar local saying. They also tilled the fields on the hillsides by day and were permitted to voice one note only, one note of finality—"Demain nous mouririons." Then they would retreat into their strict and more familiar world of impenetrable silence.

The bleak, endless winters, which resembled an old, faded rotogravure, were only relieved at day's end by an occasional Slavic sunset.

My mother, about the time she was a VAD *in World War I, France*

A *later picture of Mother as I knew her*

They were all most Chekhovian in atmosphere but much too long, and I never stopped whining. No one paid any attention, of course, so at an embarrassingly early age, I began to hit the sauce. Booze was a national sport up north. It was essential!—(a) to keep you warm, (b) to keep you from going mad, (c) to keep your madness going. How often as a mere teenager, tanked to the gills on cheap rye whiskey and Molson chasers, did I stagger home in the blinding cold. One night, stewed to the gills, I lurched off the road and completely passed out in a snow drift! I remember nothing except that I woke up in my own bed late the *next afternoon*! My mother, after hours of searching, had finally found me pickled and frozen, asleep in the snow and had half carried me home. She'd actually saved my life! A deed for which she was never quite forgiven.

The great blues singer Gertrude Niesen sang on my gramophone, *I got Harlem on mah mind / I've a longin' to be lowdown,* and the feeling was mutual. I'd found myself caught in a web of good manners and suppressed emotions—a late version of la belle époque which hung on in the colonies long after the auld country had abandoned it, as if trying to force good appearances upon an upstart age. "Rags to riches" could never then be my road, rather the reverse, with an exceedingly strong leaning toward the gutter. In the beginning, I had no struggle; I didn't know what it meant. Not exactly coming from the streets, there was no urgent need to improve, no clear path up which to climb.

> *"Roundabout," said Peer Gynt. "Backwards or forwards,*
> *it's just as far, out or in it's just as narrow."*

Well, the gutters and pavements of the harsh outside world beckoned sooner than expected, for as in all fables, the magic eventually had to end, and the elder members of my family once again came to grief and began to lose control of what holdings they had, and my mother, approaching fifty and already a divorcée, was forced to go to work—in the nineteen thirties two shameful no-no's dans les salons de la politesse.

She had been a very young and decorated VAD (Voluntary Aid Detachment) nurse in the Great War in Ypres, Rouen and the Somme; was exposed to deadly gas; tended soldiers whose faces had been blown away; helped amputate, without anesthetic, limbs rotting with gangrene; witnessed the results of shell shock. So with all that tough backlog of horror behind her, she admirably braced herself for the onslaught. Many a time as a boy, I watched Mother, in her fifties, skiing at breakneck speed straight down the Laurentien hills on her long Norwegian hickories, in those days, barely a harness to speak of; her ankles strong as steel, her skis, so close together they touched; before the slalom, before the "christie," the tassels from her colourful ceinture flechée flying in the wind as she neared the bottom, only to kneel down on one ski and execute that most beautiful of turns—the graceful Telemark. She was one of the few women to pioneer that turn in our country.

Mother had such incredible energy. If she ran out of things to do, she would take a little hatchet and cut paths through the woods, and she literally threw herself into her work at McGill, assisting Polly's husband, the dean of science. Then followed the long hours late into the night which she tirelessly spent as secretary to the Canadian Handicrafts Guild, the organization that first brought to light the primitive beauty of Inuit sculpture. In spite of all this, she always had time for me and never lost her patience. Even on bird-watching expeditions, deep in the forest when I, as a brat, would selfishly demand not just water out of nowhere but a *glass* of water, she would quietly remind me, "You have nature all about you—drink *that* in, while you can."

Mother never stopped doing things for people. She never sat down, but now she was older and slightly stooped—no one except Polly had really accepted her or made her feel comfortable, and life was taking its toll as she trudged through the snowbound city streets to her work while the other family members continued on, stubbornly salvaging their pride—defiant, in a fool's paradise.

My grandparents had held hands since they were twenty; now, in their late seventies, they were still so madly in love that though time was passing them by they hardly noticed it. But Grandad was deteriorating rapidly—his memory had failed him; he was hallucinating dreadfully, dangerously courting senility. Staring out the window he would shout, "Who are these people on the lawn?"—no one there, of course; or convinced he was on the yacht sailing down to Tadoussac, his custom for many a summer, he would gaze out the same living room window and demand irritably, "Haven't we passed Les Eboulement yet?" Though little ol' me wasn't supposed to know it, my grandfather had been ruined. His supposedly loyal partner of over forty years, a Frenchman, had gradually managed to embezzle most of the funds, leaving the old man high and dry. One tense and ominous day, my grandmother summoned the little embezzler to the country house, where she met him privately outside in the garden.

A proud and warlike Campbell descended directly from Sir Colin "the Wonderful" in the fourteenth century and the ancient lairds of Ardkinglas, she wasted no time; her revenge was sweet. I hid under a nearby pine tree and listened, my heart pounding, as, leaning on her cane, she let him have the tongue-lashing of his life! Though he deserved it, my heart went out to him; I couldn't help it—he was shaking just as I was from the deep hurt her words inflicted as they cut the air like a scythe. She could be pretty awesome, my granny, when angry—even the flowers seemed to bow their heads in shame.

When she had finished, he still stood there, hat in hand, head bowed, motionless, in what seemed the most prolonged silence I have ever known. Then, he slowly turned and walked away. Someone told me that about a month or so later he took his own life. I think I knew why. I had witnessed, at its fiercest and fullest force, the terrible rage of righteous indignation—and I would never forget it.

Grandad was now confined to his room. He could no longer talk—he just made little wheezing sounds. He would lie in bed, eyes vacant, staring at the ceiling, recognizing no one, not even Granny, who never left his side. His face was so thin and ashen; his frame sagged appallingly—he looked like someone else altogether, a complete stranger. I missed the dapper, kind, gentle man I once knew. I missed the sound of his rich, contagious laughter as we read reams of Stephen Leacock aloud to each other, falling about, not able to go on. What I saw now was a husk—a shell—and there was a new smell about the room too, an acrid smell, dank and clawing. I never went back inside.

The day after they buried him, his sister, a perky little old lady of about seventy-eight with a bustling good humour, came, not just to live with us but to fill our lives with laughter again.

> Dear old Aunt Harriet, up in heaven she be
> Can't afford a chariot, . . .

Everyone called Aunt Harriet "Aunt Baby" because (a) she was a wee baby of a thing, (b) she was the baby of her family and (c) a lot of the time she behaved like a baby.

She introduced us to a strange pastime called jip-norring, a very nineteenth-century English exercise indeed; it could have come straight out of *Alice in Wonderland.*

She would carry a sort of pogo stick, dig it in the earth and then catapult herself all over the grounds. Hard to describe—it was a mixture of skipping and pole vaulting, and she insisted it got her places far sooner than other more normal modes of travel. When she wasn't thus engaged, she would bird-watch, read everything, including the *Book of Common Prayer,* tell quaint little stories and listen to classical music on the radio or gramophone. In fact, while Grampa was alive, we had regularly gathered round to hear the Saturday afternoon Metropolitan broadcasts only to be swept clean away by the celestial voices of those two Wagnerians, Flagstad and Melchior. One matinée, we sat in horror as the famous Giovanni Martinelli ruptured his voice reaching for a high note in "Veste la giubba" from Pagliacci. Suddenly over the airways came this screeching sound as if a goose had been strangled. The Met audience gasped audibly and the mellifluous Milton Cross announced to a puzzled nation that the tenor had burst the blood vessels in his throat. They pulled the curtain down—Frederick Jaeger was summoned and escorted by motorcycles from Long Island (we could hear the sirens over the air), finished the performance and overnight, became a star. But the great Martinelli never sang again.

In spite of being weaned on bagpipes and the sound of the reel, Granny did appreciate "serious" music when she wanted to, but there was little patience left in her for anything anymore. Aunt Baby, on the other hand, was devoted to music, passionately devoted. As youngsters, she and her sisters had studied composition and the piano in Berlin and Paris under some grand old masters. For many years, she had served on the committee that sponsored Montreal's Ladies' Morning Musical Club—a prestigious recital series that attracted a great number of internationally known artists, in spite of their being expected to perform at eleven in the morning. "It was somewhat different," Aunt Baby recalled, "the day Chaliapin was engaged." It appears the demand for tickets was so overwhelming, there was no space in their regular concert hall, so they were forced to rent the Forum, similar in size to Madison Square Garden. The vast audience, many of whom had camped out the night before, was there at eleven sharp, eager to hear the great Russian—a once-in-a-lifetime experience. It was two full hours before he appeared. When he finally arrived, my grandaunt and several of the committee firmly chastised him: "You have kept the audience waiting, Maestro. You were to sing at eleven o'clock; it is now one!" "Seeng?" boomed the world-famous bass. "At Eelavan? Modom, I don' speet before twalve!"

She was always encouraging me in my love for music and the piano. She would jip-norr into the living room whispering loudly that Heifetz or Rubinstein was playing or that Gigli or Schipa was singing on the radio and Mother and I would run up the stairs two at a time where the three of us would press our ears close to the speakers, the sound turned way down, terrified of being rebuked. We could hear the thump of Granny's cane on the tiled floors below as she restlessly prowled about the house like some obsessed warden! Poor Gran! She'd lost her man and she'd lost her temper at one and the same time, and it seemed only a matter of days before she would rush from our midst with the speed of a comet to be by his side once more.

WE WERE NOW down to one gardener, quel tristesse, who also doubled as chauffeur, butler and just about everything else. He'd been with us forever. His name was Louis Brunet. He was a French Canadian of the old school who, as a boy, had been in service to my great-grandfather. He was remarkably handsome but had spent most of his life outdoors in the rough, raw winters, so his face was ruddy, gnarled and weatherbeaten, and his teeth were quite black from chewing tobacco. Louis was in his late seventies; I was nine or ten. I whiled the days away as he worked in the garden, madly chatting to each other, comparing Charpentier to Joe Louis or Max Schmeling. I will never forget the explosion his laugh ignited.

Although he was poor as a church mouse, he was gentler and had more impeccable manners than any of our so-called grand friends, and he carried his pride to the point of exasperation. He had no car or bicycle of his own, and although he was offered the family car, he would not hear of it, preferring to walk back and forth to work at dawn and dusk the whole two miles to his house in the village. One day the news came that his wife of fifty years had suffered a fatal attack and was dying fast. We insisted on his taking the car. Too proud, the old man, as always, refused and ran the whole way home. We followed him in the car and drove alongside—he looked neither right nor left but straight ahead, his cap held tightly in his hand as he ran on, his face streaming with tears. He was rewarded, though, for she had held on—she had waited for him, waited to slip away in his arms. I loved that man. He was a friend to whom I could tell everything.

At any rate, it was all just about over—the beginning of the end for anglicized Quebec. The infamous Durham Report of 1839 demanding English monopoly in everything had crushed French Canadian hopes and sowed early seeds of discontent. Although the older lot had tried to keep intact the "Two Solitudes," they couldn't manage it and they'd been misunderstood. The younger generation of French Canadians had lost patience with their Anglo contemporaries, who did nothing but patronize them, take them for granted, many not even bothering to speak their language. It was as if a disturbance under the Plains of Abraham had caused its surface to separate and the shades of Wolfe and Montcalm, old and battle weary, now stood as before, glaring at each other across the chasm. A new era was sweeping its way over the province, sweeping away the old, and the old couldn't keep up with it. Like the dinosaurs, they had no inkling they were to become extinct, soon to be washed away with the snow.

Sometimes there is a ghostly rumble among the drums that swings me back to those memories. No matter how dim and far away in my mind they lie, the romance of that lost time remains as clear as if it were yesterday. It all seems so foreign now, but it was quite wonderfully theatrical in its way; and there was something else about it, something I can never explain that touched me to the core. To the end of my days, I shall be grateful for that curious link with the past, to that other universe of grace and values—and to my quaint old family, for if there is the merest smidgeon of decency in me at all, it came from them, and without doubt, though they never would have guessed it, they gave me my imagination.

CHAPTER FOUR

*. . . will you see the players well bestowed? Do you hear,
let them be well used, for they are the abstract and brief
chronicles of the time.*

— HAMLET

The first play I ever saw was at school. It was James Barrie's *Mary Rose*. When the offstage shot rang out at the end, I was absolutely certain that someone had really died. All the rest of the children filed out of the hall, not in the least taken in, but I sat where I was, motionless—my eyes locked on to the asbestos curtain. You see, I knew, as sure as eggs is eggs, that behind it, there had been a death!

One day we were hustled into the school's assembly hall to watch some old-fashioned thespian gentleman whom I seem to remember,was Bransby Williams—very British, with long hair, who rolled his Rs and wore a monocle. He was well known for his "Characters from Dickens" and managed quite brilliantly at least a dozen of them simply by altering his voice and changing hats in the twinkling of an eye. In a flash, he was Fezziwig, Macawber, the Artful Dodger, both Scrooge *and* Marley, and, of course, Sidney Carton intoning heroically, "'Tis a far, far better thing I do than I have ever done . . ." and so on. The entertainment continued as he offered some rather singsong Shakespeare and ended with a splendidly declaimed, "Once more unto the breach . . ." from *Henry V.* I was naturally captivated but, strangely, so were *all* the children present, even the most blasé among them. The old boy was, to say the least, a bit of a ham, but by God those stirring words found their mark that happy morning.

Not realizing it, I was being hooked! In those days I fancied myself as a mimic of unusual brilliance and with the help of one other wayward classmate, young Kasatchenko (a natural comic everyone called the "Mad Russian"), would entertain the class during breaks with unflattering imitations of our various masters. Our French master in particular. Tall and angular, he would enter the room with a kind of goose-step and in a very deep voice would call us to order by barking, "All right la classe!" All good stuff to mimic. One day, Kasatchenko goose-stepped in shouting, "All right la classe!" I followed suit behind calling out, "All right la classe." Then someone behind me also echoed, "All right la classe." Guess who! Invariably, we were caught thus and publicly given the strap!

However, mightily inspired by the old ham actor's rendition of *Henry V,* I committed "Once more unto the breach" to memory and at the next day's first recess, hurled at my captive fellow students a barrage of pentameter I was determined they'd never forget. It must have had some impact for they rallied at the end, the good little scouts, with some pretty convincing war cries of their own. I'm not sure, but it must have been then that I first felt the future nudge me in the ribs.

This sudden flirtation with the arts was surprisingly not to be discouraged, least of all by my mother. "Mater" had been a lucky girl. She had seen Nijinsky, Pavlova, Isadora Duncan and Diaghilev's splendid company of dancers. As a youngster she had watched the great Sir Henry Irving and Ellen Terry, Sir Johnston Forbes-Robertson's gentlemanly, beautifully spoken Hamlet, the triumphant Sarah Bernhardt, the revolutionary Eleanora Duse and Daphne du Maurier's father, Sir Gerald, the man who had introduced a fresh, conversational style into the British theatre. Mother's first cousin Gwen Price had married the playwright Guy du Maurier, Gerald's brother, so however distant, there was some theatrical connection there, to be sure.

Mum managed to meet many such luminaries at after-theatre parties in the houses of friends, particularly at the grand house of her friend Martha Allan—the impressive Raven'scrag I often mention. She marveled at John Martin-Harvey's blinded Oedipus being led across a huge ramp extended from the stage to the back of the theatre—one of Max Reinhardt's bold and daring innovations! She waxed adoringly over the great Scot Harry Lauder and his song "A Wee Doch an' Doris" and Maude Adams in Barrie's *The Little Minister* and *Peter Pan.*

She wanted me to be just as fortunate, so with a determination that would have reduced Boadicea to a mere wallflower, she took me to *everything* that she could and could not afford! By the time I was thirteen, I had seen the Ballet Russe de Monte Carlo; I had watched Massine, Ulanova, Dolin, José Limón and Kurt Joos. I had seen *and* heard Galli-Curci, Martinelli, Tibbett, Pearce, Richard Tauber, the glorious Jussi Björling and "Ol' Man River" himself, Paul Robeson. The great crusader had just returned from Russia embraced by socialism and fresh new propaganda for liberating his race. He had more education and intellect in his pinky than all the painted papillons and dilettantes that patronized the Ritz-Carlton put together; yet simply for being black he was denied entry there.

From the early eighteen hundreds, at least twenty-five theatres were open for business in Montreal, some of the best known being the Hayes Theatre, l'Académie de Musique, Theatre Montréal, Le Théâtre des Variétés and Le Monument-National. But a lot did not survive. Long gone was the Mechanics' Hall (1854) where our own Emma Lajeunesse warbled her way to world fame as the great Albani. Long gone too was the Theatre Royal, also known as the Molson Theatre, named after the beer family. Edmund Kean had played there, as had John Wilkes Booth, Charles Dickens and William Charles Macready.

Sarah Bernhardt arrived in our fair city, couvert en gloire, but did not endear herself to the church with her racy production of *Adrienne Lecouvreur*. Apparently, this didn't faze her, for up till 1917, she returned to Montreal at least nine times. Taking up her cue, another great Parisienne, Réjane, followed in her wake. Yes, we'd had a rich theatrical past and it was still with us by the time I came on the scene, but mostly visible in only one precious old structure. From the balcony of His Majesty's Theatre on Guy Street, I had gazed admiringly down upon Edwige Feuillière, Jean-Louis Barrault, Yvonne Printemps, Sacha Guitry, Donald Wolfit, the young Gérard Philipe and that bewitching Viennese imp Elisabeth Bergner.

I can still see her poised at the top of a steep flight of stairs catching sight of her long-lost stage lover waiting below and literally floating down to him in one joyous flight of ecstasy. The play *The Two Mrs. Carrolls* couldn't have been more trifling, but that tiny moment and the magic she brought to it earned her an ovation and stopped the play. She was so delighted, she improvised in her seductive Austrian lilt, "O, I like zat very much—I sink I do zat again," bounded up the stairs, turned and once more floated downwards with a mischievous toss of her head. Another ovation! A shooting star no less!

Donald Wolfit, a beefy warhorse, well known for touring Shakespeare to the English provinces, was one of the last leading players to cling to a nineteenth-century style of acting. His career was irreverently described as not a "tour de force" but "forced to tour." His reputation for chewing scenery had preceded him, and his outrageous curtain calls alone were worth the price of admission—the sad picture of a tragic figure breathlessly hanging on to the tabs for support, the epitome of exhaustion following triumph. Quel ham bone! In his large repertoire, which included a superb Volpone and a delicious Bottom, he had disastrously miscast

himself as Hamlet, which he
played at such speed, it gave the
impression he had a far more
pressing engagement elsewhere.
Brooks Atkinson of *The New York
Times* had written of this performance, "O to be in England now
that Wolfit's here!"

He did, however, move me to
unashamed tears when, as King
Lear, he ended the famous curse
and with one crack of his gigantic
bullwhip enveloped the Fool and
sent him spinning like a top into
a corner of the stage. Hurling the
whip aside, he lifted the terrified
Fool into his arms with such tenderness, I held my breath; his
voice broke—"O fool, I shall go

*Donald Wolfit — one good old-fashioned,
leafy war horse*

mad!"—and covering him like a baby in his cloak carried him out into
the waiting storm. Wolfit had used London critic James Agate's extravagant quote in large print beneath his name on the marquee—"the finest
actor since Sir Henry Irving"—a fair conceit indeed. But that night, no
one had questioned the accolade; he had earned it and more, for I remember to this day what it felt like to be, for the first time, in the presence of
greatness, no matter how coarse.

From my little seat in the "gods," I had marvelled at John Gielgud's
immaculate and definitive *The Importance of Being Earnest;* I had seen the
Abbey Players (Arthur Shields, W. G. Fay, Sara Allgood); Micheál
MacLiammóir and Hilton Edwards's Dublin Gate Theatre and Barry
Jones and Maurice Colbourne's company parading their specialty,
George Bernard Shaw. And the actress-specialist who all by herself
became a thousand people before your very eyes—the invincible Ruth
Draper. Mother took me backstage (my *first*) to see the great lady,
whom she had known in London. Miss Draper had been famous for her
salons there, where intellectuals and artists the world over gathered to
mingle with society and, if the mood was upon them, to occasionally
perform. One night when Mother was present, Rachmaninoff and
Kreisler got up and improvised for hours together and of course she
never forgot it! Then I was spirited off to concerts—Heifetz, Ellman,
Szigeti, Milstein and an extraordinary woman, a Mrs. Rosen, also

Mother's friend, who played the theremin. When the beautiful Mrs. Rosen died, she willed her estate outside New York, named Caramoor, to be used as a festival of music, which has since become world famous and where, many decades later, I was privileged to give a concert.

Then off we would go to see the pianists—Horowitz, Backhaus, Casadesus, Egon Petri and Jesus Maria Sanroma! Montreal's distinguished music critic Thomas Archer, who valiantly tried to persuade a wartime populace that just because Wagner was German, he wasn't necessarily a Nazi, was a tall, cadaverous Englishman who loved his drink. Once, after a full dinner, he went to hear Horowitz and before the concert began, promptly dozed off in his seat and slept throughout the evening. To conceal his embarrassment, he gave Maestro Horowitz the next day a glowing review describing every nuance in minute detail. To his horror, he discovered too late that Horowitz had cancelled at the last moment and had been replaced by someone local.

The Australian, Percy Grainger, for whom Grieg had written his Piano Concerto in A Minor, came to town very often—declined hotels and insisted on sleeping on his piano in a studio at Steinway Hall. He was most eccentric and would play only two encores, "The Man I Love," as if Grieg had written it, and his own "Country Gardens." I was also scared out of my wits by the angry pounding of Malcuzynski and Brailowski. I even saw Rachmaninoff when I was almost too small to remember—a very tall, sad-looking man with enormous hands towered over the piano, glowering at the audience for what seemed hours, till they'd stopped coughing. The rest was hazy, but the moment I heard him on disk with his magical touch, I bought all his records (charged them to Mother, of course) and would cart them to Polly's Island—and Polly and I would listen all day long. I would imagine he was the last of the romantic composer-pianists and we were the last romantics listening to him.

It was Rachmaninoff's fault that I fell for the keyboard! Instantly, I saw myself as "le Grand Pianist" with leonine looks and dazzling arpeggios! I slaved away under several long-suffering piano teachers but was much too impatient. Why take lessons when I could pick it all up by ear?! Gradually, I found I was able to emulate the left-hand harmonies fairly accurately, and though my meager but growing repertoire may have been in all the wrong keys, I could duplicate some of the great concerti and solo pieces adequately enough to fool at least a quarter of the people a quarter of the time. I could also play my own arrangements of popular tunes and jazz. This questionable talent rescued me from having to fox-trot or jive at kids' parties where I was so terrified I would

Proud Oscar Peterson with offspring

freeze on the dance floor. I should have had a plaque hung round my neck saying, "Please don't save me this dance." So making a beeline for the piano, I would improvise madly. It worked! This is how I could get the attention I wanted—and girls!

I decided I'd do my practicing on the school grand at recess. Miracle of miracles! Soon I'd attracted a crowd of fellow students. One of them, a big, stout black guy wearing pants a little too short for him, shoved me off the piano stool and had the audacity to start playing himself. This routine became a daily occurrence. I'd begin—he'd shove me off! I wondered why he was drawing much larger crowds, but put it down to the fact that the collective tastes of the assembled multitude were far too bourgeois for my loftier contributions. Though I fumed with jealousy, I had to admit he played some pretty mean jazz, as well as classical. Everybody was calling him Oscar. "Sorry I didn't quite catch your *last* name?" I condescended from some Olympian height. "Peterson," he quietly replied. We formed a truce and struck up an acquaintance. He was most complimentary about my "doodling" and insisted I come to all the Saturday night dances, where he played for the school band. It was known as the Montreal High School Victory Serenaders. "You'll love the trumpet player," he said. "He's just great! His name's Maynard." "Maynard who?" I asked. "Ferguson" was the cool reply.

I often went downtown late at night to hear Oscar play at the Alberta Lounge. He also played intermission piano at a place called the Penthouse Club. The headliners were two fairly well-established comedians but the audience was restless and talked a lot through their act.

The moment it was time for intermission, instead of going out they stayed in their seats, listening enraptured to Oscar, then very much at the foot of his rainbow. So it was not too far-fetched to assume that one day he would bring the house down at Carnegie Hall.

Besides Oscar and Maynard, there was a considerable amount of raw talent about—hogging most of the spotlight! Darling little exhibitionist that I'd become, I vowed to do something about it. With my obnoxious gift for mimicry, I spent most of my time emulating others. I would ape their dress, their mannerisms, their voices—even their tennis strokes. I would sneak in and out of movie houses convinced I was Gable, Ladd, Colman, Bogie—even Peter Lorre and Sydney Greenstreet. I also knew most of their dialogue—God knows I'd seen those films over and over!

FOR SOME TIME NOW I'd become fascinated by the libido. No doubt it had unconsciously begun several moons back when I'd had a nanny called "Mademoiselle." She was French, of course, a handsome woman in her early thirties—very proper and correct. I must have been eleven or twelve. I kissed her once because I thought she looked so pretty. By mistake, it lasted a little longer than I'd intended. However, I rather liked it as, it seemed, did she. So it became a regular ritual. We began to look forward to these harmless little kissing sessions. One day she kissed me very hard, full on the lips, and her mouth opened. So did a door behind her and one of my aunts appeared. I never saw Mademoiselle again.

As a family, we were always paying visits to the museum. In fact, Mother insisted on enrolling me as an art student. I couldn't wait to sneak into the rooms where all the nude statuary was kept, where, like a dirty old man, I'd caress the stone teat of some unsuspecting Venus. Not too far down the road that same thrill would be multiplied a hundredfold when I was able to hold a real live one in my hands—but for the moment, alas, I was to be content with stone.

It was about this time I became seriously distracted by my body! In fact, I thought about my body a lot and wondered what the hell to do with it. I started getting unexpected erections in the most awkward places—on trains, at public swimming pools, in hotel lobbies. Sitting with my family in a front pew at Christ Church Cathedral, I would stare up at the stained glass windows, mesmerized by their colours, and was just about to climb into one and disappear forever back through the centuries when bang! A great organ crash and everyone was on their feet singing Hymn No. Whatever and in my row, two soldiers standing at rigid attention—me and the one in my pants pointing heavenward. Regaining my seat, I naively supposed no one would notice as I piled every prayer book, hymn book, religious pamphlet I could find onto my lap to hide the embarrassment. It wasn't so bad in class when the teacher wasn't looking 'cause you could take it out and give it some air. All the guys would follow suit and at recess we'd bundle off to the locker rooms to compare our various sizes. This subject was discussed with clinical gravity, our voices at least an octave lower than normal to ensure masculinity and assume a carnal indifference.

Girls took on an altogether new and different look now that they had something to challenge them, I smugly surmised. What taxed most of my brain power was what they would look like without any clothes. Each one I passed on the street, no matter what age, I would rape with my eyes, positive that whatever she was wearing would instantly fall from her like lead and there she would stand, for all the world to see— Ha! Ha! without a stitch!

News of massive import hit Montreal High School like a tornado that one of the girl students across the quad wore no pants. It turned out she herself was largely responsible for this hot little scoop as she never ceased to inform the world of that fact. She was raunchy, petite, cheeky with a galvanizing little body and was thoroughly enjoying wreaking havoc with the male students and their concentration. One day, a bunch of us fellows passed her as she was reclining on the school steps, smoldering away seductively to herself. She saw us ogling her and at once began sinuously to spread her legs, lifting her skirt ever so casually at the same time. At the apex of two pale, graceful, well-shaped young limbs was the biggest black bush anyone is ever likely to see. On such a tiny creature, I couldn't believe it; it wasn't possible, but I was burning with envy, for when I got home and checked in the mirror, my own, compared to hers, was sadly sparse and inadequate. I rectified that at once. I ran to the fields, and after slicing off blond strands from the ears of corn, I hastily pasted them just above mon région pays boisé. When corn was not in season, I would draw them in with a dark pencil or paint them on one by one with black paint from my paint set. Of course, it took forever to remove. What a lot of exhausting work! I couldn't wait to come of age. O, to be hirsuite now that Pan was here!

I started dating girls by taking them to the movies, what else? And afterwards I would cunningly lead them behind some convenient shrubbery and spout dialogue from love scenes between harmless kisses. Most of them got pretty fed up and left in a huff. I wondered why. A rather lovely, languid lass, a fugitive from the school play (one of the Bennet girls to my Darcy in *Pride and Prejudice*) proved much more in tune and cooperative. A would-be actress, she would strike all the appropriate poses, leaning against a tree, affecting a most tragic line whilst I, besmooching betimes, wouldst transform myself into Laurence Olivier in *Wuthering Heights,* showering her with such Brontë-saurean gems as "You're still my queen?" or "Why isn't there the smell of heather in your hair?" Though her dialogue recall fell far short of mine—she was most helpful, never once allowing the spirit of the moment to flag but skillfully and breathlessly coming in on cue with the occasional "Heathcliff!—Oh! Heathcliff." Alas, our potential love tryst, which had reached the boiling point, was to be nipped in the bud, for by this time I was deeply immersed in my character—I was in full swing—I played *all* the parts for her. In fact, I did the whole damn movie while she sank to the ground, speechless, a look in her eyes that could only have read, "What have I got here . . . some kind of schmuck?!"

THE DAMSEL of the Black Bush was chummy with another lass, her roommate, who was reputed to have "jousted" with most of the young knights in the school. Whether she was a student, a hanger-on or simply a "pro" no one quite knew, but she was decidedly a damsel in distress. Famous about the campus as the local nympho, raver, sex fiend, you name it, she was tall, skinny, long of leg, not pretty, but outrageously kinky! Having exhausted the majority of my male contemporaries, she finally got around to me. "Come over to my joint—no one's home," she offered subtly. Cursed by bad timing and my infatuation for celluloid, I suggested we see *Laura*—just out, and one of my favourites. Already I'd seen it six times and could give a pretty first-rate imitation of Clifton Webb and some of his sparkling dialogue. All that week, I'd worked overtime at becoming Clifton, dressing up like the dandy he was, sporting my grandfather's cane, très dégagé, generally exuding sophistication and chic. "Okay," she had said, "but let's sit at the back of the balcony." It appeared she didn't have the time to be impressed by Otto Preminger's stylish opus; her hands were everywhere, her tongue beating at the door of my taut, terrified mouth as I squirmed in my seat fighting to catch a glimpse of the screen.

I walked her home. It was a cold, bitter winter night. She said she had no gloves and could she put her hands in my pants' pockets? I wondered how Clifton would have reacted, but nevertheless, I acquiesced. She reached in and what she didn't do with her fingers as we waddled along the streets was nobody's business! I wanted so much to let go and relish the novel adventure, but Mr. Webb had taken over almost completely, and I heard myself saying priggishly, "Young woman, you must gain for yourself a modicum of control." We'd arrived at her front door. She stormed in shouting, "You selfish fuck! All you think of is yourself!" Then Waldo Lydecker, Webb's character in the flick, threw back his retort—a direct quote, "Yes. I find no other subject quite so worthy of my attention." She slammed the door and a frustrated Clifton Webb was left standing all by himself shivering in the Arctic night as dry and celibate as the ice under his feet.

CHAPTER FIVE

Jusqu'à la fin du monde
Jusqu'à la fin du monde
Nous dormirions ensemble la
Nous dormirions ensemble
— ANCIENT GALLIC SONG

In my green years, long before the threat of separatism, we had been so close—the French and us—there was so much we shared. Our "Belle Province" offered every sort of distraction imaginable. If we felt inclined to skip school, we could always catch a matinée at the old Gaiety Theatre and ogle the great Queen of Strip herself, Lili St. Cyr (a daring, most erotic strip behind an umbrella and one unlocking a chastity belt). Or if we preferred sport of another kind, there was always skiing—skiing out of the crib, skiing to school, to church, slaloming through the trees, under the chairlifts, pulled by horses or across the ice-bound lake by Catamaran. We would all chip in for lessons from Lugi Foger, that pioneer of the stem turn who was the first to mount a camera on the back of his skis and who was always spouting his little jingle—"Bend ze kneece; vatch ze treece; seex dullahs pleece." We even learned under Emil Allais, the great French champion who was visiting Tremblant, and once I won a case of Molson's for coming first in the Hill 70 downhill dash at St.-Sauveur.

Lili St. Cyr, the Queen of Striptease,
a true artist in her field

There was also hockey, of course ("Away, Away"—Boom Boom Geof-frion, Hull, Orr, Cournoyer), snowshoeing, lacrosse and that holdover from Scottish rule—curling. Many of us Anglos annually joined the sacred St.-Jean-Baptiste Parade and before the spring melt, our annual "sugaring off" would take place—the celebration of the first maple syrup with breakfasts out in the snow, sausages, bacon and eggs and "gummette" (the first oozing syrup that freezes like candy on the bark of maples) all mixed together—the best! In the Laurentiens, at St.-Agathe-des-Ments, St.-Marguerite or Tremblant, high on the hills, we rested on our poles and listened to the church bells far below us. We could just make out little dots of habitants—old men driving their horse-drawn sleighs, the same old men, the same sleighs with which our top painters, the famous "Seven," had peppered their landscapes. Later, when we became young blades, I remember bashing down those very slopes at hair-raising speed, soused out of our minds, once, immaculately attired in full evening dress! (I've always wanted to see that in a movie.) We did most everything together, the French and us, conspired together, laughed and fought together; we opened our veins and marked our allegiance; the two languages melted into *one,* no thought of parting *ever.* It was just *"us"*—nous deux—that made our space unique in the world, *us twain* that will keep it that way—if only someone will listen!

> *D'où viens-tu bergère*
> *D'où viens-tu?*
> *Je viens de l'étable*
> *De m'y promener*
> *J'ai vu un miracle*
> *Ce soir arrivé.*
>
> —ANCIENT CAROL

And then Christmases in Montreal—engulfed in snow drifts as high as tidal waves, we tobogganed all the way down from the top of Mount Royal, screaming like banshees, shouting every old Norman curse word we could think of! Even the priests joined us on their skis, barrelling down the hill fully decked out in their cassocks, looking like a flock of blackbirds. Then at night, the little blue lights, *always* blue, on all the Christmas trees, in a long never-ending line up the side of the mountain where they joined the stars in that northern sky—the darkest starlit sky of all—and music, music everywhere; French carols ancient as the hills, glorious concerts at Notre-Dame Cathedral—full orchestra, choirs and organ resounding around the Great Altar as it would continue to do right up through the Pavarotti years.

Hochelaga was the old Indian name for Montreal. I linger here far longer than I should perhaps, simply because a lot went on in this lively northern town most people today know nothing of. In the thirties and forties, when I grew up, it was the second-most important city in the British Empire. It literally ran Canada from St. James Street. Being a seaport where many languages moored, it was a hotbed of international trade. It had more continental atmosphere than any other town in North America. It was cosmopolitan, stylish, sophisticated and fast!

News came in two tongues. On the English side, the *Gazette,* the *Herald,* the *Star*; and on the French, *Le Devoir, La Presse, Le Canada.* The phone book read like a romance: names such as de Frontenac, de Repontigny, de Lotbinière, de Boutillier, de Gaspé Beaubien, des Rivières, and

Boucher de Crèvecoeur de Perthes peppered the pages alongside Athelston, Mount Stephen, Featherstonhaugh, Shaughnessy, Knatchbull-Hugessen, Hamilton Gault, even, believe it or not, a Smellie-Bottomne or two. The brewery families were represented by Molson, Dow, and Dawes. Then the great Jewish names Sassoon, Sebag-Montefiore, de Soula, the Davises, the Josephs, the Judahs and the latest and most powerful of the new arrivals—the phenomenal Bronfmans, from bootleggers to billionaires. This somewhat mixed bag of local éminence grise would convene regularly at a cheeky little boîte known as Café Martin. I would hang in there after school and soak up the atmosphere.

I once got a tremendous thrill when our great World War I flying ace Billy Bishop, then over seventy, sashayed into Martin's replete with boutonniere, homburg angled over one eye and two delectable blondes angled over each arm. At the bar, huddled together in intrigue, two young avocats, Canada's future political icon, Pierre Elliott Trudeau, and his mortal opposition, René Lévesque, probably carving up the country between them.

It was Mark Twain who said that you can't throw a brick anywhere in Montreal without breaking a church window. That also could have been said of its nightspots. There was an old saying around town that you could enjoy a different nightclub for every day of the year. That wasn't far wrong, for our unique metropolis with a lascivious wink could smugly boast that it never closed, that it had more clubs, casinos and whorehouses than you could shake a stick at, where jaded New Yorkers—especially during Prohibition—who had run out of trouble could be easily replenished by simply staggering across the border.

In an abortive attempt to clean things up, Quebec's ruthless and humourless premier Maurice Duplessis passed an edict which became known as the Padlock Law. He ordered the police to close down every house of ill repute in the city. It was such a profitable business, however, attracting so many important customers, including one or two Supreme Court justices, that the police, principal profiteers themselves, had to come up with something. They did. They locked up the front doors of the whorehouses but left the back doors open.

Entertainment was at a premium, and with all those languages floating around, we got the best and the tackiest imports and I was determined to take 'em all in with a vengeance. My mother worked late every day at the Handicrafts Guild and would come home and cook us dinner, but the minute dinner was over, I was out of there—no thought in my head that she might be hurt or concerned. I was on the move; there was too much temptation in that town. I had fallen in love with the night.

Down the street from Mum's flat was the exclusive privately owned Ritz-Carlton Hotel. Charles Hosmer, with the support of Sir Herbert Holt, Sir Montagu Allan and other wealthy Golden Milers, pigeonholed the famous Cézar Ritz of Paris to give the proposed building his blessing and his name. He did so and on its completion in 1912, it became the second-oldest Ritz on the continent after Boston's. At fifteen years old, I used to monopolize its Maritime Bar, guzzling freshly opened Malpeque oysters by the baker's dozen, washed down with Molson's or Dawes Black Horse Ale as I ogled local society scampering past. Conveniently across the hall from my perch was the elegant Ritz Café. There the accent was on sophistication so we got Lucienne Boyer, Mabel Mercer, Jean Sablon, Charles Trenet, Jacqueline François and Carl Brisson; then the pianists, Shearing, Fats Waller, Errol Garner, Art Tatum and, of course, Oscar, who by now had securely planted his star in the firmament. I sat marvelling at George Shearing, whom I later befriended. I was astounded that someone so totally without sight could play with such dexterity and so beautifully. He made blindness seem an asset and, being a true musician, his imaginative arrangements of "Tenderly," "Roses of Picardy," "Lullaby of Birdland"—anything he chose to give us—had a musical style quite its own. Classically sound, he would occasionally color his tunes with the harmonies of Debussy, Ravel or Satie in a most witty fashion. He also interspersed his sessions with some very clever repartee and with that exquisite touch of his he could silence a room at once. When, very rarely, people at the back tables continued talking during a number, George would stop dead, stare them down (he could always tell where they were) and remark with acid politeness—"Oh, do go on, please. I was only playing softly so I could hear what you were saying."

All season long, our own Johnny Gallant presided at the Ritz piano, smoothly accompanying regulars Suzi Solidor, Hildegarde, Celeste Holm, a sleek Anne Francine and a beauty with ebony tresses and a sultry voice named Monica Boyar. There was also on view the striking, very cool blues singer Josephine Premise. I had such a crush on this beautiful black lady, you wouldn't believe, so I turned myself into a sort of groupie—her veritable man Friday. She let me sit and watch her act every night as her guest and then she would join me at the table. I thought my golden moment had come, but all she wanted to discuss was how crazy she was over Frank Sinatra, with whom she had shared a tryst. She transformed me into some sort of personal telephone operator whose sole mission was to reach Ol' Blue Eyes at all costs from her hotel room nightly. Tough assignment, considering he was in Africa madly chasing Ava Gardner.

Along with my school chum young Lynch-Staunton, who always had an "in," I would crash as many parties as I could around town where I might rub shoulders with the local legends. Montreal's leading impresario, Jean Lallemand, a strutting peacock of a man who dressed his chauffeurs in the same matching colours as his two-tone Rolls-Royces, threw fabulous after-concert suppers. He had great flair and they were very grand indeed. I was present one night when Leonard Bernstein, then in his twenties, a guest piano soloist with Les Concerts Symphoniques, was feeling particularly boisterous. He promptly sat down at Lallemand's precious grand, took off his socks and proceeded to pick out with miraculous dexterity some intricate tune with his bare feet. Monsieur Lallemand, not amused, muttered to anyone in earshot, "He ith rooinin' my betht peeano!" Leonard, ignoring him, explained to the room that it was being treated to Bernstein's Concerto for Right Foot.

Next, I'm nursing a beer at the Chez Paree, gaping openmouthed at the young Billy Daniels, Sinatra (back in town at the request of mobster and owner Harry Shipp), Tony Martin, even Judy Garland. Sinatra, if not in the right mood, would sometimes "throw the show." He would publicly humiliate the band and merely phone the whole thing in. On one such night, some of "the Boys" were out front. Afterwards, so the story goes, they went backstage and offered to take him for a "ride" if he didn't shape up. For the remainder of the gig, Frank sang like an angel.

Then I would sneak into the El Morocco to watch Milton Berle or Sophie Tucker; Dede Pastor and Charles Aznavour were visible in les boîtes on Rue St.-Laurent. Edith Piaf sang at the Sans Souci—tiny Edith, a pathetic birdlike figure in a simple black frock, her pale white face and matted hair illuminated by cruel lighting, let loose her songs of the streets and sent shivers down your spine. There was a bitterness, a bravery and a poignancy about them; that such an outpouring of sound and passion could come from such a minute frame boggled the mind. I would haunt Edith, wherever she sang, for the rest of her life.

How lucky I was at my age to have seen Louis Armstrong, the great Ella, Lady Patachou and the fabulous Kay Thompson. And over at Carol's Samovar, although I never saw her, a young chanteuse regularly appeared named Angela Lansbury. Then at Chez Maurice, all the big bands—Basie, Miller, Dorsey, Kenton, Cab Calloway—and the jazz, the jazz! I was swept away by a tornado of talent, all of which had an immense impact on my life. If they could hold a rowdy crowd filled with drink spellbound—the hypnotic powers necessary to our profession were worth investigating. After every such nocturnal adventure, I would walk home acting out everything I'd seen, singing at the top of my lungs all the material I'd memorized, shouting it out to the tall cathedral spires along Sherbrooke Street—my only audience.

The real downtown (Vieux-Montréal itself) was where the future was on the boil in tiny clubs and holes-in-the-wall—the French Canucks emptying their hearts, folk singers, revolutionaries, the political satirists—the true rebels stirring up a new anger, the poets of the night. And in the wee hours down at the old Martinique among a crowd of beer-swilling toughs the great Mistinguette at age eighty was still giving us her apache dance and showing her "million-dollar legs"!

We all sat there waiting for la Grande Dame to make her entrance. What a surly lot! Every drunken, brawling backwoodsman was there that night. The noise was earsplitting—it wasn't possible that this rabble could ever be silenced. All of a sudden, there was a skirmish directly behind us at the entrance doors to the club and a lot of screaming. The bouncers were trying in vain to evict an old bag lady who was yelling a lot of French cusswords the likes of which I'd never heard before in my life! "Sortez, Madame! Sortez!" they shouted, and she would scream back in a guttural, whiskey voice—"Bien non! Non! Je veux chanter! Je veux chanter!" They tried to explain to her that only Mistinguette was allowed to sing here, but it was too late. The old bag jostled and fought her way past them and was now staggering between the tables on her way to the stage. She was a ghastly sight to behold, decked out as she was in all her filthy rags. Suddenly a blue spotlight hit the old crone full in the face. She stopped dead in her tracks at the center of that motley multitude and began to sing "Mon Homme," the song that had been written for her so long ago. The silence was deafening—in one second she had us *all* in the palm of her hand—there was not a dry eye in the house.

That was what it was about! That was a star! It was Mistinguette herself all right! And moments after, she had quick-changed out of her rags and was being hurled about in the apache dance wearing a skintight leotard that showed off her hourglass figure and those incredible legs. Not bad for eighty! Sometimes the lowliest of dives can give birth to the loftiest of memories—for that entrance of hers and what followed was certainly one of the most astonishing coups de théâtre I have ever witnessed!

A COUP DE THÉÂTRE of another kind was about to make itself known—for one day, Miss Diana Barrymore came to town. She was

Diana with her father, the great John Barrymore

doing a nightclub stint at the old Mount Royal Hotel. A friend introduced me and I was knocked out of my socks to meet the great John's
daughter! I didn't realize she was on the skids and doing this hard-sell
tour to pay her drinking debts. She was truly a *victim,* was Diana. Most
of her act was pretty awful — some not-too-terrific imitations of famous
personalities (including her dad) and some exceedingly off-colour jokes
and jargon. People came to see her because of the legendary Barrymore
signature, but Diana was generally pretty inebriated and would stop in
the middle of her act to reprimand the waiters in her father's stentorian
tones if they so much as rattled a single dish. Because of her eminent
family the promoters had insisted on modestly billing her as "The
Crown Princess of the Theatre." She was only in her late twenties and
although neither of us had the faintest clue then, time for her was
swiftly running out.

> *J'ai ta main dans ma main.*
> *Je joue avec tes doigts.*

She had a dark animal look about her, not beautiful, but sensual, arresting, and she sang songs in French—vraiment comme une ange! I am positive that had she known what discipline meant, she could have been a really wonderful actress, for she was riddled with hidden talent. By now I was a grown-up sixteen and sorely stuck on her! The rebel in her appealed to me divinely—she was "real wicked *bad*"! I never paid for anything, meals or drinks—she was one of the kindest women I've known. I guess underneath the bravado she was a lonely soul and liked the attention a worshipping idiot swain like myself lavished on her, so I was allowed to hang about. When I was fourteen, I had just about memorized cover to cover Gene Fowler's *Good Night, Sweet Prince* about John Barrymore's dynamic career and outrageous high jinks. It was the book that decided me on my future.

One of Barrymore's many wives was a stunningly striking and eccentric lady of means called Blanche Oelrichs who preferred to be known as Michael Strange. Diana was their offspring. I shamelessly showed off my knowledge of the Barrymores to her and in return she would regale me with a delicious lot of family dirt, especially concerning her father. She seemed quite obsessed by him. We would drink, smoke and talk for hours in her hotel room, she, sultry and brooding, a Madame de Montespan, draped seductively over her bed, naked as the day she was born and I, in a chair opposite her, bolt upright, fully clothed, ridiculously formal, pretending I hadn't noticed.

One night she was asked for after-dinner drinks by some very posh people in town who had known the Oelrichs side of the Barrymore clan. She instructed me, in no uncertain terms, to come along as her escort. Diana had already primed herself for the evening and was well on her way. So indeed was I. When we arrived, I realized that my hostess was a friend of Mother's. My God! What was I to do?! Although very polite, they were an awfully stuffy lot and they looked at the two of us as if we were from outer space. In order not to panic and to somehow justify my presence, I boldly sat down at the piano, hoping to accompany Diana in a French song or two. She hadn't known I could play—was very surprised and mightily relieved. She winked at me and took up the cue. As was her custom, she had decked herself out in a daringly revealing low-cut dress. In the middle of a song in order to emphasize a phrase, she made a sweeping theatrical gesture, miles over the top, when suddenly, not just *one* but *two* glorious breasts popped out in full view and stayed out for the rest of the number. Even after it was over, they were still out—I suppose Diana was too far gone to notice. Gauche was my middle name as I tried to revive the old gag about the waiter with a warm spoon, etc., etc.—there was nothing but deadly silence! They finally found their manners again, that poor shocked little gathering, and were nice enough to give us some mild applause as we bundled ourselves together and made a hasty retreat into the snow and to the nearest pub where we could drown our questionable triumph in a gallon of stingers.

DUE TO MY appalling sense of timing and the fact that I was somewhat underage—I just happened to miss the Second World War (a rather embarrassingly large chunk of history to let slip by, you might say)!—I felt a little left out, for at the time my cousins and older friends were "over there" getting decorated on a regular basis for acts of bravery and derring-do whilst I had to be content with sitting at home for the entire duration—listening to the whole damn thing on the radio!

We lived by the "wireless" then. I had barely stopped teething before I'd heard George V's garbled Christmas messages crackling over the airwaves, Edward VIII's rather weak but terribly human abdication speech, Roosevelt being very impressive, our own dry little prime minister Mackenzie King doing his pedantic best—then George V's amazingly sombre and grandiose funeral service echoing through the Abbey; and following hot on its heels, the halting, stuttering, gentle George VI trying valiantly to assume control of his speech and his nation.

We heard the slimy voice of "Lord Ha-Ha," Hitler and his bad German, the piercing oratory of Herr Goebbels and, of course, Churchill—Churchill and then Churchill—Pickwick as the God of War or a militant Falstaff, cheering us on with his great command of the language and its wit. We sat, tensely listening for the daily "missing" lists—the horrors of Dunkirk, the disgrace at Dieppe. Then Big Ben, sonorous but comforting; *L for Lanky,* the serial made in Canada about life aboard a Lancaster bomber; the utterly unruffled-by-war programme *The Archers,* produced by the BBC, a comforting and affectionate part of one's daily life.

Then on the home-front stations, we could hear our own mayor, Monsieur Houde, urging everyone in Quebec not to join up—"It isn't our war"—a bit late as everybody had been embroiled in it from day one! Camillien Houde was fat, ugly, bombastic, full of oozing charm and a two-faced bully. He was also notorious for continuously making insufferable faux pas. At a banquet at Montreal's Windsor Hotel in honour of Their Majesties George VI and Queen Elizabeth, Houde,

Mayor Houde with their Majesties — good luck!

according to my mother, who was present, concluded his welcoming salutation by saying in broken English, "Your majesties, I wan' to tank you from de bottom of my heart—and Madame Houde—she tanks you from her bottom too!"

When conscription was in full flower in Quebec, everyone got religion. The priesthood was suddenly bombarded with applications from young men running away from the draft. There were more priests than ever—thousands—beneath every cassock, a draft dodger. You could see them in winter joining their brethren on their skis, clogging up the hills—there was hardly room for anyone else. If you stood at the bottom, there they came, barrelling down upon you, so close together they looked like a Breughel painting in an earthquake. Then Mayor Houde tried to stop conscription altogether ("Why should we fight d'ere warr—it's none of our business?") but nobody listened anymore and in a matter of days he was safely in Sing Sing. The irony was that Les Fusiliers de Montréal and the famed Régiment Vingt Deux, two of our crack French Canadian battalions, had already proved themselves some of the toughest and bravest fighters on the European and African front. Well, that was my war and I'd missed it, just as I'd missed my baptism, my catechism, probably my circumcision—and God knows what! It couldn't help cross my mind—was I to miss college as well?

I blindly recall my entrance examination to McGill! There was that moment of ghastly tension and unbearable suspense as the questionnaire was being passed around—the same tension I was to feel in later life in those few moments before watching my first "corrida." No difference really—in both cases, I was about to witness death! The questions blurred and ran into each other as I stared vacantly down at them; I felt a mounting nausea, so I averted my eyes and looked out the window. One of those perfect spring days was in progress—with the tiny crocuses and trilliums peeping so optimistically through the rapidly melting snow.

It was all too inviting. I exchanged glances with my ol' pal Lynch-Staunton, a few "pews" away. He had just recently appeared with me in an amateur production of *As You Like It,* in which he contributed hugely. Though he had no lines to speak whatever, he came on wearing several dead branches as a headdress by which he represented the entire Forest of Arden. I liked him for the simple reason that he was out for a good time. Over the shaky scholastic years we had shared many similar tests of terror at cram schools such as "Jenning's Hoscatorial" or "Barney's Barn for Backward Bastards." So, "Who the Christ needs this?!" was obviously the question on both our minds. After all, with his mum's money he could probably *buy* McGill, and with my talent and genius it was all redundant anyway! We both grabbed our pens simul-

"John Five" (the once and future senator)

taneously, scribbled across the answer foolscap in huge scrawl, "I HAVEN'T THE FAINTEST FUCKING IDEA!"—and ran from the room out into the warm and, in our case, exceedingly *brave* new world. I think we both turned out okay in the end, in spite of it; I was to enjoy some success on the stage in the Theatre of Starvation, and he, out of the woods of Arden at last, on the Senate, in the Theatre of the Absurd.

CHAPTER SIX

She speaks poniards, and every word stabs:
if her breath were as terrible as her terminations,
there were no living near her;
she would infect to the north star.

— MUCH ADO ABOUT NOTHING

Cachow! Thwack! A hot burning stab in the neck and the sidewalk came up and hit me—my nose indented in the pavement like a Grauman's Chinese imprint. Not for long. I was roughly jerked back onto my feet; a burly, smelly, tattooed arm encircled my jaw in a pressure hold, which gave me a lip any Ubangi would have killed for! My leathery, swollen mouth still locked in that massive grip rendered conversation a definite no-no, I just managed a faint gargle as with one swift jab in the coccyx I was shot through the air into a waiting sedan. My female companion was faring somewhat better—she was still giving the other goon an evening to remember! Already she had winded him severely with a karate chop to the food basket—now, she was working on his groin. The two goons, by the way, were plainclothes city cops, my formidable lady friend, none other than the Founder/Producer/Designer/Builder of The Mountain Playhouse, where I was currently appearing in support of that funniest of ladies and niece of one of America's first cardinals—young Elaine Stritch. The performances were being given in summer atop Mount Royal.

Joy Thompson Asselin was one of those heroic, once-in-a-lifetime creatures who knows no fear, rides horses bareback, shinnies up flagpoles, wrestles, heaves the shot put and generally makes most strong men look like sissies! Behind this bionic facade she was exceedingly feminine—warm, gentle, kind and painfully shy. Because of her shyness which was agonizing to the point of speechlessness—she drank! She drank enough for twenty stevedores and then, God love her, no one was more hilarious, eccentric, daring or dangerous! This female Rambo, with her own money, energy and love, was one of the prime innovators and pioneers of professional English theatre in our country. An extraordinarily talented designer of sets, she insisted on building and painting them herself, working right through the long nights to meet her own hair-raising deadlines. She never slept. She chose the plays, directed them, bought old warehouses, converted them to workshops, gave encouragement and employment to young talent from all over Canada and imported her "stars" through her connections with New York's famed Irwin Piscator Institute where she studied with and had become close friends of Stritch and Marlon Brando. In fact, she was built very like the young Brando—muscles rippling on a superbly circus-trimmed torso, Grecian in its perfection, not an ounce of fat anywhere! Strong as an ox, she was not one to be on the wrong side of; if she liked you she'd fight to the death for you, which, as it happens, she was doing at this very moment. The goon she was busy mauling finally managed to disentangle himself and join his partner in the front seat as our car lurched forward, tires screeching, its solitary prisoner, me, with the big lips in the back. Through the rear window I watched my female protector become a tiny dot in the distance, still covered in paint, still shouting obscenities!

After that night's performance everyone in the cast had hit the town. Joy T. and I, the last upstanding braves, had ended up doing the "wee hours" joints. Outside a favourite slimeball dump called Aldo's, we had both made a horrific scene 'cause the bouncer (a newly hired baby-ape) decided I was too young, wouldn't let us enter and called the fuzz! Hence our predic!

Well, back at the ranch, the goons, positive they could simultaneously win at Indianapolis and Le Mans, were hurtling me to a station way out east of the city, bien loin, where they locked me up. Not wishing me to feel lonely, the sweet things thoughtfully paid me the odd visit every now and then just to rough me up again. I was getting pretty tired and bloody and couldn't understand why "disturbing the peace," which was what I'd been charged with, warranted all this violence. With every poke, punch and pummel they would shout in my

Joy Thompson with a young John Gielgud

face "Fargole! Faggot! Faggot!" I couldn't understand that either till I caught sight of myself in the cell's broken-down mirror. Christ! In my haste to leave the theatre, I had not only forgotten to remove my costume bottoms (tights, that is) but my makeup as well, so my face, what was left of it, was entirely smeared with lipstick and rouge! I looked, my dear Oscar, like some rumpled mangled version of your poor friend Dorian Gray!

It was now 8:oo a.m. I could barely stand, bruised and beaten as I was by Montreal's "finest," when I heard a familiar voice yelling in the street outside. My heart leapt for Joy (no pun intended)! She'd found me! but how? Then I remembered her other last name—Asselin! Of course! I'd forgotten, she was still married to "Big Eddie" Asselin, Montreal's commissioner of police. In a flash I was released, doors unlocked, boots echoing down corridors, heels clicking, goons bowing and scraping effusive apologies as Madame Asselin and her charge made their sweeping exit. It wasn't as smooth and sweeping as we might have wished, however, for Madame had brought a flask along to keep her spirits up and by now was completement blotto! We kept ricocheting off the walls of buildings as we groped our way along the courtyard and she would every now and then turn back to scream at the goons, sheep-

*Critic Herbert Whittaker, who gave us would-be
young artists such confidence*

ishly but suspiciously watching us, "I'll have your jobs in the morning you bastards—you sons of bitches—you filthy . . ." I can't go on. At one point, her anger having stirred her to a new peak of frenzy, she started back toward them, threatening to have their lives all over again. My heart sank, for I knew we'd both be locked up for eternity. With all my remaining strength I roughly pulled her back, and the two of us, our heads splitting from the night's revels, staggered out into the punishing morning sun, which like some harsh and unforgiving judge, granted no mercy in its rays.

A TINY NUCLEUS of such dotty and dedicated "angels" with their hearts in the right place did their level best for the arts in English-speaking Montreal. With loving care they managed to keep the standard of theatre, for instance, in spite of its being mostly amateur, remarkably high. Herbert Whittaker, the devoted reviewer on the *Gazette* (later, *The New York Times* and Toronto's *Globe and Mail*) gave me a most encouraging notice for my Darcy in *Pride and Prejudice* at

Montreal High back in 1945. It instantly went to my head. But I wasn't alone. He literally scoured the country in order to discover and promote new talent and bring it to the fore. Herbie did something few critics ever do; without once forsaking his pen he became a "straddler." He boldly climbed over the footlights onto our side and before you could say "George Spelvin," he had established himself as a first-rate director and one of the country's best set designers. He directed and designed productions for the Montreal Repertory Theatre, McGill's Moyse Hall, and the Trinity Players; he paid equal attention to the creative ethnic development in the city, serving the local Negro Theatre, the Young Men's Hebrew Association and a French Canadian company called L'Équipe where he staged plays of quality in French. In a land consumed with reticence toward its young artists, Whittaker stood by and encouraged all of us beginners. He did this both as a journalist and man of the theatre.

> *While most all local "crits" were busy snappin' at our ass*
> *Dear Uncle Herbie made us feel that we could be world class!*

Another faithful supporter, my own high-school English teacher, Doreen Lewis, ran the Montreal Repertory Theatre (MRT) where, recommended by Whittaker, I began. The MRT had been created by Mum's friend Martha Allan many years before, but now Doreen managed it as smoothly and professionally as if it had been the Theatre Guild. I made my debut there, age sixteen, in François Mauriac's *Asmodée,* directed by a young genius only two years older than myself— a poet and writer who ran the aforementioned Théâtre de l'Équipe. His name was Pierre Dagenais and with his pale complexion and flowing scarves he resembled the dying Chopin or the young Coleridge. He once went to jail for refusing to pay the outrageous entertainment tax. Pierre, precocious from birth, would have inspired Rimbaud had they known each other and, like Rimbaud, he was taken from this earth disastrously young. I don't recall how he died, but I'm sure it was from something characteristically romantic. There was a madness and an innocence about his prodigious talent that was pure gold and Canada is much the poorer for his absence.

Two years later, at the MRT, I played Oedipus in Cocteau's *La Machine infernale.* "Un acteur de grande classe—une interprétation magistrale," the critic from *La Presse* wrote. Because of this extravagance, my head had now swelled to grotesque proportions, and I had

My first Oedipus, age nineteen, in Cocteau's La Machine infernale

also collected along the way a few more devils of my own. To quell them I began to drink more heavily than usual.

One night, young Oedipus turned up at the stage door, eyes like sockets blind before his time, far too inebriated to go on. When admonished, Oedipus made a terrible scene, insisting he was in peak condition and quite capable of being more brilliant than ever. I don't really know what happened—they probably made an announcement of some sort, but I don't recall—the whole night remains an utter blank. All I do remember is that the next day I knew I'd let down a lot of good people who had faith in me and had given me a chance—especially my mother. As usual she never showed it, God bless her; she was always so tired at the end of a day's work, but I was slowly getting the message that she was worried sick.

In the eastern townships at Knowlton Quebec, Madge and Filmore Sadler, loving fans of the stage, ran a semiprofessional summer theatre called Brae Manor, which gave to a lot of talent its first thrust. A very young *me* replaced an ailing actor overnight as Faulkland in Sheridan's *The Rivals.* I crammed in the car on the way out from the city, learned most of it, but once before an audience I dried up completely and utterly! In desperation, throwing all cares to the wind, I departed considerably from the elegant Restoration style and shouted at the cute lit-

Young Mordecai Richler, satirist extraordinaire

tle babe prompting in the wings, "What the hell's the line, darling?" It brought the house down. I gained my composure and carried on, but the prompter, who had been shamefully perusing a comic book instead of the text, was so taken aback she passed out!

Poets and writers of English prose furtively lurked behind the scenes before bursting out all over as did A. M. Klein, Irving Layton and a young up-and-coming Leonard Cohen. Straight prose on both sides was represented by the senior Hugh MacLennan, the younger Mavis Gallant, Gabrielle Roy speaking out so touchingly for the working-class French and, about to raise his head above the Jewish ghettos of St. Urbain Street, the youthful satirist Mordecai Richler, whom I was lucky enough to get to know. He was poised, ready to give us his *Son of a Smaller Hero* and *Duddy Kravitz*, warming us up for an abundance of treasures to come.

As far as English theatre was concerned, there were many basements and caves from which it fought to emerge, but the leaders of the artistic community were, quite naturally and quite properly, the French. Not as constricted as we "maudit Anglais," they were far freer to express themselves. They also had quite considerable cause to gripe politically, which gave birth to a stable full of extremely gifted authors and playwrights. Quebec Province began to pour out French-language films of high quality and originality. In this regard, they were streaks ahead of the rest of the country.

Quite naturally I began to savor the Gallic flavour more than any other and became a staunch follower not just of the local films but of the great cinema from France in the thirties and forties. I would spend most of my time in movie houses mooning over such gems from Paris as *Un Carnet de Bal, La Règle de Jeu, La Grand Illusion, Les Enfants du Paradis* and all the Pagnol masterpieces. They were my inspiration. Instead of Gable, Tracy and the old gang, I now saw myself as Fresnay, Gabin, Raimu, Blanchar, Brasseur and Philipe all rolled into one! So, armed with this gargantuan and repellent confidence, I boldly planted both feet firmly upon those very "boards" where no man who has a modicum of wisdom in him should ever tread.

AN OFFSPRING of the Clouston dynasty, another child of Boisbriant, with the tuneful name of Rosanna Seaborn Todd, had formed a secret alliance with Mother to encourage me toward the stage. God knows they had to, for I was useless at anything else. Rosanna's Cree blood (Swampy Cree, that is) had given her face its darkly striking beauty, but her personality left very little room for doubt that she came out of the womb "acting"! As a teenager with oodles of time on her hands, she had thrown herself passionately into directing, writing and "starring" in home movies, which boasted such epic titles as "Gone with the Birth of a Nation" and "Passionate Prairies"! In her formative years, when not enjoying a brief but successful sojourn on the London stage, she would restlessly roam the globe as a permanent unpaying guest carelessly dropping bits of her considerable wardrobe all over the floors of such houses as Max Beaverbrook's, the Maharajah of Jaipur's or her school chum Doris Duke's. In her later years, she adopted a grande manière, part chatelaine, part film star. Lunching with her in a restaurant was like sharing a snack with Eleanor of Aquitaine. But I was entranced by her "glamour," her theatricality—she was fascinating to watch and to listen to. No one so far had made the world of make-believe sound so magical.

Full of energy and enterprise, Rosie started her own theatre (also on

Rosanna Seaborn Todd,
who convinced me the theatre had magic

Montreal's mountain) which she called The Open-Air Shakespeare Company. It was modeled after Robert Atkins's famous Regent's Park Theatre in London and similarly dedicated to the Bard. She then assembled an astonishing assortment of youngsters, some who would become well-known names later in life, and managed to employ one or two distinguished directors from England to help polish us "rude mechanicals" from the colonies. But "Rose-Pose" insisted on playing all the leading female roles. Well, why not? After all, it was her show! She had an exquisite speaking voice, but her acting style slightly out-Pola'd Negri and out-Gloria'd Swanson. Although Shakespeare had furnished her with some fairly adequate material, the way she insisted on helping him along seemed to indicate it wasn't quite good enough. As an entrepreneuse and rallier of spirits, however, she was splendid—a veritable Lilian Baylis! She also paid some of us—just as Joy T. had done. Think of it, at seventeen I had turned pro!

As I was just too young to own a license, Rosanna became my chauffeuse, giving me lifts back and forth from the theatre every night. Though she drove very slowly indeed (too busy talking to drive fast) she never stayed very long on her side of the road and, gesturing extravagantly, her hands off the wheel, she was too caught up in her own world to notice oncoming cars swerving crazily to miss us. One night, on the way back from the theatre, having had a tad too much booze, I suddenly felt somewhat overly affectionate. As any brash, lecherous seventeen-year-old would, I put my hand firmly on her leg, considerably above the knee. She froze and I instantly withdrew my paw. That seemed to be her only reaction except that the car had now left the road entirely and we were bumping along most uncomfortably through an adjacent cow pasture the entire rest of the way home in a tense and thoughtful silence.

"SWIFTER THAN ARROW from the Tartar's bow," the next year and a half (overcrowded with incident) simply flew by!! One of Rosie's "distinguished." Brit directors, a dishevelled old sheepdog called Malcolm Morley, put me on the payroll (twenty-five bucks a week) at Canada's only year-round professional repertory company, the new Stage Society, later the Canadian Repertory Theatre. The job—dogsbody, propman, small parts as cast; the location—a place once called Bytown, now Ottawa, the nation's capital. Press fast-forward—sweet innocent little town on a windy hill, whose idea of sin was taking tea with a nun at the Bytown Inn. Two or three tall parliament buildings on its summit, that's about all, except for tacky dilapidated old Catholic Académie La Salle (a school for priests) now quite properly converted to a theatre, my new home. One snag—the priests had to be consulted on censorship; they got to read all the plays first! The programme—a play a week; the company—very good-grand old refugees from Broadway, London and Dublin's Abbey and a sprinkling of Canucks. Me a complete cretin as propman soon shared leads with fellow wetback Derek Ralston, a dazzling light comedian on- and offstage. Derek and I became partners in crime—did the town (what there was of it, nothing to do but drink)—found it easier across the bridge in neighbouring Hull (part of Quebec), open twenty-four hours a day—we worked like hell and lived like Hull! Always in debt—oh well, charge it to Mother—our memories began to collapse—we were so damned mixed-up—how could you learn *Glass Menagerie* and *Private Lives* at one and the same time? It got to the point that onstage, we couldn't look each other in the eye without corpsing—how about giving bits of *Hamlet* and *Charley's Aunt* in *Room Service*? So we fell about giggling. The poor weekly audience had by now caught on and forgave—result of confusion, we learned to ad-lib superbly, Derek quite spectacularly deft at handling his props, a veritable Cary Grant; my other favourites—sweet little Amelia Hall

(Canada's Helen Hayes) and a comforting old sod named Sam Payne who could charm an audience out of its socks even when talking rubbish, which he mostly did—"We get our kicks from Sam Payne, dear Millie Hall doesn't thrill us at all, so tell me why should it be true, that we get a kick out of you!" Not true. Millie did thrill us—a dynamo as an actress.

"Millie" Hall, an early boss of mine, as Maria in Twelfth Night

Theatre now began running out of money. I was down to two suits (to be used in every production—and fifty more roles to play—Jesus! I got cunning, thrifty, wore my shirts back to front when portraying clergy, slept in my nicely pressed suit to crumple it up for geriatric parts (hated playing my own age, much better at crumbling decrepitude). As an ancient vicar (*The Passing of the Third Floor Back*), I gave my best, unrecognizable eighty-three one dreary matinée when the assistant stage manager (ASM) whispered a man named Plummer wanted to see me backstage after the show—Christ! It must be my father! We'd never *met*, never even *seen* each other! Hot damn! He must have been having a stroke out there watching his prematurely decayed offspring, an old bent wreck of a crone with white hairs, looking years older than himself!

We met—hemmed, hawed and shuffled in embarrassment as I feverishly smudged away the filthy greasepaint to reveal my seventeen years. Much relieved, he managed to stammer a few incomplete sentences—the suspense was awful—I felt so sorry for him. God! It took guts to show up! I took him to the unglamourous beer hall for supper. Things looked a little better, except, still nervous, I started to get diarrhea of the mouth. Now it was his turn. He fed me tidbits of Plummer family history I knew nothing about, assuring me I was not the only thespian in the family. My cousin Sir Michael Bruce (baronet and journalist), who resided in Vancouver, had a brother called Nigel, my second cousin. Nigel was that well-known character actor, hugely entertaining as a bumbling Dr. Watson opposite Basil Rathbone in the Sherlock Holmes films. Nigel "Willie" Bruce was also a member in good standing of the so-called Hollywood Raj in British-dominated Tinseltown of the thirties and had made heaps of movies, among my favourites *Rebecca* and *Frenchman's Creek.*

It appeared the Plummers and the Bruces were old mining families in Britain and Canada, and Michael and Nigel with their highly coloured Bruce tartan careened directly back to thirteenth-century Scotland and King Robbie the Bruce himself—not exactly an anemic bloodline! At this knowledge, I downed a few more—in fact, we both got a tad tiddly. I think he started to have a good time. He was a nice guy really—I was beginning to quite like him—another time, ah well—it was all too late and we both knew it. Our paths would cross once or twice again in our lifetimes and then no more—no big deal, no sweat.

On rare breaks I took the train to New York to "second act it" at most of the shows and caught some late nightlife. Armed with an introductory letter from his aunt I met fellow Montrealer Robert Ward Labatt Whitehead, who had become a big hotshot Broadway producer (at that moment presenting Julie Harris and Ethel Waters in Carson McCullers's *The Member of the Wedding*). Kindness itself, he showed me his plush offices, presented me to his partner Oliver Rea, told me he had nothing to offer me, sent his love to his aunt and showed me the way out. Later I became attached to Oliver and his warm, delightful wife, Betty, and of course Robert, or "Ratty," as he is now affectionately nicknamed, was to be a lifelong ami-propre. Always dapper, handsome, replete with old-world charm and a ferret nose for business, his expression every so often took on a sudden faraway look of longing as if yearning to break loose—very much a characteristic of the Rat in Kenneth Grahame's *The Wind in the Willows,* hence "Ratty." I left the then-mighty formidable Ratty and snuck off with Marian Seldes to watch Maurice Evans and Edna Best in Rattigan's *The Browning Version* which we would do back in Ottawa in two weeks time—me causing a small stir as the old professor simply because I cheated disgracefully by giving a direct and rather accurate imitation of Mr. Evans, if I may say so myself!

Some saint called Southgate saw to it we pull through financially for a while longer. Amazingly the loyal little audience still supported us—they'd got used to us by now. Also it was way below zero Fahrenheit in Ottawa—maybe they just came down to the academy to snuggle up with us and keep warm. I fell in with a crinkly loveable curmudgeon, Budge Crawley of Crawley Films, a true pioneer of the cinema, who gave me my first film part in one of his "short" subjects. Crawley had

Robert "Ratty" Whitehead, Broadway producer extraordinaire,
handsome dog, a friend and fellow Montrealer

started his career with another great camera pioneer, Robert Flaherty (*Nanook of the North*) and had since garnered an Oscar or two for his courageous documentaries, one of them *The Man Who Skied Down Everest.* He also fathered the National Film Board. I was thankful for his belief in me, but ungraciously and stupidly, I shunned celluloid and adopted toward it a repulsively snobbish disregard.

Anyway, I was frightfully busy now—sorry, my time was not my own. You see I was having my first real *serious* love affair—not smooth! She was married—and what's more, her husband was always around. She was several years my senior. She was also the leading lady, so sometimes we met only onstage. God! I was hooked! I now knew what jealousy meant. When she went home to him at night, I paced up and down outside the house for hours, mumbling abusive threats, sobbing loudly like some mooncalf, vowing that I'd kill myself. I actually was plotting how best to kill him! When we were together, though, in private or public, we couldn't keep our hands off each other—it was so urgent, so new—we touched all the time—oh the pain of it! Of course, we "did it" everywhere, anywhere we could—in the dressing rooms, backstage, in public conveniences, at the back of cinemas and cars, even at parties. One night, at one of those large dress-up soirees, she was on my lap and I was inside her, her evening dress spread out over us for concealment when her husband walked in! We stayed exactly where we were, having the pleasantest of chats, the three of us, he none the wiser, while she and I slowly, gently, carefully moved our imperceptible way toward an absolutely expressionless, silent but nonetheless blinding climax! A grim lesson in underplaying. He still none the wiser, or was he? I guess I'll never know.

Lover now discovered her life was with hubby, went back to him. I was desolate, though not for long. The pain was amazingly brief. It was not the end really—the world was a big place, so I threw myself back into the arms of Thespis, the only real therapy I knew. The company was running out of money again; the saints began to scrounge. My suits were worn out and my contract was up so I took my leave of Bytown, not such an innocent little town after all, with perhaps a touch more stage savvy, considerably less virginal and gripped with the shattering revelation that the gap between Theatre and Life is remarkably infinitesimal.

CHAPTER SEVEN

Fear no more the heat o' the sun,
Nor the furious winter's rages.

—CYMBELINE

Fyodor Komisarjevsky vas vun beeg feesh and Rose-Pose Todd had caught him. "Komis" or "Kommie," as he was known to his intimates, was one of the twentieth century's most influential theatrical gurus. The famous Russian director-designer had begun in his very own theatre in St. Petersburg in the early nineteen hundreds and soon became head of the Imperial and State Theatres of Moscow. He then immigrated to Paris and London where his massive staging of operas and his presentations of the plays of Chekhov and Shakespeare were controversial and legendary. This visionary had breathed a refreshingly new and vivid life into the classics and treated them with the same sort of revolutionary irreverence with which Tyrone Guthrie was to treat them decades later. But he got there first! He had produced most of the

*Fyodor Komisarjevsky of Moscow's
Imperial Theatre and London's Old Vic*

top classical stars of the time—John Gielgud had called him "perverse, but the most contradictory and fascinating character I have ever met." He designed London's Phoenix Theatre and introduced Chekhov to British audiences at the little theatre in Barnes. His leading actress on these occasions was the young (Dame) Peggy Ashcroft, whom he subsequently married.

All his life he had remained in direct opposition to the Moscow Arts and the methods of Stanislavsky. Now I am not one to denigrate and criticize the hallowed Method, dear Lord no! It is extremely useful to actors who are lost and floundering in their interpretations and need a private source of experience to draw from but Kommie made a great deal of sense when he wrote, "An imaginative actor needs no naturalistic copies of the environment of his personal life to help him to act as he is able to transform any object before him into anything he chooses to make it. If it were possible for an actor to act by means of pure remembrance, his rendering of a character in any play other than one written by himself for himself would be a complete distortion of the work of the playwright."

Kommie had just completed his Broadway production of Dostoyevsky's *Crime and Punishment,* which starred John Gielgud and was produced by Ratty Whitehead and "O." Rea. He quite clearly missed his Shakespeare, which he hadn't presented for some time, so Rose-Pose, taking advantage of this, had the whopping great chutzpah to lure him into our midst. Here he was then, quite literally, in our neck o' the woods, up to his ears in flora and fauna and eager Montreal talent. A pixie of a man in his midseventies, he looked and behaved like an aging faun—his perpetual sly grin gave the impression he could and would, at any moment, play some wicked practical joke. His celebrated power/magic combination had, I imagine, diminished with age but even an untutored eye such as mine could detect the odd flash of creative madness that had made him such a force and a legend.

Rose-Pose had engaged him to launch her Open-Air summer season with a production of Shakespeare's *Cymbeline* with which quite obviously he had a field day. For some curious reason he set the not-too-frequently staged opus about ancient Britain smack in the middle of pre–Second Great War, and among many a controversial piece of stage business in this never dull production he ended the unwieldy play with the entire cast tramping up a little hillock and disappearing over the other side, singing full out, "We're off to see the wizard!" I had the good fortune to be cast as the leading juvenile Posthumus. I remember Kommie saying to a chap playing one of the kings, "You don't hyave to ect kink. You do notting, pliz. I vill hyave everyvun roun' you make you look like kink!" (One of those early useful zingers!) Rose-Pose gave us an Imogen full of piss and vinegar and the part of Cloten was played by Kommie's favourite of all—un autre comédien Montréalais comme moi, William Shatner.

The future Captain Kirk and I "beamed up" together in many a production in our hometown after that and particularly on radio in both French and English. Even this early, Shatner showed great promise with his versatility and light touch. Our competition for all the key principal roles was a wondrously powerful young tragedian of Latvian descent by the name of John Colicos. His voice could shatter glass and its range was unimaginable! In years to come he would play a twenty-two-year-old King Lear at London's Old Vic (their youngest Lear ever) to sensational press, and would eventually emerge as one of the theatre's very finest classical actors. But we were riddled with envy and admiration back then as he continued to steal all the cream! Radio, of course, was where the money was and bilingual radio was a thriving art industry in those days—with weekly hour-long dramas, musical extravagan-

John Colicos as Lear, age twenty-two at London's Old Vic

zas, and at least ten soap operas a day. Can you imagine an actor—and a teenage actor to boot—actually complaining that there was too much work to handle?! But there was! Shatner, Colicos and I were regulars on Rupert Caplan's weekly Bible series plus special two-hour-long Wednesday night dramas such as *The Trial* by Kafka and dozens of similar classics. Great stars such as Paul Muni would cross the border and play leads for us. I was in an English soap called *Laura Ltd* and once had the pleasure of appearing briefly on the top French serial, *La Famille Plouffe.* The little boy with the cracked voice I had listened to I don't know how many times was to my astonishment played by one of the most beautiful of dark-haired demoiselles, the French actress Ginette Letondal. She would one day be my "princess"—onstage, of course.

I became busier than a bird dog doing several other soaps for the French network, and was making pretty good money, but still dear Mum was stuck with most of the bills. She had always given me so much rope but by now she had come to the end of hers. I vowed that as soon as I'd acquired sufficient capital, I'd buy her a house. Instead of hanging out with my usual racy friends, she and I would do the town together—she'd be my date. She wouldn't have to work anymore. I'd look after her for the rest of her days. Fortified by this resolve I threw myself into my work with renewed vigour, but the excitement of it all got the better of me and my good intentions were soon forgotten.

There was a time when I was in so many soaps in both languages all at once, my calendar became so confusing that I'd forget to show up. I was enjoying a lengthier lunch than usual, one day, when it hit me in the face like a bunch of icicles that I had completely missed an entire episode in French. It was too late to run for the studio as the show was already on the air! My evil friends couldn't wait to turn on the restaurant's radio and force me to listen. I sat in dumbfounded horror as I heard my fellow actors (improvising frantically, of course) inform the listening and, I hoped by now, mourning public that *I* had tragically been killed by falling down some old deserted mine shaft! The sad thing about that scene was that it was "off mic"—I never got to play it. My timing was obviously so bad I had missed my own death.

Radio was everywhere then and it had to be, for apart from the two railroads (CPR, CNR), it was up to the Canadian Broadcasting Corporation, which was founded in 1936, to connect our oversize country and bring it closer together—and bring it closer, it did. It was the medium of the moment—how I loved it and how I miss it. I began to commute to Toronto. Now Toronto in the late forties was about the dullest city on this planet. You really *did* have to go to Buffalo to have fun. Not now, of course, for present-day Toronto is one of the finest of modern North American metropolae. But then it had nothing in it save a bunch of complacent Presbyterian-Protestant Babbitts who lived by a set of rules familiar only to the Roundheads. There were also so many bigoted bylaws and drinking restrictions one couldn't possible remember which to obey.

"Dry Toronto," Stephen Leacock had called it, or "those who live in Central America . . . Dry Tehauntepec." Leacock writes, "I found it impossible that night—I was on the train from Montreal to Toronto—to fall asleep. A peculiar wakefulness seemed to have seized upon me [and] the other passengers as well. . . . I could distinctly hear them groaning at intervals. 'Are they ill?' I asked . . . of the porter as he passed. 'No, sir,' he said, 'they're not ill. Those is the Toronto passengers.' 'All in this car?' I asked. 'All except that gen'lman you may have heard singing in the smoking compartment. He's booked through to Chicago.' " Leacock was right, and even when I arrived in the much later forties, the town still smelled of Prohibition. Toronto did have one thing, though—one redeeming thing. It had, quite possibly, the very best radio drama in the world!

For years the CBC had been thrust into war reporting and very little else until suddenly in 1944 the Stage Series hit the airways and Canada, at last, had its very own homegrown entertainment. Under the supervision and direction of an absolute master called Andrew Allan, a small exclusive group of brilliant young writers and talented character actors (boasting at least twenty-five different voices each) had begun by making extraordinary magic over the airways and sustained it for at least a decade. As one writer put it, "They managed to shatter the awful silence that characterizes Canada." They had successfully burst the bonds of nationalism and had gained recognition way beyond our borders.

Andrew was a civilized creature, stylish and urbane, and it was just the moment in our history when someone with these qualities was sorely needed. He wasted no time in organizing with Val Gielgud (head of BBC Drama and John's brother) an exchange arrangement with the "Beeb's" Third Programme. His guest artists were legendary, but for the most part he stuck to his little "team"—that homegrown ensemble that was nonpareil, unbeatable. Writers such as Lester Sinclair, Len Petersen, Harry Boyle, Jo Schull, Reuben Ship; actors Lorne Greene, Frank Peddie, Bernard Braden, Tommy Tweed, Bud Knapp, Lloyd Bochner, Don Harron, Mavor Moore and a gem of a talent, John Drainie. Orson Welles took me aside many years later when he learned I was a Canuck and pronounced stentorially that John Drainie was the best radio actor in the world. He was right. John had the gift of making his characters jump right out of the wireless and grab you where it hurts. His were documentary performances of stark reality—his hayseed farmers; his high-camp Restoration buffoons; his dry, tough contemporary heroes; and his heartbreaking Richard II all still live on in the Temple of the Ear.

There were always new works as well as classics to listen to— original productions could range from Joseph Conrad's *Heart of Darkness* to Conrad Aiken's *Mr. Arcularis* to Reuben Ship's *The Investigator* (the well-known satire on Senator McCarthy's Communist witch hunt). John Drainie's superb mimicking of McCarthy cross-examines Socrates, Milton, Spinoza and Luther and finds them all guilty. Then the episodic broadcasts—Dickens's complete *Nicholas Nickleby* and *Pickwick Papers* accompanied by a full orchestra playing Lucio Agostini's specially composed and incredibly descriptive music. His witty, bubbling score for "Christmas at Dingly Dell" was as close to the true spirit of Dickens as any music can get.

The productions had a vitality, style and urgency that never slackened; there was an ever-present sense of occasion about them. In a desert of stifling impotent conservatism where the natives wasted every waking hour wondering if they were "Brits" or "Yanks" it was an oasis of originality and daring creativity. Many Canadians had been seeking a cultural liberation from their British heritage for years and it was Andrew's sensitivity to this plight that gave us for the first time in the lively arts a real personal identity of our own—he had changed Canada's cultural scene forever.

I was so happy and privileged to work with Mr. Allan and his band of brothers. I had found a professional home there, far more exciting and comfortable than my own but, as luck would have it, it was all soon to be taken away. For that monster "Cyclops," or the "Boob Tube," or, as Don Harron more aptly christened it, "Summer Stock in an Iron Lung," had begun to rear its ugly head! The fickle government, ignoring everything else, had decided to turn its attention to this newly adopted impertinent child, so all that was left of Andrew Allan and his golden gifts to a world whose imagination he had so eloquently enriched were a few faded worn-out cylindrical discs, some saved, many rusting with age, hidden away forever, in some remote forbidden archive.

THE OFF-MICROPHONE everyday life in stultifying "Muddy York" (Toronto's original name) was considerably livened by the turbulent presence of one of the most unusual characters I have ever had the questionable fortune to encounter. His name was Kane. It could have been Charles Foster Kane (as Welles had played him)—his personal charisma was just as formidable—or the *other* Cain, for there was enough darkness in him to have done away with twenty Abels, but no, it was simply Kane. Unlike his biblical namesake, however, he was very much his brother's keeper for the small band of devoted slaves he had gathered together to form his "cult"; he protected and cared for them as fiercely as he could make them jump. I am ashamed to say I was one of them—but I wouldn't have missed it for the world.

He was in his late twenties, tall and handsome, had served in the war in the air force and at one glance he could have been taken for any successful young man on his way to a lucrative career. But his looks belied him, to put it mildly, for among his many personalities one could detect without much difficulty a Mesmer, a Pied Piper, an Aleister Crowley or a Groucho Marx. He would go to the very limits to use his demonic persuasive powers on the unsuspecting, which usually resulted in sidesplitting chaos! He was both frightening and shatteringly funny and had been blessed with enormous charm.

Professionally, Kane was a radio announcer-cum-narrator-commentator both in the United States and Canada, not particularly famous but certainly one of the best in the business. He regularly commuted between New York, Montreal, Toronto and Chicago—his polychrome voice floating over the airwaves, seductive and soothing. He made a very good salary indeed but never seemed to have any money, partly because of his enormous family of kids (some adopted), partly because he always gave it away to drunks, bums, nuns, cripples or simply burnt it whenever the mood of protest took hold.

He had left his hometown, Montreal, a bit of a war zone after his many pranks, fed up and seeking change. He had been demoted by an angry producer he thoroughly disliked who one day discovered a horse in the control booth just minutes before air time. Of course he knew at once who had done it. Kane had bribed the "boys" downstairs to put the beast on the freight elevator and take it all the way up to the third floor. As usual, he was fired on the spot. Chastised, Kane found himself deejaying a late-night "pop show." After a raunchy old recording of a lady blues singer wailing away in a dirty, cracked whiskey-soaked voice he would announce, "And that was Eleanor Roosevelt with her version of 'One for My Baby,' " or after some red-hot mama had belted out her mean jive or skat, "There goes Helen Keller doin' her thing again." He got his revenge but, further demoted, he was promptly sentenced to the lowest rung—the final insult—doing early-morning interviews out in the subzero wind and slush: "And how are you, sir, this fine morning? What do you do?" In those days the outdoor mikes were connected to power within the building by a cord fairly limited in length and Kane, in order to get out of the cold, would follow his interviewee onto a bus or streetcar, still talking. The door would close, the mike cable would snap and Kane, toasty warm at last, would not be seen for the rest of the day.

He never once ceased in his cause to fight for freedom of the spirit, his or anyone else's, but his windmills had been invisible. Now in Muddy York, then the capital of conformity, he at last could see them as plain as pikestaffs and with renewed relish began his attack. He would prowl the streets (me tagging along as a fledgling Sancho Panza) and address the tight-lipped citizens, depression written all over their long, downcast faces. "This is National Smile Week in Toronto, folks—come on, you can do it! Give us a smile." In supermarkets he would give away carton after carton of cereal or anything else to be found on the shelves, saying they were all gifts from the store "just for a smile." They smiled all right, perhaps for the first time. Then we would quickly slither out a side door to the street and gleefully watch the crowds lumbered with hundreds of cartons trying to explain to the outraged manager and cashiers that it was "Smile Week" and they'd been told everything was free.

He loved public transport—any kind, because of course the audience was captive. Out of nowhere from the back of the bus Kane would scream at the top of his lungs, rush forward to the front crying out, "Rape!! That dreadful woman tried to rape me. Driver, stop the bus and let me off—I can't stand it. Let me off now!" The driver happily complied and the bus moved on, everyone staring at a perfectly innocent-looking nun and wondering what hidden unleashed lust lay beneath her habit. One of his disciples, a pudgy, good-natured kid whose dark skin and thick hair could place him anywhere along the Gaza Strip, was called Irving Lerner. Far from stupid, Lerner could, however, make his rubberlike baby face assume the dumbest and most cretinous of expressions. Kane took instant advantage of this. He announced to an embarrassed and crowded bus that "Bongo" had just got off the boat, didn't speak any language known to man, was extremely susceptible to appearances and could express himself only by laughing or crying; if he thought someone was ugly he would laugh—beautiful, he would cry. "Bongo! That woman sitting in the corner—what you think of her?" Bongo would fall about the bus laughing hysterically.

I once was on the same sardine-packed streetcar as Kane and Bongo. They were hanging on to their straps, looming over a sweet little old lady armed with parcels who had finally found a seat. Kane began regaling the old dame with an endlessly complicated but heartrending spur of the moment histoire of Bongo's miserable and tragic life. When it was over the old lady was so overcome she got up and offered Bongo her seat. Kane took it instead, explaining that because of a rare jungle-related bone disorder caused by ill nourishment due to abject poverty, Bongo was more comfortable standing.

There was an orchestra conductor in the "light entertainment" section of the CBC not too many people warmed to—he was rather brash, loud, low on sensitivity and taste and exceedingly pleased with himself. Kane took matters into his own hands. He started spreading the totally false rumour that "higher echelons" were busy interviewing conductors from far and wide to possibly take the fellow's place. As no one at the station recognized me, Kane decided I was to be the prime contender! I was to be the new boy wonder from Vienna, the next Mahler—the messiah the music world had been breathlessly awaiting. To make the stress even more emotionally charged, I was to be blind. (He even provided a white stick.) Every time we came upon the unfortunate conductor, on the street, in the studio corridors, anywhere, Kane would whisper in my ear the command "Blind," and I would immediately go into my silent act, tapping my stick, as Kane slowly and gently led me by. This happened over and over again—in the most unlikely places. I was becoming exhausted. Once at a major hockey game we were venting our spleen at the opposing team when Kane (who had eyes in the back of his head) hissed, "Blind," and I was forced to miss the rest of the match by having to become yet again that goddamn unseeing child-genius! It eventually drove the poor man (who was not overly endowed with grey matter) to utter distraction and I believe he sent in his resignation at a later date, possibly to save himself the embarrassment of dismissal.

Kane was brilliant on the telephone. He would pick a name at random from the directory, make the call and keep the unknown person on the line for as long as he wanted. If it was an odd name, a name that tickled his warped sense of the macabre—woe betide its owner. His improvisational powers were so extraordinary he could have, had he wished, started a war. He actually did once. He picked two names, both of them men, and phoned each one as the other. He continued this at intervals until he had managed to stir up such animosity between them that to settle the matter a meeting had to be arranged. Standing on the other side of the appointed street corner, Kane watched as the two perfectly innocent, complete strangers proceeded to beat each other to a pulp.

He had invented a smooth character for himself for these phone escapades whom he christened "Harrison Martins," a cool cat who probably wore shiny suits and lifts in his shoes. Harrison and I would get on the blower, arrange assignations and work our way miraculously into the houses of people we had never set eyes on in our lives. We got to meet a lot of ladies that way. Even though these situations were fraught with danger, Harrison never did anything harmful; his only challenge was to see how far we could go. There was clearly not a lot to do in Toronto the Good in them there days—one had to search rather hard for diversions, but for a youngster like myself, trained to suppress emotions, being around this particular citizen Kane was certainly an early lesson in free expression, if nothing else.

One day Kane left Toronto—you could almost hear that old Mausoleum of Morality sigh with relief. It seemed, at the time, he had gone for good. His parting gesture was entirely in keeping. The producer and crew of his least favourite programme assignment reported for work early that morning to discover not a trace of Kane but in his place half a dozen sheep standing around the piano with a formal farewell note tied to one of them. I wondered where he'd got to and if he had taken his brood with him, that long-suffering family who adored him but who were forced to share him with his other much larger family— the lost and the downtrodden. In spite of his cruel streak, he had a huge and generous heart and would at a moment's notice turn his home into a soup kitchen for the derelict and the homeless. In the shaky postwar days he proved, as the Brits would say, damn good value. He was not afraid to be free or to free others who were afraid.

The last I heard he was living with his family, his animals and God knows who else in an old abandoned railway coach on some deserted field outside Quebec City. I know it wasn't because of hard times— that was far from the case—but because it appealed mightily to his strong sense of the bizarre, the eccentric. Before any self-righteous bigot could pronounce his doom, he had already sentenced himself to this cozy exile, locked away in his little fortress of protest, away from the world outside, which, freed from his tentacles for a while at least, could return uninterrupted to its former, more comfortable routine— dull and safe.

CHAPTER EIGHT

Bonjour ma Belle Province
Vous m'avez sonné?

It was high time for me to leave as well. I made my way from that shadowy town which had yet to come out of the closet, back into the light—the light of my very own province where I could feel the pulse of the country; and my city, my welcoming city of sin, where it was always cocktail hour, where I could find at least some madness and laughter, the serum I craved. Like a man possessed, I went from dive to dive—every one of my favourite haunts—determined to make up for lost time. My frenzy continued far into the night and ended as it always ended in the first light of dawn way down in the bowels of the town, that final call to arms, that last little outpost of sound and fury—Rockhead's Paradise! Even though it was falling to pieces, it hadn't changed. It never changed. There he was, old Rockhead, waving you in and that sly Jamaican roué "Lord Caressor" still rhyming his raunchy calypso, along with Josh White, classic, dignified, tickling the ivories till dawn, the cabaret stars, their gigs over, would appear and start to improvise. Huddled in a corner, looking somewhat used and bleary-eyed, a little cluster of carriage trade in all their furs and finery, desperately drinking their way out of an era—the local vampires who came out only after dark.

I had met them on their decline. (My bad timing again!) It didn't matter a damn, however; I was drawn to them as if by maggots—or magnets—I never know which. They were the outcast offspring of wealthy socialites (French and English, "Franglais" to be exact) who had gone astray. They'd never worked a day in their lives—you could call them failures, you could call them losers, but, at least, they were determined to "go out" in style. Their dialogue was a mixture of Coward, Rattigan, and Maugham, with distinct Rabelaisian overtones. Their biggest enemies, besides themselves, were the philistines of this world and they worshipped everything that was rebellious, left of centre or off the wall. *Time* magazine had called them "The Naughty 10." Chic, theatrical prancing peacocks, they were early pre–jet-setters bent on terrorizing the globe, but now, no longer flush, their range was limited to café-society Montreal—the only stage left to them on which they could dance their somewhat depraved dance.

Two of the more formidable among them, the leaders of the posse, were women. One was a tall, fair, strikingly beautiful ex-debutante named LaFleur—with a shock of golden tresses and legs that went on forever. Somewhere within her, there lurked a jolly, fiendish dybbuk who gave her a maniacal wit and a danger that was as lethal as the sparks she ignited from a sinuous and quite stupendous body. When LaFleur was bored or had run out of invention, she and another ex-deb, a dark-haired beauty called Rita, would prop themselves up at the bar at Carol's Samovar or any exclusive nitery, and pose as high-class hookers,

Ma grande amie, LaFleur, a mixture of
glamour and fire

just to see which of them could maka
da mosta moolah in one night! They
always managed to follow through
and quickly became the favorites of
the visiting business elite, much to
the chagrin of the *real* prostitutes. I
wager, in a dull month, had they
wished, the two of them could have
gone through a goodly portion of corporate Europe and America. If any
lady at the bar became jealous and
began asking for trouble, LaFleur
would quietly and neatly place her
unfinished martini into her bag — zip
it up for safety's sake — and engage
her heckler in a boxing lesson she
would never forget!

The other considerable force to
contend with in the group was my
favorite. Her name was Nanette. She
was in her sixties. She was small, slim, soigné, dressed to perfection but
with a face that not even a mother could love! It was the face of a comic
and inspired nothing but laughter, so it was not surprising to discover
that her beau ideal was none other than own our homegrown Beatrice
Lillie. She had been married to a homosexual alcoholic called Stanley
who played café-society piano. She had kept him for years. He had died
writhing in agony from cirrhosis of the liver. Nanette was the biggest
drunk I have ever known! By now she had squandered most of the fortune she inherited from the family steamship lines so the trust had cut
her off with a mere piddling allowance and put it all aside for her two
sons. "Not mirages dawling — they're really mine. Poor Stanley — I had
to prop it up with matchsticks but we managed!" When relatively
sober her humour was gossamer, mercurial and excruciatingly funny.
Her bon mots would be delivered in a voice that out-Talloo'd Tallulah.
She made me laugh till I cried. *But,* one rye on the rocks, her eyes
revolved back into her head, and she would slide, silently, on some
invisible bobsled under every table or barstool across the city. Most bar-
tenders in town could tell you she had no control whatsoever over her
poor old pins, which she affectionately referred to as "Legs by Bech-
stein." In this state, no piano legs *they;* they had to have belonged to

some worn-out rag doll and were so wobbly it was impossible for one man to lift her (God knows, I tried!) so that several waiters had to be regularly commandeered. One could never say that Nanette was *thrown out* of a bar—for as she was gathered up, her exits had all the dignity and precision of a military funeral.

Part of the summer Nanette would disappear to the coast of Maine and sit on a beach with a picnic basket and a shaker by her side, sipping martinis all day long. She told me Stanley and she used to do this together every summer at this very same spot, but now she was doing it alone. I think she missed the old sot. "There was this rather dishevelled-looking seagull that kept hanging around me and my picnic basket all day long. Each time I'd appear on the beach, that same seagull would stride up and just stand there with its head on one side and stare at me. I threw everything I had at the stupid thing but it wasn't interested in food—only the martini. It loved martinis! It became a ritual. I brought two chilled martini glasses to the plage, poured one for myself and one for the seagull. This went on for a whole week! One day the seagull didn't turn up. I was relieved 'cause I'd have all my martinis for myself, yet a little hurt because it didn't seem to care. At the end of the day I decided to fill one last shaker for the road and take a quick dip. Just as I was staggering back up the beach I saw the damn bird. He was on my rug, weaving about unsteadily, pissed out of its skull! It had lapped up the entire shaker of martinis! I always knew that Stanley would come back as a fucking seagull!"

I was crazy about her! She was kindness itself to me—we did all the nightspots together and she taught me how *not* to drink! Nanette was a total tonic to be with, for she saw the ridiculous in *everything* and *everybody* and most of all, which was as hilarious as it was redeeming, in herself!

SEAN O'CASEY might have been describing the Naughty 10 when he coined the phrase "wincing worms in a winecup," but they were better than that. There was a reckless bravery about them—they had tremendous guts—you couldn't take that away from them. The further they fell from grace, the more they stuck together; and when they replenished their coffers by selling their souls, they reformed ranks and like a pack of wild beasts, tore the city apart and once again left it ravaged! If they liked you, however, and you were in trouble, they would give you the shirt off their backs—a gesture which LaFleur by the way was only too happy to offer quite literally, at any given time and preferably in public. She owned a fabulous collection of furs from lynx to sable under which she very frequently wore nothing at all; so when the going got tough at the bar and the customers objected to her increasingly foul language, with an imperious gesture she would let the furs fall to the floor while she remained elegantly perched on the bar stool, magnificent in her alabaster nakedness—a veritable Godiva—gleaming in the soft, dim light. She had often thus reduced the room to a shocked and paralyzed silence and her musical laughter only made her more ravishing than ever, as she threw back her head in a taunting mockery of triumph.

Well, the Naughty 10 slowly began to "drop off the twig" one after the other, and like their cousins, the ten little Indians, soon there would be none. I guess they'd somehow got the scoop on what was coming—the close of their particular chapter in history—and they weren't going to stick around to pick up the pieces. They were the last dregs of a fading society—they knew it, and their moment was over. I suddenly felt deserted; it scared the hell out of me and like the cowardly rat that I was, I too turned my back on them.

Several months had gone by and I was trudging home unusually sober along Sherbrooke Street about 2:00 a.m. in a blinding snowstorm. The road was dark and deserted. Except for the street lamps, the only other lights came from the Ritz-Carlton on the opposite corner. No one was about—the doorman had long since gone home. Suddenly there was a squeaking noise, and the revolving doors began to move. I stopped dead in my tracks. I couldn't see distinctly, but it seemed that a figure, on all fours, was laboriously attempting to push it around with its head. Finally it won! The figure emerged—it was Nanette! She had obviously been denied her last drink, her legs had given way and she was politely seeing herself out. She found the sidewalk and continued on her way. It was quite a sight. Swathed in full-length chinchilla and jewelled turban, the old lady crawled on her hands and knees through the deep and driving snow, her purse between her teeth, all the way down to the next pub, determined to get there before it closed. I stood in wonder, the snow covering me like huge dandruff—I couldn't move. Was this how it ended—that vanishing "style"? Nanette, the last of the Furies, could no longer postpone her rendezvous with Death. She had owed him too much and he would soon bury her in the snow.

There had been quite a few deaths lately. My erratic so-called career, for one. At this stage in my own country I'd gone as far as I could. The

Wasps that remained still thought that "theatre" was something you did in your spare time. The more artistic Jewish community was too occupied in rising like a phoenix from the dying ashes of racial intolerance to take up the slack at present. And radio? Well, English radio at least was soon to become about as dead as the dodo and all that was left of my wartime buddies was a collection of medals. I had been a witness to the death of vaudeville, a sad gap in the world of mirth; the imminent demise of cabaret was just around the corner and so too the slow lingering death of jazz that I have mourned the rest of my life and which left me with only a few precious old seventy-eights for memories— smashed to pieces one drunken night, the sole survivor, ironically, a warped, badly scarred single of Benny Goodman and Teddy Wilson's unforgettable "The World Is Waiting for the Sunrise"—and then, last of all—the death of my mother.

The news came to me as I suppose it sometimes does to the young as a kind of callous thrill, a quick rush of adrenalin, a momentary high as if it wasn't at all real or serious, or final but just a cruel and thoughtless game. Evidently, she had suffered a small stroke, fallen and cracked her head on the bathtub. But nothing would convince me. I was too late of course; she'd gone before I'd reached her. They had put her in a cold, heartless little room at the back of the mortuary and I asked if I could be with her alone—if there was time. Time? All the time in the world, son, but somehow I felt pressed, that I must hurry. There was something I had to say to her. What a selfish thing it is to wait for someone to pass on before realizing you need them so terribly. I gazed down at her lying there. She looked pretty today—not a trace of the blow that had killed her—she'd wake up in a minute, I knew it. As I kept staring, I became a child once again, and she was reading *Peter Pan* to me just as she used to, and I could hear her say so clearly, like Peter, "To die will be an awfully big adventure!" So it was a game after all and at any moment now it would be all right—she'd open her eyes and wink at me. Embarrassed, I turned around to see if anyone was looking, but we were alone. I bent over her and whispered something I can't remember, but it sounded strange and false like someone else's dialogue; I touched her cheek with my lips, but all I felt was cold marble—and then I knew she wasn't there anymore.

IT TOOK ONLY forty minutes to get to Polly's island by train. The skiff was on the other side moored to the landing so I knew she was home. I rowed a little flat-bottomed boat across the bay and walked slowly up toward the house. Polly saw me. She knew, of course; it was she who had found her and she did the right thing—she always did the right thing—she left me to myself, just me and the island. I dreamed again that it was mine—that it belonged to me forever. Then I sat on a rock looking out across the lake and the floodgates opened.

Back in the city, I insisted on taking charge of the funeral. I wanted no one's help. I went at once to Christ Church Cathedral where our family, for such a long time, had been so much a part of its history; so much so, in fact, that we'd come to think of it as our very own. I tried to get old Canon Whitley who had known all of us, generations of us, to take the service—she would have loved that. But he was far too aged and failing miserably; he couldn't make the trip. There was a new dean now, very polite but aloof and indifferent who didn't seem to know who anybody was; also, a new organist. I asked him if he wouldn't mind playing some of Wagner's "Liebestod" from *Tristan and Isolde,* a favourite of my mother's, just a few bars would do but he shrugged and said he didn't know it and couldn't play it. The church was surprisingly packed when the day arrived. I was so proud for her as I sat alone in the front pew. The event proceeded smoothly and professionally but there wasn't much heart in it, nothing personal about it really, just clear-cut and cold. Even the voices of the choir seemed faraway when the final hymn was sung as I looked around the old church with its beautiful stained glass, the great Gothic arches, the massive stone columns, and at their feet, the casket patiently waiting to be borne away. For a moment it seemed that everything was as it should be when suddenly out of the corner of my eye I saw the dean. He was stifling a yawn and looking at his watch. Somewhere deep inside a door slammed shut and the past closed around me. Although Mum's death left me emptier and more helpless than I could ever have imagined, it at last gave me the anger for which I'd been searching so long—and the wings on which to bear it away.

IT WAS A LATE AFTERNOON in winter. I took up my skis for one last run down Mount Royal. I stopped by the great stone wall of Raven'scrag and waited. I suppose I was half hoping to catch a glimpse of that woman I'd seen standing there once so many years before, the woman that might have been her—but there was no one. I made my way around the mountain to the other side. The sun was setting over

Fletcher's Field. The last priests were skiing down the northern slopes, their black robes billowing out in the wind behind them as they headed back to chapel. It was a lovely sight, but there was no one there to paint them.

Now it was dark, and the moon came out and bathed the snow-covered mountain in a soft white light as I crunched my way to the top. A single dog barked somewhere far away, but the night air was so cold and dry, it could have been right beside me. A slight breeze began to shiver and make a gentle rustling sound through the furs, like a secret, whispered. Or was it a rebuke? "You don't have to remind me," I thought. "I know my city is beautiful." I looked up at the lighted cross on the summit, a symbol of patience as it watched over the restless town—the Sentinel on the Crest. For a moment I was mesmerized and once again felt that awful pull, but with all the might I could muster I tore my eyes away.

I looked down the hill on the other side directly below me, where the grand old mansions rested sedately among the trees, then beyond, farther down, where shone the flashing lights—the bad times, the honky-tonk, the seedy side of life, God love it!—and beyond that *still,* out, across the river, the frozen St. Lawrence, *out* into that hazy uncertain future I was now obliged to crash and, apart from some rather heavy unpaid bar bills—and a nagging sweet pain and heartache that will stay with me till the day I reach Valhalla—the dream had cracked; I had broken free.

BOOK TWO

CHAPTER NINE

A BERMUDA SHORT

The button clicked open in the control booth.

"Where did you say you were going?"

It was Andrew Allan, in aspic or behind glass, whatever—his clipped English tinged with even more precise Highland Scot. He'd cut me off in midphrase, a cunning little habit he had of changing the subject when things weren't going too well. It was a radio rehearsal, of course, and I was mouthing with much difficulty into the microphone a torrent of Restoration ribaldry from Etherege's *Man of Mode.*

"Bermuda," I gulped.

I could see his eyebrows arch higher than the steepest Grampian hill.

"And how do you intend advancing your avocation 'mongst the 'still-vexed Bermoothes'?"

"There's a year-round rep company there, Andrew," I stammered, already preparing my defense.

A unanimous intake of breath silenced the studio as everyone glared at me in disgust.

"So we have a deserter in our midst?" was the curt dismissal.

The button clicked shut and we resumed our high-flown duties. But there had been a wicked glint in his eye, so, in a way, I felt blessed. It was just Andrew, after all, running true to form—his way of saying good luck!

MY MOPED was purring me along, up quaint, narrow carless roads which rose gently away from a clear turquoise sea. The soft breeze bathed my face in a welcoming warm spray, and there was something agreeably sensual about the air that reminded me I was in a strange new land. I noticed too a slight irregular rhythm in the revolution of my

Marian Seldes, our leading vamp

rear wheel, where some small bits of Marian Seldes's skirt still stuck to the spokes: some days before, she had been riding behind me, holding on for dear life, when her dress caught in the wheel and ripped right off, leaving me in a ditch and the tall, lanky actress sprawled rather unceremoniously in front of the posh Princess Hotel, practically "starkers" from the waist down. Otherwise, most trips had been smooth, and by now I was becoming quite fond of my trusty little motor. Although I'd not slept the night before (I was never to sleep on that island), I felt curiously buoyant as it contentedly buzzed me away farther and farther from what I had conceived to be the loftier reaches of Art toward the more earthy world of light entertainment commonly known as "stock."

The year-round rep theatre that had engaged me as its bushy-tailed resident leading man was snugly situated inside Hamilton's Bermudiana Hotel, perilously close to the bar. It was run on the star system (the theatre, not the bar) which meant established, slightly aging idols of stage and screen would sneak a quick island hol' while performing in plays of their choice while we, the resident company, shakily but bravely supported them. My "resident leading lady" was a very young, very perky Kate Reid. Marian Seldes (daughter of distinguished New York critic Gilbert Seldes) played every femme fatale of the season; also from New York, fabulous old Ruth McDevitt, who took care of the characters; and from Canada—in charge of all *low* comedy—hilarious

Kate, my surrogate sister and friend,
as Mary Stuart

Barbara Hamilton. To keep us in order was a gifted and sensitive Norwegian, Johann Fillinger, who acted as director–cum–scout leader and claimed Henrik Ibsen as an ancestor—don't they all?! Among others there was a sneaky scene-stealer called Eric House and a merry, sexy little fifteen-year-old apprentice named Waverly (stepdaughter of John Steinbeck and daughter of film star Zachary Scott), whom Kate at once took under her protective wing. And then there was Mister Billie.

Mister Billie wasn't part of our company, though he might just as well have been. He was certainly a member of our "family"—in fact he helped make us a family. Mister Billie worked for the hotel. He was a tall, fine-looking black man of indeterminate age (somewhere between forty and sixty) and always jolly and smiling. His effusive greetings as we arrived each day for work never failed to start life off with a bang. He had a habit of whistling all day long wherever he went. It could have been most irritating but it wasn't, because Billie knew how to whistle—it was quite beautiful, really, soft and musical. The hotel had no need of an aviary. It had Billie.

He ran the elevator during the day and was our "front of house" man at night, making sure the audience was settled in their seats before sending us back the signal for the curtain to go up. He looked after us as if we were his brood, often mixing his special concoctions to start our hearts whenever we felt under the weather. He also tended the bar after the performances. Billie did everything and was always smiling, always whistling. I'm sure he never slept. The hotel was his life. He loved the hotel, and the hotel loved him. I'm certain it couldn't wait for the very last guest to retire to bed so it could share its secrets with Billie. Far into the night, Mister Billie would shuffle through the empty hotel whistling softly to it and telling little stories, and the hotel would listen until it felt quite calm again, and then it would fall asleep. But damn it, if Billie wasn't there first thing in the morning to wake it up.

One thing was crystal clear. The semitropics did not inspire work — hard or otherwise. I quickly began indulging myself in my latest ambition to become a thespian by night and a beach bum by day. If I could accomplish both, then — by Setebos, it would indeed be a perfect world!

The isle is full of noises
Sounds and sweet airs that give delight and hurt not.
Sometimes a thousand twangling instruments will hum about mine ears.
— THE TEMPEST

The night before, we had all gone to Myrta's house. Myrta's parties were the best — somewhat bizarre — but the best. Myrta was himself somewhat bizarre. In fact, I don't believe the shutters in his somber, old colonial mansion had ever been opened. Myrta never chose to rise before 6:00 p.m. There is no doubt about it, he lived for the darkness — Myrta was a creature of the night.

Myrta Guinness, eccentric, reclusive, one of the more obscure members of that large illustrious family, lived alone on the island, except for a few shadowy figures one took to be servants. In this "Villa Dolorosa" Myrta would lose himself amongst an extensive assortment of elaborate mechanical music boxes of all ages and sizes, some reaching to the ceiling; added to which, piled on shelves and in glass casements, his pride and joy, probably the world's largest and most unique private collection of baby coffins.

Myrta was a hopeless dilettante — a harmless voyeur; he loved, above all else, to have the young about him, especially young artists whose talent he admired. He entertained on a lavish scale and was gentle and generous. Myrta hardly ever spoke a word. He was, I discovered, a sad, shy and lonely soul, bereft of purpose and blessed with no particular gift of any kind save one: he played the musical saw more brilliantly and more hauntingly than could be dreamed possible. He would wait till all the trilling, tinkling birdsong and little mechanized marching bands from his massive music boxes had come to an exhausted halt, and then, in the half dark, he would bend that menacing saw over his knee and with his bow delicately brushing the shining metal, he would transport us to another world, a world of high-pitched unearthly beauty. It was the song the Sirens sang—it had wrecked ships, it had lured men to their watery deaths. As he played, an extraordinary thing happened—his face visibly altered, he was suddenly vibrantly alive, he had brought his own youth back.

BERMUDA in the early fifties was much less tightly packed than it is now, but it was a small world. One needed only to stay for little more than a weekend to discover who the key figures were on the island— the Triminghams (at whose well-known shop I instantly began running up bills) or the Butterfields or the Farnsworths, and so on. One very quickly got to meet most of them.

One young ne'er-do-well scion of an established Bermudian family was a Michael Somers, whose distant ancestor, Sir George Somers, had been wrecked off the island at the turn of the seventeenth century, the incident which most probably gave Mr. Shakespeare the idea for his *Tempest.* M. was camp as a row of tents, definitely in the fast lane, and threw round-the-clock soirées by the baker's dozen. If the drinks were slow in coming, he would scream in a kind of high-pitched bark at his black "houseboy," "Goose the Guests" while delivering a vicious karate chop-kick to the old man's derrière with a dexterity Bruce Lee would have envied. Long experience had taught the ancient retainer to ward them off with equal dexterity by swiveling his bottom from side to side in what resembled a geriatric version of the hula-hula.

An annual tradition of his young master's was to drive his speedboat (a sleek cigarette with a knife-sharp prow) late at night at full throttle straight into the large cruiser *Queen of Bermuda,* habitually anchored in Hamilton Harbour. Having accomplished this mission, he would speed away undetected leaving a great gaping hole in the ship's stern, forcing the tourists on board to be detained indefinitely while the damage was being repaired. Had he ever been caught, the headlines in the local papers would simply have read "Queen Rams Queen."

There was no doubt about it—the atmosphere down in them islands was soporific to a degree. No matter how hard you tried, you couldn't buck it. When one wasn't forcing oneself to summon up enough energy to commit words to memory, there wasn't an awful lot to do really, except get into trouble—gentle, harmless trouble, that is. The few nightspots, dotted sparsely across various towns from Hamilton to Somerset to Paget Sound, were for the most part considered out of bounds. They were largely attended by the local black population, who were warm, friendly and kind—a sunny contrast to the somewhat uptight, stuffy whites. At that time the island natives were pretty much kept at bay, shown little regard, made to feel subservient. Notwithstanding they seemed fairly content—any sign of anger or dissatisfaction was barely apparent. We thespians and some local playboys were just about the only white trash who visited those boîtes of the night. Mister Billie had put us on to them.

To while away lunch breaks or free evenings, Kate, Barbara, Marian and I would hang about "21," the smart harbour-front restaurant in Hamilton, where the action was, and watch the big private yachts glide in and come to rest. We would establish beachheads at the bar and mingle with visiting VIPs. Everyone who was anyone paid court at "21," particularly during the famous Bermuda Cup races. Errol Flynn's yacht was regularly moored out in the bay but only occasionally was one lucky enough to get a glimpse of the man himself, surrounded as he was by so many cronies plus entourage. We were never to get even close.

There was tennis on the Princess Hotel courts, of which I took daily advantage; and in the big white house on the hill above, which the Farnsworths had lent us for our digs, we could eat, sleep and gossip in the damp, cloying rooms, compare notes and organize hanky-panky. Button-nosed Kate Reid was a marvel of morale-lifting joy. A combination of finishing-school deb, tomboy, Mother Earth and imp, Kate was prodigiously talented for one so young. She was already an expert at her own brand of light comedy, but every so often one could detect a vulnerability creeping through—a hint of the pathos which was to flood her work in later years.

She was then married to the theatre's founding partner, a tall, handsome Irishman who seemed more interested in upgrading his social status than lavishing his young spouse with attention. It was, I suspect, his method of running away. She was clearly too much for him to handle—her effervescent charms and rollicking sense of fun embarrassed him a little, and although I know they were happy for a while, their drifting apart seemed inevitable. I am not suggesting Kate was in the least promiscuous—she was above all else a one-man girl, but there was too much going on in that head and heart of hers to suffer such a tepid alliance.

Kate had started to booze quite heavily. She was not an unhappy drinker—she enjoyed it immensely. Gradually however, this became an addiction. I have always thought in her case it was inherited, for her attractive mother, nicknamed "Babby," a wonderful character with a fierce generosity of spirit, quite obviously had, for some time, a serious problem with drink. They were great together though, always holding up the hotel bar, singing songs till all hours with Mister Billie egging them on. They were terrific buddies, inseparable, always laughing. This drinking did not seem to affect Kate in the slightest; after all she was still young and pretty—it was much later that it took its toll, marking the last years of her life. She never lost her sense of fun right up to the end but back then, boy, was she a riot!

I remember waking one Sunday morning, the air heavier than usual, the sultry breeze blowing through the windows, particularly warm and seductive. I sauntered into Kate's room rubbing the sleep from my eyes; both of us confessed to feeling decidedly turned on and vowed then and there to take a stab at it. It began fairly smoothly, promising all the earmarks (if you'll forgive the phrase) of success. Our kisses were becoming quite passionate when I, fancying myself as some irresistible Don Juan, a master of technique, must have made some clumsy, overly calculated "paso dobles," for suddenly Kate burst into loud, uncontrolled laughter. I was mortally wounded, my libido quite deflated. To save face, I instantly feigned hearty indifference and, ignoring utterly the mating call of the tropics, joined in, as we rolled over onto the floor together, giggling away like fools. The noise must have raised the others, for it seemed the entire company was standing in the doorway leering at us in mischievous derision. That moment sealed our friendship, Kate's and mine. Romance was never again broached and for most of her life we remained, like brother and sister, warmly and deeply close.

Kate's supreme creation that year was her transcendent Pegeen Mike in Synge's loquacious verse drama *The Playboy of the Western World.* She was to give us a loveable Gabby, a tough but touching barmaid in *The Petrified Forest,* and acquit her bubbling self well in other fairly undemanding roles, but her Pegeen was the first clear affirmation of just how strong and powerful her real gifts were and how far they could take her should she wish to go the distance. Burgess (Buzz) Meredith was the transient star that week and a much too old Christy Mahon. It mattered not a jot however for his quixotic, pixieish charm, his speed and tenacity, convinced all about him that he could pass as a plausible but somewhat lived-in thirty.

Buzz was then in his late forties, Kate in her early twenties, but as the ill-fated lovers they made a dynamic duo not easily forgotten. The part of Old Mahon, Christy's father, was played by me. At twenty-one or -two, I was hardly the obvious choice. It was Buzz's fault entirely; he had cast me. Christ! Here I was again—old before my time. But it was exciting to say the least, for it was the closest thing I had ever been to a really fine theatre actor—and there was one hell of a lot to learn from him. When as Christy he was roused, his intensity was electrifying. He was a mini tornado. With imperceptible ease he could switch from the lowest, most intimate conversational tones to soaring lyrical heights— all which this play demanded. He also had the confidence and experience to milk the big moments without ever spilling over into mawkishness. Buzz was American to the core, but with his instinctive musical sense of lilt and ear for cadence, he was born to interpret the great poets of the Emerald Isle.

Our season was by now well under way and the celebrities who graced our stage included Jeffrey Lynn, Constance Cummings, Kay Francis (the Hollywood comedienne who could never pronounce her r's; she insisted on calling herself Kay Fwancis) and the extremely bright playwright actress Ilka Chase. All were skillful, slick performers who delighted the audience and warmed them up for the rest of us; but the sun really came out the day Edward Everett Horton rolled into our lives.

His polish and indisputable mastery of timing were light-years ahead of the rest of them. The response he drew from the public was extraordinary. They were drenched in affection for him. It was as if he had bought the entire audience and given them to us for a Christmas present. It was a constant challenge to keep Mister Billie away from him. All Billie did was to point at him and dissolve into helpless laughter. Luckily, E. E. stayed an extra week or two, for he had brought two plays with him—his old warhorse *Springtime for Henry,* which as a touring vehicle over the years had made him his second fortune, and a new play, an English version of André Roussin's Parisian farce *Nina.* In

Edward Everett Horton, the best double-taker in the business

Springtime, of course, he played Henry and he cast me as his crony and comic foil Jelliwell—a part that had been created many years before in the much straighter London original by my cousin Nigel Bruce. Not having a clue what to do with the role, I did the unforgivable thing and simply imitated Nigel. (I had seen enough of Nigel in the movies to sense how he might have sounded as Jelliwell.) Edward Everett didn't seem to mind in the least as long as I accomplished to his satisfaction all the intricate "business" he had invented for Jelliwell to set up his laughs. There was so much "business" and precise timing to perfect, there was very little time left to learn the lines. It was my first taste of what vaudeville must have been like to rehearse and how painstaking the process; but Eddy's style, though he had been trained by the great team of Weber and Fields, was several notches higher than vaudeville.

The prime lesson to be learned from Mr. Horton, I discovered, was just how real, natural and true one had to be in order to make comedy the supreme art that he proved it was. Those familiar with his delicious portrayals on the screen in the Astaire-Rogers musicals, bantering with Eric Blore, rolling eyes at Carmen Miranda, or in the early classics such as *Ruggles of Red Gap,* have simply no conception of just how much finer an artist Eddy could be, unless they had seen him on the stage. Although he quite clearly prepared his performances from the outside in, comfortably relying on a stupendous technique, ironically the results were quite Stanislavskian in their spontaneity and freshness. It was as if Eddy, like Gerald du Maurier before him, had anticipated the Method.

I don't think Ben Levy, the British playwright and MP, ever forgave Edward Everett for transforming his rather ordinary comedy into a howlingly funny solo vehicle—but Eddy's tinkering had virtually guaranteed *Springtime*'s huge success on the road, the royalties of which had helped fill Mr. Levy's coffers. So somewhere along the line, he must have been grateful.

E. E. had outrageously interpolated into the text several lengthy moments of silent clowning. Every night when I wasn't on, I would stand in the wings and watch one particular mime sequence which was supposed to last approximately four minutes, but counting the public's raucous reaction, would inevitably stretch to eight.

Alone on the stage, he would sit absolutely still on the couch waiting for his attractive lady secretary and become suddenly fascinated by a small ball of fluff on one of the cushions. He would scrutinize it intensely from all angles, pick it up, examine it at much closer range, then finally pop it in his mouth and eat it. Increasingly bored waiting, he then started telling himself little stories under his breath which he obviously found excruciatingly hilarious, for he would buckle over in paroxysms of silent laughter. Tired of this, he began tapping his foot in growing impatience. Still tapping, he would then look around to see where the tapping was coming from. Was someone hammering outside? Tapping still and more irritated than ever, he would hold his hand out—was it raining in the room? Giving up the tapping, he unconsciously set about drumming his fingers on the table beside him and with his other hand turned up the lapels of his jacket, clutching them tightly together to avoid getting soaked by the gathering force of an imaginary downpour. He would take a sip of water from a glass and put it back on the table with a rather too-violent crack—scaring himself to death, convinced someone had taken a shot at him. The next few moments were spent in gingerly, ever-so-carefully searching for a wound. During all this he never once left the couch—it was a brilliant bit of improvisation, silly beyond all silliness but so intensely real. I can't think of anyone else getting away with it and every night along with the convulsed audience, I nearly expired in the wings.

Nina, our next project, was a slightly updated Gallic imitation of *Design for Living.* Marian Seldes was the apex of the triangle (the Bermuda Triangle, we called it), I was her lover, Gerard, and Edward Everett played her husband, Adolphe. As it was new to all of us, Eddy couldn't find the time to decorate it with his customary frills. Instead he attacked it with a genuine conviction that made this modest bit of fluff all the more plausible and humorous. I couldn't wait to walk on stage and play a scene with Eddy; he made it all so relaxing, so effortless. Sharing a dialogue with him wasn't "acting" at all; it was simply a pleasant chat with an old friend.

E. E. was a specialist, a unique specialist. He had not only invented his own style; he had invented himself. He took infinite pains to make certain the motive that drove his kind of comedy was always crystal clear—a man of logic and precision hurled into indignation and confusion by an unruly, unpredictable world that was neither logical nor precise. Whenever a little order came his way and restored the balance momentarily, his disbelief, gratitude and wonder were overwhelming, and for a second, we were touched beyond measure. Eddie was one of the great clowns. He had shown us the map of our journey, he had given us a reason to do what we do and the day he left the island, we aimlessly wandered about for some time after—lost children—wondering about our future and how we could manage it all without him.

HOPE SPRINGS ETERNAL. The gap was about to be filled, or at least partially filled, for help was on its way in the shape of two ministering angels. They didn't manifest themselves both at once, thank God—they came "single spies," each in her own inimitable form. In fact, that very morning my trusty little motor was delivering, none too smoothly, me and my extra-heavy head into the presence of the first visitation—a dark apparition clearly possessed of ancient, unknown powers, named Florence Reed. As I came through the lobby Mister Billie looked as if he'd smelled voodoo. She must have spooked him senseless! A fiery little witch, Florence was well into her seventies. Everything about her was black—her flashing raven's eyes, her hair, her dress, her stockings, even the silver-headed cane she brandished about her like a scimitar. If we had not known she was the famous

Florence Reed

stage star who had been storming Broadway for decades, she could have been mistaken for an aged Spanish duenna or the mother superior of some old, obscure religious order. She had the deepest, most resonant voice I have ever heard in man, woman or beast—deeper than Paul Robeson's, I swear. Rumor had it that Florence had taught Tallulah Bankhead how to laugh, but Talloo's famous whiskey-barrel guffaw was a schoolgirl's giggle beside Florence's warlike roar. If Miss Reed thought something was *really* funny, her rumblings became phenomenal, and we would pretend to run—"Watch out for the rocks, guys. It must be a landslide!"

The school of acting she suggested was that of Ada Rehan, Réjane or Modjeska—dark, forceful, tragic. She was about to rehearse us in Edna Ferber's *The Royal Family,* a play about America's famous acting clan, the Barrymores. I was cast as John Barrymore (alias Tony Cavendish). Florence herself ferociously gnawed the scenery as old Mrs. Drew (Aunt Fanny Cavendish). The Barrymores had fascinated me, and will for a long time, and here I was playing John, dear Diana's father, that mythical rascal and great actor. I had a marvelous time making myself up to look exactly like him—our profiles were not dissimilar, so it was fairly easy, and when I wasn't spending time practicing his voice I would stand in front of a mirror for hours hopelessly trying to raise one eyebrow in quizzical hauteur. I gave up, shaved my eyebrow and drew the damn thing in.

Finally, I felt ready for the onslaught, convinced I was Mr. Barrymore's living reincarnation. God, how proud Diana would be if she could see me now, I thought! Florence, on the other hand, was far from proud. She constantly accused me of mumbling. In front of the audience, she would cut across the scene and frequently shout, "Speak up—speak up—no one can hear you!" or "Louder boy—louder!" rapping my knuckles or giving me a massive crack across my knees and shins with her cane. By the end of the week's run, I was black and blue. Yet I was crazy about the wicked old thing for apart from her hostile, warlike attacks, she had a big heart and her conversation was full of wonderful stories about the theatre and the Barrymores, particularly Jack.

"That bastard," she boomed and objects on tables began to rattle in terrified anticipation. "One minute he could be so marvellous and sweet and the next a monster from Hell! We were in *The Yellow Ticket* together in Chicago decades ago. I was manager and star—Jack was in second place. In the story, our characters had met already, had fallen in love, and I was waiting in the living room set where we had arranged a clandestine meeting. One night, I speak the cue that signals his entrance—no Jack! I go through my soliloquy one more time as slowly as possible, arrive at the cue—still no Jack! Now, his dressing room is right by the stage, so there's no excuse for a late entrance. Suddenly I hear emanating from that room a stream of the vulgarest, lowest, filthiest cusswords I have ever heard shouted at the top of his lungs. The poor audience down to the last man cannot help but absorb it all—every syllable. It was Jack—totally inebriated. He had obviously passed out on the dressing room floor and the frenzied stage manager who was shaking him into consciousness became the object of this abuse. I tried singing—shouting—anything to distract the people, when just as suddenly as it had begun, all noise ceased.

"There followed one long and awful silence. I was frantic. I started telling stories, but quickly ran out of ideas; I was just about to sit down at a piano which was mercifully part of the décor and play something—God knows what—when Jack appeared, at last, in the doorway. He was reeling badly, holding on to the doorknob for support. Half dressed, half undressed with a stupid leer on his face, his glazed eyes finally focused on me and, arching his eyebrow in that familiar manner of his, he said very slowly and very grandly, 'Who the hell are you?' I walked to the wings and snapped, 'Take down the curtain' and flounced into my dressing room. The theatre manager came out and announced that there would be no more play because Mr. Barrymore had regrettably been taken ill. Only too aware of the situation, the audience exploded in laughter.

"A year later, a very great friend who was ailing asked me to accompany her to a matinée of *Pelléas and Mélisande,* which was starring Jack and Constance Collier. I told her—not on my life. Never! Wild horses couldn't drag me within miles of John Barrymore. She was dying to see it however, and had no one else to take her, so I relented. The curtain went up. I was fuming inside. All the past horrors with that rascal came back to me as I waited—dreading his entrance—but when Jack walked onto the stage that tense afternoon in winter, he brought such magic and beauty with him I not only forgave him everything but fell head over heels in love with him all over again—that goddamn son of a bitch!" To emphasize this last expletive, she cracked my shins once again with her cane. It was only then that the relieved objects on the tables settled down to rest.

Florence had been a ripe, old-fashioned powerhouse as Aunt Fanny Cavendish, but now it was time for her to make her exit from our lives. I was to miss her badly and her tales of a hundred and one theatrical nights. I would even miss her bruising, disciplinary broomstick. We all expected her leave-taking to be ultradramatic; either the ground would open and she'd be swallowed up or she would vanish in a puff of smoke—preferably black—but no. When Florence walked through the lobby to the hotel's front door, she was just a tough old gypsy going to her next gig, full of spunk, still very much in love with her profession, who couldn't wait to lacerate the next young Tony Cavendish about the shins.

SHE HAD BARELY checked out, when hard on her heels, like a tropical squall, came the second angel. From some aerie in the clouds, on a rush of wings she blew in, scattering all before her. With a final flap, she folded those wings and deposited one bewildered and bewitched husband, enough luggage for a tsarina, a maid, a cook and a pre–jet-lagged dog. Her soigné manner and extravagant turn of phrase left no one in doubt she had owned a castle in Spain, flew her own plane, was bosom

*Ruth Chatterton, a great star of early talkies and the stage,
for me the epitome of glamour*

buddies with Amelia Earhart and had, since the twenties, reduced the
Atlantic and Mediterranean oceans to mere commuter hops.

Back in the teens, she had reigned over Broadway as a popular star
(among her vehicles Barrie's *Little Minister* and *What Every Woman
Knows*) and as the mistress of famed producer Henry Miller.

She had been a silent-screen star in Hollywood and when talkies
emerged (because she was one of the few who could speak the King's
English) she became for a spell First Lady of the Screen and the highest-
paid woman in the United States. "She reeked with chic, her hat of the
week cost sixty-four courses, three runaway horses," and her name was
Ruth Chatterton. Ruth wore many hats. She was a novelist, a director
and a producer. Besides being an aviatrix, she was a tennis player, a
golfer and a skier. To say she was emancipated and a pioneer of sorts
would have been a gross understatement.

Ruth might have been created by F. Scott Fitzgerald and Sinclair
Lewis. In many ways she personified the twenties but now had mellowed considerably and though still a whirlwind of energy, there was an
aura of seductive world-weariness about her that made her Regina in

The Little Foxes so deadly frightening and so very much her own. This was the play she was now directing and acting for us so brilliantly. Lillian Hellman, who wrote it, told me years later that of all the Reginas, Ruth's was by far the best. Of course, it was universally known that its creator, Tallulah Bankhead, and Lillian were mortal enemies, so Miss Hellman may have been somewhat prejudiced. Nevertheless, Ruth was superb, and Mister Billie, who stood at the back and watched, said he was mighty impressed, and that was good enough for us.

There is a moment just before Regina decides to kill Horace when she is alone on the stage. I shall never forget the frightful effect Ruth produced to make that moment stay in the mind forever. Like a panther she prowled about the stage. Arriving at her decision, she came to a dead stop. Her absolute stillness and repose when she knew the dreadful moment had come were terrifying and beautiful both at once. This vampire became, before our eyes, silkily feminine, soft, almost innocent. Then with two sharp little clicks of her fingers that rang through the theatre like gunshots, she softly whistled a little tune between her teeth, silently turned on her heels and slithered up the stairs towards her kill.

Ruth had discovered late in life that she could direct. What a loss for the theatre up to then! She was absolutely marvellous at it. In contrast to her rather carefree, high-flown manner, she possessed quite profound insights into the human psyche. Johann just stood by and watched—a glorified stage manager. She brought things out of us we didn't know we had. I played Regina's older brother Ben, a wonderfully rich character I enjoyed immensely (adding a soupçon of Lionel Barrymore to taste, I shamefully admit). I was really becoming quite adept at these old codgers, but when the hell was I ever to act my own age? Ruth, however, thought I was the cat's whiskers (lucky for me) and both she and her husband, Barry Thomson, lavished me with unbelievable kindness and attention. Barry, an extremely handsome older Englishman with a kind, soft nature, played Horace whom Regina totally dominates (precariously close to their real lives, I couldn't help thinking). Marian Seldes was a heart-wrenching Birdie; Eric House, a tight-lipped, perfect Oscar. We were a pretty good group altogether and the loyal little audience sat up and took notice. That week we surpassed anything we had attempted before and it was all due to Ruth, her drive and her inspiration. She had turned us into a proper company of players and, God forgive us, we had, for that moment at least, earned the right to be proud.

After the curtain call on the last night of *The Little Foxes,* Ruth took me aside. She held both my hands in hers, leaned very close and whispered, "The first thing you do when you come to New York is to look me up. I'll take you to dinner—there are some very important people I want you to meet." When she spoke in low tones, she had the most beautiful voice and I felt the effect of it all the way down my spine. She may have been accused of being a bit piss-elegant, as Guthrie McClintic once described her, but by God, she had the gift of making you feel you were the only man in the world. I stood there reeling, quite giddy and light-headed, enveloped in a mist of expensive perfume.

The Chatterton contingent left the next day. After much kissing, hugging and elaborate promises of eternal love, I watched them go. Through the hotel lobby at the head of her host swept The Archangel, her little regiment of supplicants trailing behind her in single file— the frightened, bedraggled dog, already hating the awesome journey, taking up the rear. Whether it was the sudden lump in my throat that made me turn away or whether I just couldn't face the dreaded moment when she would gather them all up, I'll never know; but I found myself clapping my hands tightly over my ears to shut out the fearful rushing sound of her wings as she flew them away.

OUR LITTLE COMPANY was never to be quite the same again. The breathless tension that had been created for us was gone—we'd become a bit complacent, too comfortable with each other. Bad habits were forming. We were too relaxed, too easily distracted. Our eyes began to wander—mine particularly. Fifteen-and-a-half-year-old Waverly, our adopted mascot, had blossomed considerably; there was no mistaking it. The slight crush I already had was growing rapidly by the moment. Kate, however, always the chaperone, in her best Mother Cabrini, wagged a "Don't touch" finger at me and I was forced to play possum. The fact that Waverly's father had arrived to be our new "star" made any sort of tryst all the more unlikely, so I transferred my attentions to a much easier target, the voluptuous young assistant stage manager with the great boobs who provocatively made it her constant practice to sit on everyone's lap.

Zachary Scott, darkly handsome, the Hollywood star known for his slippery rich boys and rather too-smooth villains (in company with Peter Lorre and Sydney Greenstreet in *The Mask of Demetrios,* etc.) turned up trumps! He became the leitmotif of the season on and off the

*Zachary Scott — the playboy of the Western,
or* any *other world*

stage. Zach was more fun than a picnic. A picnic to him (had he ever deigned to attend one) would have meant copious hampers of gin and vermouth for martinis, Jack Daniel's for juleps, tequila for margaritas and very little else. His humor was high camp, shaken not stirred, with a whiff of wit passed over ever so lightly for taste. To punctuate his many bon mots he would raise one shaggy eyebrow heavenward and let his mouth sag in imbecilic incredulity at their unexpected success.

A Texan from old Austin stock, his manners were genteelly Southern and his low, deliberately languid drawl had oil and honey in it. He was the first heterosexual I had yet seen to sport an earring. Waverly worshipped him and I could understand why. This of course could have made me exceedingly jealous, but for the fact that Zachary and I became close companions in crime and loyal-to-the-death drinking partners. He was married most happily to Ruth Ford, the onetime famous Vogue model of the thirties—sleek and elegant, with whom the author William Faulkner had fallen in love (he wrote *Requiem for a Nun* for her). Zach and Ruth together made a stunning couple. Avid art lovers (an astounding Tchelitchew collection) and superb hosts, they saw themselves as the younger Gerald Murphys, ultrasmart, internationally accepted citizens of the world. Wherever they went, heads would turn. But Ruth was not here with him now, to keep order or to help turn heads, so his sky knew no limits.

Zachary gave a very smooth rendition of Sam Behrman's *The Second Man.* He had been performing it for some time on the "summer circuit" and could play it backwards—which one day, quite unintentionally, he managed to do. I remember being most impressed with his expertise in handling props—very Cary Grant–ish. He was able to light countless cigarettes for everyone while spouting rapid small talk, or cradle with ease two or three telephones at once while dealing with several separate conversations. Cool, Dad, cool! When I practiced this privately, the telephones would drop on my toes with a painful thud, and the matches would burn my fingers to a cinder. I worked at it for years afterwards — I'm still working at it.

> *So we sailed away*
> *For a year and a day*
> *In a beautiful pea-green boat.*

There it was, waiting for us at the jetty — a gorgeous speedboat all in green, with a chauffeur in attendance touching his cap to us. We had been summoned to a scrumptious, private island out to sea far beyond Hamilton Harbour. It belonged to the enormously wealthy diamond king Stanhope Joel, who was our little theatre's principal backer. He had commanded us to a pre-Saturday matinee fête consisting of a quite sumptuous breakfast-cum-brunch.

> *We had dolled ourselves up in our best bib and tucker*
> *And devoured with a vengeance the food, drink and succor*
> *Stanhope was, I admit, a great host, the old — —!*

Of course, we all got pretty squiffed, on extra-lethal Buck's Fizzes and French Seventy-Fives, but Zach, in spite of his usual capacity for the booze, became quite bouleversé'd, paralytic! When the time arrived to head back to shore for the matinée, we had to lift him into the speedboat — an utter deadweight. He instantly revived and, pushing Mr. Joel's chauffeur almost overboard, insisted, above all protestations, that he drive us back full speed. "Ay'll getcha theah on tahme," he slurred and while Kate, Barbara, Marian, Waverly and I huddled together in the stern, petrified out of our wits, Zach, with the steering wheel between his two bare feet, drove us at hair-raising speed, his arms clasped behind his head laughing and singing deliriously all the way like some demented merman. Once safely back in the hotel, he collapsed and we carried him to his dressing room, where Mister Billie poured gallons of caffeine down his throat while some of us struggled to help him into his wardrobe.

Zach hardly offered anything from the text that afternoon. Not exactly in control myself, I was forced to recite most of his dialogue as well as my own, take all his phone calls (fortunately remembering the gist of most of them) — in fact, I just spent a great deal of the time talking to myself! Quel horreur! And all afternoon Zach quite affably allowed me to propel him around the stage looking as dapper and debonair as ever with a ridiculous, inane grin permanently painted on his accursed mug! God love him! I'm not sure if we ever actually finished the play; I suspect the curtain was prematurely lowered and the bamboozled audience shuffled home in morbid silence as though having just left a funeral.

Zachary recovered significantly to get through the evening performance without a single hitch, and when that exhausting day was finally over and all of us had no other thought but for our beds, he came out of his chrysalis once more and fresh as a daisy cried, "Alrahght, you mothahs, wheah's the pahty?"

He had been such a tonic to us, none of us wanted him to leave, but when Old Kaspar's work was done and all that, there was nothing left for him but to rush back to the Big Apple, the Dakota apartments, his Tchelitchews and Ruth. I suggested that he try driving the little speedboat with his bare feet all the way back to Manhattan, and, I swear, by the look in his embryonic eye, he'd already thought of it.

FRANCHOT TONE was the last celestial being to visit our modest little island home. At one time, not too far into the recent past, he was considered by critics, pundits and public alike "the bright white hope of the American theatre." As a young leading man on Broadway, he had shown staggering potential in the famed Group Theatre days. That revolutionary establishment had brought to the fore such luminaries as Harold Clurman, Elia Kazan, Cheryl Crawford and Clifford Odets. Franchot, with his and his family's money (they had inherited the Carborundum electric company) had largely financed the Group Theatre from its inception. So it would not be an exaggeration to surmise that almost single-handedly he had oiled the machinery for the great New Wave movement which signalled the arrival of John Osborne in England and Bertholt Brecht in America and was to have such a lasting influence on theatre everywhere.

But Franchot had a weakness for the movies and a penchant for domineering, glamorous women—Joan Crawford was one spouse among many—need I say more? Only once, maritally, as in the case of June Walker, did he really strike lucky. Each one more beautiful than the last and each matriarchal to a degree, none stayed with him for long. He seemed to search for this kind of self-destructive alliance, an alliance that could not but help inflict certain pain. Indeed, Franchot Tone was a handsome, sensitive, highly educated and tremendously talented gen-

*A principal founder of the Group Theatre
and once the stage's young white hope*

tleman who was, nevertheless, motivated and driven by pain. His hard living had somewhat diminished his former brilliance, but every so often his work showed strong evidence of great depth and nobility of spirit. Franchot was part French and he used to scream French Canadian invective at me whenever he could in perfect "Joal." His sense of humor, as one might guess, was seeringly self-deprecating, drawn as always from this inexplicable inner torment. These vulnerable qualities were to make his Chekovian performances (*Uncle Vanya* and *A Moon for the Misbegotten*), both of which I later saw, so memorable—a rare combination of lightness and poignancy.

Franchot had brought to Bermuda Robert Sherwood's famous *The Petrified Forest,* and he and Johann hit it off splendidly as codirectors. They cast Kate as Gabby the barmaid, whom Bette Davis had played on the screen, and myself as the mobster Duke Mantee, made famous by Humphrey Bogart both on stage and film. Franchot, of course, played Alan Squier, the Leslie Howard role, but was streaks ahead of Mr. Howard in emotional power.

Squier, the intellectual cynic, near the play's end rounds on Duke

Mantee, the gangster who holds him hostage, begging to be killed to save both their souls. He confesses his love for Gabby and why he so desperately yearns for his own death:

SQUIER: *I want to show her that I believe in her—and how else can I do it? Living, I'm worth nothing to her. Dead—I can buy her the tallest cathedrals, and golden vineyards and dancing in the streets. One well-directed bullet will accomplish that. And it will gain a measure of reflected glory for him who fired it and him who stopped it.* (He holds up his insurance policy.) *This document will be my ticket to immortality. It will inspire people to say of me: "There was an artist, who died before his time!" Will you do it, Duke?*

DUKE: (Quietly) *I'll be glad to.*

Franchot directed this to me every night and every night his conviction was extraordinary. Here was a man already dying it seemed—still praying to be snuffed out. I no longer was convinced it was Squier, but Franchot himself pleading for his death. It was eerie, too close, almost too real, and shattering, shattering.

He brought a substance to the play it didn't quite deserve, and though his pace became slower each successive night (he would kill an entire bottle of Stolichnaya on stage at every performance), he managed at times to lift the piece far above its ken into the loftier spheres of O'Neill.

Duke Mantee made Bogie a star, but it sure didn't make me one. It was a marvellous role—I should have been grateful—but I was a disgrace. No, not entirely true. I wasn't too bad in the early scenes (they are a bit of a gift anyway) but I never could learn the last few pages, which had to be delivered at enormous speed—a series of barking commands, cold and steel-like, all difficult to learn under any circumstances and, in my defense, I had only five days to do so, but still it was no excuse. I was to be saved, however, for the luscious assistant stage manager/prompter came up with a sensational solution. She positioned herself snugly against the window on the offstage side while I sat on the ledge *on*stage—we were literally inches apart. She would whisper each command to me very quickly, and I would repeat it immediately afterwards. Our proximity also gave us the chance to smooch a little, unseen by the audience—my body was "on," my head "off." I would lean out the window, deliver a command and get a French kiss delivered straight back to me, another command, another kiss—a fair exchange. As there were numerous commands, we got a lot of smooching done. One night while Duke was peering out into the darkness, this cuddly little ball of flesh had unbuttoned her blouse, exposing a voluptuous young breast, which I stroked with one trembling hand while scanning the horizon with the other. Out of the blue, Duke Mantee had become, need I say, one of my very favorite offstage roles.

Each night after the performance we would celebrate in the bar. A fresh bottle of vodka would be opened for Franchot and I would sit at the piano improvising for hours, my scotch beside me, watching Franchot, Mister Billie and Kate gabbing away to their hearts' content. Franchot thought the world of Billie and wanted him to leave the island and work for him as a butler back home, but Billie always politely declined. Franchot was also crazy about Kate. Here was a girl to respect, talented, bright, who wanted nothing else from him but to make him laugh.

Like Kate, Franchot was so much a part of my early memory and like Alan Squier and Duke Mantee, we shared an unspoken bond. We were both romantics—incurable to the last—and our separate upbringings shared the same confusion of identity. He may have seen in me, occasionally, his younger self. I'm not sure and I wouldn't wish it on him; but I saw in him someone I could perhaps one day aspire to; not the hidden sad, pained man that was part of Franchot but the part he couldn't conceal, no matter how hard he tried, the part that was refined, noble and infinitely kind—the man of golden promise.

FRANCHOT'S leave-taking was the cue for a number of departures. Johann went back to his trolls and the magic of Norse mythology; Ruth McDevitt to New York and a new Broadway play. Ditto Marian. Kate's mother, Babby, having demolished a tray full of Manhattans, took the next plane home, and others had fled to employment far afield, but employment nonetheless. And I, the leading man, the jeune premier, "the offspring of David and the bright and morning star"? What of me?! I had *nothing* to go to—nada, ninch! I was about to seek out Kate, Mister Billie and the few little loyal stragglers that remained and drown my sorrows—when the telegram arrived.

> My dear Gerard. On expiration your Bermuda engagement report Chamberlain/Brown Agency W. 42nd Street N.Y.C. sign contract U.S.A. tour Nina commencing immediately your arrival. Your friend Adolphe—signed Edward Everett Horton.

God bless Eddy! I always knew somehow he'd come through! My American career was about to be launched! I'd be costarring with that fabled old genius of comedy—my pal Eddy. I didn't walk or strut or saunter—I *ran* to the bar, knocking into half the audience on the way. I couldn't wait to tell Kate—in fact, I didn't—I shouted the news at the top of my voice. The bar was packed that night, and they all put down their drinks and gave me an ovation. The bar was almost always packed now. The audience had accepted us finally, and many of them usually stayed behind to mingle—hangers-on included. In fact, I think we got a bigger attendance at the bar than in the theatre.

There was one rather strange young lady from New York staying at the hotel. For two or three weeks now, she had attached herself to the company. She was in her midtwenties—good to look at, deeply tanned, had jet black hair and was the proud owner of two gorgeous, nut-brown legs. She hung about the lounge perfectly content to listen to our gossip without contributing anything herself in the way of conversation. What she did contribute was purely visual. She had the purest, softest of faces, yet there was a toughness, a hardness about her, a restlessness that was most unnerving. She was also a diabolical tease. Scantily clad always, she deliberately never wore underpants and made certain that wherever she sat, on a bar stool or on a couch, she positioned herself in such a way that everyone could get a first-class view. We christened her "Miss Snatch."

That night I noticed for the first time that Miss Snatch was missing. Someone told me she'd packed her things that very day and had left the island in a great hurry. We decided there had always been something a little shifty about her, a girl her age, traveling alone, and so on. She looked so dissatisfied, so discontented most of the time, okay—she was after something all right. Whether she ever got what she came for, I'll never know; but I was to know one thing for sure—she got Billie.

THE NEXT MORNING walking through the lobby, my telegram still clutched tightly in my fist, I felt there was something different about the hotel. It was quiet, deadly quiet; it seemed to know something but wouldn't tell. And then I knew why—there was no whistling. I began looking all over for him, in the kitchen, in the washrooms, by the pool, everywhere—not a sign. I went to the front desk and asked one of those faceless, tight-lipped colonials:

"Billie? He's in prison, sir!"

"Prison! Where? Where can I find him?"

"You can't sir—no one is allowed sir."

"What on earth is he in prison for?"

"He's awaiting trial."

"Trial? What happened, for God's sake? What did he do?"

"We are not permitted to say."

It didn't take me long to find out. It seemed our young lady friend had enticed him to her room on some pretext or other. Once he was inside the door, she must have flashed him and I guess poor Billie couldn't help himself. I know as sure as I know my name that Billie was too shy with the ladies, too simple, too innocent, to have done anything harmful or rash—he probably just touched her where he shouldn't have and that was all. Whatever happened, when he left the room, she called downstairs to the desk, threatened the hotel with one hefty lawsuit and demanded the police. When they arrived, she told them he'd raped her.

We felt we'd been kicked in our stomachs. We knew there could be no trial. A black man charged with rape? On that island, at that time? No way. He wouldn't see the light of day again. He would live and die in whatever hole they'd shoved him in. It was over for Billie. His curtain had come down.

FROM THAT MOMENT ON, things started to deteriorate. The season was over anyway. Most of the paying public had gone from the island. There was only a staunch little band of them left and, on matinées, the same eight old ladies more or less. There were no more "stars" so we played our last play as a company. It was that dreadful old warhorse of a domestic comedy, *George and Margaret*, a perennial summer-stock standby. Barbara, Kate and I were so tired and played out that whenever we made eye contact onstage, we simply corpsed. I don't honestly believe the eight old ladies knew the difference or gave a damn. I hardly think it mattered. We knew we had come to the end of our rope—it was the moment to leave.

> *We shall lose our time,*
> *And all be turned to barnacles, or to apes.*
> — *THE TEMPEST*

IT'S A PARADOX. Whenever I'm about to say farewell to a place in which I've lingered too long, and know I must get out—damn it, if I don't get hooked. I'd known all along that these jewels set in azure waters were a romantic group of islands whose history was as baffling and mysterious as the triangle that bears their name. If Bermuda had been created by any other than some sea god, it had certainly been christened by a force called Shakespeare. If it had been born merely in a poet's mind—a poet who had never seen it—what a rich, magnificent birth. But it did exist; it *was* real. In the beginning of time, the sea had belched it forth. It was Caliban's island, wild, lush, painfully beautiful—I suddenly wanted to stay:

> *I'll show thee every fertile inch o' the island . . .*
> *I'll show thee the best springs, I'll pluck thee berries . . .*
> *I prithee let me bring thee where crabs grow . . .*
> *Wilt thou go with me?*
>
> — CALIBAN

THE FEW FREE DAYS that remained would find me on my well-worn moped covering the countryside for all I was worth searching for more "subtleties of the isle," afraid lest I should ever forget. I would scour the reefs in glass-bottom barks gazing down into the laser-clear depths watching the big lazy morays undulate slowly, seductively— their mouths opening and shutting in silent screams.

I would watch for hours, paralyzed by the underwater beauty of countless fish of all shapes and sizes and the never-ending sunken gardens reaching to infinity—radiating colors too unimaginably rich ever to describe.

> *Full fathom five thy father lies;*
> *Of his bones are coral made;*
> *Those are pearls that were his eyes . . .*

Our little trio, Kate, Barbara and I, would try to relive nostalgic moments at "21" over evening cocktails, not succeeding too well, invariably falling back into long pensive silences. Even the sight of Errol Flynn one lunchtime, standing at the bar sans entourage and quite accessible, didn't cheer us up much. Then I would go up to "Ariel's nest" and sit, snuggled among the rocks, the wind whistling about me. I would squeeze my eyes tightly shut till I swore I could faintly hear Prospero's voice echoing against the cliffs:

Thou hast done well . . .
Thou shalt be free
As mountain winds.

I THREW MY CLOTHES into my suitcase. They were so damp from
the cloying spring I could have wrung them out—and they stunk of
mildew. Brand-new clothes from Triminghams I had yet to pay for, and
I'd never worn them! They looked like secondhand junk. Two official-
looking men from the tourist board, dapper in shirts and ties, long
kneesocks and those hateful Bermuda shorts, drove us to the airport—
at least we were going out in style. I kept looking out the back window
to make sure I wasn't being chased by bailiffs or salesmen brandishing
chits. So far so good.

When we arrived on the tarmac, Kate, Waverly and Zachary, who
had come back for her, were all there to see us off. Waverly made a
quick dash for the plane—she suddenly wanted to come with us (that
would be awfully nice, I thought), but Kate pulled her back and Zach
in the background just stood there making outrageous comic faces. We
settled in our seats. I looked out the window. Kate had turned away and
tears were streaming down little Waverly's face. Inside the plane, we all
seemed pretty controlled, if a trifle tight-lipped. I was thankful we
were able to hold it in and that Waverly was doing the crying for all of
us. The doors shut with a clang. No gendarmes—no militia to cart me
away—I'd made it! We took off.

My body was transported through the first bank of clouds but my
mind was still on the ground. I began to think back. I thought of the
hotel—the cozy, old hotel with the pink stucco walls—and the endless
days and nights I'd spent there. It had been our ship—our vessel. It
had sailed us safely through many a storm. We had worked hard there
and played even harder. We had met some extraordinary people and had
learned much—a lot of growing up had gone on within its walls. So it
came as a special shock when we heard only a few weeks later that the
hotel had burned to the ground. It had burned so rapidly that nothing
was saved. It had gone to grief on its very own reef.

Had I been any god of power, I would
Have sunk the sea within the earth, or ere
It should the good ship so have swallow'd.
— MIRANDA (*THE TEMPEST*)

We would joke amongst ourselves, long afterwards, that it was the audience who had done it—that they'd had enough of us dumb actors, so they torched it to prevent any more such punishment. But that was just to cheer us up. I think most of us pretty much shared the same view—that the day Mister Billie went to jail, the old hotel gave up its ghost and decided one night when no one was looking, to set itself on fire. For with no more Billie to care, no more whistling, laughing and singing in the corridors, no more shared secrets in the dead of night, no more whispered stories to send it to sleep—the heart had gone out of it—it just wanted to die.

CHAPTER TEN

AN AMERICAN DÉBUT

Gingerly I climbed the long, creaking staircase. Once at the top I stood for a moment in order to get used to my gloomy surroundings. With all the bric-a-brac on the walls, the heavy volumes and papers bulging the shelves, I could have wandered straight into Ye Olde Curiosity Shoppe. The scent that greeted my nostrils was the musk of ages. From behind a lopsided old rolltop at the far end of the room through a thick curtain of dust rose a tall cadaver in a shabby ill-fitting cardigan I doubt had ever seen better days. A few wisps of straggly hair tried unsuccessfully to hide his parchmentlike temples, but his ears, for some obstinate reason of their own, sprouted voluminous tufts of healthy dark fur—a most unsettling sight indeed. In a clawlike hand, he was clasping some documents, which he abruptly thrust toward me—"Plummer?" echoed a voice from somewhere inside that hollow frame and without waiting for an acknowledgment, it snapped—"Sign here!"

There was no doubt I was in the presence of one Lyman Brown, the other half of that ancient firm of Broadway flesh peddlers—the Chamberlain Brown Agency—so old and timeworn, in fact, it was said that

John the Baptist had once been a client. Certainly they had managed Edward Everett Horton from his earliest vaudeville days right up through the Hollywood years and Eddy, being such a grateful and loyal gentleman, had never left them. Indeed, he was probably one of the only clients they still had and, most likely, the sole reason for their very existence. From this room, at one time, considerable power had been wielded, but now it was a dead and creepy place. I eagerly signed but before the ink had dried Mr. Brown was loftily dismissing me— "Edward Everett instructed us to look after you while you're here," he hissed; "now run along and don't keep him waiting!" My audience was over.

I couldn't believe the cab driver didn't get out to help old Eddy hump his many pieces of luggage. Ed caught my look of astonishment and immediately rebuked me, "Oh, you won't get that here. Oh, dear me, no. This is New York, sonny; this is New York," and we sped off to our season of *Nina* and my introduction to that long-abandoned but much loved tradition—the "summer circuit." And a glorious summer it was as we hopped from one country town to another—Cape Dennis, Falmouth; Stockbridge, Massachusetts; Sea Cliff, Long Island; Ogunquit, Maine; etc., etc. *Nina* proved perfect holiday fare—light and frothy. Marta Linden, a lady of glamour, sophistication and real warmth, took Marian Seldes's place as Nina and at each theatre the resident leading man would play the small part of the butler. When we reached Niagara-on-the-Lake, the role was played by a Canadian ex-army fella from the war who had decided to become a professional actor. His name was Bill Hutt. Not too far down the road he would one day be known as the great William Hutt, one of our finest classical actors.

The theatre at Niagara-on-the-Lake was run by Franchot Tone's aunt, Maud Franchot, a passionate patron of the arts and a generous friend. Everywhere we played we were wonderfully welcomed and, of course, everyone adored Edward Everett. All the rich old ladies in each town knew him personally; he had been charming them for years, and they were all quite dotty about him. They would throw these sumptuous after-theatre suppers for him, great spreads they were, but he stubbornly refused to go unless all of us, the entire cast including the stage management, were invited. A democratic star if ever there was one. Before the curtain went up each night, not thinking of the play at all, he would rub his hands together with great relish and announce, "Oh my goodness! Are we ever going to have an elegant supper tonight! Mm-Mm! Elegant! Oh my!"

Eddy Horton, Marta Linden and me
on the road in Nina

For a man in his seventies Ed possessed a superhuman, almost obnoxious energy. He organized everything—our days, our nights! Marta finally got so wrung out she began to feign various illnesses to escape his tenacious schedules. For instance, he insisted I play tennis with him every day at 9:00 a.m.—rain or shine (I began to think he'd hired me only because I was good at the game). He would appear on court clad in something which resembled Churchill's boiler suit but turned out to be his long winter underwear (quite a sight first thing in the morning) and he demanded I hit the ball straight to him at all times so he would never have to move. This applied to rallies as well as actually playing a set. If I hit one out of his reach by so much as a yard he would stamp his foot, flounce off the court and go sit in the clubhouse and sulk. It only took about fifteen minutes till he deigned to speak to me again and then, with great renewed enthusiasm we would return to this very original form of play.

The only private recreation I had any time for was a short-lived caprice with two lesbians. A girlfriend of mine turned up one night with this very pretty, very wealthy young lady. I hadn't realized she basically preferred the fairer sex. "Little Miss Rich" owned a huge sleek Caddy convertible which I was longing to drive. So after the show we would pub crawl—she'd throw me the keys and I'd drive, while they necked. We would sometimes go back to their hotel room, where only occasionally was I allowed to participate in any way, but most of the time, I would just sit and watch the two of them go at it, hammer and tongues! I need hardly have complained; I just felt a little left out!

Ed, through Lyman Brown, had now extended the engagement to include Portland and San Francisco. So, packing my duds, I decided to write a farewell note to the two little dikes which I signed, "I shall always remain, erotically yours, The Lone Ranger."

Portland was largely memorable for its hospitality and its Olympia oysters. But San Francisco in 1952 produced a spectacular impact. It was an elegant, chic, breathtakingly beautiful city—a far cry from what it is now. We played the Alcazar for almost a month. I lived over in Sausalito for most of the run with my old producer friend from Montreal, Joy Thomson, who owned a house there. Her brother Harrison, one of the world's great skaters (star of the Ice Follies and Ice Capades) had retired and was running a lively bar-restaurant on stilts by the water called the Glad Hand, just a few hundred yards down from a famous old whorehouse, the Valhalla. Sausalito was mercifully uncrowded then and very bohemian—artists of every shape, size and specialty living on the water in barges to escape the tax—the whole place sizzled with atmosphere.

In San Fran itself I also had a marvellous time—what variety! On my night off I saw Jussi Björling, my favourite tenor, and the great Renata Telbaldi sing at the Opera House. On another, Ed took me to see Danny Kaye in his miraculous one-man show. Kaye burst onto the stage singing "Jambalaya an' a codfish pie-a." He made us laugh, cry and scream for more. He brilliantly mimed, playing a harp to Saint-Saën's "My Heart at Thy Sweet Voice"—his body and hands creating a ballet of their own. And then he would follow it with some sidesplitting nonsense by his wife, Sylvia Fine. What an extraordinary versatile talent—much more apparent from the stage than on the screen! As he bowed to the audience at the end he noticed Ed and, beaming from ear to ear, he pointed to him and beckoned us both to come backstage. Did I ever glow with pride?! Danny quite obviously had been a fan of Ed's from infancy and he invited us over to the original Trader Vic's where he had a special table and treated us like visiting royalty!

One evening Ed took us to the very popular Top o' the Mark for supper. He had no reservation. God knows he never needed one. On arrival we discovered the entire roof restaurant was shut down. The maître d' at the door, recognizing Ed, apologized profusely, explaining it had been taken over for a private party. We peered through the glass partitions from which one could see the whole room—it seemed absolutely empty. "But there's no one in the place," sputtered Mr. Horton with growing irritation. "Oh yes there is, sir, over there," corrected the maître d', pointing to a solitary couple seated far away in a corner surrounded by a phalanx of attentive waiters. It was a very young Debbie Reynolds and her host, Howard Hughes, who had bought the whole place out just to serenade her—a quiet tête-à-tête à deux!

After the show, some nights I would join forces with Joy and Harrison. Together we would do the clubs. Edith Piaf was in town so, of course, as usual, there I was worshipping at her feet. La petite oiseau with that call to arms in her voice would always be Jeanne d'Arc to me, and I would follow her to the death anywhere—into any battle— wherever she might choose. Eddy took Marta and me to Finnochio's one daring evening and afterwards I revisited it on my own whenever I could. Finnochio's had just about the best female impersonators in the world. I marvelled at those truly remarkable men who were able to transform themselves into such beautiful women so effortlessly. No matter how close one sat there wasn't a flaw—they were perfection. I met some of them backstage and was amazed to learn they were married, had children and led quite normal lives. Yet here they were, sewing away at their own stunning dresses which they so painstakingly had designed and made for themselves. I suppose for them all this was a mere living. For us, it was a faultless art.

Then there were the strip joints. Oh boy—the strip joints! I would toddle along and pay my respects (without Eddy and Marta), but Joy or Harrison sometimes joined me late into the night. The exotic "Tempest Storm"—a grand exponent of that ancient practice—was currently the toast of the town. Once her star turn was over, the rest of the act consisted of introducing fledgling strippers in their late teens who were now ready to graduate, rather like putting out young bulls in Pamplona. One stripper in particular caught our immediate attention. She wasn't in the least coarse like the others; her features were delicate, fine. She had pale skin and long blonde tresses, and from head to toe she was perfectly formed. The very picture of a tiny angel untouched, unsullied, she was, as Keats might say:

Full beautiful, a faery's child,
Her hair was long, her foot was light,
And her eyes were wild.

She must have lied about her age—she was only sixteen, the waiters told me. The other novilleras, when strutting their stuff, assumed expressions of world-wearied boredom, which made them appear oddly stiff and inhibited. This nymph who seemed so pure and innocent would not have recognized an inhibition had she met one head-on. Someone was obviously grooming her for stardom, for she'd been given a solo spot all to herself. I've never seen anyone attack her work with such passion and fury. She clearly couldn't wait to take everything off as she tossed aside each minute particle of clothing with careless abandon and instinctive grace. The combination of devil and saint was proving too irresistible—it was most apparent her intentions were not just to taunt us but herself as well and the crowd began to see signs of approaching turbulence. If San Francisco was a breeder of earthquakes, please let them be like this one. Caught up in our excitement for her, she would dance this mad dance of hers, naked as nature had made her, or slither and roll along the floor, reflected in its shiny surface striking every suggestive pose imaginable; she had to have been triple-jointed for she was able to do the most amazing and unprintable things. We were out of our seats! She was shocking, fearless, shameless, and she was laughing with sheer joy at our celebration of her body. Of course, she had broken all the rules, she was quite out of control but we didn't care and neither did she. She was flying now, doing her favourite thing, bringing herself to her particular state of grace, right there before our disbelieving eyes and suddenly the room wasn't a room anymore; we were all together in some forbidden jungle—wild, primitive and free.

On the marquee outside in very small print, she was billed quite simply and appropriately "Sorry." I was certain I had fallen in love with Sorry. As if craving some drug, I went back several times in the hope of seeing little Sorry perform again but she wasn't there anymore. They had taken down her billing. I had a horrible fantasy that in a dark alley on some black Walpurgistnacht, her fellow strippers, those older vultures, mad with jealousy, were violently pecking her to death.

TO FAN my unrequited passion, there was always a brisk breeze that cut like a knife along by the cliffs which overlooked the sea. I would go there sometimes alone to get windburned and watch the hordes of sea lions and seals barking at each other on the rocks. Or were they laughing at me? If so, I certainly deserved it. But the late-summer sun was soon to set on the Golden Gate Bridge and on *Nina* as well. Eddy and Marta, who both had houses back east on Lake George, kindly offered to put me up for a little holiday and a good-bye celebration of sorts. Eddy's house was a wondrous old pile hidden by huge trees just above the lake, full of character of course, and typically him. I moved in with Ed and his formidable mother who had just batted 101, God rest her soul. I saw at once where Eddy got his energy and endurance. Then during the day I would join Marta, her husband, and their daughter, Barbara, for boating and picnics.

We had built a strong little unit together, Marta, Eddy and I, during that lovely fleeting summer. So it was far from easy when the time came to say good-bye. Neither was it made any easier to know that the dawn of my American début had quickly turned to dusk. I was now unemployed and just about dead broke. So it was with certain trepidation that I made my solitary way—a Dick Whittington without portfolio—to that behemoth of cities whose jaws, I was convinced, would open and swallow me up. But all was not lost. For deep down in one of my pockets on a crumpled bit of food-stained paper, still damp from the islands, was a telephone number. I had no choice. I rang it.

"THOSE ARE ALL my husbands on the wall," sang out Ruth Chatterton, breezily. I was dying to paraphrase Robert Browning's acid line—"looking as if they were alive." We were in an elegant eagle's nest somewhere high above New York's Park Avenue. She was showing me her apartment which was, just as I expected, very posh indeed. This was the master bedroom. Above the bed, in a large elaborate frame, were set-in circular cutouts resembling miniatures, photographs in sepia of at least three Mr. Chattertons. There was George Brent, Ralph Forbes and the current, Barry Thomson. In the center, dominating all three, her original mentor and lover—the Broadway impresario, Henry Miller. He seemed to be glowering downwards in general disapproval, particularly at the present successor as he lay there nursing a raging cold. Poor Barry, I thought, what a horrible fate to be constantly haunted like that in bed. Under such critical surveillance, how could he ever possibly perform?! I was astounded too at Ruth's total disregard as she blithely chatted away moving swiftly from one non sequitur to another. "She's leaving Barry to die in there all by himself," I mused, stumbling after her into the living room like a pet dog. The houseman poured us drinks as she outlined my itinerary for the next fortnight—they were not exactly suggestions; they were orders, gilt-edged commands.

To say dear Ruth had kept her word would be the decade's most glaring understatement. Her thoughtfulness was quite beyond belief. With that familiar little snap of her fingers she got me into parties I would never have dreamed of crashing. At the mere mention of her name, people became at once attentive. Through her I met authors, producers, actors, musicians, painters and society—top-drawer, café, even cafeteria society. But the best thing she ever did was to bring me to a woman way past middle age who, for years to come, I would respect, admire and love to the end of her days and beyond—my friend and very first real agent—Miss Jane Broder.

> *She has a touching way*
> *Of backing a man up against eternity*
> *Until he hardly has the nerve to remain mortal.*
> —CHRISTOPHER FRY

A full-fledged legal-beagle was our Jane. More judge than lawyer, perhaps, since her strict sense of fair play was her creed and the guiding force of her life. An older and wiser Portia she was indeed, a "Daniel come to judgment." The integrity she had built around her was an impenetrable fortress. Part purist, part puritan, her occasional outbursts of righteousness could be a trifle irritating, but there was generally a pretty firm basis of truth behind them and they always cut to the quick. If Jane had ever looked Sin straight in the eye, Sin would have just wilted away, riddled with remorse. In composing her ironclad contracts, however, she was more ruthless and thorough than any lawyer or agent I have ever known. Her speech was hard-core New York Jewish. She began most of her sentences with "Now listen, honey." But she was in love with talent—that was the soft side of her. If Jane thought you had talent, she was a pushover and she'd do anything for you. A surrogate mother and Golda Meir rolled into one, she would have made a damn fine prime minister of anything. This rotund, affable lady who wore a hat and veil at all times, even in her office, had once created and managed the foremost independent theatrical agency in New York.

Along with Ruth Chatterton, she had looked after a young Bette Davis and a younger Rosalind Russell, and among others she served were Marjorie Rambeau, Eva Le Gallienne, Gladys George, Paul Lucas, Frank Morgan and Paul Muni. Many of Broadway and Hollywood's brightest luminaries had, in their early years, passed through her door.

Untypically for an agent, she was also a brilliant casting director for such powerful men as Herman Shumlin, Kermit Bloomgarden and the writers Elmer Rice and Maxwell Anderson. These men valued her wisdom and trusted her above all others. It was quite clear that Jane had known what it felt like to be First Lady of the Admiralty in command of a huge fleet. But the much larger corporate giants were beginning to dominate the ocean (MCA, William Morris, CMA to follow) and her battleship was now severely reduced to rather cramped quarters—three poky rooms and a waiting room on Forty-ninth and Madison. Her present band of clients, loyal to the death, were young artists George C. Scott, Colleen Dewhurst, Stephen Elliot, David Wayne, Anthony Perkins, Richard Kiley. Older character actors included Eva Le Gallienne (still), Anne Shoemaker, Aileen McMahon, Lucile Watson, Shirley Booth, Kent Smith and John Williams.

Now most 10-percenters reel off the same old familiar spiel to the young and eager. "We can't do anything for you till we've seen your work—when you do something let us know." Jane at our first meeting virtually echoed the same phrase, "Listen, honey, I don't take people till I see their work." She must have clocked my hangdog look of disappointment, for she followed up with, "But I'll tell ya what I'll do. I'll get you some work so I can come see it!" That was Jane. She called her old friend Morris Carnovsky, that pillar of the Group Theatre, who was organizing a reading of Montherlant's darkly purple piece—*Queen After Death* at the ANTA Playhouse. The part of the villain was still open. My long radio training stood me in good stead. I read the pants off it. Jane came backstage afterwards looking like the matriarch of all Yiddisha-Mamas. She gave me the fiercest of double whammies and said, "Honey, you got yourself an agent." From that moment on I was never out of work.

THE "GOLDEN AGE" of live television in New York's early nineteen-fifties was the wackiest of wacky times. To say there was an immediacy to it would be far too tame—idiocy, perhaps, describes it better. No one ever knew what was going to happen next. Most of the time we did nothing but bump into the furniture, the roving cameras and each other, all at once. Even so, some pretty marvellous work was done between mishaps: writers were really writing then, richly, deeply; there was a whole new breed of them, busy as bees, creating little gems of true substance for an upstart medium that should have been very grateful—it still owes them a lot—Horton Foote, Alvin Sapinsley, Paddy Chayefsky, Reginald Rose, S. Lee Pogostin and James Costigan among them. Comedy was being churned out by Mel Brooks, Carl Reiner, Larry Gelbart—all top-class stuff. Comics Jack Benny, Phil Silvers, Sid Caesar, Imogene Coca and Mr. Berle ("Uncle Miltie"), while searching for their light, were being exceedingly funny, if a trifle static. This was understandable, for if they got carried away and actually moved a few feet to the right or left—there was no more set—they had banished themselves to oblivion.

Journalists Edward R. Murrow, Charles Collingwood, a young Brinkley and Cronkite, even Alistair Cooke, had no choice but to become expert ad-libbers and improvisors to get themselves out of trouble or just to keep the party going. Scriptless, they could extemporize for hours, adding to the "You Are There," accident-prone quality of early television that made us feel we were living on the edge. Interviewers John Freeman in London and Mike Wallace in New York discovered that the camera could prove a perfect ally when humiliating their celebrity guests. To extract on-air confessions from them, they reduced them to tears in full view of the public, bombarding them with delicate questions they were ill-prepared to answer. That was the cruel side of the medium—probably what it did best—its very purpose for being, to expose the raw nerves of humanity. Nothing could have better illustrated this than the notorious Army-McCarthy hearings we devoured daily in bars, offices and store windows all over the city. Horrified, hypnotized, we watched grown men behave like nasty little boys, supposedly distinguished senators make utter fools of themselves. It unfolded before our eyes like some bad melodrama—the good guys and the bad guys shooting it out to the death—and in the end, it was not the court but the cameras that made the final judgment as to who would win or lose.

Those were the early warning signs that this explosive new invention was about to get out of hand and go too far, that one day soon it would tell us how to eat, how to dress, how to live. Drunk with power it could dictate policy, bring down corporations, swing elections, topple governments. Newscasters were turned into opinionated superstars. Nothing would be sacred anymore, neither the dignity of high office nor the sanctity of the ruling classes. All would become an open book—what was caviar to the general was now popcorn for the masses. Today we have become quite accustomed to being fed intravenously with third-rate dogma; like some insidious germ warfare it all seems painstakingly planned, carefully calculated. Oh, sometimes something fine comes along to momentarily redeem it, but not often enough.

In the early fifties, however, television promised everything. There was nowhere it couldn't go; its horizons were limitless. It was also wonderfully brave, young, fresh, even innocent.

"GEORGE HAS SOMETHING FOR YOU," called out Jane from her inner cubbyhole as I waited in the foyer. "I don't handle television, honey. Let George do it—go see George." The very smallest of the three small rooms was occupied by a chubby sheepdog of a youth who belonged to that newly discovered species—the television agent. George Morris was a whiz at it. He had managed to wangle me the lead in Rudyard Kipling's *The Light That Failed* for the most prestigious drama series on the air—Studio One. The big boss of Studio One, Worthington Miner, was a good-natured, powerfully built man with a rich, rumbling belly laugh which identified him at once as a member of the old boy's club. Both "Tony" and his wife, actress Frances Fuller, were very like protective parents to me in those early days. I shall be forever grateful to them. The distinguished cast in the Kipling piece included that famous D'Oyly Carte star from England—the man with the monocle—Martyn Greene, and the richly talented fugitive from *Citizen Kane* and Mercury Theatre days, Everett Sloane. The show's sponsor was Westinghouse, who went totally ballistic when they realized it was far too late to change the show's ads, which ironically read: "Westinghouse Electric Presents *The Light That Failed.*" Though for me it was a most auspicious debut, I'm afraid the show will be mostly remembered for that unfortunate gaff.

Work began to come thick and fast. George got me a steady job on a daily soap opera where I met new friends like Robert Webber, Audrey Christie and Connie Ford. Not the glamorous separate soft-porn worlds they have become today, where soap stars are turned into gods and do nothing else; soaps then were looked upon by hard-working Broadway actors as merely a means to an end between serious stage work. There was a new episode every day so we all got up at an unheard-of hour of the morning to rehearse and of course we never really *ever* knew our lines. So we invented and mastered a new technique, which was to wink at the camera operators whenever we were in deep trouble, and they would move past us and shoot a blank wall or a painting or two while we snuck a quick gander at the text.

The most famous soap opera writer of the day was a lovely older lady with a shock of gorgeous white hair, a big heart and a sunny charm. She was a great hostess and her name was Elaine Carrington. The soaps she was famous for were *Pepper Young's Family* and *Life Can Be Beautiful*, among others. They had run for years successfully on both radio and television and had made her an absolute fortune. I became friendly with her son Robert, a would-be producer, so I was always asked to her legendary shindigs which she threw like clockwork at her house on the sea at East Hampton or her penthouse on Fifty-fifth Street in the city. Everyone in and outside the business was in attendance, Noël Coward a frequent guest. Marlene Dietrich would appear quite regularly, occasionally accompanied by her daughter, Maria, but more often she would bring her friend the delightful Marti Stevens, for whom I have always had the greatest affection. Judy Garland and Gene Kelly came and went and at one party I was introduced to a pert young lady with a brush-cut hairdo and a ski-jump nose who had a penchant for wearing raccoon overcoats with very little underneath. Her name, which could easily have come from the pen of Charles Dickens, was Tammy Grimes.

THANKS TO JANE AND GEORGE I never stopped. Still "soaping," I also found time to do all the major shows—Philco Television Playhouse, Kraft Television Theatre, Robert Montgomery Presents, Camera Three and a weekly marathon aptly called Broadway Television Theatre, the brainchild of Warren Wade, a fat little man who always wore an oversized fedora. It was like doing summer stock with cameras—we played the same show nightly—we even did matinées. It was really quite bizarre. Ex-Hollywood icons who had a taste for theatre would fly from the coast to play the leads. I was Sylvia Sidney's leading man twice—in *Kind Lady* and *Dark Victory*. Sylvia, who was a superb actress, had large, deep pools of eyes, which right on cue would overflow with tears gushing from their ducts like waterfalls. "She Could Cry on Demand" should have been the show's new title.

In *Dark Victory* the part of her faithful butler was played by a onetime silent screen star from the Cecil B. DeMille epics. Ian Keith was a

Young Sylvia, my favorite picture of her

handsome, rugged American with a beautiful speaking voice. He resembled a much taller John Barrymore, was just as big a bon viveur and had a daredevil quality to him, that even in his late sixties, was most attractive. When England declared war on Germany in '39, Ian left Hollywood, went straight up to Canada and enlisted in the Black Watch.

At the end of each show, which was sponsored by General Motors, the three leading cast members were obliged by contract to stand beside the latest car, usually a Ford, and in a few choice words extol its praises. It was humiliating and awful, particularly for important stars like Sylvia, but we gritted our teeth and did it. On the first night of *Dark Victory* Ian, whose appearance was over in the first act, went out and got drunk. Professional down to his little toe, he returned promptly at the show's climax to do his bit for Ford. Slapping the brand-new vehicle with a good whack, Ian, in that booming voice of his, shouted, "I want to tell you about my new little MG. She's the best mistress I've ever had. Goddamn! I do love that car. If she was just a tad smaller, why, hell, I'd take her to bed with me. She sure beats this old piece of tin!"

Warren Wade stamped on his fedora and hit the roof. Ian was reported to AFTRA and banned from ever working on television again. My heart went out to him. That lovely old rebel had done something we all had secretly longed to do but didn't have the guts. He had separated art from advertising and mocked commercialism with its self-imposed pretensions. Jane insisted I go down to the union meeting and testify against Ian and his dastardly deed. "You've got to go, honey. He's put us all in jeopardy." I suppose she was right, but I didn't have the heart—I never went.

There was no end to disasters on TV in those days. My next assignment was opposite that beautiful Swede from stage and screen, Viveca Lindfors. *The Riddle of Mayerling* was a half-hour drama for Robert Montgomery Presents. It dealt with the suicide pact of those two famous lovers, Crown Prince Rudolf of Hapsburg and his mistress, Baroness Maria Vetsera. The show's only set was the interior of the hunting lodge where their stormy deaths were to take place. The assignation arranged, Maria paced up and down the room waiting for her prince to arrive. On air night, Maria paced up and down for a much longer period of time than had been rehearsed. In fact, the entire show was running out of time. The reason? I couldn't find my entrance. It was so pitch-bloody dark behind the set, there was nary a door or window in sight—no floor manager—no one to help. I panicked. Suddenly I saw a light in the distance, coming through what looked like a very low opening; with great relief, I made for it at once. It must have looked very strange indeed both to Maria and the nationwide audience when the crown prince in full dress uniform, jangling with medals, sporting a fur-collared Magyar cape greeted his lover by entering through the fireplace.

The producer, Marty Manulis, normally a quiet and civilized man—turned into a mad, screaming banshee when the debacle was over. Martin had a walleye which always looked past you so you never knew who he was giving shit to. That night there was no mistaking the object of his abuse. He was so angry I thought at one point his eye would pop out like some frightened Pekinese!

"Why the fireplace? Why the f-f-f-fireplace? Why come through the fucking fireplace?" he sputtered.

"You're fucking lucky I came through anything!" I hollered back. Afterwards, I was to see Marty every now and then in California. We always exchanged pleasantries. But I never worked for him again. I wonder why.

A series of small Dunkirks occurred almost daily in our newfound medium—there was such intense pressure and so little time. I remember walking through an entire show on the air, cool, calm and relaxed only because I thought it was the dress rehearsal. I was not, however, TV's only victim. Lloyd Bridges, after a sterling performance on some hour-long drama, upset over a minor catastrophe, let fly a barrage of four-letter words, not realizing the sound switch was still on—and the entire country listened, wondering if it was their fault.

For some obscure reason, producing Westerns suddenly became a fad and the big studios in Brooklyn transformed themselves into little "Devil's Gulches" or little "Black Rocks." They also had room to stable horses. Most New York actors were not exactly trained to be cowboys so things got a little hairy down at Studio A. On one disastrous occasion, the cameras were forced to cut away from the main scene to a bunch of hams dressed as wranglers not knowing what on earth they were supposed to be ad-libbing. It was all too late anyway, for what the audience had just witnessed was Lee Marvin, on horseback, riding straight through a papier-mâché mountain and his frightened nag taking an instant dump at one and the same time.

I once appeared in a quasi-classical Western written by the gifted Alvin Sapinsley. I played the male lead opposite Lee Grant. The rest of the terrific cast was made up of Franchot Tone, Boris Karloff, Frank Overton and a young Jason Robards. I remember we all kept getting our spurs caught in everything. Sapinsley had centered his main theme around some familiar lines of Swinburne and actually borrowed his title from them—*Even the Weariest River.* The poem would act as an off-camera prologue and epilogue to be spoken by Boris Karloff. Though he read it beautifully, of course, it was not the most ideal exercise to give Boris considering his famous lisp. This is how it came out:

> *That dead men rythe up never;*
> *That even the wearietht river*
> *Windth thumwhere thafe to thea.*

I remember watching Maurice Evans give us his live television presentation of Hamlet for NBC with Ruth Chatterton playing Queen Gertrude, her last performance. When Mr. Evans, who was a most distinguished Hamlet, arrived at his famous soliloquy, "Now I am alone . . . ," he wasn't. In mellifluous tones he continued to emote, blissfully unaware that only a few feet behind him in full view of the camera was a beefy, unshaven stagehand peering around a pillar chawing at an oversized deli sandwich. Whenever Mr. Evans decided to move, so did the stagehand. So did his sandwich. In fact, the entire solo piece became a trio. The hungry grip must have been thinking, "Who da hell's dis weirdo wearing tights and a wig walkin' around in my lunch break talkin' to himself?"

Frayed nerves and dementia were commonplace—especially for movie actors unaccustomed to learning long passages of dialogue. Noël Coward, producing and starring in a TV version of his own play *Present Laughter,* stopped the dress rehearsal dead cold and gave Claudette Colbert a severe dressing down for continuously muffing her lines. Miss Colbert flew into a rage. "If you ever speak to me like that again, I'll throw something at you!" "Good. Why not start with my cues?" retorted the Master.

The advertising world had by now completely taken over this over-grown monster of an industry and was bringing with it, rather inconsiderately, a horde of new young executives and so-called producers who knew next to nothing about the business of drama and were equally ignorant as to who anybody was. It was only certain casting directors like Marion Dougherty and Rose Tobias Shaw who, with extreme tact and knowledge, would eventually set them straight. Up to then, famous stars of stage and screen were forced to suffer the indignity of being interviewed, even auditioned by these ill-informed arrivistes. One young whippersnapper of that ilk, armed with an overextended ego and no past, theatrical or otherwise, had the temerity to ask Helen Hayes to describe her long career. "Please, Miss Hayes," he whimpered, "tell us what you've done?" "After you—" invited the great lady with a gracious smile.

Mildred Natwick, a much-respected character actress on both coasts, known for her quick wit, was being similarly interrogated by some other erstwhile executive. "And tell me, Miss Natwick, what have you done?" "About what?" replied Millie with a querulous look of wide-eyed innocence.

My friend, the rebellious old dog Ian Keith, had become quite used to these humiliating sessions. At one of them, a cheeky young director of little experience (over at Kraft Theatre) asked Ian the same worn-out standard—"And what have you done?"

Ian decided to have some fun: "I don't believe you caught my name, sir."

"No, sir, I didn't."

Picking one at random, Ian chose a celebrated classical actor from a distant past. At his most grandiloquent, relishing every syllable, Ian pronounced magisterially, "My name is Holbrook Blinn!"

None the wiser, the director barrelled on, "And what have you done Mr. Blinn?"

"I'm dead, you son of a bitch," Ian tossed over his shoulder as he swept from the room, unemployed but triumphant!

Occasionally into this sea of chaos, redemption like an angel came with such chef-d'oeuvres as *Patterns,* produced by Fielder Cook and sporting a gem of a cast headed by Richard Kiley and Ed Begley. *The Whooping Cranes* in which E. G. Marshall as an old lighthouse keeper pines for that moment once a year when the birds fly over. (E. G. had me blubbing on the floor like a baby.) Rod Steiger gave two superb accountings of himself—one as the crippled genius Steinmetz and the other as Marty, Paddy Chayefsky's touching study of a loser. Like vanishing phantoms, the Lunts were fleetingly caught by the roving lens. Shirley Booth and Maureen Stapleton brought us to tears, each in her own way, and Martha Graham and Fred Astaire separately awed us with their inventiveness and grace. There was brilliant work from the directorial batons of Sidney Lumet, Franklin Schaffner, Dan Petrie, George Roy Hill and the old-guard producers who actually knew what they were doing—Fred Coe, Robert Saudek, David Susskind and Hubbell Robinson chained themselves together like watchdogs to keep integrity from rusting.

Live cameras candidly captured golden moments: cryptic old Joseph Welch's famous rebuke to "Senator McCarthy (Have you no sense of decency?") as he quietly swung the nation against the boorish Commie-baiter from Wisconsin; white-haired Toscanini in fiery old age, whipping his NBC orchestra into frenzies of excitement; Leonard Bernstein on Omnibus informing, with great charm, millions of average North Americans that classical music did not begin or end with Tchaikovsky and Rachmaninov. TV's doctor of divinity, Archbishop Sheen, like some lisping medieval priest, filled our eyes and ears with his low-key fire and brimstone. For world coverage on an epic scale and as educator and guide in the right hands, early television promised to be of the greatest value in years to come; and even though it was just as fond of making messes as would any unruly child growing up too fast, there was one glaring truth which nobody could dispute—it was a bloomin' miracle!

"I Wasn't Born; I Was Squeezed out of a Rag at Sardi's Bar"

OLD SARDI, Vincent Junior's father, who ruled his domain with an iron hand and a steel fist was, to put it in the mildest vernacular—some hombre! Sardi's—which winked at you from the far end of Shubert Alley and warmed the cockles of your heart on bitter winter nights with its red-trimmed front door, before which stood a doorman all in red and behind which a sea of red-uniformed waiters swarmed like bees—was the city's foremost theatrical meeting place. It catered to audiences and performers alike and made damn certain they got in and out on time. Top artists, musical and "legit," who had made it on Broadway, ate and drank in the front room, their recently drawn caricatures resplendently in evidence on the walls above them. They sat basking in the adoration of ever-loving fans and the public, who were

relegated to the very rear of
the establishment. Sardi's was,
in those days, the louder, live-
lier version of London's Ivy or
Le Caprice. It played host to a
constantly buzzing theatrical
Who's Who from Europe to
Hollywood and back. In fact it
was, in many ways, the theatre
itself.

Of course, at my stage of
life, I shouldn't have gone
there at all—I could ill afford
it. But once a headwaiter or
two took pity on me and
grudgingly let me in, I slowly
became what could be de-

One smart, funny lady

scribed as a poor man's regular. Though way out of my league, at least
it made me look and feel that I was a success like the rest—that I had
reached a higher rung. I particularly loved lounging at the bar rubbing
shoulders with Robert Preston, Gig Young, Bernie Hart, Harold
Kennedy, Rex Harrison (whenever he was in town) and that duffle-
coated raffish "Trupshawe" of an Englishman—old "Cootie"—Robert
Coote. Elaine Stritch, representing, all on her own, most of the actresses
in Equity, proved once again that she could drink all of us stalwarts
under the table and still be the leitmotif of the room. Martyn Greene,
whose throne was at the north end of the bar, took special pains to
include me and make me feel I was "one of the boys." With that big
monocle in his eye and bigger heart in his chest, he never stopped
introducing me to my favourite bartender, Cappy, who was part French
Canadian, part "Stromboli" and part saint. My two actor pals, Robert
Webber and Val Avery, were my faithful guides and ever-ready seconds
should any unforeseen troubles arise.

Old man Sardi was astonishingly kind to actors, young and old. Even
when they were too proud to admit penury, the old man could smell it
a mile away and would permit them to run up tabs indefinitely. He
always managed to forgive and forget. Whenever I was lucky enough to
eat there, I was generally herded into the back of beyond next to the
kitchen, where the lesser tourists sat. One day down the road I would be
swept to my table in the A room as close to my own caricature as discre-

tion would allow, but now, as I munched gratefully on my hot Shrimp a la Sardi, far away in Siberia, I could only dream such things as with each mouthful my credit rapidly slipped away. I was now so much in debt, it was far too humiliating to face Mr. Sardi so for the longest time I didn't go back. One day I gathered up enough courage to fight my way through the crowds at the door and the first person I fell upon was the old man himself. "Mr. Sardi—," I began, sheepishly, my voice breaking ever so slightly, but before I could say another word he was all over me with that expansive bonhomie of his. "Come in please. You've been away too long—you are always welcome here." "But Mr. Sardi—" I tried again. At that moment his son Vincent, who had already inherited his father's celebrated hospitality, came over and whispered in my ear, "It's okay. Jane Broder was here. She settled everything."

All the way from Fortieth to Fifty-fourth streets going north and from Sixth to Tenth avenues going west, there were hundreds of cafés and bars, a great many of them Irish and French, but mostly French from good old Café Brittany on down. It was as if every Frenchman who ever stepped off a boat onto the dock had instantly erected a restaurant right where he stood. There were also numerous tiny watering holes where actors and dancers could hang out. Those who didn't wear ties, jackets or skirts and couldn't afford Sardi's generally convened at what was probably the smallest of the lot called, not too originally, the Theatre Bar. Squashed tightly between several other dives on Forty-fifth Street, it was, in its day, the most popular joint in the district. Two tough guys from Central Europe (if you could find them in the crush) ran the place like a soup kitchen. No one could ever remember their surnames—they were known simply as Patsy and Karl. They loved us gypsies and understood that most of the young ones were struggling and ten times out of six would buy them dinner—"Don't vurry—eets all on us. Pay next time."

I practically lived there with Val Avery, Bob Webber and his wife. Stritch would be there with that wonderful raucous cackle of hers dropping one-liners by the bucketload at one end of the counter, while Jack Warden, just out of the marines, was busy getting laughs at the other. Maureen Stapleton and a statuesque Colleen Dewhurst (O women of Thebes) were sure to be present and accounted for. George C. Scott, about to explode upon the scene as one of the best actors America has ever produced, was forever getting into scraps of the most heinous variety. With his dangerous stare, smoldering passion and quick wit (generally mistaken for cruel sarcasm) he was the likeliest candidate in the room to start a brawl. Though everyone was terrified of him when he had a few too many, surprisingly, he ended up the loser every time. I don't think George C. ever believed he'd really had a decent evening unless he finished it up on the floor in a pool of blood.

Most of the others in the room were out-of-work stage actors waiting for their next gig, so there was a lot of pent-up anger and envy floating around; there was also an additional warlike atmosphere due to the two separate "schools" mingling at such close quarters—the Method boys from the Studio, the exponents of street acting in Brando-like T-shirts and torn jeans, and the more polished classical brigade, who dressed fairly well and spoke even better—each snubbing the other in utter disdain. It was a riot, and it wasn't in the least surprising that fights would break out, with Patsy and Karl always in the middle—two refugee referees—trying to separate these frustrated, hot-tempered pugilists. Of course, when Lawrence Tierney (wonderful when portraying violence on-screen) appeared bombed out of his skull, the police automatically were called in. Like a madman, he would clear the bar of all glass and cutlery and, breaking a bottle over the counter, would threaten everyone in sight. This could happen late at night or early in the evening, depending on Mr. Tierney's mood, so it was not much of a welcome for unfortunate audiences who had sauntered in for a quiet drink at intermission, only to encounter a drama far more petrifying then any they might have just witnessed on the stage.

But thank the Lord for Patsy and Karl for keeping us alive. Their proud little warren could never be called dull and, looking back, I can't believe what an astounding amount of talent was squeezed together in that narrow, sweaty little room. If someone had ever decided to hurl a grenade through its front door, the future of the American stage might have been erased forever.

"WHERE ARE YOU LIVING NOW, honey? How can I ever get you—you never tell me where you are!" It was Jane Broder on the warpath again! Of course, she was quite right—though I had steady work from my soap, I was living ridiculously beyond my means, partying way into the night drinking and dining at hideously expensive restaurants (Le Volnay, Le Chambord) and, because of my early passion for clothes, running up accounts at Brooks Brothers, Tripplers and Weatheralls. Overextended beyond credulity, I kept checking in and out of cheesy hotels (the Van Rensselaer, the Pickwick Arms, the old

Edison). If I couldn't pay, I just left my clothes and moved to the next one; when I ran out altogether, Bob Webber and his wife, Sammy, took me in or if there was no room there I would end up on the floor of Jack Warden's pad. When I'd finished confessing all this to Jane, she lost her patience completely, took me by the scruff of the neck and marched me straight down Forty-fourth to the Algonquin, made a deal with the manager and I was in like Flynn.

"I can keep track of you better here, honey," said Jane as she left me at the front desk. I didn't move; I simply stood in wonder as I marvelled at the dark mahogany panelled lobby vibrating with the presence of the living dead—its Round Table truer and more famous than Camelot's. The spirits of Dorothy Parker, Marc Connelly, George Kaufman, Robert Benchley, Robert Sherwood and Alexander Woolcott, much to my relief and joy, seemed more than alive and well—in fact they had never left. O'Neill had once been a fixture of that lobby, as had the Barrymores and Tallulah and Jane Cowl and all this was recorded for posterity in James Thurber's and Al Hirschfeld's witty caricatures scattered at random on the hotel walls. The Algonquin was now a favourite stopover for the visiting British acting-producing hierarchy—Donald Albery, Henry Sherek, Binky Beaumont and of course, Olivier, Richardson—most of the theatrical knights. Writers like Tennessee Williams, W. H. Auden, T. S. Eliot and Norman Mailer lived there on and off. Robert Roark wrote one of his novels there. Oscar Levant came and went, as did critics Elliot Norton and Kenneth Tynan. It was quite amazing and uncanny but the past was so very present, there wasn't much difference between customers alive or dead; they were simply guests getting along quite splendidly as they mingled together in that smoke-filled paneled lobby.

Like some powerful elixir, this heady atmosphere had quite obviously inebriated the staff as well, who moved about the rooms with an extracharged energy and urgency as if floating six inches above floor level. Those wonderful bellhops and waiters, who never saw the light of day and never went to bed, would become my pals for life. So would Robert, the headwaiter in the Rose Room, or old Charlie, the busboy, an ancient Chinese rumoured to be in his midnineties who never spoke but smiled inscrutably as each day he performed his sole duty— placing a fresh rose in every finger bowl.

The hotel was nicknamed the "Gonk," or, when particularly effete members of our profession were in residence, the "Alicegonquin," but what's in a name?! This wonderful old inn was to be my new home, my headquarters for years to come. I couldn't believe my luck. Immediately, I took advantage, establishing for myself a tiny beachhead in the lobby. I must have made a total nuisance of myself, but I was deliriously happy. The place spelt Broadway and The Theeahtah in capital letters—even the smell of it made me long to get back on the boards. The mad rush of television work was not only unsatisfying, it had quieted down considerably; my role on the soap had inconveniently run out; the little bank account Jane had arranged for me at Chase Manhattan was looking very sparse and I was overspending so horribly in my newly discovered haven, I found I wasn't able to settle the tab. So one afternoon when I went up to my room, I couldn't get in. Outraged, I ignored the elevator and ran down the stairs to the front desk three at a time. "Why is my room locked?" I demanded in a towering rage. The rather prissy new manager who had replaced the late Frank Case (famous for his patience and generosity) responded most unceremoniously, "We will keep your things here till you pay your bill. And I don't want to see you till you do! Now go!" He turned his back on me and flounced away, leaving behind him a shower of dandruff which slowly fell to the carpet like snow in a crystal globe. I couldn't think of where to go and I certainly didn't dare tell Jane.

I don't remember where I spent the next several nights (some kind-hearted sucker like Jack Warden must have offered me shelter) but one morning window-shopping along Madison, I bumped into her. "The McClintic office called. They seem interested, honey. Get over there first thing in the morning!"—and she was gone. Well, this is it, I thought, this is it! I'm going to make it! Now I could thumb my nose at the Algonquin, at television—at the world. Here was a summons from Broadway's highest peak. The Titans were calling. With a majestic thunderclap, the clouds had parted and, at last, I could see Olympus. Permit me then to jump several months ahead, if I may, in the same state of impatience and excitement with which I ran, like a long-lost son, toward the first stage door I could see.

CHAPTER ELEVEN

A CANADIAN WETBACK AT MCCLINTIC'S COURT

S pring 1955: New York–Paris flight. Four-engine Constellation. First-class cabin. Sole occupants—Judith Anderson, Stanley Gilkey (a theatrical manager), one rich American playboy, two snobbish Afghan hounds, Guthrie McClintic and me. Trip's purpose— to present McClintic's famous *Medea* by Robinson Jeffers at Théâtre Sarah Bernhardt with Anderson at her demonic best and me opposite her as a ludicrously far-too-youthful Jason. It's probably McClintic's seventy-fifth Atlantic crossing. This one takes fourteen hours—we're into our sixth—McClintic still entertaining the cabin, regaling us from his bottomless trunk of sidesplitting anecdotes. Aided consider-ably by a half-killed case of Scotch, we're all falling about in the aisle— all, that is, except the disapproving Afghans and Miss A., who somehow left us way back when and seems to be floating on nuage numéro neuf! With all the dignity we can muster the four of us hoist the great actress into her upper birth (a bizarre conceit of early first-class air travel) as McClintic, still absorbed in deviltry, never draws breath. While we lift her he is telling us how he and his producers— Robert Whitehead and Oliver Rea—finally dissuaded an adamant Miss A. from performing her tragic heroine authentically bare chested! "She may be getting on and she may have the face of Mrs. Danvers, but she's still got two of the firmest, most remarkable boobs and she was dying to flaunt 'em! If I'd let her, she'd have closed every goddamn the-atre!" Twenty-five vulgar stories later, exhausted from laughter, we report to our first Paris répetition—a line rehearsal. Location? The ultrachic Ritz bar. Elsa Maxwell holding the book.

THE LAST FEW rehearsals back in New York had been, to say the least, chaotic (Miss A. condescending to appear only occasionally). Even the presence of witty Mildred Natwick, who played the nurse, didn't help cheer me up. I would stand on the stage, a woefully under-rehearsed Jason, staring into the wings waiting for the Goddess of Thunder. I could see her sitting on an offstage bench casually going through her morning mail while emitting the two unearthly howls that preceded her entrance. She was of course merely "marking" it, but even at half speed those ear-piercing cries that daily rent the air at 10 a.m. never ceased to send shivers down my spine.

I had tried so hard to hold my own and give the impression of masculine power in that improbable, wimpish role Mr. Jeffers must have bored himself to death writing. To look Greek I had gone to some sleazy salon to have my hair dyed blond. They had merely succeeded in singeing my entire head with second-degree burns. I was relieved I'd forgotten to have my chest hairs dyed too, and they remained a thick dark brown. Too cowardly to shave to make all consistent, I would have to spray them nightly with gold dust. At any rate, the new Jason came out looking like a plucked chicken with alopecia—the only albino in the brood!

The final run-through at the old New Amsterdam Roof before the cream of Broadway theatrical society (the Lunts, Helen Hayes, George Abbott, Katherine Cornell, Josh Logan, Ruth Gordon and Garson Kanin, Gilbert and Kitty Miller, etc.) was when Judith decided to pull out all the stops! She was electrifying! Attired simply in black sweater and black tights she prowled, stalked and slunk about the stage—hissing, spitting, breathing fire like some enraged dragon. She splashed the canvas of her extraordinary voice with every colour in the spectrum; now, soothing, seductive—now commanding, tempestuous—a cadenza of sounds culminating in a finale of frenzy! Truly, we were in the presence that day of a tragedienne of the first order—upon whose shoulders would surely fall the mantle of Rachel or Madame Georges.

But, hélas! Once in Paris all was to change. It was the height of Le Festival International. Every theatre company of stature in the world was present—the Brecht Ensemble, Italy's Piccolo Teatro, the Chinese Peking Theatre and the Kabuki from Japan. From Paris, there was the TNP, Jean Vilar's great classic company, and to heighten tension even further, yet another Medea in the person of France's own Marguerite Jamois. Normally this wouldn't have disturbed Miss Judith for a second. Why, even without an appetite she could consume *twelve* Marguerites for breakfast! But on the Place du Châtelet at the famous Théâtre des Nations, now named for la Bernhardt, she was to inherit the Divine Sarah's massive dressing rooms with their ornate double doors leading from the antechambers into the hallowed sanctum sanctorum still richly reverberating with memories of passion and glory.

Judith stood in the midst of her vast new domain staring at the bare walls, the great windows and the high ceilings. Gone were the sumptuous Oriental rugs, the chaise longues, the chandeliers; gone—the majordomo admitting adoring kings, presidents and ambassadors; gone—the powdered, liveried footmen flinging wide the doors for "la petite Juif" to step forward, still in full costume and proffer her hand for their homage and obeisance. Nothing left now but the empty echoing rooms and far away in a distant corner under a single electric lightbulb, the meanest, most insignificant makeup table imaginable! Judith must have felt at that moment very much alone, a stranger with nary a friend in sight. She may have thought of her newfound home, America, the scene of her many triumphs; her native Australia and of course, England, where she had scored such successes at the Old Vic—three countries she was, in a sense, about to represent here in the city of light. Unwarranted as it may have been, the considerable weight of all this suddenly descended upon her—and that morning, the tough little sheila from dahn under—lost her voice.

"Medée," sans sa voix, est une image pitoyable—sans majesté, sans puissance. Throughout the Paris run the future dame of the British Empire never once regained her vocal powers but valiantly croaked her way through each performance—a pale shadow of her former self. The French press were glacially polite and loftily patronizing. Was this the famous Madame Anderson from whom they were to expect such marvels?! The frailer her voice box the more mine grew in strength, but it didn't save me from the critical lambasting I rightly received. What the hell was a snotty-nosed college kid doing cast as the noblest Greek of 'em all? Was this a mate to match the Gorgon, the swarthy hero of the Golden Fleece?

Guthrie was remarkable! He wasn't going to take any of it lying down. He ranted and raved, defiantly defending us to the death, and he was wonderful to her. He filled her days with private viewings at museums, delectable lunches at top Parisian restaurants, arranged a meeting with Monsieur le Président, threw parties for her at both the French and American embassies (which I was allowed to attend) and showered her with gifts. He even found time to take me along with him to see the current plays—Gerard Philippe in *Le Cid,* Jean Vilar in Pirandello's *Henri IV* and Pierre Fresnay in *Les Oeufs de l'Autruche.* This was showing at Fresnay's own charming little theatre La Michodiére which he co-owned with his wife, the famous chanteuse Yvonne Printemps. Guthrie took us backstage to meet Fresnay, who had once reduced me to tears as St. Vincent de Paul in a film called *Monsieur Vincent*.

Guthrie also introduced me to the "Sardi's" of Paris, the Elysées Matignon, where I met the two young farce writers who had penned *Occupe-toi d'Amélie* now known as *Look After Lulu* in which my then current girlfriend, Tammy Grimes, was to appear in New York under Noël Coward's direction. I was hardly listening to what they were saying—I was too busy gawk-

MEDEA

THE PLAYBILL

FOR THE ROYALE THEATRE

ing at a very young girl who was making her way towards the bar. She was blonde, wore no makeup, was dressed in the shortest of short skirts and was fairly bursting out of a dangerously low-cut blouse. She was so beautiful—she stopped my heart. "Qui-ca?" I asked the two playwrights. They turned to look, shrugged indifferently, and one of them said, "C'est une petite vedette quelconque. Je croix que son prénom est Brigitte, je ne connais pas l'autre." "Bardot peut-être," gruffly offered the other, and they quickly dismissed this nouvelle arrivée and returned to the subject at hand.

Judith had sent for a close friend of hers from the States, Anne Hunter, to console her and keep her company. She was cast as one of the Greek chorus. Anne was an exceedingly attractive woman in her forties, but when she arrived Judith was so busy being fêted that Anne was literally left on her own. We became friends at once. She knew Paris like the back of her hand and took great delight in showing me the sights—the Opéra, the Louvre, the Crazy Horse, Maxim's, la Rive Gauche and all the little cafés, clubs and boîtes famous and infamous. She loved her food and drink so we had a fabulous time guzzling our nights away with gallons of wine, regularly staying up to watch the

*Judith, dressed as Medea, in Sarah Bernhardt's dressing room;
the lady behind her is Alice B. Toklas.*

dawn creep over the Seine—surely one of the world's most haunting
sights. We watched it from a different "pont" each morning, and we
would hold hands and feel very romantic, and that is as far as it went.
She was so grown-up, kind and wistfully pretty. I would like to have
gone further; it would have been the correct and natural thing to do in
Paris—but I was shy and wary that her friend the Gorgon might have
me boiled in oil! So Anne was mercifully spared.

The festival at last came to an end. For a parting fling, Guthrie threw
a lunch party for Judith at the famous Grand Véfour. The party
included Stanley Gilkey, Judith, the manager of the Bernhardt theatre,
Millie Natwick, John Cabot Lodge, Anne and me. The Grand Véfour is
that ancient restaurant that had been the gathering place for France's
literary giants since the eighteenth century. The tables along the wall
had golden plaques encrusted in the backs of the upholstered
benches—a famous writer to each table—Balzac, Alfred de Musset,
Alexandre Dumas among them. We sat at Victor Hugo's table and

Guthrie ordered an enormous repast which included canard pressé with all the appropriate grands vins. It was a bubbling success—and as some flaming concoction to climax the meal was being prepared at our table, the maître d' explained that the more recently honoured literary figures such as François Mauriac and André Malraux were relegated to the rear of the room—the latest and farthest-away table of all belonging to Jean Cocteau.

Just as he was pointing towards the darkest reaches of the grand old restaurant, a tall, elegantly slim figure arose and emerged from the shadows—a tall figure with a leonine head and flowing hair, cuffs rolled back over his coat sleeves (the very signature of the man), a tall phantom heading straight for us and Victor Hugo! He only had eyes for Judith. Ignoring us, he came up to her, took both her hands in his, bent low, kissed them tenderly and in a soft melting voice murmured just loud enough for all of us to hear, "Ah madame! Thank you! Thank you! You make life!"—and then he was gone. It was Cocteau himself.

That lunch and that moment alone had made Judith's trip worthwhile. She just sat there speechless for the remainder of the meal. Her face shone with gratitude and pleasure—the powerful Medusa who could turn an audience to stone with one quick sharp glance had now become a little girl again, exposed and vulnerable, and she began to laugh as tears of joy ran down her cheeks. It was the kind of occasion that Guthrie conceivably might have choreographed—he was most assuredly expert at this sort of thing. It has always been my suspicion that on this instance he was guilty.

A few words about Guthrie and the not-so-tiny empire he created upon which for some considerable time the sun never set.

1926. The curtain has just rung down on the out-of-town opening night of one of his first major Broadway productions. Instant crisis! The wunderkind knows he must fire his leading lady, that legendary megastar of bygone theatre glory, Mrs. Leslie Carter, making her long-awaited comeback but not knowing one word of the text! New York looms—he has no choice. Stealing himself for this daunting task, the youth breaks the sad news to the old lady in her dressing room. Without turning a hair she waits for him to finish, takes his hand, pulls him provocatively close to her ravaged, overly made-up face and whispers in a thick, whiskey-coated voice, "You always were a sensual little bastard!" Guthrie told me later, "I don't think she *ever* once knew who the

*Guthrie McClintic, a theatrical wizard
and an early champion*

hell I was." He replaces her with Florence Reed, who instantly becomes a star all over again. The part—Mother Goddam. The play—*The Shanghai Gesture.* The rest—history.

The brash young satyr from Seattle continues to take Broadway by storm. Adventurously he introduces new writers such as Maxwell Andersen and Sam Behrman, even early Tennessee Williams. The guttural-voiced pixie with the explosive temper holds the key to the magic box. He seems born with most theatrical tricks already up his sleeve. As a director, he stages beautifully and has an impeccable eye for casting, but his biggest talent is for producing. He is a true entrepreneur. With uncanny instinct, he knows how exactly to present his star—preserve the mystique, nurture the myth. He even marries her—the light of Broadway, the famous lady under Michael Arlen's *Green Hat,* Katharine Cornell. Together, they form a partnership that takes them to the summit of their profession. For almost forty years North America is entertained by their sumptuous productions. Guthrie even takes time to produce, among others, John Gielgud's Broadway *Hamlet* and of course, Dame Judith's triumphant *Medea,* but it is on his very own "Miss Kit" that he most lavishes his care. He knows better than anyone around how to compliment her, make her stand apart, caress her with lighting, protect her from public scrutiny, keep Hollywood from her door, sustain the image—the image of a pure star of the stage and just about the last of the great actress-managers.

Like a kid on a spending spree he rents her the most expensive and most talented "toys" for support. Bernard Shaw has called Miss Kit his ideal Candida so when she plays the role, Guthrie gets her two Marchbanks—the first, Burgess Meredith; the second, young Marlon Brando. When she plays Juliet he sends to England for Maurice Evans as Romeo, Edith Evans for the Nurse and Sir Ralph Richardson as Mercutio. Filling out the rest of the cast, he procures young Orson Welles for Tybalt and in smaller roles, Tyrone Power and a very thin Kirk Douglas. He also presents his lady as Masha in Chekhov's *The Three Sisters,* her two others being Judith Anderson and Gertrude Musgrove— Natasha is played by Ruth Gordon. For Behrman's play *No Time for Comedy* he gives her as her leading man—Laurence Olivier. Raymond Massey plays opposite her in *The Doctor's Dilemma,* and now Guthrie mounts an entirely new treatment of *The Barretts of Wimpole Street* with Miss Kit literally playing herself as Elizabeth Barrett Browning and Brian Aherne playing himself as Robert Browning. The jeune homme terrible continues to spoil his beloved star with such grand and glorious concoctions as *Antony and Cleopatra* with Godfrey Tearle and *Antigone* with Cedric Hardwicke. They are not all winners, however. *White Cargo,* a new play set in the South Seas, a pale imitation of *Rain,* has the usually dignified Cornell playing the native girl, wearing nothing but a sarong. She is also required to speak the deathless prose with "forked tongue." There are three acts. The curtain comes down on the second act as she crawls across the stage towards some hard-nosed missionary pleading, "Me Tondelayo, me good girl, me stay!" Robert Benchley, reviewing it for *The New York Times,* headed his column with:

> *"Me Tondelayo, me good girl, me stay."*
> *"Me Bobby, me bad boy, me go."*

Guthrie instructs his office to never let Miss Kit see a bad notice— the reviews are kept from her. She sometimes wants to leave the stage door, like any normal person, wearing slacks and sweaters for simplicity and comfort. He screams at her, "You are a star. When the public sees you, you must look like a star." He dresses her in Mainbocher, Schiaparelli, Balenciaga—the world's leading designers make her clothes. To design her sets, he lures the brilliance of Oenslager, Melzinger, Robert Edmond Jones and Oliver Messel. When they travel they travel like royalty in their own private railway coaches—one for them, one for the company, one to sleep and a separate dining car for all of *us*. I happen to know 'cause I was there.

"THE KATHARINE CORNELL SPECIAL"

I SAT AWESTRUCK in the observation car as I chugged along across the vast and endlessly flat Midwest, through the Colorado mountains,

Miss Cornell, the last of the great actress-managers — and my sponsor

the Rockies, staring in wonder at the noble snow-capped peaks floating by with such dignity until I finally caught my second glimpse of the distant Pacific. By the tour's end we were to play all the main houses across the country: the Curran in San Francisco; the Biltmore in Los Angeles; the Shubert, Chicago; the National, Washington; the Colonial in Boston and many more such historic buildings, some sadly no longer standing. The play *The Constant Wife* was a dated bit of froth by Somerset Maugham, but a suitable vehicle for Miss Kit and her staunch troupe of seasoned players. This included two elderly actresses well into their seventies, both British and very grand—elegant, soft-spoken Margery Maude, and a tiny creature known as Eva Leonard-Boyne, a chirpy little bird in full plumage with an enormous milk-white *poitrine* and a definite past who sported a monocle on and off the stage. We were positive she even wore it to bed; John Emery, a lovable Yank and very funny to boot, cursed with bad ulcers caused by a marriage to Tallulah Bankhead, who had once in the sanctuary of their bed informed him quite firmly, "I don't go down anymore dahling; it gives me claustrophobia." John also admitted that occasionally, when he was attempting to excite her, she would invariably show indifference by singeing the tips of her pubic hairs with a lighted match.

Then there was Gertrude Musgrove, a delectable lady of considerable style, an expert at light comedy with a ribald sense of humour for whom I was developing a rather large crush. She became my constant companion and partner in crime. My heart was gladdened too at the sight of young Anna Cameron, my pal from Canada, playing the ingenue and who, like myself, was understudying the major roles. Dear Anna had discovered the Method and would on occasion take it to the extreme. She was convinced her character came to life in the dressing room. Her role in *The Constant Wife* was a good one, but brief, and at each performance, before her entrance, she would talk quite loudly to some invisible creature offstage before opening the door. Cynical old Eddie Bayliss, Guthrie's principal stage manager, thinking she had gone quite mad, asked her if anything was wrong, and, if not, who the hell was she talking to? Blithe as ever, Anna replied, "Oh, I was just telling my chauffeur downstairs to wait for me as I won't be long." Making up our dangerous quartet was a dear, daft lost soul of an Englishman named Peter who played the butler and had a disastrous problem with hootch. Being his understudy, I lived in a permanent state of terror as I knew at any moment I would have to go on.

The train was much like a travelling boardinghouse reeking of

Gertie (seated) in The Three Sisters *with Cornell and Anderson*

intrigue and at "lights out" Gertrude, Anna, Peter and I would snoop up and down the sleeping car trying to ferret out *who* was in *whose* upper berth! The four of us squatted down outside Eva Leonard-Boyne's curtained compartment muffling our mirth as the old lady, whose prolonged snoring was invariably interrupted by some late-night fantasy or autumnal wet dream, cooed and gargled her way to what seemed a wistful aging climax.

Way into the night we sat, Guthrie occasionally joining us, telling endless stories—one of them Gertrude's romantic tale of how she first met her husband, the late great set designer and painter Vincent Korda of the celebrated Hungarian film family (the subject of her son Michael Korda's delightful book *Charmed Lives*). It appeared she was a mere teenager of about fifteen attending a private girls' school somewhere in the mountains of Switzerland. Every morning the students, wearing their regulation school uniforms, took a recess and went outside to play.

One such morning Gertrude, standing a little apart from the others, noticed a tall man of middle age, dark and swarthy, walking up the hill towards her carrying an easel over one shoulder. The bell rang for the girls to return to their classes, but Gertrude lingered behind. Sometime later, privately, Gertrude finished the story for me: "There was something about that man that riveted me where I stood—something hypnotic in the confident way he approached me. He walked up to me, put down his easel, gently, slowly, unbuttoned my pinafore and gazed for the longest time at my breasts. He then gave me the tenderest, warmest smile, refastened my blouse and, taking me by the hand, said quite simply, 'You're coming with me.' I went with him—I knew I had to. He led me away—out of my world into his—a world of love, passion and art. But wherever we went he always made sure to enroll me in some school or other in order to finish my studies. When his celebrated contemporaries came to supper he would banish me upstairs. 'You vood be so bored, dahling; zey are all too old for you'—but I didn't mind. I would sneak out onto the staircase balcony and peer down at them through the banisters. One night when Winston Churchill, an old friend of Vincent's, arrived to dine I curled up for hours on the landing in my nightie, hugging my knees, my eyes popping out of my head trying to hang on to every word." How ironic, I thought, as I listened to Gertrude—there she is "the Constant Nymph" appearing in a piece called *The Constant Wife.*

Now, there are some who insist that this is not true. That she met Korda many years later on the set of Charles Laughton's *The Private Life of Henry VIII,* which Korda had designed. Well, I admit Gertie was prone to embellish on a grand scale and she could have been putting me on. But this was the story that she told me and I want so much to believe it that I'm sticking to it. Besides, Gertie could have made me believe anything really, because, you see, I was hopelessly infatuated.

Guthrie could never turn Miss Kit into a great actress. No matter how skillful his presentation of her—she remained always the same—fine, noble, sympathetic, in everything she portrayed. But by bringing those qualities of hers to the surface he had, intentionally or not, turned her into a great star and a great "boss." She ruled her little kingdom like a queen and as she worshipped goodness to obsession, so she believed everyone in it to be good. When one of her lambs decided to stray from the path of righteousness, she simply refused to believe it; and if some outsider dared criticize her "brood" she turned a deaf ear and a cold shoulder.

Now the time had arrived for Miss Kit to be tested in the extreme, for the "butler" decided to go on one hell of a long binge. Poor Peter was in bad shape that week. He had hit the sauce with a vengeance, run out of booze money and had started in on the methylated spirits (a bottle of witch hazel wasn't safe to leave around). So it wasn't exactly a picnic the night I arrived at the theatre a little after the "half hour" to be told by the stage manager that I had to go on because the butler was bombed and had passed out in his dressing room.

"Does Miss Kit know?" I stuttered, beginning to shake like an aspen leaf.

"Not yet, she doesn't" was the ominous reply.

"Give me a minute," I said as I rushed to get Anna and Gertie. The three of us barrelled into his room, bolted the door, slapped him around, poured gallons of coffee down his throat and threw him into his butler's weeds. He seemed to be recovering slightly and I prayed like hell, for the last thing I ever wanted to do was go on in that fatal part. At least he was able to stand, though somewhat shakily, and we pushed him toward the stage. Apart from walking smack into a couple of stage flats, he was doing pretty well.

Now the butler's role was complicated to a degree. He was required to make countless entrances merely to announce various people and then retire, but all with split-second timing for each announcement was meant to cut across specific discussions of a most private and intimate nature. The curtain went up. Peter, though he slurred a good deal, seemed to be doing not too badly and Miss Kit, who never left the stage, noticed nothing out of the norm. But Peter, still basically sloshed, suddenly got a second wind and began to get bubblingly overzealous.

With an aggressive insistence he would appear onstage whenever he felt the urge and stand there weaving about dangerously, announcing with stentorian defiance a host of arriving visitors, not all of whom belonged in the play. He was so enjoying himself, in fact, that he would interrupt crucial scenes by announcing guests who had already been onstage for some time. As a capper, Peter finally decided he had had enough of his butler role so upon his very latest entrance he pulled up a chair, sat down in the center of the stage, joined the family and nodded sheepishly at everyone in the room *and* in the audience, a silly, grinning, vacuous expression frozen all over his exceedingly purple face. The act one curtain came down with a louder, more final thud than usual. I replaced Peter in the second and third, Anna pushing me on when my cue came. I was frightened out of my wits, but I made it. By

Miss Kit, la chatelaine at Martha's Vineyard with friends

the time the last curtain fell, I had become a hero—a minor hero, perhaps—but a hero nonetheless.

BEING A NOVIERO of fair standing at the McClintic-Cornell Club meant positive, nay, guaranteed reemployment and almost certain promotion. Brashly confident that this would occur and banking on it utterly, I ran back to Mother Earth (Jane Broder) for some interim financial replenishment. She had already anticipated me, calling her old friend Eva Le Gallienne who responded by promptly giving me my Broadway debut. God bless Miss Le G! I was twenty-four.

Miss Le Gallienne or "Le G" as she was affectionately nicknamed, was not just one of the theatre world's supreme figures, she was a woman of exceptional intellect and individuality who could draw with ease from her rich ancestral link with the literary past. Her father, Richard Le Gallienne, was the celebrated English poet and friend of Oscar Wilde and therefore exceedingly close to the center of that buzzing elitist society of Victorian letters. Her mother was Danish, a language that Eva understood—she also spoke perfect French and a little Russian. So it was not surprising that Le G was more than capable of tossing off new, fresh working adaptations of the plays of Chekhov and Ibsen, which she not only translated but also adapted from the original Russian and Norwegian. An actress of high intelligence and power, she was able to further ensure their success through her unforgettable inter-

*Miss Eva Le Gallienne, or "LeG,"
as we all affectionately called her*

pretations of Mrs. Alving, Hedda Gabbler, Masha and Madame Ranevskaya.

Le G sported a withered arm and hand and one eye that tipped slightly askew, some of which she had received when long ago, risking her own life, she carried to safety the near-asphyxiated young actress Josephine Barrington from the top of a burning building. It was this same courage and determination that made her such a force as an advocate and champion of women's rights and fervent supporter of the plea that lesbianism be treated with compassion and understanding—not brutally suppressed and outlawed. At a time when every conceivable obstacle barred the way to such a cause, she quietly fought to dignify her beloved sex not with the objectionable militance we are sometimes confronted by, but with a grace, wit and humility that were astonishing in their effectiveness.

With her friend Margaret Webster, she also had the guts to manage a most ambitiously mounted repertory company smack in the very heart of Manhattan called the Civic Repertory Theatre. Surrounding herself with a talented rostrum of players, she gave many innovative presentations of new and experimental works as well as classic revivals of top quality. Though she mostly became Ibsen's champion, she assumed such diverse characters as Lewis Carroll's Red Queen, Émile

Zola's Thérèse Raquin and Rostand's Chantecler. Sadly, several years later the theatre, financially insolvent, closed but it had gained for Miss Le Gallienne not just a multitude of adoring fans but also a firm place in the history of the American theatre. She was in many ways responsible for what is now considered Off Broadway. Now, after much too long an absence from the very public she had created, she was at last making her comeback!

The play of her choice, *The Starcross Story,* which she had engaged me for, was a dated English piece of little merit, not in the least worthy of her and it opened and closed in one night! One solitary night! But what a night! As many as possible of her loyal supporters who could cram themselves into one building were in attendance! I shall never forget her entrance—that modest woman tiptoeing onstage to one of the most memorable receptions I have ever witnessed. Like the disciples of some archangel, they rose in a body to welcome her—cheering, yelling, screaming, throwing hats and programmes into the air! I thought it would never cease—they refused to let her begin—the noise was deafening; no end seemed in sight, so she did the only thing she could to stop them. She acknowledged them. Slipping completely out of character (something Le G would normally frown on), she bowed low to the waist and held that bent suppliant position till I thought her spine would snap—waiting for them to calm down so that the anticlimactic play that followed could be allowed to proceed on its mediocre course. In our time, that sort of adulation occurs only at the opera or rock concerts, but I'm glad I was standing on that very same stage next to Miss Le G amidst all the frenzy she had stirred, in the days when it *could* happen in the theatre, and *did* and *should.*

But one night?! Please! I was convinced my career, Broadway or otherwise, was at an end! This was it! Jane snapped me out of it, of course, and pushed me forward into a new production the Theatre Guild was presenting. So after all I was to have another chance. I kept searching out Miss Le G, however, regularly attending her master classes. She was, as might be expected, a brilliant teacher—an inspiration. Although I was to see her again only at odd brief moments throughout her long and distinguished life, I shall never forget that brave lady and her relentless, steadfast quest to fight conformity and despite a somewhat cold, academic exterior, how curiously, how strangely alluring she was, with her beautiful speaking voice, her superior mind, glowing inner spirit, her little crooked smile, her flashing eyes, her floating hair.

At least the new Theatre Guild production of Irish actor-playwright

Walter Macken's *Home Is the Hero* enjoyed a slightly more respectable run at Broadway's Booth Theatre (three weeks) and brought me some kudos in the small but meaty role of Manchester Monaghan, a sleazy spiv, replete with winkle-pickers and knuckle-dusters. The play's director, Worthington Miner, television's drama chief, was once again my angel of mercy. It also gave me the opportunity of renewing my old friendship with Donald Harron (playing the lead); laugh at his quips, get to borrow his makeup; develop a crush on Peggy Ann Garner (the soubrette), who in turn had a crush on Don but decided to marry Albert Salmi—oh well! What the hell?!

After the closing performance we all hit Patsy and Karl's with a vengeance and the next day (which I could barely recognize) brought me my invitation to rejoin the McClintic-Cornell establishment. Climbing into my best blazer, shirt, tie and grey flannels, I reported to rehearsals for Christopher Fry's pastorally poetic *The Dark Is Light Enough.* The story recounts how an aging countess at great risk to her life harnesses her own horses and rides through the Hungarian winter into enemy lines in order to rescue a young deserter she believes in and bring him to her castle, where she hides him from certain death. The play took as its theme and inspiration those lovely lines of Fabre's:

> *The weather was stormy; the sky heavily clouded; the darkness . . . profound . . .*

> *. . . It was across this maze of leafage, and in absolute darkness, that the butterflies had to find their way in order to attain the end of their pilgrimage.*

> *Under such conditions the screech-owl would not dare to forsake its hollow in the olive-tree. The butterfly . . . goes forward without hesitation . . . So well it directs its tortuous flight that, in spite of all the obstacles to be evaded, it arrives in a state of perfect freshness, its great wings intact . . . The darkness is light enough . . .*

Guthrie presided over the gathering like some great pasha— a Cheshire cat who had just swallowed a dozen canaries; Stanley Gilkey stood as usual, smirking in the background; Oliver Messel, present with his *muy elegante* costume and set designs accompanied by his nephew Tony Armstrong-Jones (yet to meet HRH Margaret); John Williams, debonair, polished light comedian (British and a poppet),

*Me as Count Zichy — the hard-set jaw line shows how much
I want the "other" role.*

who would become a dear friend; Tyrone Power, looking exactly as a
Hollywood film star should, about to attempt the principal role of Gettner, a role I coveted more than life; and apart from the surrounding
cast, retainers and numerous staff whispering in hushed tones—Miss
Cornell herself, her tall frame reclining à la Madame Récamier in what
could have been a throne, graciously offering her cheek for anyone who
felt so inclined to kiss. But sadly, no Gertrude Musgrove this time
'round. She had tired of me by now and the prospect of giving up the
theatre for marriage to an old staunch friend she had known for years
separated us for good. I missed her dreadfully—she had stolen an enormous chunk of my heart. Gertie was so kind to me, so caring, and for a
short while had been one of the most powerful romantic influences on
my life, and I'll never forget her.

My supporting role of Count Zichy was a damn good one and I

should have been grateful, thankless twerp that I was. But I was dying to get my tongue around those word gems Mr. Fry had given Ty Power to declaim, so after some whining and pleading I was made Mr. Power's understudy as well (a closer, more convenient position for a hit man) and had I not been so fond of Ty, who was such a gent, I would gladly have had a contract out on him. Of the two guards cast to keep Gettner prisoner, one was a young Sydney Pollack, a warmhearted chap with a lightning-quick mind and a terrific dry humour whom I liked enormously and who, since he has become in our present time one of the screen's top directors (*Out of Africa, Tootsie,* etc.), has *not once* offered me a job—the mensch! What did I ever do to *him*?

There was also Don Harron for good measure again—I couldn't believe it! Pundit, wit, author, actor, Harron had been a crackerjack student with a staggeringly high IQ and a Rhodes Scholar to boot. Because in the world of theatre I had chalked up a few more national tours across the continent than he, Don patronizingly dubbed me the "Road Scholar." I was glad he was going to be around, not just for moral support, but because he was great fun in a cryptic sort of way, though his penchant for puns could at length drive one bananas. He had just invented his hayseed farmer from the sticks—his alter ego, Charlie Farquharson, that rustic master of malapropism who suffered from a "mis-spelled youth." (My wife, Valeda, "was a Drain on her father's side.") One day Charlie would become a national figure on the lecture circuit, a permanent fixture on *Hee Haw* and a shedder of new light on the history of the Bible.

THE BOOK OF JENNYSEZ

The Moon and Stars worked nights and the Sun was put on the day shift.
God thot that set-up should work out all right.
That was yer fourth day.
God sed, Look here there's nothin' doing in these waters.
Better stir things up a bit, git some creechers moving.
Air's kind of empty too. Might as well fowl it up.

Don or "Charlie" was always good for a touch. He helped me out of many a scrape, and with a great deal of sufferance, he allowed me to borrow his makeup. His daughter Martha's biography of him has a running gag throughout, a series of montages of me stealing Don's "five and nine," which he kept in an old cigar box town after town. She was

Tyrone Power — as Gettner — a true gent!

right. In my whole damn life, I've never owned one. I thought a cigar box was for cigars! Where is it now when I need it?!

Rounding out the group was the Bad Influence himself—Michael Laurence (a principal understudy) a tall, lanky Irishman from the Abbey and the Dublin Gate—lugubriously cynical and wickedly tongued. Raffish and oh so evil, he was like the trouble-stirring fox in Disney's *Pinocchio,* and I was his willing accomplice. When we were not busily occupied in painting "chaque ville a vivid rouge," he would lead me with great care into the kingdoms of Joyce, Synge, O'Casey, Desmond McCarthy, Eliot and Auden. You had to forgive him for that. Being Irish, he had, from birth, fallen in love with language. So had all our company. It's as well we took advantage and indulged while we could, for the demise of Mr. Fry's poetic reign was sadly just around the corner. All too soon his wit would be extinguished—his brilliant verbal extravagance a victim of change.

Off we rumbled, once again across North America's vastness—a questionable little band of pioneers on luxury wagon wheels. Familiar towns flashed by, having been regaled with heady verse, now far behind us, more confused, more provincial than ever. Only when we hit the high spots—Chicago, Frisco, Los Angeles—would snorting ol' Guthrie come aboard to amuse us and keep us from going spare. In Los Angeles, we spent more time, our run being somewhat longer. On my nights off, I would sometimes visit my friend, the actor Robert Brown, whose house was just down the beach. In those days, Malibu was wonderfully uncrowded and unspoiled; there were at least fifty or seventy-five yards of plage between houses. Bob owned two enormous concert speakers from London's Albert Hall, which he had acquired at an auction. We would have dinner and then play classical records at full mind-blowing volume, sipping our stingers as the Pacific surf rolled in unheeded.

One night, while we were indulging in all this sound, there was a loud knock on the door. A man who looked somewhat familiar politely asked if we could turn the music down as he and his friend were practicing for a concert and couldn't concentrate. We stood openmouthed—it was Jascha Heifetz! The penny dropped. Of course—the next house belonged to the renowned cellist Gregor Piatigorsky! We turned everything off, grabbed our container of stingers, ran down the beach and spent the rest of the night sitting on the sand, listening to two of the world's greatest musicians as they serenaded us with their glorious Bach. Even the surf had subsided to a peaceful calm, no doubt out of sheer respect.

During our Los Angeles engagement, one realized the extraordinary drawing power the double-star combination of Power and Cornell possessed, for all of "haute" Hollywood came through that stage door—Cary Grant, Brian Aherne, Ronald Colman, the Hollywood "cricket team" (the British contingent with its captain Sir C. Aubrey Smith), my coz Nigel "Willie" Bruce (who I still hadn't nor ever would meet), and Basil and Ouida Rathbone. There was Gladys Cooper, Doug Fairbanks, Jr., his stepmother, Mary Pickford, and one glorious night the great Garbo herself.

Then all glamour would vanish and back we would hipoccata-poccata to the next set of towns. Charlie Strakosch, Miss Kitt's tour manager, a tough old hombre, crustier than Long John Silver, had been

terrorizing the theatre and opera world since the days of Chaliapin and
Caruso. Between bouts of poker on the endless rides, the stagehands
teaching me how to cheat, Charlie would have one too many and tell
the same story over and over again; how he buried the famed old opera
star of yore, Madame Nordica, at sea during a vicious transatlantic
storm. She had died en route and because there was little room, Charlie
and the captain were forced to lower her into the potato hold. The
image of that grand old diva, Nordica, with her voluminous poitrine
lying in regal state among all them spuds, has kept me smiling ever
since.

Our rails now bore us shakily across the border into Toronto the
Good almost right up to the very stage door of the Royal Alex itself. As
I renewed my acquaintance at lunch with Herbert Whittaker, now
major critic for the *Globe and Mail,* I exuded a repellent confidence.
One of the few critics then in Canada to be genuinely proud of any of
his young countrymen's success on foreign soil, Herbie had given me a
glowing notice. Nevertheless, thankless git that I was, I had the gall to
insinuate how far superior I would be at filling Ty Power's shoes—in
fact, I practically performed the entire bloody role for Herbie right
there in the restaurant—how gauche! Suffering no fools, Herbie
smiled compassionately as if humouring some escaped inmate.

The Toronto sojourn came to an abrupt end and, packing to leave, I
realized to my horror, I couldn't reenter the States—I had no visa! I
never had one to begin with! Oh Christ! I'm caught—this is it. I'm not
only finished—I'm illegal! So I confessed this to the partner and lifelong friend of the McClintics—a wonderful lady called Gert Macy. She
promptly called her closest relative, Harry Hopkins, who just happened to be a close adviser to the president of the United States, and in
a few high-powered seconds my reprieve was granted. Adequately
armed, I could skip jail *and* pass go! From a distance, however, I noticed
that Miss Kit began to be watchful, concerned. Could God have possibly sent her yet another wayward son?

The tour resumed. Guthrie visited an understudy rehearsal, saw me
do Gettner—grudgingly admitted he was proud—gave me the high
sign. I glowed!—but with the kind of flame that promised to spread
out of control. Ah, will this unattainable role ever be mine? Every line
of the part carried with it, for me at least, a stabbing, personal message:

GETTNER: *For how much longer, I wonder, am I to be
Kept standing in the pillory?*

While the prospect of Gettner distanced itself further and further, Ty and I became really good pals. The glass of fashion and the mould of form, he was a prince among men. How annoying! How awkward! But what could I do? He invites me to supper with his lady friends and always makes sure I have a date. Ironically, this Beau Brummel's taste in ladies was always a mite off-colour—all statuesque courtesans, all beauties, but a trifle on the gamey side. He sent for them in every town and as swiftly as they gratified him—just as swiftly he discarded them. Some fell for him hopelessly and lingered behind, seeking me out for consolation. A few tears on my shoulder—and lucky me—I've inherited his castoffs! But I'm a real Eve Harrington. I had to wear his shoes as well—I had to get Gettner's garter! There was no contest—the dude had to go.

John Williams, Mike Laurence "the Fox," Harron and I plotted murder plans that would make Agatha Christie and P. D. James seem like amateurs, but these sessions had the habit of always ending in hilarity and anyway how the hell could we ever harbour such thoughts?!

Little things began to irritate in performance. A well-respected American actor, Arnold Moss of stentorian vocal powers had a quirk that drove me crazy—he enunciated everything he spoke in the same pompous, heavy-handed manner. No matter how I changed my readings or lowered my voice to bring him down to some level of intimacy, it was in vain—he would shout louder than ever. Williams whispered in my ear, "A roaring Moss gathers no tone" and I almost collapsed on the stage. One night while spouting a particularly lyrical passage, Ty Power belched in my face midphrase. Ever the gent, he promptly said with the same projection, "Excuse me," disastrously breaking up Mr. Fry's precise meticulous meter and my poor self, totally unable to go on.

Everything started to fall apart—the boredom and frustration of the tour caused me to stay up nights later than ever—the Fox, my constant companion, screeching passages from *Finnegans Wake* or "J. Alfred Prufrock" as we crawled from bar to bar.

> *Let us go, through certain half-deserted streets,*
> *The muttering retreats*
> *Of restless nights in one-night cheap hotels.*

It all came to a crunch in Seattle—that culture-loving town I shamefully hadn't the time for, being too busily occupied on the longest binge of my short life. I had not slept since I'd arrived—

indeed, quite sleepless in Seattle. I remember sitting at a bar in broad daylight, my only company some feline, dark-haired creature I wasn't getting anywhere with, who eventually turned out to be the bartender's dog: booze was clearly beginning to affect my eyesight. I had long ago in the distant evening given up scotch and was nursing what was probably my seventh Bloody Mary, mostly vodka—feeling decidedly cosmic. I thought I could just make out a somewhat familiar form looming over me in a kind of mist. It was Keene Curtis, the stage manager, no less! What was he saying? Something to do with the fact that it was very late in the morning, that because Guthrie had praised my Gettner, Miss Cornell had come to the understudy rehearsal to see for herself but *I wasn't there* was I? and if I didn't come with him now, I would miss the matinée as well! I struggled to my feet, I could hardly stand. Keene propelled me across to the theatre. It was way after the "half hour" when we arrived—did I even have time to get into my costume?! The first person we bumped into was Guthrie, purple with rage, who growled some indecipherable invective, jerking his thumb in the direction of Miss Kit's dressing room. Ty's door was open as we passed and the dear man winked ominously and with fingers crossed gave me a good-luck sign that didn't hold much hope. Keene pushed me on. My legs turned to jelly as we finally reached the boss's door.

It opened. There she sat, as in a painting, robed, dignified, before her mirror—the perfect chatelaine. Her maid, Evelyn, was furiously combing her long, dark tresses. I'd never known Miss Kitty had so much long hair, reaching right down her back, and for a moment I was pleasantly distracted. Keene had left and I was alone now in the doorway staring into her eyes—those huge, slanted eyes that belonged to some wild Tartar queen. Her face, which seemed pulled back through tiredness, gave her an unusually vulnerable appearance and those famous, broad, voluptuous lips of hers were quivering with hurt and rage. Not just the Magyar countess alone was to pronounce sentence upon me. I had roused the ire of Candida—I would feel the strength of Masha, the wrath of Antigone—I would bow in shame before the Serpent of the Nile.

She began to speak. Her tone was low, quiet and deadly. Her voice, always beautiful and rich, seemed distant as if it came from another room. As she spoke, Evelyn's brushstrokes became more rapid. I was electrified. I'd never seen Miss Kit like this before. This was a revelation. She was straightforward, direct, utterly simple—intensely and marvelously real. Her looks cut to the quick; her words pierced my gut.

She was letting me know in no uncertain terms of her great disappoint-ment; that she ran a family of professionals and I had let them down; that my behavior was unforgivable, my discipline nonexistent; and that under the circumstances, she could not take me to Broadway and that after this very matinée, in fact, I would be replaced!

When she had finished, an interminable silence fell upon the room. I found it difficult to breathe. Evelyn had long since ceased her brushing. In fact, nobody breathed; nobody moved. Only the Hungarian snow began to fall softly about us. I felt suspended as one does after witness-ing some magnificent performance. A sudden flood of admiration and wonder rushed through me and I wanted so much to blurt out, "You've never been better," but I couldn't of course because, although I didn't know it, I was crying. I heard myself stutter some inane useless apology, but the axe had truly fallen, and I moved away from the door, carrying my severed head up the stairs.

In my modest cubicle in the sky, someone poured coffee down my throat. I was made of rubber and it took me forever to pull on my boots. Not for the world could I think what I was going to say. Ah well—it didn't matter; it was too late anyhow. I found the stage. Each entrance I made, the boss stood in the wings to watch me make a fool of myself. Though I went through the motions and mouthed the lines I was hear-ing someone else, someone I didn't know playing my part. I hadn't a clue where I was. At last the curtain came down on that horrid after-noon. What was I to do now with my life?! I wasn't trained for any-thing else. The Fox had cleaned out my dressing room, good scout that he was, and had packed all my things into a satchel. All I wanted was to see no one, say no farewells, just get out that's all—out! As we descended the stairs, I heard Gettner's lines in my head:

> *I shall go back to the journey I was making*
> *In no direction in particular*
> *Where the dark makes no false promises . . .*
> *And this time ride through the nightmare and not turn back*
> *Your days are well rid of me, and so, goodnight.*

We reached the ground floor. Miss Kit's door was ajar. She was enter-taining visitors. Like two cat burglars, we tiptoed past so as not to be heard or seen. "Oh, Mr. Plummer?" said a voice. One of the cat burglars turned around. "Thank you, I so enjoyed your performance." It was a friend of Miss Kit's—but I wasn't looking at her—I was looking beyond, at that tall, imposing Amazon smiling broadly in agreement and when, with her thumb and forefinger, she made that little circle of approval in my direction, I knew she had forgiven me.

I rushed out into the street and threw my arms around Michael in relief and joy. One more pardon! One more chance!

"Let's have a drink to celebrate," wisecracked the wicked fox.

"Tea anyone?" I rather prudishly suggested.

NOW FOR THE EAST — just two more stops before Mecca. I was back in the fold, a pack member once again. The long train ride rocked me to sleep at last, the sleep of the dead. I woke in Baltimore, overwhelmed by excruciating pain and nausea. In my hotel room, drained from non-stop vomiting and diarrhea, I was sure I was dying. Some kind Samaritans rushed me to Johns Hopkins, where I was told I had the severest form of infectious hepatitis—not so curable back in '54. I would be grounded three weeks to a month—if lucky, bedded down—out of the show, no chance of opening. My punishment had come. On the third day, my bottom a pink pin cushion from all the hypodermics and my body covered with more tentacles than a giant octopus, from the intravenous tubes they'd attached me to, I slowly came round. I had the vague impression of a nurse standing over me. "You have a lady visitor," she said. Then I heard the unmistakable footsteps echoing down the corridor toward me.

> GETTNER: *I'd have prayed and begged and bullied her to fetch*
> *me . . .*
> *There was no one else I could believe would come;*
> *Except the firing squad, which I was not*
> *In the mood to welcome.*

With the blood of Florence Nightingale coursing through her veins, Miss Kit was at my bedside every other day. She brought me radios, books, presents of all sorts. She showered me with kindness. She had even found a motive for all my past conduct. She had convinced herself that I was not just a twenty-four-year-old drunk after all—it was the hepatitis which had caused my strange behavior! Hers was an executive pardon on the highest level. Guthrie too, who had not a shred of patience for illness of any kind, came to pay his respects, sit on my bed and make me laugh till it hurt. He told me that Ty Power had also been struck down with the same virus, was hospitalized, and that they would postpone and reopen when we both recovered. Some chutzpah, I thought.

They waited; we recovered—we opened. It was a brief but distinguished New York run—the "crickets" were respectful—my Zichy was praised. I even won a trinket or two and was dubbed most promising newcomer along with Barbara Cook and Julie Andrews. But everything was breaking up. Fry's sun and moon were on the wane. Tyrone Power was going back to lotusland. Guthrie was busy concocting new theatrical soufflés—in short, we were closing. Miss Kit called me into her theatrical boudoir once again (I couldn't believe it—Evelyn was still brushing her hair) and told me she was taking the play on the road to a few major cities as a triumphant finale, but she didn't have a leading man. Then she dangled the carrot in front of me—Gettner! Oh, how I had dreamed of that chance but I had dreamed too hard—it was too late; the thrill was over. I yearned for some new adventure and Guthrie, bless him, took up the slack—flew me to Paris, to the deeper but nobler gloom of Greek tragedy and a little Tasmanian devil called Judith Anderson. From a captain in the Hungarian army to captain of the Argonauts. Not too shabby after all!

KIT AND GUTHRIE—a mythical pair indeed. What a startling contrast they made, the two of them! She—a monument, beautiful, remote, seeking solace among her women; he—feisty, promiscuous, the court jester shocking all and sundry with his acid tongue, an ageless and irreverent schoolboy let loose in the Temple of the Muse. Their house at Snedens Landing became a haven for the glitterati of the time, which ranged from the Sitwells to Gertrude Stein, Scott and Zelda to Stravinsky, the Gerald Murphys and Eleanor Roosevelt to Amelia Earhart and Helen Keller. On a single weekend one could have easily collided with Alexander Woollcott, the Lunts, Noël and Gertie, Larry and Vivien, Garbo or Kirsten Flagstad and in the center of them all—Guthrie—the gregarious raconteur stage-managing life as one long party.

But the party which he had helped to keep fresh was just about over. A coarser, far crueler era was fast approaching, and wise old Guthrie had seen it coming long in advance and braced himself for it like some irascible Quixote. He lost, of course, saved from bitterness by his innate sense of puckish glee. I think towards the end it was cancer that forced his low profile, but one day he just vanished completely from our midst as undetected as Houdini.

He truly was the most entertaining of men. His reign had been solid, enduring, vastly successful, even dazzling. And when it ceased, a certain grace, elegance and glamour left the American theatre that has never been captured since. I'm grateful beyond measure I was there at the end to wave it good-bye. Will it nae' come back agen? Ach! I ha' ma doots! For the lad wi' the magic box has swallowed the key.

CHAPTER TWELVE, PART ONE

TWO STRATFORDS
What they gonna keep under there—snakes?

Yep! That's what a lotta the town folk were askin'. Too wary and suspicious to get near and find out for themselves, they made damn certain to give it wide berth. Oh sure, they knew somethin' was goin' on all right; a tent was being put up—that's what. A whoppin' big tent—right out there, see, on the edge of town, by the river? Some guys all the way up from Chicago—Ringling Brothers was it? And that world expert on tents—that wiry old boss man himself with the battered ten-gallon hat climbing all over the canvas—Skip Manley? What d'ya make of him, Chrissakes? And who were all them strangers comin' inta town—all them big fancy chauffeur-driven cars? Why, one day someone said they saw the governor general's limo with all his flags flyin' and a motorcycle escort whisk by! And those consarn newspaper men from all over Canada, even the U.S. of A., not to mention yer jolly ol' England—what were they doin' here? What did they want anyway? Was this a takeover of some sort? And what about our quiet little town where nobody bothered us—what about our peace of mind? Hell! What about our jobs?

Of course, they didn't know it but just a few years down the road, those same guys and damn near every Tom, Dick and Harry like 'em would triple their businesses and the sleepy little railroad town of Stratford-on-Avon, Ontario, which they called home would boom and boom big! And it was all the fault of one of their own. Yep, a local journalist just back from the war, a small natty man in love with bow ties, with a feisty charm and a head full of dreams by name of Tom Patterson was to blame. Yessir! If you wanted to lay it all at someone's feet it would be Tom's all right. You see, Tom was makin' trouble again. Somethin' weird had come over him—he even looked funny—he must have been having another of his "inspirations." Only this time he'd gone too far—this time he was downright certifiable. Tom had simply wondered why North America didn't deserve a great classic theatre like the famous one at Stratford-upon-Avon, England? And why couldn't it be right here in the little Ontario town, his town, that bore its name?

Well, there were no white-coated attendants with straitjackets; no one summoned the sheriff. Instead, a loyal little steadfast group of town folk got behind Tom and swore allegiance to the death. They even raised enough money for a telegram or a phone call to anywhere in the globe. Who was the best and most acknowledged master of the classic theatre in the English world that could head this impossible dream? That's what Tom wanted to know and someone called Dora Mavor Moore told him. Tom telegraphed to northern Ireland—would this outlandish scheme ever light one tiny spark of interest?

The postman in Doouaght, County Monaghan, jumped on his bicycle and pedalled furiously up the hill to a large rundown estate known as Annaghmakerrig, which smugly boasted no telephone. The owner, a tall man of six foot five or over who looked somewhat like an eagle, mounted his bicycle, accompanied the man down the hill, picked up the post office phone and called Tom. All Tom heard were just four words—"When do we start?"

The gods had responded. Patterson had hit the mark for the great man himself. The Good Doctor, Tyrone Guthrie, was as big a dreamer as he, and, as a bold adventurer in the world of make-believe, a veritable Ulysses. Decades earlier in London under the strict regime of Lilian Baylis, "the ol' gel from the Vic," he had become Peck's bad boy of the stage shocking traditionalists with his unorthodox treatments of the classics. After Miss Baylis died, the doctor, firmly tucking the Old Vic under his own wing, whipped up many irreverent but highly spectacular concoctions igniting the young careers of Laughton, Olivier, Richardson and Guinness; in fact most of the top British talent of the early twentieth century had grown up under his thumb.

The little maker of miracles

A Tyrone Guthrie production was more of a "happening" than an evening of theatre—banners flying, flags waving, whole multitudes masterfully choreographed, sweeping across the stage, scenes changing at staggering speed and then, suddenly, in stark contrast, at his command, the absolutely still moments of great beauty and simplicity. He was forever adding new feathers to old wings and there was never a dull moment—his failures were as big as his successes. Apart from his ringmaster's instinct for the circus which he never lost, theatre to him was a place of worship, of ritual, a religion, perhaps the oldest of all. Glaring proof of this were his extraordinary productions of Chaucer's morality plays, called *A Satire of the Three Estates,* at the Edinburgh International Festival, and a mammoth *Tamburlaine,* of Christopher Marlowe's in London starring Sir Donald Wolfit. Both had put the theatre on another plain—both had made theatrical history.

For *The Three Estates,* the brilliant designer, Tanya Moiseiwitsch, had transformed the interior of Edinburgh's Festival Hall into a kind of theatrical agora—an open apron stage flanked by four central pillars, as simple as it was ingenious. Tanya would join Dr. Guthrie on his trip to "Beaverland." The doctor (who much preferred "Tony" to the more high-flown "Tyrone") was, to say the least, a hilariously entertaining companion on any trip, but until you knew the man, he would remain lofty, remote, the quintessential loner. Like most true innovators, he detested being thought of as fashionable and when his own triumphs became overly popular with press and public, rather than bask in that glory, he knew it was time to move on—the further afield the better. He was as much at home at Israel's Habima or later at his own theatres in Australia and Minneapolis as he had been at the Vic. Wildly eccentric, caring not a hoot what he wore (old running shoes in church—that kind of thing), he blissfully roamed the earth in search of new battle grounds, toujours, un voyageur sans baggage, just his own special genius to declare.

Patterson's accidental timing was perfect. Weary of metropolitan sophistry and fed up with trendsetters, the Good Doctor longed once again to be amongst raw undiscovered talent, unshackled from convention, so, brimming with fire, enthusiasm and a full heart, he welcomed this tiny chink of chance to conquer a new world.

They descended from Olympus—the three tall Graces—Tanya, Tony and Judy. Judy had, it seems, been Tony's wife since childhood, a mere inch or two shorter than her towering husband, just as eccentric and a striking cross between a Celtic goddess and Edith Sitwell. It seemed the Goddess had invented chain-smoking, for pack after pack were inhaled and consumed daily. In the midst of many of Judy's amusing anecdotes (as I was to witness later) she would invariably halt in midsentence as a series of hacking coughs like thunderclaps seized her, wracking her whole body in massive spasms. The room would freeze, poised, terrified, in fear for her very life—until the fit finally ceased and a nonplussed Judy would casually pick up precisely where she had left off as if nothing at all had occurred.

Out from a great cloud of Judy's smoke emerged the little town of Stratford. They fell for it at once. They fell for Tom's dream. They fell for Tom. They even fell for Tom's tiny group of followers who would one day become the Board, the best board anyone could ever want—not exactly equipped with the greatest clout and connections in the world but blessed with the kind of guts, faith, intelligence and passion that money couldn't buy. There they were—Alf and Dama Bell, Archdeacon Lightbourn, Mr. Showalter and good ol' Dave Ray—their uplifted faces telling the whole story, ready to go to work, ready to go to any lengths for their new messiah, ready and willing, waiting for the Word. The Word came—and everything spun into action.

Money! Raise it! Going to need a lot of it. You'll get rejected—never mind—rise above! That hill overlooking the river? That's where it'll stand; not to worry, you've already got your swans. Dig a hole—

*Left to right: Judy Guthrie, Tyrone Guthrie and
Tanya Moiseiwitsch, three tall legends*

make it a semicircle like an amphitheatre. Tanya will design it. Then
we'll put a tent over the whole thing—cheaper that way. If no one here
knows about tents, we'll get that chap from Chicago—Skip Manley—
that his name? I'll choose the plays and the actors, but you'll need a
star; I'll find one—ditto, a lady warhorse. I'll bring a manager from
London, Cecil Clarke—v. good at running things—he'll start us off,
then train the locals to take over. Don't forget costumes—find a
space—gather every seamstress you can. I'll send Ray Diffen, best cut-
ter there is—he'll make 'em. Tanya will design 'em; v. essential—give
jobs to the locals—stir them up, enthuse them. They'll love it; and
whatever you do, remember—get the town behind you. It's all going
to be theirs you know—back in a few months—good luck!

Tony was true to his word. He delivered the goods and the goods
arrived intact. From Blighty came Sir Alec Guiness, gung ho to take on
Richard Crookback—ditto, Irene Worth for *All's Well That Ends Well;*
Dougie Campbell, a gruff Scot from the Glasgow Citizens' Theatre who
you could trust with your life, would take charge of major characters
and be Tony's chief whip. Cecil Clarke (the new manager), Ray Diffen
and of course, Tanya, followed hard upon an assembled band of top

Tanya's stage and the tent going up — will it all be ready?

Canadian talent, including my old pals Bob Goodier and Don Harron, were waiting to welcome them. The race was on!

Rehearsals and building took place simultaneously, the noise was deafening—actors in mufflers and duffle coats, their lips chapped and blue trying to mouth iambic pentameter as the bitter April winds whistled under the tarpaulins—Tony like a demented Toscanini barking commands and beating time. Shapes were beginning to emerge—the ensemble was slowly forming a personality and style of its own, and Tanya's platform had already assumed a timeless dignity. There was a long way to go, but enthusiasm showed no signs of flagging when, suddenly, disaster! Everything came to a halt. No more money! The town cynics, egged on by rumours, chanted, "Told you so—told you it wouldn't last!" Everyone went into shock—everyone, that is, except Tony, who tore about like some possessed emu screeching, "Rise above! On! On!" as Judy huddled in a backseat somewhere nonplussed and stoic as ever—a lighthouse surrounded by an ocean of cigarette butts. It was hard to rise above, there was no getting away from it—all building had ceased, the decision to abort was at hand, the time was out of joint, the race was done.

Then something remarkable happened. Whether it was Tanya's unfinished Doric columns bathed in moonlight silhouetted against the night sky that evoked the aura of ancient Greece and a promise of glory, one will never know; but the spirit of Marathon had undoubtedly descended, for the foreman, Oliver Gaffney, offered to finish without pay, and the workers came slowly back. High up on a rigging, Skip Manley, wearing his olive wreath proudly if slightly askew, called down, "We'll finish yer tent for ya—pay us when ya can!"

The games were on. The athletes had left the palaestra and had gone onto the field; the race was resumed—the torches passed—the finishing line was in sight; and so, on the evening of the thirteenth of July, 1953, a fanfare of blaring trumpets greeted a large, eager but somewhat apprehensive international audience. If you searched carefully amongst them, you'd have found Alf and Dama Bell, Archdeacon Lightbourn, Mr. Showalter and good ol' Dave Ray, battle wearied, with one long powerful story to tell; and, oh yeah, there was Tom Patterson, looking kinda funny again, his dream waiting for him, just around the corner. And whose big limo was that drivin' up with flags flyin' and an escort? Why, by God, if it wasn't the governor gen. himself getting out and the lieutenant governor and the mayor! Hordes of critics and journalists from Great Britain, the U.S. of A. and Canada were pushing their way toward the doors, some of 'em wondering why the hell they'd been sent to the sticks. But, once inside, they sat waiting, humbled and spellbound by the purity of the noble structure Tanya had created. Somewhere up on the hill behind a cannon boomed—a hushed silence fell over the multitude—the long, low resonant sound of a gong gave the signal—the runners came out into the light and the finest damn classical repertory on the whole North American continent was up and away.

> "This small town has gone so giddy with success that it doesn't bother to turn the street lights off in the daytime."
> —WALTER KERR, *NEW YORK HERALD TRIBUNE*

> "The Stratford Festival of Canada has been born with a silver spoon in its mouth."
> —*THE CHICAGO AMERICAN*

> "This is the sort of stage that lovers of Shakespeare have often dreamed about and seldom seen."
> —BROOKS ATKINSON, *THE NEW YORK TIMES*

"The most exciting night in Canadian theatre. The Guthrie
touch has not failed to summon scenes of momentous splendour."
— HERBERT WHITTAKER,
TORONTO GLOBE AND MAIL

"The town is still trying to accustom itself to the idea that
something possibly unique in North America has happened
within its bounds."
— *THE TIMES* (LONDON)

And for beloved Tanya, the heroine of the hour:

"Tanya Moiseiwitsch, a designer whose special interest is in open
platform work and has given her mobile figures such grace and
strength you begin to wonder why anyone even bothered to
invent scenery."
— WALTER KERR, *NEW YORK HERALD TRIBUNE*

FAR AWAY, deep in Manhattan's theatre district seated at Patsy and
Karl's Bar, I was busy digesting all this when my heart jumped. More
than anything I suddenly wanted to be there. Funny, wasn't it? All my
young life I'd tried running away from home to get the attention of the
big world elsewhere. Now, all at once, the big world's attention was on
the home I'd just run away from.

Like everyone else, I had already strutted my stuff long ago for Dr.
Guthrie in a boardroom at my old school—Montreal High. My friend
Dick Gilbert and I had chosen Brutus and Cassius's famous tent scene
as our audition piece and had given it all we had for the great director.
We were quite confident—there were no hitches—I know we were
good. I'm quite sure he thought so too, for he was most charitable and
complimentary. It is a sad irony, however, that one's own hometown is
possibly the last place one should ever look for support. Due to my
wayward escapades as a youth there, I had gained for myself a fairly tar-
nished reputation. A quite powerful aging radio producer who often
employed me and with whom Dr. Guthrie had consulted concerning
local talent clearly was not my ally. So convinced was he that I'd been
doing "baddies" with his favourite lady soap opera star and mistress of
many an organ-backed moon, this Judas of Montreal willfully pro-

ceeded to brand me a womanizer, a libertine, a drunk, totally irresponsible, undisciplined and a black influence on any company. This all sounded most exciting. Under other circumstances, I only wished it had been true. True or not, my report card had been taken seriously — I was turned down flat, not just the first year but the second and third as well!

Now these carpings may seem petty and hardly worthy of mention but to a young artist, impatient to crawl up the ladder, such obstacles were crucial. They meant the difference between discovery and obscurity, life and death. I confess it — I was bitter and jealous. Bravely donning the mask of nonchalance in front of Patsy and Carl, I chased down my inconsolable rye whiskey with a somewhat more encouraging ice-cold beer.

CHAPTER TWELVE, PART TWO

STRATFORD-ON-THE-GIN-'N'-TONIC

The muddy Housatonic River lazily winds its way through southern Connecticut, settling momentarily in and around yet another Stratford — a harmless blue-collar town of little personality and less potential. In the late spring of '55, the river gurgled and spluttered along in customary fashion, blissfully unaware of the proud new erection resembling London's old Globe Theatre which loomed imposingly over its banks. Nor was it any less indifferent to the illustrious company that on a Saturday some months before had assembled there for the official "breaking of the ground," and now, once again, stood in a tight little group staring up at the completed masterpiece of weathered wood that would call itself the American Shakespeare Theatre.

There they all were: the founder of New York's famed Theatre Guild, Lawrence Langner; his regally attractive wife, the gracious Armina Marshall; Theresa Helburn, a feisty, white-haired, little old lady (the

Guild's principal Queen Bee); and an assortment of other luminaries, Maurice Evans (Shakespearean actor), Lincoln Kirstein (patron of the arts) and the man who got me there in the first place, Raymond Massey. They had all gathered for the glory of God, New England and the Bard of Housatonic, gloating with satisfaction over the spanking new monument they were convinced was to top their already established rival — the two-year-old, much more modest but miraculously successful Canadian upstart.

Whether it was the bizarre and hysterical opening night performances (*Julius Caesar* and *The Tempest*) a few weeks later that churned the perpetually sluggish river into a torrent of distemper and distaste, I am not at liberty to say, but obviously it had had quite enough and decided to boil over, contributing to the worst floods Connecticut had seen in many a decade. No matter how catastrophic the outcome, I was most thankful to be a part of this festival's inception if for no other reason than to thumb my nose at my northern friends across the border who had so rudely ignored me.

THE 10:07 for Connecticut was about to leave Grand Central on a warm spring day. I had just thought of boarding when a young man with a quick step and quizzical look, carrying more camera equipment than seemed possible for one so slight, came hurrying over in my direction.

"Plummer?" queried a light, musical voice mixed with overtones of Aberystwyth and MGM. I nodded.

"McDowall here."

"R—Roddy?" I gasped. "Roddy McDowall?!"

I had instantly turned into the village idiot—my big mouth gaping wide in dumbfound stupidity. I somehow couldn't fathom that standing before me was the grown-up version of that little boy, for whom I, as a child, had cried so often in tearjerkers like *How Green Was My Valley,* and, of course, *Lassie Come Home.* Yet here we were standing in the station staring at each other—and just about the same age. With more than one hundred films to his credit, Roddy was one of that rare breed of child star (Dean Stockwell, Elizabeth Taylor, Peggy Ann Garner were others) to have actually made the successful transition from infancy to maturity, becoming in the process a fine actor of both stage and screen.

"Don't tell me—I know," he said. "You're to be Mark Antony and

Ferdinand and I'm Octavius ("Ricky-Ticky-Tavy"), Caesar and Ariel! God help us both—" and with a horrendous giggle that splattered like machine-gun fire, he shoved me onto the already moving train, scrambling up behind me, nearly losing in the process every expensive camera known to man. We spent the whole journey standing on the outside landing between the cars, the cool breeze swirling around us most agreeably. Like some crazed paparazzi, he began at once to photograph everything in sight—me, the conductor, the pistons and anything that flashed by—the tracks, buildings, trees, cows, all the while merrily chatting away. We hit it off instantly. Roddy was a very funny fellow— loved a joke and was passionately fond of limericks, particularly unsavory ones. It was he who that day taught me one of my favorites:

> *From the depth of the crypt of Saint Giles*
> *Came a scream that was heard for miles*
> *Cried a brother, "Goodness gracious*
> *Doesn't Father Ignatius, know that the Bishop has piles?!"*

Together, we straightaway invented two greasy, grizzly goons, Max and Schultz, seedy Hollywood producer-moguls (nightmare images from Roddy's West Coast youth) replete with bulbous noses, swollen lascivious lips, slovenly slurred speech—not just hair lipped, harebrained! I was Schultz; Roddy was Max. We represented the ultimate sleaze of our profession. Sweaty, obese, repulsive, both studio "heads" would scream at each other in rasping, cheap-shyster, show-biz diatribe, which invariably ended in Max whispering with nauseating intimacy down my ear, "Nether mind, Schultz—jutht kith me!" at the same time emitting a large wad of drool which slobbered and dribbled slowly and deliberately down his stubbled chin. Over the years, whenever we met, Roddy and I automatically went into this routine without even thinking. But the day of that train ride saw the birth of these two monstrous moguls.

We were fast approaching our destination; there was one more stop. Roddy put down his cameras, commanded them to stand easy and, in a low, confidential tone, began to set me straight on what lay ahead. "Now don't jump off the train—wait till you hear the cast of the century! Guess who's playing Brutus and Prospero—none other than ol' Abe Lincoln himself—Ray Massey." (Roddy here launched into an accurate stuttering imitation of dear Raymond.) "And the lean and hungry you-know-who? Yes! Jack Palance will be our Cassius. Fritz

Roddy, the welcome court jester!

Weaver [best young classic actor around] will be Caesar, a newcomer stand-up comic, Jerry Stiller, and Rex Everhart will play the funny men and Hurd Hatfield [famous for the film *The Picture of Dorian Gray*], who looks just like his mother, will tackle Julius Caesar, and then Julius Caesar will look just like Hurd Hatfield's mother! Well, that just about wraps up the main team! How about that gaggle of strange bedfellows? Would you say this promises to be an ensemble renowned for its cohesive style?! Vee are doomed, Schultz; vee are doomed!"

If I ever felt in need of some delicious gossip or some subtle information I couldn't for the life of me find elsewhere, I called Roddy. He was a veritable font of potted knowledge. His theatre memorabilia and his phenomenal collection of old and obscure films are legendary. He had the memory of an elephant and had simply known everybody from Lauritz Melchoir to Noël Coward, Howard Hughes to Marie Dressler. If he knew the Gish sisters, then he knew Lugosi and Karloff, and he could give you the number of a man who once did the makeup for George Arliss and John Barrymore. Perennially youthful in appearance, he really was Old Hollywood to the marrow—he had rubbed shoulders with many a great star of the silent screen. He had a direct line to the past. If someone was to tell me that Donald Crisp or C. Aubrey Smith were his uncles or that his godmother was Mrs. Patrick Campbell, I wouldn't be at all surprised. Roddy knew where most of the bodies in our profession were buried, and he treated this sacred knowledge with affectionate discretion. He was the good serpent, Ka—guarding the treasures of our history.

Someone yelled, "Stratford—watch yo' step," and gathering up his cameras, "Max" impatiently pushed me down the stairs. As the train pulled away, we stood alone on the empty platform, and I found myself wondering what exactly to expect of the long, hot summer ahead; but Roddy had set the stage like a true magician, and I knew, whatever happened, it was going to be one big howl.

CONNECTICUT'S BRAND-NEW TEMPLE to Gloriana with insignia and flags flying looked mighty handsome from the outside. It was the interior that left mucho to be desired. The cast seemed to spend most of its time wading in and out of their new basement dressing rooms ankle deep in mud. Our vast intelligence told us they had been built well below the water line. I had premonitions of eventually swimming from room to room in order to wish everyone "Merde" in a kind of choked gargle. Under such circumstances, "Merde" was the most suitable and floatable salutation. It was just a bit unnerving to round a corner in those dark passageways and bump into all seven feet of Jack Palance with that great mask of a face of his, hissing away like a cobra about to spring (actually he was only just going over his lines).

AMERICAN
SHAKESPEARE
FESTIVAL THEATRE

STRATFORD, CONNECTICUT

The proud new building

Upstairs onstage, things were a little drier, but by no means better! Lawrence Langner, the "Godfather," never stopped telling us to speak up—he couldn't hear a goddamn thing! He was, of course, quite right to do this except he'd forgotten his architect had neglected to consult a proper acoustics expert, so the whole place was cursed with "dead spots." He had also forgotten he was hard of hearing.

The Julius Caesar set was nothing but a huge ponderous staircase reaching the heavens, massive in structure. Stretching the entire width of the stage, it was solid, permanent and unbelievably cumbersome. It gave the impression it had once been used in the D. W. Griffith film *Intolerance* and was rejected as being too heavy. Its designer, who had put the theatre back at least a hundred years, left us only the meanest margin of flat surface down front upon which to perform. His general design had also forced him to build a replica of the massive staircase behind the existing one so that we could all descend the other side and disappear out of sight. To make matters worse, all the Roman cloaks were made of the heaviest velvet stretching out in a long train, so if anyone turned left or right, the cloak simply stayed where it was as if anchored to the ground. One could have concealed several dwarfs inside to help maneuver the damn things. (Follow the actor, munchkins; follow the actor!) Of course, we all complained bitterly amongst ourselves, swearing eternal revenge, but no one actually spoke out.

Once, during a mournful lull, I pulled Raymond Massey aside. Raymond had known my father at school so there was an unspoken bond between us. I pleaded with him, as he was the top headliner, that he should speak up for us all. "We can't move in them, Ray; you know that; we simply can't move!" Iago-like, I began to slowly stir him up into some sort of appropriate rage. Now Ray was a gentleman of impeccable manners, never complained, never swore, so at first he was reticent: "Oh—uh—they'll be—uh—all right I'm sure—uh—we'll get used to them—uh—they just need working in—uh—that's all—and—uh—"; then suddenly, releasing all his pent-up indignation, he boomed out to the power committee seated in the darkened auditorium, "Now—uh—just—uh—look here, all of you—uh—Judas Priest! Let's—uh—try—uh—using the brains the good Lord gave us and—uh—git these gol-darn costumes together and—uh—uh—make 'em spell 'mother'!" I collapsed onto the not-too-solid stage in helpless silent laughter, rolling about in my cloak till I got caught up in the frigging thing and almost suffocated to death.

Mr. Massey's outburst had done some good. Our trains were briefly trimmed and everyone was looking a bit better already—Hurd Hatfield—splendid as Caesar (as long as he didn't try to move). Hurd actually did have his mother in tow—she never left his side—and Roddy took reams of snapshots of her together with Hurd in his costume. "You see, you really can't tell which one is Caesar, can you?" he whispered in an evil aside. Then someone came onstage and said, "You've all forgotten to wear your hats," and handed us these huge, floppy velvet things that made everyone suddenly look like Rembrandt! In fact, there was now so much velvet being worn that you couldn't see the actors at all. Roddy stomped off the stage, breezed past me and said, "They're not going to come near me in *The Tempest*—those horrible people from wardrobe. I tell you Schultz—they're not going to touch Ariel! *I'm* designing *and* making my very own costume and that's final!" Which he proceeded to do and superbly. He painted his entire body, which was clad only in a skullcap and loincloth, an azure blue and covered everything including his face in thousands of multi-coloured sequins stuck together, and when he had added several delicate fishlike quills to his arms, hands and head, the effect was extraordinary—he looked like a psychedelic seahorse! But we still had to get *Caesar* off the ground, and anticipating physical disaster, I rid myself of my cloak altogether and played the whole thing in open shirt and tights, trying to look as sexy as Brando in the Mankiewicz film.

I loved Mark Antony and I loved playing him. I was glad too that he was a lone shark, independent of other characters in the play—his big moments being the soliloquy and the familiar oration and that was the extent of it. He could come on with his own style, do his own thing and be gone. The British director Denis Carey, who had both talent and sensitivity, could not—no matter how he tried—control the two big guns, Massey and Palance, whose chemistries were so diametrically opposed. So he left them to their own devices. Except for a few shining talents, all the way down the line to the smallest extra there was this same unevenness of style—different accents and backgrounds all sharing a glaring inexperience in the classics. So having to make do with what he had, poor Carey could only present a very stolid and conventional production.

But the Ides of March had come. There were to be no more excuses—the great Caesar was to be assassinated in full view of a real paying public—the dreaded "first night" was upon us. America's latest new cultural institution was to be unveiled. The occasion was both solemn and grave. Besides all the critics, there was to be a glittering array of stiff-shirted, black-tied, jewel-encrusted, overfed, overboozed penguins, rich and impenetrable—who would, as sure as pie, sit on their hands. The hierarchy of the theatre would be there, of course, as well as beaucoups des socialites and sitting in the front row dead center, as was her custom at every opening, that blinding apparition—Hope Hampton—clothed in white samite, peroxide hair to match and simply smothered in diamonds. There was a saying among us actors that should your lighting designer be overly fond of the back-lit dim romantic look and it is a trifle tough to be seen, all you have to do is walk down stage center, stand directly in front of Hope Hampton and you'll get all the light you need!

It was one hour before "curtain up." I walked onto the stage to go through my silent paces alone as would be my custom for the rest of my life, but there was already someone there. It was Jerry Stiller, bless his heart, trying out new routines for his Trinculo in *The Tempest* scheduled to open the next night. Jerry was a workaholic—he never stopped—a fact that paid off very soon thereafter when he was to become a star comedian with his wife, Anne Meara. Even then, Anne was always at his side, inventing new sketches, new routines, a devoted audience and a staunch partner. She was there now, somewhere in the dark theatre, invisible as always, watching over him. I stood quietly on the side till he finally noticed. "Okay. Anyone in J. Caesar has priority—Mazel Tov," he shouted and relinquished his space.

"BEGINNERS—PLACES, PLEASE!"

Moments later in full costume, the scent of battle in my nostrils, I stood on wooden slats in my cubbyhole to keep dry, listening to the Tannoy. Ready? I should think so—this was the fattest role as yet in my cheeky little repertoire! But why did we not begin? Oh, that's right, the speeches; I'd forgotten—my God—the speeches. They'd already begun. Outside my door I heard a strange noise like escaping gas. I opened it a crack and peeked out. It was Jack Palance hissing away, pacing up and down the corridors, furious at the delay. I didn't blame him. The Bard must have been thinking of Jack when he described Cassius:

> *Seldom he smiles, and smiles in such a sort*
> *As if he mock'd himself and scorn'd his spirit*
> *That could be mov'd to smile at any thing.*

Every dignitary present up there in front of the curtain felt impelled to give his two cents' worth—first—Lawrence Langner, who deservedly was given a standing ovation for his new toy. (I felt like shouting, "Speak up, Mr. Langner, speak up. We can't hear you.") Then, one after another—on and on, the rhetoric spewed out into the night. Everyone seemed to have forgotten that there was a play being presented. It was the monument, the temple, the crucible of culture they had come to worship. The poor little rich audience, not too good at listening in the best of times, were by now, I imagined, half asleep—in fact I swore I could hear snoring over the Tannoy system. How in hell were we *ever* going to wake 'em up?!

The great new curtain, with one gigantic sigh of relief, finally rose, but it rose on a company drained of feeling who had simply waited too long. We went through our paces like so many sleepwalkers, except that Caesar, or his mother, I can't recall which, gave us a spectacular death rolling down the huge flight of stairs. The evening limped on, nothing particularly eventful occurring till Brutus, on the eve of the battle of Philippi, called for a taper and a stool to be brought to his tent.

> Now sit we close about this taper here
> And call in question our necessities.

The stool forthwith being brought, Brutus missed it completely and his butt hit the hard stage floor with a sickening thud. One snide local critic later suggested that perhaps the venerable Mr. Massey had had a few too many before the performance—that the camp near Sardis was more like the bar at Sardi's. But the truth was that Jean Rosenthal's lighting was so minimal, so "artistic," that if you held your hand out in front of your face, you couldn't see it—you couldn't even see Hope Hampton in the front row—no hope from Hope.

The only other dramatic occurrence that night was the late arrival of my then girlfriend, Tammy Grimes. She had been at a grand party in faraway Long Island and had forgotten she was supposed to attend my opening. In a panic she remembered. Hard up for transportation to cover the long distance in time, she left the party and hired a private plane—a Cessna. Just she and the pilot. The plane had trouble coming down over the local airport, missed the runway and crashed in a nearby field. Tammy emerged without a scratch except that her exorbitantly expensive evening dress had a small tear in it. Outraged, she strode up to the cockpit and let the pilot have it with full barrels as the poor man sat speechless, crumpled in his seat with both arms and collar bone broken. She had missed the play, but she made the party.

The press came out. As was expected, the building got all the notices. You might say that "Caesar" had suffered another assassination. Roddy, Fritz Weaver and I came out of it smelling of roses, but the headliners, Massey and Palance, fared not so well. The papers were icily polite to the distinguished Massey but devastatingly rude and cruel to Mr. Palance—how unnecessary and unthinking to an extraordinary actor who, though a stranger to the classics, had obviously worked so hard and cared so much.

Second night—opening of *The Tempest,* which weathered its own storm admirably. Palance made a wonderfully sinister and touching Caliban (those hisses of his appropriately hitting their mark this time). Roddy—a glimmering firefly as Ariel. Massey a ducal, resonant Prospero. Myself—a miscast Ferdinand, but Jerry Stiller—a complete tonic as an endearingly funny and most original Trinculo. Ditto Everhart as Stephano.

It was the third night and second opening of *Caesar* (this time before the magazine and television critics) where everything came apart at the seams, and we all took a giant leap into Grand Guignol! Well into act 1, I enter as Mark Antony, shake hands with each conspirator, as directed, pretending I was on their side all along—but where was Cassius? No Jack to be seen. Then I spot him in the distance near the very back of the set stage left. I walk the long walk up to him and offer him my hand. He stands there, a mad look in his eyes, breathing heavily, and does nothing for the longest time. He eventually takes it, but he flings it away from him in disgust and loathing—something he has never done before. I turn back to the dead body. Now it is time for the senators to mount the stairs and leave me alone with Caesar. They do so, like tortoises dragging their heavy shells behind them. I am just about to begin my soliloquy when I realize I am not alone. I hear the familiar hissing sound directly behind me. It is Jack. Beads of perspiration have begun to pour down my face for he seems perfectly content just to remain there at my back forever. Doesn't he know that a soliloquy means one is alone? This is getting serious. The hissing becomes louder as he circles me like a hungry panther and when he arrives at Caesar's corpse, he straddles it with both legs and stands there in triumph, his arms folded across his chest—those strange eyes boring into me!

The prolonged silence was beyond endurance. The audience had begun to mumble and murmur among themselves. The pause was so long in fact that I had started to get hungry. Just when I thought I had no choice but to speak my piece—Jack left the stage. I held my breath. I could hear him mount the stairs. Everything was going to be all right. I even had the confidence for a second to turn and look. On the third step, he tripped on his robe and fell. Instead of recovering as if nothing had happened, he got to his feet, tore off his entire cloak including his doublet, rolled it all into a tight little ball and, with all his might, threw the whole cockamamie thing into the wings. Cassius, wearing only his 1955 T-shirt with a gaudy pair of suspenders holding up his tights, now stomped noisily up the rest of the long staircase—hissing all the way. I turned around to open my mouth, when I remembered that once he reached the summit, he had to go all the way down the other side. I decided to wait another agonizing few seconds, wisely as it turned out. I listened as he clanked his way down. Then his sword must have caught in something, for he ripped it from his belt, scabbard and all, and threw it full force down the remaining stairs. The noise it made as it bounced off each step could be heard in New Haven and, like the junk in Fibber McGee's closet, it didn't stop. The audience sat stunned, dangerously quiet. Any second the volcano might erupt, so I decided it was time to speak:

> *O pardon me, thou bleeding piece of earth,*
> *That I am meek and gentle with these butchers.*

I learned only afterwards that during my long-awaited solo moment, the drama offstage was by no means over. For as Palance came fuming down the backstage stairs, kicking his sword with each step, an intense young Englishman by name of Roger Hamilton (Cinna the Poet) stood watching, horrified, in the wings. As stormy Jack came nearer, Roger, summoning all the ire and British indignation he could muster, spoke out loud and clear:

"I say, have you ever been on a professional stage in your life?"

"S-S-S-S-what did you s-s-s-say?" hissed Jack in white heat.

With no change of inflection, the challenge was repeated.

"I say, have you ever been on a professional stage in your life?"

There is, I swear, a definite imprint to this day in the upstage left wall of the body of Cinna the Poet as it was hurled with superhuman force into the still-damp concrete.

The night of the long velvet robes was now at an end for the new curtain, looking much older and wearier than when it went up, came crashing down. During the pathetic curtain call, Roddy, his chin moist with slobber, turned to me and whispered, "Get the movie rights for dis turkey; vat you vaiting for, Schultz? Dis gonna be beeg hit!"

> *Either there is a civil strife in heaven,*
> *Or else the world too saucy with the gods*
> *Incenses them to send destruction.*

Ah oui, bien sur—pour après tout-ca—le deluge! Having patiently waited for the climax of the opening weeks, the troubled local Tiber "chafing with her shores" decided to reek revenge upon us. All across the peaceful Laurel State the rains came! With no mercy the swollen rivers overflowed the countryside, families evacuated their homes, houses stood half submerged in water—everything turned to liquid chaos:

> *I have seen tempests, when the scolding winds*
> *Have rived the knotty oaks, and I have seen*
> *The ambitious ocean swell and rage and foam*
> *To be exalted with the threatening clouds.*

The content of Shakespeare's play juxtaposed with the long, wet summer was too coincidental, too close for comfort. Nothing this bad had been written about us.

> *Have you not made an universal shout,*
> *That Tiber trembled underneath her banks*
> *To hear the replication of your sounds?*

To get to our basement dressing rooms we now were almost obliged to swim ("Help me, Cassius, or I sink!"). The costume department wasted most of their time keeping those dreadful robes from getting soaked (save the clothes; drown the actors). At every performance when Ray Massey with heavy but poignant deliberation spoke Brutus's lines:

> *There is a tide in the affairs of men*
> *Which taken at the flood leads on to fortune.*

we nodded together in little groups, sage men deep in accord. There were so many references to climate in the text that the play became a nightly weather report, and we were its anchormen.

> *Dars't thou . . . Leap in with me into this angry flood*
> *And swim to yonder point?*

The good news was that everyone in our brave little company rallied pretty well—Jack Palance, above all, coming up absolute trumps. Not only did his performances become richer by leaps and bounds but he exhibited a side of which we hitherto had been ignorant—namely a deliciously macabre sense of humour. Also hugely generous, he threw us parties, showed us his current movies (*Panic in the Streets, The Big*

Knife) and generally behaved in such a manner that no one could help but warm to him. One night after the show, we were recruited to appear in some distant town on a TV "save the flood victims" marathon. While waiting, we all got pretty well swacked. Who could blame us? We didn't go on the air till about 3 a.m.! What we said once on I shudder to remember, but I do recall that the drive back in the limousine was so endless we ran out of gas. The driver pulled up at the only gas station we'd seen for miles. Everything was, of course, dark as pitch but the desperate driver nevertheless banged loudly on the door and woke the enraged owner who, throwing a coat over his pajamas, walked straight up to the limo and screamed at us: "You know what time it is, you bastards? You woke me up—get the hell out-a-here—we're closed!!" Just as he was about to indignantly turn on his heel, a back window of the limo rolled down and a terrifying white face appeared, glowing like phosphorescence out of the dark. The face said nothing but the expression on it was so frightening that it stopped the man cold in his tracks. His own face was only inches away from the face in the car, which now leaned forward ever closer and in the low hiss of an anaconda issued forth one stinging command:

"Gassss-s-s-s-s-s-s-s-s-s-s-s-s." Just that one word, no more. I've never seen anyone move so fast. Lights were immediately switched on—everything went into warp speed—pumps began to pump, petrol flowed like Niagara herself, and before one could say "Caesar" we were filled up and ready to go. God bless Jack! As we drove off in the limo, I caught a glimpse of the gas station owner from the rear window. He was still bowing, scraping and genuflecting like a wound-up mechanical toy.

New Haven was close to Stratford, so one day Ray Massey drove me up to meet Noël Coward (godfather to Ray's son Daniel), who was rehearsing Tammy in *Look After Lulu*. Ray introduced me to the fabled Master, who at once made me feel I was a long-lost friend. "Your gal is going to be a star, dear boy; she has the same spark Gertie had when I first knew her." He was referring, of course, to Gertrude Lawrence, whom he discovered and had groomed for her special place in history. It struck me at once how secure in himself Mr. Coward was, how he wore fame as comfortably and as elegantly as one of his familiar dressing gowns and how easily his generosity became him. I was instantly jealous of Tammy. I would gladly have changed places with her just to be around that sunny, witty "old pro." I thanked Ray for thinking of me—he was full of little kindnesses like that.

There is no question that even the smallest disasters invariably bring people closer together. In that funny, sad, soggy summer of '55, we became a tight little family and I have nothing but the warmest memories of them all. My regret is that I never again performed with Fritz Weaver, one of America's finest, nor with Jerry Stiller, that jolly good fellow and expert comic. I am forever grateful for the lifelong friendships I was lucky enough to have made with Raymond Massey and, of course, that wise and witty imp—dear Roderick "Max" McDowall.

I magnanimously forgave the season everything. After all, let's face it, it had been pretty good to me. Cheers to Armina and Lawrence Langner and good ol' Ray for thinking of me—I owed them a lot. I even forgave my northern friends. The same press that had praised them were now praising me—the hatchet was buried. Basking in the tiny pinpoint spot of temporary glory, I must have seemed utterly obnoxious; but I was sure having the time of my life. My Mark Antony oration was the top spot on the Ed Sullivan show—I was getting attention from all quarters—offers of work as well as "play." Female companionship was hardly wanting; even a couple of Ty Power's ex-courtesans turned up to pay their respects (for this relief, much thanks!), and now that the summer was over and Stratford-on-the-Gin-'n'-Tonic was no longer a festival but just a good old-fashioned drink, I was free once more.

The Langners, founders of the Theatre Guild and
for a while my stage parents

Two tempting engagements beckoned from the horizon: José Ferrer's *Cyrano de Bergerac* for television in which I would play Christian opposite the beauteous Claire Bloom, and for Broadway *The Lark,* Anouilh's play about Joan of Arc, which was to star Julie Harris (I would be cast as the rugged, romantic Earl of Warwick)—neither exactly chopped liver! For an old man of twenty-five, my career wasn't doing too badly. All at once everything seemed to fall into place when, quite by accident—my number came up.

There on the front table of my digs sat the fatal envelope. My heart in my mouth, my hands trembling, I tore it open. Had I dreamed it once? Perhaps once, but I'd put it aside. Now in the glaring light of day—here it was, staring me in the face. It seemed the United States Army could not carry on any longer without my services. The Korean occupational forces would tarry no more. Can you imagine my bile? A peacetime army at that! There wasn't even a proper bloody war going on! Yes, you guessed it—I'd been drafted! My second in the sun was eclipsed. I was on my way to the scaffold.

GOVERNORS ISLAND is not in the least exotic. It is not a winter playground for the rich. It is what it is—a cold, forbidding island just offshore from Gotham's concrete city somewhere between two other such unpreposing islands—Rikers and gloomy Ellis. During my detention, it felt more like Alcatraz!

All draftees with recorded previous illnesses were bundled off there to be checked on—examined. We would be classified A1 or 4F. I was banking heavily on 4F. Ever since I'd received the initial call-up, jolt or kick in the arse, whatever, I'd been frantically analyzing my status which was quite simply—"Situation Intolerable." Even though I was not a citizen but a mere resident "alien" (I love that term), in other circumstances I would have served the country with a clear sense of duty and adventure. I was no conchee—not on your Nelly! But a peacetime army with nothing in it for me but six long years of boredom and disillusionment was to waste my precious youth—literally finish me off! Besides, I was only one year under the cutoff age. What a catastrophe—I had to get out of it somehow.

Then I remembered I'd had hepatitis, and hepatitis then was a definite no-no in the army. I'd been supposedly cured of it but the disease still stays in the blood, and its symptoms can, with a little effort and the proper neglect, be drastically revived. So I had put down my shameful confession on the medical form and proceeded with profound dedication and deep commitment to enjoy a monthlong binge. José Ferrer had promised to wait at least a few weeks more. I had warned my nearest and dearest ones that I wouldn't see them again for a long stretch; that I had something of great importance to attend to—I bade them a tearful farewell, and turning my face toward Soho, I left for the Crusades. Malt, plonk, pocheen, vodka and brandy were my only companions—my only sustenance. "If that doesn't stir up the liver, poison the blood, discolor the urine, bring back the yellow jaundice," I said to myself, "then I'm a Chinaman!"

I had just come out of the showers where, the past couple of repulsive days, I had spent a good part of the time in the buff—rubbing buttocks with at least a hundred other such naked, smelly youths. We'd been told to line up. There we stood, our wet, shiny bodies shivering in the cold, waiting for some uncouth military goon to squeeze our testicles till we winced and then screech in our ears the only word he knew in the English language: "Cough."

Now it was time for the blood tests. "Git ya head down between ya legs," growled another animal who began blindly jabbing me with a needle so old, dirty and blunt it refused to penetrate. This jabbing continued repeatedly—my veins and arteries by now black, blue and swollen, till the good soldier Sweik at last found some he hadn't yet mutilated, and with several brutal final thrusts made his triumphant connection. I just about collapsed in an unconscious heap at his feet.

Now the long wait. Climbing into my shroud that resembled death-camp prison gear, I sat myself down in a sort of solarium and began to read the only book I managed to smuggle in—Budd Schulberg's latest hit, ironically titled *The Disenchanted.* Now and then I would look up and through filthy, smeared windows catch a glimpse of the distant Statue of Liberty. "Liberty?" I thought—"that's a laugh." Every young punk around me seemed happy as a clam—probably the happiest they'd ever been in their lives. They couldn't wait to be accepted by the army! They couldn't wait to be shipped forthwith to sultry, glamorous Korea! Poor and unschooled, they had at last a purpose to their lives, whereas mine had just been taken away. So eager were they to be soldiers they were already practicing forming fours, doing drills, marching goose-step fashion up and down the halls, playing war games and generally behaving like little gangsters. I overheard one say, as he nearly knocked me off my chair, "Who's the old guy?" Jesus! I guess he was right. I *was* old. I was a decrepit twenty-five and they were all an obnoxious seventeen or eighteen—and these were to be the majority of the inspiring young comrades with whom I would be forced to keep company for six long years! What a suicidal thought!

I began to hallucinate. I fantasized that the beauteous Claire Bloom (whom I had never met) was at this very moment languishing in some sad, empty hotel room, all alone with her embroidery, pining after me, waiting breathlessly for my return. I had just reached the point in Schulberg's book where F. Scott Fitzgerald, alias Manley Halliday, is suffering from delirium tremens when the little posse arrived and told me to get dressed. "Where are you taking me?" I stammered as they one-armed me down the long Kafka-like corridors. "Ouda-here," they snarled, and I realized I was on my way back to Manhattan, back to my four walls in the Hudson where I was to await my fate. I turned the key in the door of my "suite" and was just about to open the window and throw myself out when the phone rang. A dry, disgruntled voice at the other end told me in the manner of one who is dismissing a leper that I was 4F. Yeee-aow! It had worked! My liver had destructed! I waited till I'd caught my breath and then feverishly dialed a number: Mr. F-F-F-Ferrer?" I stuttered. I'm f-f-fine, I'm f-f-f-four F, and I'm f-f-f-Free!"

CHAPTER THIRTEEN

NEW YORK AND THE LARK

New York had all the iridescence of the beginning of the world.
— F. SCOTT FITZGERALD

That's exactly how it appeared through rose-coloured spectacles when you were young and even moderately successful. Once it decided you were worth recognizing, what you had taken to be an essentially heartless city suddenly opened its doors, and before you could say Damon Runyon—presto!—it had adopted you! The island of Manhattan had become the Island of Bad Boys—you were as gullible as Pinocchio—and all its shining treasures were yours for the taking. If it had ever been cynical and cold it had most certainly earned the right. No other metropolis in recent history had played host to such greed — had been so generous with her favours. What's more, it seemed most of her customers were visitors from other planets. Where the hell were the natives? Was there such a thing? A true New Yorker was as rare in New York as a blond Athenian in Athens. Everyone had migrated there with no other purpose in mind but to rob the old harlot of her riches. This achieved, she would be discarded without so much as a nod of thanks, tired and used, yet still resilient enough to come bouncing back for more.

Of course, none of this occurred to me when, as a youth, I gazed hungrily upon the Big Apple and took my first bite. Although the delirium known as the Age of Jazz was an age long gone, there were still in the midfifties echoes of it everywhere (you could always reach me at Birdland) — precious pockets scattered about from Harlem to the Village to remind us it had once succeeded in freeing the slaves, shaking up the Puritans, and that its glorious past had not been in vain. Fitzgerald, that era's definitive spokesman, though long dead was still fairly popular amongst the college set; but besides jazz, there was a new sound now with which to contend. With the coming of the Pelvis, "Heartbreak Hotel" and "Blue Suede Shoes," we were about to witness the dawning of the Age of Rock and the birth of the teenybopper. Young James Dean had just immortalized himself by crashing his car, Martin Luther King, Jr., was about to begin his crusade and the latest D. H. Lawrence was a witty White Russian who proved he could play wondrous tricks with the English language and also manage to beat the censor with a racy little novel called *Lolita*. After the Cold War impotence of the McCarthy era, a slice of beautifully blended spice was a welcome aphrodisiac. Nabokov's brilliant satire of nymphet America seducing decadent old Europe filled the void admirably and turned us all on again.

Having occupied a tawdry variety of roach-infested, "one-night cheap hotels," I decided to upgrade myself and moved back into the Alice-gonquin. This time I could afford it and with some supportive words on my behalf from good old Jane Broder, I was able to hold my head up high and for a change make my entrance through the front door. There was new management, and the old staff, which was still there, if they indeed remembered my questionable shenanigans and reputation for unpaid accounts, didn't give a rap and were as charming and accommodating as ever. Bob, the delightful maître d', who knew everybody's name and business, and good old Charlie the Chinaman, ageless as ever, still feeding each finger bowl with a rose.

The autumn smells of New York, which for Broadway meant the

Rites of Spring, were some of the most pungent on earth. They were the signal for the Season's excitement to begin. The latest luxury in our profession was taped television (which meant one could do it again if it wasn't right) and, courtesy of Edmond Rostand, Mr. Ferrer and the Dupont Show of the Month, I had been rescued from the twentieth-century military draft and inducted into that seventeenth-century regiment of crack guards—Les Cadets de Gascoyne! And how could I ever forget the lady?

> CHRISTIAN: *"Yes, yes, yes, who—tell me, oh my knees are knocking."*

She was a pure-skinned, raven-haired, Semitic beauty from Blighty and her name was Bloom. Not the Molly Bloom of *Finnegans Wake* nor the bloom of lilacs in Walt Whitman's dooryard, but a fresh, young bloom called Claire—une véritable Claire de la Lune Bloom. She was nineteen or perhaps twenty, spoke verse like an angel and could already claim as her leading men Charlie Chaplin, Laurence Olivier and Richard Burton. At a glance she was everyone's idea of Jessica, Nerissa, Perdita, Ophelia—even Juliet—so it wasn't too tough an assignment for my Christian to make an utter bloody fool of himself over her Roxanne.

A demure demeanor disguised, I suspected, a good deal of fire and brimstone and she had a coquettish custom of lowering her eyelids and tilting her head sideways at an angle so that masses of black tresses cascaded forward, half concealing her face, like a mantilla. She was mouthwatering—I was entranced, struck dumb! Nothing ever happened between us, of course, her aura had so shackled me it was not possible to make a move, and the fact that her overprotective mother was more than frequently present hardly induced encouragement or invited opportunity.

I took Claire, her wimple at a rakish angle, to a few speechless dinners and that was about it. I must have been the dullest company—I could do nothing but stare at her. Two such shy ones accompanied by no other sound but the nervous clink of cutlery had the effect of canceling each other out. I was quite honestly relieved when she went back to Blighty and my poor cracked heart, which she had unwittingly cut to pieces, was permitted to mend on its own.

José Ferrer was at the very height of his career. His Cyrano de Bergerac had earned him an Oscar and a Tony and he was now prepared to reap all the television awards as well. Although the production was

José Ferrer, my languid self and Claire Bloom

generally supervised by Kirk Browning, Jo directed the major scenes himself. Most of the cast had been with him since the beginning, on stage and screen—Jo being both loyal and practical—so they all had weathered many campaigns together. Rehearsing with this lot was a bit like being in boot camp—*Stalag 17* with plumes.

Jo was a very fine director with a particular penchant for farce. He was both tough and sensitive. He quickly saw my lovesick predicament, took me aside like a proper sergeant major, drilled the wimp out of my Christian, gave him back his balls and made a man out of him! And out of me! Thank you, Jo, for that. When I wasn't gaping at Claire, I watched his Cyrano most carefully. I admired tremendously the comic force with which he attacked it and made many a mental note which helped a great deal when, one day, I was lucky enough to play that God-given character myself.

I think this production of Jo's came off pretty well on the "box"— I can't quite remember—it all went by so quickly. But triumphant or not, it was television after all, and like yesterday's newspaper soon to be forgotten. It was really the theatre that year that took hold of my life, pushed me several more rungs up the ladder and made me feel, perhaps for the first time, that I belonged on the "street" and that that throbbing city with all its glittering lights swimming in my eyes had allowed me to stay.

ONE OF THE LAST FEW remaining seasons of quality and quantity on Broadway was that of 1955–56. When one examines the present state of commercial entertainment in these sparse, uncertain times, it is heartening to look back to a time when the American theatre was still rich in invention, when there was an equal representation of original works by major writers both foreign and domestic and where there was always a healthy traffic jam of out-of-town tryouts waiting in line, frantic to move into their final New York parking space.

This was the year of *Pipe Dream, The Most Happy Fella,* the Lunts in *The Great Sebastian,* The D'Oyly Carte Opera Company, *La Comédie Française,* Michael Gazzo's *A Hatful of Rain* with Shelley Winters, Ben Gazzara and Tony Franciosa, Shirley Booth in *The Desk Set,* Edward G. Robinson in Paddy Chayefsky's *Middle of the Night,* Joyce Grenfell, gently satirical in her own revue—Maurice Chevalier at one theatre—Marcel Marceau at another. There were also Tyrone Guthrie's productions, *Tamburlaine the Great* and *Troilus and Cressida,* Sammy Davis, Jr., in *Mr. Wonderful* and Sean O'Casey's *Red Roses for Me.* Jayne Mansfield's magnificent chest had its "coming out" party in *Will Success Spoil Rock Hunter* while an accident-prone Orson Welles gave us his sometimes magnificent King Lear in a wheelchair.

And, by the way, these were just by the by. The ten top new plays of the year were Arthur Miller's *A View from the Bridge,* Giraudoux's *Tiger at the Gates, The Diary of Anne Frank* which made a star of Susan Strasberg at seventeen, and *No Time For Sergeants,* which marked the debut of that charmer Andy Griffith. *The Ponder Heart* by Chodorov, *The Chalk Garden* by Enid Bagnold, Thornton Wilder's *The Matchmaker* with a towering comic performance by Ruth Gordon and a pixie performance by Robert Morse—and Bert Lahr, equally brilliant in the American première of Beckett's *Waiting for Godot.* There was a little-known musical that snuck in called *My Fair Lady* with Rex Harrison and a young newcomer from Wimbledon named Julie Andrews and lastly, the first big success *I* was ever in—*The Lark.*

The Art of Producing by L. Doherty is a biography of the late Kermit Bloomgarden, who presented *The Lark.* It is aptly titled for if ever there was a man who made producing an art—it was Kermit. He had gathered and brought before the public most of the top playwrights of our time and had the theatrical knowledge and professional wisdom to guide them through the work process with devout expertise. His record of original productions speaks for itself: *Deep Are the Roots, Another Part of the Forest, Death of a Salesman, The Crucible, A View from the Bridge, The Diary of Anne Frank, Look Homeward Angel, The Most Happy Fella, The Music Man, Toys in the Attic* and *Equus,* among others.

Brooklyn-born Kermit was a tough hombre but unlike most of his fellow producers, he admired and respected actors and writers. "We should interfere as little as possible with artists—just throw out sparks that will stimulate them, to make better use of their own creativity." The antithesis of the unruffled, old-fashioned impresario whose suits were never rumpled nor ties ever out of place, he sweated his way through every production in his shirt sleeves as if he were delivering his very own baby. He knew everyone's function, could do just about everyone's job—an expert on all aspects of the game, yet he still never interfered. He was, in fact, exactly what a producer should be and rarely, if ever, is.

And now here he was presenting Jean Anouilh's *The Lark,* adapted by Lillian Hellman, music by Leonard Bernstein, settings and lighting by Jo Mielziner; and here was I staring at him across his desk. It appeared that the British actor rehearsing the part of the Earl of Warwick was to be replaced, and I was the main candidate. Jane, Kermit's old casting director, had cunningly arranged the meeting and insisted on bringing me along herself. "Honey—you gotta do this, and I'm coming with you to see that you do!"

Kermit, successfully covering up a soft heart, sat unsmiling, gruffly introduced himself and, jerking his thumb in the direction of a rather small older lady seated nearby in a wing chair furiously chain-smoking, muttered matter-of-factly, "And, by the way, this is Miss Hellman."

The lady at once took command. She must have been referring to me, for without removing her cigarette from her lips she mumbled out of the corner of her mouth, "Oh yeah, he'll be fine." Then in a few seconds she'd explained the play, its characters and the style in which they should all be performed. I wondered why I was so immediately disarmed, but soon realized it was the natural tone she adopted—low, intimate without artifice—a secure woman in a man's world but able to beat most of them at their own game. It was a reassuring manner which at once put me at ease, but as she spoke I was reminded of a wonderful actor called Robert Pastene who psychologically had suffered a

Lillian Hellman — in a man's and woman's world, she was herself

nervous seizure in the neck, permanently paralyzing it at a very crooked angle. I asked a friend what had caused this unfortunate handicap and was told, "Oh, didn't you know? He was working for Lillian Hellman." I was never to see that side of her, however, if indeed it existed at all— I was lucky to remain on her good side for all the time I was to know her, but that morning in Kermit's office there was no doubt I was in the presence of one strong lady.

Lillian was the furthest thing from being pretty but that had never stopped her. Her amazing charisma and high intelligence had seduced a great many influential, creative men who seemed to fall for her as regularly as clockwork (Herman Shumlin, Dashiell Hammett, William Wyler, among them); she had them dangling from her bracelets. Based on her reputation as one of America's great playwrights (*The Children's Hour, The Little Foxes, The Autumn Garden*), Lillian was still at this time an exceptionally powerful force in Hollywood and on Broadway. At the time she was certainly the most dominating writer of either gender—

the only one to have total casting approval over all her scripts. Major Hollywood stars were required to audition for her; she made Paul Lukas read for his part in her film of *Watch on the Rhine* even though he was a big star at Warners and had already enjoyed a huge success in the same role on Broadway. Profoundly motivated politically, she was, as everyone knows, a considerable and controversial force in the House Un-American Activities hearings. Whether one agreed with her principles or intentions, one could not deny her courage in taking the Fifth and categorically refusing to name names.

Besides her writing gifts, her intellect and the effortless way she managed to accumulate power, one of Lillian's greatest gifts was her clarity. She had an uncanny ability to cut straight to the chase. It took only a few rehearsals, therefore, to observe the director Joseph Anthony (a nice gentleman somewhat frightened by Stanislavsky) make several ill-conceived suggestions before Lillian decided, not too subtly, to take over. We would all assemble on the stage after each out-of-town performance to receive our notes from the director—a normal custom in the theatre. But Lillian had beaten him to it. A chair was brought out in front of us, and ignoring all protocol, Miss Hellman promptly sat down and firmly announced, "I shall give my notes first" (and this with ill-concealed sarcasm); "then, uh, Mr. Anthony can give you his." Lillian's only took a few minutes. They were clear and concise. Joe Anthony's went on and on into the night—obscure and uninspired. I'm afraid we only really listened to Miss H. Her criticisms were often cruel but always frighteningly accurate; her suggestions, constructive, enlightening.

LILLIAN STRUCK IT LUCKY with her cast. A company of players made of sterner stuff would have been difficult to find. Theodore Bikel, newly arrived from Israel's Habima, and a wonderful little celluloid import, *The Kidnappers,* took the small but telling role of de Beaudricourt and made a succulent meal of it. A talented musician, Theo also played the guitar and sang a number of French, Spanish and Israeli songs with a great deal of charm—many of which he composed himself. Every night, one could hear him strumming and singing away in his dressing room, and at parties his "companion" never left his side as he explained in song: "Ma Guitar et Moi, Nous ne Nous Quittons Pas."

JOSEPH WISEMAN, who was from my hometown, played the Inquisitor with a sinister stillness that was remarkably chilling. A taut,

Joseph Wiseman as The Inquisitor in The Lark

highly tuned, highly strung stage actor, he had electrified audiences and gained considerable distinction with eccentric performances in the films *Detective Story* and *Viva Zapata!* We shared a dressing room on the road and at the Longacre Theatre in New York, whose meager quarters reflected the disdain for actors common to theatre owners and architects. Wiseman was a fiercely intense creature who always gave people a wide berth, didn't care to be touched and rarely spoke to anyone. He seemed continually in a state of monastic meditation as he glided about obsessively immersed in his role. At rehearsals when his turn came the cast would retire to lie down or take a welcome cigarette break, for we knew these analytical sessions would last most of the morning.

Thrown together as we were, Joe and I, it didn't take me long to discover that behind the impenetrable mask lurked a maniacal gallows humour. One night while we were putting on our "slop," I complimented him on his extraordinary performance opposite Marlon Brando in *Viva Zapata!* "Oi—uh—my Gott, what a trial, how unpleasant, people staring in stores, in restaurants, for days, for weeks maybe. How embarrassing it was—oh Gott! One evening, some young animal, God forgive me, approaches me in the street. 'Mr. Wiseman,' he begins. 'Don't come near me. Don't touch me,' I say. 'Mr. Wiseman—' I turn; I walk away down the street. Can you believe the gall? He starts coming after me, the fresh meshuggener, 'Mr. Wiseman,' he shouts, 'I just want to ask you something—please!' 'No autographs—get away from me!' I shout back, breaking into a run. He runs after me screaming, 'Mr. Wiseman! Mr. Wiseman!' Doesn't the mensch ever get tired? I run across Broadway down Forty-fifth to Eighth—turn right—up Forty-sixth, back to Broadway, turn left, left again down Forty-seventh. The young fool is gaining on me—I duck into an alley—he's right behind me! Ah well, Joe, I say to myself, be fair; come on, he's a nice boy— maybe a little crazy, wants to pay a compliment, maybe an autograph. It's not the end of the world—let him. By now he's almost on top of me. 'Mr. Wiseman, Mr. Wiseman,' he gasps, out of breath, exhausted. I stop. I turn around, at the end of my rope, weary, resigned, but forgiving. 'Yes?' I ask gently, quietly. 'Mr. Wiseman,' he says, 'what's Marlon Brando like?' "

During the pre-Broadway tour in Boston, one night after the first act I flounced back to our dressing room at the Colonial, frustrated and frankly pissed off. The actor playing the principal monk was notoriously slow in his delivery and habitually kept us all waiting simply "covered in egg." His heavy deliberation particularly affected Joe and me. Slamming my sword and gauntlets on the table, I blurted out, "Goddamn! What are we going to do about M? He's holding up the whole works! And look what he's doing to *you,* Joe—he keeps you hanging forever before you can respond. He's forcing us to pick up the slack of the entire evening!" Exasperated, I kicked the door several times with my boot. Joe, ever benign and philosophical, gravely shook his head.

"Chris—look—be nice. Learn patience, my friend. He's a good boy—he's talented—he takes his time. He's searching; he'll pull it together, but, in the meantime, why the fuck should we sit around looking like schmucks while that *selfish prick* learns on our time?! Fourteen trucks I could drive through his pauses! If he doesn't get his finger out, I'll stick a red-hot poker up his arse already! No! Better *he* burn at the stake instead of Joan!"

I was crazy about Joe Wiseman—he was so contrary but was always loyal and caring. Known to most as a performer who specialized in kooks and weirdos, he oddly enough possessed a strange and mesmerizing lyrical quality. He had a poet's head and a beautiful speaking voice, which, when combined as it was with the suppressed violence he kept

Boris, the gentle giant

simmering so near the surface, could have made him, had Fate pointed in another direction, one of our most passionate romantic actors.

The character of Bishop Cauchon who presided over the trial, and Boris Karloff who brought him to life as such a moving and sympathetic figure, were interchangeable. They were really one and the same man and for everyone of us a kind of Father Confessor. Boris the giant — who had been used and misused in early silent pictures, cruelly taken advantage of, made to suffer grave physical hardships for little money, and then, surviving all, to carve for himself a celebrated career out of terror and pathos — was the gentlest of men. He even walked with an apologetic stoop as if he wished not to overwhelm with his massive frame and imposing presence. I don't think Boris ever knew how blessed he was with that most extraordinary face, nor how handsome — he was so completely without vanity. When he spoke, his famous baritone voice with its attractive lisp was not in the least frightening but soft, musical and mellow.

On-screen the world affectionately admired him as "the Monster" but most of it would never know how marvelous he was on the stage. Boris cared deeply for a thousand things, but one he cared for almost more than any other, except his darling wife, Evie, was cricket. He himself was an expert at the game, and as part of Hollywood's Raj in the thirties, a valued member of their famed cricket team. Wherever he went one could see the English newspapers with the latest scores peeping out from every pocket; and he longed for those breaks when he could get back to England and watch the test matches at his beloved Lords. Boris asked for very little in life and was the kindest, most selfless and modest man. No small wonder then that each member of our large cast made it a ritual to call out goodnight to him as they passed his first-floor dressing room every evening. The old man regularly turned up at the theatre an hour before the curtain and all through the play's lengthy run never once missed a performance.

One night, after the half hour had been called, there was no sign of Boris. This was most odd as he was always so prompt. At the fifteen-minute call—still no Boris. Joe and I, worried sick, came out of our dressing room and gazed down toward the first landing below, waiting for news. The stage manager was outside in the alley pacing up and down, beside himself. Just for a second, I chanced to look up and there, above us, on the next four landings every member of the cast from featured player down to the smallest soldier, monk or "walk-on" was similarly peering over the balustrades, tense and anxious. Boris was our tower of strength, you see; we not only needed him, we already missed him. Just then he lumbered in through the stage door and, as one man, we gave him a rousing welcoming ovation. He looked up at us, beaming, with that wonderful twisted smile of his, and we all went back to our rooms as if we'd just been given a present.

As I was struggling into my armour it came to me like a ray of truth that there are only the rarest few born into this world who are truly good humans and, I realized, with a sharp little pang of sadness and envy, I could never be one of them.

THE MAID OF ORLÉANS with her proud standard held high was reincarnated in the form of a little star called Harris. A will-o'-the-wisp, surprisingly fraught with fire, the freckle-faced gamine who as that captivating waif Frankie in Carson McCullers's *Member of the Wedding* had stolen everyone's heart and had also shown her soignée side in

I Am a Camera was at last challenged by the range required of St. Joan. She met it head on, in a performance beyond praise. Not as demanding as Shaw's maid, perhaps, nor as high-flown (Anouilh's heroines are mostly cast from the same mould—subtler victims, whom critics impishly nicknamed "Little Orphan Anouilhs") but it was still a substantial workout for an actress. Julie Harris was the Lark, and for more than two hundred nights she flew to Heaven's gate and back with matchless conviction.

There is a moment in the play when Joan, reliving her memories at the trial, suddenly bursts out screaming blood and encouragement to her soldiers on the field. In one swift movement she jumped onto her little stool as the lights went out on everyone leaving only a single spot on her. Julie shook her fists at her imaginary army and called out into the darkened theatre, the tears glistening on her cheeks while we stood there each night, spellbound in the dark around her. I made the ghastly blunder of letting her know how telling that moment was. She rounded on me and told me to shut up—that now I'd made her aware of it, she could never do it again. I learned a valuable lesson—but it did cross my mind that if ever one wished to ruin a performance, all one had to do was to constantly compliment it. Of course nothing could have ever shaken her commitment—it was grounded so solidly in truth.

Julie Harris was and is the Peter Pan of actresses—she makes us all feel like children when we watch her on the stage and her special light has never been extinguished. She received the Tony Award for her Lark as best actress of the year and has since won more Tonys than most actors. The United States finally recognized her by presenting her with a Kennedy Center honour. For she is, without question, a national treasure and for more than fifty years has continued to illumine, strengthen and hold together what has now become the fragile fabric of our theatre. Anything short of canonization would be a colossal snub.

I was to have the great joy of working with Julie on many another occasion, but during *The Lark* run we made our first television appearance together for Hallmark Hall of Fame in *Little Moon of Alban*. James Costigan had written a very touching story about a young Irish nun and a dying British soldier during the early uprising. The sister tries vainly to nurse him back to life and in spite of their differences, they fall in love. Julie (miraculous as usual), James and I were nominated for Emmys. Julie and James won for their pains but that year the categories were strangely conceived and muddled beyond comprehension—the best actor category suffering the most confusion. This was the lineup:

Julie, a most memorable Joan

Rod Steiger, Mickey Rooney, Paul Muni (all superb), me and, for some inexplicable reason, Fred Astaire, whose performance had not included acting but purely singing and dancing with his new partner, Barrie Chase. I sat (black tie) in the audience in New York awaiting my fate watching two screens representing both coasts—what a mess! Fred Astaire won! Now I'm his number one fan, but this was too much—the audience couldn't believe it—neither could Fred, but it was too late. Outside in the street afterwards I bumped into Rod Steiger who with a wink and a shrug quipped, "Well! See you tomorrow at Arthur Murray's."

CHAPTER FOURTEEN

HENRY V

KING HENRY: *What treasure, uncle?*
EXETER: *Tennis balls, my liege.*

The day I shouted, "Once more unto the breech," at my fellow students somewhere back in the mists of the ninth grade, I would never have believed that ten years thence I'd be the youngest of my country to lead Canada's Stratford on home ground and at the Edinburgh Festival as Harry the King himself. There was justice after all—I'd been paid back in full.

A considerable amount of time had gone by since Laurence Olivier's mighty motion picture established Shakespeare as a first-class screenwriter. Richard Burton at the Old Vic had soon thereafter made a sonorous, rough and ruthless brawler out of the young king, but no other major production of the work had since been given. Times had changed. Henry would have to change with them.

This attempt of ours, therefore, became the tale of an angry young rebel reluctant to shed his youthful debauchery for a throne he didn't particularly cherish, only to discover on the eve of Agincourt he had grown up, not just another brawling soldier, but a king—and a king with some conscience. There were still heroic remnants of Churchillian propaganda which England in its finest hour had demanded of Olivier's film—after all, it is a concerto for trumpet and orchestra. But it was also raw and very right for the midfifties—the emergence of Osborne, Arden and Wesker, the growing influence of Brecht and the birth of the antihero. Whatever it was, who cares—I had some of the best times of my life in it—it was like quaffing gallons of champagne.

What made the production particularly unique was that our director and new boss, Michael Langham, had invited Quebec's celebrated French company, Le Théâtre du Nouveau Monde (TNM), to perform their repertoire of Molière farces, on condition that they also play the

My new and lasting mentor,
Michael Langham

French court in *Henry V.* It was a bold move and a fortunate one for, alongside our own rough-and-ready English, this stylish company brought to the play not just an added elegance, but a whole other life—a whole other world. This ingenious coup of Langham's was a triumph both politically and artistically and marked in the arts the most significant and successful marriage of our two cultures within memory. Would that such a rare alliance had continued on an annual basis.

The TNM was a thriving concern under the baton of two complete opposites—Jean Gascon and Jean-Louis Roux. Quebec Province was home base, but they toured their company extensively in Europe, especially through Belgium and France, where reports spoke goldenly of their bawdy and roistering Molière interpretations. As opposed to the static, somewhat lifeless Molière that La Comédie Française had recently been feeding everyone, theirs thrived on the kind of free spirit of improvisation and broadness of style that most likely would have been closest to the master's heart. Les deux Jeans had collected a first-rate group of highly skilled exuberant Frenchmen, rich in comic invention, swift of speech and agile of movement. One or two members were from France—Guy Hoffman for one—a small, rotund creature with a mooncalf face and tragic eyes, a great clown with an irresistible sweetness about him who was now loyally bound to the New World.

The difference between the two artistic leaders was vast. Roux was a fine director and a subtle actor of steel-like precision—an introvert and academic whose taste impeccably helped guide the troupe's choice of repertoire. Gascon, gregarious with a gargantuan charm, an extrovert in the extreme, had an astonishing instinct for theatricality. A monstre sacré, he was an imaginative director and an actor of great artistic size in the vein of Pierre Brasseur and Harry Bauer. (He had begun in life as a doctor of medicine and had since been awarded honorary degrees from various universities.) He would impishly weave this information into one of his speeches from Molière:

Je suis Docteur!
Je suis le premier Docteur des Docteurs!
Je suis touts les Docteurs á touts les Docteurs!
Je suis le Doc de les Docs!
Je ne suis pas une *fois Docteur!*
Je suis undeuxtroisquatrecinqsixsepthuitneuf
DIX FOIS DOCTEURS!

Gascon, in appearance, was a cross between Pantagruel and François Premier. I am happy to say he became one of my closest and dearest friends and his great spirit and even greater heart was a constant source of joy to me and to all who knew him. He loved life as passionately as life loved him. I can still hear his rich voice with the touch of whiskey blanc in it bellowing Racine and jaunty French chansons. As the Constable of France in *Henry* he glided across the platform with an insulting pantherlike grace and that same rasping voice boomed over the audience with savage power. His presence and that of his entire company on our "battlefield" was utterly and wonderfully alien. But what

Jean Gascon, Renaissance figure who brought
all of life to the stage

was abundantly clear was that Michael Langham had become the festival's sole lifeline. If Guthrie's genius and panache had given the enterprise a champagne start, Langham was to mature it into a robust, enduring burgundy.

All summer I dangerously shared a flat on Stratford's main drag with my old pal Bob Goodier, who was the Duke of Exeter, my uncle in the play. Bob was in his late forties, a trifle portly but still an extremely handsome dog who loved the ladies. He nicknamed himself The Great Satisfier—and I don't think for a moment he was exaggerating. Thanks to my lord of Exeter, the flat was always supplied with plentiful entertainment, and I fear that my role *off*stage was as boisterous and disreputable as the real Prince Hal's. There was wassail all as the floorboards groaned night after night. Campbell, Gerussi, Hutt, Helpmann, Follows, formidable actors all, made me walk the plank. I was the new boy—it was tough being accepted into this fraternity.

Touts les nuits, the French connection, who by now seemed joined to us at the hip, behaved just as badly as we, if not worse. It was war between the Gauls and the Brits to see which side could outdance the other. Between us we had collectively consumed a great amount of sugar, so we could actually exist for quite long periods of time without much food. It was just as well for the choice of restaurants in the town was, to put it mildly, limited. There was the Golden Bamboo and Ellam's Diner, and that was just about it. The Golden Bamboo was a Chinese restaurant which had not improved since the owner's ancestors built the railroads. In fact, we occasionally took our washing there, justifiably mistaking it for a laundry. But when we did become ravenous, Gascon and his beaux frères would take turns cooking for us, whipping up sumptuous tourtières, cassoulets or pissaladières.

That pure Protestant, Presbyterian town suddenly reeked with garlic. Things were looking up. The local liquor store (called a liquor commission, which was government-run) housed a pretty pathetic assortment of wine (Blue Nun and Manischewitz being their grandest offerings) so the sneaky Gauls, grace de Dieu, imported for the entire company proper vino from Quebec Province (multiple choice) which we downed with grateful gluttony. The French boys quickly made friends with the liquor-commission lads, slowly but surely coaching them in the Art of the Grape so that by summer's end the store was stocked to the ceiling with profoundly drinkable plonk, Pontet-Canet, Chambertin, Haut-Brion—all "Mis en bouteille au château."

Gascon and Jean-Louis Roux, overcome with summer madness, decided to put me in one of their Molière plays on my days off. I would take on an old man called Villebrequin in one of the farces. Ninety or thereabouts, he staggers on at the end of act 2 with a startling revelation that tears the plot to shreds and brings down le rideau. Now I'd played in French a few times before, but never Molière, and certainly not *this* Molière, performed as it was at such breakneck speed. There was wall-to-wall laughter from the audience, and the actors spoke so fast, I couldn't hear my cue let alone understand it, so I had to be pushed on. The boys were so free, loose and funny in this mad farce, it was a joy to be onstage with them no matter how briefly.

I shall never forget those chers méchants—when a few years later at a reunion party in Montreal, they presented me (maudlin tears running down our faces) with an award for my "courageous interpretation of Molière and Shakespeare." I was convinced it was called "Le Prix Marc l'Escargot" and I thought it was all in jest. I even made a quip about the prize being named for some chef, until a friendly soul, to save me further embarrassment, set me straight. It was l'Escarbot with a *B*. It seems that on November 14, 1606, Marc Lescarbot, a young French nobleman, had written and produced the first known theatrical performance in our country on the eastern part of the Acadian coast. The occasion was to welcome both the recently appointed governor of New France and Samuel de Champlain, founder of the colony. French and Indians made up the cast, speaking in verse, some in standard French, some in Indian dialect and others in broken French. It signaled, quite unconsciously perhaps, the early bringing together of a bilingual populace and its presentation was clearly miles ahead of its time.

Every time I look upon this handsomely mounted plaque, I am touched all over again. Because it was given in such a spirit of light-heartedness, this fraternal gesture made me feel more than ever a part of French Canada, and I cherish it above almost any bauble that has come my way.

THE RIDE THROUGH that summer had its share of turbulence—it wasn't *all* the "brightest heaven of invention." Stiflingly hot under the tent flaps, especially when sporting Tanya Moiseiwitsch's superb but heavy costumes, most of us lost a good deal of weight. After all, we had covered quite a few miles during each performance. Just about my favorite section was the night scene before the battle and that quiet moving soliloquy of Henry's—"Upon the king . . ." But inevitably, when the most intimate moment of the speech arrived, the loudest train whistle would shatter the silence of the night. This happened repeatedly at every performance in precisely the same spot. It never failed to obliterate the famous words, reducing the scene to a shambles. Faking a tantrum, I shouted at Tom Patterson, the theatre's founder, demanding he instruct the station to forbid the train from whistling. I couldn't believe what happened. He did! He called them up and accused them of desecrating Shakespeare. They not only stopped the whistle—they changed the time of the train!

PART OF THE THEATRE'S PROGRAMME was a music festival of short duration but considerable prestige. It was much loved and enjoyed great success. On an average clear day, one might find oneself in the Golden Bamboo staring across a table at Yehudi Menuhin, Dave Brubeck, Wilbur de Paris and Julian Bream munching their egg rolls. Or, out shopping, the person next to you could be Inge Borkh, Maureen Forrester, Paul Desmond, Rostropovich or Erroll Garner.

Upon leaving the stage door after an evening performance, in the pitch black I accidentally bumped into a tall grey-haired man in a white dinner jacket. He was pacing furiously up and down, humming away to himself and wildly gesticulating. I couldn't see who this madman was—it was too dark—so I got as close as I politely could. He must have recognized me, for he greeted me enthusiastically with "Vat great evening! Sank you! I yam cawmpawzeeng Henry Feeft piano concerto—fentesticle play—fentesticle!" Conducting an imaginary orchestra, he scurried away up a grassy knoll. It was the renowned pianist Rudolf Serkin.

AFTER A PARTICULARLY sleepless night, I was jolted out of my bed with a call from Kay Brown in New York. She was informing me that David O. Selznick and his wife, Jennifer Jones, were flying in from the coast to see the Saturday matinée of *Henry V* and would like to get together with me afterwards to discuss my future. Would I please arrange a meeting place? It would have to be a large house over a certain square footage, secluded from view with at least two acres of surrounding grounds attractively landscaped, including a swimming pool. The owners would be required to vacate the premises until the Selznicks decided they were ready to leave. It would also be necessary for some staff to be left available in order to serve drinks and hors d'oeuvres. The owners, of course, would be handsomely remunerated—money not being a concern.

David O. Selznick and his wife, Jennifer Jones, about to offer me the world

Land's sakes, Miz Scarlett—What waz ah gwanna do?! A wealthy community Stratford was not. I called Tom Patterson—and, bless him, he came up trumps. The richest couple in the vicinity seemed to have just the ideal spot, and as romantic as one could find. They not only agreed; they offered the whole place scot-free for as long as the Selznicks wanted it. It appears they had furnished one of their rooms with several tables, chairs and other artifacts from the set of their all-time favorite movie, *Gone With the Wind,* at the famous MGM auction. To them, David O. Selznick was God and Jennifer Jones was Saint Bernadette and the Virgin Mary combined. I couldn't believe my luck.

D-Day arrived. The Selznicks just managed to make the matinée as the opening fanfare was being played. They had expressly asked for everyone to be discreet concerning their visit, but when they came backstage after the performance, the whole damn place was jammed with press and photographers from far and wide—David directing them like so much traffic, explaining to the world as the three of us squinted into the blazing lightbulbs that I was to be his new male star! Later, on the lawn with tea, champagne and sandwiches, the three of us alone at last, he laid out before me my entire programme for the next few years—my life seemed no longer mine.

First on the agenda was F. Scott Fitzgerald's *Tender Is the Night.* Jennifer and I were to impersonate the Divers (Nicole and Dick). Rosemary, with whom Diver has the torrid affair, would be the sought-after ingenue Hope Lange. Katharine Hepburn had agreed to play Baby, Nicole's feisty elder sister. Tommy Barban, the soldier of fortune, would be Vittorio Gassman, and for the wisecracking, piano-playing Abe North it was a toss-up between Noël Coward and Oscar Levant, depending on availability. Both wanted to do it. Ivan Moffat had written the latest screenplay which would, no doubt, be under heavy Selznick scrutiny and John Frankenheimer, the hottest, most provocative new television genius, would be our director. "I want his first motion picture to be mine. I am not interested in the older establishment for this—I want someone young with an unruly imagination." David was uncannily right—Frankenheimer had an edgy, stylish way with him and a subtle sense of tension that was right up the Fitzgerald alley.

Selznick was still talking—enjoying his grandiose plans. He would insist we migrate in early summer to the French Riviera, where he had acquired a massive villa. We would reside there for one whole month at his expense for the mere purpose of soaking up "atmosphere"—then we would begin shooting both there and in Switzerland. My next two projects we would discuss at a future date, but he could tell me now that the first was most certainly Hemingway's *The Sun Also Rises*. The two leads would again be Jennifer and me. "The very first thing you must do, however," David concluded, "is to get a new set of teeth. Yours are awful—impossible to photograph—I can't even see them!"

The tea, sandwiches and champagne had not yet reached my stomach. They were stuck somewhere between my throat and my chest. David, I could see, was a past master of persuasion and there was no denying it, he certainly never thought small. I glanced at Jennifer Jones, who was sitting slightly apart. Yes, she was attractive all right, even beautiful in a sensual, neurotic way. The huge myopic eyes, the pouting mouth, gave her a look of despair that was strangely desirable. Yet every now and then her face would tighten as if betraying some disturbing inner secret, forcing the long tendons in her neck to stand out just as I remember them on the screen. She was looking away nervously toward the pond below us and I couldn't possibly divine what thoughts were going through her head. Although she was perfectly polite and warm, she spoke very little, nodding approval only occasionally— clearly distracted. She was unquestionably a star and able to set up pictures on her name alone (David had seen to that); but was she not a trifle old to be a Fitzgerald or Hemingway heroine? And was she capable of acting those complex, difficult women? More to the point, though I was the right age for Dick Diver, was *I* not too youthful for *her*? Yet the whole project was tailored for Jennifer. David would do anything for her. This was the lady for whom the most powerful mogul in filmdom was willing to throw away his kingdom. Trilby had hypnotized Svengali. David Selznick was blinded by love. There was another Jennifer he saw—and it wasn't the one sitting next to us in the garden.

I woke from my reverie. The enormity of the offer had hit me with no mean force. Here I was, midtwenties, being presented on a platter with the main characters in two of America's best contemporary novels! I was among the anointed—my future guaranteed—fame a certainty. But Langham had already promised me Hamlet for the next season and the formidable Tyrone Guthrie, who had crossed over to my side of the fence, likewise—Aguecheek in *Twelfth Night*. I was torn. How could I throw aside my chance, boring young fart that I was, of improving my craft in the best schooling there is—playing the great characters around whom playwrights of the past had built their tallest tragedies and highest comedies?

The afternoon sun was disappearing behind the trees and the car had arrived to take the famous pair back to the airport. I muttered weakly something about my duty to continue my stage career. As they were climbing into the car, David threw over his shoulder, "Well, we'll do *Romeo and Juliet* first then, you and Jennifer. We'll do eight weeks on the coast. I'll get Paul Scofield to play Mercutio. You can keep your hand in any time you want—before we do *Tender*. Think about it!" And showering me with compliments that would have turned anyone's head, and certainly turned mine, they were whisked away, leaving me dazed in the middle of my newly borrowed driveway. I had hired Finn Diehl, a local man whom everyone trusted as being the safest and most cautious driver in town. Finn told me later, "You know that Mr. Selznick, eh? He was so dern anxious fer to ketch his plane, eh? He kept shoutin' at me to git a move on, drive faster and he never stopped hittin' me over the head with his newspaper till we got there!"

I TELL YA, Emma, this was some dilemma! I wandered about for days, my heart in the classics, my head in Hollywood, not knowing where to turn. There was only one thing that was going to make me forget this mess—I had to get laid! Freud or Kraft-Ebbing could explain it away till kingdom come, but the truth was that every time I came up against an impossible situation—I had to get laid! I spent the night with a local girl I'd met at a bar. I'd never seen her before in my life but she was warm, understanding, loads of fun and by God was she good at it! What was it with this small town anyway? It had lousy food, and it rolled in the carpets annoyingly early, but surely there must have been a school for lovers somewhere nearby, for this young lady had graduated Magnus Come Loudee!

It was just what the doctor ordered. I woke up alone the next morning and had just started to roll out of bed when I keeled over onto the floor. The pain was all around my groin and lower abdomen—sharp and jabbing. It made me instantly nauseous. There was no way I could get up. I managed to knock the phone onto the carpet and breathlessly called the taxi service to take me to the hospital. They came right away, carried me into the cab, propped me up on the backseat, where I immediately doubled up and fell on the floor into my own puke. *That* made them put their foot on the gas and as they tore through the peaceful town I started to whimper like a whipped dog. "So this is what syphilis is like?" I thought. "I suppose I deserve it, but Christ, how the hell was I to know?" Obviously I had syphilis on the brain because *Henry V* in the fifteenth century had contracted the dreaded disease and had passed it on, considerate fellow that he was, to Katherine, Princess of France, and it ultimately killed her. This, then, was Katherine's revenge. It had taken her five centuries but she'd finally done it!

They carried me into the hospital, still raving, where a man in a white smock shot me full of morphine. I zonked out and woke up much later to find someone standing at the foot of my hospital bed busily shaving away my pubic hairs. It was a male orderly. Well, I'm not certain—male is perhaps not too accurate a term. It seemed to be wearing a red wig slightly askew, was chubby, with fat little hands, had albinolike skin covered in freckles and was very, very nervous. Every time it shook, its hands slipped, taking another jab out of me with its razor. I looked down. I was bleeding away happily in several areas.

Also the orderly never stopped talking—it simply wouldn't shut up. "Lithen, I wouldn't wanna be thtuck with what *you've* got! You've gone and got yourthelf an iddy-biddy nathty kidney thtone up there. I bet I know whooth not gonna by playin' Henry The Fiff tonight? Yeth thir! You're gonna thtay thtuck in your bed and retht and firtht thing t'morrow you're goin' to be thtrapped thtraight onto the operating table where they'll thtick a long thin peeth of wire up yer lil Henry the Fiff. Oh yeth—*that'll* get rid of the lil thun of a bitch, you'll thee!"

I was at the miserable creep's mercy and it was enjoying every minute. The job accomplished, the creep finally minced out, leaving

William Shatner, my rebellious understudy

behind a trail of cheap, heady perfume that lingered in the room long after with a suffocating stench. I glanced down at my war wounds. My God! I didn't know guys also had a mound of Venus! I felt thoroughly emasculated and it began to sink in that I was really going to miss tonight's performance and that William Shatner, my understudy, would have to go on. The thought of Shatner or anyone replacing me in that part instantly brought back my pain. I screamed for a nurse who jabbed me with more morphine. The shots must have found their mark for they discovered me just in time as I was about to exit the hospital's front door. "Where do you think you're going, dear?" said Edith Cavell. "I've gotta p'foramze," I slurred as she dragged me back to my room where I, at last, passed out.

My periwigged orderly friend had been right. The next morning they strapped me to the table with great leather thongs which pinioned my arms and legs in a vice. They then began rubbing some sinister ointment on and around my genitals, which was laughingly supposed to ease any pain. Then, to my horror, I saw the High Priest insert a long, thin bit of barbed wire with a hook on the end slowly up my poor, unsuspecting Henry Fiff. Jesus! It didn't stop; it continued on and on, farther and farther up as far as my heart I was certain, as I lay there paralyzed.

When it could go no farther, the Marquis de Sade left the room instructing his vultures to keep me in that position, absolutely still, till he returned. The vultures folded their wings and surreptitiously stole away, leaving me alone on that hard, cold slab—my only companion a young student nurse who had been ordered to hold on to my dick for dear life. She was obviously terrified, poor thing, for each time the nerves in her fingers twitched, I would cry out as the jagged wire sent a fresh spasm of pain straight through me. I slowly moved my head to one side to catch a glimpse of her. Behind her mask she looked really delectable—Oh God! Chris! Don't even think it! If you get excited now, you fool, you'll pass out for good.

After what seemed an hour, the Marquis returned and very slowly withdrew the long instrument of torture from its bruised and tender scabbard. O rapturous day! Niagara poured out of me. The never-ending stream didn't cease. Respighi's Fountains of Rome flooded my brain and borne away on the gushing spray of Old Faithful even the weariest offending stone within me was hurled somewhere safe to sea.

Later, over coffee in the canteen, someone told me that Bill Shatner had scored full marks as Henry. Ignoring all my moves, he had made sure he did everything I didn't do—stood up where I had sat down, lay down where I had stood up. He refused to copy—he was original to the last. I knew then that the SOB was going to be a "star."

A FEW DAYS LATER, I married Tammy Grimes. There seemed to be a matter of some small urgency. I learned this from her mother, Wool-lie, who had telephoned me and tactfully suggested in clear, nautical terms that it might be appropriate if we tied the knot. She's probably right, I thought, for having children out of wedlock was still fairly frowned upon in those days. Now Tammy and I were quite dotty about each other; after all, we'd lived in and out of each another's pockets for some time—she made me laugh a lot and I think once or twice I even managed to squeeze a couple of giggles out of her. "Ah well," I thought, rather ungracefully, "marriage will be a new experience—why not? I'm game!"

Tammy happened to be in Denver, Colorado, playing Anne de Poitiers in *The Lark,* which was touring the country with Julie H. She had called me to tell me that because she was so large with child her breasts, which had swollen to more than generous proportions, kept frequently popping out of her low-cut bodice in full view of the paying public, thereby authentically duplicating de Poitier's famous portrait from *Très Riches Heures.* Wow! We'd better get a move on, I thought. I had only two days off from *Henry,* so I took advantage and flew to Denver.

Tammy, with her usual sangfroid, had conned Tweet Kimball Ruddock (a wealthy acquaintance of a friend) to lend us her castle for the wedding. Cherokee Castle had been built entirely of Colorado stone. It stood five thousand to seven thousand feet above sea level on ten thousand acres of rolling mountainous country. Tweet had bought herds of Santa Gertrudis bulls from the King Ranch in Texas to see if they could survive a colder climate at such high altitude. She grazed them there on her land and the experiment proved such a success it was not possible to judge who became the more famous—Tweet or her bulls! Now exaggeration was quite common with our Tam, so I took all this with a grain of cattle salt—until I was driving up a long steep road in the foothills outside Denver. In the distance on top of a small peak—sure enough—stood a gorgeous and imposing heap, crenallations and turrets pointing to the sky, straight out of some faery tale! The rays of the sunset which bathed the mountain in a luscious warm light washed its walls with a staggering pink. It took my breath away. Good ol' Tam, she'd done me proud!

As I recall, it was a tiny, private ceremony, only five of us present. Tweet and two of the Ruddock family had remained behind: one, to give the bride away, and the other to take charge of the food and booze. What turned out to be a Ruddock relation of sorts offered to marry us. He was the local honorary sheriff and as such had the authority to act as justice of the peace. He reeled off the service by heart, but it was not one I was familiar with. I could understand very little of it and was wondering to what denomination the justice belonged when I noticed the scriptures he was holding were upside down. The man was clearly pickled. Tammy and I froze. Our eyes met—signalling an unspoken vow to give each other a cue when we thought it was the moment to respond. There was but one thing on our minds. Was this a ghastly omen? We didn't dare look at each other for fear we might burst out laughing. Luckily the bizarre Brueghel-like ceremony was soon over, and we were alone in our turret chamber—a ravishing circular tower room with a spectacular view of Pikes Peak.

Sipping champagne before a roaring fire in the beauty of that room we said little, lost in the awesome realization that our Gordian knot was firmly tied and that Team Plummer was officially on the score-

A rising star and my first wife to boot

board. The deep stillness of the mountain night took pity on us and a shyness that was both awkward and tender overcame us in a way we had not known before.

IN ACT 2, SCENE 3 of Henry V, the Hostess at the Boar's Head Inn says of the dead Falstaff:

> *Nay, sure he's not in Hell; he's in Arthur's bosom,*
> *If ever man went to Arthur's bosom.*

Come season's end our gallant company had crossed the pond and relinquished Arthur's bosom for Arthur's Seat. There could not be a more conspicuous spot for Arthur to show his seat. Permanently exposed, prominent by day, floodlit by night, it sits atop the famous cliff by the castle overlooking the lovely old town of Edinburgh for all its good burghers to gaze upon. Homage is paid at the famous festival's conclusion with a spectacular and moving ceremony complete with son et lumière and bagpipes called a tattoo. I often wonder who it was that knew Arthur had a tattoo on his bum.

While the rest of the troupe were searching for digs, Uncle Exeter and I decided to damn the expense and rustle up a suite for ourselves at that quaint old railway hotel, the Caledonian. The living room and bedroom were high-ceilinged and vastly spacious and we concluded at once that as a beachhead for after-hours entertainment, it was right on the money. The Scottish lass that curtsied us in informed us politely and shyly that she would get us anything we set our hearts on.

"We'd love some scotch for starters."

"Certainly, sairs, wut kaind o' wesky?"

"Oh, a couple of bottles of Glenlivet and some glasses."

"Cairtinly sairs." (She stood there, stoic, immobile.)

"Could you get it for us now please? We're parched."

"Ah noo sairs a kin nai du that forr ye masell."

"Why not?"

"You'll huff t' tailaphun doon stairs."

"Right," we said, picking up the telephone.

"Ah noo sairs, y' kinna tailaphun doon yet sairs, y'll haff t'wait."

"Why, for God's sake?"

"Cuz a haff t'go doonstairs t'ansair the tailaphun."

We knew then we were in store for a lot of charm but a lot of trouble.

Everything was swiftly taking shape—the two Jeans and their henchmen had located one or two acceptable French restaurants in town. We were busy getting used to our new stage, the old Assembly Hall which Tanya Moiseiwitsch had transformed into a most impressive playing area; everything was a-bustle with activity. The festival's manager was a tall, pompous young reed called Ponsonby. Academically snobbish, he had the patronizing manner of a petty civil servant. He probably had every good reason but he took an instant dislike to me. Ponsonby's first name, believe it or not, was Harry and I couldn't wait for the dress rehearsal at which he was present to let it rip:

> *The game's afoot:*
> *Follow your spirit and upon this charge*
> *Cry "God for Harry Ponsonby and St. George!"*

Our company's other offering was Tyrone Guthrie's amazing production of *Oedipus* (surely one of this century's most original) with Douglas Campbell, William Hutt and Douglas Rain giving particularly shining performances. Together, *Henry* and *Oedipus* were just one more testament to Tanya's genius as a designer—her extraordinary uses of fabric, her courageous blending of colours, her insistence on creating clothes, not costumes. As always, she offered a brilliant study in contrasts from the intensely human look of the homespun English and the over-popinjayed elegance of the French in *Henry* to the tall, stark figures in *Oedipus* mounted on stilts beneath their gowns, the masks of birds and animals concealing their faces, making of the tragedy a pagan ritual of solemn barbaric grandeur.

It is not surprising that Tanya has taught and influenced some of today's top designers both in theatre and film, who gave anything then to work as her assistants. She had made me a special Order of the Garter for *Henry* to wear on his tights, just below the knee. I could never, for the life of me, remember which was the right side up—until one night the Princess Royal, aging Princess Mary, came backstage all alone except for two of her detectives. She was most complimentary but explained she really had come back because she wished to show me how I should wear my garter. I was still in costume and she asked me to put my foot on a chair so she could reach my knee. The old lady then removed her gloves and began working away at the offending garter, twisting and turning it until she was quite satisfied she had made the correct adjustment. I bowed my eternal gratitude and she left with the sweetest smile, quite content that royal protocol had been maintained.

Edinburgh, even at festival time, closed pretty early so relaxing or partying after a performance was not made easy. The only place where drinks and food flowed with any regularity was the Press Club. But what to do after it shut down? Uncle Exeter and I soon found that our good ol' Caledonian Hotel had the answer. They held to a strangely archaic rule which forbade you to drink in your rooms after midnight but allowed you to imbibe all through the night in the hotel lobby and as long as you were a guest you could invite any number of derelicts you wished—comme c'etait bizarre! Robert and I began to ask the odd friend back, but pretty soon actors from every visiting company in town had caught on, and there was a fresh free-for-all each night as the numbers increased. Unfortunately, as Uncle Exeter and I were the only residents, a great majority of the bar bills landed on our tab. It took months afterward to sort the whole thing out but Robert and I were for the most part forced to split the expense. Why we never hit skid row, I cannot fathom.

One morning around ten (with only a couple of hours' sleep under my belt), the telephone rang. I woke in a haze, reached out and knocked it onto the floor. "Yes?" I barked angrily, leaning over and shouting down into the receiver.

Bob Goodier — the great Satisfier

"This is the Countess of Harrington speaking. I've just had a delightful letter from your aunt who told me you're here. Can you come up and spend next weekend with us in the country?"

"Oh, fuck off, Bob," I said. "I'm trying to get some goddamn sleep!" Robert was always playing tricks like that, calling from outside pretending to be someone grand—his idea of a joke. I was groping around to find the cradle so I could hang up when I saw him. There he was, dead to the world, fast asleep and snoring in the next bed. It was too late for redress. That was just one more stately home I wouldn't be visiting!

Apart from these wasteful nights and days with a little Shakespeare thrown in for good measure, I was not unmindful of my surroundings: the somewhat sad stone beauty of Edinburgh—its graceful grey streets, its wondrous castle, the mystery of Holyroodhouse—but there was little time to venture beyond its gates. I reconciled myself that I would have to wait for some future opportunity to be hypnotized by the mists and rugged beauty of the Scottish countryside from whence my forebears had come.

Now that we'd been given a few days off, Robert, Jean, a brace of females and I all made an immediate beeline for Londontown and a

busman's holiday. It was a rich, full few days. The whole face of the theatre was changing, as was London and the country. It was a must, therefore, to see John Osborne's *Look Back in Anger,* one of the leaders of the
new trend, with Mary Ure, Kenneth Haigh and a young Alan Bates in
the cast. Other waspish trendsetters were Angus Wilson's *The Mulberry
Bush* about prewar progressives losing touch with reality and Joan Littlewood's wonderful production of Brendan Behan's *The Quare Fellow,* a
remarkable play by a remarkable new playwright. Geraldine Page
weaved her particular magic in *The Rainmaker,* and I was able to renew
my acquaintance with that talented and zany lady.

But what made the London trip so memorable, that obliterated
everything in sight and would live in my memory for the rest of my life
was the Berliner Ensemble in three of their great Brechtian productions
Mutter Courage, The Caucasian Chalk Circle and *Trumpets and Drums.*
Never before or since have I witnessed such perfection in ensemble
playing—every player a star actor in his own right. Brecht had just
died that very summer, and his widow, Helene Weigel, had taken up
the reins. Weigel, a tiny woman with the bone structure of Martha Graham, was a force of nature and a great actress in the bargain. Seared into
my mind forever is the unforgettable moment in *Mutter Courage* when
her son is executed. She suddenly opened her mouth to its fullest, held
it open for some seconds, but made absolutely no sound at all. The
effect was devastating, for it was as if all the blood had left her and her
face had become a mask. It was a numb, completely mechanical reaction, yet *we* the audience screamed for her nonetheless—*we* supplied the
missing sound within.

"Skepticism moves mountains" was Brecht's dictum and Epic Theatre was his platform. His theatrical technique as a writer-director was
to pick a quarrel with the spectator—to incite argument, even alien-
ation; he detested reverence from the public, and little attempt was
made at realistic illusion. He wanted to remind you that no matter how
moved you could become, you were still sitting in a theatre and it was
all effect. Watching Ernst Busch, the chef in *Mutter Courage,* peeling
potatoes with the speed of light as he tried to tell a sad story, or Eck-
hardt Schall, that fabulous young German actor, do his violent sword
dance as cleanly as any samurai warrior, were enriching, breathtaking
experiences. In *Caucasian Chalk Circle,* the ensemble baffled and dazzled
one even further by illustrating they could perform in two contrasting
styles at the same time, the realistic German School and the high pan-
tomime style of the Peking Opera.

Just as critics Clement Scott and Bernard Shaw had anticipated the new wave of Ibsen at the turn of the century, so Eric Bentley in America and Kenneth Tynan in Britain heralded the importance of Brecht's impact upon the Western world. Writing of *Mutter Courage,* for instance, Tynan states:

> . . . the production achieved a new kind of theatrical beauty—and the broad canvas and the eagle's eye view of humanity were restored to European drama after too long an absence.

At any rate, I had found a new force in the theatre to worship, and with the clanging of Asiatic bells and horns, the splashes of vivid color on vast, bleak canvases and the image of that brave gnomelike creature dragging her little cart across the battleground forever branded in my memory, I went back to Scotland and the last few performances of *Henry*—a chastened, humbled servant who now felt very small indeed.

Confidence gradually returned when, swept along on the glorious tide of Shakespeare's verse, I began to enjoy myself once again. But it was all too brief, for now the hour had come to put Henry Plantagenet in mothballs for the time being. It was not good-bye, for at various intervals throughout my life the old warhorse was to cross my path and invite me to take up arms once again. Pistol said it all for me:

> *The king's a bawcock, and a heart of gold,*
> *A lad of life, an imp of fame;*
> *Of parents good, of fist most valiant:*
> *I kiss his dirty shoe, and from heartstring*
> *I love the lovely bully.*

Looking back to those days in the midfifties and their all-too-vivid growing pains, I am nothing but eternally grateful to Harry and his followers: "The poor condemned English" lads that made up such a happy band of brothers—"the confident and over-lusty French" whose joie de vivre I was fortunate to share, and the brilliant Scotsman, Michael Langham, who had made it all possible to begin with and who never once wavered in his trust; for they all gave me a fighting spirit I'd never known before and helped bring down the curtain on my youth.

CHAPTER FIFTEEN

SETTLE DOWN? NOT BLOODY LIKELY!

Tammy lost no time. She had found and furnished a home for us both when I returned from the land of the kilt. It was a charming house on Bank Street in Greenwich Village just a couple of doors away from ye olde Waverly Inn. We had the top two and a half floors, our own entrance and use of the garden. Her wily charms had managed to persuade the owners from whom we rented (a remarkably docile pair) to retire to the basement apartment where they burrowed molelike, only occasionally surfacing for air. Diagonally opposite was a convenient garage several stories high (corner of Greenwich and Bank) with private self-operating elevator, where I could park my sparkling new convertible MG—Tammy had not yet acquired the objects of her taste (gull-wing Mercedes and Ferrari). The garage was used by a variety of citizenry and several members of our profession, including my friend with the Gilbert and Sullivan monocle, Martyn Greene.

In the wee hours one morning after some late partying, Mr. Greene drove his car into the elevator in order to park it on an upper floor. As the elevator ascended, slower than any tortoise, Martyn decided to get out, monocle and all, and look under the chassis for a suspected fuel leak. Stretched out on all fours, his legs dangling over the elevator's edge, he suddenly heard a crunching sound and a searing pain shot through him. One of his legs had got caught between the wall of the building and the lift and the crunch was the elevator jolting to a dead stop. There was no one about in the entire building or in the area, for that matter—it was so late. For hours, Martyn must have been calling for help, lying as he was, pinioned, unable to free his leg.

An eternity had passed before a man drove in, found the elevator stuck on the fourth story, left his car and walked up to see what the trouble was. Looking down from above, he saw the awful predicament

Martyn was in and managed to climb down onto the elevator itself. By ringing the down button, he released Martyn's leg and pulled him to safety. Martyn was now delirious, could hardly speak, and the man, who luckily turned out to be a doctor, set about to examine the mangled leg. To his horror he saw at once that gangrene had set in and was spreading fast. There was no time, no choice—it had to be done—he must remove the leg now, right here in the elevator, or it would be too late. He quietly informed Martyn of this, apologized, said he had very little equipment with him, only a knife and no anesthetic except for a full bottle of brandy in the car. Would Martyn be very brave and give him permission? It was life or death! Martyn agreed.

The very nickel of a modern Major General

Several weeks later, I saw Martyn at Sardi's bar, chipper as ever with his sawed-off leg, his crutches and monocle, looking for all the world as much the "Ruler of the Queen's Navee" he always was. The medical authorities had barred the doctor from his profession, claiming he should never have performed such a delicate operation under such reckless and barbaric circumstances. The fact that he had saved a man's life didn't enter into it. For the next several years, Martyn fought to repair that doctor's reputation and did not flinch till he had done so.

Not every happening on Bank Street was as sensational but it was a fairly accident-prone area nonetheless. Soon after the Greene incident, I carelessly put my arm through a glass door, blood spurting out as if I'd opened a hydrant, and if St. Vincent's Hospital had not been just around the corner, I could have quite easily bled to death. George C. Scott turned up at our doorstep one morning at 4:30 a.m. looking most sinister and as usual dripping blood from head to toe. "I want a shower," he rasped in typical George C. fashion. Tam, whom he'd known at college, hid under the bedclothes while I showed him the bathroom, and after the last of the blood had washed down the shower hole à la *Psycho,* and he'd rested a little, I drove him to his television rehearsal.

Nothing much else would have made local headlines, apart from a few knockdown humdinger fights between Tam and me, except that our Trinidad maid, Dessa, who quite obviously was obsessed with voodoo and would, during thunderstorms or at any given hour depending on certain vibrations, insist on lying supine on the floor in a state of transcendent karma. One day I came down the stairs to find several rather elderly relatives of Tammy's from Boston sitting in the living room staring down at the hapless form of Dessa lying across the rug in front of them, moaning like a sick cow. "The weather must be changing" was my lame explanation.

Tammy's talents did not necessarily embrace the kitchen. I had once taken her to Henri Soule's superb Le Pavillon, where she ordered bacon and eggs. She could, however, if roused, rustle up a mean Sole Amandine or Véronique, but that was it! That was her limit. For a brief spell, she took domestic delight in cooking for her "man" at home, so we alternated these two culinary delicacies with such furious regularity that I began having recurring nightmares of being chased by oversized soles hurling giant almonds and grapes at me till I screamed for mercy. Soon Tammy became bored and there were no more home-cooked meals—the nightmares ceased, and we took to eating out. We had already begun to drift apart—we were seldom alone—but I thoroughly enjoyed being with Tammy when we could be together. She was one funny lady, a madcap, her eccentricities were delightfully catching, and she was, after all, carrying our child.

There was a Baldwin grand in the living room upon which I could pound to my heart's content on those lonely nights while "she" was busy doing her act at the Plaza or The Blue Angel. Her career as a cabaret-chanteuse-comedienne was rapidly zooming and already she was earning considerably more than I, so a kind of competitive game began to be semiconsciously played between us. Her cracked voice and farcical timing made her unique along the nightclub circuit and the little, quirky ski-jump nose gave her a kind of childlike pathos that, for a while, put her in a class by herself. We were two fans observing and admiring each other at forty paces—hardly the stuff to secure a union; we were having too much fun enjoying our separate ascendancies— much too immature to take on the twin responsibilities of marriage and raising a child. We were also far too young.

> There was movement at the station, for the word had passed around
> That the colt from old Regret had got away,
> And had joined the wild bush horses — he was worth a thousand pound,
> So all the cracks had gathered to the fray.

I NEVER HEAR those words of "Banjo" Paterson's but tears are in my eyes, for they put me in mind of a fella who was forever declaiming them as the two of us lurched from one Gotham bar to another all through the long, warm Babylonian nights. It was not always just us twain, for this descendant of the Pied Piper coted many a rat old and new along the way. I met him for the first time that very winter. We were both in a live television broadcast (most undistinguished)— I played an elegant jewel thief; he was my disreputable but willing tool. The liaison we formed was wonderfully disastrous. The only thing that mattered, of course, was that we became friends for life!

Jason Robards, Jr., was an angular young man, slightly stooped, who loped rather than walked, was quick and deft in movement like an athlete and possessed even in his young years one of the great craggy faces of memory. Huge, hurt eyes gave him his vulnerability and his popularity. Every woman within wooing distance wanted to coddle him, convert him (from what they knew not) or, at the very least, spare his life, even if it wasn't in any particular danger. Of course, when he gathered all these qualities together and put them on the stage, the effect was irresistible.

At the end of the Second World War, Jason had come out of the navy not knowing where to turn. Some good Samaritan informed him the American Theatre Wing in New York was offering a special deal for returning servicemen—a year of free tuition in the arts. Jason jumped at the chance and enrolled. He chose singing. History proves he did *not* become the world's leading countertenor nor a major authority on lieder. Instead, he became, thankfully for us, an actor. At the time of our meeting, he had just made a phenomenal success of Hickey in *The Iceman Cometh* at Circle in the Square in one of the most dynamic and shattering performances I have ever seen. His explosive combustion of pain and laughter hit me with such force as I sat glued to my seat, I utterly forgot I was in a theatre and could do nothing but helplessly succumb to his desperate outpourings as if they were mine alone. With this moving creation, he had seriously revived the real spirit of O'Neill and would become in our time that author's most famous and definitive interpreter. I am certain that had O'Neill lived to see Jason perform, he would have cast aside his customary melancholia and leapt for joy.

Robards, in my thinking, belonged to a generation of American actors long gone. They were part of a Golden Age of theatre in this country, around the turn of the century or even much before. Had he been alive then, he would have felt much at home with either of the Booth brothers, the Davenports, Joseph Jefferson, Edwin Forrest, the

Me, Julie, and Jason

senior Tyrone Power or any of the Barrymores. He would also have given them a hell of a run for their money. Though he played realistically, he was always larger than life and completely instinctive. He gave naturalism a classic proportion. Already back then, he knew, perhaps too well, the hidden soul within him and could release his demons and pixies at will, they were all so perilously close to the surface. Advantage was often taken of Jason's innocence, openness and deep generosity: he wore his heart upon his sleeve for daws to peck at.

The Palace Bar and Grill on West Forty-seventh Street was a favourite hangout of ours; I don't remember it ever closing. It was a narrow room with a long, unpolished, peeling mahogany bar which ran the entire length of it. When empty, it was seedy and depressing as hell—when full, it was the richest, warmest room in town. It resounded nightly in jubilant celebration and its regulars were characters that could have dripped off the pen of William Saroyan. Donald Voorhees, Gene Kelly, Adlai Stevenson, Bernie Hart, Ben Gazzara, Maureen Stapleton and dear Stritch often dropped in and paid their respects. Gene Kelly had affectionately remembered it since his early Broadway dancing years. The rest of the mob that frequented it were actors and journalists and a quaint assortment of ancient fugitives from the Lambs' Club. Whatever desperate secrets had brought them together, they were neither resigned nor morose. They were determined at all costs never to go gentle into that good night.

Sol, the bartender, owl-like, soft-spoken, with a sympathetic ear, was master of ceremonies—the attending High Priest poised to give us final absolution. No matter how big the congregation, it seemed that everyone was biding his time, waiting for Jason to appear before the evening could be called complete. Through the heavy smoke and deafening din, he would make his entrance shouting an old Russ Columbo favourite, "Just friends, lovers no more." Without warning, it was a habit of Jason's to burst out in a sudden flood of verse from the works of Patterson, Service, Drummond and other such semiclassicists. At the drop of a drink, he might let fly all forty verses of "Eskimo Nell." He also possessed a charming whiskey baritone, and later in the early morning hours, when the room had subsided to a mellow calm, accompanying himself on the guitar, he would softly chant in torpid nostalgia, "Summers in Bordeaux, rowing the bateau, where the willow hung, just a dream ago, when the world was young," over and over, bridge and all, to some private and misbegotten moon.

"IF ANY OF YOU BUMS wants a line change, I'm charging eight-fifty a word." Up spake Arch Oboler, writer, from the rear of the stalls.

Yes, I was back on "the Street"—once more under the caring banner of Kermit Bloomgarden; and yes, this time my name was above the title and, would you believe it, in lights as well. I circled the block till I wore out the pavement staring up at the marquee to make sure my eyes did not deceive me. They didn't. Jane Broder had once again fought valiantly—bless her. I was not alone up there, mind; my two partners (not to be sneezed at) were Claude Rains, the old master himself, and that character from Hollywood with the offbeat charm and whimsical light touch—Wendell Corey. The two remaining cast members were, in their own right, just as impressive—Dick York (later famous in *Bewitched*) and Martin Brooks. Our ill-fated company of five was stage-managed, mothered and coddled by Elaine Carrington's no longer wayward son, Robert; and the director, once the boy Jesus in Max Reinhardt's production of *The Miracle* who, still very much in character, continued to suffer all us little children to come unto him, was Sidney Lumet. The play was *Night of the Auk*.

Perhaps the most accurate assessment of the work and the tidiest

Claude Rains and me in The Night of the Auk,
directed by Sidney Lumet

summation of the audience's general perplexity came in the form of an opening-night telegram sent to me by the actor Jack Warden. How he got it through the mail service, I'll never know, for it simply read, "What the fuck's an Auk?!"

The play's action concerned a rocketship returning to planet Earth after man's first landing on the moon. On the journey back, the crew learns that atomic war has broken out on Earth and that their ship is almost certainly doomed. Prophesying an atomic age that could leave man as extinct as the auk, Mr. Oboler couched his potentially interesting idea in sententious blank verse that gave the colour purple a deeper, more pungent tone than usual and offered, as one critic opined, "ten frills for every frisson."

Yet there was a pioneering spirit about it, a sense of being in front of its time. It anticipated Bradbury, Roddenberry and a goodly number of sci-fi chefs that would soon monopolize the market. If only Arch had not persisted in impressing all and sundry with his pretentiously elaborate and subhuman English! Kermit made many a constructive suggestion to remedy that, but Oboler would only turn a deaf ear. Claude Rains, who had the longest speeches, went about his masterly business as usual, never complaining and managed to make it all sound like Milton or Wordsworth, but Wendell and I had the much more difficult task of trying to make our stilted brief exchanges sound contemporary and natural. While attempting at rehearsal to underplay a scene particularly overloaded with rodomontade, Oboler would interrupt us and yell out, "That's about as exciting as watching Jeff Chandler and Sonny Tufts." Theatre protocol generally frowns on playwrights who voice their opinions loudly during a rehearsal—after all, that is a function of the director. So to cover the embarrassing silence caused by the clumsy gaffe, Wendell and I shook hands and introduced ourselves: "Hi, Jeff"—"Nice workin' with you, Sonny." The author was not amused.

Arch Oboler was a squat, gnomelike figure who wore expensive leather Windbreakers and narrow-brimmed porkpie hats. He continuously wisecracked in rather coarse one-liner quips which gave the impression he was auditioning for the Catskill circuit. He had been one of radio's most prolific writers and among the first to make a feature film in 3-D, the film process introduced into cinemas for which you were forced to put on goggles of dark glass in order to view the images on the screen. Looking like an early motorist, you would watch the action in laser-sharp relief leap out at you in aggressive three-dimensional proximity. That was all very fine, but upon removing the offending spectacles you became strangely disoriented, a trifle dizzy and, in some cases, engulfed in nausea. After my first 3-D encounter (*Bwana Devil*), there was no other. I had, in fact, been quite seasick. I told this to Wendell who, every time an altercation arose with the stubborn little author, would whisper violently in my ear, "Go on! Quick! Tell him you puked at his film! Tell 'im now!"

Of course, Arch had become quite wealthy in the process so he went out and bought himself a small mountain he could call his own—somewhere in Nevada, Colorado or Montana (I'm not sure which)—probably one of the Tetons. Each day, he became more and more obsessed with atomic war and convinced that at any second the world was about to end, he had his mountain excavated in order to create what was possibly the first private bomb shelter in the United States.

One day, his little boy was playing dangerously near the mouth of this man-made crater, when he slipped and fell to his death. Instead of taking at least some of the blame for this awful tragedy, Arch went about righteously exclaiming to the world in general that his child had been the first victim of the Atomic Age on home ground. Bloomgarden, by now fed up to the teeth with Arch and anything to do with him, could be heard muttering under his breath, "The wrong Oboler went down the hole."

There was nothing to be done. No miracle could save us now. Not even the boy Jesus could raise this dialogue from the page—it was deader than any sea scroll; so the whole debacle came to a merciful end after a week's run at the Playhouse in spite of a sensitive and beautifully spoken performance by Mr. Rains. No one was sorry—not even Kermit, who had taken such pains to raise the money. Arch Oboler didn't even bother to hang around long enough to say good-bye. The only element of the play that survived the closing and enjoyed a little "hit" run of its own was Howard Bay's remarkable set; for the rocket ship's interior, complete with Perspex floors, on different levels lit from beneath, multiple control panels, blinking lights—everything representing the highest of high tech—seemed the only live creation on the planet. Young Bob Carrington bought the whole caboodle, shipped it out to his mum's estate on Long Island, charged admission and probably made more money than anyone remotely connected with the play.

THE BOY JESUS, in all his bountiful mercy, took pity on me and as a consolation prize hired me for his next film, already in production, the remake of *Stage Struck*. It was my Big Screen debut and I played a very young writer in love with the female star—eighteen-year-old Susan Strasberg. The boy Jesus had recently stumbled onto his eleventh commandment—obeying it most successfully, "Thou shalt become a director of film and thou shalt not suffer anyone to covet thy editing room." With fiery determination, he immersed himself in everyone's problems—the little Messiah seemed to be everywhere at once—in fact, this year was turning out to be very much a boy Jesus year.

Sidney "Keep 'em in the East" Lumet or "Bubuleh" as he was affectionately known to most of us, was a stockily built little firecracker who tirelessly worried over his brood, rabble-rousing us like some possessed cheerleader. A street-smart young filmmaker with a mission, who loved New York, he *was* every kid on the block and stubbornly refused to film anywhere else. He felt it his duty to keep Manhattan the moviemaking town it had always been, particularly as Hollywood was stealing everything away from it, including his other toy, television. And the powers that be let him! For young Sidney was just about the hottest director around—his *12 Angry Men* had already made history on its own. He was especially good at gathering together great casts—most of the top tough-guy actors in town had worked for him but with *Stage Struck,* a romantic comedy, he was on slightly foreign ground. So to give it the proper patina, he hired Herbert Marshall, that distinguished British arbiter of gentlemanly elegance and the veddy Bwitish and veddy eccentric comedienne Joan Greenwood (*Kind Hearts and Coronets, The Importance of Being Earnest*). The required American star name that rounded out the dramatis personae was graceful Henry Fonda.

Susan Strasberg had just scored a New York success by creating the role of Anne Frank. I got an instant crush. Though we giggled a lot together, she scarcely noticed, being too busy basking in adulation or taking notes from her ever-present mother and coach—Paula. Paula was a nice lady, warm, intelligent and was probably one hell of a good coach, but she drove Sidney crazy because she made Susan listen only to her. One morning, tearing his hair out of its roots, Bubuleh whispered (he never screamed), "She's keeping all of us waiting! Everyone—crew, actors, producers—while she and that mother of hers are locked in the bathroom giving each other acting lessons!" Paula was unintentionally naughty that way—she never ceased to indulge her already overly indulged daughter, carrying the Method and its message to unprofessional extremes. She would say to Susan, "Stay in your room and don't come out till you feel you're really ready—they can wait." She gave the same sort of advice to Marilyn Monroe whom she coached in *The Prince and the Showgirl,* which similarly drove Laurence Olivier (its director and costar) around the bend.

Memories of the year of boy Jesus come in quick flashes—Sidney's vast collection of hats and caps from which he chose a different one for each hour; I can see so clearly that wonderful handpicked crew of technicians who did all the top films from New York (I was to work with them a lot). I'm positive they themselves had invented the motto "Keep 'em in the East." They had a mock disdain for the West Coast that was hilarious and not without reason, for Hollywood during that period was for the most part grinding out cutesy Doris Day movies, while they were making *On the Waterfront, Panic in the Streets, A Streetcar Named Desire*—works of some stature and substance. They had been very much

Elia Kazan's boys, had taken turns with George Roy Hill, Franklin Schaffner and of course, Sidney.

A tight-knit family, professional, quick, efficient, they still found time to horse around which kept morale high on those cold, windy Gotham nights. I remember them all with affectionate glee—"Salty" the prop man who was always complaining he had nothing on his truck and at the very last tense moment would produce miracles out of a hat. Bill Garity, Charlie Maguire (ADs) always laughing, always long-suffering, always enthusiastic. Robert Jiras (B.J. for short), makeup man extraordinaire, and my good friend, was cursed with the severest case of self-deprecating humour I've ever come across. I suppose it was his Hungarian blood that inspired such madness. Apart from being tops in his field, he was exceedingly bright, an erstwhile producer and writer.

He had already written a script, his *Place in the Sun* as he called it, which was titled *The River*. Shrouded in mystery, it was so special, so different, the plot so delicate, the subject matter so sensitive, that I don't think anyone had dared read it nor was allowed to. It was always just about to be "picked up," but not yet produced. The whole thing became a running gag—the entire crew were in on it—and all B.J. had to say was, "I've got this script called *The River*," and everyone, including B.J., would fall on the floor. The remainder of the crew were the Flaherty brothers, chief grip Jack and his fast-talking comedian brother Ed, the "intellectual" grip who amusingly defended all the world's losers. Both spoke a separate and most original jargon which kept us permanently convulsed. Boris Kaufman, the brilliant but aging cameraman, fell off his perch one day with a heart scare. As he lay there heaving and pale, Jack (head grip) shouted to Salty, "Brandy on the double." When it arrived, Jack took it, downed it in one gulp and quipped, "Now get one for Boris!"

I remember how impressed I was with Herbert "Bart" Marshall's smoothness as an actor, his effortless technique (a later Gerald du Maurier) and his very great personal charm. He was famous for his limp, the result of a botched amputation by German doctors when he was held prisoner in the Great War. They had severed his leg in the wrong place, stitching the nerves together. What courage he exhibited, never letting us be aware for an instant that he was suffering permanent pain.

I recall with amusement and gratitude my friendship with tiny Joan Greenwood, whose low, deep voice resembled the cooing of doves. She always came into a room sideways in a kind of shuffle-off-to-Buffalo

Herbert Marshall — the epitome of civility and polish

move. She was so eccentric one thought at first it was all put on—but indeed not! I'm convinced that she'd emerged from the womb side-saddle. That great lady and actress, Cathleen Nesbitt, had loaned Joan her apartment while she was away and the two of us used to end up there occasionally after work.

Miss Nesbitt, as everyone knew, had, as a young girl, been the lover and mistress of the poet Rupert Brooke. He had written most of his famous love poems for her—it was she who had inspired them. "Listen, dahling," burbled Joan one evening, "I know exactly where Cathleen hides all her love letters from Brooke—I've found the keys. Let's get ourselves nicely tiddly and burrow our way through them, shall we?" Mischievous Miss Greenwood, batting her eyelids with schoolgirl innocence, proceeded to rifle Cathleen's dresser drawers, spread the yellowing letters on the floor and together like two ravenous Peeping Toms, we devoured their romantic contents. They were absolutely extraordinary in their beauty, so intimate, so very private. And as we made love on the floor among them, I felt we had stolen into some forbidden garden and had come upon the secret of passion itself.

IF THE REAL JESUS had ever married, it might conceivably have been to Gloria Vanderbilt. After all, very few needed to receive as much tenderness and mercy all the days of their lives as did Gloria, whose past had been so plagued with pain and public scrutiny. Sidney seemed to care for her as gently as if she were a precious gem. Gloria, who was going through her "thespian" period, must have been both grateful and content that in the arts they shared so much in common. Gloria was beautiful, vulnerable and intensely shy. Yet in spite of this shyness she was certainly one of the most dynamic of hostesses. She packed her parties with everyone that mattered in the theatre, ballet and music worlds and her exquisite apartment on Gracie Square literally jumped the whole season long. It seemed there was a party every week and she and Sidney sweetly saw to it that I was always included.

You would find Marilyn Monroe sitting at the feet of Isak Dinesen, Oona O'Neill and Sydney Chaplin in conversation with Harold Arlen and George Balanchine. There, in a corner, would be Truman Capote mesmerizing a little adoring group with his high nasal twang and at the piano, Leonard Bernstein, once again getting laughs with his "Piano Concerto for the Left Foot." Adolph Green and Betty Comden spoofing their own song "It's the fuckiest fuck of the year" from *Bells Are Ringing* while its star, Judy Holliday, collapsed laughing on a nearby ottoman. Fritz Loewe and Alan Jay Lerner watching Sammy Davis and Miss Monroe, she looking more edible than ever, singing duets accompanied by Jule Styne. There was almost more entertainment going on between those walls than in the Big Apple itself.

Carol Grace Marcus, twice married to William Saroyan (soon to marry Walter Matthau), was one of Gloria's best friends. Pert and attractive, she had shocking red hair and ivory-white skin, which she daily powdered clown white in the thirties style of Lady Diana Manners. Her transparent looks and breathless twitter made an outrageously amusing contrast to her conversation, which was generously peppered with four-letter words. Carol told me when she first made Gloria's acquaintance they were attending acting class together and that one day Gloria asked Carol to pick her up at her apartment but when Carol arrived, Gloria had already left. A creature with long, floating white hair wearing a floor-length bathrobe came out onto the balcony and relayed Gloria's apologies. When the two girls later got together in class, Carol told Gloria that a most dignified older lady ("your grandmother or aunt, perhaps?") had spoken to her to which Gloria replied, "That wasn't my grandmother or my aunt. That was my husband—Leopold Stokowski."

Sidney, who gave me my first movie role

At one particular soiree at the Lumets', I was at the piano accompanying Jack Warden, who was doing some very amusing patter. My weather eye kept wandering toward Syd Chaplin, who was ignoring us completely. He was lounging on a sofa too busy insulting a couple of gorgeous dames (who were, of course, loving it) to take notice. Warden and I were eighteen sheets to the wind (everyone was that night—there were strange vibes in the air) when I suddenly got it into my head that Mr. Chaplin was deliberately sabotaging our "brilliant" double act. I stopped playing, rose, staggered over to him and requested that he step outside. As "outside" meant stepping into a very small elevator, it was a tad ridiculous. Besides, I was so far gone, all Syd had to do was touch me and I would have hit the deck. However, I had thrown down the gauntlet and there might have been a confrontation of sorts had not someone stepped between us and led me away, where I burst into angry sobs of frustration, muttering through my drunken tears, "That-ne'er do-well-dilettante-nothing-son-of-a-*great man*!"

The next day I delivered a bottle of champagne with my apologies to Syd in his dressing room after the *Bells Are Ringing* matinée and I soon came to learn that the shoe was indeed on the other foot—that Charles Chaplin had treated Sydney abominably, shamefully inhibiting him at every opportunity—that the "great man" in his case only existed on the silver screen. Real life had painted quite another picture.

Later in the sixties when I was living in Europe, I got to know Sydney considerably better. He was running a restaurant in Paris called Moustache and a gambling establishment on Curzon Street in London called the Pair of Shoes. As a chum he was staunch, loyal, extremely sensitive and one of the funniest human beings I have ever met—a drawing-room comic con cojones!

GLORIA VANDERBILT'S talents were not just restricted to writing some enchanting poetry; she had an eye for detail and decoration that was exceptional. Her tastes were liberated, her imagination boundless. Not because she was bored but because invention never let her be, would she change the apartment for each season—yet another colour scheme, yet another theme, and at Christmas it all fairly burst with a dazzling richness and warmth. I also remember the great Georgian-silver wine coolers and her exquisite collection of Louis Quatorze seashell chairs.

Then, though I'm certain she never noticed, I would find myself staring shamelessly at Gloria's beauty in repose, touched by that haunted, lost look of hers—the look of a startled fawn. It was hard to believe in the midst of all that surrounding gaiety that her life would again be scarred with more tragedy to come. Yet here was a born victim with an invisible, built-in toughness and bravery that has, over the ravages of time, managed so splendidly and gracefully to see her through.

NOW IT WAS TIME to postpone the good life, go back to television and what is laughingly called a living. The first assignment was a crisp little comedy which I shared with a very pretty Sally Ann Howes. It was a trifling romp mostly made memorable by the presence of Buster Keaton in a small role. The great silent-film comic was in his sixties, absolutely delightful, never said hello or good morning, but instead would launch into a stream of anecdotes which he occasionally punctuated by executing perfect somersaults from a standing position.

The second gig that winter was perhaps more my line of country—Mark Twain's *The Prince and the Pauper* for the DuPont Show of the Month. My first DuPont appearance had been in support of José Ferrer. This time I was the star. My lady partner was that exquisite jewel from Britain, Rosemary Harris, and between us, we had the supporting cast of our dreams: mad marvellous John Carradine, Victor Jory, Sir Cedric

Hardwicke, young Rex Thomson and a little scene-stealer who could have been anywhere between the ages of eight and twelve named Patty Duke. Our producer, David Susskind, welcomed us by making the most sanctimonious and pompous speech, saying how privileged we should all feel to be part of a great classic and that he hoped we would rise to the occasion and do it justice. This in front of all these distinguished professionals. The speech was greeted with stony silence broken only by Sir Cedric whose noble organlike voice rang out loud and clear, "I've closed in better shit than this!" It was, however, just as Susskind had ordered—a resounding success.

Robert Saudek, a gentle academic who ran the prestigious Omnibus programme that employed crusty Alistair Cooke as its commentator-host, invited me to play Oedipus Rex, Sophocles's young king, who, in a moment of inexcusable carelessness, had murdered his father and married his mother. Talented Alan Schneider (later killed by a car when crossing a London street looking the wrong way) presided over the production and good ol' Bob Goodier and Donald Davis were sent down from Canada to give the support some strength and stature. During the "dress," not content with plucking out my eyes in the last act, I twisted my cartilage as well, wrenching my knee out of its socket, sending it all the way round to the back of my leg. We were to air the show the following day! In a panic, they carried me on a stretcher into a van which trundled me through the streets to an address on the East Side. On the way, to distract myself from the pain, I busily pulled out the latex prosthetics from my eyes till they resembled long stringy bits of cheddar.

Dr. Max Jacobson, or "Miracle Max" as he was more commonly known, was a cross between Conrad Veidt and Martin Borman. His reputation for getting people who were near death's door back on their feet in a matter of seconds was the talk of the town. This had earned him his nickname. Opera stars who had lost their voices, politicians who had lost their nerve, dancers, actors, athletes, all plaintively knocked on his door begging for the "cure." He was also society's darling—they called him "Dr. Feelgood." Later President Kennedy would make him part of the White House inner circle as his private saviour, summoning him for treatment whenever or wherever he felt pain or flagging energy.

"Vell? Vat happent to you?" this darkly sinister man shouted at me. I felt I was in the cabinet of Dr. Caligari.

"I put my knee out, Doctor."

"I know vat you dit. I asked you vat happent?!"

My second Oedipus, *CBS Omnibus*

I told him the whole grisly story, adding that I had to perform the next day. He didn't even wait for me to finish. He was out of the room in a flash. I could hear him bellowing at some frantic oversized diva, whom I had recognized as I was being carried in. He reappeared a moment later mumbling to his nurse, "Zere iss notting wrong mit dat stoopit bitch—tell her to go away!" He was brandishing two long, thin sticks with cotton wool wrapped at the tip, one which was soaked in some liquid substance, the other covered with white powder. With no explanation, he stuck them both so far up my nose I heard it crack.

"But Doctor Jacobson," I stammered, "it's my knee, not my nose!"

"Shaddup undt mindt your own business," he retorted as he shot me at least six times around the knee area with several ominous hypodermics.

"Now stand up! On your feet! Undt get outta here!"

I didn't walk. I strode—I ran—I leapt. I was Superman!

True to his name, Miracle Max had done me proud.

We were to learn later he would come under investigation by federal authorities for suspected misuse of amphetamines and that his license to practice medicine was revoked by the New York State Board of Regents in the midseventies. How shortened our lives might have become under his care, one will never know; but whatever joy juice Dr. Feelgood Caligari had pumped into me that day, I could have played Oedipus at Colonus, Oedipus at the Olympics, at least ten more "Eeda-pussies" all at once and still have enough energy left to seek out my old troubadour friend Jason and celebrate with a vengeance, gouged eyes and all, my new bionic state.

THE POLICEMAN ASSIGNED to the West Forty-seventh theatre district was a particularly agreeable fellow and, luckily for us, an avid fan of showbiz! On horseback, he regularly patrolled the street at night, checking out the Lyceum, the Ethel Barrymore, the Cort, etc. After "curtain up" like clockwork he dismounted outside our beloved Palace Bar and Grill, tethered his horse and wandered in for his usual libation. All of us this particular evening were well on our way so the rousing greeting we gave him was several decibels louder and more boisterous than normal. One could hear Jason's powerful voice topping the rest of us as he instructed dear ol' Sol not to serve the cop unless he brought his horse in with him, insisting that the long-suffering beast deserved a drink just as much if not more so than his master. The cop obliged. There we were, all of us, standing at the bar—horse included! Jason bought the first of many rounds—triple Jack Daniel's for both cop and horse. We tenderly held the glass to the horse's lips as he gratefully joined in. He seemed to be hooked and clearly wanted more, as the evening became more obstreperous with much singing and shouting of old shanties. Suddenly the cop realized the shows were over and he was embarrassingly late getting back to his beat—but there was a prob-lem! How to get the horse out of the bar, up the stairs and into the street! The room was so narrow—it couldn't possibly turn around. After much grave and slurred discussion, we decided to take the beast out through the back alley where the rubbish was kept, turn him around there and then walk him out the front door. This took an eter-nity but finally success was achieved as we toasted the departing pair, horse and cop, returning to their duty, both totally bombed out of their skulls.

Later that year the cop, we were happy to learn, was promoted to captain, but I don't think it was for anything that occurred on that dubious and extremely shaky eve. His partner, I should imagine, is by now safely confined to a home for alcoholic nags.

SOMEWHERE IN A HOSPITAL on the other side of town, poor Tam was going through the tortures of the damned. She never did have a very high threshold for pain and her labour spasms were becoming increasingly unbearable. They had filled her with drugs which made her hallucinate badly and her screams were heartrending. There was little I could do—she didn't even know who I was, so, coward that I am, I'm afraid I couldn't take any more and left. A sympathetic nurse assured me it would be all right to come back in a little while.

The nearest, most soothing room I knew of was the lounge at Regent House on Sixty-fifth and Park. I made a beeline for it, ordered a stiff drink and set about tranquilizing my jangling nerves. Two gentlemen at the next table invited me to join them—one turned out to be Budd Schulberg, author of *On the Waterfront, What Makes Sammy Run* and *The Disenchanted,* and the other, his partner and friend, a comforting whiskey-voiced Teddy Bear of a man by name of Harvey Breit. In fact, they both rather resembled Teddy Bears and when I told them what the Plummer ménage was going through, they made all the appropriate Teddy Bear noises and ordered champagne.

After the first toast, Budd told me that Harvey (a well-known journalist and Bear of Very Big Brain) was adapting Budd's book *The Disenchanted* for the Broadway stage and that I, though a little young, would be very right to play the leading protagonist—Manley Halliday. That made me feel considerably better. So we toasted that idea, and Budd, with that soft-spoken charm of his and delightful stutter, which he has spent his life timing to perfection, suggested I also play the lead in his next film about illegal egret hunting in the Florida Everglades. That talented maverick of movies, that rebel with or without a cause, Nicholas Ray, was to direct. Several toasts went by and the afternoon rolled on in much mellower fashion as both Bears continued to recount wonderfully tall tales of the newspaper world, the fight game and, of course, Old Hollywood.

Budd's father had been head of Paramount Pictures in the twenties and early thirties and one of the West Coast's most powerful figures. Every year, according to Budd, the Schulbergs would embark on a long European excursion—a most orderly ritual—everything meticulously managed. They would leave LA by train to New York—then New

York to England or France via ocean liner. Two Rolls-Royces would pull up at LA station, one carrying Mr. and Mrs. and offspring, the other containing spanking new luggage filled with every conceivable object they were convinced was suitable for each country and climate. "P-p-poor f-father," Budd stammered, "he had no knowledge whatever of European c-c-customs." One year, limousine number two fairly burst at the seams with innumerable cases of liquor. "What you got in all them cases, Mr. Schulberg?" asked the conductor as they were loading the train. "Scotch," said the mogul. "Gosh! You must be goin' a long way, sir. Where is it this time?" "Scotland!" was the brusque reply.

Now it was Harvey's turn. He was just about to launch into some yarn when I jumped out of my chair. My God—I'd forgot! Tammy must have given birth by now. I waved good-bye to my two Teddy Bears and didn't stop running till I reached New York Hospital. But I was too late—my cursed bad timing again. I had missed the moment. I wasn't able to visit Tam—she was sleeping the whole thing off, but there, behind glass, was the tiniest, smallest-boned creature I'd ever seen. Automatically I glanced at my watch. It read the twenty-third of March, 1957. I just stood there in a haze—the room spinning around me. Did someone speak? I wasn't sure. It must have been the nurse. I couldn't quite hear what she was saying if indeed it was the nurse at all, but a voice that came from very far away was trying to tell me I was now the proud sire of a wee elf in search of a name.

AS IF THAT WASN'T exciting enough, David Selznick had just flown in from his chalet in Switzerland and had taken over most of the top floor of the St. Regis Hotel—Jennifer and he in one suite, the children and nanny in another and the remaining rooms were reserved for secretaries and staff. They had barely unpacked before the receptions began. David was almost as brilliant a host as he was a producer and had a passion for collecting people—new faces—new talent. It gave him the greatest of pleasure as he lavished his attentions on them. The latest of his "finds" this particular year were a young, fresh-faced, boyishly sexy Jane Fonda and me. Jane, who unquestionably had a direct line to fame and like a feline leopard could change her spots to suit the latest cause, would rise like a phoenix to the top of the class with a will that exceeded Eva Perón's; as opposed to my subplot of a career born of self-inflicted doubts, and strange loyalties, which up to now could be simply described as an "Enigma Variation."

While I ogled Jane in the distance, David pounced on me and propelled me around the room. Some people I already knew, but not John Huston, with whom I was now shaking hands, nor Irene Selznick (David's ex and daughter of Louis B. Mayer), nor Jock Whitney, who had backed *Gone With the Wind.* I renewed my acquaintance with Hank Fonda and we sashayed over to a large group who stood hypnotized, listening to Truman Capote. Truman was recounting how he once watched a chain gang in the South working on the tracks, each man's leg bound to the other, on a stiflingly hot summer's day in, let's say, Hades, Mississippi. All of a sudden a great number of cranes flew overhead, their graceful flight a thing of beauty to behold. All the men stopped work, dropped their picks on the ground, stood absolutely still and watched those cranes till the last one had disappeared over the horizon. The look of longing and of envy that filled their eyes told its own story and Truman would never forget it. I suppose the anecdote was made all the more riveting because Truman's supreme gifts as a raconteur were enhanced by his high-pitched tones, which resembled the wailings of a theremin.

As the thought of that ever-looming seven-year contract with David again crossed my mind, I too identified strongly with those poor convicts and I swore to myself that the next day I would tell David—No. On the morrow I found him wandering back and forth from one suite of rooms to another in an elegantly cut grey flannel suit sporting a cane and wearing no shoes. He was wildly dictating some of his now famous "memos" to a slew of overworked sleepwalking stenographers. As I sauntered in, he smiled that beaming smile of his that made the whole world look rich and successful. "Let's go across the street and grab some lunch." The waiters at the Côte Basque bowed low and swept us to our table. They even bowed to me, obviously convinced that anyone with David could be nothing short of a tycoon.

At lunch, David became the Three Tempters under one skin. As he made my future sound more and more lush, I bided my time. I thought of what Jane Broder had told me after she had called an old colleague of hers in LA—that David O. was now a dollar-a-year-man as far as the government was concerned, so that his huge expenses could be resolved, and that he had sold most of his interests—Selznick Studios among them—and that he no longer owned the world rights to *Tender Is the Night.* I knew too that the days of long-binding contracts were to be a thing of the past and that the old studio system would soon give way to the "Independents." So bracing myself, I thanked Mr. Selznick from the bottom of my heart, said I was sorry but I was off to play the

Great Dane himself for at least twenty-five cents a week plus a maximum guarantee of obscurity. We sat in silence.

It's a rare thing in life to meet someone who really believes in you. Here was a man with a huge heart—a hero of mine, the man most likely to film my dreams, whose style, taste and judgment had been nigh impossible to match in the movie industry, and he'd gone to battle for me—he had genuinely believed in me and I'd cast him aside. Was I insane? David thought I was and told me so—not just that day at lunch but years after in his biography—and the look of disappointment on his face when I told him made me want to crawl under every table in the Côte Basque. Yet at the same time I knew he understood. For behind all the mogul-mania, David's real wealth and power was his artistry. He was a consummate artist, a master craftsman—intensely dedicated and intensely human. Yes, he understood all right.

So with a final salute to one of the last great romantics, ruler of a vanished cinematic epoch I would have been much more comfortable in, I cut my chains, gathered up my tiny offspring, waved good-bye to my fellow convicts and joined the wild cranes as we flew to our northern outpost, a summer of poetry and a newfound freedom which, ironically, I had never really lost.

CHAPTER SIXTEEN

"KRÖNBERG-ON-AVON"

Stratford's tent had been struck forever and with it a wonderful sense of living dangerously. Now, everything would be "safe"— perhaps too safe. At last we could boast a roof over our heads; in fact, we were permanent; the only "established, permanent crap game" of its kind on the continent. Our cocoon was sealed. Except for the few free spirits who knew they must one day cut the old umbilical—the future seemed assured.

To celebrate the new structure there was a series of gala functions and two strenuous opening performances of *Hamlet* and *Twelfth Night*. The affirmation of several seasons of glorious work came on the second night with Tyrone Guthrie's magical production of the latter when an international audience, as one body, gave the new enterprise a jubilant welcome. Our revels had by no means ended. Most of the company went way over the top—the festivities continuing far into the next morning—not just on the banks of, but deep in, the Avon River itself; drunken heads bobbing up every so often to shout triumphant obscenities at the indifferent sky.

It had completely slipped our minds of course that the dear, inconsiderate management had scheduled a matinée of *Hamlet* that same day at 2:00 p.m.! Puce with rage, we dragged ourselves from the murky shallows, bedraggled swamp creatures, sodden with lake water and booze, and dutifully reported to the theatre, where we began pouring ourselves into our gear. My old friend, that bruiser of an Aussie Max Helpmann (who played the Ghost), had actually never left his spanking new dressing room—in fact he'd been quietly celebrating there for days. Max was the swarthy brother of the famous ballet star Robert Helpmann. While Robert spent the war years grand jeté–ing his way to fame on at least four continents clad in a variety of toe shoes, Captain Max amused himself during battle breaks in the Pacific campaign by driving motorcycles off the decks of aircraft carriers into the sea far below. A daredevil, cursed with shyness, you couldn't find more of a man's man if you tried. A veteran in the theatre of war and a warring veteran in the theatre, he was a seasoned expert at burning candles at both ends. At this moment, true to form, having downed his last drink, he was just packing up to go home and pass out when we arrived to break the sad news. "Turn around, Max, you're going the wrong way."

Poor Max, in this rigid state, struggled manfully into his heavy fiberglass armour and ghastly green makeup and glided rather unsteadily onto the stage—"my father's spirit doomed for a certain term to walk the earth." "Hearsed in death," he looked like we all felt. I could have sworn I heard Hamlet, perhaps it was me, shriek, "Go on, I'll follow thee" as I crawled after him up the steep staircase. We were on our precipitous way to the little balcony on high where we were to play the famous scene between Hamlet père et fils. The balcony had no railings, and there was barely enough space for two—certainly no room for a waiter with a tray of much-needed Fernet-Brancas. A tiny spot lit both of us—the only light source, everything else in stygian gloom, including the audience. Below us, nothing but a gaping hole—not even a trace of the stairs we had just mounted. From the way Max was

Max Helpmann — a woefully hungover Ghost

swaying up there, the lines he was spouting—"List, list, o list"—took on a fresh and special significance.

"Brief let me be—" insists the shade and proceeds to unfold one of the longest and most tortured tales in theatrical literature. I know one is not supposed to touch a ghost onstage or off, but as "Dad" rambled on I had no choice but to grab hold of his legs to keep us both from hurtling to certain death. Rivulets of escaping booze poured down his face melting his deathly green makeup until he resembled the decomposing Mister Valdamar, but he managed to get to the end of his lengthy message quite superbly and without a hitch! "The glowworm shows the matin to be near" was his cue to take leave of the platform and glide gracefully and soundlessly down into the enveloping darkness. Max gingerly began his backward descent into the black. Oy! Could he have used a glowworm! With his first "Adieu" he made the top landing but there was a tremendous thud as he collided headlong into a pillar—the balcony shook. I was certain I would never set eyes on my friend again. I could hear him swearing all too audibly as he feverishly groped his way about. My poor old specter was irretrievably lost. I prayed his undercarriage would lower and he could land safely.

Finally he decided to give up being a silent ghost altogether and began to stomp angrily down the rest of the staircase in his clanking boots of mail. This phantom was taking forever to disappear and advertising every step of the way. To cover its uncertain journey it kept repeating "Adieu" and "Remember me" many more times than the Bard had intended. At long last I heard him reach the apron of the stage. All he had to do now was to tiptoe unseen down the ramp and be done. I steeled myself for my soliloquy, which would follow ("O, all you Host of Heaven . . ."). The earth gaped, the Hosts of Heaven were poised, all Hell was standing by waiting to be coupled. I was just opening my mouth to let fly Hamlet's exclamation of release when with a prolonged clatter much like the sound of garbage cans colliding in a tin laundry chute—my father's spirit catapulted and ricocheted down the ramp and disappeared far below into the cellarage. There was a long, deathly silence. Then a pitiful little voice from somewhere in the subterranean bowels called out one last "Remember me!"

Remember thee? How could I fucking forget?!!!

AH, MES AMIS, 'twas by no means the finale of that wacky afternoon! For a while at least, things began to resume their normal expectancy and settle down. Hangovers were being sweated out one by one and, for a spell, most of the large ensemble managed to get back on track. Then a sudden sea change occurred, for the general pace now took on a most alarming speed. Clearly there was but one thought on everyone's mind: to get shot of the damn thing as quickly as possible. It was a race to the finish. To a man, each actor seemed determined to get the hell off before the next guy. This new, unexpected attack gave the performance a certain urgency and passion not experienced before.

It is now the graveyard scene. Hamlet leaps into the grave gathering the dead Ophelia in his arms:

> *Forty thousand brothers*
> *Could not, with all their quantity of love,*
> *Make up my sum.*

Our grave was an open trapdoor in the center of the stage. At the scene's conclusion, I would climb out of the trap and slam it shut, on the lines:

> *Let Hercules himself do what he may,*
> *The cat will mew, and dog will have his day.*

It was necessary to close the trap in order that the remainder of the play could be performed on the full stage. That day I was not the only one to leap into the grave. A young and overzealous French Canadian lad (un véritable étudiant du drame) who played one of the monks, had, in his religious fervor, leaned too far forward, lost his balance and dove in with me. This would have been perfectly okay had he climbed out when I did. But, not wishing to distract, humiliated beyond repair and out of a certain deference to the leading player, me, the damn fool remained down there out of sight. No urgent eye signals from me could persuade him otherwise. I had no choice but to slam the trap on them both! There was a low rumble of stifled amusement from the audience and for the rest of the afternoon the only thing they could think of was "What the hell was a young monk going to do for the rest of his days shut up in a grave with the dead daughter of Polonius?" The answer was all too obvious—necrophilia!

The afternoon limped on, teetering as always on the edge of disaster. Was this the Hamlet I had grown to imagine would perhaps, in the annals of theatre, be a tiny milestone? Was not New York opening its widespread arms? After all, there had been rumors on the street that I might be the awaited Prince—the Dane of the moment. Managers, producers, promoters were on red alert for the signal that would be their assurance of a Broadway production. One of them, Roger L. Stevens, had arrived the night before for the opening of *Twelfth Night* and would stay over to view *Hamlet* this very matinée. Roger had always shown great kindness to me over the years since he coproduced Miss Cornell's *Dark Is Light Enough* and the Paris *Medea* of Judith Anderson. We had been drawn closer together because of my long-standing friendship with his partner and pal Robert "Ratty" White-head. Yes, if anyone was to produce my Hamlet, he would be the one!

Roger was a laid-back, speechlessly shy American businessman who became very rapidly one of the most significant theatrical patrons in the United States, and principal advisor on the arts to several presidents (Democrat and Republican), starting with his old friend John F. Kennedy. He also founded the Kennedy Center in Washington, D.C., and was a prime mover in real estate both in Washington and New York City. In his long and distinguished career, it could be said of Roger that he never rose—he was always up there! He was on so many boards it was sometimes difficult for him to remember of which ones he was chairman! In fact, he had already earned the somewhat endearing reputation for being irritatingly vague and absentminded.

Once, so the story goes, he was forced to entertain some high-powered, out-of-town executives who insisted they be taken to El

Morocco, the then-exclusive New York nitery. Now, conservative Roger, who had at one time owned the Empire State Building and several other such landmarks, never went to nightclubs—indeed he hardly ever went out at all. He certainly had never been inside El Morocco. When supper was over, he called for the bill so he could sign it. The management was sorry, but they didn't know him and would he please pay cash or cheque. Too shy to tell them who he was and make a scene, he admitted he had no cash or cheques with him. The out-of-towners he had entertained so lavishly had had such a great time ogling all the glamorous ladies they fought like terriers over the bill, insisting they take *him*. Roger was mortified. The next day when arranging with his secretary to reimburse them by mail, he told her of his predicament with El Morocco's manager. The secretary, dumbfounded, could only say, "But why didn't you tell him, Mr. Stevens?"

"Tell him what?"

"That you own that building."

That was Roger. So it didn't come as too much of a surprise when I learned what had happened. Fighting as hard as I could through last night's vapors to give him the best Hamlet I knew how, I might as well have been baying at the moon. Our man wasn't there! He'd forgotten to come. In fact he hadn't even been to bed! The previous night's celebrations had got to him as well and he was still partying away over at Siobhan McKenna's house. The captivating Irish actress and nighthawk who played a wonderfully lyrical Viola in *Twelfth Night* had the day off and was taking full advantage of it! And Roger was smitten! Here was his new star! Good-bye *Hamlet*! So long, Broadway! While I was vainly acting my heart out, the absentee entrepreneur and his newly discovered Colleen at midafternoon were shouting Irish ditties at each other in raucous disharmony, which the loudest cannon in the Elsinore artillery could not have silenced!

TYRONE GUTHRIE must have still harboured suspicions about me, for early on in the *Twelfth Night* rehearsals, he couldn't resist the odd dig or two. He had damn good reason to put me in my place for, playing the plum parts that season, I had become very much a Cock-o'-the-Walk. One morning I arrived embarrassingly late—at least an hour! I had totally forgot that my Aguecheek scenes were to start the day. When I entered the rehearsal room the entire company was sitting around in silence and there was a table set up on the empty stage with coffee, toast and eggs. "We thought you might like some breakfast," said the Good Doctor, seething with sarcasm and he made me sit down, utterly mortified, and told me they would not proceed until I'd finished every mouthful. I choked down my coffee and toast as everyone just sat and watched.

The day Siobhan McKenna arrived for her first rehearsal as Viola was especially tense. A star from Ireland who had made considerable waves in Dublin and London's West End, she would quite naturally expect to be rather envied and resented by a resident company which had not yet been introduced. Not knowing the town at all and with no one to guide her, she had every reason to be late and late she was. Dr. Guthrie, to my great surprise and horror, berated her most severely in front of everyone. "But Doctor Guthrie," she stammered defensively in that beautiful Irish lilt of hers. "Discussion over! Waste of time! Press on!" snapped the great man. None of us could believe this treatment of a visiting celebrity, so at the first break we rallied around her in support and gave her the warmest welcome we knew how. She was so overcome, she burst into tears. As I passed Dr. Guthrie, who was seated apart watching the whole scene with owl-like satisfaction, he gave me an evil wink and out of the corner of his mouth said, "That's got 'em on her side. They'll do anything for her now!"

Tony Guthrie, as a director, was an audience of a thousand people. He had a special genius for getting the very best from his actors— goading them on to be more inventive than they ever dreamed possible. Dougie Campbell (Sir Toby), Bruno Gerussi (Feste) and I were trying outrageously over-the-top bits of business one night at rehearsal. The Good Doctor finally yelled at us from the back of the stalls, "Much too much! Very bad taste! Keep it all in!"

Sir Andrew at one point during the carousel scenes with Sir Toby Belch and the Fool says wistfully out of the blue, "I was adored— once!" Tony, in a matter-of-fact manner, said simply, "After the word 'once,' why don't you fall down the trap and don't come back up for at least a minute?" That piece of business became my whole characterization in one stunt and never failed to capsize the audience. I confess I also used Tony's voice for Aguecheek, which he pretended not to notice.

In spite of such tomfoolery, Tony never once neglected the depth of his characters, poignantly bringing out the sadness and loneliness of the comics; sharply accenting the bitterness of the Fool and the cruelty with which he treated Malvolio in prison. All the silly stuff about mistaken identity near the play's end he made us take at a tremendous

*My Aguecheek, with Douglas Campbell's Sir
Toby and Siobhan McKenna's Viola*

clip—drilling us till we dropped—bringing the audience to its feet;
and in the autumnal scene at the very end, the Fool's song ("The rain it
raineth every day") became an unusually hard and cynical lament, so
painful and sad that autumn had quite suddenly turned to winter.

IT WAS ABOUT A FORTNIGHT into the run, when making my
entrance as Aguecheek, capering down the aisle convinced I was the
funniest thing since Grock, that I accidentally turned my ankle on a
step and hurtled forward onto the stage flat on my face. I had unintentionally brought down the house sooner than expected but my foot was
quite seriously broken. After what could be accurately described as a
staggering performance, I sought out the brilliant Tanya Moiseiwitsch,
who straightaway ordered her minions in the costume department to
construct a fiberglass cast so decorated to look like part of each costume
and carefully weighted to take pressure off the foot. Good old Tanya—
ahead of her time as always.

The next day was yet another *Hamlet* matinée and my understudy
would, of course, have to take over one Dane while the other Dane
retired whimpering to his truckle bed. My understudy was William

William Hutt as a most original Eskimo Lear

Hutt who already was busily occupied in giving a rich and witty characterization of Polonius, avoiding, with his inherent good taste, any hint of the accustomed buffoonery indulged by lesser players. Now, even as far back as 1957 Bill Hutt was immensely experienced and would go on to become probably Canada's all-time most versatile classical actor. He was equally adept at low, high or medium comedy, tragical comical, comical pastoral, tragical-comical-historical-pastoral. He was also good fun to be with, had a wicked sense of humour and an explosive laugh that could trigger any electric appliance for miles around—you name it. However, genial though he was most of the time, he could upon occasion become extremely pompous and rather grand. "Grand as in Grand Rapids," one wag put it.

The matinée in progress, I restlessly tossed and turned in my bed, scowling at my fiberglass cast, hoping against hope that I was not at that moment being outshone by Mr. Hutt. The matinée over, two of

IN SPITE OF MYSELF

my "spies" arrived at my bedside armed with their secret information. Both moles informed me that Bill had been absolutely wonderful all afternoon, cool as a cucumber, completely in control; that the audience had risen to the occasion and that even the production's playing time had been reduced considerably. I was just about to gnash all of my teeth at once and grind them to dust when the more sympathetic of the two moles assured me that towards the play's end Bill's nerves had, for a second, got the better of him and he had made one glaring, monstrous gaffe. Hamlet grabs the poisoned cup from the dying Queen and, as the text has it, rounds on the King:

> *Here, thou incestuous, murderous, damned Dane*
> *Drink off this potion . . . Follow my mother!*

It was only the *f* he had trouble with after all—it was hardly enough to mar his career—no real grounds for early retirement, but when the phrase escaped his lips, a flood of Freudian connotations of the most suggestive nature were at once let loose upon the poor, unsuspecting public. For Bill, cursed as he was with impeccable diction, could not conceal the enormity of his boo-boo:

> *Here, thou incestuous, murderous, damned Dane,*
> *Drink off this potion . . . Swallow my mother!*

Hideous jealous toad that I was, I lay back against the pillows, blowing kisses at my cast, my smug face wreathed in a smile of petty and repugnant victory!

I CAN'T REMEMBER whether it was Shlegel, Hegel or Bagel who said, "Hamlet is a tragedy of thought inspired by a continual meditation on the dark complexities of human destiny calculated to call forth the same meditation from the minds of the audience." It matters not, but it was damned good stuff anyway, even if it didn't offer much practical assistance. Then I rather took a fancy to that old poet laureate, John Masefield's view:

> Life who was so long baffled only hesitated . . . Revenge and
> chance together restore life to her course, by a destruction of
> the lives too beastly, and of the lives too hasty, and of the lives

too foolish, and of the life too wise to be all together on earth
at the same time.

Then there was my favourite of all humourists, Professor Stephen Leacock, who simply clarified the entire thing:

> "Hamlet" is not to be confused with "Omelette" which was
> written by Voltaire.

I suppose the real story is of a great and fearsome action imposed upon
a gentle, thinking soul who might indeed be perfectly fit to perform it
but whose wisdom renders him impotent. At any rate, no matter what
precept you follow, Hamlet remains a dilemma, a universally challenging dilemma. Most think of him as a sort of Everyman, that there is a
Hamlet within all of us. But all of him in all of us? Hardly. Very few of
us could ever be as cultivated, refined, noble or scholarly. Neither could
we be as polished or courtly, nor as remote from the world as he until
the world made itself known to him and kicked him in the chops. The
big obstacle the actor faces when he walks onto the stage as the Dane is
that the audience already has its own preconceived notion of what its
Hamlet should be. The time is very out of joint for any Hamlet who
falls into the trap of whining; it is extremely hard to avoid—Hamlet
on the surface seems to whine a lot:

> HAMLET: *Denmark's a prison.*
> ROSENCRANTZ: *Then is the world one.*
> HAMLET: *A goodly one; in which there are many confines,*
> *wards and dungeons, Denmark being one o' the worst.*

Of course, this is meant to be witty whining but it's whining, like it or
not. And then from the very start—concerning the world in general:

> HAMLET: *'Tis an unweeded garden*
> *That grows to seed. Things rank and gross in nature*
> *Possess it merely.*

Himmel! He kvetches a good deal! Shakespeare must have intended
these carpings to be sincere philosophizing sans malice, otherwise our
protagonist would garner nothing but irritation from the reader or
spectator. Hamlet, therefore, surely must view life with both an acade-

mic's insatiable curiosity and a student's innocent wonderment. Although abounding in sardonic humour, he should remain at all times above cynicism! There needs always be present a generosity of spirit. No matter how fond the world is of corrupting itself, Hamlet must always support it as a miraculous creation. Michael Langham had a wonderful suggestion that before each critical pronouncement, I should think the unspoken thought—"Isn't it extraordinary?"—then deliver the line so that even Hamlet's death phrase, "The rest is silence," becomes a scholar's very last revelation of discovery and wonder.

One thing is certain—you sure have to win 'em over when you first appear or you're dead! How on earth do you achieve that? It's a cinch! Break your foot—and—wear a cast! It worked! The second I limped on, by God, I had wrung their sympathy. They instantly pitied me. Even as the season went on and my foot was perfectly healed, I still insisted on wearing my cast! Oh, yes! I wasn't taking any chances. I was cruelly snapped back to reality, however, at summer's end by the school matinées! What a shock! Children of a certain age are, to put it mildly, merciless—the hideous fiends—and when there are a lot of them together, they instantly become a lynch mob. They certainly had no time for my indulgences, no room for pity in their hard little souls.

There are two facts children refuse to put up with in the theatre—love and death. They don't believe in them; they want no part of them. So, of course, there were just as many cat calls when I didn't kiss Ophelia as when I did. What's more, when the King, Queen and Laertes are all lying prostrate spread out across the stage, dead, can you imagine the merriment and joy with which this was greeted? And a few moments later when Hamlet says softly to his friend Horatio, "I am dead," the entire mob of hoodlums fell out of their seats hooting with laughter. But that's not the end of it—poor Hamlet doesn't give up! Once again he persists in informing those around him who are still standing that he is dead, and finally, just before he actually does leave this world, his last heaven-sent speech begins most unfortunately with the words, "O I die Horatio." Of course, by now audibility was no longer possible for a roar of thunderous proportions that could be heard in the next town exploded in the new auditorium, drowning all further dialogue. As far as we Danes were concerned the rest was indeed—silence.

It was one of the final run-throughs before the opening. I have always been paranoid (still am) of strangers wandering into rehearsals, asked or unasked. On this day I noticed a man sitting all alone about halfway up the aisle. I stopped after the first scene and asked Michael to come down to the stage. "Could you please ask that person to leave," I said rather

Frances Hyland's most exquisite Ophelia to my Hamlet

grandly; "his presence throws me. I find it impossible to concentrate."
"Why don't you come and meet him," suggested Michael gently. He
brought me over to a most imposing and distinguished-looking black
man of middle age. "May I introduce Duke Ellington," said Langham
politely with a triumphant gleam in his eye. My jaw dropped. "He is
composing a jazz scenario on Hamlet and is watching our rehearsals to
get some ideas." I couldn't believe it! I retired backwards down the
aisle, bowing and scraping as I went.

A year or so went by before Ellington's wondrous pastiche came out
on LPs. It was called *Madness in Great Ones* with Maynard Ferguson
playing the meanest, maddest trumpet in my memory and is dedicated
to our Stratford Festival and my Hamlet. What a piece! I treasure it to
this day.

LANGHAM'S PRODUCTION was romantically conceived, somewhat
static, but always highly intelligent and crystal clear. There were also

some fine performances in it but the one that was to attain true tragic heights was the Ophelia of Frances Hyland. I have never yet seen a finer rendering—it was a privilege to be on the same stage. As usual when witnessing something rare, the public was not quite sure how to react but they nevertheless went away—shocked and much disturbed. The press were more certain. Brooks Atkinson of *The New York Times,* drained of all superlatives, simply called her Ophelia the finest of the century. She seemed to have all the qualifications, the looks, the grace, the emotion and the range to cope with that subtle and tricky exercise. A rare piece of porcelain, infinitely breakable, I was afraid to hold her—she was so tender, so brittle, yet no one was fooled for a moment that within that frail little body beat a heart as big as an ocean.

Frannie also had a big voice for such a little throat with an enormous range at her command. It was at the conclusion of her agonizing outpouring for Hamlet, "O what a noble mind is here o'erthrown," that Frances chose to collapse. She spoke the passage exquisitely and most musically with not a vestige of self-concern. Upon reaching the line, "That unmatched form and feature of blown youth/Blasted with ecstasy," her voice moved into a disturbing upper register as if stifling a scream and on the last syllable of the word "ecstasy" it snapped, culminating in a long soaring glissando as though a bow had brushed across a broken string. I stood offstage each night, marvelling that only such a prodigious technique as hers could produce consistently the same extraordinary freshness.

Later in the play, there was an ecstasy in her madness that is quite unexpected—startling; in fact if anyone should have been "blasted with ecstasy" it was Frances. This Ophelia had long since left us revelling in her very own newly discovered world, happy beyond measure— such a giving little soul—and one can only surmise that she went to her watery death, not with the violence of some deranged harpy but with the same delicate precision with which she lived her short life, just one last duty she must perform. "Drowned," echoes the Queen much later, "drowned." And we were—in our own tears.

Some scientists, wacky or not, insist that without doubt, sound is preserved through the ages; that the air around us is filled with centuries of encapsulated voices; that one day we may be able to hear the Gettysburg Address, Oscar Wilde delivering his witty lectures, Napoleon rallying his troops or even the Sermon on the Mount (God, I hope it's not dull). Perhaps because I want all this to be true, I am inclined to believe in it. If we had performed *Hamlet* in the tent, I fantasize that the sounds we made (rude or otherwise) would have disappeared forever through the open flaps, but that in the new building with its solid four walls they too might very well have found a permanent home.

Sometimes when I visit Stratford I sit all alone in Tanya's beautiful empty theatre. I stare up at the dome and if I concentrate very hard I can almost hear the voices of my actor friends who have created such memorable moments there; and above them all, Frannie's voice—"like sweet bells jangled out of tune, and harsh" as it chases across the ceiling, trying to escape, but the building won't let it. Like some devoted guardian of precious memories it holds her in bondage for eternity, proud of its prisoner. If it has done nothing else, it has served its purpose.

CHAPTER SEVENTEEN

EVERGLADES AHEAD

The only snakes I know are on Madison Avenue." The man in charge of reptiles was expounding his intimate knowledge of their habits sexual or otherwise and lecturing us on the docility and sweet naturedness of the slithery creatures. It was a swelteringly hot day in a large dilapidated room at the famous old Rod and Gun Club which stands in the swamps of Florida's Everglades and we'd been firmly requested to listen to this fellow. He was in a shirt of indescribable filth open to the navel, had several days' growth of beard, smelled of something so disgustingly pungent it could only have been snake piss and was wearing, what he obviously considered the height of fashion, an enormous live boa constrictor wrapped several times around his neck.

We were all there to film Budd Schulberg's *Wind Across the Everglades*, which soon would be affectionately known among us as "Breaking Wind Across the Everglades." "We" were the cast and a motlier crew has never been assembled under one very badly leaking roof. These were

Budd, a loyal friend

the players: MacKinlay Kantor, the novelist; Tony Galento, the wrestler; Sammy Renick, the welterweight; Burl Ives, the folk singer; a Seminole Indian called Billy One-Arm; and Gypsy Rose Lee, the stripper. The only actual actors in the film were Peter Falk in a small role, Pat Henning, George Voskovec, Howard Smith and me.

Budd Schulberg, "O Jephtha, judge of Israel" had, in his mind, justly metered out his two sentences, one to me, the other to Jason Robards. Mine was the young Audubon official whose mission was to roust out egret hunters, the somewhat colourless leading juvenile of this fated film; Jason's was to play Manley Halliday in *The Disenchanted* later on Broadway, the assignment I had really coveted and would have much preferred. I believe Jason won a Tony for playing *my part*—blast his hide!

Attempting to keep us cool, the ancient ceiling fans creaked away, hopelessly inadequate, as the snake man droned on. He was telling us that as there were to be snakes in the film, we should come over to his shack any time we wished to familiarize ourselves with the little darlings, a huge variety of which he kept in his bathtub. His diatribe finally wound down with the assurance that snakes if you treat 'em right are the safest things around and that in all the twenty years he had enjoyed the privilege of working with them, not once had there been an altercation. Our confidence was hardly bolstered when he waved to us in a farewell salute and there was only one finger on his left hand.

Budd's story had painted a potentially atmospheric picture of one of America's last frontiers at the turn of the twentieth century and, photographically, it could have brought to the screen a kind of desolate beauty. But there were so many eccentrics involved, real and imagined, and the doomlike locale itself which made us feel we had gone there to drown in quicksand, infected everyone with such malaise that there was more drama offscreen than on.

One of the most affected by this spreading sickness was Nicholas Ray, the director, only he'd already had a head start. He had just arrived from the Libyan desert where he had shot a film with Richard Burton and while there had formed a none-too-savoury alliance with a young girl half Libyan, half French, who, if she didn't push dope, pushed just about everything else. She was certainly feeding Nick with something for to those on board who had known and respected this gifted man he most certainly was not himself. His eyes were always running, the pupils strangely dilated—he would stare vacantly into space. Half aware of this he began to wear a black patch over one eye so that he resembled that famed rebel director from the recent past André De Toth.

Nick and his girl were never apart. She stood close to him on the set, never took her eyes off him. One could sense there wasn't much tenderness there; they seemed shackled together in a love-hate bondage that could only end in despair. I began to liken their relationship to those famous lovers of literature who tragically end their days in the desert. If they too had wished for the same fate, they had come to the right place, for the Everglades offered a perfect alternative setting. The girl had a sexy, pouty look of discontent about her at all times—we at once nicknamed her "Manon."

Whenever actors were about to do an important take, Nick would put his arm around them and take them for a long walk. He called this ritual "agitating the essence." On these instances, he could be at his most pretentious. Only too occasionally would flashes of talent show through and then he was both lucid and helpful. On one such journey, however, just before one of my close-ups, he spoke of my character as if it was Hamlet or Oedipus, flavoured slightly with a touch of Kraft-Ebbing and Kierkegaard. I told him I didn't think "Bird Boy" or "Buoyed Boway" as the local crackers had dubbed me warranted such depth of scrutiny.

On another of our endless walks, the camera crew patiently waiting, we must have travelled at least four hundred yards in utter silence before he finally stopped, turned to me and said, "See what I mean?" Things were getting a little scary. Once we caught him describing the action to a bunch of actors who weren't even present. I needed help. I got it from my good friend B.J., who was again my makeup man or The Powder Puff, as he called himself. B.J. became my surrogate director. Whenever he saw the whites of my eyes just before an offending take he would call out, "You'll need a little more K-fourteen," or "K-two moving in." And while everyone silently waited, he would apply the cosmetic, which of course I didn't need at all, and whisper invaluable instructions into my ear, literally saving my screen life. Sometimes B.J.'s wacky humour spilled over and when he had no advice to give, he would come up just after they had called "Roll it" and say, "Don't shoot. Moving in with a bissel spritzel," and spraying a little sweat on my face, he'd whisper in my ear, "I have this script I've written. It's called *The River*"—and that's all he had to say. I would just lose it—completely broken up—gone for the rest of the afternoon.

Our real director, Nick Ray, had been one of the groundbreakers for the new wave of filmmaking in America. A disciple of Grotowski in the theatre and Godard and Kazan in film, his attitude toward the cinematic process was keenly European in its approach and his presence on the American motion picture scene was refreshing. He was, in his way, an early exponent of nouvelle vague, or French New Wave. On this film, however, whatever he was doing was assuredly more "vague" than "nouvelle."

Nick cut a handsome figure; he was a very sensual man—attractive to both men and women. He was also gifted with a vivid imagination. Some of his photographic setups and angles in *Everglades* were most interestingly conceived. There was never anything conventional about Nick; he had a touch of the poet about him. But this time around he was not a happy camper. He was also fed up with my own inexperience as a film actor and my sheer arrogance and intolerance toward him. Exasperating though he was, I was far too immature to have compassion for him, so instead I relentlessly patronized him as he in turn would patronize me. Had I not lacked confidence I might perhaps have exercised some restraint. But others were just as bad as I was. B.J., Peter Falk, Bill Garrity, and others formed little "Anti–Nick Ray" cliques, anything to cause trouble. Gypsy Rose Lee kept saying, "I think you're all acting in the most unprofessional manner!" and would turn her back on us in a huff. She was probably right, but there wasn't much else to do in swinging downtown Everglades City which in those days was made up of three or four huts, a corner store, one bar, the club and a local jail.

The Schulberg brothers, Budd and Stuart, stood patiently by as they watched their chef d'oeuvre proceed down its rocky path. Budd had started on the vodka at ten in the morning and by late afternoon was still standing, believe it or not, quite sober, even writing copious pages of new dialogue—what a constitution! By the end of the shooting day we would all head for the hills which in Tony Galento's case meant Miami and the dog races. "I'm goin' to da dawgs! I'm goin' to da dawgs," he rasped in his gravel-like Bronx bark. I once went with him—once was enough. He drove at one hundred miles an hour down the Tamiami Trail, then one of the world's most lethal highways—dangerously narrow with nothing but swampland and alligators on either side. "Slow down, Tony, please." "Whazza madda wit ya? I godda a governor on da car for Chrissakes—I godda governor!"

Because he lived in Sarasota, Budd Schulberg started importing all his friends from that town and putting them in the film. For some story purpose, I can't for the life of me remember what, he hired part of the Ringling Brothers circus. They were marvellous people, tough hard-core professionals, devoted to their work, their various skills handed down generation to generation. There was a girl in the troupe whose specialty was to hang from the high wire solely with her teeth and perform all sorts of hair-raising calisthenics high above the ground without a net. From a distance she appeared a tiny graceful sprite—up close she was a huge woman built like a decathlon champion, rippling muscles sculpting her arms and legs.

Well, for some strange reason she got a crush on me, the poor deluded thing. I can't think why—she probably thought I was some superstar. I was terrified; she was much too much woman for me or any other man, for that matter. And those teeth! Those powerful fangs—petrifying. Eons before Peter Benchley ever thought of his book, we were already calling her "Jaws." She followed me everywhere. B.J., brother John and Falk acted as my bodyguards and spies: "Look out, she's coming down the street—duck!" I'd jump into the front seat of my Thunderbird convertible with our little mascot, an adorable black-and-white mutt, a stray, who had adopted us and would do absolutely anything he was told. I would put him in the driver's seat with his two paws on the wheel, me on the floor under the dashboard steering from below and we slowly glided out of town. It was my only means of escape. No one could see me at all, just the dog, all alone, driving the car. This had been B.J.'s inspired staging. Sometimes the crew would play diabolical tricks such as placing Jaws right in my line of vision during a take. Those unforgivable swine! There she stood, grinning at me, with all those thousands of teeth, ready to snap.

At last the day came when the circus left town along with my erstwhile somewhat empty-handed paramour. Although I'd been spared possible permanent teeth marks, I kind of missed this Powerful Katrinka and the excitement of the chase.

Budd, his cup of kindness brimming over, kept inviting more of his friends down to watch the shooting, including several pugilists (Budd is an incurable fight fan), among them the famous Roger Donahue. He also had the good taste to employ a young dark-haired beauty from New Orleans to play the part of Memory Mellons, a half-breed native who wasn't required to speak or be spoken to but only to be looked upon. This turned out to be no chore, for with what she had to offer, and what she was wearing, she became known to all of us as "Mammory Mellons." Her real name was Cynthia and she was eighteen or thereabouts. Sometime after the Everglades saga was just a mammory, Cynthia and I became good friends and to this day, we still are.

Peter Falk turned out to be a wonderful ally and supporter of the Manon-des Grieux opposition team and kept our spirits from flagging with his cynical offbeat humour. Peter had only recently become an actor. He had started out in life, unbelievably, as an accountant. From an accident as a youth he wore a glass eye and just before a take he would call out to the makeup man, "Heh! you forgot to spray de eye! Spray de eye for Chrissakes!" He also loved to shock every now and then by popping the eye out and placing it on a rock as he gleefully watched people, suddenly overtaken with nausea, about to keel over. Something told us he'd be a star one day.

On a Saturday morning, our day off, while I was dozing in a chair on the club balcony, the delightful sound of clinking ice roused me from my torpor. Budd sauntered up with his usual morning vodka in an oversized milkshake carton. "I've g-g-g-gotta—I've hired a launch and we're g-g-g-oing—we're off to an island miles out in the gulf. They say a hermit lives out there all alone with his dogs. C-c-c-come on then.

G-G-Gypsy Rose, B-B-B.J. and Stuart are all coming. So let's g-go!"

It took forever, but at last the
island appeared in the distance. We
anchored and waded ashore. A
scruffy old man was standing on the
beach while two unidentifiable mon-
grels ran up and down yapping at us.
The old man's eyes were like deep
holes, and he stared at us as if he'd
never seen another human. He said
nothing but beckoned us to follow
him. It was a tiny island—no evidence of a hut or anything; he obviously slept with his dogs in the
shelter of the rocks. However, there
was a verdancy about the place, so we
concluded he must exist on berries
and what fruit and vegetable growth

Peter Falk, "Heh, makeup! Spray the eye, guys!"

it had to offer. There was very little else to see so we told him it was time
to go, thanked him and bade him farewell. None of us knew what language the man spoke, if indeed he ever spoke at all. After all someone so
unused to people had no need of speech. He may indeed have been mute
since birth. As we started wading out to the boat, he suddenly spoke.
His voice was a mixture of Gabby Hayes and Walter Brennan:

"Yoush-goin' back-t'town-ish-ya?"

"Yes," we answered.

"Could-yoush-gimme-a lift?"

"But," we all stammered at once, "you-you-you-you're a—you're a
herm—herm . . ."

He interrupted us. "It getch awful lonely out here sometimesh."

We took him on board. As we left the island, the two dogs ran
around in circles on the shore, barking their hearts out. Gypsy and I
stood at the railing in the boat's stern watching the island become a
tiny speck. We couldn't see the dogs anymore but we could still hear
them—barking away faintly in the distance. "It's so sad," I ventured.
"I bet those dogs are going to miss him like hell. That's what that barking is; they're saying, 'Come back, come back!' " "They're not saying,
'Come back, come back,' you schmuck," corrected Gypsy firmly;
"they're yelling, 'Phoney hermit! Phoney hermit! Phoney hermit!' "

To while the days away and relieve the idiotic chaos, B.J., Falk and I

Gypsy Rose — a "pro" to her fingertips

would very often wait until dusk and take one of those flying boats that skim over land and water far out into the lagoons. There we would stop the boat and sit in awed silence as we watched nature triumph over man. Millions upon millions of water birds—herons, egrets, bitterns, tropical exotic wild fowl, every known variety flying home to their water beds for the night. This was what the Everglades was all about. This was their kingdom. No notice was taken of us; we were invisible, insignificant. Those evenings made us forget not just *our* silly world but the *whole* silly world—a magical and cruel reminder of just how little we matter.

Then on our return home to the club, we'd sit on the balcony and Burl Ives would take up his guitar and sing songs in those special mellow tones of which he was the only master. The ease with which he weaved his spell as he gently rippled off "Jimmy crack corn and I don't care" or "A little bitty tear let me down" made one feel that he alone had invented folklore. Even the fireflies hovered longer and closer.

THERE WAS ANOTHER BUD in our midst (with one *d*) who was warden for the Everglades Park. He was also our technical advisor, and Bud Kirk's job was to watch over us, make sure we didn't drown or get swallowed up by quicksand. It seemed a trifle odd when Burl Ives and I were doing our final confrontation scene, wading chest-deep in alligator-infested waters, that Mr. Kirk, who kept calling out instructions such as, "I think you should move more upstream; there's less chance of gators that way," was sitting on a chair, fully dressed, on a bank several yards away from any danger. Was there something wrong with this picture?

He did have his useful side, however. He knew just about every rock, cranny and cave in the surrounding islands. Outside the Everglades themselves was a spit of land called Chokoloskee Island. In the nine-teenth century it had been inhabited by poor Polish outcasts who had copulated with the natives there including some of the Seminole tribe, producing illegitimate half-breed offspring. These offspring in turn intermarried, transforming the island into a haven of inbreeding and incest. They had eked out a living selling egret feathers, pirating and robbing the mainland. By now, however, most of them had become pretty lazy, content to hang around dealing with trouble only if it came their way.

A posse of them had been hired to play the villainous egret killers in the movie. Anne Roth, the cute, young, stylish costume designer, who always smoked from a cigarette holder and who would become the Anne Roth of Hollywood and Oscar fame, didn't have to worry. The clothes these crackers wore daily hadn't changed since the century began and, by the look and smell of them, didn't need to be broken down either. The Chokoloskee boys had a strange custom they couldn't wait to practice. For a fortnight or so they would leave their women and go off on a huntin', fishin', drinkin' spree of unusual violence. At night they would engage in a ritual they called lip fighting. They would lie together on the ground like lovers and furiously bite each other's lips until they bled profusely and swelled to an enormous size. They would hold on in this death-lock sometimes for hours on end, ominously sug-gesting a kind of cannibalistic sex.

Tosh Brown, the leader of the pack, was rather more passive than the rest and tried to keep a semblance of law and order among them. At least he could read whereas the rest of them were pretty illiterate. Tosh played himself in the film. He also sang rather nicely some incompre-hensible local dirges while accompanying himself on the guitar.

There was a little eating hole in the marshes just across from Chokoloskee Island on the mainland. Dreadfully ramshackle, it was built on stilts and had cardboard walls, but it offered some of the

Nicholas Ray — an immensely gifted maverick

best fish 'n' chips I've ever consumed. It was also the Chokoloskee boys' favorite haunt. We began to dine there regularly, bringing our own booze. Bud Kirk insisted on accompanying us even if he didn't partake. Though you never saw it, he always packed a gun. One Saturday night, eight of us had arrived there feeling no pain. To make things more stylish, we decided to dress up in our Sunday best. B.J. kidnapped James, the bartender at the Rod and Gun, to come along in his white coat and serve us the club's champagne throughout the meal. James couldn't have had a better time—chuckling away most of the evening—he got such a kick out of this performance.

The joint that night was packed with the Chokoloskee clan. Our table was in front, and right behind us sat Tosh Brown and his cousin, one of the seediest-looking male creeps I've ever set eyes on. "Coz" started singing in a very bad off-key monotone some ghastly drunken madrigal. He kept on and on like a broken record—the whole room now forced to listen. I heard Tosh make a swift movement behind us. I didn't want to look. He had obviously grabbed Coz by the throat; I heard Tosh say very slowly, very gently, "You stop that now, ya heah me? Ah, don' laik that sawng." There was quiet for a while then Coz began again. Our own table was now getting quite rowdy—we'd forgotten the incident; more champagne corks popped, and everything was getting back to normal when suddenly Bud Kirk appeared from nowhere and in an urgent whisper said, "We're leaving now—pay up and let's get outta here." "But," we protested, "we haven't even started." "Do as I say—now! I'll explain later." We paid up, walked down the rickety steps, Bud herding us all the way to our cars which were parked some twenty-five yards up a dirt road. We could still hear that awful wailing sound emanating from Tosh's cousin. Then we heard a shot, followed by silence—an awful stillness. It was broken a moment later by the whirring of a great flock of exotic birds flying away from the surrounding trees. Clearly, they too had had quite enough.

A few days later, another violent incident occurred. Manon, it seems, had tried to kill Nick. In the dead of night she had left their bed, Nick still sleeping, got into the big Cadillac convertible, backed up several yards then gunned it at full speed straight through the wall of their bedroom. If, seconds before Nick hadn't got up to pee, he would surely have been a dead man. We saw the cabin the next morning which looked like a collapsed accordion.

Manon disappeared never to be seen again and Nick, badly shaken, did not report for duty with much regularity, so a few days later he was dismissed. What gave the whole farce a bizarre ending was that when Nick was being driven to the airport, he lay on the backseat so that no one would see him go.

Years later in London I got to know this bright, talented maverick a lot better when we were both staying at the Connaught Hotel. He was a different person altogether and we had such a pleasant time, never once referring to those days in the swampland. I still felt a certain guilt over my uncooperative behavior toward him, but he'd obviously forgiven me or else had more than likely blocked the whole weird experience from his mind. He continued to do some fine work, in Europe mostly, and characteristically spent the remainder of his reclusive days at the end of the world on an island off the northernmost tip of Denmark.

BUDD SCHULBERG, Charlie Maguire and Bill Garrity finished the movie, but it was all a bit late—nothing much they could do. Gypsy Rose Lee, her engagement completed, stayed on as a sort of wardrobe woman emeritus, mending and repairing costumes. "June and I were taught to do this when we were both on the road with mother. We sewed; we stitched; we made all our own costumes." This valiant lady, a true professional, had most certainly learned all the tricks of the trade.

B.J., Memory Mellons, Falk and I were all that was left of the group except for the little mascot who, for laughs, still drove the Thunderbird with me on the floor steering. And then the inevitable day arrived when we would bid adieu to the old Rod and Gun. We absolutely emptied the place. James, the kidnapped bartender, was broken up. "What am I gonna do now?" he moaned. No, things would never be the same. The Hermit, who hated being alone, now had a permanent address in Everglades City with his two dogs, and the snake-man who was always getting beaten up in bars and always drunk spent most of his time in jail. He's probably still there.

My sidekick, the indescribable B.J., went back to Vermont and his manuscript *The River,* Memory Mellons to New Orleans and Budd Schulberg, the film under his arm, left for the nearest editing room where he would try to extract some sense from the botched-up mosaic of his story. And me? With my tail between my legs, I went back to Manhattan and the real snakes of Madison Avenue with whom I had always felt far more comfortable to begin with.

CHAPTER EIGHTEEN

WHAT'S IN A NAME?

For the next hectic weeks, nay months, I stewed and fretted over what in God's name to call my pixie offspring. Of course it mattered not a tinker's damn what she might want. After all she only had to live with it for the rest of her life. Why should she have a choice? I had always been rather partial to masculine nomenclature for girls, convinced that it lent a certain flair and challenged them to be feminine at the same time. I especially liked Sidney, Hilary, Steven, Frances, Leslie, Georgie—names of that ilk. This would of course be her middle name; the principal one, without question, would have to be ultra-feline.

Tammy wanted Amanda. She liked the aristocratic English sound. She also loved the Amanda Coward had created for Gertrude Lawrence in *Private Lives.* She was to play it herself more than once, winning a Tony for it. Well, if it was to be Amanda it was okay by me, though I was fearful she'd be called "Mandy" for short. But what boyish appellation, which I seemed to think so stylish, could complement it? When I badgered friends for suggestions, some jeered at me; others merely looked at me as if I'd gone mad. Jack Warden scoffed, "What about Howard or Marvin? How about Moishe?"

Then I remembered a fresh-faced beauty who once served as a very young apprentice at the American Shakespeare Theatre that crazy summer when it began. She was sixteen or seventeen, was madly in love

*Jason Robards, Jr., one of the very best
Hotspurs I've seen*

with a handsome young actor, Peter Donat, whom she later married, and her name was Michael Learned. (Yes the same Michael Learned from the Waltons who became such a fine actress.) There it was—Michael! And it sat perfectly on her; God knows there was nothing tomboyish about Miss Learned! So, screaming bloody murder as she was dipped into the font by Archdeacon Lightbourne at St. James Anglican in Stratford, Ontario, one beautiful but very noisy afternoon, our offspring was christened Amanda Michael Plummer—satisfying all and sundry.

But there must have been some mysterious potion lurking in the rough waters of the font that day; some "eye of newt" or "tongue of dog," for a little demon grew up inside Amanda that would bring forth in her later youth a talent, deeply intense, utterly original, which could, if it had a mind to, stir up the "terrors of the earth."

WELL, VERY NEARLY ALL the cracks had gathered for the fray. The little church was fairly bursting with joy, and with her christening, so was the summer christened. It was a summer of children, of comrades and some pretty proud work—it wasn't all spit and polish, but, by God, it was alive.

> *Rare words! brave world! Hostess, my breakfast, come!*
> *O, I could wish this tavern were my drum!*
> —FALSTAFF (*HENRY IV, PART I*)

Jason Robards, after another triumphant O'Neill performance as Jamie in the world premiere of *Long Day's Journey Into Night,* drove up from New York in his "Red Ding-Dong," a large, loud fire-engine red station wagon. He brought along his dad, Jason, Sr., a delightful charmer who had once been a leading man in Hollywood silents. An old naval salt, he was instantly dubbed the "Admiral," Max Helpmann, another navy man, was the "Commander," Jason, Jr., the "Captain" and I guess I must have been the ship's MD, for they called me "Doctor."

Jason gave us his Hotspur, and Doug Campbell was a rich and robust Falstaff, both in *Henry IV, Part I*; Tammy relinquished her musical-star status momentarily for the small comic role of Dorcas in *The Winter's Tale.* The West End star, Eileen Herlie, a warm and brilliant Scottish lass who had been Olivier's Queen Mum in his film of *Hamlet* was Paulina from the same play and also Beatrice to my Benedick in *Much Ado About Nothing.* It was playing Benedick that freed me from all outward influence and for the first time I was able to find a trust in myself. Michael Langham's witty and very human production received unanimous praise on both sides of the border and we, the actors, didn't do too badly ourselves—our ensemble had never been stronger. For a moment our little northern company appeared unchallenged anywhere. To top it all off, the French brought back their Molière for a brief but exhausting visit and the Press Club, our only after-hours green room, rang out louder and longer than all the carillons of Notre Dame.

Almost everyone who loved the theatre was in attendance that season. Polly left her beautiful island on the Lake of Two Mountains and brought her brood with her. From New York came Zachary Scott, Ruth Ford, John and DeeDee Ryan, Paul and Joanne Newman, Alec and Hildy Cohen, Rod Steiger—always Ratty Whitehead and Roger Stevens. Maurice Evans drove up bringing Margaret Webster. Tony and Judy Guthrie arrived from England, Nicholas Monsarrat (*The Cruel Sea*) ditto. Iris Mountbatten and an old lady came and went very quietly from Cooksville near Stratford, where she lived in very modest circumstances indeed, the Grand Duchess Olga (sister of Czar Nicholas II), a lonely survivor of the doomed Romanov dynasty.

Another royal in the petite form of Princess Margaret was brought up the Avon on a launch to see *Winter's Tale,* and we were presented afterwards. She was pretty, wickedly funny and had star quality in spades. Years later she told me, "I thought you were all terrific. I didn't like the play very much." The summer of '58 was one long children's party—our being the children, grown-ups and babes alike—no one could tell us apart; always a little out of control, a little too fond, living just on the edge and oh so flammable.

JASON'S HOTSPUR was the best I've ever seen. Olivier's, years before, had been marvellous too, of course, with his inspired idea of faltering on any word beginning with *W* so that when he died he would die on a stutter.

> HOTSPUR: *No, . . . thou art dust,*
> *And food for w-w-w- . . . (dies)*
> PRINCE HENRY: *(finishing it for him)* For worms, brave
> Percy.

But Jason's was remarkable because he achieved the impossible. He made us believe Hotspur would rather fight than talk. I don't think he had ever played a major Shakespearean role up to then, but he instinctively used his hesitancy with the language to great advantage by saving all his emphasis and effort to attack the parenthetical sections of his text. This had the very plausible effect of illustrating a rough soldier's habit of overblowing the importance of little things, leaving the big ones to take care of themselves. This Hotspur rode his wife as he rode his horse—a coarse fighter whose biggest battle perhaps was the battle to express himself. But when Jason as Percy grasped at straws he could recognize and hold on to, the sheer tenacity of his quest for truth and glory freed the poetry in him and when he reached for the sky "to pluck bright honour from the pale-faced moon," he was unforgettable.

King Polixenes as a role is of course nowhere in the same league as Hotspur. It is not one of Will's gems. Jason knew this and took a much-needed vacation while performing it. He would mock his opening speech by speaking it as Jimmy Durante. It had all the right Durante rhythms:

Nine changes of the waddery stah hatt bin
Da shepherd's note since we have left our trone
Widdout a boiden

Tanya Moiseiwitsch had dressed the king in a long gown and, if you took a peak underneath, you'd see Jason had kept his street clothes on, pockets filled with packs of Marlboros and wearing a heavy Rolex, ready for a quick getaway.

In the play's last scene, Leontes, in guilt and despair, stands over the stone effigy of his dead wife. For a moment he believes she could be breathing and says, "Methinks, there is an air comes from her!" On the first few performances, as I spoke the line, I made the mistake of bringing both my hands to my face—a gesture innocently intended to express awe and wonder. Jason, quick to notice, immediately farted. The whole assembled company corpsed. It was a slow, soft, lingering release (Jason could supply a variety of speeds and volumes at will). The audience couldn't remotely believe they'd heard what they'd heard; the possibility would never have occurred to them, but *we* certainly heard! Every night we visibly tensed in anticipation of the dreaded moment and every night he did not disappoint us.

Eileen Herlie brought a good deal of emotional power to Paulina and as Beatrice she was a sheer delight, saving that very power solely for the famous church scene. Dame Sybil Thorndike and Sir Lewis Casson, Dougie Campbell's in-laws and grand old pillars of the British stage, came to see the *Much Ado* dress rehearsal. Sybil was in her late eighties, Lewis in his nineties and very, very deaf. They sat at the back of the theatre holding hands as they had done rain or shine since the day they fell in love. We are now in the midst of the church scene. Beatrice berates Benedick before the whole congregation in her famous speech which begins, "Princes and Counties!" Eileen really let it rip that afternoon, pulling out all the stops. A long silence follows before Benedick can speak. In that pause, Sybil, from the last row, in a voice that could be heard across the plains of Saskatchewan shouted at Lewis, "I said— she's got the guns for it, hasn't she?" We had the devil of a time trying to continue with straight faces, but that pronouncement made Eileen's summer.

Tanya, as an opening-night present, gave me an LP of one of her father's last concerts before he died. I had once owned some rare seventy-eights on which he exquisitely played the Fourth and *Emperor* Concertos of Beethoven, so this was a treat. Benno Moiseiwitsch, in his time, was

Eileen as Paulina in The Winter's Tale

one of the world's great pianists and a bosom friend of Rachmaninoff. He also lived gregariously and loved his food and drink. "You'll enjoy this, I think," said Tanya. "He was quite tiddly when he recorded it and makes ghastly mistakes all over the place. You can't drink and play at the same time, you know." I reminded Tanya that I could barely sit down at a piano unless I was bombed!

Running out of things to do in the brief spare time there was, our dreaded little quartet (the Admiral, the Commander, the Captain and me—the ship's doctor) had arrived at a dead impasse. We needed new inspiration; we craved new blood. We found both in a young man called Peter Hale who was playing small parts that season and doubling as an assistant stage manager. We at once detected great promise in the youth. He had a completely natural and unaffected penchant for deviltry, a real down 'n' dirty glint in his eye and a talent for improvising wickedness that was prodigious in the extreme. Because he was ASM on *The Winter's Tale* we christened him "Winters Hale." Winters boasted a large two-wheel motorbike which could fit three, so two of the "fraternity" would take turns and jump on behind Winters as he madly drove that devil bike through the black night in search of trouble.

The latest sport we had invented was to visit our actor friends in their rental houses or flats, complain bitterly about the quality of their furniture ("How can you expect decent men to drink amongst all this Swedish G Plan?") and proceed to throw every chair and table out the window. This would occasion a kind of desperate and hysterical laughter from our hosts, especially when after the last piece had disappeared we followed suit and threw ourselves out. Needless to say, the Admiral did not participate in the acrobatics, he just observed, drink in hand, an expression of total satisfaction painted all over his face.

As we got more confident, these feats became all the more daring, especially when the windows were four stories high. One of us always had to gather up the poor unfortunate who had landed on his back in a small tree or bush. We got to be quite expert, however, and Winters was clearly the most nimble for he executed it all with the dexterity of a stuntman and his timing was superb. After a while, he didn't even bother with the furniture gag anymore. The moment he entered a room he simply threw himself out the window. We gave him a new nickname, "Windows Hale."

As the summer limped along, Jason and his old man, the Admiral, never stopped quarreling—in bars, on the streets, at parties—morning, noon and night. It got worse. They were actually enormously fond of each other, but the Admiral, who'd been with Jason since New York, matching him drink for drink, showed no signs of leaving and stayed on and on. This got on Jason's nerves and although the Admiral was proud as Punch of his son's success, he was also, I think, a little jealous of it. The fights were loud, overplayed, sometimes funny, sometimes horrific. They came straight out of an O'Neill play.

Once when Jason ran out of horrible names to sling at his dad, he ended up calling him an old "poofinjay." This marriage of Elizabethan and contemporary slang was a clear indication that, in Jason's case, "art" was influencing life. Finally, Jase persuaded the Admiral to check into a clinic in nearby Guelph so that the old man could dry out, sober up and fly right. Though we sorely missed him, the seas, I must admit, became a lot calmer. But not for long. Jason firmly announced that on his day off he'd be driving to Chicago to see his wife and would be back in time for the next show. "Wife?" We were dumbfounded. We had no idea he'd married again.

A native of that toddlin' town, her name was Rachel Taylor. We had already made her acquaintance; she was a good girl, but we didn't think she was right for the Captain and I believe we even told him so—can you stomach our gall?! Actually, we just didn't want him to leave; he was too much fun. Nothing could dissuade him, however, and after much celebration, deliberately organized to delay his departure, at 3:00 a.m. on the appointed day, he fell into his Red Ding-Dong wearing a helmet from *Winter's Tale,* brandishing an enormous sword and carrying a shield that Leslie Hurry had designed for *Tamburlaine* with the grimacing head of Medusa on the front. Thus fully caparisoned, he drove off down the street shouting those immortal lines:

> *One, she was my wife*
> *Two, I was in a perverse mood*
> *Three, I had a Byronic complex*

He managed to cross the border either because the customs officials thought it wiser to humour this deranged Quixote and let him pass or Jason had simply showed them Medusa's head and they'd all turned to stone.

"GIB" JARROTT was the kindest man around. He lived in Sebringville, a few miles outside Stratford on beautiful rolling farmland whose hills and fields dominated the countryside for as far as the eye could see. Gib and his wife, Elizabeth, devoted patrons who loved the theatre, literally gave us actors the entire run of the place of which I'm afraid we took full advantage. In his sixties, Gib was a semiretired doctor but no one could figure out when he found the time to practice—he was always too busy looking after us. Jean Gascon affectionately called him "le médecin malgré lui" and Jean would go out there and cook for them occasionally and we'd sit around noshing on the terrace while the strong scent of garlic pleasantly hung in the evening air.

That summer Gib's birthday came around on a Sunday—our day off. Jean, in a moment of inspiration, called a meeting. "We're going to give Gib a surprise party," and he proceeded to unravel his plan. He would borrow some of the festival orchestra, hide behind the farthest hill along with most of the company. He would also con Jean-Pierre Rampal (the world's greatest flautist, conveniently giving a concert here) to join in. A few of us would be delegated to stay at the house and at a given time would see that Gib came down to the pool which had a spectacular view of the hills beyond. Everything worked according to plan. Our small but diverse group gathered at the pool—the Guthries, Michael and Helen Langham, Marcel Marceau (doing his clown "Bip"

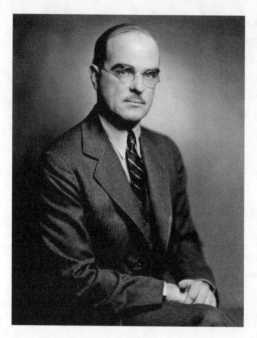

The amazing, whimsical Mr. Wilder

for the festival); the pixieish Thornton Wilder (staying with the Guthries); Jason Robards; Liz Jarrott; Tammy, who was still friendly; me and the unsuspecting Gib.

From at least a mile away the sound of fife, flute, trumpet and drum echoed down the valleys and there suddenly on the horizon appeared the little band. They were playing "Happy Birthday," "La Marseillaise," "En Roulant," God knows what else all at once. And there was Jean-Pierre Rampal tootling away with the rest; out in front, Gascon, a Callot drawing in animation, wearing a long false nose, doing his crazy swaggering walk, and behind, in one long line, the rest of the company carrying all the food and wine, singing their hearts out. The sight of them lit by the afternoon sun, coming down the slopes, through the golden fields and up the final hill, sent tingles down the spine; and dear old Gib couldn't stop laughing and crying for the rest of the night.

MALHEUREUSEMENT, the Molière season came to an end—it was time for the French adieu. We fêted them with champagne at my pad the day they left—that gallant company. After many promises of fealty, they poured themselves into two cars which bulged at the seams and set off for the long journey to Montreal. They drove down the street shouting bawdy French chansons and Québecois obscenities, but moments later they were all back on our front porch giving the same farewell speeches, and poured themselves back into the cars once more, screaming and shouting till they were out of sight. A full fifteen minutes went by when, would you believe it, there they were once again repeating the same performance.

Thinking we had seen the last of them and weak from laughter, we went into the house for a much-needed rest. At least an hour had lapsed when I thought I heard in the distance the sound of approaching horns.

I rushed out onto the porch and Tabérnacle! Sure enough, the whole street resounded with an ear-piercing din as those maudits habitants came back for more. They had to have been at least a quarter of the way to Montreal when Gascon blackmailed them into turning around for one last exit—this one the grandest of them all. Good ol' Jean, he would go to any lengths for a laugh.

> Farewell, thou latter spring! farewell,
> All-hallown summer!

CHAPTER NINETEEN

THE POET AND THE REBEL

Lounging in my digs one languid afternoon, I was jolted from my reverie by the sound of the telephone. It rang with a rather more joyous peal than usual, and by God! if it wasn't Archibald MacLeish!

> Quite unexpectedly as Vasserot
> The armless ambidextrian was lighting
> A match between his great and second toe
> And Ralph the lion was engaged in biting
> The neck of Madame Sossman while the drum
> Pointed, and Teeny was about to cough
> In waltz-time swinging Jocko by the thumb —
> Quite unexpectedly the top blew off.

—A.M.

Well, my life was considerably brightened by that call, and the voice on the other end was the youngest voice I had ever heard in a man of his advanced years. He was saying that someone had suggested I play the

Devil in his play *J.B.* for New York, which would be directed by Elia Kazan and could he fly up and meet me?! Now I had never set eyes on Mr. MacLeish and as I listened to that youthful voice, I couldn't help imagining that in spite of his long, rich life and the great abundance of literature and poetry he has given us, he must, by the sound of him, be just a mere boy, and when I finally met him, to my sheer delight, he still was!

Archibald MacLeish, who died April 20, 1982, just short of his ninetieth birthday, was a playwright, lawyer, teacher, journalist, a librarian of congress and an assistant secretary of state. Amy Lowell was his mentor; Ernest Hemingway, Dean Acheson and Judge Learned Hand were among his closest friends. He worked for publisher Henry Luce and President Franklin Roosevelt; at one point Adlai Stevenson worked for him. He was called a fascist by Communists and a Communist by Senator Joseph McCarthy. The author of more than forty books of poems, plays and speeches, he won the Pulitzer Prize three times as well as the National Medal of Literature and the Presidential Medal of Freedom. He was one of the most remarkable men of his time and, above all, he was a poet—in spirit and in dress.

Because he was both bohemian and conservative, I secretly nicknamed him "the Poet with the Vest." Pretty soon I was calling him "Archie." His youthful spirit, his genuine enthusiasm for everything was utterly contagious. He made me feel one hundred feet tall. Age and experience notwithstanding, there was not a hint of cynicism in him, no side. He appeared unsullied, pure, as if already adorned for immortality. Yet there was always an irreverent glint behind those kind, gentle eyes. About this country—his country—Archie had always been honest, tough and loving:

> *It is a strange thing — to be an American.*
> *Neither a place it is nor a blood name.*
> *America is West and the wind blowing.*
> *America is a great word and the snow,*
> *A way, a white bird, the rain falling,*
> *A shining thing in the mind and the gulls' call.*

> —"AMERICAN LETTER"

I was so impressed with this dapper older man who had exiled himself to Paris in the golden twenties, had lived through the age of Dada

One of the great unsung poets of America

and had known Picasso, James Joyce, Scott Fitzgerald, the Gerald Murphys, Gertrude Stein.

> *Fame was what they wanted in that town.*
> *Fame could be found there too — flushed like quail in the*
> *Cool dawn — struck among statues*
> *Naked in hawthorn in the silver light.*

—"YEARS OF THE DOG"

Well, he'd come to see my Benedick, had given me his seal of approval and was now leading me onto the murky stage of Forty-second Street's New Amsterdam Roof. A woman with a hat and a veil emerged from a dark corner. It was Jane Broder carrying all my contracts. "I want you to sign these right now; then I'll get out of your hair, honey." There were various people sitting in a line waiting for Archie, who was going to read his play to us—Pat Hingle, that titanically talented Texan who would be Job; my old friend Raymond Massey (I suspect he'd recommended me), who was to play God; Jimmy Olson, Cliff James, Janet Ward; Christopher Walken, a decadently handsome boy of fifteen who would play one of Job's children; and several older, crustier characters from Laura Pierpont on down, representing survivors of bombed out Second World War London.

Ray came over and together we lamented the recent death of Ty Power during the filming of *Solomon and Sheba* in Madrid. Ty had suffered a heart attack while carrying the buxom Gina Lollobrigida up a long flight of stairs for take after take. Wandering in and out, looking quite incongruous amongst us working stiffs, except for Massey who always dressed like a successful CEO, was Alfred de Liagre ("Delly"), the play's producer, attired in beautifully cut country tweeds from Savile Row, greeting everyone as if they were in a play by John Van Druten or Terence Rattigan.

At a little table facing us sat Archie, Bob Downing, the stage manager, and a stocky, ruggedly built man in his fifties with dark penetrating eyes and a mass of thick hair growing almost to a point on top of his head. He had not yet spoken, but already he radiated an electric tension of such voltage the whole building seemed to vibrate from it. So this is Elia Kazan, I said to myself! There sits the current most powerful world influence in theatre and film; the man who gave us Tennessee Williams and Arthur Miller at their best, who changed America's identity by creating two major folk images—the sullen, angry rebel symbolized by Brando and a new kind of phenomenon, a young man with a brain who dared stand up to his elders and challenge convention in the person of James Dean. Whether intentional or not, Kazan had succeeded in inducting these two monstrous forces into American mythology, cementing forever this country's obsession with youth.

"Mornin' Gadge." Some of the stagehands and carpenters—the pride of the Union—had gathered around to do obeisance. "Mornin' boys," he jovially snapped back, passing around oversized Cuban cigars. This would become a weekly ritual. Mumbling their gratitude, the "boys" retreated into the darkness. There was no doubt who was the Godfather around here. With a single gesture from Kazan, Archie began to read the play in that light soothing voice of his and we were soon lost under its spell.

J.B., when it first played at Yale some months before, had been rated by Atkinson of *The New York Times* as "the greatest play of the century." It wasn't, nor would it ever be, but the presentation by Gadge, the amazing set by Boris Aronson and the intensely felt performances made it seem more than worthy and lent it a borrowed majesty that concealed its weaknesses. It offered considerable theatricality and there was some occasional noble language, but Archie the playwright could never match Archie the poet. It was almost a foregone conclusion we would be a hit in spite of a crippling newspaper strike on the opening night in New York. For the mystique of a Kazan production plus the fact that the theme was Biblical and that God, Job and the Devil were in the cast, overawed a certain segment of the press when they finally did review us and we sold out solidly for over a year.

Elia Kazan was certainly the very greatest director of tragic drama I have ever worked with. Having charged through the Group Theatre days as a character performer of exceptional power, he spoke the actor's language, understood our foibles, found our Achilles' in a flash, thus cutting through all the baloney and coming straight to the point. Uncannily, he would uncover layer upon layer of depths within us till we stood before the public naked as plucked chickens. Sex, racial intolerance, politics and human sacrifice were the passions that ruled his work, that drove his life and he was relentless in his pursuit of them.

My role of Nickles, the young actor who would be taken over by Nicodemus himself, was in my view the best-written part in the play. Devils are always more interesting than angels and Archie obviously had the most fun writing this character:

NICKLES: *I heard upon his dry dung heap*
That man cry out who cannot sleep:
"If God is God, He is not good,
If God is good, He is not God;
Take the even, take the odd—"

I also had the most terrific time rehearsing my Nickles. I was so anxious to show Kazan I could be as "Methody" as the next guy that I overdid everything in rehearsals, going way over the top, working far too hard. One day, he shouted at me, "Relax! For Chrissake, relax! Sixty percent, Chris! Sixty percent." With great relief I realized he could be as technical as anyone else. I once asked him who the most exciting actor was he'd ever directed, spurred on by the faint hope it might be me. I should have known he would answer "Marlon Brando." Through gritted teeth I asked him why. "Because I never knew what he was going to do next. Whenever he picked up an object from a table I was sure at any moment he might throw it at me."

Gadge was a bundle of energy; he was everywhere at once and the air about him was always charged. If you really caught fire during a rehearsal he would run down from the stalls, jump up onto the stage

Archie, Alfred De Liagre, Jr., and Elia Kazan

and like a basketball or hockey coach, stand right in front of you and yell, "That's it. Come on! You've got it! Come on, kid. Come on!" He also had a diabolical method of playing one actor off another to get the desired effect—defying discretion to provoke confrontation. To get more anger out of Massey in *East of Eden,* he had goaded James Dean into hurling insults at him from off camera. It worked—but at what price?!

Gadge, however, could be conciliatory and ingratiating if the urge took him. At rehearsals, Raymond as Zuss (Zeus) sat in the little God-box Boris had designed for him high above stage level, patiently waiting for his scenes to come up. Gadge, with a slight smirk in his voice and an overembellished politesse, would call out: "You all right there, Ray? Send Mr. Massey a chair and some water up to his crow's nest. Sit down, Ray—relax—be with you in a minute." Yet he always demanded more of himself than anyone else. I once caught him all alone on the darkened stage sitting cross-legged on Job's sack cloth quietly playing the role for himself in order to give Pat Hingle some fresh ideas. He was clearly chief cook and bottle-washer; that's how he liked it and that's how it was going to be.

His complex Central European background (part Armenian, part everything else) made him several different people at once—all things to all men. Elia Kazan was a taut spring—a fuse. By turning an invis-

Ray Massey, me and Pat Hingle

ible knob he could make your blood pressure rise and fall at will. If you weren't careful, this chameleon of chameleons might change into you, wear your skin and if you let him, like the real Nickles, steal your soul.

"Tell the little Turk to be more polite," Ray Massey rumbled into his beard as he left a rehearsal one day. Andy, the stage doorman, an old ex-vaudevillian, called out after him, "Oh yeah, shooah, Mr. Massey, no sweat. I'll be da foist ta tell him—da foist!"

WEST FIFTY-SECOND STREET—third time at the ANTA Playhouse—my home for a year!

"I sit in one of the dives/On Fifty-second Street . . . ," wrote W. H. Auden,

> *Faces along the bar*
> *Cling to their average day:*
> *The lights must never go out,*
> *The music must always play.*

It was as if Auden's ghost had bequeathed the street to MacLeish— one poetic legacy to another:

Lest we should see where we are,
Lost in a haunted wood,
Children afraid of the night
Who have never been happy or good.

Well, we may not have been exactly *good* little boys and girls, but we were certainly *happy;* and, far from afraid, we relished the nights that good ol' street would offer us. There was Roseland for ballroom dancing, La Scala for food (Arthur Miller's and Ezio Pinza's favorite), Confucius for drinks and light Chinese, a great after-show pickup joint; then Jilly's right across from our stage door—Sinatra's bar, run by his dogsbody Jilly himself and inhabited mostly by dear old Andy our stage doorman, who once played piano for Jimmy Durante. Whenever Ol' Blue Eyes turned up, tension reigned. At any moment he might order Jilly to eject some poor innocent whose face he hadn't particularly taken to. Fifty-second below Eighth had one or two excellent French bistros and above Broadway it continued eastward in lively fashion all the way up to the "21" Club.

One of the "observers" on the production who also assisted Kazan was a young James Baldwin, whose book *Giovanni's Room* had made him famous as a pioneer for many black causes. James hung out with all of us. He was witty, delightfully angry, clever as paint and great company. We didn't have to travel far to have fun—it was right there on our street. *Gypsy* had just opened on one side of us and around the corner on the other *West Side Story.* We had a collective ball with "above the salters" Jule Styne (who was always so good to me), his best girl Sandra Church, who created the role of Gypsy, and Steve Sondheim, who had been a classmate of Tammy's at Stephens. And all those girls!

Confucius was jumping with them. I occasionally dated one of the chorines from *Gypsy,* who was so tall I had to climb onto a chair to kiss her. I made good friends with Lee Becker, delectably small and athletic—she was a regular companion; Lee, a superb dancer, assisted Jerome Robbins on his *West Side* choreography and originated the role of Anybody's. She literally bubbled with humour and talent.

One night at Confucius, my favorite of Ty Powers's rejects turned up, the sinewy blonde Slav with whom I had once shared quelques moments passionels. She had broken up her European marriage and was suggesting that we revive our relationship of old. Tempting though it was, I am relieved I didn't take her up on it, for as I later learned, my lovely friend of the smooth unblemished skin, innocent eyes and soft

Slavic tongue was, to put it quite simply, a shark. From a fairly tender age she had run two very successful high-priced prostitution networks, one in New York, the other in Chicago. She herself had been a prostitute and a madam and had nearly killed a certain young president's campaign election chances by threatening to expose their torrid affair. Think what I'd have learned if I'd stuck around. She certainly could have taught Mata Hari a thing or two.

AFTER WE HAD OPENED *J.B.*, Kazan began rehearsals for Tennessee Williams's new play *Sweet Bird of Youth.* Just before their out-of-town opening they held their last full run-through without costumes at the New Amsterdam Roof. Gadge invited our entire cast. Also in attendance that afternoon were most of theatre's top brass—the usual suspects—Josh Logan, Helen Hayes, the Lunts, Lee Strasberg, Cheryl Crawford, Lillian Hellman, Ruth Gordon, Garson Kanin, etc., etc. Not a large group but mighty potent. Gadge got up and announced that they would have to wait to begin because Tennessee had not yet arrived. "Tennessee, as you know, has his own rhythm," he quipped, not without edge.

Finally, it began. The exceptional cast included Paul Newman, Rip Torn, Sidney Blackmer, my Montreal friend Madeleine Sherwood and, of course, Geraldine Page in the leading role of Princess. They were each in his or her own right first class, but that afternoon belonged to Geraldine, for before our lucky eyes we were watching her, for the first time, discover her own performance. Gerry was flying! God knows Tennessee was a marvellous writer and there was fine writing in this, but Gerry lifted the whole thing to another level—she was transcendent! When it was over you could hear a pin drop. We were not just transfixed; we had been seduced.

Gradually we pulled ourselves together and began to shuffle out. No one spoke. Just then from the balcony in that rasping voice of his, Tennessee started shouting. I couldn't quite make out his gist but it seemed to convey that we had all just witnessed the total destruction of *Sweet Bird of Youth,* and it was all Gerry's fault. Gerry was the sole culprit. "She's ruined mah play! She's ruined mah play," he kept yelling. He must be drunk, I thought, or ill. No one seemed to take much notice, or pretended not to, and as Gadge passed me in the aisle I tugged at his sleeve. "What's the matter with Tennessee?" I asked. "My God! It's been such a glorious afternoon." "Oh, don't worry," Gadge replied, "she's just taken his play away from him. It's hers now—it doesn't belong to him anymore and he knows it."

AFTER A *J.B.* PERFORMANCE one evening I wandered into Michael's Pub on the East Side to have a late snack and watch George Shearing make magic on the ol' "Joanna." A lady seated at one of the tables called out, "Oh, Mr. Plummer, I have a message for you." It was Viola Rubber, the famous agent-cum-entrepreneuse who managed only the elite such as Bette Davis or Greta Garbo. She cut a very domineering and imposing figure in her mannish suit and close-cropped pepper and salt hair. "I ran into Diana Barrymore the other day and she wants to see you. She has something to ask you."

Now I hadn't set eyes on Diana for over ten years; I had only followed her sad antics and disastrous public exhibitions in the tabloids. Gruesome photos of her, bloated with drink, fighting in the street with her numerous undesirable male friends, appeared every once in a while on the back pages of the sleazier rags. Rumour had it that she was wiped out—dead broke. She had asked for help from her aunt Ethel, who refused even to see her. It was a tough question, but I had to ask it, "How is she, Miss Rubber?" I said, expecting the worst. "Oh, she's absolutely come around; didn't you know? She looks wonderful and hasn't touched a drop in months. She's clean—a complete cure. Here's her number." Reassured, I called Diana and we made a date. Miss Rubber was right. She looked absolutely wonderful—slim, trim, tanned— the same darkly sexy girl I had met there many years ago, only she looked even better, even younger. After a few laughs (she never lost her humour) she became uncharacteristically shy, leaned forward and whispered, "I want you to do the biggest favour for me. I want you to persuade Mr. Kazan, whom I don't know, to let me audition for Geraldine's part for the National Tour of *Sweet Bird.* I want that part so bad! I'm right for it; I know it. And besides, I've already learned every word of it." I looked at her. All her usual theatricality had vanished and she was suddenly very honest and very real. Yes, she would be quite wonderful as Princess, I thought. She has all the right fire and passion. And it is scarily close to her own life. It could bring her a whole new career, give her some dignity again and some pride. "I can't wait to ask Gadge," I said; "I'm so excited." The radiance came back into her cheeks, and at that moment she looked positively beautiful.

Two nights later I saw Gadge and told him the story. "Oh, not a Barrymore," he said. "Preserve me, not a Barrymore. That's all I need!" "But Gadge, she's kicked the habit; she looks terrific and she'll work like a Trojan, I know it. And she really needs it. It'll save her life. Please see her—please!" I could tell his heart wasn't in it, but he agreed to let her audition. I called a jubilant Diana and the appointment was arranged. Several weeks went by and I'd just about forgotten the whole thing when one night Gadge wandered in for his monthly "look" at the show and we went out for a drink afterwards. "By the way, did Diana Barrymore ever audition for you?" I asked. "No," Gadge replied. "No?" I repeated incredulously. "Oh, she turned up all right. She was on time and all that," continued Gadge, "but she was so goddamn drunk they had to help her out of the theatre." My heart was in my mouth. I wanted to cry or be sick, but I couldn't do either because I was in shock. Poor darling Diana. She must have been so frightened. It had meant too much. She'd just taken one for Dutch courage and that was it—she was right back on it. A couple of months later, she was dead in her early forties.

J.B. RAN ON INTERMINABLY. It's all very well to be in a hit, one should be grateful, but—please—there is a limit! The first six months go by fairly speedily, but the next six are like pulling teeth from a dinosaur, and they begin to infect the mind. Strange things started occurring. I was standing in the wings one night whispering to Bob Downing, our stage manager, and noticed that nothing was happening on the stage. It was as if the play had stopped dead—no one was speaking. I muttered to Bob, "What the hell's going on out there? What's with that endless pause? Why is everybody standing around doing *nothing?*" "They're waiting for you," Bob replied and pushed me on.

In the Bible poor Job endures the longest, most miserable bout of suffering imaginable. As a result, to put it mildly, he is not a bundle of laughs. MacLeish's Job is an even longer role than the Good Book's and the burden of playing him over and over was taking its toll on Pat Hingle. During a matinée as I, the Devil, curse Job, pointing a menacing finger at the pathetic creature huddled in his rags, I happened to look down—no Job in sight! I had been cursing a perfectly clean, empty stage! Pat, taking his rags with him, had rolled off it, straight into the audience. I must have looked pretty stupid standing there with egg all over my face, but was momentarily saved when two hands suddenly appeared, grabbing hold of the apron, and Pat, sheepishly, climbed back on.

Two things happened to relieve the monotony. I bought myself a neat little Jaguar convertible sports and Windows Hale joined our jaded company as the new ASM. This head Boy Scout in charge of light entertainment was much needed to brighten things up. Jason Robards was just down the street in *The Disenchanted* with Rosemary Harris and his dad the Admiral in the cast, so Windows, Jimmy Olson and I would roll down there of an evening, pick him up and do the town. As well as actors, the *Disenchanted* cast also included a collection of very appetizing-looking society girls hired as extras to give the play an authentic Scott Fitzgerald look.

One such socialite who became my close friend was a statuesque, handsomely structured figure of a woman called Dorothea. She had an entrancing smile and her prematurely greyish-white hair, which was closely cropped, had a stunning effect on the natural beauty of her face. When she spoke it was in low musical tones, but because she was by nature shy, she didn't speak too often—she just looked wonderful and laughed a lot. Dorothea loved a good time more than anyone. I can't forget the image of her perched on the hood of my Jag—a noble figurehead on a ship's bow, sweater rolled up, magnificently bare-chested, laughing into the night wind as we drove hell for leather down New York's one-way streets in the wrong direction.

The Disenchanted was playing at the Cort Theatre. Many a night we sat in Jason's room discussing battle plans. Unanimously we agreed that if we systematically destroyed our separate theatres we wouldn't have to show up anymore. Whether it was to pay homage to the wild rip-roaring twenties of the Fitzgerald era or whether we were just simply Disenchanted with our lot remains a mystery, but we started with Jason's dressing room. Windows, Jason, Dorothea and myself, reviving the old "get rid of the ugly furniture" gag, one by one we passed pieces out the window onto the street below—I believe we also did the same with the carpet. It was, of course, a most satisfying experience, everyone doing his part, except Dorothea who just stood there laughing. When the room was finally emptied of everything but the bare walls, Windows for tradition's sake helped lower us one by one through the window and, grateful for a good job done, we groped our way down the street and into the night. I'm positive the old management is still looking for us.

To further relieve the monotony, I rented a house near Weston, Connecticut, by a running stream so that cast and friends could live it up on summer weekends. Ray Massey owned a marvellous old country house

*Ray, my staunch and loyal friend, in his crow's nest as God,
me below as the Devil*

and some forty acres on nearby Honey Hill Road. The property had belonged at one time to Lawrence Tibbett, the great Metropolitan Opera baritone of yore. Its main living room was a converted barn with high ceilings and a minstrels' gallery. Dorothy and Ray, who nicknamed me "Ignatius" (from that old dirty limerick Roddy McDowall had taught me), kept asking me out on days off and at last I gratefully accepted.

Ray drove me after the show that night in his dignified old Rolls-Royce and the moment we arrived I was introduced to Bungie—"Ignatius—Bungie! Bungie—Ignatius"—one of the greatest dog friends I ever came in contact with. He was an oversized Golden Lab and quite the stubbornest and most adorable of canines. Gregory Peck had given him to the Masseys as a present and no better present could any man give. That night, after Bungie and Dorothy had retired, Ray cracked open the grand old malt and we played darts rather shakily till the early hours of morning. I woke up in a huge four-poster bed to find Ray standing at its foot attired in full business suit, complete with vest and watch fob. I thought he looked a little pale. "Where are you off to, Ray?" I said. "I thought we were going to sit by the pool all day. Look out there how beautiful it is." "Last night Pat Hingle fell down an elevator shaft, and he's on the critical list." Then Ray paused, looked longingly out at the sun-drenched day and said the most typically actorish thing, "And Gol darn it, we're going to have to go in and rehearse." He didn't mean it; it just came out that way, but of course he was the first to visit Pat and continued to do so at least twice a week from then on.

Hingle had been at a party the night before, and when he left, the very overcrowded elevator he was in got stuck between floors. Feeling no pain and dying to play the hero, Pat volunteered to save the day. Just below the floor of the lift was a small opening. Pat was convinced he could crawl through it and go for help. On the way through, however, the raincoat he was wearing caught in the cables. Attempting to wrench it free, he slipped, grabbing the cable with his hand to save himself, but in the process his little finger got torn off. Letting go because of the pain, he fell at least thirty-eight feet into the machinery below. It was a mercy that he was inebriated for he fell loose and though he broke a lot of bones and was seriously concussed into the bargain, he was still miraculously alive.

Ford Rainey went on as his understudy and James Daly took over permanently, but it wasn't the same. We missed Pat's stoic magnificence in the role and his contagious Texan charm. Our little sessions in Ray's dressing room at intermissions and after shows when his dresser poured endless drinks for all of us, continued as usual, but there was a hole where Pat had been.

Now another blow hit us, for Ray's contract was up, and he was off to the West Coast to play Dr. Gillespie in the vastly successful Dr. Kildare series. "There is a young man called Richard Chamberlain in it — most promising," said Ray. "Where are you going to live?" I asked. "Oh, I'm going to have to sell the house here and live there I suppose," he answered with a wistful sadness in his voice. I could not imagine Dorothy, Ray and Bungie leaving that beautiful spot in Connecticut. It wasn't right — they belonged in the East; they were such New England people. "Why don't *you* buy it, Ignatius, and keep it in the family?" I laughed hopelessly and bade him good night; I was too choked up to stick around.

Dorothy and I put our heads together and threw him a surprise party on his last night. It was to be in the basement of the theatre and after the show we'd all coax him down there on some pretext or other. It was a huge hit. Ray was overcome—he was much loved by the company. The food was cooked at La Scala and all their waiters came and served it with scrumptious Italian wines and cases of Veuve Clicquot. The whole cast was there, Andy the doorman, Gadge and Molly Kazan, Archie MacLeish, Martin Gable, Arlene Francis, Sir Cedric Hardwicke and David Niven (both old friends of Ray's), Jason Robards, Basil and Ouida Rathbone (Basil took over from Ray), and wouldn't you know Pat Hingle was wheeled in. Some thoughtful soul (Dorothy, in fact) had arranged it with the hospital. Last but not least Bungie—Ray couldn't believe it, the tears gushing down his face. We had rented a barber's chair and we put Ray in it. Sir Cedric took one side, I the other and together we shaved his beard off—David Niven offering outrageous instructions. Everyone soon forgot why they were there and we had the time of our lives. I swear old Andy, who cleaned up the next morning, was still finishing off the liquor.

Raymond Massey has meant a great deal to me in my little life. He has always been a complete man—no frills, no fuss. From early pioneer stock, Quakers and United Empire Loyalists, who settled in Canada he, like they, steered his course by the Good Book. His prominent ancestors had gained fame and fortune manufacturing farm equipment which they supplied in great abundance to the world (Massey-Harris, then Massey Ferguson). There was no need to turn their weapons to ploughshares for ploughshares were their weapons, the weapons of wealth and power.

Raymond therefore enjoyed the required grounding, a gentleman's education—boarding school, a commission in the cavalry and chambers at Balliol College, Oxford. Yet there was no side to him. His happiest moments were when he was immersed in his carpentry or reading Trollope or merely exchanging amusing nostalgia with his cronies. As I watched him pack his things from his dressing room, it crossed my mind that this well-read, highly intelligent man, with all his background, could have been anything in life but an actor, a successful banker, lawyer, a captain of industry or, perhaps, like his brother Vincent, a governor general. Of course he would have hated all that and I was relieved, for instead I was sitting with Hamlet, Ethan Frome, Strindberg's "Father," Henry Higgins, Black Michael, Prospero, Brutus, Cardinal Richelieu and a host of such warhorses including his touching Abraham Lincoln. He had starred in some groundbreaking British films, *Things to Come, A Matter of Life and Death* and *49th Parallel.* He ran his own theatre in London, the Apollo, where he produced

With an older Ray and Joseph Cotten

the world premiere of Sean O'Casey's *The Silver Tassie;* he also directed a young Laurence Olivier in *The Rats of Norway,* wrote his own plays and even found time to sire offspring of which two, Anna and Daniel, would be counted amongst the finest actors of the English stage.

And then one day he found his last leading lady in Dorothy Ludding-ton, a lawyer by profession, whose clear sense of judgment and quick sharp wit kept him for the remainder of his days on the edge of his seat. Together with Tyrone Power, Greg Peck, Martin Gable and David Niven, they formed their own rat pack of which I was a proud mem-ber—a mysterious secret society known as IGGUMFOO (IGMFU) which literally means "I got mine fuck you." It is not quite the Fellow-ship of the Ring, the Order of Freemasons or a membership at White's or the Hell-Fire Club, but it is an affectionate nonsense and a bond.

Dorothy, Bungie and Ray are long gone now and I miss them all, but I miss him most—he was very special to me. I have often secretly thought of Ray as the likeliest candidate to play the real-life father I never really knew. But then that would make him too old. No, I shall simply continue to remember him with affection as a warm, talented, extremely lovable, slightly naughty bigger brother.

BASIL RATHBONE GAVE, in his own way, a wonderful rendering of Ray's old role. Even though he was in his seventies, Basil was in fabu-lous condition, thin, tall, athletic—after all he'd been a world-class fencer all his life. He also had tremendous energy—that old-school energy that is largely missing from the theatre today—and, of course, a glorious speaking voice. He valiantly carried on the Massey tradition— his dressing room was always open to the company and he loved telling stories—but it wasn't quite the same, it wasn't as warm. I think it tickled him pink to learn that Nigel "Willie" Bruce (his Watson in the Sherlock Holmes films) was my "coz," so for a while we got on like a house on fire.

But Ouida didn't take to me—she hadn't liked me from the start. She was outraged that my name appeared before her husband's on the theatre marquee, and she was probably right to feel that. I don't think he gave a damn—in fact I know he didn't—but she resented it bitterly and gradually saw to it that Basil and I could never be friends. Sad, but no spilt milk. It's all over now. They're gone as well and with them a whole era of Hollywood glamour.

Gone too is the great Gadge Kazan, who lived out his retirement with his books and his demons. His naming of names at the McCarthy hearings must still have plagued him as he gradually slipped into Alzheimer's. I regret that a man of such scope as a director never attempted the classics. He came close to putting on *Othello* with Sidney Poitier, even promising me Iago. But it was never done; both Poitier and he got cold feet. What an excitement of riches he could have brought to plays like *Othello, Lear,* the Greek tragedies and Chekhov, Ibsen or Strindberg. But the finger he so accurately placed on the public pulse belonged very much to his own time. He was far too busy galvanizing the contemporary theatrical scene into a significance it had not known before. He had arrived on these shores a wide-eyed immigrant in a country of immigrants. The language he knew was the rough-and-tumble language of a raw new world and he felt his duty was to paint that world as vividly and honestly as his passion would drive him.

And gone is Archie MacLeish of the light step and the quicksilver mind who lives on forever in his poems. I am never without them. No one knew better than Archie that "a poem should be motionless in time / As the moon climbs." Long after *J.B.* had closed, I recorded some of them, and he wrote me the loveliest letter. It is one of my treasures. And then to celebrate his memory years later, Alfred de Liagre asked me to write and perform a solo tribute to him at the 92nd Street Y's Poetry Center in New York. I was thrilled and honoured, and I think it is one of the happiest things I have ever done. The last thing he ever said to me was, "Be careful crossing the street."

It was hard to reconcile Archie leaving this world—almost impossible. I think it must have surprised him too; he had always remained so young. "I have the sense of infinity about me," he once wrote, and he was right—and we expected it of him.

> Dying shall never be
> Now, in the windy grass;
> Now, under shooken leaves
> Death never was.
> —"AN ETERNITY"

CHAPTER TWENTY

"CALL TO ME ALL MY SAD CAPTAINS— LET'S HAVE ONE OTHER GAUDY NIGHT"

The swan song of the fifties and the birth of the sixties were to me indistinguishable. Two whole years had joined at the hip to become one chokingly overcrowded season. And it wasn't just me; everyone I knew felt the same need to hold on to a gloriously entertaining decade that was rapidly slipping away. We all must have sensed that New York City's theatrical community would perhaps never again produce such an abundance of life, that soon its creative juices were to flow less freely and the next ten years would do little else but slowly drift into fantasy and war. So in a kind of panic we began to stretch our beloved fifties to the very limit just to see how much work and pleasure we could squeeze out of them before they became history. We saluted them at every opportunity and nowhere were these celebrations more in evidence than at P.J. Clarke's on Fifty-fifth and Third.

This already familiar watering hole had been made even more famous by the great Billy Wilder, who had shot his film The Lost Week-

end there in the midforties. Owned and operated by that big-hearted, booze-loving, horse-bettin' pussy cat, Danny Lavezzo, P.J.'s became our sentimental headquarters. It was a regular diversion for the most bizarre assortment of night owls. Dress code was wildly optional—tux, white tie and tails, dungarees, jeans, plunging necklines—even drag. P.J.'s might as well have been my permanent address. Every chili con carne, bacon cheeseburger or London broil (the best in town) should have been accompanied by special P.J. stationery. The front room and the bar often overflowed with team members of the Giants, the Knicks and the Mets, and the tough, wiscracking waiters knew everyone by name and doubled as nannies and bouncers. Of course, there was always "21," "Cheerios," Malachy's, Allen's, Jim Downey's, Harold's Show Spot or distant Harlem, but the infinite variety at P.J.'s never staled and most of us found ourselves nightly homing in on it, like bees to their queen.

In the back room, which had its own entrance, no tourists or strangers were permitted. There was always some good-natured Cerberus on duty to screen all oncomers and the big round table by the bar, Danny's table, the "in" table, was the constant focus of attention. Danny kindly saw to it that I always had a seat, so I'd usually find myself rustling feathers with a gaggle of fast-living, fun-loving geese. My favourites: Elaine Stritch and Ben Gazzara—a new item and a good rowdy one at that—Robards, of course, Jack Warden, Peter Falk, Gig Young and sometimes Rosalind Russell's husband, Freddie Brisson, that sly, conniving Dane who was wickedly nicknamed the "Lizard of Roz." On the music side, I'd find myself sitting next to Gerry Mulligan or Stan Getz; the great baritone from the Met, Robert Merrill, or Leonard Bernstein with his serenely beautiful better half—Felicia Montealegre. Several well-known pugilists had adopted it as their second home, as had the odd New York Ranger and, once or twice, baseball hero Joe DiMaggio, with breathtaking Marilyn on his arm.

Other visitations were from the fresh new comedy team of Nichols and May (Mike Nichols and Elaine May), who had taken the town by storm, and the captivating British pair Flanders and Swann, two gentlemen famed for their witty song and patter routine; Mr. Swann—the silent one—and stout Mr. Flanders, who, oblivious to the wheelchair to which he was sentenced for life, merrily tossed about epigrams like so much confetti. Also producers Alexander Cohen and his wife, Hildy, Ratty Whitehead and Morton Gottlieb—writers Arthur Miller, Tennessee Williams, Truman Capote and Gore Vidal, quelques fois but never at the same table if possible. Ever present was a young Johnny Carson before he ruled the late-night airways and dear Joe Allen, poised to launch his worldwide empire of checkered tablecloths. Shelley Winters with Tony Franciosa would sashay in as would playwright/actor Mike Gazzo (A Hatful of Rain), the great Zero Mostel, comic Milton Berle (when he wasn't at Toots Shor's), Sid Caesar, Art Carney, the perennial Steve Allen and Jules Munshin.

My pal Jones Harris, Ruth Gordon's son, occasionally brought his famous dad, Jed Harris, producer extraordinaire and the onetime terror of Broadway who, by now, had disappointingly mellowed. The caustic Jonesy, champion of mockery, cunning mixer and first-class troubleshooter, had inherited his father's legendary rudeness. Born illegitimate, he derived a macabre pleasure from playing his bastardy to the hilt. It would have disgusted him to learn we'd found a soft spot in him, that beneath the ice was a warm world smoldering away, anxious to melt the surface but rarely succeeding. I think he enjoyed "slumming" with us theatricals because he was, in many ways, an artist manqué. Quick-witted and stimulating, he kept us, conversationally, on our toes, always taking the opposite view, and he got a particular kick from our irreverent imitations of well-known personalities—mine of Ray Massey and Peter Lorre and Jason's of Humphrey Bogart and Ralph Richardson.

At the end of that old British film chestnut The Four Feathers, Richardson, blinded in battle, sitting in his London club, tired and alone, despairs that all his favourite Bengal Lancers have perished in the war. At that moment, news arrives that two of his closest comrades from the regiment have survived. Rising unsteadily to his feet he exclaims in a voice that captures the entire Edwardian era and the glory of the Raj in one magisterial inflection: "Peter alive?—and Willoughby??? Peetah alaive?—and Willowbay-ay-ay???" As only he could do it, Sir Ralph stretched out the line to infinity and beyond. We got to be quite expert at it and it became a sort of private code between the three of us. Once, when running for my life to catch a plane, an announcement came over the Tannoy: "Would C. Plummer report to the information desk at once. There is a most urgent message for him." It sounded pretty ominous so I doubled back as fast as I could only to discover it was from the diabolical Jonesy and it read: "Latest dispatch—no need for alarm—Peter's alive—and Willoughby." I missed my plane.

A permanent fixture at P.J.'s was killer columnist Dorothy Kilgallen, queen of gossip, with her sharp little pointed face and even sharper little pointed pen. Her darting lizard eyes scanned the room to see who was having who so she could embarrass them in print. No matter who you were with, to Miss Kilgallen it was an assignation of the most lecherous nature. You could be sitting next to a nun or even your grandmother—you were dead meat! Her insinuating ink never dried. And representing her male opposition were Earl Wilson, always with some tall showgirl–enfant prodige; the eccentrically lovable Leo Lerman (*Vogue*), a cross between Oscar Wilde and King Farouk; sometimes Walter Winchell; crusty old Ward Morehouse; society columnist Doris Lilly and Leonard Lyons of the *Post* on his "rounds," the fairest of all showbiz reporters, who loved and protected our profession with an aggressive and genuine zeal—a true gentleman of the press.

Amongst the steadiest customers (though not always so steady on their pins) were producer-actor Martin Gabel of cynical wit and stentorian tones and the talented and magical Robert Preston, just about the best friend anyone could ever have, who will always be sorely missed along the "street." Very frequently, stunning Vivica Lindfors would drop by with her fun-loving Hungarian spouse, playwright George Tabori, and the two teddy bears, Budd Schulberg and Harvey Breit habitually checked in; Harvey and his exotic wife, Pat Rinehart, owned the most elegant little Rolls-Royce I have ever seen—a miniature Phantom from the thirties in black and garnet with the chauffeur's seat open to the sky. Quel bijou! I leched after it madly and every time I saw it I tried to kick a hole in my poor inoffensive little Jag.

This was the dimly lit den where I began my pleasant associations with that beloved pillar of Broadway itself, caricaturist Al Hirschfeld, set and costume designers Oliver Smith, Boris Aronson, Ben Edwards and Jane Greenwood, Peter Larkin, Ringling Brothers' elegant Miles White of the long cigarette holder and Ann Roth, pert and delectable, brandishing hers, the splendidly mad Irishman Sean Kenny, an aspiring cohort, and once in a blue moon, languidly lolling beneath his wide-brimmed picture hat, the very grand but warmly disposed Cecil Beaton. Superstar press agents Ben Sonnenberg (J&B whiskey, ocean liners, world governments and, it was widely rumoured, Mussolini had been his clients), Richard Maney, Henry Rogers, Warren Cowan, the smooth, laid-back Rupert Allan, who would one day look after me, and the infamous Jim Moran, who had once hired numerous bald-headed men and deliberately placed them in the Metropolitan Opera's orchestra seats one particularly chic opening night in such a way that to the entire audience gazing down from the tiers above, they spelled S-H-I-T.

As if we all came from the same side of the footlights, theatre critics could be seen hobnobbing with us actor folk—John MacLean of the *Daily News,* Henry Hewes of the *Saturday Review,* Kenneth Tynan (*The New Yorker*) and the *Herald Tribune*'s Walter Kerr. Two of F. Scott Fitzgerald's mistresses visited P.J.'s separately, the diminutive and deceptively young Anita (*Gentlemen Prefer Blondes*) Loos and the much-lived-in Sheila Graham (Hollywood columnist and author), who was a poppet and very kind to me. In that age of heavy gossip power, it was necessary to have someone like Sheila on your side to rescue you from the claws of such predators as Louella Parsons and Hedda Hopper.

Lillian Hellman occasionally slummed it, as did her archenemy, novelist Mary McCarthy on the arm of her brother Kevin. The wonderfully deranged Trevor Howard (brilliant British actor and friend) was there, outconsuming everyone from his customary place in the front bar which never lacked for action—the football teams heavily immersed in disagreements, every now and then a minor scuffle breaking out but always Trevor's voice rising above the din barking mock military commands and greeting everyone with a jovial, "Ah, there you are—Sporting!" It wasn't such a great idea to get into a sports debate with the boys in the front room. Once, a few years later, when Attorney General Robert Kennedy came in with Marilyn Monroe (there were more secret service than waiters), one of his security guards got into an argument at the bar and was thrown clean through the front door right under what used to be the Third Avenue El.

As part of the passing parade you could easily bump into Steve Sondheim, Harry Kurnitz, Adolph Green and Betty Comden, and of course Billy Wilder, who had more right to be there than anyone. Like a clap of thunder, a deep resonant voice behind me yelled out, "ALLO! Mon T'i Coq! Camaw Sa Vaw! Chris de Calvert." It was Franchot Tone in his best French Canadian joual accent, sharing a table with his latest demoiselle in distress. They were all so beautiful, Franchot's ladies— the price he paid for having his heart slowly eaten away. And then all the city's top cops it seemed made P.J.'s their hangout, heads of the vice squad, inspectors, homicide chiefs. The charming lopsided old brick building so bulged at the seams with constabulary, it was solidly guaranteed never to close.

I remember one late Saturday night bash in the "after-hours" room below street level at which beloved composer Jule Styne shared the piano with Jack Lemmon, all of us belting our current favourites until 8:00 a.m. Sunday morning when, collectively, we melted into the streets like zombies under a blinding sun. Jack insisted on going straight to Mass. He was adamant! Not having a clue where to go, he staggered off in no particular direction. "But Jack," we called out after him, "you're not even Catholic!"

For after-the-show pub crawls I sometimes forsook my Jag for Windows Hale's motorcycle, he being the designated driver. Jason, who, with Maureen Stapleton, was currently starring in Lillian Hellman's *Toys in the Attic,* or "Toys in the Cellar," as he called it, would join us and we would hold on for dear life as Windows hurtled us through Gotham's streets at warp speed. On one particular occasion, anxious to get to P.J.'s, the three of us decided it would expedite matters if we drove the bike right through the back door straight to our table without hurting anyone. This might have been accomplished with a certain flourish had not the bike hit the unyielding pavement with such jarring force we were instantly catapulted through the door and landed with amazing accuracy into three conveniently empty chairs. Without wincing or skipping a beat, we ordered triple Jack Daniel's with beer chasers, the crippled bike still rattling about in agony on the pavement outside.

AS EAGER TO WORK as I was desperate to play, I threw myself at the boob tube with a great assist from the ever-watchful Jane Broder. Young George Morris from her TV department had quit and left her in the lurch so the aging yet dynamic Jane, swallowing her pride, resigned herself to the shame of handling television which, of course, she managed as expertly as she managed everything else. *The Autocrat of the Breakfast Table,* a TV study of Oliver Wendell Holmes and his austere father, united me once more with Sir Cedric Hardwicke (playing Dad) and introduced me to my beautiful new leading lady, Anne Francis, the prettiest robot the screen has ever produced (*Forbidden Planet*). The iridescent Julie Harris and I did two shows back-to-back—Ibsen's *A Doll's House,* in which, as Nora, Julie touched all hearts, and *Johnny Belinda,* where she was equally moving as the deaf-mute. Desperate to differ from Lew Ayres in the movie version of *Johnny Belinda,* I played the doctor with a French Canadian accent you could have cut with a knife. The ever-faithful and tasteful George Schaefer, who directed both, had assembled for *A Doll's House* Jason Robards, Eileen Heckart and Hume Cronyn, each one a superlative complement to the piece. Due to an overly long night, Jason and I missed the crucial camera walk-through

The cast of A Doll's House —*Robards, me, Julie, Eileen Heckart, Hume Cronyn*

on the show date, throwing everyone into a conniption, but wreathed in a profusion of apologies we made the 'air' all right and a slice of television history into the bargain.

Anthony Hope's Ruritanian romance *The Prisoner of Zenda* in which I portrayed the dual roles of Rassendyll and the king, as close to Ronald Colman as I dared, brought me together again with my old friend John Williams, who had just recently as the inspector in *Dial M for Murder* successfully stolen Hitchcock's film. My lady this time was the Swedish beauty Inger Stevens, the first girl I'd ever met who'd been forced to pay alimony to her husband, a somewhat sleazy Hollywood 10-percenter. I vowed if I ever met the cad, I'd nickel-and-dime him to death. Next came *The Philadelphia Story,* with that charming, gifted bounder, Gig Young, whose throwaway humour both on- and offscreen made him, in my view, the best light comedian in America after Cary Grant. The gregarious Fielder Cook was our director and, in the Katharine Hepburn role of Tracy Lord was pert, adorable Diana Lynn, whose prodigious accomplishments on the piano could, had she wished it, have rewarded her with a brilliant concert career.

It seemed that every major television drama was conceived in that ramshackle old building on Second Avenue and Seventh known as Central Plaza. Like one big happy family we all worked, horsed around and practically lived within its peeling walls and often late into the night we would return there to hear Conrad Janis on his hot trombone pucker up some mean jazz with his group, which he called the Tailgate Five. Central Plaza was owned by a fellow called Bernie (no one ever seemed to know his last name) who, in the spirit of an old retainer, tended to our every whim. Everyone would gather at the end of a day's work and crowd into his tiny office on the third floor where he kept an open running bar day and night. Perhaps he just wanted to be around show people; I don't know and I don't care, but Bernie to me was one of the kindest souls I've ever known.

Everything was available to us at Bernie's Second Avenue headquarters: Ratner's downstairs for great kosher lunches thrown at you by traditionally insulting waiters; ancient Moscovitz and Lubowitz down the road for delicious Polish Jewish nosh; Jon's on Tenth for Italian and up the street historic McSorley's pub (men only) which offered sawdust on the floor, cheese and onion sandwiches and a veritable Niagara of beer on tap. The best restaurant by far, however, was Luchow's for top German and Danish cuisine, every known herring, every kind of aquavit, smoked sturgeon, succulent bratwursts, weiner schnitzels and a rich wine cellar. José Ferrer had introduced me to it, and it's the one establishment I think I miss most in New York with its big round tables, its high beamed ceilings, dark panelled walls and the long ornate oak bar framed in gleaming brass.

This whole section of town all the way down to the Bowery had once been ruled and dominated by the Yiddish theatre. These were the streets upon which Jacob Ben-Ami, Maurice Schwartz and the famous Adler family had all made history. This is where I had seen the fabulous Molly Picon, mama of all vaudevillians, and that slippery smooth comic, the sour cream on the Borscht Belt circuit, Myron Cohen. There were one or two derelict old theatres still standing, but most of them by now had gone away with the passing of tradition.

Out from this cabal many years past had emerged the young Muni Weisenfreund, better known as Paul Muni, the Academy Award winner famous for portraying biographical figures. Mr. Muni had now decided to slum and do television. It was called *A Letter from the Queen* and both Polly Bergen and I played the young leads. It was fascinating to watch Muni's work process. Now that he was older, he learned his lines by listening to a tape of himself reading the role. He brought this recorder to rehearsal and would stop every few moments to replay bits over and over again. Once in the studio, however, Mr. Muni came into his own—he took over. He knew every light on the set and where they should be directed, often suggesting adjustments himself. Though he was quite frail and extremely deaf, he still gave a really strong and remarkably touching performance, doubly moving because he paused before his every line and the expressions that chased across his face told stories of unimagined suffering and pain. Actually, the pauses were there simply because someone in the control room was reading each of his lines into his earphone before he spoke them. Muni was a master at hogging screen time—what a devilish old trickster he was! So indeed was Polly Bergen, for when it was all over, she instantly became a star turn on her very own TV show.

I remember a TV adaptation of *The Oresteia* of Euripides, in which I essayed both the roles of Orestes and Agamemnon—my Clytemnestra, that powerhouse of lady performers, the statuesque Irene Worth. Irene, who spoke the English tongue with more precision and perfection than most Brits, was, ironically, an American, born in Nebraska, who had begun as a schoolteacher. This had not deterred her from taking out British citizenry and becoming one of England's very finest classical actresses. Much later she would grace the Honours list as a Dame. There was still a residue of the schoolmarm about her, however, for when I resorted to some four-letter words in her presence, she chastised me by snapping, "Christopher, go and wash your mouth out with soap at once!" That was small-town Nebraska coming out and a trifle unfair, I thought, for just the day before I'd caught her using language that would have made a coal miner blush.

THOUGH I WAS AS BUSY as a bird dog—actors live to be busy—I suppose I didn't have much center in my life. I was about as restless as the time I was living in, driven along, God knows where. Sometimes I would go home to Bank Street, now mostly empty except for little Amanda and the nanny when they weren't at her grandmother's. Otherwise, I would stay at the Algonquin. Tammy, too, was rarely at home—we had really distanced ourselves and, after all, she was at the moment being the toast of the town. She was packing them in at the Plaza and

Amanda P. about to leap into the world

the Blue Angel and Meredith Wilson's *The Unsinkable Molly Brown* had opened to raves and had made her a Broadway star. She was to win all sorts of prizes, and Walter Kerr in his *Tribune* review had suggested that for everyone to be happy they should have a Tammy Grimes at home. Well, I had a Tammy Grimes at home and that was terrific and we'd had a baby girl and that too was terrific, but the theatre and our careers consumed our attention and we'd now grown further and further apart. I was a lousy husband and an even worse father and Tam's and my life together was clearly over. In fact, she was now quite serious about someone else.

In the Algonquin lobby, I bumped into Kenneth Tynan. He was then drama critic for *The New Yorker* and was temporarily staying at the hotel. "I h-hear you and T-Tammy are separating," he said with his famous stutter. "Well—" I began. He cut across, "So are w-we." He was referring to his wife, Elaine Dundy, a bright young American writer, who had had her moment in the sun with a little book called *The Dud Avocado.* I couldn't help thinking how like two dud avocados we both must look, and I think I said so.

I had always admired Ken Tynan even though he represented the enemy. He'd been most complimentary to me in print upon occasion which, of course, made me admire him even more. His knowledge and intellect were streaks ahead of most critics, and as a master of prose he rivalled the great James Agate and Alexander Woollcott. Reading a Tynan review was sometimes far more entertaining than the show he was critiquing. When Vivien Leigh played a very slight, barely audible Cleopatra opposite her towering husband, Olivier, he wrote, "I am dying Egypt—dying to hear what you're saying." He had once aptly described Sir John Gielgud as "the glass eye in the forehead of English acting" and Noël Coward as "the monocle of all he surveys."

But now here we both were, at our most vulnerable, staring at each other in the lobby and Ken, a connoisseur of food and wine, took charge: "Let's indulge ourselves in a g-great d-dinner! Afterwards, I'll show you the f-funniest man I've seen in a long time." The Forum of the Twelve Caesars was a hot, new and outrageously priced eating hole with a different course for every Caesar. Feeling sorry for ourselves, and ravenous, we demolished all twelve Caesars and staggered down to the Village Vanguard, where we sat, waiting for the hilarity to begin.

Professor Irwin Corey, billed as "The World's Foremost Authority," was one of the funniest clowns on the scene. His irreverence for the audience, his rubber face, his outlandish clothes and his wicked mockery of all that smacks of pretension were, in themselves, a tragicomedy of gargantuan proportions. His lectures on the Bible, for instance, were masterpieces of sacrilegious nonsense. His opening alone was worth the price of admission. He enters and stands by the piano, hopelessly attempting to speak. His expressions change from confusion, longing and pain to complacency, boredom and exasperation. For a solid five minutes at least, there is utter silence until he finally breaks it with one single word—"However." It seems another five minutes before we stopped laughing. In return, I took Ken to hear Mabel Mercer, whom I'd worshipped since Montreal days. She had her own "room" in town, which was filled to capacity every night with a loyal and elegant clientele. Mabel was a short stocky black lady who spoke in a broad North Country dialect which was as delightful as it was unexpected. When she sang, however, her velvet tones were cloaked in a highly sophisticated style—her phrasing quite unique and wonderfully off the beat. Often I would see Sinatra, Mel Tormé or Perry Como sitting amongst the crowd, listening intently, admirers all. Many of the great songwriters had written specially for her, Cole Porter among them, and when she sang her own particular favourites such as "Did You Ever Cross

Over to Snedens," "On the First Warm Day in May," "Wait Till You See Her" or "Blame It on My Youth," New York belonged to her.

Kenneth and I had one or two more dates together as bachelors out in the cold, but it was getting depressing—it reminded us both of our losses. Was I to spend the rest of my nights dating male critics? I don't think so! Tammy had found someone she cared for, so it was high time I secured for myself a steady companion from the ranks of the fairer sex. I found her—on the slopes of Hunter Mountain.

SHE WAS RESTING on her skis—straight and tall, her ski poles in one hand. It struck me what great poise she had, unlike most girls her age or even older; and those wise, seductive, knowing eyes gave the instant impression that she had seen the world. Susan Blanchard Fonda was the daughter of Dorothy Blanchard, a warm, strikingly lovely Australian lady, who had been happily married to the legendary Oscar Hammerstein. Susan was, therefore, Oscar's stepdaughter. I had met her once before under somewhat strange and unpleasant circumstances. It was at the height of a very large and rowdy party and in the middle of all the raucousness stood this patrician beauty looking on with detached amusement and a dignity far in advance of her years. She was a trifle deaf, I discovered, and in order to speak to her I had to stand quite close, which was, to put it mildly, not the most unpleasant thing in the world.

I asked if she was by chance related to Henry Fonda and she answered softly, "I was once his wife." Having had several drinks too many, I did something so inexplicably rude and rash that I have never really lived it down. Spotting Hank Fonda in the distance standing at the bar, I grabbed her by the hand and pulled her over to him, saying boldly and loudly, "May I introduce you two? Susan—Henry, Henry—Susan! What the hell did you ever leave her for? She's gorgeous!" (or words to that effect). Hank let out an ear-piercing scream of half-mock horror and I felt Susan's hand leave mine as she turned and walked away. What came over me, I'll never know! I was drunk, of course, and I suppose I had wanted to show off in front of her or get a laugh or something. I can't imagine what, but never before had I felt quite so stupidly young. I left the party.

It was becoming frigid on the slopes, and it was my one and only chance. Apologies poured out of me as I tried to find excuses for my repulsive behavior on that embarrassing evening. She looked at me for the longest time. The cold didn't seem to affect her. There was an aura of serenity about Susan. She gave me the most wonderfully slow, forgiving smile and together we skied back down to the hotel.

HUNTER MOUNTAIN was more of a hill than a mountain, but steep enough to warrant chairlifts and a couple of decent runs for skiers who didn't want to always travel up to Snow Ridge, Stowe or Lake Placid. It was literally a snowball's throw from Manhattan. Jimmy Hammerstein, with a few pals including Larry Hagman and John Mckay, had bought the mountain and converted it into a miniature ski resort complete with artificial snow, some cabins and a ski lodge. It was all rather "in," everyone mostly knew everyone else. Susan and I saw a lot of each other up there that winter, and back in Manhattan, she took me to all sorts of parties—she was the most sought-after young lady—she even took me home to meet Dorothy and Oscar, who instantly made me feel I was part of the family. Susan was passionate about painting, cooking, music and theatre. She was terribly intelligent, marvelous company, listened so beautifully, fed the ego, and there was something deep inside her that was most calming, reassuring, comforting. I confess—I was smitten!

The pace and urgency of that season had inspired other such partnerships. Jason and Lauren Bacall had now met, formed an instant tryst and seemed distinctly marriage-bound. Laurence Olivier, sans Vivien Leigh, had fallen in love with Joan Plowright, who had been playing *A Taste of Honey* in New York; they too were ready to tie the knot. Sometimes the six of us shared late after-show suppers at Orsini's, watched over by its owner—that handsome princely Roman, Armando Orsini. Jase and Betty never ceased to jostle and maneuver the subject of marriage in Susan's and my direction—once going as far as suggesting a double wedding!

Susan came with me to California, where I was to play Black Paquito opposite Greer Garson in the Hallmark Hall of Fame's production of Shaw's *Captain Brassbound's Conversion*. Dear, generous Greer, one of my favourite movie stars ever (*Pride and Prejudice*, *Random Harvest*) was a most remarkable woman; her ceaseless work for charity and the joy she got out of life were staggering. She kept saying how our little company of classically trained actors—George Rose, Liam Redmond and I—reminded her of being back at the Old Vic. "I started there, you know," she said with great pride. Greer never stopped asking me to visit her and her husband, Buddy Fogelson, at their enormous Texas ranch and I

Greer Garson, George Rose and me in Captain Brassbound's Conversion

could kick myself that I never was able to do so. Greer wrote me the most wonderful letter of encouragement I have ever received—I still keep it safe, under lock and key. This is one lady I wished could have been my friend. Of course, Greer instantly bonded with Susan, as I knew she would, and took up our cause at once, matchmaking with a vengeance. Poor Susan. I really couldn't judge how she felt; she was always so quiet about private things—in fact I don't even know if the subject had ever entered her mind. I knew she would make someone the most unselfish and devoted wife, but I also knew I wasn't worthy of her. I needed to be made of sterner stuff. Still inclined to sow my wild oats, I simply wasn't grown-up enough for the truly serious commitment she rightly deserved.

So climbing down from our fictitious wedding cake, we remained instead, I like to think, the best of friends.

"I GOTTA CALL from Alan Jay Lerner, honey. He wants to know if you'd like to be in his new musical." It was Jane on the telephone. Alan

Alan Jay Lermer — determined to have me sing. Brave man!

had always seemed to like my work, for some reason, and I wasn't about to give him an argument. It all began when, in 1956, he, Frederick Loewe, Herman Levin and Moss Hart asked me to do a number from *My Fair Lady*. They wanted me to take over Rex Harrison's role of Henry Higgins in New York and then do the national tour. I had just seen this miraculous new hit a few nights before and had been swept away by it. It is still, arguably, the most perfect musical ever conceived. One moment of supreme theatre magic occurred when a young Julie Andrews as Eliza stands on the stage, alone and vulnerable, in a single spot and softly sings "I Could Have Danced All Night." It was as if she'd flown all the way up to the balcony where I was sitting and sang to me alone.

The other fascination was watching the polished Mr. Harrison give the performance of his life. The part of Higgins fitted him like a glove; he owned every Anglo-Saxon attitude of it. Rex's rhythms were imbedded into the score forever. For Lerner, Loewe, Hart and Levin, I was to perform "I've Grown Accustomed to Her Face." What the hell was I to do? There was only one thing—sing where Rex talked and talk where Rex sang! It worked. The famous foursome were most complimentary until they were reminded I was a tad young at twenty-six, so we mutually parted company.

Now Alan Jay was after me again. This time it was *Camelot*. They had not begun rehearsal and at this point it was titled "Jenny Kissed Me." The whole thing was inspired by T. H. White's *The Once and Future King*. Richard Burton and Julie Andrews were set as King Arthur and Guinevere and I could play Lancelot if I was a good boy and my singing passed muster. They first showed me the extraordinary costume designs the great Adrian had created. They were fascinating, subtle, mystic and distant—the watercolours of the Russell Flint illustrations. Lancelot had a dark swarthy look and, true to Arthurian legend, sported a withered arm. I was, needless to say, somewhat keen. In contrast to Burton's conversational style, my songs were to have a wider range—but how on earth was I to manage this? Determined to give a good showing, I worked like a dog on "Till There Was You" from *The Music Man* helped along by a whip-cracking coach.

The day arrived—I walked out onstage. Moss Hart greeted me like an old friend (he was such a gent); Alan and Herman waved to me from out front and "Fritz" Loewe was seated at the piano. I got through it the best I could, and when it was over, to cover the pause that hung in the air, I asked Fritz in what range he would place my singing voice. He looked at me with those wicked, cynical Viennese eyes of his and said, "Somewhere in ze middle—no highs—no lows!" Of course, it was all so foolish; I could never have achieved the operatic range the role demanded—I could just about carry a tune, for God's sake—but I like to think that I pushed Robert Goulet into stardom. Goulet, mon compatriot Canadien, opened as Lancelot to popular acclaim, his powerful baritone soaring above the jousting fields like a windswept banner; dear Roddy McDowall wittily played the villain Mordred; Burton rumbled magnificently as Arthur and Julie A. was a Guinevere as fresh as an English rose. But sadly the great Adrian had passed away before the production had time to flower and his inspired, darkly muted designs were forsaken for a rather garish chocolate-box look that only put the accent on the word *future* in *The Once and Future King*.

MEETING KATHARINE HEPBURN is like being hit by a warm sirocco. She is as natural a phenomenon as the Great Geyser or Old Faithful himself. I was summoned to her house in Turtle Bay on Manhattan's East Forty-ninth, a street I knew well, for Garson Kanin and Ruth Gordon lived next door but one, and I had visited there many times. Tea was being served and Miss Hepburn rolled in wearing a safari suit and sneakers. As it's not possible to try to match a quarter of the force of her personality, I sat quietly like a marooned sailor and let the storm wash over me. She was about to play Cleopatra to Robert Ryan's Antony and wanted me for Enobarbus; and though it would have been a rare experience to work with her, the truth of the matter is, I had better parts offered to me that summer. I was mulling this over and wondering how I could tell her when I remembered the story of how John Barrymore and she were at each other's throats during the filming of *A Bill of Divorcement*. On the last day of shooting, as the story goes, Hepburn had allegedly said, "Mr. Barrymore, I shall never act with you again," whereupon he allegedly responded, "Miss Hepburn, dahling, I didn't know you had!" I also remembered once thinking that in an ideal world, what a marvellous Mark Antony Barrymore would have made—a ruined crater of a man. I mentioned this to Miss Hepburn and she curtly nodded in agreement. I then boldly inquired if there was any truth to the rumour that they were always feuding. Her voice became a tone higher. "Absolutely none whatever," she flung back at me as if to close the subject forever. "John Barrymore was one of the gentlest men I have ever known, and he couldn't have been kinder to me!"

She continued, wound up now, in that famous voice of hers with its ever-present tremolo. "I was very young and had the lead opposite a man that every actress in the world would have given her eye teeth to work with. I had not yet met him—indeed I wasn't to meet him until the day we shot our first scene together. George Cukor [the director] told me not to wear shoes as I was taller than Jack, so I complied and when everything was ready, I waited breathlessly for his entrance." In the scene, Barrymore, as her father, comes home after being released from a sanitarium where he has spent many years with a severe loss of memory. He walks into the living room and carefully examines the objects on the mantel, photographs, knickknacks, anything that can remind him of where he is and who he is. He turns and suddenly sees a girl sitting on the couch. After a long and searching pause, he says, shakily, "I'm not sure but I think you're my daughter."

Kate Hepburn waited as Jack's stand-in rehearsed all this business over and over—still no Jack. Then finally it was time for the first take and at last Barrymore himself came into the room. Kate was on tenterhooks. He repeated the business exactly as his stand-in had rehearsed, turned, looked at Kate, said his line and she immediately burst into floods of tears. "Why? Because he was so marvellous?" I ventured. "No," she replied, "because he was so bad. He was awful, mechanical, just going through the motions, and he looked so spent—so embittered. Cukor said, 'Cut,' and Jack came over to me, saw the look of disappointment on my face and said, 'Young lady, I do believe you really care.' Then he turned to George and said, 'I want to do it again.' He did the same thing and though I wasn't supposed to, I cried all over again because this time he was absolutely wonderful! From that moment on, he went out of his way to let the camera favour me—he did everything he could to get the focus on to me. 'It's your picture,' he kept saying. Dear, generous Jack—he helped make me a star."

Well, I had been properly chastened, and as I sat in that living room listening to Miss Hepburn tell her stories and weave her particular spell, I realized that this one afternoon with her alone was worth ten Cleopatras and that I would never forget it.

THRUSTING MY REGRETS ASIDE, I opted for another dose of Shakespearean medicine at my favourite northern Stratford, this time as the Bastard in *King John* and Mercutio in *Romeo and Juliet*. To travel the nine-hour journey by road, and to satisfy my lifelong passion for cars, I bought myself a classic gem called an Invicta. Created in the twenties through the joint forces of Railton and Bentley, it was the first British car to reach 100 mph. Mine was a later model—a 1931 touring open sports E type classed as vintage—long, low and sleek. It was black with red upholstered leather interior, red spoked wheels and shiny chrome accessories. Its chassis was made of a metal as soft and malleable as suede and, with the exception of one Aston Martin carburetor, its otherwise original engine purred with authenticity, incredibly allowing the car to gather speed going up hills in high gear. I had paid a mere twenty-five hundred dollars for this museum piece from a madman called John Stix, who claimed he needed the money for analysis—I could understand why. For a spell, I derived great delight from driving it around Manhattan, stopping traffic all over town. At every red light people would come over and demand to know what it was. I finally got so sick of this that I mumbled incoherently to anyone who asked that it was a "Motherfucker 31."

Vincent Sardi, who collected antique cars, put me in touch with a master mechanic, the British racer Stirling Moss's right-hand man, whom *Time* magazine had just named "Mechanic of the Year." He happened to be working at Inskip (MGs, Rolls-Royces) in New York, so I brought him my beauty to look at. He approved, gave it a thorough once-over, told me to call him every so often and report progress. Too nervous to swing it alone, I commandeered Windows Hale to take turns driving and be my support. Good old Jane Broder, who had little or no interest in automobiles of any kind, gave it and me her blessing, waved good-bye and called out, "I'll track down some warehouses, don't you worry, honey, when you get back, it'll have a roof over its head."

We had hardly reached the New York Thruway when the rains came! Like an idiot, I'd left the side flaps behind and though the hood was up it made no difference—we were drenched. The roads began to seriously flood but the old car behaved impeccably, even passing brand-new Cadillacs and Mercedes pulled over on the side. The sun came out around Binghamton, dried things up a bit, but suddenly blue flames began to spurt from the engine. I was sure we were about to blow up so, pulling over at a gas station, I called Moss's man, as promised. "Stick wads of chewing gum in the exhaust," the mad genius barked into the phone. Hardly convinced, I nonetheless obeyed orders and, wouldn't you know, we rolled on without incident all the way to Stratford town as smooth as silk!

HALFWAY THROUGH the rehearsal period, I was leaving the theatre one night when I noticed an attractive dark-haired girl sitting by the stage door. "Don't you remember me?" she called out as I passed. I looked back—by God, if it wasn't Memory Mellons from the Everglades in person! It had been only a year and a bit, but she was prettier than ever and, my, how she'd grown up. "Who are you waiting for?" I asked. "Who do you think?" she replied with that taunting little rebuke of a smile I remembered so well. Her deep tan looked oddly out of place beside us pale-faced theatre-bound victims, and clothes-wise she was clearly ahead of her time, for the briefest of skirts she was wearing anticipated the much later arrival of the infamous hot pants and mini-jupe. Of course, it was not solely for this I was glad to see her but for the casual and undemanding companionship she was to offer me, which turned out to be as natural and as effortless as waking up in the morning. My roommate for the second time, Uncle Exeter (Bob Goodier), whose wisdom in such matters was exceeded by none, gallantly withdrew, and I happily settled down to a summer dominated by my three romances—Shakespeare, Memory Mellons and the black and scarlet winged chariot that had so nobly borne me to it in the first place.

King John is another of Shakespeare's few plays that could have been written by committee. There is little of the familiar flow of language; it is staccato throughout. There is also at times an unaccustomed coldness and a totally foreign style. My character, the Bastard, though great fun to play, seemed not to belong in the story at all—there was no way to link him convincingly with the rest of the characters. Very much an outsider, he continuously comments in a series of tongue-in-cheek soliloquies on the play's action rather like a cynical Greek chorus.

A gentleman in a white tropical suit seated in the very front row one night was following the play by reading a copy of the *King John* text while we, poor sods, were trying to act our hearts out. It was clear that our performance meant nothing to him, for the moment we stopped speaking he would look up and the moment we spoke again he returned to the text. As there were several major textual cuts in our production, the gentleman had terrible problems keeping up with us and would constantly lose his place; he would then make the most appalling racket as he violently turned his pages in a frantic effort to get back on track. This had begun to irritate the audience as well as ourselves. Not able to take much more of it, I waited till I was alone for one of my many soliloquies; then in the middle of it I walked up to him, snatched the offending text from his hand, held it up on the point of my sword so the entire audience could see, then with a great flourish, hurled it down the tunnel. I got an instant ovation and when the applause had died down, I looked back but the man in the white suit had gone.

How things backfire! I later discovered that after leaving his seat, the gentleman had sought out the theatre manager, apologized profusely for the disturbance he had caused and asked if there was anything he could do to make amends. It appeared that he had just recently been released from prison for swindling a large amount of jewels, had loved the theatre all his life and that *King John* was the first play he had attended in all the years he'd been behind bars. It was one of the works of the Bard with which he was not familiar, and so the better to understand it, he had brought along his text. Well, I need hardly say, I felt so small I could have donned an archbishop's mitre and walked upright under the pope's cassock.

King John will never be a crowd pleaser simply because its main line is obscure, and the enigmatic central character (in our production wonderfully played by Douglas Rain) can wrest little sympathy from the audience. I confess I prefer A. A. Milne's more touching nursery rhyme concerning poor unpopular King John, who, finding his Christmas stocking always empty, climbs onto the roof and leaves a message for Santa propped against the chimney:

> *I want some crackers,*
> *And I want some candy;*
> *I think a box of chocolates*
> *Would come in handy;*

> *I don't mind oranges,*
> *I do like nuts!*
> *And I SHOULD like a pocket-knife*
> *That really cuts.*
> *And, oh! Father Christmas, if you love me at all,*
> *Bring me a big, red India rubber ball!*

ONE GLANCE AT *Romeo and Juliet* and there can be no doubt as to the identity of its author. Here is Master Will in all his youthful glory—the surges of poetry and passion that erupt on every page are there for all to see. The story is built on many tragedies, Mercutio's being one—the man of dazzling promise, reckless humour and mercurial imagination. It is this shimmering imagination, his greatest gift, that lifts him to the clouds but because he is without love he cannot pierce them. The two youngsters overtake him in this, for the very enmity and violence that engulfs them creates a love so overwhelming it whisks them through the clouds toward the many suns and moons it has invented for them.

Julie Harris, in her thirties, was of course technically too old for Juliet, but because of her will-o'-the-wisp appearance, her celebrated vulnerability, her tiny features, her plaintive voice and her youthful vigour, there were moments when she could have passed for fourteen. Her reaction to drinking the Friar's potion was to me the highlight of her performance. Her hallucinations were vividly terrifying and appallingly real. When she saw Tybalt's ghost—so did we. Watching her face as the drug possessed her, we knew that, for a moment, she had looked into Hell. It was a remarkable rendering. Bruno Gerussi was a loving and desperate Romeo and Kate Reid, in one of her finest characterizations, pulled out all the stops as the Nurse. Padded to the eyeballs, she transformed herself into this rotund, moonfaced duenna, coarse, vulgar, big-hearted and caring—Falstaff as a woman.

Mercutio dies early in the play. Ralph Richardson, when he played the part in the thirties, famously remarked, "The biggest problem with Mercutio is to stay sober from the time he dies till the curtain call." Hear! Hear! I eventually solved this by simply *not* taking a curtain call, but I enjoyed having a go at this wonderful creature, particularly his dueling sequence, which in our production was most spectacular.

As the season dragged on, Memory Mellons got the wanderlust and frequently disappeared without explanation. Although she always came back, there were still great gaps of time when I was without a security guard. My friendships with Kate, Pat Galloway and Julie H., of course, kept me going, but they were involved in their own lives, and gradually I fell back into the rut of parties and deep booze-ridden sleeps. After one particularly heavy night, I awoke to find my right hand was totally numb and fast asleep. Normally that wouldn't have fazed me in the least, but when at five o'clock in the after-noon it was still asleep I began to worry. A local doctor told me I had what is known as Saturday Night Paralysis. Rummies and Bowery bums frequently fall prey to it by sleeping heavily in one position on a nerve, in my case the radial nerve, which is then deadened for a fairly

Kate, both bawdy and touching

lengthy period of time and can become permanently paralyzed. They gave me some archaic exercises such as picking up pins off the floor. Talk about limp wrist! I couldn't shave, run my hand through my hair, drive my Invicta, nor, for that matter, fence. I loved my duel—so determined to save it, I found that by guiding my helpless right hand with my left I could simulate the movements to good effect, gathering speed as I practiced it night and day. I even got to like it better than the original choreography. People would comment on it afterwards: "What a great idea for Mercutio—a unique fencing style for a unique fellow."

The visits continued—Jason and Betty Bacall had tied the knot and on his night off from *Toys,* he brought her up, bless him, and we had a blast. The ever-faithful Polly again arrived with the usual Senneville contingent following like a train behind her. I also cheered up consider-ably when Memory came back, looking cuter than ever, this time smok-ing a pipe. Robert Goodier, who had made an eloquent and noble impact in the double roles of Chorus and Prince in "R and J," one night near the season's end, feeling a little the worse for wear, spoke the last two lines of the play with his usual resonance, but with a slight change of text:

> *For never was a story of more woe*
> *Than this of Romiette and her Julio!*

For that one glorious slip of the tongue, we will love him forever!

Julie Harris's Juliet cradling Bruno Gerussi's Romeo

Noises off and murmurs from London across the pond began to come my way. Tyrone Guthrie wanted to produce me as Hamlet on the West End. He was already negotiating with the great French tragedienne Edwige Feuillère to play the Queen when a severe heart attack of his cancelled the project. A young Peter Hall, who had taken over Strat-ford-upon-Avon Warwickshire and turned that theatre into the Royal Shakespeare Company, asked both Langham and me to come over and join their season. Things were happening—we were running out of time. I had to get back in the action, back to the Great White Way and P.J. Clarke's to find out what the world was up to. My steering hand had now recovered, so Windows and I brought the Good Ship HMS *Invicta* back safe and sound, and there was the First Lady of the Admiralty Jane Broder waiting for us. A four-gun salute to Jane—she'd arranged a space, all was well. She now had become an expert on antique automobiles. "You should put it on blocks, honey, when you're not using it," she announced with great authority and, adjusting her veil, she added, "Oh—by the way, I have another offer for you!"

THE WINDS OF CHANGE had almost blown the fifties clean away, and the western front was starting to undergo open-face surgery. Castro had taken over Cuba; in Canada, Prime Minister Diefenbaker ("Deef the Chief") had been overwhelmed at the polls by a far more intellectual and liberal-minded Pierre Trudeau; in the United States John F. Kennedy and his clan were closing ranks and the Age of Aquarius was about to dawn. Political satirists who had graduated from San Francisco's hungry i, such as the nonsubversive Mort Sahl, no longer had a right-wing establishment they could attack—only zanier creatures like Lenny Bruce survived by taking satire on to a wider, more universal route of conscience. With the dawn came the invention of panty hose heralding a whole new age where sex would openly dominate politics for years to come. This was the time when the greedy television giant Cyclops continued to swallow everything in its path, including a grateful *me,* who, God knows, always needed the money!

The offer Jane had mentioned came from Hallmark Hall of Fame's prize director George Schaefer, who for years had shown me nothing but the sincerest kindness and loyalty. The piece on this occasion was Anouilh's *Leocadia,* or *Time Remembered.* I was to enact the leading male role, Prince Albert; the family ward and my amoureuse propre was to be Janet Munro, a delectable tomboy of an actress from Britain who had enchanted audiences in the Disney film *Swiss Family Robinson.* Offscreen Janet and I teamed up successfully as a couple of playful brothers under the skin; there was an impish glint about her that was most appealing. Now sat expectation in the air as we both waited for the late arrival from London of my aunt, La Duchesse, played by none other than that most sublime of actresses, Dame Edith Evans.

In walked this wonderful white-haired lady in her vigourous seventies wearing a Second World War RAF bomber's jacket and huge fur winter boots. Her face, which shone with a certain open-eyed spiritual innocence, was far from beautiful—one eye drooped rather comically and quizzically below the other—yet there was a beauty about her nonetheless which Ken Tynan had once described as "tilted and slightly askew." Here was a lady who in 1917 had shared the music halls with Ellen Terry and who had helped William Poel revitalize and revive the open Elizabethan stage. Here was the grande dame for whom George Bernard Shaw and James Bridie had written plays. In 1922, Edith had made theatrical history as the definitive Miss Millamant in Congreve's *The Way of the World,* and from the moment she walked onstage as Lady Bracknell in Wilde's *Importance of Being Earnest* she owned the part for eternity.

The experience of playing opposite her was inspiring and whimsical both. This big-boned, lopsided figure of a woman surprised one with her consummate grace. Her acting touch was as light as gossamer and she made everything look so easy—oh, so easy. Her supreme instrument was her voice—it could do anything; she is known to have said that once she got a beautiful word in her mouth, she couldn't bear to let go of it. How lucky I was to be able to marvel at such close range not just at the faultless execution of her craft, but at the immense joy and abandon which accompanied it. That old lady was and still is the youngest actress I have ever worked with.

When it was all over and we were saying our farewells, I told Dame Edith I'd been asked to become part of the Royal Shakespeare Company that next season. Like a little girl starting out on her career, she blurted out, "Oh goodie! Do come—I'll be there too." And then they drove her to the airport all bundled up in her RAF gear. I'd like to think when she got there she disdainfully waved aside the brand-new passenger jet in which she was to travel first class and insisted instead on the rough and ready comforts of a good ol' Spitfire or Mitchell bomber!

"WHERE'S JASON?" It was Betty Bacall on the other end of the line. She'd taken the words right out of my mouth. "Have you seen Jason?" she repeated in that deep, sultry voice of hers. But there was an urgency behind it. This was a dialogue that would take place more than frequently between Betty and myself, and I'd invariably end up the volunteer in search of Captain Spaulding, the African explorer. I certainly knew all his favorite haunts, so it wasn't difficult to find him. Even before I got there I could hear through the swinging doors that gruff croak of his which resembled a soused grackle:

> *The Red Socks were jamming at Fenways*
> *Every girl was an Irish Colleen —*

Poor Betty was concerned, but it was all very harmless really; he just loved to spread himself around. When I found him I would sit with him and join the fun, forgetting entirely the reason for my mission. Together we drifted away the nights just as all my chums were drifting away the rest of the decade, the last Golden Age of theatrical New York. We had left loads of lost time behind us and an abundance of folly, but the years had not been wasted—we'd worked as hard as we'd played. The boozy and smoke-ridden fifties had established us, taught us our craft; out from their fumes had emerged a splendid lineup of young talent who for years to come would form the bulwark of America's theatre.

The older generation of artist had left us something glorious to aspire to. They were the last of their breed. The directors I had been fortunate enough to work for—Komisarjevsky, Elia Kazan, Tyrone Guthrie—were the greatest of their day; also the crusty McClintic and the scholarly Langham had helped immeasurably to ease my growing pains. Each of them had taught me how to hold a stage, carry an evening, orchestrate the grand roles and never to become the slave of caution. With rapt attention I had attended the classes of Eva Le Gallienne and Harold Clurman—Eva, the brilliant purist; Harold, the aggressive, energetic master, surely one of the finest critics and theatre analysts of his or any other age. I had observed the dour and awesome Lee Strasberg conduct his Actors Studio sessions with the solemnity of a High Lama, but in his home discussing music I have seen him become a boy of twelve bubbling over with excitement as he proudly showed off his vast collection of priceless recordings. I bore witness to the once precocious prodigy Orson Welles as King Lear on television, and later in the theatre watched while Orson directed Orson as King Lear.

And no theatrical experience of mine could exceed the Berlin Ensemble season masterminded by that tiny giant Bertolt Brecht, who single-handedly rid the stage of elitist indulgence and brought it back to the marketplace. At the White Horse Inn, a disciple among disciples, I have sat at the same table with Dylan Thomas, listening to that tousled genius, permanently pickled, hold forth on any subject in that deep Welsh organ of a voice—his normal conversation as rich and pungent as his poetry. I thrill to the memory of Thornton Wilder bending my ear, a man who, as Tyrone Guthrie once described him, might easily be mistaken for the local country doctor if one hadn't known he'd already claimed classic immortality and was fluent in several patois of Chinese. I had proudly known and worked with the last actress-managers of their day and on my fast-growing résumé, I could now boast that I knew an aging sprite of unparalleled energy called Edith Evans, the greatest female exponent of the art of high comedy in our language.

Me and the supreme Dame Edith Evans in Time Remembered

Music too, a permanent part of my consciousness, had treated me to some very special live memories; watching tiny Edith Piaf taking command by merely standing still and relying on a sound that could rattle the tumbrils on their way to the Bastille; I had seen the magnificent Björling, the magnetic Callas, the celestial Tebaldi; I had watched Toscanini tear his passions to tatters; I had even seen Rachmaninoff once when I was too young to spell his name; and I had by now quite convinced myself that one twilit evening on a beach in Malibu, the great Jascha Heifetz had played to me alone.

FEELING A TRIFLE SMUG that so far I hadn't done too badly, I found myself walking in the direction of no. 14 Bank Street. I had not seen Tam for some time now nor, for that matter, little "Manders"— a visit was more than due. It would be pleasant to share a jar or two and recapture old times. I also longed for my old bed. I rang the bell and a face that definitely wasn't Dessa's appeared in the doorway. The new maid was informing me in no uncertain terms that Bank Street was no longer my address and that all my belongings had been sent to the Algonquin Hotel. In a daze I made my way to the old "Gonk." The bellhops greeted me with mischievous knowing grins on their faces and even the normally jolly maitre d', Robert, came out of the Rose Room and stared at me as if he'd seen a ghost.

I took the elevator up, turned the key in the lock of my new abode and stood there struck dumb. Tammy had with evil humour picked the smallest room in the hotel: all my things were piled up in cartons on the bed and on the floor—there wasn't an inch left in which to move. I couldn't help feeling I'd deserved it—that justice had been done! I looked at this collection of rubbish strewn about me and I started to laugh. Was this all I had to show for myself? Were these few pathetic items my worldly goods? I was thirty years old and had amassed nothing but junk? By the time I'd stopped laughing I had made up my mind.

> *Doth Fortune play the huswife with me now?*
> *Old I do wax and from my weary limbs*
> *Honour is cudgelled . . .*
> *To England will I steal, and there I'll steal.*
> — PISTOL *(HENRY V)*

I left everything where it was—I quit the hotel—I sought out Jane—I handed in my green card. I blew a kiss to my lost twenties— waved good-bye to America—and determined to follow Dame Edith's little Spitfire on its flight path to London, I climbed aboard the first big Iron Bird I could find.

BOOK THREE

CHAPTER TWENTY-ONE

THE MIASMAL SIXTIES

Here's your damn uniform! Go and make it yourself, you bloody Colonial!" This abrasive outburst came from Maurice Angel of Angels, London's celebrated military costumier. From the wings of the Memorial Theatre, Stratford-on-Avon, he had just hurled the offending unfinished jacket onto the stage right smack at my feet! We were in the midst of our first dress rehearsal of *Much Ado About Nothing*. Once more I was playing Benedick and my leading lady this time was one of England's finest light comediennes, Geraldine Mc-Ewan. Humiliatingly, I was the only member of the company without a costume. I had complained at all the former dress parades that mine still didn't fit and I suppose Mr. Angel had never been spoken to like that by a mere actor, so consequently he had seen red and gone quite berserk. Noel Willman, a civilized man of exceptional intellect and directorial talent who was playing Don Pedro, stopped the run-through, strode to the apron and demanded of Peter Hall (the Royal Shakespeare Company's new boss) that he request an immediate apology. "This behavior is most unprofessional, insolent and beyond belief insulting to a visiting artist!" I was overwhelmed! Dear, mild-mannered, gentlemanly Noel, furiously standing up for my punctured dignity, God bless him—I would never forget it.

Peter Hall had taken over the *Much Ado* production from Michael Langham, who one day in rehearsal went into serious convulsions caused by a nasty polyp that had to be removed. He was forced to be hospitalized for some time and suddenly I felt deserted, for Michael and his wife, Helen, had so kindly smoothed my way onto foreign soil and now I was to be truly on my own. But I liked Peter—he was young, just a couple of years my senior, and had a boyish charm that was most reassuring, so I slowly began to feel more at home. Here I was a "bloody

Geraldine McEwan, my new Beatrice in Much Ado

Colonial" playing the most attractive leading parts that season in the country of Shakespeare and Milton. I was indeed fortunate and was beginning to have a good time despite a mild patronizing resentment from certain quarters that clearly showed how insularity can breed contempt. I had every reason to be cocky and if cockiness and arrogance were to be my defense, then go to it, I said to myself with all guns blazing! At every local pub I visited I had such wicked fun adopting the harshest North American Midwestern twang. People would actually come up to me and say with customary British tact, "How could you possibly play Shakespeare with a ghastly accent like that?!" "Just wait, you fools," I thought to myself.

I hadn't much time, for already the season had begun. And what a season! The newly named Royal Shakespeare Company could hold its head up very high indeed. Its youthful members ranged from a whimsical Geraldine McEwan, a magical Dorothy Tutin, a young and glorious Vanessa Redgrave to Ian Bannen, Eric Porter, Ian Richardson, Roy Dotrice, Colin Blakely, Richard Johnson, Peter O'Toole, down to the very youngest of them all, Ian Holm, Diana Rigg and the adorable Judi Dench. Each one became a star in his or her own right and collectively they would form the very spine of British drama for the next thirty years. To add to this illustrious roster, the older guard were splendidly represented by Dame Peggy Ashcroft, Margaret Leighton, Dame Edith

Evans, Esmond Knight and Sir John Gielgud. And I had garnered most of the plums! From the crass New World, I had crossed the ocean to take the wind from their sails, beat 'em at their own game—I was insupportable!

MOST OF THE THEATRICAL cognoscenti are aware that apart from being perhaps the greatest verse speaker of the last century, John Gielgud was also notoriously and endearingly guilty of hundreds of delicately mistimed and embarrassing faux pas, boners, gaffes, bloopers—call 'em what you will—that have, by now, become part of stage history.

Example A. Having lunch at The Ivy in London many years ago with Bobby Andrews (Ivor Novello's new male lover), John suddenly spots Novello making his entrance through the revolving door and turning to his companion whispers, "Ah, there's Ivor! All alone for the first time without that dreadful little bore, Bobby Andrews!"

Example B. After a Hamlet performance by Richard Burton (which John has directed) outside his dressing room about to take Burton to supper with friends: "I'll wait for you out here, dear boy, till you're better—I mean—ready—I mean, oh never mind."

Example C. The late George Rose told me of this exchange between Sir John and himself while Sir John was directing him as the grave digger in Hamlet.

SIR JOHN: *Could you hold the skull a little higher so we could all see it, dear boy?*
GEORGE: *Yes, of course.*
SIR JOHN: *By the way, did you see Paul Scofield's Lear?*
GEORGE: *Yes.*
SIR JOHN: *What did you think of it?*
GEORGE: *I very much preferred yours in '52.*
SIR JOHN: *Mine? My Lear? Did you see it?*
GEORGE: *I was in it.*
SIR JOHN: *Oh! What did you play?*
GEORGE: *Oswald.*
SIR JOHN: *Of course you did. And how very good you were too!*

A champion of faux pas named Sir John
At shocking his friends truly shone
Not intending to sting

He would say the wrong thing
And wonder why they'd all upped and gone!

Anyone who knew John is, of course, pleasantly aware that there was not a malicious streak in his entire makeup. I had worked with him on several films since and can gladly add my twopence to the hordes of actors who have already donated theirs that he was possibly the most modest and least selfish of performers ever to grace our profession. These qualities have surely contributed to the noble and elegant manner by which he reached his exalted age. In his midnineties, he still strode rapidly forth, ramrod straight while, one by one, his close contemporaries and those younger still, fell by the wayside.

Back in 1961, however, I hardly knew him. I was a distant admirer and was familiar with most of the funny anecdotes concerning him, but that was all. One day I passed Sir John in the corridor waiting to rehearse his Othello in the room which I, as Richard III, had just vacated. He was leaning against the wall with a casual grace, an elegant scarf in loose folds about his neck, a hat tilted at a jaunty angle, looking for all the world like a stylish Edwardian dandy. Pleased with my progress as Richard, and very full of myself, I gratingly greeted him with the gruffest of modern-day catcalls, condescendingly slapped the great man on the back and wished him the best of much-needed luck, as if he were appearing in some minor church-basement offering down the street. As I passed, he quietly readjusted his clothes to their original splendour and in a voice so compassionate, so beautifully modulated, but not without the slightest hint of edge, said, "Ah, Christopher, and how are *you* in your own small way?"

I would like to think that was one of his bloopers—but I don't hold out much hope.

ANNE HATHAWAY'S cottage was always excruciatingly cold, even in the daytime when tourists came to gape. I had a room there in which sat a pathetic contraption called a gas fire with a meter into which one inserted a shilling to receive any semblance of what was laughingly called heat. A very comely but skinny lass who assisted in "wardrobe" and who lived in even colder digs than I, agreed to share my bed. In return I fed her as much as I could to fatten her up but to no avail. We clung to each other through the bitter nights and though her insatiable appetite for grub never gained her an ounce of weight, she certainly made chez Hathaway a lot warmer, bless her rattling bones! This partnership was alas short-lived (when the costumes were complete, her job was over), and I moved into Avoncliff—an old mansion that belonged to the Flower family, who owned Flower's Ale and employed most of the town. Sir Fordham Flower, whom we all called "Fordy," was the industry's current CFO and also president of the theatre's Board of Directors. Peter Hall, his lovely wife, Leslie Caron, the film star, and their children occupied most of the house and I was relegated to the Billiard Room, large enough to swing several cats in but every bit as congealing as the cottage. When I wasn't witch hunting for witches to help warm it up, I spent most of the time warming up at a famous pub called The Black Swan, better known as "The Dirty Duck."

It had recently been taken over by an attractive, outgoing married couple, Ben and Margot Shepherd, who turned it into the coziest and most fun hostel, I venture to say, in the entire county of Warwickshire. The fact that it was the actors' pub and diagonally across from the Memorial Theatre was its main attraction. A faithful few from the town's locals and stragglers from the audience patronized it but it belonged mostly to us theatre folk and the Shepherds saw to it that it stayed that way. They would throw out the public at "last call," shut the doors, reopen the bar and the snack kitchen and we would stay all night long, a great deal of booze being consumed "on the house." The walls of the main bar were completely covered with photos of actors and directors who had worked on that Stratford stage since its beginnings and all of us were up there on the wall too, including Sir John. A while back, when John had been famously arrested in London for exhibiting his homosexuality, the then owner immediately took John's picture down from the wall in self-righteous disapproval. So respected and loved was Sir John that every living actor represented on that wall removed theirs as well in defiant protest. They even blackballed the pub. John's photograph was instantly remounted and gradually the gallery became once again complete. But the publican responsible for such bigotry left under a considerable cloud and it was Ben and Margot, the two good Shepherds, who soon gathered their newfound flock around them and gave us all a home in which to graze.

The late-stayer-uppers I befriended included an aging musician-composer Alec Whittaker; two gregarious character actors—one Patrick Wymark, and the other a robust old comic straight out of Dickens named Newton Blick. Then there was Ian Richardson, later well known for his portrayal of Nehru on television and for his hilarious

Ian Bannen, a mythical creature and a comrade forever

BBC series *House of Cards,* whose speech, the drunker he got, became more and more precise and perfect Highland; and my newest and closet friend of them all — that other mad Scot, Ian Bannen.

Ian, who was so marvellous recently in *Waking Ned Devine,* his last film before he died in a tragic car accident, was for me back then the perfect companion replacement for Jason Robards. Although as men they were poles apart in most aspects, they did share two enviable gifts — prodigious talent and great freedom of spirit. Also, as coincidence would have it, Bannen was Britain's answer to Eugene O'Neill, having achieved great success in the identical roles Jason had performed in America. Ian was a handsome dog, thin and wiry with sharp, fine features, a noble brow and a voice that resembled the soughing of winds across the moors. He lived a life of complexity, a life mixed with gigantic gusts of joy and long walks through dense mists of gloom and despondency. There was absolutely nothing English about him; he was pure Norse. He also loved classical music and at parties when most youths lined up to play the latest pop tunes on the phonograph, Ian would move into the queue clutching his favourite grand-opera LPs guaranteed to kill the evening outright, much to his diabolic delight and mine. Ian that season had quite typically taken on much too much, encumbering himself with an exhausting repertoire that would have killed a man half his years. Orlando, Buckingham to my Richard, Mercutio and two of the longest parts ever written — Iago *and* Hamlet — all in one summer!

He moved from one rehearsal to another nonstop in a kind of daze and was invariably at the wrong play at the wrong time. One morning he was a whole two hours late and when he finally arrived, with great courtesy he announced to the entire company who'd been sitting around waiting: "I'm so sorry, hearts, but I spent an inordinate time shaving this morning." Common sense would have told him to live near the theatre, considering his daft schedule, but his love of romance made him choose to live several miles outside Stratford at Hampton Lucy, the famous old Elizabethan estate belonging to the ancient Lucy family, where Shakespeare had once been arrested for poaching and where, as a result, *Twelfth Night* was conceived and its setting established. Ian adored the eccentricity and mystery about the old place and haunted it as if he were a bewitched Andrew Aguecheek.

His Hamlet, directed by Peter Wood, opened early in the season and we all went in a group to see it. It was, to say the least, frenzied but in many instances quite remarkable. It was not necessary for this Hamlet to feign madness before the court—he was quite bonkers already. His rendering of the "O, what a rogue and peasant slave" soliloquy was particularly unnerving. On his scream of "O, vengeance!" in the middle of the speech, he leapt into a trunk of props the players had left behind. It was an exciting and imaginative bit of business and would have proved most successful had he not chosen to close the lid after him. For a few seconds one could have heard a pin drop as the audience stared dumbly at the solitary trunk in the center of the stage. Then they began to titter nervously, for Ian, God love him, had waited a trifle too long before flinging it open and appearing once again. Unfortunately, when he did appear, his next line was, "Why, what an ass am I!" which, of course, brought down the house. Somehow, he miraculously managed to get them back and the play resumed its frantic pace, at all times bordering on the brink of recklessness. One went away from the evening wondering if perhaps this wasn't the way one should always play Hamlet— unhinged from the start.

The dry old mausoleum of a theatre was considerably brightened that year by an unusual wealth of directorial talent: on the menu we were offered three Michaels—Michael Elliott, Michael Langham and, from France, Michel Saint-Denis; three Peters—Brook, Wood and Hall; one whiz kid from the Royal Court Theatre—William Gaskill, and, from Italy, a young and precocious Franco Zeffirelli. Franco's production of *Othello* was the next opening I was to attend. Gielgud was the Moor, and Ian played a strangely lovable and dippy Iago. He was by now completely and understandably exhausted from all the memory work he had undertaken, so a lot of his lines that night eluded him. Cassio had barely begun speaking when Ian wandered onto the stage and casually departed from the text by informing us that Michael Cassio was dead and then, realizing his blunder, made matters considerably worse by adding, "Uh—nearly dead." Otherwise, his immense charm carried him through unscathed.

John Gielgud was the antithesis of Othello, far too refined, too subtle and much too nineteenth century a man to ever suggest that great and passionate African general. Although he spoke the golden verse beautifully and with great authority, his light string instrument of a voice, when angry, rose to a high-pitched shriek where the sound of trumpets and trombones are required. He was badly miscast and John, with all his intelligence, knew this, of course, but with his usual bravery was determined to take a crack at it. John confessed that he was always hopelessly nervous on first nights, so on this occasion, he was quite naturally more nervous than ever and at one point swallowed half of his false mustache.

The play seemed longer that night than I ever remember it due mostly to Zeffirelli's heavy, elaborate settings, which he insisted on designing and building for almost every scene. Each change, therefore, took so long (they'd not been properly rehearsed) that the audience, thinking they were intermissions, filed out into the lobby. They then had to be herded back each time before the act could resume. When the real intermission finally arrived, it was of necessity so short, they had no time to even leave their seats. I remember Sir John at season's end giving a farewell speech to the audience, gratefully praising places such as Stratford "where we are permitted to experiment, make fools of ourselves and forever learn."

Coming to his senses, Ian Bannen had begun to cut down on his workload by giving up Buckingham. He was replaced by Eric Porter. I missed Ian a lot at rehearsals (we'd had such fun), but Eric was terrific and a marvellous actor. I was rehearsing Richard III by day and playing Benedick at night. One night after the *Much Ado* performance, I was about to remove my uniform when the stage manager called to me: "Keep your uniform on; Field Marshal Montgomery was in the audience tonight. He's in the VIP room now, waiting to see you." I ran down the stairs, doing up my tunic as I went, knocked on the door and entered. A very small, natty man stood before me with salt-and-pepper hair, a tiny military mustache, wearing a double-breasted grey flannel suit and leaning on a cane. "Plummer, is it?" he barked at me in a whiny, clipped little voice. "Yes, my lord," I mumbled apprehensively. I kept clicking my heels together automatically (I'd been doing it all night on stage). "You were splendid—splendid," he said. "Thank you, sir. I uh—" but he interrupted, pointing at me as if he remembered something. The corners of his mouth twitched slightly into a kind of smile. "Weren't you—ah?" the field marshall began. I knew what he was going to say so I thought I better stop him, "No sir, I did not serve under you; I was not at Alamein or anywhere else, sir; I was too young for the war, sir!" He looked terribly disappointed and slightly annoyed. "Strange. I could have sworn—" Then a beat: "You're Canadian, aren't you?" (He'd read my bio in the programme.) "Yes, sir," I replied. "They were all with me in the desert, you know." Then he pinned me with those sharp, narrow little eyes of his and said, "Great killers—the Canadians." I couldn't exactly respond to that, but as it happened, I didn't have to for he'd already gone.

THE DESIGNER OF *Richard III,* Jocelyn Herbert, had sewn an enormous hump in the left shoulder of all my tunics to give the impression of great deformity. To exaggerate this even further, I limped through rehearsals with one shoulder higher than the other and a brace around my left arm to make it appear shorter. In fact, I spent most of my days walking about in this manner. There was only a week and a bit left before we were to open when suddenly my whole left side seized up in a vicelike cramp. I found it difficult to breathe and the pain was excruciating. Richard is just about the most exhausting of all the great roles from the vocal point of view as well as the huge physical energy that is required. This is due to the fact that the Bard (who wrote the play when quite young) never gave his "star" the necessary "rests" throughout the evening. All the relentless vocal pyrotechnics occur in the first quarter of the piece, then Richard has a very short break or two until the end when the pyrotechnics reappear, this time performed in a white heat. Not satisfied, the author makes poor Richard fight an unconscionably long and fearsome duel before he finally and mercifully expires. To render this all the more tiring, John Barton had choreographed a brilliantly grotesque and terrifying duel for me by tying a long and heavy spiked ball and chain to my withered arm which I could lash out with at intervals whilst with the other I brandished a huge oversized broadsword. But now that I could hardly move, all seemed lost.

1st Costume
Jocelyn Herbert
Richard III

Michael Langham had recovered from his polyp surgery, and he and
Helen were staying in town. Helen took one look at my paralytic plight
and insisted I see her doctor, Tibor Czato, at once who, as luck would
have it, happened to be their weekend guest. I had already visited the
local doctors, and one specialist from London had been brought in courtesy of the theatre—but none knew what was wrong and were of no
help at all.

Tibor, quite obviously, was a Hungarian and had the most comfortable bedside manner I've ever known. A man in his sixties with a graying mass of hair, he dressed more like a great painter or poet than a
great doctor. He always seemed to have egg stains on his clothes and, at
all times, gave the impression of organized chaos. Yet, a great doctor he
surely was, one of the very best diagnosticians in England and quite
possibly Europe as well. He had been the family doctor and friend of
the Hungarian film magnate Sir Alexander Korda, his famous brothers,
Vincent and Zoltan, and their separate offspring for most of his life. He

was also Picasso's doctor, and, as most of the time he refused payment, Picasso instead paid him with his own paintings and drawings so that Tibor's consulting room and his home proudly displayed wall-to-wall Picassos. He took one look at me and said in the thickest of Magyar accents, "Krees, yoor awnly breezing oud ov *von long!*" And then he named some unpronounceable disease and gave me some shots. In no time I was back in action. This miracle medicine man, whom I would call upon again much later, had in a brief second taken charge and, as one good thing breeds another, Florence Nightingale in the person of Sue Fonda showed up at the theatre all the way from New York, just in time to help nurse me back to health.

The tensions of Richard were momentarily relieved by Vanessa Redgrave's Rosalind in Michael Elliott's supremely pure and shimmering production of *As You Like It.* During the early spring, I made friends with "Big Van" (as Ian and I called her) on the tennis court. We had hit a lot of tennis balls together. She was the only company member who played. Had she not been so nearsighted, she could have been a wonderful player—she was tall, athletic, with lovely, long natural tennis strokes and had the form of a champion. It was on the stage, however, that she really ruled as a champ, and during that dress rehearsal we watched her become a star before our very eyes—a quality of beauty, magic and potential greatness that was simply indescribable. When she made her entrance, for the first time dressed in women's clothes at the play's end, it might as well have been Garbo herself.

If Vanessa represented greatness in the young, the essence of true greatness in age and youth combined belonged undoubtedly to Edith Evans. One observant critic described her acting as "a succession of tremendous waves, with white-caps of pure fun bursting above them." I could never get used to the fact that I was a thirty-one-year-old Richard III in that principal and showiest of roles, and Dame Edith was supporting me in the small but telling part of mad Queen Margaret. Early rehearsals were in progress. Gaskill was directing. Heavily under the influence of the Method, he insisted we spend the first few days improvising the play. For a while we all complied—all, that is, except for you know who. Edith, who had in the distant past willingly stood on her head for William Poel, Harley Granville-Barker and Bernard Shaw, this time politely demurred, "I don't think I'll join you, if you'll forgive me, dear Mr. Gaskill, but I find it quite difficult enough to put across the real words as written without making up a lot of rubbish of my own." With a certain relief we were permitted to return to our

Me as Richard III in the wooing scene

texts. Soon, of course, we would drop them and begin to test our memories. Edith, for the first time without book, delivered Margaret's long soul-wrenching curse. She began slowly and quietly, hypnotizing us with those dark, measured tones of hers, then switched to an even more somber rush of intensity, a gathering storm that promised terrible devastation. As we listened, we were all turned to stone. Then suddenly she paused and, speaking quite conversationally out into the empty house and to anyone in particular, said, "It's no good. I can't do it. I simply can't go on cursing like this forever. It's all much too long! Katina Paxinou should play this part. It's in her blood, you see—she's Greek, you know—they can go on cursing all night long without taking a breath, those Greeks. I'm Anglo-Saxon. I'd have to stop in the middle and have a cup of tea." And then in tones of such power they shook the building and nearly blew me off the stage, "Besides, I haven't the voice for it."

It was now dress rehearsal. We were to hear the background music for the first time. The composer, we were told, was very progressive, very fashionable, and was watching from "out front." The lights went down. I stood in silhouette, my back to the audience, my hump elongated in an enormous shadow against the backdrop waiting for the opening bars to end before I was to speak the famous speech, "Now is the winter of our discontent."

The music began. Progressive? Fashionable? Musique concrète? Hell no! A musical concrete jungle. A pretentious twelve-tone wank! The introduction played on and on; I was so long standing there, I practically lost my hump! As I listened, I could tell that the composer was giving away the whole story of the play—the seduction, the coronation, the fight to the finish and Richard's death. There was no need for Shakespeare or any of us to be present at all! Finally, the ghastly overture came to an abrupt end like a frightened hiccup. I couldn't resist it. I turned around and uttered my first line, "Now is the winter of our discotheque!" There was an ominous silence; no one seemed amused, except for some muffled giggles coming from the wings. It was Edith, her eyes gleaming like a rebellious schoolgirl as she gave me a gleeful little round of applause and a mischievous wink of approval.

As the rehearsal progressed, we discovered to our horror there were similar musical introductions for each major character as they first appear. "If this is allowed to go on, for the love of Will, the play will run six hours!" When Edith's entrance music began, we all crowded into the wings to watch her reaction. A blast of hideous oscillators clanked together so unspeakably cacophonous that even Stockhausen would have cried out in pain, "Where's the tune? Where's the tune?!" Edith as Queen Margaret stalked majestically onto the stage and, precisely in rhythm to the musical horror, danced, for our benefit, the dirtiest, meanest version of the Twist I'd yet seen. The powers that be got the message—the music was cut and Richard and I went limping on quite happily *without*—thank you very much.

RICHARD opened successfully, but a few nights later our madly complex duel at the play's climax came to grief. Right at the start, Brian Murray and I both skipped a beat, failed to count correctly and froze! But the force of Richard's adrenaline drove me back into action and I began to flail away with sword, ball and chain, improvising wildly. Brian simply stood still, every now and then attempting lamely to parry in self-defense. This was rather unfortunate as Richmond must be the victor. It was the opposite scenario to the famous *Macbeth* story of the well-known actor who, playing the tortured Thane, went so berserk in the duel one night, chasing Macduff all over the stage, that the stage manager had to yell at him from the wings, "You've got to lose!" In my

Dame Edith (center) *as mad Queen Margaret*

case, I found myself hissing at Brian, "Kill me! Kill me, for Christ's sake; you've got to *win*!" I finally decided to make one last desperate sword cut before pretending to run onto his blade. A great gash appeared where his left eye had been and blood literally burst from it like a fountain. With an agonized scream which was more than real, I pinioned myself onto his sword, fell back and died. Richmond then speaks the long victory speech that closes the play. Brian delivered it with an amazing authority, all considered, as I lay there not daring to open my eyes for fear he had lost one of his own. When it was all over he came to me offstage and told me it was all right. I had just missed by a hair. He was still bleeding profusely. The stage was, by now, covered in rivulets of red. I guided Dame Edith on for the curtain call. She tip-toed through the splatters, stepping high to avoid the gore (Lady

Bracknell slumming it on Bosworth Field) and with grand hauteur whispered in mock disapproval, "A trifle eager tonight, were we?"

Personally, there was nothing grande dame about Edith whatsoever. She never seemed to have lost her childlike innocence; in fact, she was rather an untidy concoction of shyness and skittishness, fiercely practical on the one hand, deliciously potty on the other, and a bit of a flirt. But a very private person—after the performance each night she would return to the tiny little two-room mews house they rented for her, cook herself supper all alone and go to bed.

The closing night of *Richard III* was Edith's final performance of the season and the last time I was ever to see her. As the curtain fell, she asked me if I was hungry and, if I was, to come home with her and she'd make me something to eat. She'd always kept an eye out for me, convinced I needed saving from myself. I accepted with glee. It was fried! Fried eggs, fried bacon, fried sausages, fried bread, fried tomatoes, fried potatoes—the best! As the pan sizzled and we sipped our whiskeys, she rattled on a mile a minute telling me wonderful stories of the theatre and the extraordinary people and places she'd known. She also bombarded me with questions; she was always so interested in others. When we'd eaten, she shoved the whiskey bottle toward me and said it was mine to finish if I wished to. I fairly glowed. It was cozy in the little room tucked away from the crippling damp of Warwickshire. I began to regale her with some endless histoire and was having a whale of a time, when I turned to see how she was taking it—by God, if the old lady wasn't slumped in her chair fast asleep. She'd been asleep all along! The little room was dead quiet except for a ticking clock somewhere and the crackling of the dying fire. I suddenly felt as if I'd lost a friend. It was all quite simple, really—she'd had a good time and then she'd had enough of me. There was no other way but to leave. As I reached the door, I looked back. She was still sleeping peacefully—all alone with her great art. With a new surge of energy, I ran out into the night.

BECKET by Jean Anouilh, adapted by Lucienne Hill—a scene near the end of the play, Thomas à Becket and King Henry II are on horseback in the middle of the plain, the winter blizzard wails like a shrill dirge beneath their words.

    KING: *You look older, Thomas.*
    BECKET: *You too, Highness. Are you sure you aren't too cold?*

KING: *I'm frozen stiff. You love it of course. You're in your element, aren't you? And you're bare-footed as well.*

BECKET: (smiling) *That's my latest affectation.*

KING: *(he cries out suddenly, like a lost child) Becket, I'm bored!*

BECKET: *My prince, I do so wish I could help you.*

KING: *Then what are you waiting for?*

BECKET: *I'm waiting for the honour of God and the honour of the King to become one.*

KING: *You'll wait a long time then!*

BECKET: *Yes. I'm afraid I will.* (A pause. Only the wind is heard.)

I shall always be grateful to Peter O'Toole for ditching the RSC in favor of a camel on the Sahara desert. He was to have played King Henry that year, but now, bless his heart, he was playing Lawrence and so Henry was mine! The London premiere of *Becket* at the Aldwych in the Strand proved the success of the season, and my Henry is probably one of the best things I've ever done. With the help of Eric Porter, who splendidly partnered me as Becket, Peter Hall's free and sweeping production and a cast that represented the very finest in British acting, my modest invasion of the Sceptered Isle was at last justified. I won London's Evening Standard Award for best actor of the year. (Big Van won best actress for her Viola in *Twelfth Night*.)

At the ceremony, Sir Donald Wolfit, the very first Shakespearean actor I had seen in my young Montreal days, presented me with my prize. Now the cycle is complete, I thought—how strange and how right. He gave a rather bitter little introductory speech saying he was sure he was merely a replacement for Sir Alec Guiness who was too busy sitting on an elephant making pots of money in *Lawrence of Arabia* where every other member of Actors' Equity seemed to be employed. Then with deep Shakespearean intonation he informed us all that he had tried hard to see *Becket* but couldn't get a ticket (what bullshit, I thought) and then very magnanimously followed up with: "And I have never seen Plummah act, but I understand that report speaks goldenly of his profit" and so on and so on. I'm afraid I did not accept it very graciously; he had put me into such a blue funk. I heard myself say, "But I've managed to see Sir Donald many times on the stage, with no trouble at all getting tickets." I didn't feel too bad, however, because later that night his behaviour remained consistent. He was insufferably rude to Eric Porter for when Eric greeted him with, "Hello, Donald, remember me? I played in your company for many a season," Wolfit looked

The lovely Diana Rigg in her late teens and me as Henry II

straight through him and said nothing. And when Eric asked after his wife, Rosalind, and where he might write to them both, the old ham bone responded, "Ah, my dear boy, you'll find all that sort of thing in *Who's Who*," turned on his heel and left. But the rest of the night was a blast. I sat with Vanessa, Anna Massey and Eric—we all got smashed, and I promptly lost my award. My actor pal Peter McEnery found it much later somewhere and kept it for two whole years.

I loved *Becket*. It is still one of my favourite plays. Fictitious in most respects, it remains, however, a witty and passionate story of an extraordinary relationship between two demigods who, in their separate ways, ruled a great part of the medieval world. As many scenes take place on horseback, the use of hobbyhorses fully caparisoned, controlled by ourselves the actors wearing built-up bootlike hooves hidden under our robes, was an inspired piece of imagination and served to give the evening much added theatricality and panache. In the film, made some years later in which O'Toole marvellously reclaimed his role of Henry, it was, of course, necessary to use real horses so that much of the story's originality and style went by the wayside. Anouilh's light touch is very French and very theatrical. The reality of the film made it all seem too literal and at times inclined to take itself too seriously.

All sorts of celebrated people came backstage to compliment me: the Oliviers, the Nivens, Ralph Richardson, even Donald Wolfit, who had finally got himself a ticket. I now felt most welcome in England. One

Me in Becket *and Vanessa Redgrave in* The Shrew —
was I ever in good company!

night a rather posh group had assembled in my dressing room when suddenly O'Toole himself burst in. "What are you doing here?" I asked. "I thought you were in the desert." "I have a week off from the bloody camels. They made me ride the buggers bareback." As he said this, he proceeded in front of the speechless, po-faced group to pull down his pants and show us his ass. It was absolutely raw and riddled with welts. "Look at this," he screamed. "It's all your fault, you colonial prick. You're playing my part and this is the thanks I get!" The horrified little posse quickly dispersed and Peter and I went to the nearest pub and got pie-eyed.

Images of our production stay with me: young Ian Holm's vital and touching performance as the little monk; the crude rough Barons led by George Murcell; the hilarious power squabble over Becket between Roy Dotrice's Pope and Murcell doubling as the Cardinal, both armed with thick Roman accents; young and beautiful Diana Rigg as the Welsh girl; Gwen Ffrangcon-Davies's Queen Mother; and Esmond Knight's King of France. It all looked muddy, cold and very Middle Ages but moved with a swooping swiftness and boisterous humour that carried the actors and audience along with it. And Peter Hall had seen to that.

Young Hall was then just about the hottest item on the British theatrical scene. Running both the Royal Shakespeare Company in Stratford-on-Avon and London's Aldwych Theatre, he juggled several seasons in one with the utmost "cool." There were rumours that the BBC was courting him for their next Lord and Master, and many of us believed he might even make a fine prime minister. After all, he was young, progressive, politically astute, a skilled diplomat, an exceptional administrator and one who could "walk with Kings nor lose the common touch." Already he was being feted in high circles and there were instances where important celebrities would turn up to watch our rehearsals. I remember Margot Fonteyn visited more than once and Princess Margaret with her Tony Armstrong-Jones in tow attended a run-through, Eric and I clowning away like mad for their benefit. Hall was also becoming a major director and one year hence his famous collaboration with John Barton on the entire Shakespeare historical cycle would place him at the peak of his profession.

There was one small habit he was guilty of in rehearsals, however, that was slightly offputting—he very often neglected to watch what we were doing onstage and instead buried himself in the text. We would be working away feverishly up there and he wasn't even looking. Were we that bad? Or did he not give a damn? What could we do to arrest his attention? Eric and I put our heads together and came up with a plan. One morning when we were on a roll and going at it full throttle, we happened to glance out front and, sure enough, Peter, eyes downcast, was busily immersed in the script. Without pausing, we unzipped our flies and took out our penises, letting them dangle in the open air while we proceeded to finish the scene. Surely, we thought, this ought to get some reaction. He never once looked up! As there was never enough heat in those freezing London theatres, we couldn't wait to tuck them back inside before they shrivelled away to nothing.

H. M. Tennant Ltd. in the person of Hugh "Binkie" Beaumont was the foremost producer in the London theatre. He dealt only with the top playwrights, top stars, directors and designers and all his productions bore that unmistakable "Binkie" stamp of elegance, stylishness and chic. *Becket* was doing so well that Binkie, forming an alliance with Peter and the RSC, transferred it for another few months to his own West End theatre, the Globe on Shaftesbury Avenue. There would be a hiatus, so we could all take a much-needed break before reopening. I looked at my pale body, which I had to bare down to my tights each night for the flogging scenes, and decided I deserved some sun. I had

With Peter Hall, the charmer

not a clue where to go that was close to English shores. I had only ever been to Paris and didn't know the continent at all. They all told me to see Binkie, who knew the world and had amazing connections.

His offices were on the top floor of the old Globe, so up I went to see him. As soon as I stepped into the rickety lift, all those legendary stories came back to me. The lift was so narrow it could only take one customer comfortably — if there were two, they would have to squeeze in to each other so tightly and closely that their faces and bodies would stick together like glue. Binkie, who was camp as a row of tents, used this as a means of recruiting young actors who hopefully were as gay as he. The easiest way to find out was to stick 'em in the lift with one of his gay stage managers who then would give the master a full report. Every ambitious young gay actor in town, talented or not, who knew about that lift looked upon it as their bread, bed and butter. This same scenario was hilariously parodied many years later in Mel Brooks's classic film comedy *The Producers*.

On the other hand, to hire the heterosexual hunks, Binkie employed a woman called Daphne Rye, a brilliant and notorious casting-coucher. No one could say that Daphne did not enjoy her work as she was reputed to have bedded most of the young studs in London — actors or otherwise. A lady approaching middle age, Daphne, I was told on good authority, was exceedingly proficient in a variety of adventurous sexual tricks and, it seems, was a bit of a contortionist to boot. These images

Janet Munro, a fine actress and my tomboy friend

couldn't help but play in my mind as I went up in the little lift, mercifully alone. When I got there, Binkie could not have been more charming and suggested North Africa as a holiday, recommending Tangier,
Casablanca and Marrakesh. He would get someone in the office to make
the arrangements and would himself call the hotels. I couldn't wait to
corral my little tomboy friend, Janet Munro, and together we set off for
the plane.

Casablanca was a big letdown. It was dirty, uninspiring, no obvious
action to speak of and absolutely none of the anticipated mystery or
glamour. Tangier, on the other hand, was fabulous. Even though it had
long passed its international glory days, it was faded and beautiful,
simmering with intrigue, wildly decadent—a place where one was
much more likely to come across Sydney Greenstreet and Peter Lorre or
Bogie and Bergman fanning themselves in some suspicious hidden café.
There was also a shocking amount of poverty. I had never seen so many
beggars; deformed children crouched in crumbling doorways and children whose desperate parents had purposely broken their limbs to make
their begging more profitable. But there was sufficient beauty about to
draw the eye away. Situated on a steep hill, the city commands a clear

view of distant Gibraltar and from certain vantage points one can see where the three seas meet by their changing colours. The red of southern Spain is just across the water and from the dining room on top of the Hotel Velasquez, where we stayed, we had a spectacular view of the Riff Mountains; I expected, at any moment, to see Nelson Eddy burst into song.

Janet and I made this our nightly tryst because of the food and the romantic sunsets, but our private seraglio was soon to be discovered, our caprice cut short, for two tables away from us sat none other than that zaniest of British comics, Tommy Cooper. He was with his wife and was waving madly at Janet. He obviously recognized her from her films and was signalling us to come over and as we were both admiring fans, there was nothing to do but join them. Tommy summoned the maître d', a White Russian whom he immediately christened Rachmaninoff, and we ordered sumptuously. That was it! From that moment on we were never alone—we became the Four Musketeers. With his outrageous Cockney humour, his silly stories and his spur of the moment improvisations, Tommy never stopped entertaining us. And the thing was—we couldn't get enough of it! When Janet and I hit the sack at night we were too exhausted to even think of making love.

Every toddler in England could have told you that Tommy's famous act was that of a magician whose tricks never work. But instead of acting angry or hurt, as many comics might have done, he greeted each disaster with wonder and joy as if they had been major triumphs. Only he could have got away with this, for there was about Tommy Cooper an inexplicable bravery and pathos that made him one of the very few great clowns of the twentieth century. Of course he had to have been a skilled magician in the first place to be able to effect such glaring and difficult mistakes, but he was away from the stage now, and we were being treated to his real-life magic, as indeed were the peasants in the streets who followed him wherever he went. This tall, kind jolly man who always wore a little fez much too small for his big head, became overnight the Pied Piper of Tangier. Beggars followed him, not just for money, but because he made them laugh. Street children in rags clustered about him screaming for more tricks as he gave away all his brightly coloured handkerchiefs. He would stand on top of the city steps looking down upon the masses of Muslims below him dressed in their turbans and djellabahs and yell out, "Awright then, spray the extras!" He would joke about the hundreds of carpet sellers who pestered one everywhere and never took no for an answer. "One followed me up to me 'otel room last noit," or "When I get back to bloody London there'll be one of 'em waitin' for me in me flat!" And then, in a flash, as swiftly as he and his long-suffering wife had taken over our lives, as swiftly had they gone. Saddened yet relieved, Janet and I wondered if we should check into a hospital for a long, much needed sleep, but we opted for Marrakesh instead.

France no longer ruled Morocco, but there was still an inherited formality that intruded upon life there. The Hotel La Mamounia, outside Marrakesh, was a massive elegant Edwardian-cum-Moorish pile which stood all on its own in the middle of the desert with nothing around but a few scattered mosques and minarets and far away in the background the deep blue hint of the majestic Atlas Mountains. With its high ceilings, Moorish arches, columns and glittering chandeliers, the dining room of the hotel belonged in a palace. At night people moved silently about like graceful shadows; most wore evening dress—black tie was still, upon occasion, mandatory. Year after year, Winston Churchill had come there to stay and to paint. There was a suite named after him. It was all quite incongruous really—all this grandeur, in the center of nowhere. But the climate was ideal, particularly in January, hot and dry in the day, cool at night, fanned by the sensual desert winds. The jaunts through the souk in Marrakesh, a thriving bustling throwback to the past, and our excursions to the hills beyond, home of the Berbers, were romantic adventures set amongst stark but staggering beauty. I was to go back there many times in the years to come, drawn by the haunting deep magenta colours at sundown as the high-pitched wail of the muezzin ushered in the impenetrable African night.

Janet and I, by now copper toned, reluctantly flew back in our time machine to twentieth-century London, feeling decidedly out of epoch and quite unprepared for what was to greet us. The so-called swinging sixties had already begun!

THE SECOND WE TOUCHED DOWN on English soil we were swept up in Beatlemania and Rolling Stonery. Suddenly London was leading the world in fashion, pop music and theatre. The fashion headquarters was Carnaby Street. For women's designs, Mary Quant was all the rage. For men, winkle pickers and drainpipe trousers (required dress for "Teddy boys") were out and bell-bottoms were in! We abandoned ties in favour of flowing scarves, grew our hair and sideboards long in order to affect a Byronic look and merely succeeded in resembling rather revolting early Britons. Following Warhol's dictum that a Coke bottle was a thing of beauty and a joy forever, Yoko Ono, chalking one up for freedom of expression, rigged together a few brightly painted ladders, stuck them in a shop window and called 'em Art. Musicals no longer belonged to Broadway. London's own Lionel Bart gave us *Oliver!*, Tony Newley and Leslie Bricusse *Stop the World: I Want to Get Off*, Joan Littlewood's *Fings Ain't Wot They Used T'Be* and *Oh! What a Lovely War* were the latest in musical satire, and Shirley Bassey, Tom Jones, Petula Clark, Dusty Springfield and Engelbert Humperdinck were among the new hot songbirds.

The sedate, old carpeted and panelled restaurants were giving way to sparklingly clean tile floors. The trattoria takeover, institutionalized by those creative Italians Mario and Franco, Alvaro and San Lorenzo's very own Myra, was teaching Londoners that bright atmosphere and light fare could make eating decidedly more attractive. The King's Road, Chelsea was the hip street on which to cruise with its trendy outward facades but little substance within. Discos for the hoi-polloi began to thrive from Pimlico to Soho and the Garrison, the Saddle Room or the Society in Mayfair were their upgraded versions for "Hooray Henrys" to let down their hair and their upturned noses. Gambling which took place mostly in the privacy of drawing rooms was coming out of hiding into the limelight of Crockfords, the Curzon Club and the Clairmont.

It was the decade of offshore accounts and discretionary trusts. Chubby Checker's Twist was the preferred dance, and two young ladies called Christine Keeler and Mandy Rice-Davies, using the corridors of power as their beat, jumped into bed with a few "toffs" from Top Brass, not to mention a couple of spies, and together they brought down the entire Tory government.

PATRICIA AUDREY LEWIS (TRISH) was a leading entertainment columnist working for the Beaverbrook Press in London. Her column was prominently featured in the *Daily Express;* she was a favourite of the Old Beaver himself, and as a writer of talent far beyond her requirements she was as popular with her readers and her fellow workers as she was with her competition, reporters such as Marjorie Proops and Jean Rook. American and European stars loved being interviewed by her, not just because she was attractive, witty and fun to be with, but because she never once printed anything that was, in any way, salacious. By that I don't suggest her column was tepid or dull—au contraire—

it fairly sparkled with edge and bite, but never went out of its way to sting.

She had already written a more than flattering piece on me when I first joined the Royal Shakespeare and I like to think we hit it off from the start—I know I was very much taken with her. Trish was half Welsh, sported a permanent golden tan, had thick black hair and two of the most enormous dark pools for eyes. Exceptionally well read, she was as fully cognizant of the opera, ballet and theatre world as she was of politics, pop music and film. She had met and interviewed many a famous author, some of whom had become her friends, as loyal to her as she to them. She was as much at ease with Robert Ruark, James Michener, James Clavell or the poet Robert Graves as she was with Hope, Crosby or Sinatra. Through the influence of her column and by regularly confronting producers, she had helped a considerable number of talented artists—amongst them a young Sean Connery, whom she ceaselessly pushed for Bond, going as far as insisting that Saltzman and Broccoli watch a kinescope of his performance in *Requiem for a Heavyweight*. That was one of the clinchers. A grateful Mr. Connery sent her a case of glorious "bubbly" when Bond came his way. In short, Trish Lewis could with ease sniff out London town blindfolded.

I soon discovered we had a lot in common, food and wine near the top of the list, and together we enjoyed culinary solace at the White Tower or L'Etoile restaurants on Charlotte Street and for simple steaks and chops (the best in London) at the Guinea on Bruton Place. She could whip up a mean Lancashire hot pot at her flat when the mood struck her, but most of the time we hit the town.

Every so often Peter Finch, the Australian actor, would join us. I suspected he had once been a lover of Trish's so I hid my jealousy as best I could. Trish adored driving and driving fast. She took her little Triumph Herald convertible to the very limit, tearing through London streets at hair-raising speeds. Once, on our way home, the three of us packed like sardines into her "machina" as she called it, I picked a fight with Finchy. "Stop the car," I slurred. "We'll settle it right here on the street." "Roit, mate! You asked for it, punk!" snapped Finch. Fed up, Trish stopped the car and ordered us to get out. Ready for battle, we clambered out and blimey! if she didn't drive off leaving us stupidly gaping at each other in the pitch dark somewhere outside Hyde Park— the nerve of the woman! Finch broke the tense silence. "There's no point in going through with this without a fuckin' audience. Come on, let's have a drink instead!" From that moment we were friends!

Trish was always dragging numerous visiting VIPs to see me in

Becket. Anthony Mann, the Hollywood director, was about to make a film in Spain and dear Trish began her campaign on my behalf with a vengeance. She also introduced me to David Pelham, an American living in London who had produced John Osborne's *Look Back in Anger.* David was a vastly amusing entrepreneur-party animal who loved sprinkling his evenings with the likes of Judy Garland, his great friend whom I first met at his flat; the two Margarets, Margaret, Duchess of Argyll and HRH Princess Margaret (though never together); Noël Coward; Cecil Beaton and whatever film star happened to be in town. Through Trish I met and made friends with one of my very favourite "bad boys"—the talented Scots author, James Kennaway, who, along with his novels *The Bells of Shoreditch* and *Country Dance,* had written a stylish film about a Highland regiment, *Tunes of Glory.* I would soon become part of Jimmy and his wife Susan's lives.

Through Joan Collins and Trish I came to know Leslie and Evie Bricusse who one Sunday organized an excursion to visit Beatrice Lillie and her manager, John Phillips, for lunch at her house on the Thames. Miss Lillie had, by that time, become more eccentric than ever, and didn't appear until lunch was almost over and when she spoke, which was seldom, it sounded like some foreign code. We spent the rest of the day on the water in her tremendously long and narrow electric canoe, Bea pressing buttons and steering from the stern, reclining on a fur rug, looking very much like a slightly tipsy Queen of Sheba.

THE ESTABLISHMENT in Soho was the latest, hottest club to hit London. It offered a bill of provocative entertainers, political satirists and review artists—it was out of the ordinary, clever, upscale cabaret. Trish and I went almost nightly, usually joined by Peter Coe, the director, and my mad Irish friend Sean Kenny. Far and away the most fun, it was run by Peter Cook who, with Alan Bennett, Dudley Moore and Jonathan Miller, had written and performed *Beyond the Fringe,* their witty evening which everyone in the city was clamouring to see. At the club I met Dudley and Jonathan. Dudley, who had his own combo, played jazz and classical piano with equal zest. Sometimes he took pity on me and allowed me to strum the keys, but only if everyone was too pissed to listen.

It was there I saw Lenny Bruce perform his one and only British engagement. He was certainly the most original, uninhibited, off-the-wall messenger of derision England had seen and perhaps ever would see. All his dark humour and ugly cynicism was simply a screen which masked the awful truth behind. One critic summed him up by saying he had the heart of an unfrocked evangelist.

Trish and I attended his second night—his opening the night before had been even more sensationalized when an outraged Siobhan McKenna and her noisy party got to their feet and loudly protested his attitude toward the Roman Catholic Church. As they stomped out, Peter Cook tried to calm her down but only got slugged for his pains. Trish and I had been waiting at our table at least two hours for Mr. Bruce to appear. We wondered if he would ever show up again after the first night debacle. Peter Cook assured us that sort of thing only whetted his appetite and added that the reason for his lateness was that he was finding great difficulty in getting his "fix."

At long last he walked out onto the stage carrying a tape recorder which he promptly turned on, explaining that he was playing us last night's show in case we had missed it and that a great part of it featured "one of your country's most distinguished actresses." The irony was not lost on us as we all listened to a tipsy Siobhan venting her self-righteous vitriol. It was a cunning way of getting the audience on his side. When he'd had enough he turned the tape recorder off and began improvising on religion, politics, sex, the inhumanity of his fellow man—any subject that was open to destruction. He was obscene, vulgar, unforgivably out of line and absolutely brilliant. At one moment, entirely missing the point of Bruce's harangue, a rather stiff British army officer type accompanied by his wife and children, rose in outrage, shouting, "I've never heard such filth, it ought not to be allowed—there are decent people present!" With that they made their exit, loudly protesting all the way. Bruce waited patiently till they reached the back of the room before calling out: "Be careful! There are twelve Doberman Pinchers outside waiting to bite your balls off!"

Now that he had tasted blood, he was on fire. No philistine, prig or bigot was safe in that room. On a soaring, inspired flight of language he carried us away with him with his biting truths and made us laugh at our shameful selves till it hurt. He finished the exhausting evening by changing his mood completely. We sat in shock as he profusely thanked us for being there in the sweetest, gentlest curtain speech in my memory, and then with such a heartfelt, beatific smile that a Carmelite nun might have forgiven him anything, he told us all to go fuck ourselves!

ONE EARLY MORNING, around 2 a.m., several weeks later, Trish and I had just left the Establishment and were heading home to her flat.

She was driving. The roads were still slick from a late-night rain and as we sped down the Mall far too fast to make a left at the circle in front of Buckingham Palace, the little Triumph Herald went into a skid and lost all control. Nature takes over at moments such as these and, in a way, prepares one for what's to come. A sinister calm prevails, which enables you to see things with slow-motion clarity. "We're going to have an accident. Don't worry. Just hang on," I heard myself saying as in a trance. "The big light posts are quite far apart; there's lots of space between—we're going to miss them and go straight up onto the pavement. You're all right." I was wrong.

The next thing I remember, I was standing on the street staring at the figure of Trish lying facedown in a pool of blood. The police and medics were taking charge and administering to her. They must have been right behind us all the time. I looked over at what was left of the little Triumph. It was squashed up like an accordion; to this day I cannot fathom how we ever got out of it. I must have been thrown clear and had unbelievably escaped disaster, for I only had a scratch on my neck. Trish, on the driver's side, had collided smack into one of the pillars, receiving the full impact of the crash. A policeman came up to me and gently took my arm. "We're taking her straight to St. George's Emergency—come along please." We all crowded into the ambulance.

It seemed forever before someone came out of the emergency room. "We think you should call her parents." My heart sank. "She's broken her jaw in many places and has an overly large clot on her brain. We can't do anymore here. We'll have to take her to Atkinson Morley to set the jaw and remove the clot." I called her parents in Brighton. I'd never met them and they didn't know me from Adam. I had my work cut out. I rang off and went with Trish in the ambulance to the suburbs, terrified that every jolt on that bumpy ride would dislodge her jaw all over again. Atkinson Morley looked like a temporary Quonset hut in a military outpost on foreign soil. No one could imagine that some of the world's best brain surgery took place within its shabby walls. The morning brought her parents with it—an ordinary decent aging couple who were justifiably proud of their daughter's journalistic prowess but not so enamoured of her life in the fast lane, as they conservatively thought of it. As for me, I was a total stranger to them for whom they had no knowledge and less trust. Nevertheless, as I was Trish's only friend present, they had no choice but to accept my credibility. As Trish lay there in a deep coma, I could see that one ear had been severed and was hanging by a thread of skin and her face, still covered in dried blood, was so misshapen and swollen she was virtually unrecognizable. This was the sight that greeted them. Of course, they were understandably distraught, but the mother soon became quite hysterical and it took all my courage to persuade her to think positive thoughts so that Trish, comatose though she was, would not sense negative vibes that might challenge her will to live. My improvised Zen lecture worked and from then on, both parents behaved like good soldiers.

The nurses bandaged her ear onto its proper place. "It'll grow right back—you'll see—good as new," a nurse chortled rather cavalierly, I thought. But there was a problem. The blood clot had now covered her entire brain and had to be removed before any work could begin on her jaw. This delay might cause the jaw to set in that unfortunate position and make it impossible to restore it to its natural shape. All we could do, the three of us, was to wait and pray.

The London police were wonderfully sympathetic. They drove me back to the Globe Theatre so I could resume my duties in *Becket* and told me they would drop all charges of inebriated driving. The first two performances I went through the motions as if I were sleep-walking. But people who'd read about the accident started coming backstage to cheer me up—friends and complete strangers both. Van Johnson, who knew Trish and had heard of her plight, was playing *Damn Yankees* down the street. I didn't know him at all, but he came back to tell me not to worry. He had had the same operation on his brain, and "Here I am, large as life," he affirmed with that sunny smile of his. People were so caring and generous, but nothing could stop my anxiety. I called Michael and Helen Langham for advice. "I don't know what to do. I'm going crazy. The doctors don't know me; they think I'm just a date of hers—I can't get any information." "Call Tibor Szato," they said. "He knows everybody and everybody knows him. He'll keep an eye on things." Tibor was incredible. "Don vurry, Krees. I know zeez doctors. I vill monitor ze whole sing. I vill tell zem you are her fiancé, and I am your spy."

They operated and the clot was removed, but though she was still alive, Trish had not come out of her coma. I was going spare. News that Tammy had obtained a Mexican divorce and I was free didn't exactly cheer me up either. Rex Harrison's son Noel and his wife, Sarah, looked after me throughout this ordeal. I slept at their place; they would pick me up at the theatre, take me to their house, listen to my ramblings and leave me with a bottle of Scotch so I could drink myself to sleep. They were absolute saints; I'll never forget them.

On the third night after the operation, one of the nurses called to say things had not changed. Trish was still unconscious and that was the last I heard—no more information was forthcoming. I was by now feeling no less than suicidal. Instead of going directly to the Harrisons' after the show, I went on a solitary pub crawl. Noel found me and joined me drink for drink, bless him, as we sloshed our way into the night, ending up around 2:30 a.m. at Alec Stirling's club. Alec had also been a sympathetic friend and he had given the hospital his telephone number. He was just about to close when the phone rang. "It's for you," he said; "it's urgent." "Hello?" I began, shaking in every limb. "Ees zat you, Krees?" And in that comforting soothing Hungarian drone like the sound of cellos, Tibor was saying, "Everyteeng's all right now. Trish just voke up; she vants to live!" Good old Tibor! I could have kissed him. I kissed the phone instead.

She was moved to yet another hospital, this one on the west side of London where they operated on her jaw. For the first time I was allowed to visit her. She was sitting up in bed beaming from ear to ear, the old and the new. The nurse was correct; the right one had grown perfectly back on—absolutely normal! But she was a sight to behold—bald as a coot (her head had been shaved completely) and her face, which was still enormously swollen, had been skewered by a huge primitive-looking steel contraption, presumably meant to hold her jaw together. She was the spitting image of a Martian with a telephone implant. I don't suppose she had been able to utter a word to anyone for the longest time, but the moment she saw me she managed to blurt out, "I can get Tokyo on this thing!" Trish was back, all right!

Many weeks of slow recovery followed and many setbacks. It was like watching a child grow up. Several times they had caught her in the hospital corridor trying to escape with that damnable thing stuck to her face. Once she managed to get as far as the street in her nightie before they hauled her back inside. But the closing of *Becket* and her final release coincided beautifully. The "telephone" had at last been removed, her hair was growing back in a promising little fuzz and on one rainy afternoon in the cozy chambers at the Marylebone Registry office—I married Trish!

CHAPTER TWENTY-TWO

PETER O'TOOLE'S GIFT

The very next morning I boarded the big iron bird for Canada leaving my bride behind. "The baked meats that furnished forth the marriage tables" had been barely sampled as I sped away toward the younger Stratford, blowing grateful kisses to Peter O'Toole at every lurch of the plane. Michael Langham was about to put together a terrific season with me as Macbeth and O'Toole as Cyrano de Bergerac. But *Lawrence of Arabia,* bless its overbudgeted heart, still held Peter, along with his raw camel-sored arse, hostage in the African desert. As with most David Lean movies, the end seemed never in sight, so he was forced to pass and I ended up playing de Bergerac! Ah, Peter! May Allah look kindly on you. You gave me King Henry. I won the prize—and now Cyrano! O light of the desert. I'll clean your sandals and carry your cigarette holders wherever you may go.

But first, let us brace ourselves against the heavy weather. I am referring to *The Tragedy of Macbeth,* or the "Scottish Play," as it is known in our wary profession. The doomed masterpiece spells from the start Trouble in River City. Shrouded in superstition, it is famously cursed. Dire happenings are supposed to occur to anyone involved and usually do, and there is an unspoken rule that an actor who utters the name "Macbeth" or any line from the play in his dressing room must leave the room at once, spit and turn around three times before reentering. My friend Eric Porter, about to rehearse his Macbeth at Stratford-on-Avon, was startled out of his wits by a telephone call from England's head witch—Dame Olwyn, who assured him everything was all right; she had checked, and he could proceed unscathed!

The Thane of Cawdor, as a role, is fraught with problems, not just supernatural but psychological and physical. There is a well-known theory that a large chunk of the play's early scenes has been missing for centuries, a chunk which, if ever discovered, might help us better understand Macbeth's hasty decision and his overly swift journey into darkness. It is, suspiciously, the shortest of all Shakespeare's plays and the huge transitional leap our protagonist must take from the moment he leaves the three weird sisters is precipitous indeed, almost implausible. It is as if a whole reel of film had been stolen from the lab. Anyway, that's my excuse and I'm sticking to it!

To add another troublesome ingredient to that greasy cauldron, the Macbeth of medieval Scotland, though highly placed in the land, must have been nothing more than a coarse, brutish peasant warrior—completely uneducated, illiterate—never read a book in his life and who even in his most inebriated state would never be caught spouting such lofty utterances as

> *Come, seeling night,*
> *Scarf up the tender eye of pitiful day.*

or

> *Pity, like a naked new-born babe,*
> *Striding the blast, or heaven's cherubim, horsed*
> *Upon the sightless couriers of the air.*

It is conceivable that the lowliest Manhattan cabbie from Hell's Kitchen might pull over for a few moments and hold his customer captive while he recites selections from Milton's *Paradise Lost,* but in this instance our author has put into the mouth of his unwashed Highland jock some of the greatest, most soaring poetry ever written. The combo I don't buy—sorry! To make this futile exercise work is, of course, its eternal challenge and good bloody luck to anyone batty enough to undertake it. With masochistic relish, we actors hurl ourselves into the fray seduced by the majestic verse, hoping to God the audience doesn't notice our physical shortcomings. As it is, Macbeth would really do best on radio, where the poetry would be isolated, the actors heard and not seen and the listener's imagination allowed free rein.

At any rate, with a foolhardy resolve, I squeezed into my Scottish woolens, held my nose and jumped in feet first. I don't think I was very good. I spoke the verse well because that I can do, but in my desire to stress the Thane's "vaulting ambition" I became far too neurotic to be a convincing leader and that very ambition Macbeth talks about in my

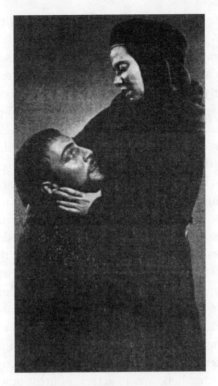

Mr. and Mrs. Macbeth, with Kate Reid
as the missus

case literally "o'er leapt itself and fell on the other." I also allowed myself to be dominated far too much by that bullying better half of mine, Lady Macbeth. Thus the story unfolded as a sort of mother-son relationship in the manner of Ibsen's *Ghosts* rather than that of a man catapulted into action through the monstrous gathering strength which his lady had been feeding him.

Ellen Terry had described Henry Irving's look at the end of the play as that of a "famished wolf" and it was just that sort of seething state one must achieve in order to do the Bard's great horror-drama justice. Also I confess, I was jealous of Kate Reid. It didn't take me long to realize what a workhorse role Macbeth really is and what a cool "star" part the author gave to his leading lady. She swans in, confident and relatively uncomplicated at various key intervals, wrapping every moment she's onstage—takes a long pleasant sabbatical in her dressing room and then, after a breathtaking sleepwalking scene, decides to expire comfortably offstage while her poor overworked husband never draws breath, endlessly eulogizing her after she's gone. The lady has barely exerted herself the entire evening, and has taken all the glory! Thankless bitch!

Of course, it was a joy to be reunited with dear Kate, my surrogate sister, no matter the circumstances, and she was quite wonderful in the part—a glowingly warm and melting siren on the one hand and a vicious strident viper on the other. Peter Coe, the West End's new hot young director, had come over from England to stage the play and possibly take over the festival after Langham's rumoured departure. Heavily influenced by the Berliner Ensemble as was almost everyone at the time, Peter made the production very stark and realistic, punctuated by Germanic lighting characteristic of a Fritz Lang movie. He clearly wanted to emphasize the dank, dour atmosphere of uninviting empty hovels where we sat around on our haunches huddled together in tight little clusters, presumably to warm ourselves from the frigid Scottish air. The whole mise-en-scène had the look of a Breugel painting. His was an interesting take on the play, but lacked the loftiness which I'm afraid was largely my responsibility to supply. However, there were some affecting moments; a tall, striking young lady called Martha Henry, making her Stratford debut, came on with all guns firing as Lady Macduff. Her grief over the murdered children was devastating, and one could see that here was an actress of great power; the staging of the phantoms on the moors that haunt Macbeth was remarkable— glowing forms appearing from under the stage as if from the cauldron itself.

In spite of my shortcomings, I did, at least, come up with one or two bits of "business" I can claim as my own. At the beginning of the play, when the witches first encounter Macbeth, they prophesy he will become Thane of Cawdor, adding, "Thou shalt be King hereafter." I decided to react by laughing uproariously for the longest time as if it were the funniest joke I'd ever been told until it struck me like a thunderbolt that they were telling me everything I wanted to hear. At that point I choked on my laughter and, quite shaken, sat on the ground beside Banquo (played by William Hutt) as together we shared several moments of stunned silence. It worked well and was most effective. The second innovation was more of a trick than a true expression. Always anxious to show off my athleticism, I picked the famous banquet scene as the moment to surprise the audience. Upon seeing the ghost of Banquo suddenly appear seated opposite me, I hurled myself at him across the table headfirst, clearing it and landing smack on the empty chair, then began strangling it in impotent rage as I brought it crashing to the ground. This didn't always work and I frequently grazed my groin rather badly in the process—not a stunt to be recommended to anyone who might have ambitions as a sought-after stud. Instead of using the traditional broadswords for the scuffle at the play's end, a rather original knife fight was choreographed by Paddy Crean, an expert fencing master from England, very pukka sahib indeed. Paddy, who had stepped right out of a Rudyard Kipling tale, had staged many a celebrated duel and had once or twice doubled for Errol Flynn in his Hollywood epics. True to the bad-luck theory associated with the play, I consistently cut myself in the fight, almost every other night.

The most unorthodox thing that occurred during all this was that Kate and I were to go down in history as the first actors in North America to appear on satellite. Satellite was a new phenomenon then and we were asked to play a short scene from Macbeth, which would follow a speech by President Kennedy—what a non sequitur! We shot it from the Stratford stage on our day off and had to wait several hours for the beam to appear. We got so nervous waiting that we hit the vodka big time and the world watched through a mercifully grainy picture the two alcoholics, Mr. and Mrs. Macbeth, teetering unsteadily around their living room.

Our brazen production received vastly mixed reactions from public and press alike. They either hated it or defended it—both vehemently. But Macbeth as a work is so strong it makes phantoms of its actors and somehow plays itself. And the controversy famously associated with it always manages to put asses in the seats and we sold out for the entire season.

My real-life better half finally arrived from London looking very much herself again. Her hair had grown back completely and there was no longer any trace of swelling in her face—but she was far too thin and needed serious fattening up. We set up shop in a ground-floor apartment on a quiet street shaded by huge trees. Away from the bustle of sixties London, I was afraid Trish would be bored out of her wits, but she made friends easily and the company would come to like her enormously. One day, we both stumbled upon a fully grown young crow who had presumably fallen out of a tree. He had been obviously shunned by his family and was limping quite badly. As if guided by some unseen force, we took him into the house, fed him, his health improved and he lived happily with us for the rest of the summer. We called him, quite fittingly, Caw-dor. Cawdor never stepped talking— we were nearly driven mad. He would perch on the top of the bedroom door and imitate our entire conversation in his scratchy, gravelly fashion. ("The raven himself is hoarse / That croaks the fatal entrance of Duncan / Under my battlements.") We could hardly get a word in. Whenever we came in from being away, he would fly down from his perch and berate us in a lengthy salvo of vitriolic rebuke. Of course there was a lot of ornithological pooper-scooping to be done, but we managed and really became most attached to the silly thing.

At parties after the performance we would give him a little whiskey in a cup which we placed on the floor. He would eagerly lap it up, being careful to spread his wings and cover the cup with them so no one could see him drinking. Obviously, the bird was a victim of Ontario's puritanical liquor laws. After imbibing thus, Cawdor would stagger about a little, looking quite skwiffy with a stupid vacant expression on his face. He loved his hootch, of that there was no doubt, so we nicknamed him the Secret Drinker. Shakespeare consistently refers to ravens and crows throughout the play and Cawdor's presence among us seemed uncannily if appropriately timed—almost sinister in its implications. I was convinced it was Dame Olwyn in disguise. As all the horrific action in Macbeth takes place after dark, so did Cawdor favour the night. He came alive, a true night-bird down to his last ruffled feathers. After all, he was just following the text:

> . . . and the crow
> Makes wing to the rooky wood:
> Good things of day begin to droop and drowse
> Whilst night's black agents to their preys do rouse.

THE ELEMENTS now began to behave themselves. The mists of Scotland lifted, the sun came out, the champagne corks popped, I glued on my oversized false nose and Edmond Rostand's inspired creation, Hercule Savinien de Cyrano de Bergerac, became, over the next several years, my other self.

At first I thought the nineteenth-century classic would seem to a sixties audience old-fashioned, flowery, overly romantic. It had had no major revival since José Ferrer's well-known rendition in which I had played Christian, on television, and that was back in the early fifties. Now, things were different; times had changed. I had convinced myself it wouldn't work. How wrong I was! Soon Rostand's impeccably constructed, ageless opera buffo was sweeping us along at a high voltage.

Michael Langham's production glittered with wit and style—real cannons fired away at the Battle of Arras, punctuating the melodrama, and the pathos of the last scene, with autumn leaves falling all around the dying Cyrano, wrenched everyone's heart and brought the crowds to their feet.

English versions of the play, no matter how good they may be, can never approach the natural beauty of the original French. Nonetheless, Langham had cleverly mixed a direct translation with the famous Brian Hooker adaptation, which garnished the enterprise with a much more genuine Gallic flavour. This was also enhanced by Louis Applebaum's background score with special songs written for les Cadets de Gascoyne, sung in French by Quebec actors from the Théâtre du Nouveau Monde. At the end, when Cyrano addresses the heavens: "I take one thing away with me tonight," instead of Hooker's "white plume" Michael restored Rostand's original word "panache":

CYRANO: . . . *et ce soir, quand j'entrerai chez Dieu, Mon salut bailaiera largement le seuil bleu, Quelque chose que sans un pli, sans une tache, J'emporte malgré vous, et c'est . . .*
ROXANE: *C'est? . . .*
CYRANO: *Mon panache!*

The very words "chez Dieu" are untranslatable. One can only say "before God" or "in God's house" or "with God." None comes anywhere near the closeness and holy intimacy the French words suggest. It was fascinating, too, while researching to read Rostand's stinging reply to the Académie Française after the first Paris performance. They had challenged him as a fellow member to explain his meaning of the word "panache." We know it to suggest flair, style and a carefree nonchalance in the face of adversity, but Rostand's explanation, too long to print here, is a masterpiece of verbal gymnastics.

Cyrano of the huge nose and the grand soul is perhaps one of the starriest, most spectacular characters in all romantic drama and one must take full advantage if given the chance. Though I'd admired José's performance very much and at such close quarters, I also learned from him what *not* to do should I ever attempt the role. He was so stunning in the comic scenes but towards the end, far too sentimental. Someone said quite accurately that he cried so much at his own death there were no tears left for anyone else. I came to learn from Michael Langham that Cyrano dies ecstatic and that is what is so infinitely moving. After all,

Rostand's stage direction, before the last words "mon panache" is quite simply—il dit en souriant.

I had every reason to smile, being blessed with a most wonderfully skillful cast. The masterful John Colicos with his great voice, urbane, sardonic, deliciously frightening as le Compte de Guiche; William Hutt's inimitable presence and humour infusing much style and military dash into his Carbon de Castel-Jaloux; a dark-haired beauty, Toby Robins, made a charming Roxane very easy to look upon and just as easy to fall in love with. Douglas Rain, about to voice his memorable HAL the Computer in Kubrick's film *2001*, made an equally memorable Ragueneau the pastry chef—abandoning his usual remote self— utterly endearing. In designing and staging the duel that accompanies Cyrano's famous improvisation in act 1, Paddy Crean completely outdid himself with a very complex and brilliantly funny flourish of swordplay. Every night, it brought down the house. *Cyrano* quickly sold out as had *Macbeth* but this time the reactions were overwhelmingly positive from every local paper, also the *Herald Tribune* and *The New York Times;* even Québec's French press gave it full marks. Everyone in the cast down to that irreplaceable character actor, Eric Christmas, as Montfleury, was right on the money. It was one of those once-in-a-lifetime lucky moments where everything falls into place and joy takes over. I was so proud of our illustrious company in that short season and in that small distant town away from everything, and so sad that when it was over they must break up and go their separate ways and that New York or London was never to see this gem of a production.

Late autumn winds blew in a piercing cold through those last few days of the season. Trish had gone back to London for medical checkups and left Cawdor and me all by ourselves in the flat. Cawdor had made a rather grumpy companion but had grown quite used to us, as we had to him. Dame Olwyn or no Dame Olwyn, I believed he had brought me some luck along the way. And now our relationship was over. What was I going to do with him? I couldn't set him free—other birds would smell the scent of humanity and peck his eyes out. Vic Polley, the theatre's veteran general manager, the "fixer" of all our problems, said, "Give him to Rob Miller, the swan man; he takes in all sorts of strays." Rob had made it his job to look after all the swans in the winter months. He got them out of the river, walked them up the hill to his place, kept them under cover and when spring came around he walked them back down again. This had become such a ritual that the swans were actually piped down to the river by a Scots Highlander in full kilt and tartan—much to the delight of the tourists. Rob, I discovered, was a gruff old soul of very few words whom you could trust with your life. When I told him I didn't know how to bring Cawdor to him, he grunted something disdainful and said, "Aw heck. Jis leave the front door open. I'll come and get him—he'll be all right."

Much relieved, I went back to the flat. The moment I got through the door he flew down from his perch, landing on the back of a chair where he could look me straight in the eye. He must have sensed something was up for he greeted me with the longest, loudest barrage of guttural obscenities I had ever heard coming out of that beak of his— it was an explosion! He must have used every swear word known to the grackle tongue; he would not stop. I vow he was telling me in no uncertain terms that he would put a curse on me and my family, that he was in league with every warlock from Scotland's southern tip to the Hebrides, that he was Macbeth's very own crow and that if I left him, we'd both die! I poured some Johnnie Walker Black Label into a shot glass and put it on the floor. He never turned down booze and this was his favourite drink—so that shut him up. Spreading his wings around the glass, he began to sip. I poured myself a stiff one too—damn it, I was going to miss this crazy bird! We toasted each other. Then I couldn't take it anymore. I ran out of the house down to the nearest pub and waited till he was gone.

Well, I did do *Cyrano* in New York after all—and this time on television once again. George Shaefer, director of the prestigious programme Hallmark Hall of Fame, had seen the show at Stratford and decided that in conjunction with the festival he would film it. There were sadly very few of the original cast left and there was to be no vital supervision from Michael Langham, who had gone back to England. There was no Colicos so Bill Hutt became de Guiche. My pals Bob Goodier and Bruno Gerussi remained on board. Ken Campbell stayed on mercifully as de Valvert so that very difficult complicated duel did not have to be redone. Donald Harron was our new Christian and the beautiful Hope Lange from the movies was Roxane. The whole thing worked up to a point. Dear George did all he could to remain loyal, but it came nowhere near the magic the stage had brought to it. It is not possible to squeeze that sprawling romance into the meager confines of the boob tube. Plus the fact it so badly needed a live audience to help sweep it along. Besides I was disappointed in everything, including my own performance. I was having too much fun being back in New York and staying up every night drinking far too heavily. It slowed me down—I was not at my best.

I had moved into the old Algonquin and the moment I checked into my room the phone rang. It was Lauren Bacall—how did she know I was there? Did she think I was the hotel's permanent resident? "Where the hell's Jason?" she demanded. "I haven't a clue, Betty, I've just got here." "Sorry, I thought he was with you," she went on out of the corner of her mouth. "He hasn't been home for the last two days!" I went out in search of him, checking all his familiar haunts, finally locating him at the White Horse Tavern down near the docks. We had a great reunion and the next several days, after my rehearsals, we pub-crawled through the East Side, taking along the beauteous Hope as my date. To our great surprise, she matched us drink for drink, which came to a considerable total (in fact, she rather outdid us and never once turned a hair—just as pretty and fresh as ever). I had always felt close to the Lange family. My friendship with David, her brother, and her sister Minelda, whose husband, Bob Jiras, the "Powder Puff," still whispered in one's ear at every opportunity, "I've got this script called *The River.*" I was particularly fond of Mrs. Lange, their mother, who was so good to me. And Hope? Well, of course, Hope is always "the thing with feathers." Is she not?

Before embarking for England, I found myself one evening at The Players Club on Gramercy Park where I had been a member since 1957. This old house of Edwin Booth's (the nineteenth-century actor) had been turned into an artists' club—one of the most beautiful and most charming in existence. That evening there was a lot of laughter at the bar. A crowd had gathered round a very tall, graceful young man immaculately dressed with a shock of golden blond hair. Damn it if it wasn't Peter O'Toole holding court. I couldn't believe it. He had finally finished *Lawrence,* and brimming with Irish whimsy, a Jameson in one hand, his cigarette holder in the other, he was busy regaling them with tales of the desert.

One in particular dealt with Peter taking a lunch break, his camel by his side, on the sweltering sands with no cover in sight. It was too far to go back to camp as they would be resuming photography after lunch way out there in the dunes. David Lean had taken shelter in his air-conditioned Rolls-Royce shooting-brake and there was no one around except Peter, his camel and several Arab riders in the distance waiting on their horses, bored and restless, looking for entertainment. Seeing that Peter (the infidel British actor) was alone in his robes, they decided

The young Cyrano

to scare the daylights out of him. Screaming their high-pitched battle cries, they charged him at full gallop. His heart in his mouth, Peter saw there was nothing for it but to lie flat on the sand. The riders were almost upon him when a miraculous thing happened. The camel walked up to Peter and stood over him, straddling him so that he was completely protected. The furious riders made a V, rode past and no one was hurt. I know this tale to be true as there had been witnesses on the horizon. The story over, I went up to him, gave him a hug and thanked him for Cyrano. With his usual sweeping largesse, he loftily quipped, "I heard you did me proud—you thieving cunt!"

Peter O'Toole is truly one of the great personalities of our time. His towering Lawrence and his delicious performance much later in *My Favorite Year* were mere microcosms of this larger-than-life creature. Fiercely intelligent, with a Shavian wit, he is also the most incurable of romantics—far more than I could ever hope to be. Though he was supposedly born near the Cliffs of Connemara, he unquestionably comes from another world altogether. Where that world is I cannot be sure, but I'll hazard a guess it is hovering happily somewhere in the air above the mists of Avalon.

Peter O'Toole — wonderfully off the planet

He had just begun to tell the boys at the bar about his camel sores. I knew he'd somehow get to it. "Show us, show us, show us," they gleefully chanted. Dragging out the suspense by taking a long, elegant sip of his drink, he gave them his most quizzical look: "Very well, you hungry peasants," and in the somewhat staid atmosphere of The Players, he began to take down his pants. I headed for the door. "Where are you going?" someone shouted at me. "O'Toole is about to show us his ass." "No thanks," I called back, colouring my voice with world-weary cynicism. "I've seen it before."

CHAPTER TWENTY-THREE

FALL OF THE HOUSE OF BRONSTON

1963. Madrid, Spain. Plaza de Toros. Four o'clock. A sunny Sunday afternoon. The great Miguelin is today's matador—how lucky can I get for my first bullfight?! The aficionados of Madrid are well known for their knowledge, cynicism and critical intolerance and are extremely vocal about it. But today's crowd is unusually hushed. There is a marked sense of impending drama in the air—a respect, even, perhaps, reverence. Miguelin enters the ring. With a disdainful wave of his hand, he dismisses the horroneadors and dazzles the charging bull with a breathtaking flurry of veronicas—man and beast so close they appear as one. There is a deep rumble of approval throughout the plaza. Now the horses in their protective padding and blindfolds come slowly into the ring, uncertain and unsteady, nervously sniffing the air. They are ridden by the picadors carrying their long lances with which to pierce the bull's neck in order to lower its head. They are barely into the ring when Miguelin, with spectacular nonchalance, dismisses them as well, the relieved horses skulking away to the safety of their stalls. A gasp of appreciation comes from the spectators—the bull is still fresh as ever and unscathed. Its head held high, the risks presented now are very great indeed.

With uncanny agility and grace our matador places his own bandilleros firmly in the bull's neck; another dizzying series of veronicas follows, the horns of the angry beast just brushing the "suit of lights." A nasty goring seems unavoidable—my heart is in my mouth. Now the beast stops charging and stands motionless, momentarily hypnotized. With supreme arrogance, Miguelin lowers the red cloth to his side, turns and, offering his back to the bull, slowly walks away. The olés from the crowd are thunderous. So far this has been a perfect day. There is only one thing left to do. The end comes swiftly. Miguelin is handed the sword wrapped in a separate cape. He calls to the bull, who paws the ground then charges him—a few more immaculately timed veronicas, the olés punctuating each swirling movement as if orchestrated. Finally, the exhausted bull is still. Only the wind is heard whistling across the ring. Miguelin slowly walks toward the bewildered beast and then, with one, two, three quick steps, the sword is out; it flashes in the sun, plunges down and, as if all four legs had been shot from under him, the bull drops to the ground, dead as stone.

The crowd goes wild. El Presidente stands with his thumbs up. Miguelin gets everything, both ears, the tail, everything—it has been perfection. Ava Gardner in the president's box is on her feet blowing him kisses and offering flowers. The dead bull is now dragged around the ring by a team of splendidly caparisoned horses, colourful streamers tied to their manes. The crowds stand in respect for the noble beast and his adversary—it has been an afternoon I'll never forget. From the moment the first trumpets sound for the corrida to commence, and the horses and riders attired in brilliant colours come through the gates out into the ring, our breathing becomes faster and everywhere there is the inescapable smell of danger, an effusion of glory and death. It was the single most theatrical event I have ever witnessed and, I confess, I was permanently hooked.

That year I also fell in love with Spain. Luckily, I was to be there for a good long spell, and I found myself greatly affected by that scarred old country, sadly beautiful, with its stark contrasts of primitiveness, elegant hauteur and ancient pride. Both the Gypsies and the haute monde alike shared that pride. You could see it in those dark, seductive eyes, a pride as fierce as the hot Spanish blood they would willingly shed for their history. The feeling was contagious and the longer I stayed in Spain, the more contagious it became.

THE FALL OF THE ROMAN EMPIRE was an epic film of massive proportions produced by Samuel Bronston (entrepreneur extraordinaire) and true to the grandeur of its title. Bronston, who had the ear of Generalissimo Franco, had cleverly found some way to make the pesos and the dollar work together compatibly and in the process had heightened considerably the value of Spanish currency. With Franco's cooperation, he played a major role in developing Spain into a European moviemaking center. Now with international backing, a considerable portion of which had come from the Du Pont family in Delaware, he was producing films on a grand scale with enormous studios at his disposal, giving employment to major artists as well as thousands of grateful unemployed Spanish.

A poor Romanian born in Bessarabia, Sam had swiftly and manfully worked his way up the ladder. He was accustomed to doing everything himself—delegating was not his penchant. You couldn't hope to meet a more modest and unassuming man on the surface, but what lay hidden within were nerves of steel. After all, had he not on his own knocked on the door of Sophia Loren's villa outside Rome asking her to play the film's female lead while simultaneously handing her a personal check for one million dollars? Such chutzpah she could hardly refuse. Back then that was very rare indeed! Only two female stars had ever earned a million a picture—Liz Taylor and Audrey Hepburn. And both those deals had been negotiated by my outrageous agent, the archbishop of Cologne's bad cousin, the insuperable Kurt Frings!

That formidable gentleman had just put me in a British flick, *The V.I.P.s,* a vehicle for the Burtons (Liz and Richard) surrounded by a cast which included the brilliant Maggie Smith. It was to be directed by Anthony "Puffin" Asquith and produced by a cultured Swiss gentleman known as Anatol "Tolly" de Grunwald. To make some elegant suits for the movie, Tolly introduced me to a Savile Row tailor, dear Max Vine, who would thereafter become my friend and regular "cloak

& suiter" for life. I was just being fitted by Max when the shop phone rang. It was for Tolly. I was salivating over a marvellous pinstripe I knew I would look spiffy in when Tolly came over. "It seems you're no longer in the film." "What?!" I shouted, reeling into Max's arms. "That was Kurt Frings. He says we're not paying you enough money so he's put you into *The Fall of the Roman Empire* instead." By some diabolical method known only to Kurt and his barnstorming techniques, he had relieved me of my obligations. He was ruthless but right. The money for *Empire* was tenfold greater than that of the *The V.I.P.s,* and the part of the young emperor Commodus, son of Marcus Aurelius, was the meatiest screen role to yet come my way. When I got on the blower to Kurt, he shouted at me like an SS Obersturmführer. "They hadn't yet put your money into escrow, those bastards, so I got you out of it. But don't thank me, thank Tony Mann."

Director Anthony Mann was an old Hollywood "pro" whose work ranged from Westerns to film noir to epic drama—among others, *God's Little Acre, The Man from Laramie, The Far Country* and the just completed epic film *El Cid* for Bronston. Unlike most Hollywood types, he loved the theatre; he had grown up in it. Luckily, he had seen me in

The Roman Senate in Las Matas, designed by Colasanti and Moore

Looks like I'm getting the better of Stephen but not so!

Becket and convinced himself that I would fit his vision of Commodus to a T. So with a little extra prodding from Trish, who as a columnist had met Tony several times, I landed the best role in the movie. I could not have been more thankful, for not only was I billed above the title in such company as Sophia Loren, Alec Guinness, James Mason and Stephen Boyd but the Roman captains under my command were to be played mostly by my old cronies from the RSC—Eric Porter, George Murcell, Dougie Wilmer and that stalwart pillar of the British stage, Anthony Quayle. The costumes and sets were lavish beyond expectation and were to inevitably steal the picture. The two brilliant designers, Colasanti and Moore, had reconstructed the Roman Senate and large portions of Rome itself so faithfully that for decades after the film was forgotten, their massive set remained intact at Las Matas outside Madrid as a major tourist attraction. Roman scholars from everywhere came to marvel at its accuracy. Gore Vidal, whose book *Julian* had just come out, was a particular admirer.

For almost a month before filming began, Quayle, Boyd and I trained in the Campo de Madrid with the horses and the chariots, Boyd

with more experience behind him as he had just handled chariots in
Ben-Hur when he played Messala. It was tough going, particularly on
the legs. One was barely protected; the small wooden chariots were
completely open at the back, and when travelling at high speeds one
could easily have fallen out. To practice pulling my chariot, I started by
reining in six horses, which would eventually be cut down to four. Our
instructors were the two Canutt brothers, Tap and Joe, with their partner, Jack Williams, all three top stunt riders from Hollywood.

After a grueling few weeks with the nags, we moved with the unit
up to Segovia to commence shooting. The battle between the Romans
and the Huns was filmed in dead winter near the summit of the Nava-
cerradas Mountains. The cold was congealing—there was nothing but
ice and snow and the roads down the mountain where Stephen and I
were obliged to drive our chariots at full gallop were curving and
treacherous. Although we wore heavy fur cloaks, which had a habit of
throwing us off-balance, our knees were bare and the wind cruelly cut
into them and turned them blue. I also had to hold on to the reins of my
four powerful quadrupeds with bare hands, as I couldn't feel them
properly when wearing gauntlets. Also the constant likelihood of being
thrown out gave me no cheer as I could have been trampled by all the
horses and chariots barrelling down behind me. "Boy, are we *earning* our
money?!" I couldn't help thinking.

The physical demands imposed on us up there in them hills would
have been unbearable were it not for three major elements. The first was
the constantly beaming face of Tony Mann, who showed great concern
for his actors, spurring us on with funny stories, loud laughter and
extravagant compliments. He was ruthless with his crew, however, and
whenever he smelled incompetence he went berserk and threatened to
fire everybody (on the second day he fired his first assistant in front of
the whole "Roman army," who I think were more scared of Tony than
they were of the Huns), but to us he was gentle and caring.

The second element that helped each day was the unbelievable generosity of Sam Bronston, who treated us like princes. I imagined it was
a bit like Hollywood in the twenties or early thirties. The principals
including myself were supplied with cars and chauffeurs twenty-four
hours a day (a fleet of Rolls-Royces to choose from) and the catered
lunches on the set were fit for an emperor. We were at least an hour and
a half's drive from Madrid, but Bronston had all the food and wine (the
best Spanish and French) sent up each day from that city's top restaurant, the chic Jockey Club, accompanied by its waiters who served us

attired in their formal livery. We consumed course upon course in a heated tent, lunches lasting two hours. Though Stephen didn't drink, I damn well did! But I was young and the bitter cold soon sobered me up as I climbed back in my chariot.

The third saving grace was the daily presence of a truly great professional who became our particular saviour and guide—I couldn't have done any of this without him. He was Tap and Joe's father—perhaps the most famous and legendary stunt coordinator to ever come to pictures, Yakima Canutt. A man of seventy or over, he stood tall and proud, but he walked with an odd rolling gait because of some early misfortune. "Yak," as he was universally known, was in charge of choreographing all the action sequences in our picture, battle scenes, stunts, you name it. In fact, he was the action director—in an epic, hardly anyone is more important. He had been equally famous in both silent pictures and talkies. He staged and drove in the chariot races of both the silent and the talking version of *Ben-Hur,* doubling for Roman Navarro and Charlton Heston. In *Stage Coach,* if you look carefully, you'll see that famous stunt where the tall man wearing black leaps onto the horses from the carriage and climbs underneath them holding on to the bellies as they furiously gallop away—that was Yak. A great many of the most dangerous stunts on film seem to have been choreographed or performed by Yak.

He was the quietest of men—he hardly ever spoke—and chewed endless wads of tobacco. Yet every morning on those snowy roads he took the time to explain to us clearly and patiently what we had to do, assuring me that his sons and Jack Williams had already tried it first; the chariot had been thoroughly checked, the loose boards tightened, the wheels examined, and there was nothing to worry about. "Tap and Jack will be riding a few yards behind you making sure it'll be all right." I certainly needed more reassuring than Stephen Boyd, but I think we were both equally grateful. Yak had the magic—he made everyone feel safe! I was fascinated by the tall, silent gentleman who'd spent his life dicing with death and to this day I remain ignorant of his true nationality. He could have been part native Indian, part Eskimo or part Ducabor—God knows what! "Dad was a pioneer, you know," Tap said to me one morning. "He's been in it since the beginning." "Why does he limp?" I asked. "His legs are shot," said Tap and then he called out to his father, "Hey, Dad, tell him the story 'bout your legs." There was a long pause.

Then Yak began his tale which he punctuated with a lot of spitting tobacco. "I was about nineteen. They were makin' a silent starrin' Onslow Stevens way back in the twenties. We were up in the canyons above LA. Onslow had to fall off a cliff (ptooy)—it was at least a damn hundred feet to the ground below. The main stunt guy didn't wanna do it. He was arguin' a lot about money and they was runnin' outta time (ptooy). 'I'll do it,' I said (ptooy). I'd never done a jump in my life for Chrissakes, but I had to impress someone! In them days we had no unions or nothin'. It was every man for himself. Well, they said okay. The plan was that Onslow Stevens would already be down the hill lying on the ground as if he'd just fallen. They would film me jumpin'. I would land just behind Stevens; then he'd roll into shot from a close-up camera and spout some dialogue. They wanted this all done in one damn take so it would look more real (ptooy). They called action. There was no time. I forgot to be skeered so I jumped. I quite liked the feelin' flyin' through the air for one hundred feet, but like a gol-darn fool I was in the wrong position to land right, so dammit, if I didn't land right on my heels! (ptooy) Mr. Stevens rolled into his shot just as planned and said his dialogue, but I had a hell of a time tryin' not to scream out. I didn't want to ruin the take for Mr. Stevens, so I bit my tongue to keep quiet. I kept goin' in and out of consciousness. I sure couldn't move and I must have been hemorrhaging. You see (ptooy), I'd driven both legs right up into my chest. After the take was over they all crowded 'round. How were they going to get me up the hill? So I had to tell 'em how to lay shats on the ground like train tracks, roll me onto some boards, tie it all to ropes and pull me up the hill that way. Consarn! That pain was killin' me. For a few years after, I was okay. I was quite good at my job (ptooy) but my goddamn pins are part wood, you know, and finally gave up (ptooy!)." Old Yak walked away—exhausted. I don't think he'd talked quite so much in years. As he limped along toward the horses he seemed a little ashamed, as if he would never forgive himself for being what he considered so unprofessional those many years ago.

At the top of one of the Navacerrada peaks sat the imposing hunting lodge of Emperor Marcus Aurelius, yet another chef d'oeuvre of Colasanti and Moore's. It was here I had several encounters with Sir Alec Guinness who played the Emperor, my father. I enjoyed our scenes together, but I had a hard time trying to figure Alec out, not as an actor, of course—in that art, he excelled supremely—but as a man; for the most part I found him remote and exceedingly chilly and quickly formed the impression that he did not like me in the slightest and why should he? The role of Commodus was gradually taking me over, making me far more brash and arrogant than I already was, but even when I jibed with him and tried to make him smile, he showed only disapproval. He was perfectly polite, mind you, but polite from a vast distance. Socially, we never managed to connect in any way. There was something sad and troubled about this tense man—as if he had a secret he didn't wish to share. Years later when his charming, witty and literate books came out, it was obvious he was determined to avoid revealing too much; and though I respect his discretion in denying us certain glimpses into his life, I think he was not entirely candid with his readers. I am sorry now. I would like so much to have known him better, not just because I admired him tremendously as an artist, but that I'd heard from several friends who chastised me for misjudging him just how kind and delightful a man he really was.

The Roman captains Porter, Murcell, Quayle, Wilmer, and a dour, acerbic Scottish actor Andrew Keir made up our after-work posse. Rounding out our group was the charming and quixotic James Mason, whom we'd christened "Jaime"; Doc Erickson, the jolly American unit manager who could negotiate European deals with his hands tied behind his back; and another ex-patriot Yank, Big John Ireland, who played the head barbarian or Hun—a terrific companion full of good cheer. At the end of each hard-fought shooting day, we would rejoice over drinks and food in the attractive little town of Segovia. There were many café-bars where we consumed calamari simmering in garlic accompanied by glass after glass of a comforting liqueur known as Chinchón. We were often joined by the young marquis de Chin-chón himself whose family estates nearby produced this cunning little liquid. He was a staunch movie buff and soon became our groupie—so naturally, Chinchón was, todos noches, very much on the house.

Down the street from the Alcázar, that exquisite Gothic castle, one-time home to many Spanish kings, was our hotel where we would return, in no pain, for the usual late supper. Occasionally, to relieve the monotony, Sophia (bless her big heart) cooked her delicious pastas for the entire gang. She had charmed the hotel chefs and taken over the kitchen completely.

Then came that insane day when, for the first time, Spain could boast its own whiskey. It was called Dic (presumably the manufacturer's name) and the locals pronounced whiskey "wickee" so we christened it "Wickee Dick!" I shall never forget the night Wickee Dick was introduced to Segovia. Never have I seen Spaniards so drunk. They were not accustomed to whiskey of any kind, really, and this particular firewater had a sharper tang to it and was quite a bit stronger than our own Scottish variety. Though it had a slight scented taste, that didn't deter me for a second. God knows what they'd put into it, but it didn't take long before the whole town was reeling. The bars and hotels were packed solid, wall to wall. I remember "Cairo Fred" (Omar Sharif), who had just come off *Lawrence of Arabia* to guest star in our film, being one of the first serious victims of the dreaded Dic. Being Egyptian/Muslim, Fred was not your average steady drinker, and the potent hooch dealt him a powerful kick. He kept harassing the local Segovians by yelling at them, calling them "Infidels, inferior Dogs!" in a rich mixture of Castilian, English and Arabic. The film's stunt men, who fortunately were always close by, formed a phalanx between dear old Fred, who could barely stand, and the drunken angry mob who would have gladly, had they got near him, garroted him on the spot!

THE FIRST OF A SERIES of wrap parties to celebrate the climax of "The Battle of the Huns" was in full swing at the hotel. Our loyal little group, now joined by Cairo Fred, was partying it up like there was no mañana. Likewise Doc Erickson and John Ireland, the well-hung Hun himself, so named because he famously belonged to that exclusive club whose membership boasted the most formidably endowed male thespians in Hollywood. John was a proud member in good standing, you might say. The loud cackling laugh in the corner came from Tony Mann, always in the company of his beloved Anna, a most attractive Polish girl some thirty years his junior who worshipped Tony and had given him the happiest years of his life. The soiree was now at its height—Sophia was there beaming that voluptuous smile, and even Sir Alec made a rare appearance. The regal Sophia retired early, but there was a plentiful number of fair "damsels" to party with except I was just too far gone to take anymore. I weaved my way to the lift, waved an overly theatrical farewell, opened the ornate iron gates, stepped in and promptly dropped two stories! There had been no lift waiting for me— it was up on the fourth floor. Luckily I fell "soft" (due to booze, of course) so no real damage was done. I looked up to see several familiar faces peering down at me, leering horribly. It had been quite a shock to feel nothing under my feet and I gave thanks to all the gods at once, Roman or otherwise, that it was only two floors! I could tell, however, by the disappointed faces above that they'd wished there had been a great deal more. I christened the lift "Miss Otis Regrets."

Spring had come to Spain at last. Like some huge sprawling army the film unit slowly wound its way back down to Madrid, where I found myself once more ensconced in the charming little Hotel Milford on Juan Bravo. With the arrival of primavera came Friedrich von Ledebur, an impressively tall man (six foot six at least) who was gracefully approaching seventy. He had a long, sad face that resembled the "Knight of the Woeful Countenance," framed by a glorious shock of white hair. Friedrich was a count from an ancient Austro-Czech family and he shared a house just outside Salzburg with his wife, the poetess Iris Tree, whenever they felt inclined. They adored each other, of course, but had long been accustomed to a regular separation of lives in their preferred Bohemian existence. Count Friedrich was content to drift around the world from film set to film set as an occasional actor (you can see him as Queequeg in John Huston's *Moby Dick*), but for the most part he was engaged as a riding coach to the stars. I don't think he needed the money—he just liked to be around actors and horses (sometimes you can't tell them apart).

Friedrich was one of Europe's most renowned horsemen and a member of the elite Spanish Riding School of Vienna; his teaching technique was the antithesis of the brash cowboy approach adopted by Tap, Joe and Jack Williams, who secretly nicknamed him "Mozart." An early horse whisperer, Friedrich's soft, low tones seemed to soothe every horse in sight. Whenever he addressed them, I swear to God, they would simper and bow their heads. He had been hired to help the principal actors and on weekends we would go for pleasant rides together through the parks and woods while Iris, carrying a long staff, was content to follow us on foot. Very much in charge, and very correct, Friedrich insisted on addressing each one of us as "Mr." Dougie Wilmer was always complaining about the leisurely pace Friedrich insisted on maintaining. "For God's sake, can't we get a move on, old boy, put on the old speed, jump some fences?!" Dougie, with all his British bombast, was not the world's greatest rider. So Friedrich would keep issuing quiet little commands in his soothing manner, "Mr. Vilmer, don't put pressure on ze reins," and as Wilmer broke away, "Don't gallop your horse Mr. Vilmer." Then, "Try to stay on your horse, Mr. Vilmer," and finally, "Mr. Vilmer—don't run after your horse."

Iris too had a fascinating background. Her father had been London's celebrated actor-manager, Sir Herbert Beerbohm Tree, whose own theatre, His Majesty's, at the turn of the century had presented many an extravaganza including the first production of Shaw's *Pygmalion* with

Tree as Higgins and Mrs. Patrick Campbell as Eliza. Iris's uncle was the renowned critic and author Max Beerbohm. So it was apparent she was most comfortable when moving in literary circles. Iris had shared her exceedingly adventurous life with her best friend, the legendary Lady Diana Duff-Cooper, who in the late twenties and early thirties with Aldous Huxley in tow travelled the world experimenting with drugs, mescaline being the latest and hottest hit on the block! You can actually see Iris reciting her own poetry at the famous party scene in Fellini's *Dolce Vita.*

Both Friedrich and Iris for some reason went out of their way to be kind and friendly to me. I remember a dinner Trish and I threw for them in the early sixties back in London. At the time, LSD was all the rage. Some well-known hosts were notorious for mixing it in their desserts, which they cruelly served their unsuspecting guests. The four of us were discussing this when I boldly asked Iris, this aging dynamo, if she'd ever taken the powerful drug. In deep rolling tones (a mixture of pukka-British with a Teutonic lisp) she replied, "Not recently. Everyone is so innocent today—so unprepared—so unresearched. I took LSD years ago with Aldous when it was called something else. One could embark on staggeringly beautiful voyages of kaleidoscopic colour if only one prepared correctly. Today all they want is to get to Paradise in a flash—so shortsighted. So dangerous! You must *fast first, my dear, fast first!"*

With the sound of flamenco guitars filling the air, Trish had come over from London to join me. The Sunday after she arrived, I took her to the corrida—her first ever bullfight. I was so hoping she would share my passion for it and have the thrill of a lifetime, but what a mess it turned out to be! There was no Miguelin this time to raise the sport to the level of balletic poetry. Instead we were subjected to an out-of-control hack, notorious in Spain for his clumsy performances. Many came to deride and mock him, but most left repulsed. El Caracol, the Roger Dangerfield of matadors, had some years back shown great promise and daring, but now had become nothing more than a sad, aging figure only marginally escaping a severe goring each time he set foot in the ring. This Sunday was no exception. The bull he had chosen was far more graceful than he. Awkward, timing all askew, his cape work pedestrian, everything about him expressionless; he merely went through the motions. And when it came time for the kill, he missed twice, broke his sword, got another and hacked away three or four times before the poor beast succumbed. I was convinced that the bull had simply died either from relief or to save El Caracol any further embarrassment.

The crowd let him have it loud and clear. Never have I heard such booing and hissing. It was then that Trish announced she was going to throw up. I led her up the stairs to the back of the grandstand where there were fewer crowds and more air. "Here—breathe that in," I said as we leaned over the back wall. But, to my horror, we were looking directly down on the slaughterhouse where they were already cutting up dead bulls—the stench was unbearable. There was nothing left for Trish but to vomit her heart out. No matter how hard I tried to persuade her that this had been a "freak" afternoon, she swore never to set foot near a bullring again. I didn't blame her in the least. When not executed by the very best, both ballet and opera can be utterly atrocious—so too can bullfights.

Those tranquil sunlit days riding with Friedrich on weekends were a welcome contrast to the weekly dangers on the set, where, for some unknown reason, our film horses continued to behave in the strangest manner. They had turned quite nasty in fact, throwing everyone including the expert stunt riders; mine was particularly willful. It was Friedrich who unravelled the mystery. "Mozart's stuck his nose into it again," Tap and Jack joked afterwards. It seemed that some of the main horses were covered in saddle sores undetected by us because each morning, the local handlers had already saddled them before we'd arrived. The culprit responsible for this cruelty and neglect was a shady character called Medina who ran the horse concession on the cheap, renting them out to films without bothering to take proper care of them. The poor beasts were continually in pain. Thanks to Friedrich who had, under cover of night, secretly examined them, they were relieved of their duties and fresh, healthy horses were obtained for our use.

By now I'd become really good friends with James "Jaime" Mason. His dry Yorkshire humour made up of witty self-deprecation was both unexpected and a welcome diversion. In contrast to his screen image as a dominating sadistic male (such as in *The Seventh Veil* when he controls the young pianist, his ward, played by Ann Todd—"I'll break your fingers, Francesca"), he was in life a pushover. There was something terribly vulnerable about him. Women went quite mad over James. They either wanted to baby him or control him. His soon-to-be ex-wife, Pamela Kellino, a part-time columnist with a vicious humour bent on emasculation, had successfully managed to send him into himself.

For a time, Jaime and I were without our wives. Trish had gone back to London and Pamela was somewhere in Timbuktu, probably suing for divorce, and so we would do the Madrid nightspots together. Spanish women when beautiful were truly beautiful, but they were either aristocrats or hookers—there was no in-between. There was a generous representation of both at those sumptuous lunches on the film set at Las Matas. Bronston loved sprinkling his table with visiting celebrities, which included la Contessa de Quintanilla and her good friend, that Titian-haired beauty, the Duchess of Alba. Once they arrived in the company of Alan Whicker, a British TV personality who hosted a monthly programme, *Whicker's World,* all about houses of the rich and famous. He was particularly anxious to photograph the duchess's Madrid house, the grandiose Lydia Palace. On the walls of the long gallery hung portraits of all the dukes of Alba, her ancestors, painted by Tintoretto, Titian, Velázquez, Caravaggio, and on and on. "How did you get her to allow your crew inside?" I asked Alan. "I promised her the very minimum of equipment. On the day, everything was ready— inconspicuous, neat and tidy. She came down the grand staircase and stopped halfway. 'What are those?' she sweetly asked, pointing at the cables. I explained they had to be there in order to light the portrait gallery. 'Oh, we can't have that,' she said and walked back up the stairs. There was no alternative; I had to take everything out. Someday, maybe I'll get my chance." I believe he actually did.

You never knew who might turn up at the lunches—Peter Sellers emerged one day armed with his camera, snapping everybody in sight, particularly Sophia, with whom he was having some sort of romance. At one lunch George Murcell's wife, that bubbly character actress Elvi Hale, was seated next to a tall, young, dark-haired and extremely handsome man whom no one had introduced. They were deep in conversation—mostly about horses. Elvie was explaining that she had kept a couple of horses of her own once and had had such a wonderful time riding them. "How many horses do you have?" she asked. "Oh, I grew up with horses," he rejoined. "My father had over a thousand." "Goodness," Elvie gasped, "What on earth did your father do?" "He was the king of Spain," said the dark stranger. When lunch was over, Juan Carlos got up, gallantly kissed Elvie's hand and joined his retinue.

Sam Bronston now whisked us off to Rome's Cinnecittà Studios to shoot the major interiors. More spectacular sets awaited us. Money clearly continued to be no object. Trish had come back from London and Sam put us up at what was to become my favourite hotel in Rome, the laid-back but charmingly elegant Hotel de la Ville, a few blocks down the hill from the Borghese Gardens. Gore Vidal, who lived nearby in a most attractive apartment halfway up the Spanish Steps, was more in evidence visiting our sets quite frequently. We would enjoy the odd get-together over supper with the visiting Newmans, Paul and Joanne, and the Wallachs, Eli and Annie.

Rome at any time of the day or night is mesmerizing, its splendour adding much inspiration to the movie, and I was having the time of my life being the mad young emperor, prancing about in one glorious costume after another. No attention to detail had been spared—even my sandals were richly encrusted with crests and jewels. Commodus, with a liberal sprinkling of Caligula thrown in for good measure, was a scenery-chewing histrionic romp, the designers going out of their way to enhance this: vertical gold sarcophagus which opened like wings to reveal Commodus inside as the deity he believed he was; a vast map of the globe as a great marble mosaic in multicolours was the floor of my throne room; on the tops of pedestals and columns, all the sculpted heads of gods were now replaced by one head only—*my* head (historically, Commodus had ordered this done the moment he became Caesar). Everything that suggested the crazed young creature's narcissism was executed in sumptuous taste and Tony Mann, who loved theatricality with a passion, was thoroughly enjoying himself staging it accordingly. There was little left for me to do—I'd been set up magnificently.

The film opened. Guinness and Mason were praised, of course, as was the British director of photography Robert Krasker for his superb camera work, and everyone acknowledged that Sophia as my sister Lucilla looked ravishing. She had little else to do but peer seductively out of various casement windows. And I came out of it fairly unscathed, enough to be able say with some conviction that my career on celluloid had begun in earnest. As expected, the film belonged entirely to Colasanti and Moore and rightly too, but at the box office it was a flop. My God! All that expense! Was the world tiring of epics? Or was it the quality of the writing that let the side down? I never understood, with all that money, why it wasn't spent on top-notch writers. There was no Dalton Trumbo as in *Spartacus,* or Robert Bolt as in *Lawrence of Arabia.* With the possible exception of Ben Barzman, there were just a few too many hacks with little feeling for period or language. The script was wooden and mundane. I remember one day we were shooting the return of Livius to the Eternal City. They had cordoned off a huge section of the actual Appia Antica in the hills above Rome. The Imperial Guard with their menacing shields and lances lined up flanking each side of the road some two hundred strong, I, as Commodus, in my chariot, waiting for Livius (Stephen Boyd) at the far end.

The action called for Boyd to enter on horseback as far away as the eye could see, ride all the way down through the ranks and, when he came close to my chariot, halt, dismount, walk the next few yards and tell me in the most stilted and unmemorable of lines—"Lucilla has returned to Rome." Setting up this "money shot" took forever—one wondered if it was at all worth it. Everyone was getting tired and hungry, Boyd especially. It was now the end of the day, the light was fading fast, there was only time for one take. Action! Boyd rides down the long path, dismounts, approaches my chariot, looks up at me and says with colloquial clarity, "Sophia's back in town." Not realizing what he'd said, Stephen's blank look of surprise was priceless. We were forced to wrap for the day, and the whole mess had to be shot again the following afternoon. Looking back on it now, I'm sure that Stephen's version was far superior.

Long after the film's opening, Tony Mann remained steadfastly loyal—his faith in me was quite overwhelming. He wanted me to costar with Kirk Douglas in his next flick, *Heroes of Telemark.* I was otherwise engaged and, sadly, unavailable. Richard Harris took the role instead. Tony, ever faithful, fought for me to play the lead in his next project, *A Dandy in Aspic,* but the studios wanted Laurence Harvey. I was never to see Tony Mann again, for before that movie was halfway completed, he was dead. Harvey stepped into his shoes and finished it for him. Dear old Tony had had a massive heart attack while making love to his beloved Anna. With tears in her eyes she told us later she couldn't bring herself to move his lifeless body away from her but held him in her arms for the longest time. With his great affinity for the wild west, it was the perfect way for Tony to go. He had truly died in the saddle.

Samuel Bronston, for a while, continued to produce one or two more films on the same grand scale—*55 Days at Peking,* for instance, all about the Boxer Rebellion, for which he had built entire Chinese villages including parts of the Imperial Court. But the days of his glittering empire were clearly numbered. His expenses had been astronomical; he had become box-office poison and there seemed no way he could recoup his losses. Some believed he might succeed. He was certainly expert at financial wizardry—a veritable Houdini at extricating himself from trouble. He had risen from the ashes before; he might just do it again. But this time his backers gave him no chance—not even a second. They moved right in. Their quest for retribution was ruthless,

Sam Bronston — a throwback to the thirties

particularly his powerful principal source, the Du Ponts. They seized his assets—his priceless art collection, his mansions, everything, even his silver right down to the tableware. There was nothing left. And Sam, with his ever-faithful wife who all his life had stood by him, vanished without a trace.

Some years later I was at a restaurant in Palma on the island of Majorca, a guest of the Domecqs, who owned and produced the world-famous sherry of that name. Seated opposite me was a most attractive middle-aged woman who happened to be one of the Du Ponts. The conversation got around to *The Fall of the Roman Empire* and, inevitably, Sam Bronston. Determined to defend Sam at all costs and armed with too much drink, I took up the gauntlet and directed my somewhat crude and lengthy diatribe straight across the table at Miss Du Pont, expounding volubly on how greedily and ungratefully everyone had behaved toward him—how shabbily he had been treated, how appalling had been his humiliation; after all, was he not Robin Hood of the Silver Screen, robbing the rich to give pleasure to the poor? Sure, he had spent other people's money, but wasn't that what other people's money was for? Surely his investors would have anticipated their losses going in. The Domecqs were clearly amused by all this. But heedless, I went on, and with daggers in my eyes concluded with, "What would you say to that, Miss Du Pont?" She smiled the loveliest of smiles—she was really a very pretty woman. Her putdown was as charming as it was lofty: "I wouldn't know," she said sweetly. "The hobby of financing motion pictures is not a preoccupation on my side of the family."

In the end, it matters not what nefarious route he had taken to get to the top of the cliff, for Sam Bronston was an extraordinary man, an impresario of the old school, a great dreamer whose heart was in the right place. And I will always be thankful to him for introducing me to the land of Cervantes, a country I loved and was to visit again and again throughout my life. I have only to hear the strains of de Falla, Rodrigo, Tedesco and Albéniz to be lured back to its shores. And who could possibly resist the ancient wild and wailing sound of flamenco that never fails to raise my hackles and turn my spine to water.

CHAPTER TWENTY-FOUR

FROM HAMLET TO HITLER

Trish and I had barely arrived in London when I began rehearsals for my second attempt at the Dane. It was the quadricentennial year of Shakespeare's birth and there were to be four major *Hamlets* to honour it: Peter O'Toole's for the opening of the National Theatre; Maximilian Schell's film version in German; Richard Burton's stage production for Broadway; and mine, an epic outdoor version for television shot in and around Kronborg Castle. It was presented jointly by the BBC and Radio Denmark, and Philip Saville, a tall handsomely urbane young Brit, whose reputation as a top TV director in England was virtually unchallenged, gave the old play a memorable new look, earning us numerous baubles and trinkets, amongst them the Emmy Award and a best-actor Emmy nomination for me. The cast was made in heaven—Michael Caine as a most touching Horatio; Robert Shaw, the best King Claudius I've ever seen, radiating a perfect blend of political and sexual power. That canny old Shakespearean Alec Clunes played Polonius as a wily politician in the early stages of Alzheimer's. Steven Birkoff did some exceptional mime as one of the players. Roy Kinnear was both funny and wistful as the Grave Digger, Philip Locke made a grandly devious Osric, and Donald Sutherland was most impressive as Fortinbras, complete with Norwegian accent.

We commenced shooting on a weekend when we could commandeer the horses for the escape to England section where Hamlet observes the armies of Norway and speaks the famous soliloquy: "How all occasions do inform against me / And spur my dull revenge!" I have always coveted and still do Sir Thomas Lawrence's famous portrait of John Philip Kemble as Hamlet, wearing a black velvet hat with feather. I'm determined to own this portrait one day, even if I have to steal it! Wearing a hat was a tradition for all Hamlets over the centuries, broken by Sir Henry Irving in the late 1800s when he discarded the hat altogether and nearly started a revolution. I thought I might start one too, by putting it back on again. I did so—no revolution, I'm afraid, not even a skirmish, but it kept my head warm out of doors and made me look suitably noble.

We used the woods near the castle and it worked well to see the prince on horseback—not a usual image. But we were under impossible constraints from the outset. The BBC, or "Auntie Beeb" as it is affectionately dubbed, is generally known for its insistence on quality, but at the same time notoriously mean and tight where budgets and schedules are concerned. Philip and the rest of us were given a mere few days to film a four-hour-long classic. Everyone had known this going in (hence the intense and thorough rehearsals beforehand) and fully expected to be cancelled the moment we went slightly over time, but the "rushes" of that first scene looked quite wonderful. Philip was capturing some awfully special material, so over our first supper together I pleaded with him to continue taking his time. "To hell with them!" I said. "Wait till they see the marvellous stuff you've got—they'll change their minds." He agreed. We were quite prepared to pack up

Hamlet in Elsinore, 1964

and leave Denmark at any time with virtually one scene in the can when the Beeb capitulated and gave us an extra fortnight. Sydney Newman, a Canadian with enormous chutzpah, was then head of BBC Drama. It was his courage from the outset that got the project launched and, once having seen the first day's results, he resolved to stand firmly behind us.

Philip's idea to have Hamlet address the invisible ghost of his father was most unorthodox, but visually effective. It meant I would be playing both parts, in other words talking to myself. I recorded the Ghost's dialogue in a much older voice. We shot the long difficult scene of Hamlet listening to his father on the cliff overlooking the sea with the castle ramparts in the background during a raging thunderstorm. I had made a "guide track" of the ghost's long tale of woe so I could react to it on camera. Loud speakers were placed at various vantage points, but the noise on the cliff was so deafening, I could hardly hear anything at all with foghorns out at sea blasting Mayday warnings one after the other. Because the winds and rain were so torrential and the spray from the ocean so powerful, I kept disappearing in swirls of wet mist. At times, you could barely see me at all—I could have been easily mistaken for the Ghost myself. The foghorns, incidentally, sounded at regular intervals every day and drove us out of our minds. We gradually learned to time our filming so that we could proceed without too much interruption, but it was a continuous nightmare.

The close-up lens, of course, is the ideal solution for soliloquies. They need only be spoken quietly and clearly for one to capture the thoughts behind the words. This is particularly applicable to *Hamlet* where introspection and contemplation are the order of the day. Kronborg Castle offered a variety of interesting arches, pillars and narrow passages as a background for such private moments. Philip Saville shot my "To be or not to be" soliloquy down long, winding staircases and the "O that this too too sullied flesh would melt" speech at the beginning of the play was filmed with me seated on the empty throne—the one and only moment when Hamlet is able to assume his rightful place. There sat I, all alone, a tiny figure in Kronborg's vast salon d'honneur. He also had me play the famous "Now I am alone" passage seated on a prop trunk (shades of Ian Bannen) left by the players out in the castle courtyard. He filmed the whole enterprise, not in the Graufstarkien nor the Elizabethan manner, not even à la Renaissance, but in the Jacobean period—the period when Kronborg Castle was conceived.

Philip could upon many occasions be most inspiring. It was quite evident from the earliest rehearsals in London that he was at one with this great play. Although a very modern creature full of new ideas and certainly in no way awed by the classics, he possessed, in full measure, all the sensibilities of the nineteenth-century romantic. He even looked like Hamlet—far more than I. And as each day went by, he seemed to take on more and more the demeanour of the prince. The intellectual brow, the slim athletic frame, the graceful movements, the soft-spoken voice, the aura of melancholy, everything was there. If I once wavered for a second from the character, I just had to take a quick glance at Philip and it all came back. Alec Clunes would walk onto the set, look at both of us and say, "Which Hamlet am I dealing with today?!"

This time around, and with Philip's blessing, I had made up my mind to occasionally assume a slight madness so that the Danish Court, with the exception of Horatio, would never quite know when I was feigning and when I was real. This, of course, worked admirably in the mocking of Polonius, the "nunnery scene" with Ophelia and towards the end when Hamlet is banished:

> *I am but mad north-north-west: when the wind is southerly I know a*
> *hawk from a handsaw.*

Ernest Milton, a famous Hamlet of the twenties and wildly eccentric, had played it this way and had caused quite a stir. He was my source and I had a great deal of fun trying it on. I do believe Mr. Milton had the right idea after all—the theatre which Hamlet so worshipped was also his escape. Like our own Prince Charles, he too would have loved being an actor.

> *Bear Hamlet, like a soldier, to the stage*
> *For he was likely, had he been put on,*
> *To have proved most royally.*

As I recall it now, my favourite scenes from the production were those with Rosencrantz and Guildenstern, the confrontation with Ophelia, filmed in Kronborg's ornate chapel, the joyous burst of welcome to the Players, the remembrances of Yorick, the duel with Laertes in the Great Hall and dying in the arms of Horatio. Perhaps my very favourite moment is when Hamlet has a premonition of his own death and bares his soul to his friend:

> *Give me that man*
> *That is not passion's slave, and I will wear him*
> *In my heart's core, ay, in my heart of heart,*
> *As I do thee.*

Michael Caine had painted such a true and moving portrait of Horatio throughout I could barely get through those lines without weeping. Caine, then a young man, was already on his way to being a formidable raconteur with his off-the-cuff Cockney humour. What surprised us, however, was the minute he put on his costume, he became this gentle, cultured aristocrat who had the look and manner of a Leslie Howard and whose speech was soft and beautifully accented. But once the take was over, out came that priceless Cockney rasp again and another

Michael Caine as Horatio

twenty-five stories would have us collapsing on the castle cobblestones. What amazed me was that Mike could, if he chose to, summon up real tears and cry his heart out at the drop of a hat. Very few actors can do this on cue, Sir John Gielgud being perhaps the guiltiest of all blubberers — but so with Mike, the underhanded scene-stealing sneak!

It was while I was busy dying that I fell victim to those tears. Hardly had I breathed my last words — "The rest is silence" — when from somewhere above, ducts opened and Niagara poured down on me with full force. Caine, leaning over me, was speaking his eulogy to Hamlet with devastating poignancy: "Now cracks a noble heart. Goodnight, sweet prince, / And flights of angels sing thee to thy rest." But this was accompanied by rivulets of water coursing down his cheeks landing mostly on mine, so that the two-shot of my death was somewhat marred by a series of facial twitches I could not control. We tried it several times, but Caine couldn't stop blubbing. No Hamlet since Burbage's time has had a wetter death.

What a glorious play it is — how golden in its sentiments, its wisdom, its philosophy, its simplicity and its staggering humility. I honestly believe no other can match it and the role, which was carved out of such humanity, remains forever unchallenged. I was considerably better in this, my second go, but only now, at my exalted age, do I think I know how to play it, and why not? Edwin Booth was still playing it in his old age!

I left Denmark and the lively jazz-filled nightlife of Copenhagen rather "fat and scant of breath." This was due to my daily weakness for open sandwiches and gallons of Danish ale washed down with yellow aquavit. It was just in time, for my costume had begun to burst at the seams. "Hamlet at Elsinore" would be good to me; its residuals would buy and pay for a charming Queen Anne townhouse in Mayfair for Trish and myself, whose main walls were richly covered in pale seventeenth-century walnut panelling. A friend, Jon Bannenberg, an Aussie with movie-star looks, restored the panelling and transformed the rest of the house for very little money with his innate taste and talent, the same talent that would sweep him along to become for a time the most sought-after interior designer of ships and private yachts in the world.

As poor Hamlet was haunted at Elsinore, so were we at 70 Park Street W1. On the top floor above the master bedroom was a small low-ceilinged attic space which we used for unwanted furniture and general bric-a-brac. There was a rocking chair, a small table or two and shelves upon which we neatly stored books and photo albums. It started soon after we settled in. In the dead of night, waking up, we could hear—clear as a bell—the sound of the rocking chair squeaking back and forth, and the next morning when we ventured up, the books and albums would be scattered all over the floor. Some of the photo albums were opened at specific pages, which obviously held some special significance. Every time we put the books back neatly—sure enough upon the next occurrence they were on the floor again! These minor hauntings happened regularly once every week, same night, same time, but they didn't get any worse and we became quite attuned.

Therefore, it was not due to this that I flew to New York soon after, but because dear Jane Broder had sent me a message that producer David Merrick and Tony Richardson, then the hottest director of the moment, both wanted me for the title role in *Arturo Ui* (the Hitler figure in Bertolt Brecht's grizzly sizzling little satire on the Nazi regime). "Honey, I think you should do this," she'd scribbled at the bottom. I accepted with enormous relish, waved au revoir to Trish and our ghost, and left the wealthy borough of Mayfair to fend for itself. It seemed only right in some bizarre way that I would relinquish Hamlet, the most sensitive of men, for one of history's most brutally minded dictators. From Elsinore to Berchtesgaden in one swift flight!

IF I WERE PLAYING the real, serious Adolf Hitler of history, it would be a fascinating exercise indeed, but somewhat gruelling I should think, as well as morbid and depressing. The führer as Brecht has written him, however, was an absolute lark to act—funny and outrageous. In George Tabori's skillful, lighthearted English translation, there is a great deal of farcical poking fun, vaudeville-sized comedic moments by the tumbril full. Only near the end is there an ominous foreboding and, just seconds before the final curtain, comes the warning, dark and sinister. Brecht got the idea when he was living in Chicago in the thirties—during the actual early rise of the Third Reich in Germany—clearly prophesying things to come and mockingly portraying the tiny Nazi hierarchy as third-rate Chicago gangsters, Arturo Ui himself a cheap, shoddy version of Al Capone. The establishment, the old guard under Hindenburg, he called "the Cauliflower Trust."

With a vengeance, I went to work on my research. I buried myself in still photos, newsreels of the period, anything that showed little Schickelgrubber, the house painter from Austria at work or play or simply showing off. What stunned me most were those astounding documentaries photographed by the famed Leni Riefenstahl—*Triumph of the Will* or the 1936 Berlin Olympics, where the führer leaves the stands in a huff as the record-breaking black runner from the United States, Jesse Owens, wins his gold medal. I carefully studied Hitler's gestures, his quirkish, almost effeminate mannerisms (was he really gay?), his playful smirk of triumph at the massive Nuremberg rally; the awesome display of celebration on Kristallnacht, the torches playing upon his expression of disdainful arrogance as he looks down at the beaten Hindenburg on the balcony beneath him; and the horrid little dance he improvised at the news of Poland's fall. Miss Riefenstahl's camera consistently flattered Hitler from below so that he loomed over everyone like the giant he was not! Everything—the salutes, the goose step, the tall banners inspired by Caesar's ancient Rome—all were dramatically lit to illustrate beyond question Nazi omnipotence. Supervised by Goebbels (Hitler's PR man), these amazing visual images, probably the greatest propaganda films ever produced, are poetic paeans to the new Aryan race, the Hitler youth and, as Brecht himself referred to it, as the "Resistible Rise" of Nazism. With their supreme showmanship, there is no doubt they successfully managed to brainwash and completely overwhelm the awestruck German youth of that time, a youth innocent of the consequences and too young to have known anything else.

Tony Richardson and David Merrick hired the talented Ruben Ter-Arutunian to design and execute the cartoonlike costumes and sets. The clothes were baggy zoot suits, loud checks, broad shoulders, wide lapels, long coats, extravagant watch fobs on long chains and pointed two-tone shoes. The sets were painted backdrops giving everything an artificial and temporary look (no way would Nazi rule last a thousand years!). It was all very much over the top on purpose, and this offended a lot of critics who called it *Guys and Dolls* without songs, many missing the point entirely. I think it worked wonders. I even think Brecht himself would have approved. After all, his preface to the work stated that he had written it for American actors to perform in the Chicago mobster mold.

As Arturo Ui, I was surrounded by a gaggle of crusty talent who represented my henchmen. Göring (Giri) was played by that wondrous curmudgeon and a survivor of the Black List, Lionel Stander, he of the growling voice and veteran of God knows how many hundreds of films. My lady friend from early Montreal days, Madeleine Sherwood, was superbly funny as Mrs. Betty Dullfeet. Elisha Cook, Jr., was Goebbels, Givola, vaudeville fugitive Mervyn Vye was Ernst Röhm (Ernie Roma) and a mélange of excellent Method actors, remnants of the Group Theatre, made up the rest. Roger De Koven played the actor who taught Hitler to speak, walk, salute and generally inspire the country's youth by his rousing theatricality. Of course Arturo himself was a complete stretch for me (something I'd never touched before)—a little guy with a Bronx/Brooklyn/Chicago rasp who rises from the gutter to become leader of the Fatherland. Al Pacino, who played the part many years later, was far more suited for it—to him it would all come naturally, but I was determined to master the school of Italian Street Acting, as my friend Jason called it, and to be as utterly unrecognizable as possible. With the help of much exaggerated clownlike makeup, hunched back and ghastly ill-fitting clothes, I managed this without any trouble. But how was I to do a convincing accent? I listened to the various "street" wood notes emanating from the company and suddenly there it was—the perfect sound to mimic—and it belonged to a marvellous little character actor called Tom Pedi. I clung to him, worked with him, drank with him, ate with him (I didn't sleep with him). What a superb coach. In fact, it was almost too much; there seemed to be two

Madeleine Sherwood (Mrs. Dullfeet)
and Arturo himself

Tom Pedis onstage. However, the result was extremely painful on my vocal chords as the sound came mostly from the back of the throat. And it was made all the more difficult at the end of the day when little Arturo, by now taken over by Hitler, has to change his voice in a flash to the barking clear piercing tones of Adolf the Orator. Even though I was about to lose my voice altogether through strain, I was saved for sadly the play closed. It had been much too uncommercial and daring for Broadway from the start. The reviews were too mixed to sustain a good run, and on the second week, as if to seal its fate entirely, President Kennedy was assassinated in Texas. Dorothea, my laughing socialite friend, had most generously lent her Fifth Avenue apartment to Trish and me, and one horrendous morning we woke up to see on television JFK sprawled in the backseat of his limousine, his distraught wife, Jackie, frantically leaning over him in her grief. No one who saw it as it happened live will ever forget it. Instantly, Public Television arranged a marathon tribute to the president on that Sunday by all the leading players in New York that season, which lasted into the wee hours of Monday morning. Improvised scenes were rehearsed on the spot. Among the many who performed, Frederic March read some O'Neill, Charlton Heston read from the Bible and I played Hamlet's death scene with Albert Finney as Horatio. When it came to the lines,

"Goodnight, sweet prince and flights of angels sing thee to thy rest," both of us could not stop the tears from coming. Once again, another wet death for Hamlet.

The moment Merrick closed the play he holed himself up in his office and was totally unapproachable. If he'd had the guts to present it on Broadway to begin with, why couldn't he bravely soldier on with it for a spell, particularly now that its underlying message was so patently apt? But because of the tragedy, stocks had seriously plummeted and there was next to nothing left in the till for the arts. To reopen the play, Lionel Stander, as was his fashion, organized a march of protest down Forty-fourth Street and up the lift to Merrick's office. He had persuaded some of the press to join our little march, so with reporters and television cameras and some sympathetic actors from other productions, we all of us banged on his closed doors. They never opened. There was some talk of resuming it *off* Broadway; even a London run was discussed, but neither materialized.

I remember the distinguished critic Walter Kerr, of the *Herald Tribune,* usually a staunch supporter of mine, not even mentioning my name in his unfavorable review. This could not have been more of a putdown as Arturo Ui is unquestionably the star part and hardly ever leaves the stage. He couldn't have missed me if he tried. What miffed him was that I had completely disguised myself; there was no vestige of my own personality peeping through. He considered it a cheap trick and decided to punish me for it. As a consoling measure, his wife, Jean Kerr, some days later sent me her new play, a most delightful contemporary comedy, safe rather than daring, which Walter would direct. This gesture seemed to say, "If you do our play and join ranks, you will be reinstated in our favour." At the time, I was convinced it was a kind of theatrical blackmail—I turned it down.

Well, the marquée lights went out at the Lunt-Fontanne, my voice restored, there would be no more protest marches dreamed up by Lionel, but there was the usual empty feeling at the end of the run and I was sad to let my little runt Arturo go. It was probably for the best. I'd enjoyed myself to excess getting more and more over the top as the days went by. Tony Richardson had been such an inspiring force, and I can't describe just how enjoyable he was to work with. Tony, who had married Vanessa Redgrave and sired their daughter, Natasha, was an exceptional man at an important time. He had encouraged and staged John Osborne's early work *Look Back in Anger,* which had changed the face of the English-speaking theatre forever. As a movie director, he had

Trying to look as small as I can

filmed Osborne's *The Entertainer* with Olivier and Joan Plowright, also a delightful pastiche of Evelyn Waugh's called *The Loved Ones* and, of course, the megahit that solidified Albert Finney's career, *Tom Jones*. In England in the sixties, Tony was there at the top. He treated his enormous success in the most casually matter-of-fact way, as if it didn't matter a damn and he made everything he touched look so easy. I was about to work with him again on a new Osborne play, but it never happened. And then, it was only a matter of years before Tony, shockingly young, left us for good. I wish he was still among us—he made our profession such fun.

And I shall ne'er forget the opening of *Arturo Ui* when that little musical dynamo Jule Styne, who had emerged from the early Chicago jazz days of his youth and who had now concocted for us a most wonderfully tongue-in-cheek score, insisted upon conducting it himself—on that first performance from the pit. It gave me such a rush to see that wide beaming face of his spurring us on across the footlights. Altogether it had been a brave, perhaps foolhardy venture, due largely to Merrick, for whom I will always bear a grudging respect, and dear cause-driven, black-listed, gravel-voiced Lionel, who looked like he could live forever with his huge sense of humanity and Pickwickian mirth. He was absolutely right when he fought for our play and the final message it contained:

> If we could learn to look instead of gawking,
> We'd see the horror in the heart of farce,
> If only we would act instead of talking,
> We wouldn't always end up on our arse.
> This was the thing that nearly had us mastered;
> Don't yet rejoice in his defeat, you men!
> For though the world stood up and stopped the bastard,
> The bitch that bore him is in heat again.

CHAPTER TWENTY-FIVE

"S & M"

Watching The Sound of Music *is like being beaten to death by a Hallmark card.*

— DOUG MCCLURE (ACTOR AND WIT)

The Bristol Hotel, which still stands in the midst of Makartplatz at the center of Mozart's Salzburg, invariably threw open its doors to artists of every shape and species, particularly musicians engaged by the world-renowned festival. The more gregarious of these, famous or infamous, regularly sought shelter within its walls. Upon my arrival at the front desk, back in the early sixties when we were shooting that celebrated film, I was greeted by a grinning desk clerk who informed me that two great nighthawks of the opera world, Giuseppe di Stefano and Ettore Bastianini (apparently steady customers), had just checked in. With the prospect of such easy access to confidential information of this sort, the Bristol promised to be a welcome change from the somewhat austere Osterreichischer Hof down the street where I had begun my Tyrolean sojourn. The instant warmth and relaxed sense of improvisation about my new surroundings made me realize at once that here I could be as free as I chose. What I did not foresee was that in the next few weeks, in spite of my obnoxious shenanigans, I would come to be treated and accepted as a proud member of the family. There is no better way to describe the old place other than to say, quite simply, that I had come home. The reason for this was mostly due to a pint-sized powerhouse of a lady who possessed two entirely contrasting personalities—a fearsome steel-like authority and the softest heart in Christendom. Her name was Gretl Hübner.

The Hübner family had, in the past, successfully owned and operated a chain of first-class hotels throughout eastern Europe. But times had changed, fortunes had been lost and they were now reduced to one, the

Bristol, which Gretl, the last of her line, had inherited and was caring for with a devotion that only a mother might have for her ailing off-spring. The hotel was, for her, both a toy and a roof over her head, which she shared with her American husband, a comfy old codger, General MacKristol, retired from the U.S. Occupation Forces in Germany after World War II. But the general rarely appeared, spending most of his days fishing at Bad Ischl and anyway, everyone at the hotel, staff and guests alike, were quite convinced that the real general was Gretl. She also ran the place as if it were a ship foundering in heavy waters, heavy waters she herself stirred up, if for no other reason than to keep things from being boring. Certainly during my stay it was far from boring. In fact, at times it rather resembled a reform school presided over by a strict, slightly wacky headmistress! Once inside the Bristol, there was something about the heady, pungent air that made you want to be naughty. Diabolically, Gretl seemed to encourage this just so she could come along later and straighten you out!

The food left a lot to be desired, but that was soon forgotten by the constant gemütlich atmosphere at the bar where schnapps, every known eau de vie, liqueur and some excellent local wines were affectionately administered by faithful old Bruno the bartender. Although the lobby and dining room were fairly shabby, a rundown look of faded red plush, it couldn't have mattered less for it was always kept fastidiously clean. Gretl insisted on dressing her clerks at the front desk, Karl (shy and slim) and Fritz (jolly and stout), in well-tailored cutaways and striped trousers—an obvious attempt to distract from the general dilapidation. But it was the people, the varied personalities and eccentricities of the staff and guests, which made the place jump. Gretl had seen to that. It was her mixture of opera divas, writers, politicians and local impoverished aristocracy that gave it its colour. And always present in the front lobby night and day was the majordomo, the most eccentric of them all, kissing hands, murmuring sweet nothings, welcoming anyone and everyone who passed through those portals. A six foot four slim, elegant gentleman in his early seventies, with a shock of salt and pepper hair, heavy, bushy eyebrows, a chiselled face and aquiline nose, he was known by everyone including the odd busload of day-trippers as the Count. Handsomer than any matinée idol, he looked much too grand to be a mere employee. So, one day, I asked Gretl where on earth she'd found him.

"It vas 1958 during ze Communist takeover in Hungary. Vun afternoon zere vas a man at ze door of ze hotel. He vanted to see me. He looked terrible. He vas very tired, filthy and starving. His clothes vere like rags. But zere vas somesing familiar about him. Zen, I remembered—he had stayed vith his family at some of my father's hotels. I couldn't believe it.

" 'Festitic? Is it you? Vat is wrong?'

" 'I have been on the road for veeks,' he said. 'I have walked the length of Hungary and Austria to get away. All our lands have gone. They have taken everything—there is nothing left. I have no money, nothing anymore. Please, can you give me a job?'

"It was all I could do to meet my payroll as it was—but I could not refuse him. 'Festitic,' I said, 'vat can you do?' He vas silent. 'You've never done anysing. Do you know even how to open a bottle of milk?' He was silent. 'No. But I can speak six languages.' Zen a light vent on in my head. 'Go up ze street to zat tailor shop. Get fitted for a morning coat. Tell zem I vill take care of it. Zen go and get somesing to eat. You have a job, Festitic! You can greet ze guests. You are my new major-domo!' "

The name "Festitic" (pronounced Festitich) in Hungary was synonymous with ancient nobility, wealth and power. Their vast estates and numerous castles made them one of the largest landowners in the country. The Count's mother had been companion and bosom friend to Austria's Empress Elizabeth. Young Festitic had grown up on equal terms with the Hapsburgs. As children, they played together in palaces across Europe and were accustomed to armies of servants. So it was all too evident that opening bottles of milk was a mysterious practice that would never have occurred to any of them.

Of course, that was another world, but here and now, at the moment of his ruin, with food finally inside him and freshly attired in brand-new tailcoat and stripes, Festitic must have looked splendidly to the manner born as he eagerly reported for duty. Excited as a baby, he had joined the workers of the world. In his autumnal years his life had some purpose at last. Gretl had made a man of him and he'd never felt so proud or so grateful. He too had come home.

Once acquainted with the background of the "inmates"—that gallant little staff (Karl, Fritz, Bruno, Festitic), all apparently on the rescue list, it took me no time to realize that I too had joined the pack of Gretl Hübner's lost children. Kind and sympathetic, they allowed me to bore them to tears with my daily trials and tribulations. During the early stages of filming "S & M" (my perverse nickname for that musical epic) I was not a happy camper. It did not promise to be one of "my favourite things." I had absolutely no right to feel that way, of course, surrounded as I was with such talented and respected company. Here was I, working with the distinguished director Robert Wise, formerly a top film editor (*Citizen Kane, Magnificent Ambersons*), a member of Hollywood's old guard and a gentleman to his fingertips; Eleanor Parker, one of the legendary beauties of the forties (who played the Baroness); the irrepressible Richard Haydn (Uncle), inventor of the comical character Mr. Carp, a "fish expert," who kept us laughing at all costs; the charming Peggy Wood (Mother Superior), who had once been Noël Coward's leading lady on the London stage; a gaggle of very personable youngsters playing the Trapp children, all highly professional; Gil Stewart, my limey drinking pal who played the butler as if he'd really done it; the writer Ernest Lehman, ace photographer Ted McCord, designer Boris Leven, the Baird Puppets, the brilliant arranger Irwin Kostal, the music and lyrics of Rodgers & Hammerstein, and first and foremost in importance Eliza Doolittle and Queen Guinevere wrapped up into one magical rosy-cheeked bundle of British pluck, my friend forever, the once-in-a-Blue-Moon Julie Andrews!

Riches such as these should have added grist to anyone's mill, but during the preproduction days back in Los Angeles things had gone badly for me from the start. Originally, I had accepted Robert Wise's offer simply because I wanted to find out what it was like to be in a musical comedy. I had a secret plan to one day turn *Cyrano de Bergerac* into a Broadway musical. "S & M" would therefore be a perfect workout in preparation for such an event. I also had never sung before in my life, not even in the shower, and obviously needed the practice. Most likely, however, it was due to the vulgar streak in me that made me fancy myself in a big, splashy Hollywood extravaganza.

Well, my first punishment came when they insisted I immediately record the guide track with Julie before shooting began, some of which would be used in the final picture. I was stricken—absolutely terrified! No way was I ready for that. Hell, I was still struggling with my singing lessons. I appealed and was denied. Twentieth Century-Fox insisted or they would get someone else to record. I saw my career as a second Maurice Chevalier dwindling fast. I threatened to walk off the picture. But my agent, the remarkable Kurt Frings, came to my aid, tap-danced his way into their hearts and saved my bacon. He also saved me from a two-million-dollar lawsuit. With a lot of persuasion from Mr. Wise, it was finally agreed that I could mumble the guide track and record properly after principal photography was complete. I remember

Darryl Zanuck's young son, Dick, who had taken over the studio, coming down onto the set accompanied by his partner, David Brown. He shook me by the hand in front of the entire cast and crew and said in soft-spoken tones but tinged with an unmistakable hint of somber warning, "Congratulations, Chris. Welcome back to *The Sound of Music.*"

The next hurdle was my role as the Captain. The part of von Trapp was all right in its way, but certainly far from exciting. The Broadway book had not served him well. Even in the screenplay, he was still very much a cardboard figure, humourless and one-dimensional. Human flesh urgently needed to be grafted onto those bare, brittle bones. Mr. Wise was kindness itself; he thoroughly understood my concerns and at once brought Ernest Lehman and myself together, made a cabana on the lot available for us and told us to stay in there until we made the improvements. Ernie Lehman was not just one of Hollywood's best screenwriters; he was a prince among men. He made me feel that all his invaluable ideas were mine alone; not only was it fun to work with him; it was an honour. Of course, it was impossible to turn von Trapp into Hamlet, but Ernie had made remarkable strides and the result was a far cry from the tepid original. At least now the poor soft-centered Captain had some edge to him.

In my way, I was grateful of course, but still felt uncomfortable generally. I was not very experienced on film as yet—one or two major roles had been thrust upon me much too soon—and yes, all right, I'll admit it, I was also a pampered, arrogant young bastard, spoiled by too many great theatre roles. Ludicrous though it may seem, I still harboured the old-fashioned stage actor's snobbism toward moviemaking. The moment we arrived in Austria to shoot the exteriors I was determined to present myself as a victim of circumstance—that I was doing the picture under duress, that it had been forced upon me and that I certainly deserved better. My behavior was unconscionable.

One morning I woke up late with a raging hangover to discover that the film company had left me no call sheet for the day's work. Had they no respect at all? Paranoid that I had been overlooked, ignored—I went ballistic! I threw my clothes on and ran all over Salzburg trying to find the unit. I finally came upon them filming a scene with Julie and the children on the outskirts of town. They were in the midst of a take, but I didn't care. I walked right into the shot and let forth a stream of abuse at Mr. Wise and everyone present for their lack of manners. My blood was racing, my heart pounding; I was apoplectic! The first assistant director, that good old pro Reggie Callow (he'd been an assistant on

Gone With the Wind) gently led me away toward a nearby park bench in order to calm me down. With the patience of a saint he tried getting it through my thick skull that no call sheet had been sent me simply because I wasn't needed that day. Ashamed and embarrassed to the point of despair, I slunk back to my hotel, my tail between my legs. I was not, to put it mildly, in the greatest of shape.

I began to hit the schnapps with a vengeance and vent my spleen on the poor innocent baby grand in the Bristol bar night after night. There was no one around to take me in hand and snap me out of it. The only ones who would listen to me were that faithful little staff who indulged me most dreadfully. As I moaned on, they sat attentive and quiet, but I knew what they were thinking: "What is this bloody idiot complaining about? He's the male lead in a big Hollywood movie, making terrific money, probably more than we'll ever see and he's young to boot! What the hell is he bitching about?" Very gradually, Fritz, Karl, Bruno, the Count and Gretl herself soothed the savage hyena in me. I slowly began to see the error of my ways. The cure was working; I was off the critical list, and pretty soon primed with beer and schnapps we were falling off our barstools laughing at the utter absurdity of it all.

Part of the problem from the start was that most of us on the film were lodged in separate hotels. The only other cast member at the Bristol was Gil Stewart, usually to be found holding up the British Empire at the end of the bar, happy in his own little world. Every now and then his loud guffaw would resound above the din—the only evidence of his presence. None of us, therefore, could really share our cares and woes so, once on the set, a certain aloofness prevailed. Probably due to an excessive number of nuns in the cast, there was also, at times, an atmosphere of overreverence which irritated me no end. I was determined in my resolve to take the opposite view, to play the cynic, to be Peck's bad boy—anything to prevent my character or indeed the film from becoming dangerously mawkish or ultrasentimental. Although Mr. Wise, true to his name, was tolerance itself, the one person who seemed to understand my motives completely and acted as if there was nothing untoward was Julie, the busiest of us all. I was so grateful to her for that, but I never told her. Away from work we hardly ever saw each other. At the then gloomy Osterreichischer Hof where she was staying, her hands were full tending to her child Emma, then a tiny tot. She was also in the midst of a painfully sad separation from her husband, the well-known stage designer Tony Walton, and of course, as Maria she was never off the screen.

All this combined to make of her life one long list of gargantuan

Julie the nun and Baron von Trapp

responsibilities; the pressures were tremendous. Yet she never wavered. Her optimism, delicious humour and selfless nature were always on parade. It was as if she'd been hired not just to act, sing and carry the entire film, but to keep everyone's spirits up as well. She did. She held us together and made us a team. Julie was quite transparent. There was no way she could conceal the simple truth that she cared profoundly for her work and for everyone else around her. I think that beneath my partly assumed sarcasm and indifference she saw that I cared too. As two people who barely came to know each other throughout those long months of filming, we had somehow bonded. It was the beginning of a friendship—unspoken, but a friendship nonetheless.

WELL, IT WAS TIME we got married—in the script, that is. About 25 kilometers from Salzburg lies an enchanting little town nestled beside a small, very beautiful lake. It is called Mondsee and it boasts a miniature cathedral built in exquisite baroque style right by the water. This is where Maria and the Captain tied the knot in one of the film's most delightful scenes. I fell in love with that little church and with Mondsee. Down the road nearby was an old castello which stood beside the lake. It was owned by Miche Almeida, a colourful, high-spirited

Apolog

Portuguese contessa who had been the mistress of Otto von Habsburg. It was rumoured he had bought the castello for her as a gift. To make ends meet she had turned the ground floor into a restaurant, not just any restaurant, but certainly one of the very best in my memory. It was known as the Castello Bar, but most visitors simply called it "Miche's." The eclectic and exclusive clientele descended upon that little haven like famished wolves. They came from all over Europe and even across the Atlantic—an odd mixture of British and German diplomats, American impresarios and deposed royalty. But no matter who, everyone was required to have some sort of entrée to Miche or they couldn't get in. I got in because of Gretl, and Julie got in because she was Julie.

Some of us would take that drive every other night for dinner; it was well worth the trip. I remember introducing "Jools" (Julie's nickname) to Miche's ultrahot peppers. Her throat was instantly on fire and she turned a deep scarlet. I explained to her that because she sang so well and I couldn't, this was my revenge. The great filmmaker Michael Powell arrived one day with his designer Hein Heckroth. They wanted me to play Caliban in their projected film production of Shakespeare's *Tempest* and wished to discuss it. I took them to Miche's, which they so enjoyed, I think they completely forgot why they'd come. The menu was always small and select and everything tasted absolutely home cooked. The fish and the meats were succulent, the wines exceptional, but it was the vegetables and the manner in which they were prepared that was out of this world. It was almost as if they'd been perfumed. I still hold on to an image of Miche, that most entertaining of ladies, who personally served at table with a smile as big as the room, bearing in her arms enormous platters of these superbly cooked vegetables— the very signature of the place. My mouth still waters to think of it.

WELL, AFTER OUR von Trapp wedding was "in the can," I was granted some time off. Several weeks in fact, a sort of lone honeymoon, you might say. God knows where my real-life bride was—somewhere in England, no doubt. Trish and I had begun to lead separate lives, our absences becoming longer and longer. So, deprived of a playmate, I indulgently took advantage of this reprieve and went on a rampage— cultural and otherwise. I headed straight for Lanz, the famous lederhosen shop, and was outfitted in two or three very smart Tyrolean coat and trouser combinations, and one particularly chic dark loden green smoking jacket. I was ready to conquer. Today Lanz, tomorrow ze world!

I border-hopped back and forth between Austria, Bavaria and Hungary. I did Vienna, beloved Vienna; went to the Büch Theatre and the opera; visited Schönbrunn, the Hofburg, the Belvedere and Schwarzenberg palaces; ditto the Spanish Riding School to watch the Lipizzaner horses pirouette to Mozart. I booked myself into the great Sacher Hotel with its quaint sloping floors, its sumptuous Sacher tortes and immovable feasts. I played the piano at the Drei Husaren while that famous restaurant's resident pianist sat nearby, his face a picture of disdainful mockery (shades of *The Third Man*). On my way to Budapest I gazed fascinated at the legendary storks perched on the steeples and rooftops of all those picturesque border towns. Once inside Hungary, I made a beeline for the Empress Elizabeth's summer palace of Gödöllö, meandered through the Esterhazy estates and strolled beside the waters of Lake Balaton. Passing through Salzburg I let the lush sound of the Vienna Philharmonic envelop me as I sat in on von Karajan's rehearsals. In fabulous old München, I gorged myself on Wiener shnitzel and weisswurst ünd kalbsbraten; in Bavaria I wandered through Mad Lüdwig's castles pretending I was Wagner and got myself in a deal of trouble with a fast young crowd led by that beautiful, decadent adolescent Helmut Berger. This wayward Adonis would later play King Lüdwig most effectively in Visconti's splendidly photographed movie. And oh, those Austrian girls! With their dark hair and deep flashing eyes — when they are gorgeous, they are fairly unsurpassed.

Then the punishment came! I must have been having too good a time, for someone had put a curse on me. In Austria, they call it the Hexenschuss — the witch sinks her claws into your back and leaves them there. In plain English, my sciatic nerve was paralyzed. For days I lay still on my hotel bed without moving. I had no choice — the pain was too excruciating. A local beauty of astonishing looks insisted upon looking after me. She came regularly to my room. This sister of mercy made sure her nursing skills went far beyond the call of duty. As I lay there, a captive corpse, at least one part of me was alive. It was much-needed therapy. I was in heavenly bondage, but during a particularly noisy session, a call sheet was slipped discreetly under my door and the honeymoon was over.

I girded my aching loins, bid a sad farewell to my bouncing Rhine maiden and emerged from the dream a little the worse for wear. The smiling faces of Fritz, Karl, Bruno and the Count cheered me up immeasurably. I was further honoured by Gretl, who came down from her rooms and threatened to court-martial me for desertion. Gil Stewart, now drenched in whiskey and more pukka sahib than ever, thundered an earsplitting war cry from his accustomed headquarters at the end of the bar. He had remained there for the duration of my absence, having not yet been called to work. "I'm vurried about Stewart," Gretl whispered in my ear; "he's looking so ill. I haf tolt Bruno to vater his drinks, but he steals ven Bruno iss not looking!" It was good to be back with Mutter Courage and her little army again. I had missed them.

Robert Wise took one look at me and turned pale. "Young man, you better go on a diet right away. How are you going to get into your clothes?" He was right—the good life was showing only too obviously. All my costumes had to be let out to their fullest, a couple of them were entirely remade and the makeup man was obliged to use an inordinate amount of dark shading as I was beginning to resemble Orson Welles.

However dissipated I appeared, I was obviously presentable enough for one person who had arrived out of the blue—the real Baroness von Trapp—the actual Maria, a jolly, chortling frau of ample proportions who could not have hidden her oversized shoes under any convent bed in Europe and escape detection. The baroness did not exactly boost my confidence by informing me how much more handsome I was than her husband. My God! What could he have looked like?! But she was very bouncy and bossy, laughed a lot and really was most likable. Incongruously for an ex-nun, she was an expert channel swimmer, a prize-winning world-class champion, in fact. All at once she announced in booming tones that she couldn't stay with us very long and I imagined that yet another channel somewhere was already bracing itself for her plunge. The baroness remained long enough to watch Julie and me shoot our first meeting in that glorious mirrored room, which had been a part of the great Max Reinhardt's old mansion on the outskirts of town. To see this buxom, bovine Maria gazing at the other Maria—her slim, trim alter ego—was quite uncanny.

The second scene on my agenda was with Julie and the children singing "Edelweiss" to the townspeople at Salzburg's Riding School. Back in the forties, Germany and Austria had barely surrendered when the real von Trapp family had given a concert there. They had not been received with the usual enthusiasm they expected. At that moment, they were extremely unpopular, having just returned from America where they had safely lived out the war while their countrymen suffered humiliation and defeat. To drive the stake in deeper, the von Trapps had insisted that the poor audience put on black tie and evening dress! But the fictional scene we were to shoot took place before the family's escape; we were all attired in more modest Tyrolean peasant costumes and the general reception was meant to be one of warmth and emotion, a Teutonic love-in, one might say. The Riding School was in the open and the dark night air combined with Irwin Kostal's lovely arrangement on the guide track gave the proceedings an aura of wistfulness that quite infected us all. "Edelweiss" was also, thank God, the easiest song of the bunch to sing, and my favourite.

Every now and then when not "on call," I would visit the set and watch Julie do her stuff. "Do-Re-Me," for example, was filmed all over Austria's countryside at various locations ending up in charming Mirabellplatz close by the Bristol Hotel. At the coffee breaks Gretl would appear accompanied by her young waitresses bearing trays of mouth-watering pastries. On the sidelines I would stand, lost in admiration at Julie's inexhaustible energy. With the help of those talented choreographers Mark Breaux and Dee Dee Woods, she made the simple dance numbers appear completely natural and improvised and that big heart of hers burst through everything she did. There was a radiance in her she couldn't suppress even if she'd tried.

In the meantime, Gil Stewart had been taken ill. It was inevitable of course. The bar was like a morgue without him. Poor old Bruno was lost, wandering aimlessly about, wondering what to do. From time to time I would catch sight of Gretl disappearing into the lift carrying bowls of soup up to Gil's room. She looked after him and cared for him so intensely that in a week she had nursed him back to health. It was none too soon for as he left his sick room and gingerly groped his way down to the bar, Fritz and Karl (Tweedledum and Tweedledee) were waving sheets of paper in the air. "Herr Stewart," they shouted. "Congratulations! Vunderbar! You are vorking! Tomorrow!" As the butler, it was to be his one and only day's work in ten weeks. Fritz, Karl, Bruno, the Count and I put our heads together and arranged a surprise celebration that would be waiting for him when he returned. Signs were made with "Welcome Home, Gil," "You Made It" and "Who Needs Hollywood" scribbled all over them. We got at least two hundred balloons to fly above the front entrance and the bar. Gretl had the kitchen prepare huge platters of cold meat and salads and two large jeroboams of champagne were put on ice. It was just going to be us five—the Bristol's skeleton crew as it were.

Wouldn't you know that Gil didn't begin shooting till 9:00 p.m.! We waited for the last customer to vacate the premises and then started to put up balloons and get everything ready. At 1:00 a.m., Gil had still not materialized. As on a ship's watch we took turns napping, Bruno nodding off at the bar, Fritz and Karl sprawled over the front desk, Festitic stretched out on a sofa. I went upstairs to lie down. About four in the morning a very sleepy Count called me in my room. "He's outside now!" "Turn all the lights out," I barked; "it's got to be a surprise." As the unsuspecting Gil walked through the door, all the lights went back on. He just stood there, gaping. Raising our champagne glasses in a toast we sang "For he's a jolly good butler" at the top of our lungs. Gretl appeared in her dressing gown. "Keep your voices down. You vill vake ze guests. Oh vell, never mind, gif me a vhiskey instead," and joining our revels, she stayed to the bitter end. Gil, completely overcome, became more British by the second, salvos of his deep basso profundo ricocheting off the Bristol's walls.

The film company shipped Gil out two days later. He couldn't handle it. As they were loading his bags into the van, he came up to me in the lobby. "I don't want to go back, you know. I've loved it here," he said. I could see that he was shaking and trying to fight back his tears. "I say, old man, do me a good turn, won't you? Tell Gretl thanks for everything and say good-bye for me. I simply couldn't face her. She was the best mother I ever had." He tried to laugh it off but was clearly inconsolable. He hugged Fritz and Karl and Festitic, then Bruno, who said nothing but whose expression spoke volumes. And then he was off for Munich airport. Bruno still stood at the bar stunned. Half an hour went by before Gretl came down in a white rage. "Vere iss Stewart? I can't find him anyvare! I'm taking him to ze airport. Vere is he!!??" she shouted at Fritz and Karl who were trembling behind their desk. Not satisfied, she added a barrage of German invectives and hurled them in everyone's direction. I summoned up my courage. "He's already left, Gretl, I'm afraid; he wanted me to say good-bye *for* him. You see—" but I didn't finish. She was slamming the car door and taking off in a horrible smell of burning rubber. Gil told me much later: "I was sitting in the airport lounge waiting to board when I saw Gretl, her graying hair wild and unkempt, racing toward me. I stood up. In front of everyone she came up to me—I could see she was crying—and slapped my face so that it stung like hell, looked hard at me for the longest moment, then turned on her heels and left. The last thing I wanted to do was get on that plane. I loved that woman, you know."

Before starting out for work late one morning I went to the bar for a pick-me-up. There was no Bruno. That was most unusual—there was always a Bruno. In fact, the bar was empty except for Festitic in a corner, puffing away on his cigarette holder. Fritz and Karl came over to me and, as always, Fritz spoke for Karl. "Bruno has not come to vork for two, sree days." "And Frau Hübner?" I asked. "She has taken to her bed; ve don't know ven she vill come down." I knew they missed the Englishman, but I had not realized how deeply.

The unit car picked me up and drove me to Bavaria, where we were to shoot the last scene of the picture in which the von Trapp family escapes the Nazis by climbing over the Alps to Switzerland, neutrality and freedom. It was now afternoon, and the sun was casting long shadows across the breathtaking hill they had chosen. A normal camera would have made it all look much too pretty and cute, like a picture postcard. But Ted McCord, our brilliant D.P., had taken care of that by inventing a special lens that gave back to the countryside all its natural beauty, just as one views it with the naked eye. I have always thought that last scene amusingly ironic, for over the brow of that hill supposedly lies sanctuary. In reality, at the top of our particular hill lay the ruins of a terrace, all that remained of Hermann Göring's home, called the "Eagle's Nest." A little way below was an empty plot where Herr Goebbels's house had stood, and farther down the hill the huge empty fish tanks of the Berghof overlooking Berchtesgaden itself—a last reminder of Adolf Hitler's private lair. So it would appear that instead of "freedom" for the von Trapps, they had inadvertently wandered straight into the hornet's nest.

Finally, the moment had come for the unit to move back to the States—time to bid farewell to our beautiful Austria. The film company threw a "wrap" party that was anticlimactic to the point of redundancy as we would all meet soon again in Los Angeles to shoot the remaining interiors. Trish and I had made another attempt at temporary reconciliation, so as I had a fortnight free, I would join her in the south of France for a brief holiday at the luxurious Hotel du Cap, Eden-Roc. I spent the last two days, overcome with nostalgia, wandering through Salzburg whispering secret good-byes to my favourite haunts. Back at the hotel I bumped into a busload of "blue-rinsed" ladies from mid-America. They had just had lunch and were standing in the lobby waiting for their transportation. Fritz and Karl were going quite spare answering a barrage of impossible questions. The noise was deafening. Festitic was hovering in the background being his usual charming self—all the old ladies had instant fantasies about him, I'm quite sure. In the midst of the fracas, I heard one woman, who was standing right next to Festitic, shout out to Fritz and Karl in a particularly harsh twang, "How much do I tip the Count?!"

Well, I knew what I was going to give Fritz, Karl and Bruno as a parting gift—money! Which was easy and which they would surely need. But the Count? What on earth would I give him? "Ach! He doesn't expect anything," said Gretl when I asked her. "But if you must, gif him a cigarette case; he doesn't own one." I went to the best shop in town and had them engrave his initials inside a very smart dark brown leather case. He bowed stiffly when I presented him with it and though he seemed grateful, I had the distinct impression that he would have preferred money.

It was checkout time. To go that short journey to the front desk was like walking the last mile. I cannot describe it. I knew exactly what Gil had gone through on his last day. It was awful. Fritz, Karl and Bruno gave me a big hug. Then I gave Fritz, Karl and Bruno a big hug. Then we did it all over again and started blubbing as if on cue. This could have gone on forever had not Gretl put a stop to it. I had sent my luggage on ahead with the unit van because Gretl had insisted on driving me to the airport. "Come on, hurry up. Ve can't stay here all day." I noticed she didn't look at me and I certainly couldn't look at her. I didn't have the control. She walked out of the hotel and waited for me in her car. Our good-byes spilled over onto the street, Fritz, Karl and Bruno following me out. I suddenly wanted to take them all with me. Festitic was standing straight as a ramrod holding the car door open for me. Elegant as he was in his morning coat and stripes, I noticed his shirt collar and cuffs were slightly frayed. It gave him a look of faded grandeur and he reminded me a little of the White Knight in *Alice Through the Looking Glass.* I was about to climb in when he grabbed my arm. His eyes were cast down and he said quite solemnly in those deep, soft accents of his: "You have been a good friend." There was a pause and then: "Vere vill you go now?" "To the south of France," I answered. He gave a little sigh. "Ze south of France," he whispered dreamily, "how vunderful." "When were you last there?" I asked. "It was so long ago. I vas a little boy." In his eyes I caught a glimpse of a little boy's longing to escape. "I'm afraid you will find it terribly changed now," I offered. "It's all become so commercial and built up. Where did you stay when you were there?" There was another pause. "Oh, I don't remember qvite," he murmured, "but it vas very beautiful. Ve vere staying vis King Edvard ze Seventh."

It was as if all the clocks had stopped and we were suspended above the pavement. It was the first time that Festitic had ever referred in any way to his former life. He was still gazing down at his shoes. There was something so absolutely fin de siècle about the old man. For a moment, he looked up but his sad eyes were staring past me into some far-distant time which no one, not even he, could possibly resurrect. I held out my hand.

"Plummer! Hurry up. Get in!" cried an impatient Gretl at the wheel, the blast of a car horn renting the air. "You'll miss your plane." And, with a sudden jolt, we were back in the present.

ON ITS FINAL LAP at the Fox Studios in LA, "S & M" sped rapidly towards its completion. It was now all work and not much play except for a few redeeming moments such as filming the Lendler, that graceful dance during which Maria and the Captain first fall in love. It was a welcome interlude in what had become a rather strenuous schedule and, in spite of my two left feet, a breeze, due to my partner's formidable expertise.

Then there was the new song Rodgers and Hammerstein had added to the film score, "Something Good," which Julie and I were to croon in soft, intimate tones as we squared off to face each other in a gazebo. McCord had provided some low filtered lighting for the nonce, which was extremely flattering and bathed us most romantically in semisilhouette. Everything was set up, the mood was established, but just as the cameras began to roll, the thought of us both singing at such close range with our noses touching suddenly struck me as thoroughly bizarre. It must have struck Julie as well, for we both started giggling shamefully. Cut! We tried again — no dice! Each column of the gazebo had been lit for moonlight effects and it all looked suitably romantic. We began singing again and everything for the moment seemed under control when two elusive carbons rubbing accidently together made a sound as if someone was prodigiously and continuously farting. We collapsed. Cut! Take twelve! By this time we were holding on to each other, clawing away at our clothes, dissolved in raucous laughter.

It was a contagious disease that was spreading fast, for it had infected the entire crew, including Mr. Wise. Our sides hurt — I'm sure thirty takes at least had gone by, none of which were printable, when mercifully we broke for lunch. Coming back to the set one hour later, convinced we'd sufficiently pulled ourselves together, we steeled ourselves for the moment and prayed for control. Jools had even taken a Valium, terrified lest she let her side down. Then the arcs began their revenge, and the farting continued. We buckled over in exhausted and helpless agony. This was getting serious. Bob Wise always had a pocket watch

Spooning "Something Good," trying to keep straight faces

on a chain, which he rubbed like a touchstone. It must have had a soothing effect upon him, like a patience drug. Not today. "Turn off the lights. We'll shoot it in the dark," he shouted. And we proceeded to play in silhouette, hoping no one would see us giggling. How we finally got it in the can I'll never know. I imagine we were just too drained to laugh anymore and had no option but to do it straight. The word "print" is a lovely word and makes a lovely sound at moments like these and our relief was well earned, for in the end result, something not bad at all had come out of "Something Good."

To further shake me up, the final recording session was upon us. Daunting is not a strong enough word to describe it. Julie and I stood side by side in a small glassed-in cubicle facing two microphones. Surrounding our prison cage sat seventy-five musicians like hungry jackals waiting to pounce, led by their keeper, Irwin Kostal. Warbling softly into a mike is far more difficult than singing full out in a theatre as I was later to discover. One is much more likely to catch and collect "frogs" in the throat, whereas projecting usually gets rid of them. I tried so hard not to look like a complete basket case. Julie, sensing my nerves, took hold of my hand and held it throughout the session. It must have taken her days to recover the use of it afterwards, I had squeezed so hard. No matter how diligently I'd slugged away at my lessons, I was still untrained as a singer. To stay on a long-sustained note was, for me, akin to a drunk trying to walk the straight white line, whereas you can bet the very first cry that Julie let forth as she emerged from her mother's womb was in perfect pitch! Listening to the playback, there was no disputing we were on separate planets. In the end, Robert Wise managed to hire someone to take care of my elongated passages, and the balance was somewhat restored.

Things had begun to markedly change on the "S & M" lot. There was a low buzz that seemed to indicate early hints of success. Reporters began skulking about; celebrities paid visits to the set. I remember a delectable Shirley MacLaine popping in quite frequently (she was on the next stage filming *Irma la Douce*). Agents and managers in growing numbers appeared more regularly. Well-respected directors would turn up to pay homage to Robert Wise. There was a distinct scent of success in the air. Julie took me aside one day and whispered, "Do you get the feeling we might be famous one day?"

WELL, THE REST is history of a kind. Here was a forgotten story that had collected dust at the bottom of a studio drawer for eight years,

Robert Wise, carefully preventing us from drowning in sentimentality

which would one day save that same studio from bankruptcy. *Cleopatra* had totally wasted the Twentieth lot and *The Sound of Music* became the Good Samaritan and put it safely back on its feet once more. I have never recovered from my shyness toward the glaring lights of a film premiere. I am a complete hypocrite, of course, torn between the thrill of mob recognition on the one hand and my aversion to the sheer vulgarity of it on the other. I therefore spent most of our premiere with a few chums including Robert Wise in the bar next door. The critics generally pooh-poohed the enterprise and it's always been my opinion they were too ashamed to admit they liked it lest their cynical, hard-boiled comrades of the press might call them sissies and banish them to the nearest convent. However, the film won the Oscar and the public, eager for a "family feature," wasted no time in boarding the speedily revolving roller coaster of praise; by the year's end, most countries had cheerfully risen to its bait. Most, that is, except Austria, which, for some time, had been fairly saturated by an onslaught of Trappamania. A well-made, detailed German documentary on their lives had been shown ad nauseam when "S & M" was a mere embryo; not to mention the family's persistent habit of yodeling themselves sick whenever an alp or two loomed into view. The Austrians too had somewhat understandably objected to the liberties taken by our costume department and regarded our apparel as so much Hollywoodized lederhosen. They also, not quite so understandably, decried the movie as being painfully schlag and sentimental, which, coming from that country, was tantamount to calling the kettle black.

More than frequently, over time, I have found myself returning to that part of the world, almost as a force of habit. I have appeared in other films made there and have visited as an admiring tourist and an avid fan of the festival. With each visit I noticed how much more prosperous everything seemed to appear, Austria having submitted to a major face-lift. No matter how modest, every schlöss had been freshly painted, their window boxes by the thousands overflowing with fresh multicolored flowers. The restaurants had made giant steps towards improvement and were booming. The hills and valleys, more alive than ever, were manicured to the bone—there was nary a blemish on the landscape. In fact it almost cried out for dear Mr. McCord, who had sadly left us to come back from the dead with his filters to make the whole countryside look less like a fairy tale. There was no doubt that "S & M" had helped turn Austria into a far richer country. Almost a billion dollars has poured in due to the avalanche of tourism the film has generated. Over the years, the people's attitude has altered considerably. They have entirely come to terms with it; there are "S & M" tours by the cartloads and Julie, Robert and I have accepted honours from both Salzburg and Vienna for our contributions to the pot. Every time I arrive there I feel rather like a Hapsburg reclaiming the throne. The old charm still exudes everywhere—the one and only disappointment was the little Bristol Hotel.

I snuck in one day to take a look. I was curious to see if any of the old atmosphere still prevailed. How I ever imagined it would beats me; after all, this was all almost forty years ago. Gretl, Bruno, Fritz, Karl and the Count were all long gone and there was little hope that they had left anything of themselves behind. I stood for a moment in the lobby with my eyes closed and tried to conjure up the smallest trace of that past which had found such a permanent place in my heart. I suddenly missed my little family terribly; I had adored my stay there, living in a crazy Ruritanian dream. It was like being part of a play of Ferenc Molnár's with incidental music by Oscar Strauss and Franz Lehar. I opened my eyes. No, there was nothing of that anymore. I didn't recognize this place at all. The Bristol was now just another hotel, any ordinary hotel, cold and heartless. I turned away and walked out into the bustling life of Makartplatz and the air that comes down from the mountains—the familiar, comforting soft air that is still part of my memory and thankfully refuses to change.

ABOUT A YEAR or so ago in Connecticut, I went to a children's Easter party. They were going to show "S & M" as an after-lunch treat. Oh, my God, I thought, how am I going to escape? My friends, the hosts, pleaded with me to stay. "It will be such fun for the kids to watch Captain von Trapp watching himself on the screen." Oh, sure, I thought, the monstrous little fiends! Well, I stayed. I had not seen the movie for years and the more I watched, the more I realized what a terrific movie it is. The very best of its genre—warm, touching, joyous and absolutely timeless. I suddenly could see why it had brought such pleasure to so many people. Here was I, cynical old sod that I am, being totally seduced by the damn thing—and what's more, I felt a sudden surge of pride that I'd been a part of it. How beautifully it had been shot, how natural the choreography, how rich the arrangements, how excellent the cast. And Robert Wise, with his innate good taste and judgment, had expertly held in the reins lest it all canter over the cliff's edge down into a sea of treacle.

But the picture belongs to Julie. Of that there is no doubt. It is her movie, her triumph. The familiar saying that the camera never lies is one I will gladly dispute anytime, anyplace. In Julie's case, no camera, true or false, could stem the flow of her particular genius. She thoroughly infused the story with her own spirit, her own enchantment. Of course, that glorious golden sound of hers still echoes in the shell, but her performance was the antithesis of a musical comedy turn. Banishing all artifice, she was real, true, funny and vulnerable. She had lit up the screen and spilt her blood. There was no turning back now; it was far too late, for before anyone could even whisper the name "Maria," a hopelessly infatuated world had already made her its hostage.

CHAPTER TWENTY-SIX

"WILL WE EVER?"

Natalie Wood picked up her knife, wiped it, and using it as a mirror, a regular habit of hers, proceeded to reapply her lipstick. Now normally, making up at the dinner table would be considered bad manners and extremely gauche. In Natalie's hands, it became a thing of beauty and more than acceptable. We were dining in a booth at La Scala on Little Santa Monica in Beverly Hills—B.J. (the Powder Puff), Natalie and I. "La Scala Good Evening" as we nicknamed it was a consistently warm and inviting Italian bistro in the days before Corporate Hollywood, when there was a lot more humour and fun about the place and stars were not averse to leaving their ivory towers and actually eating out; it was a most informal, friendly gathering place for producers, writers and actors who were not ashamed to be seen together. There was none of today's tension. We all knew each other no matter our status (even I, on the fringes, was made to feel welcome) and we would sit in dark red leather booths and throw roles or small talk across the tables at each other. It was one of Miss Wood's favourite spots and would become one of mine as well. The Powder Puff, who had

Natalie photographed by Roddy McDowall

known her for some time as her regular makeup artist and friend, beginning their relationship in Kazan's *Splendor in the Grass,* had set up this first meeting of mine with the raven-haired beauty. B.J.'s silly off-the-wall humour was at its best that night and we spent most of the meal giggling like giddy children. She had the most unabashed child-like giggle, which rippled musically through the garlic-scented room, and by the time the check arrived, I was infatuated.

Kurt Frings (still my agent) had procured costar billing for me under Natalie Wood's name for a film called *Inside Daisy Clover,* adapted for the screen by Gavin Lambert from his book of the same name. Gavin, an amusing British writer was based in Santa Monica near his mentor Christopher Isherwood. Natalie would play his heroine Daisy, a young undiscovered star in the making who was to be groomed for success by the studio head played by me—a character based on the famous young genius at MGM, Irving Thalberg. The story was very lightweight fare but with some attempt at style, and it marked Alan Pakula's first film as a producer along with his partner, the director Robert Mulligan (*To Kill a Mockingbird,* etc.). Pakula had married my friend Hope Lange (the Powder Puff's sister-in-law) so the atmosphere on the set was cozy and had a distinct family feeling about it. Robert Redford (one of his first films) had a supporting role, the great Ruth Gordon played Natalie's loony mum and Roddy McDowall was my sinister right-hand man. Added to this, Herb Ross did some choreography for Natalie, and the music and lyrics were taken care of by André and Dory Previn.

On my first day in front of the camera, the old propman, who'd been at Warner's all his life, came up to me and asked what I usually liked to drink. "At the moment it's Scotch," I answered. After my very first shot was in the can, there he was right in front of me handing me a Johnnie Walker Black Label on the rocks in a beautiful crystal glass. "What's this?" I asked, flabbergasted. "Hell, it's only 9 a.m." "It's a tradition

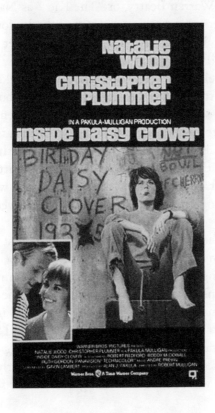

here, Mr. Plummer, for after everyone's first shot and from now on, the bar is open." The courtesy and professionalism of the entire crew at Warner's who were all getting on and had been there forever, I have never seen the likes of since. These veterans had seen everything and had some stories to tell, no question about that. How one longs sometimes for those old Studio Days to come back.

LA was a lot smaller then and the movie colony was more like a village, far more intimate, an indication of what it must have been like in the twenties and thirties. There was still in the early sixties a sense of adventure about the place, particularly as the "independents" were about to rear their heads.

With the help of a hotel PR lady, the gracious Helen Chaplin, I found myself occupying the rooftop penthouse of Hernando Courtright's Beverly Wilshire Hotel. After the last elevator stop, there was this little staircase, which led to my private aerie in the clouds. At night out of my windows I could see the canyons on one side and the Hollywood Hills and Las Filas on the other. If I wanted fresh air, I just had to step out of my cabin and the rest of the roof was mine. It was just me and the sky. Warren Beatty, or "The Kid," as Natalie and B.J. had called him often, used this charming abode for his clandestine romances. It had, in fact, "love nest" written all over it.

Trish was still in London—our marriage now seriously on the skids. I was hopelessly restless and Trish was drinking heavily again. The doctors had tried so hard to convince her that booze could damage dramatically the scar tissue on her brain. They even pleaded with me to persuade her to desist, but she didn't seem to care. So many magazines and journals had offered her some interesting positions as a writer, but since the accident she seemed to have little will to work at anything. I'm afraid I wasn't any help anymore—we fought horribly when we were together, so putting distance between us seemed the only solution.

At the time, the Daisy was the newest and hottest disco in town and I spent most of my nights there partying with Hope and Alan, Natalie and B.J. or playing pool with Peter Falk in the room next to the dance floor. The whole place vibrated with temptation. There was no shortage of beauty there and life seemed for a while wrapped in a golden haze.

On the set next to ours, Sinatra, Dean Martin and Sammy Davis, Jr., were filming some light pastiche. There was a long bar set up on the stage where drinks were flowing like water from early call till the day's wrap. But Frank was always wandering over to our set to visit Natalie for whom, like many a respectful gentleman, he nursed a serious crush. Jack Warner, the boss, would do the rounds but his favourite set was ours. He particularly admired the office the designers had built for me, which boasted a magnificent long refectory table as my desk. Warner would appear quite frequently when we were filming and chat with me in that rapid staccato rat-tat-tat speech of his. I was most flattered and quite believed he was obviously impressed with what I was doing. I was wrong. It wasn't me he gave a damn about—it was my desk. One day I overheard him bark at the production manager, "When this set is struck, I want that desk in my office."

Trish arrived for a rare visit and suddenly my little cabin in the sky was filled to the brim with the English contingent. It was fun for a while to see old friends such as dear mad Ian Bannen, but the celebrations went on much too long. The late nights were taking their toll and I had to rise at ungodly early hours to get to the studio. The brilliant Tony Hancock, one of England's great comedians, turned up one night and stayed two weeks. Like some comics whose humour comes from pain, his everyday life was a sad and lost one. He was hitting the bottle seriously and had come to LA to make a film but had never once reported for work. Roddy, who was doing a cameo in the same flick, called me. "Is Tony with you? We're all waiting for him on the set." Trish and I tried to get him into the elevator but to no avail—he would simply pass out—a complete deadweight. We finally got Security to carry him down and drive him to his own hotel. His loyal, long-suffering wife who loved him so deeply appeared SOS from London and took him back home with her across the Pond. Poor Tony never made it before the cameras, a tragic and unbelievably talented man.

Jack Warner's man Friday who arranged his entire social and business commitments was a veddy British ex-army major called Richard Sculley. He enjoyed playing Mosca to Warner's Volpone and clearly knew all the dark secrets. For some reason, Jack must have thought I too was British and an important representative of that country, for there was Richard on the blower inviting Trish and me to a small dinner for Lord Louis Mountbatten at the Warner mansion. The call caught us in the midst of a heated squabble and she yelled out loud and clear while I was still on the phone, "You can damn well go on your own!" The car whisked me up the long driveway peppered from top to bottom with plainclothesmen and police. I sought out Mr. Warner and apologized for coming on my own because my wife was ill. Not in the least concerned about her health or my apology, this highly superstitious man, looking most upset and annoyed, ungraciously mumbled under his breath, "What am I going to do, for Christ's sake, that makes it thirteen!"

Being a sort of actor manqué, Lord Louis loved Jack Warner, loved Hollywood, loved showbiz and loved the ladies, especially his date for the night, Shirley MacLaine, whose film *Irma la Douce* in which she played a prostitute had just come out. In the men's room I overheard him whisper to his son-in-law Lord Brabourne, "By God d'y know she researched it all in Paris by actually shacking up with the real whores? Can y'believe the guts?" Just before dinner I was introduced to him. He was wearing a black armband and standing beside Warner in a corner of the room towering over him. There was an awkward pause and I racked my brain for something to fill the void. Winston Churchill had just died and I remembered during that splendid televised funeral service Lord Louis had made a very stirring and moving tribute. I now gave voice to this and told him how touched I had been. Unbending for a moment and with a grandiose charm he thanked me most sincerely. Jack Warner took this as a cue for some ribald repartee, slapped Mountbatten on the back and lighting his own oversized cigar quipped, "Well, Winston tastes good like a cigarette should." I pretended to enjoy the gaffe by laughing a little too long and a little too loudly, but I caught sight of Lord Louis's extravagantly bushy eyebrow travel up the length of his ample forehead and down again.

At dinner I sat next to the new number fourteen—the dynamic and ultra-attractive Stella Stevens, one of the few Hollywood blondes with a sense of humour who could also act! Opposite me sat Mountbatten flanked by Binnie Barnes (rollickingly funny) and Shirley (ditto). Lord Brabourne sat at Stella's left and Warner took the head. The dinner service was solid gold (vulgarly pretentious as if the Pope was expected any minute) and the meal for such grandiosity was very ordinary indeed—overdone filet mignon and rather sad-looking vegetables. For some bizarre reason there was no red wine at all to quaff down the beef—only Dom Pérignon, which unsuitably accompanied every course. The dessert arrived elegantly served on smaller gold platters promising some rare and succulent creation, but on closer examination it seemed to be a collection of rather tired-looking strawberries with a lifeless runny cream a coté. Lord Louis was, by now, having fun with all this, mercifully teasing Warner, who didn't take teasing too well. "Let us consult our menu cards, shall we, to see what sort of concoction this pretends to be." There it was in exquisite writing at each place setting—

"Fraise Grimeures," looking suspiciously like made-up French. "What does 'Fraise Grimeures' mean?" asked Stella with that perpetual naughty twinkle in her eye. "Haven't the foggiest," retorted Lord Louis. "Probably should have read 'Fraise de Hier.'" There was a lot of laughter at the table and Warner, who had no options left but to join in, turned out to be a good sport after all.

We were all marched into the screening room to watch a sneak preview of *Irma la Douce*. Mountbatten and Shirley were two rows in front of me. His arm was around her and tsk! tsk! Was it the boozy haze clouding my heavy eyes or did I not catch sight of them spooning in the dark? Tsk! Tsk! When the lights came on we all attacked the after-dinner drinks with much relief. Jack Lemmon was itching to play some jazz piano. "Let's meet down at the Daisy and bring His Lordship," he called over his shoulder. Lord L. was clearly dying to break loose, so the younger group (in which I included myself) went to work on him. He pointed sadly at his armband and said, "I'd honestly love to, but my sister the Queen of Sweden died last week and I can't exactly be seen gallivanting about the town. But God love you for asking!" For a man who occasionally lost little opportunity to remind the world he was a direct descendent of Charlemagne, Louis Mountbatten was a good man underneath—handsome, witty, one of the boys, who with his beautiful late, lamented wife, Edwina, had undoubtedly helped bring an effortless glamour to the carefree twenties and thirties. When we got to the Daisy, there was Lemmon gettin' down'n'dirty on the keys, Alan Pakula, Hope, Roddy, Gavin, Matt Crowley (whose play *The Boys in the Band* had broken ground for gays everywhere), the Powder Puff and in the middle of it all, brandishing a cigarette holder, with joy sparkling in those enormous dark eyes, Natalie Wood.

Natalie was then a big star at Warner's. She deserved to be. She had weathered the storm since she was five. She had been bullied, pushed, cajoled and bribed by an overly zealous, overly ambitious stage mum throughout her infancy. "We need Natalie to cry in this scene and she won't cry—do something, can't you?!" Directors would appeal to this iron lady and she would do anything to comply, including catching butterflies and pulling their wings off in front of the child. That usually worked. Natalie told me this herself one night when we were playing True Confessions. Otherwise that was the extent of Natalie's confidences. She never betrayed her parents to anyone but always remained staunchly loyal and respectful and for years had financially supported the whole brood. Now she had built for herself a small fortune—she owned apartment blocks all over town and her money had been invested wisely. She was one hot property. She had been Jimmy Dean's on-screen girl in *Rebel Without a Cause,* Beatty's in *Splendor in the Grass.* As a star she had cornered the young market.

Nat or Natasha, as she was properly named, had a favourite colour, yellow. So yellow was always present wherever she went. Warner Brothers saw to it that yellow would be her theme. Her cabin on the lot was painted yellow, the bike they provided for her was yellow, as was the fancy little golf cart that transported her from one soundstage to the other. She was treated like a young goddess, and though she exuded great professional confidence and knew who she was, a genuine product of that industry ("I'm Natalie Vood from Holyvood," she would jest)— no one carried such success with less ego and more humility.

But the Slavic blood that coursed through her veins was inclined to induce sharply contrasting mood swings. Natalie was unpredictable. At the moment she was deeply involved romantically with a very successful young shoe manufacturer from Venezuela by name of "Lattie" Blatnik. How they had met or formed any sort of alliance I had no idea. As far as looks go Lattie was no oil painting, but he was warm and kind, slightly out of his depth and head over heels in love. Natalie, always grateful for the slightest attention, seemed to love him just as much in return. But she knew how to flirt. It was automatic—part of her woman's instinct. Of course, she must have sensed I had a crush on her, and occasionally to toss it off lightly she would play this little game with me. She would stare deep into my eyes for the longest time and then say tauntingly, "Will we ever?"—a rather cruel little game as she was not in the least serious and I was. Nat, who was always so professional, never let romance or anything for that matter interfere with her work, but the nuptials were getting close and I could see that even on the set she was becoming distracted. She couldn't wait, so she decided to throw a huge wedding party at night and the next morning to top it off—the ceremony would take place under a marquee. She had arranged for Chasen's to do the whole thing quite scrumptiously in the garden behind her house at North Bentley Avenue. Everyone from the A, B, and Z group was there. Natalie's mother, father and sister came, and Lattie's parents were flown in from Venezuela. But Natalie took no notice; she only had eyes for Lattie—nothing it seemed could separate them.

The evening was in full swing several hours later when B.J., with his usual conspiratorial manner, mumbled in my ear, "Look over there, w-what d'you think's h-happened?" I turned and saw a forlorn Natalie, all alone, sitting on a window seat, staring straight in front of her. I went up to her and asked what was wrong. There was a long pause and then she slowly turned, looked me right in the eyes and said, "I've called it off!—the wedding, I mean. It's no good. I can't go through with it!" When Natalie made a decision, there was no procrastinating.

The party had already thinned out, rather like an opening at Sardi's when the bad reviews are read out. The bridegroom, his parents in tow, had long since gone—the band was wrapping it up—the boys from Chasen's were removing the tables. "Go, g-go play something—anything," said B.J. nudging me in the ribs. I drowned myself in champagne and played into the night. When I stopped, I turned around expecting some sort of applause, but there was no one left in the room, not even B.J. Smacked out of my skull, I passed out on a couch. I woke up the next morning around ten—still no one about. I went through the house in search of Natalie. I opened every bedroom door, every closet—there was no life at North Bentley Avenue. The place was empty. Feeling quite spooked, I called the Beverly Wilshire. They sent a car over and took me and my raging head back to the hotel. To this day I'm at a loss as to what happened.

The filming of *Daisy Clover* continued on its rocky course, its story line much tamer than the one taking place offscreen. As the power-crazed studio head I had one really good scene by a pool and one or two telling ones with Daisy, but my character was mostly made out of cardboard. Ruth Gordon was amazing as the weird mother. Newcomer Robert Redford and veteran Roddy Mac were both splendid and in spite of the life going on behind the scenes we did try hard to make it work. Bob Mulligan was such a fine director, much too good for this soap opera/magazine material and rather uncomfortable doing it. Natalie, as with everything she undertook, threw herself into it whole-heartedly. Some years later she confided, "I am really just a professional—everything I do is worked out. I never had the natural wackiness to play Daisy. Tuesday Weld should have played it—she would have been marvellous in it." That sort of modesty and generosity was typical of Natalie.

Because she was in such demand she was constantly pestered by erst-while so-called producers who managed to sneak past the Warner gates armed only with their bogus offers. One in particular, a supposedly wealthy film backer from Canada, obese, loud and, quite uncharacteristic in a Canadian, obnoxiously pushy. He had taken a whole floor at the

Beverly Wilshire and would accost me at the hotel bar plying me with drinks (which I ended up paying for) and boasting about his money, his talent, his power and promising me the world. It was so transparent he was trying to get to Natalie through me, he could have worn it like a halo. When Natalie and B.J. occasionally came for drinks at the hotel, this obscene slug would come up to our booth and sit down unasked, his pudgy hands pinching Natalie under the table. Each time we had him removed, but that didn't deter him; he was soon back and at it again. One day when he was lurking around looking for us, we had to hustle Natalie through the lobby, ducking behind potted palms as we went, and when we reached Natalie's car B.J. turned back. "B.J.," she yelled. "Where are you going? Are you mad?" "Maybe he c-could give me some money for *The River.*" Collapsing in laughter, we climbed into the car. We weren't to be bothered much anymore because the loser had left town without paying his bill. I imagine all those suites were too much for him to handle. The Beverly Wilshire sent out the troops to look for him. "There goes *The R-River* again," sighed B.J. with a helpless shrug.

Just over the hill in Laurel Canyon, Roddy threw his little suppers. They were never dull! He owned probably the largest private collection of films on record, which he showed on an old-fashioned projector. In those days it was not exactly legal so Roddy, the guardian of Tinseltown Secrets, was taking a gutsy chance. Just as interesting as his rare collection, if not perhaps more so, was the guest list. Hardly anywhere else in la-la-land could you find all together in the same room Lillian *and* Dorothy Gish, Irene Dunne, Gladys Cooper, Mary Astor, Myrna Loy and dear Greer Garson. Movie history was right there in that room and they had all come out of Roddy's past. The only one not present and whom I missed most, was Lassie—or even Lassie's understudy. You'd think Roddy could have at least stuffed her and stuck her on the mantel.

It was time to go home to London. Natalie arranged little get-togethers every night as *Daisy Clover* grinded to a close. With a few belts inside her she loved to sing and always very kindly asked me to accompany her. She had a pleasant sweet voice and forgiving my occasional wrong notes she would launch into "Let Me Entertain You," "Somewhere" from her films *Gypsy* and *West Side Story* or the song André Previn had composed for her—"The Circus Is a Wacky World"—and all this while sitting on the piano bench beside me. I felt a glow at the closeness of her—she was such a magical little lady. When it was over, like a child she would gleefully clap her hands and with those huge, deep moist eyes of hers boring into me, she would whisper with a wink, "Will we ever?" and then dissolve into peals of laughter. What was the matter with me? Was I a coward? Or was I just the pitiable victim of my own polite upbringing? Why the hell didn't I just shout, "Yes!"

CHAPTER TWENTY-SEVEN

THE CONQUEST OF PORTOFINO AND PERU

Honey, I'm warning you—you might just as well turn around and come right back." It was my mother hen Jane Broder with her version of a bon voyage. "John Dexter called. He wants you for New York this year. The role is Pizarro in the North American premiere of *The Royal Hunt of the Sun.* It's the star part and it's first-class quality, honey, so take it already." Before boarding the plane I phoned him. "This time you're bloody well going to act for a change, you lazy bugger, I'll see to that," he roared in my ear with his customary rudeness. J.D. was a bustling bundle of raging talent—insulting, vulgar, irreverent, outrageous, a born leader and ruthless. And though he had the appearance of an unshaven, disgruntled longshoreman, he was totally in your face *gay*—hilariously camp—and fearlessly brave. He had risen from the theatrical ranks to become a leading director at Britain's National Theatre and not too far down the road he would assume the artistic leadership of New York's Metropolitan Opera. He was on the top of everyone's list and certainly on mine.

The moment I hit London I went to see his *Royal Hunt* production. It was beautiful to behold—on a bare-naked stage, all its startling effects created solely by the use of imaginative lighting suggesting the sombre colours of Spain and the ice-cold ascent into the Andes. This was made all the more illusionary by a mime of climbing soldiers in slow motion standing in place—a brilliant stroke of inventive choreography by

Claude Chagrin, a talented young lady from Paris. The contrast in colour and movement between the graceful Incas in their feathers and the heavily clothed plodding Spaniards with their pomp and circumstance was brilliantly effective; and against all the ruffles and finery of his fellow countrymen, General Pizarro stood apart—a rough, shabby old carcass of a man driven by his vision and a God that he'd never quite been able to trust. I still think it is the best of Peter Shaffer's writing, for although historically, Pizarro and Atahuallpa barely met and most certainly never exchanged pleasantries, their fictionalized relationship conjured by Peter was strangely moving and believable—an ancient scarred warrior, his far from solid Catholic faith shaken by the serenity of a young Inca ruler living out his fantasy as a peaceful god who worships the Sun high on the Andean steppes.

> PIZARRO: *When I was young I used to sit on the slope outside the village and watch the sun go down, and I used to think: if only I could find the place where it sinks to rest for the night, I'd find the source of life, like the beginning of a river . . . If it settled here each evening, somewhere in those great mountains, like a God laid down to sleep? To a savage mind it must make a fine God. I myself can't fix anything nearer to a thought of worship than standing at dawn and watching it fill the world . . . What a fantastic wonder that anyone on earth should dare to say: 'That's my father. My father: the sun!'*

I was immensely taken by the whole experience, both the spectacle and the substance. And I loved Pizarro—he was for me! I called Jane.

THERE WAS JUST ENOUGH TIME to spare for a short holiday so Trish and I, still going through the motions of a marriage, decided we'd try once more to salvage what remained of our fragile partnership. It was to be our last attempt. Leslie and Evie Bricusse suggested we join them and fly to Italy together. "We're staying with Rex [Harrison] at his villa in Portofino. We're there to try and persuade him to do my film, *Dr. Doolittle*. I'm going to play him the score. Come along—it'll be fun and you can help." Off we went. Trish and I booked into the Hotel Splendido, true to its name, nestled in a hill overlooking the Mediterranean, halfway up the little mountain toward Rex's domain which was perched on top—the flag of St. George flying impertinently above whenever the grand seigneur was in residence, giving the impression that Portofino was just another British colony.

The first night, we spent alone in the hotel, the sunset on the sea breathtaking. The next day we received our summons for dinner chez Villa Harrison. We took a taxi up the hill until it became too precipitous, so Rex's man drove us the rest of the way in a jeep. In attendance at the villa were Rachel Roberts (Mrs. H.), that richly talented young actress from Wales who naturally made much of my own Welsh bride; a well-known PR man and producer known as "Apjack," who had flown all the way from Hollywood to help convince Rex to do the picture and, to make up the posse, Rex's agent, a dear old Brit called Laurie Evans. After *My Fair Lady* and his Oscar, R.H. was one of the most sought-after stars on the horizon, and no one enjoyed playing hard to get more than he. The cast was assembled. We rolled into dinner, a scrumptious repast prepared by R.H.'s Italian couple, and afterwards Leslie at the piano played and sang the entire score. Rex was glowing, his excitement rising by the second—you could almost see the money clicking away in his head as he added several grand more for each new song he would be obliged to sing. We all got happily smashed, Rachel in particular (she was a very funny drunk), and Trish and I, much too far gone to stagger down the steep hill, stayed the night.

That night would extend into days, Trish and I making regular hops from Il Splendido up to the villa on the summit. Apjack and Laurie Evans had gone by now and it was just us six left. During the day we would go for speedboat rides in Rex's sleek highly polished mahogany Riva, which he'd christened *Henry Higgins II.* We'd tour the coastline as far as Rapallo where the villas of Max Beerbohm and Gore Vidal overlooked the ocean. Neither of them were ever in, of course—one being long dead and the other holding court in Rome. We ended up our trips at a favourite bar on the dock at Portofino, Radzio's. Old man Radzio, a local hood who seemed to own the town and who followed Rex around like an adoring puppy dog, served us wonderful snacks and drinks; or we lunched at Villa Harrison, looking down at the tiny speck of a port far below. "Look," screeched Rex, "it's the Burtons' yacht. It's been moored out there for days. Quick, man the telescope." We all took turns. It was already long past noon and through the powerful lens we could see Richard all alone, swigging on a vodka bottle, pacing up and down looking utterly dejected on a totally deserted deck. "Poor bastard—she's not up yet. She'll come out much later all heavily made up. You'll see. That's all he does, poor bugger—waits for her, never

Rachel Roberts (Mrs. Rex Harrison) and Rex, divinely funny;
she never stopped making me laugh.

stops drinking." I looked at that lined face through the spyglass, a bit-ter expression of regret permanently stamped on its features—regret for a wasted talent, was that it? But that's what you get when you sell your soul to the princess on the hill. They had recently completed *Cleopatra* (Rex had stolen the picture as Caesar) and the publicity of their romance overwhelmed the film completely. They had been so busy with their offscreen shenanigans that their love affair on-screen was list-less and without passion. They both had come to work literally exhausted. History's famous caprice between Antony and Cleopatra paled into insignificance beside that of Richard and Liz. Headlines in the world's press dealt with nothing else. My friend Hume Cronyn had a tiny role in the epic and I remember Milton Berle on television being asked by an interviewer if he had seen *Cleopatra*. Berle shot back, "I never miss a Hume Cronyn picture."

One day, Sam Spiegel's yacht came into view. It was too big for the tiny harbour (Sam had purchased a destroyer which he'd converted into a pleasure craft), so it had to be moored some furlongs outside. We all converged at Radzio's and Sam asked us to lunch on board. We speed-boated out and climbed up the ladder of this enormous ex-battleship. There were three or four very dishy teenage girls falling out of their brief bikinis whom Sam immediately ordered off the boat. "Alors, sortez, sortez, mes petites gigots," he shouted as they swallow dove off the bow with perfect form and struck out for the far-distant shore. "They'll be back," he shrugged with world-weary resignation. There were a few other guests on board—one of whom was my movie agent, Kurt Frings. I asked him what big film deals he was gambling away. With a licentious smile he put his fingers to his lips and gave me a con-spiratorial wink. We were served langoustines and champagne and some pasta with white truffles and I noticed a very beautiful seminude French girl seated apart at one of the gambling tables—very knowing, ultrasophisticated. "What's she doing here?" I whispered to Kurt. "Oh, her? She's a cardsharp, a pro. She's only sixteen, you know. Sam likes to keep her around when the games get heavy—and maybe for other things too—who knows?" Another conspiratorial wink. Kurt was so full of conspiratorial winks you'd think he had a nervous tic.

Sometimes Leslie, Evie, Rex, Rachel, Trish and I would turn right out of the port and boat it to San Fruttuoso, which was two or three cliff distances away. We would look for the great bronze statue of Christ of the Abyss, saint protector of divers, which in 1954 had been set in the Mediterranean at a depth of sixty feet. We would anchor and dive down to get closer looks, a daunting and amazing sight. Two rocky jutting-out points formed a narrow and treacherous harbour by which to reach the shore. The old monastery and fortress of San Fruttuoso had stood there for hundreds of years. The only way to reach it was by sea or donkey. It was the sole building on those slopes for miles, and the monks had turned the lower floor nearest the sea into a restaurant of five-star caliber. We vowed we'd pay it a visit for supper one night. The narrow harbour entry to San Fruttuoso had always been considered impassable—the winds and strong currents there were unpredictably cruel and made navigation nigh impossible. Throughout the ages, so many ships had come to grief on those rocks. So Radzio lent Rex one of his young workers, a boy of about thirteen, an expert sailor who knew those waters and would be able to get us there in the dark without mishap.

It was fairly calm when we set out, but as we entered the little harbour, the sudden powerful swells caught us completely unawares, making it most difficult to maneuver our way in. Somehow, the youngster, cool as a cucumber, managed it expertly, moored the boat and waited with it as we made tracks for the monastery. The food and local wines were superb—unforgettable. Monks had prepared it and other monks served it. After dinner as we quaffed down liqueurs of the region an elderly monk told us that before we left we must make the descent into the bowels of the old building and visit the room of the kings. Many of the ancient kings of Italy were buried below the level of the sea, their effigies lying on slabs in those thick stone walls. The monk continued in his impeccable English, "I must warn you that you will hear a thousand voices echoing through the room. Don't be afraid, it's only the ocean playing tricks as it crashes against the walls." He was right. In that vast subterranean hall the sound of human voices, some wailing, some threatening, enveloped and overwhelmed us with such tremendous volume, we had to stop our ears. Even Rex, who was pretending to be ever so nonchalant, was visibly shaken. "I think it's time to fuck off," he squeaked in a voice more high pitched than usual. "Well, you're a bloody coward," cried Rachel in her strong Welsh lilt. "But what d'you expect from the son of a friggin' Baptist minister!" She had a slight edge on the rest of us boozewise, so we helped her up the steep staircase.

When we got outside, all hell had broken loose. An electric storm of unusual magnitude had lit up the sky; the thunder was deafening and the winds were tossing the *Henry Higgins* back and forth against the rocks. The child was beckoning us to get out of there as fast as possible, and the trip back with Rex and the boy both steering as best they could with the rest of us under the hood lying on the bottom drenched was one of the scariest rides I can ever remember. The night was black as pitch and it took forever to get back as we bounced up and down on the huge waves—I was quite positive that any second we'd be introduced to Davy Jones.

Never was a sight more welcome than the wind-swept quay and the warm friendly lights of Radzio's bar. We bundled ourselves in and attacked the barleycorn. Our confidence restored with each glass, we made ready for the trip up the hill. But Rachel was having too good a time and was celebrating her escape from death with some of the locals. Suddenly, and for no apparent reason, she began howling like a wolf. It was a most convincing sound. I was to learn that these wolf howls were accustomed behaviour for Rachel whenever she'd had too much and turned the proverbial corner. "Oh, leave her here for Chrissakes," said an irritated Rex. "I'll never bloody well get her home." And Radzio, promising to look after her, drove us up in his own car. We got out at the point where no vehicle could proceed further. The rain had stopped and Rex insisted we walk the rest of the way. As we started to climb, an enormous sheet of forked lightning sizzled its way down the mountain; there was a loud crack and everything went dark. We looked down at Portofino and across to Rapallo—there were no lights anywhere. "It's another blackout," mumbled an inconvenienced Rex. For several moments, we stood still and watched the late-summer lightning illuminate the whole Mediterranean—it was a magnificent show. And after each clap of thunder, we could hear, echoing against the cliffs from somewhere in the distance far below us the piercing, agonized sound of a wolf howling. We were laughing so hard we could hardly get to the top.

The next day Evie and Leslie went back to London much satisfied, and there were four of us left in our little party. Trish and I spent every remaining night with the Harrisons. I would play the piano, and Rex would try out all the *Doolittle* numbers. Both of us had learned most of it by heart, and R.H. was enjoying himself thoroughly. But the weather turned sour and we were forced to stay a few extra days. I had by now run out of cash. Prime Minister Harold Wilson's meager allowance for British residents abroad (fifty pounds only) had become a very bad joke, so I asked Rex to lend us some money. He did so at once and with no fuss, so I challenge anyone who says he wasn't generous when he wanted to be. Rex had been at his warmest and had proved an exemplary host. He'd given us a terrific time. And of course we adored that enchanting, funny and bubbling Rachel. It was sad to leave the gorgeous coastline paradise, but back in New York, John Dexter was champing at the bit, and that crusty old soldier Pizarro, equally impatient, was waiting for someone to fill his shoes. So before I knew it I found myself Manhattan-bound.

> PIZARRO: *We're coming for you, Atahuallpa. Show me the toppest peak-top you can pile—show me the lid of the world—I'll stand tiptoe on it and pull you out of the sky.*

I parked myself at the old Algonquin. It didn't take any time at all before Betty Bacall Robards was on the other end of the phone smoldering huskily, "Where's Jason?" "Too busy to look for him just now," I said, wriggling out of the room. As I passed the hotel newsstand, every paper was announcing Rex as Dr. Doolittle. I quickened my step and went off to work. The rehearsals were thrilling in spite of being inter-rupted every so often by loud shouting matches between Dexter and the author. Nevertheless, working with Dexter was very special. He had succeeded in stretching me to the limit as he threatened he would. "Your Pizarro is proficient as in *professional*. I want you to be *terrible* as in *terror*!" I took the game to one more level—I think it worked. The first night went splendidly and all of us earned ourselves some exceptional reviews and young David Carradine, with his marvellous characteriza-tion of Atahuallpa, the Inca emperor, placed both feet firmly on his lad-der to stardom. For Peter Shaffer, it was a triumph. One critic wrote, "No Englishman in this century save Shaw and Christopher Fry has achieved such sensible beauty with words."

We had barely opened when the front desk called my room to say that some gentlemen were in the lobby waiting to see me most urgently and that my agent, Kurt Frings, was with them. "Send them up," I replied, none the wiser. I couldn't believe my eyes. The exact same cast of characters from Italy—Apjack, without Laurie Evans, Leslie and Evie Bricusse—were standing in my doorway, along with Frings. "Am I back in Portofino?" I blinked. Leslie spoke first. "Rex walked! Paramount is furious with him. We've come to persuade you to do *Dr. Doolittle*. We can buy you out of the play. There's a great cast lined up to support you—Samantha Eggar, Laurence Olivier, Richard Attenborough, Tony Newley, of course, and as Bumpo Sammy Davis, Junior. Please say yes?!" My heart started to beat very fast. This was unreal! To say it was déjà vu would be a gross understatement. I looked out the window—it was snowing. No, this was not Portofino. Kurt, with another conspiratorial wink, motioned me into the hallway. "I'll make sure you'll get paid in full no matter what." "What do you mean?" "I don't know. I smell a rat, but then I always smell rats." I spent the next few days between performances walking on air. But Kurt was right, the moment Rex heard I was going to play his part he was back on the job. Paramount had forgiven him. It wasn't the same mag-nificent supporting cast we'd all expected and the film did not do too well at the box office, but I was paid my full salary for doing nothing. Not bad for a long Italian weekend!

I SUPPOSE one has to pay in some way for such good fortune. Well, I did. I had a nasty accident onstage several weeks into the run. In actu-ality, Pizarro was a victim of some form of epilepsy, and the play demanded he fall to the ground in a semifit on at least three occasions. I took pride in knowing how to fall convincingly without getting hurt, so I purposely landed on my right knee and then quickly rolled over and I did this at each performance in the same manner on the same identical spot, night after night. Stupidly, I refused to wear knee pads, so one evening after the first act I felt a throbbing sensation in my leg. My dresser removed my boot, lifted my breeches, and there was this huge swelling the size of a tennis ball just below the knee. I finished the performance, but now the pain was so acute I couldn't put any weight on my foot whatsoever and had to be carried into a cab and then up to my hotel room. In order to sleep I killed a bottle of Scotch. The next day my right leg had swollen to twice its size and the pain, which had traveled to my chest, was unbearable. I couldn't stand up. I was bent over double. A doctor came, examined me and proceeded to shoot me full of morphine. The relief was tremendous. "You have a serious blood clot in your leg which has turned into a pulmonary embolism. It travelled straight to your left lung, just missing your heart! It's the hospital for you!" Oh God! I could have cried. There would be no more *Royal Hunt*—no more Pizarro.

I lay in my hospital bed and relived the play's entire run. Even before my accident, strange things had occurred—uneasy forebodings, portents of dark things ahead. During one performance a drunk in the audience kept shouting at the top of his considerable voice insulting, vicious assertions and criticisms of the play and the audience, but they were mostly aimed at me. The customers tried to shut him up, to no avail. After the first-act curtain came down, I had him removed from the theatre. Imagine our shock and horror upon learning that the drunk was none other than that distinguished and excellent actor Gary Merrill, who at the time was married to Bette Davis. It is an unspoken code that no one from our profession, no matter how drugged or inebriated, interrupts a fellow actor when he is busy performing. It is simply not done. Not even that mad libertine, the great Edmund Kean, would have managed to get away with it. Such boorish behavior is inconceivable—unforgivable. Days later I received the most painful and devastating letter of apology—almost suicidal in its remorse— from Mr. Merrill. I felt deeply affected by it. What an incredibly sad state he must have been in, a man of such intelligence and talent. At the time he had been running for mayor of Maine, where both he and Bette lived, a position, needless to say, this tormented man was not able to fill.

This was not the only incident that was sent to plague me, for every night for at least three weeks' duration, a middle-aged woman wearing bright red colours sat in the front row dead center and ogled me. No matter how dim the lighting, you couldn't miss her. Whenever I left the stage she would stand up and wave to me and when I returned she would do the same, this time blowing me kisses. She wasn't a good-looking woman in any way at all; her hair was shiny jet-black and she had mad eyes. And what the devil did she see in me—with my shaved head, long beard and stooped shoulders—an old wreck if there ever was one? At first it was bizarrely funny; the company would tease me rotten—"Your girlfriend's here again"—as they took turns peering through a hole in the curtain. But after a while, her continuous presence at such close quarters began to distract every member of the cast and started slowly to drive me out of my mind. Presents began to arrive at the stage door, beautifully wrapped from expensive shops. I opened one from Tiffany—it was an exquisite set of Baccarat wineglasses. Every couple of days more would come from Cartier, Hermès, Bergdorf Goodman but mostly from Tiffany. Good old Andy at the stage door warned me, "Don' open any more of dem. You'll be playin' her game. I'll keep 'em here in my cubbyhole. As soon as we gets an address I'll return 'em." I started having nightmares about her. She was like a deranged fan who at any moment could change with the wind, reach into her purse and pull out a pistol.

One night I arrived at the theatre after my usual dinner at La Scala two doors away filled with Dutch courage and determination. I went straight to the stage manager. "If she's there again tonight, I'm not going on. It's either her or me!" He went to the peephole to check. "She's there," he said. "That's it!" I barked. "Finito la commedia!" The ANTA management called the police and she was removed. I felt like a cad, but it had to be done. I watched through the curtain. She did not go quietly—screaming horrid abuse as she was literally dragged out. The whole audience watched in shock—it was most upsetting. The next day she called the New York Post and told them how shamefully I'd behaved, that I had no right to eject her. She was a member of the public—she'd paid for her seat. In fact, she had ordered that same front row seat for a whole month. This was not good press for me or the play. But Leonard Lyons, the major columnist for the Post, suspecting some sort of foul play, took my side and refused to print any of it, proving once again how staunchly he defended our profession as the actor's Good Samaritan.

By now I couldn't get into Andy's stage-door hole—neither could Andy. Presents were piled up floor to ceiling! "Hey, Chris," said Andy. "I found an address and a number. I got dis dame's sister on the line. She's comin' over tomorrow to take 'em all back. At last I'll be able to park my ass."

As usual, Andy got all the dope. It seems the unfortunate woman (according to the sister) had been in a near fatal plane crash and had suffered a massive concussion. She had sued the airline and won a huge settlement. With all this money to burn, she began having fixations about certain people and no one knew what on earth she would do next. As I lay supine in my hospital bed, my leg wrapped in ice hardly able to move, I am ashamed to say I couldn't help thinking I was safer where I was.

Leroy Hospital in the East Sixties (a haven for the ailing rich, it seemed) was so liberal it hardly imposed any rules at all. I was allowed to order my meals from anywhere I chose. Waiters from my favourite La Scala on West Fifty-second would stagger across town carrying pastas and salads with every known hot pepper I was forbidden to eat, plus bottles of their best Chianti. I even had dinners sent up from the posh Colony restaurant downstairs nearby. Vince Sardi sent gifts, messages and bottles of wine from Sardi's. As did the "boys" at P.J. Clarke's. Good old Andy would come over once a week with my mail. The nurses were great—they would do anything for me. Visitors were allowed to pop in regularly at all hours. Vince Sardi, Jane Broder—very concerned—"This is costing you, honey; take it easy." Jason would drop in with some of his drinking buddies. All the girls I'd dated at Arthurs, New York's hottest disco, would show up. It really was a never-ending party in my room. I was having myself a ball. Dexter was back in London as was Trish, but Peter Shaffer graciously came to visit and though he was sympathetic, I don't think he quite forgave me for deserting his play.

The Royal Hunt of the Sun staggered on for a while, but its producers refused to pay for a "name" actor to replace me and with just my understudy valiantly carrying on night after night, good as he was, there was no "draw" to keep it running, so in a matter of weeks this gorgeous production closed. With the play's demise, I recovered, as if a penitent Pizarro had been forgiven his crimes and released from his prison. *The Royal Hunt* had most certainly sent out strange vibrations, but by now the air had cleared. And there was a job to go to, a film in France—a good thing as I had gone through my entire salary. "You've only got

As Pizarro in The Royal Hunt of the Sun, *New York*

about fifteen bucks left out of all that," worried good old Jane. Pampering myself as usual, I booked first-class passage on the *France,* the most beautiful liner on the seas at the time with the best stabilizers in the world. Jane, bless her, came to see me off. None of my young friends bothered, but she managed it without any trouble. She looked about my lavish stateroom, and instead of chastising me for my extravagance, she said, "You deserve this, honey." As I leaned over the railings and waved good-bye, she called up from the dock and repeated her reassurance, "Don't worry about the car. I'll take care of everything, and good luck, honey."

The *France* boasted one of the finest restaurants on land or water. On the first day out, black tie was insisted upon for supper. After that we could dress as we pleased but always jacket and tie. The ship, which had everything on board—Cartier, Hermès, all the elegant shops—was run with great style and took special pride in its attractive little crush bar, which was all glass with a spectacular view of the ocean. It opened at 2 a.m. after the dance floor was closed and served mouth-watering breakfasts accompanied by champagne right through the early hours. The night before landing at Southampton black tie was once more required for supper and this time, apart from the exquisite menu, the guests were asked to order anything in the world they desired; the kitchen would oblige. Of course, all us amateur gourmets would put our heads together and ask the impossible, the most difficult thing imaginable to stump the chef. Lark's tongues, ortolans and other culinary rarities—there they were before us as if by magic. Nothing daunted the maestro. Those kitchens must have been stocked with every choice ingredient known to man.

My stateroom was on the so-called top deck, but there actually was one more deck above me—the very roof of the ship where all the pet animals (mostly dogs) were kept. Every night with my porthole open I would hear them barking against the gale-force winds. I worried about them up there on their own without their owners, but eventually the salt air sent me to sleep. Once, I was sharply awakened by a sound coming from above. It was different from the usual barking sounds and very much resembled the howlings of a wolf. In my hazy state caused by champagne overkill, I had convinced myself it was Rachel on that windswept deck with all the animals about her, letting the crashing waves know that she had just had one too many.

CHAPTER TWENTY-EIGHT

VIVE LA DÉCADENCE

I think over the years I have stayed in almost every room at the Hotel du Cap on Eden-Roc, on the Cap d'Antibes, from the most elegant suite to a toilet-sized room in the chauffeur's wing, and it all depended on how flush I was at the time, but like my favourite Parisian hotel, the Lancaster on rue de Berri, I was determined to stay there no matter how meager my financial state. This time my grand salon of a suite with two or three more rooms attached, one graced with an old Pleyel piano, looked out over the sea beyond. Always at Eden-Roc, the scent of jasmine on the salt air was overpowering and many a romance had blossomed there. Monsieur Irondel, the manager, refused credit cards and checks—only cash—and it was prohibitively expensive but, thankfully, all was taken care of by the film company which was shooting *Triple Cross,* a true story put together and coauthored by its director Terence Young, a tall, handsome Irishman who had made all the early Bond films (*Dr. No, Thunderball* and *From Russia with Love*).

Terry, who lived precipitously beyond his means, had bought a delightful villa on the point of Eden-Roc where we spent many an enjoyable evening. I grew very attached to Terry, his wife, Dosia, his daughter Julie, from another marriage, and their dearest friend, Annie Orr-Lewis. Lady Orr-Lewis was a stylish woman, extremely entertaining, with impeccable taste and a talent for interior and exterior design. Among others she had designed the attractive Lyford Cay Club at Nassau in the Bahamas, the home of Karim Aga-Khan on Sardinia's Costa Esmeralda, also Stanhope Joel's massive hotel in Jamaica. Always present either on a leash or in her arms was a shih tzu whom she affectionately called "My Little Shit." The four of us became inseparable, joined occasionally by Sean Connery, who adored the Youngs and treated them as family.

Triple Cross was a story about the shady but daring adventures of double-agent Eddie Chapman (played by me), who during the Second World War had spied successfully for both the British and the Germans. The real Eddie, who was still astoundingly alive, was to be the technical advisor on the film, but the French authorities forbade him entry into France. It seems at one point in his highly suspicious career he had managed, for what reason it's impossible to conjecture, to kidnap the sultan of Morocco!

The film began shakily in Paris. They installed me at the old George V, which I always liked, mostly because of its long bar at which sat, as if part of the décor, a number of high-class hookers of all nationalities, perched seductively on their bar stools. The first news I received on arrival was that the film had been cancelled—that the backers had not only reneged on the deal but had been thrown in jail. This sort of thing I learned was to be occasionally expected on a Terry Young film. He would try to make deals with anyone no matter how untrustworthy, living on the edge as he did, but always cunningly managed to get things fixed in the long run. The online producer told me, "Just stay close to the hotel—eat and drink all you want. It'll be covered, I promise." They had also flown over from London my old friend, the tailor Max Vine, to make me suits for the part. He stayed rather nervously in a suite next to mine, where he and his assistant began to work on the clothes. "Do you think we're all going to get stuck for the movie?" Max couldn't help asking.

By the week's end, however, a certain Madame Gouin had appeared from nowhere (no doubt charmed by T. Young) and presto!—the money was in the bank and we were shunted off on the now-extinct Train Bleu (my favourite with its famous two seatings). If you were wise, you took the second seating, then went straight to bed where you woke up le matin prochain—et voilà—la Côte d'Azur! Most of the film was to be made at the Victorine Studios in Nice. This small intimate studio had been opened during the twenties and thirties by the legendary Rex Ingram and was the most delightful I've ever filmed in. The French hours were especially civilized—one and a half hours for lunch followed by seven hours straight work with no breaks, then home in lots of time for a normal relaxed meal—and we got just as much done if not more than our normal daylong schedules. My favourite eating haunts were Félix au Port in old Antibes with its succulent sope de poisson and La Reserve at Beaulieu. The movie was not memorable but wonderful fun to make. With Terry as maestro, the life surrounding the

Gert Fröbe, Yul Brynner, and me

work was just as important if not more so, and everything and everyone involved had to be attractive. Terry was a beauty snob, may God rest his soul!

One of my leading ladies was Romy Schneider, the German actress who had distinguished herself in Vittorio De Sica's *Garden of the Fitzi-Continis* and was a favourite of Luchino Visconti's. The theatre was in her blood—her mother, Magda Schneider, had been one of Germany's greatest stage divas. I adored Romy. Always a bundle of cheer, she had the most beautiful eyes and her smile lit up the world. She had just married a charming young German writer/actor named Harry Meyen, and they seemed blissfully happy. The dashing Yul Brynner played a Nazi general, complete with monocle and cigarette holder. This was another real-life character by the name of Baron von Grunen who had fought at Stalingrad. Another leading lady of mine in the flick was the gorgeous French actress Claudine Auger. Gert Fröbe (Goldfinger himself from the Bond film) played a Nazi colonel. Trevor Howard was a "big gun" in British Intelligence; and due to Terry's fascination for the pulchritudinous female, there were any number of them present at all times. "Eye rests," Yul called them and he generally left the set each day with at least two of them on his arm.

The story needed a château which the Germans were to have occupied. So the Comtess de Villefranche (for a very modest fee) gave us the use of her enormous castle outside Paris. Her unmarried name was de Ségur and this was the home of their famous wine, Château Ségur. On the property stood another château, a smaller one, presumably used as a guesthouse. Yul, Romy and I were each given a lovely apartment there with a communal kitchen and fridge. Also on the estate, nestled in a beautiful little valley not far away, was a miniature pavilion resembling a tiny Petit Trianon, which was normally used as a restaurant for the workers on the estate. All the herbs, ingredients, meat, wine and eau de vies came from the grounds and were prepared daily for us. The lunches there were delicious, everything being so fresh. "What a peaceful oasis this is," murmured Yul contentedly, sipping his cognac. "No showbiz people—no agents, producers or PR freaks—we are away from everything here." As he said this, his face from the chin to the top of his celebrated bald head lost all its colour. "What have I said?" he moaned. "Don't look now—oh my God, what do I see?!" I turned around and in the distance, waddling down the path in their shiny black agent suits, looking lost, bewildered and totally out of place, were Milton ("Let Me Put You on Hold") Goldman and Arnold Weissberger, the well-known 10-percenters from New York! Yul, between clenched teeth, mumbled under his breath, "Madison Avenue has invaded paradise."

According to schedule, a few days of rest were coming my way, but Kurt Frings was persistent—he called me: "Listen, you bastard. Sam Spiegel wants you to play Field Marshal Rommel in his film *The Night of the Generals* starring O'Toole and Sharif. It's two days' work but it's an important picture so do it! It vill be shot close to vhere you are now. Terry has agreed to let you go." Kurt always jumped the gun like this without ever letting me know. "What am I to get for two days' work?" "No money," he snapped. "Money would be a quote—a precedent and you'd be stuck with it. So you take a car instead!" "What kind of car?" "A Rolls-Royce. Sam has agreed. I've made the deal!" So with a fresh sense of folie de grandeur, I set out for the village of La Roche-Guyon, whose local inn and four-star restaurant the great Rommel had adopted for the duration of occupied France. The veteran Hollywood director Anatole Litvak, a handsome Hungarian in his silvering seventies and a friend of Spiegel's, had a history of romantic films behind him both European and American. He was impeccably mannered, smooth and civilized and it was a privilege to work with him, if ever so briefly. Together we lunched at this delightful pension. Two of the waiters were very old and had been kept on by Rommel and both related in reverent tones that even though he was the enemy he had treated the whole

Me as Rommel

French staff with great respect. "Ah oui! Il était un homme vraiment sympatique." According to them, he had loved it here in this village and loved the inn, vowing that once the war was over he would come back and stay. He was the only good German in the military, they told us, and he was killed so soon after he left us. "Comme c'était triste—un homme tres gentil comme ça." Mr. Litvak turned to me, "You see? He was a most remarkable man." I suddenly wished that my role was a much larger one. The day I finished shooting this extraordinary character, the unit manager came up to me and asked, "What colour would you like your Rolls to be?" I must confess I had already given it a great deal of thought. My response was immediate. "The body, a deep garnet, the roof jet black, please!" Trying in vain to stifle my excitement by assuming a casually modest pose, I bade my farewells.

When I got back on the *Triple Cross* set, Milton and Arnold were still there. The untimely appearance of this canny duo turned out to be fortuitous. They had smelled a fly in the ointment and they were there to protect their client, Yul. Of course they were right—there was no more money and we were only halfway through the project. Terry confirmed this the very next day. Everybody's agent suddenly converged on the château—everybody's except mine! Where the hell was Kurt when I needed him so desperately? Were we all to walk off the picture; what were we supposed to do? Kurt's problem was he never trusted anyone but himself to do his work. He was never able to delegate responsibility—he had come to be simply a one-man band and couldn't be everywhere at once. Not good enough when one was in trouble. I called him and was told he was in Rome looking after Audrey Hepburn. I finally got him. "This is a real crunch, Kurt. I need you here!" When he refused to come I fired him on the spot. I'm sure it mattered little to him—he was so successful—but I felt terrible about it. Apart from the fact that he'd done me much good, I had grown extremely fond of that crazy German. It also hit me that I had just dismissed arguably the bravest and very best movie agent in the business.

We met in a body to confront Terry. Bluff your way out of this one, we all thought at once. He did! Smooth as silk, with no show of nerves, he announced, "I've got another backer—a Monsieur Bédas, incredibly wealthy and head of a Beirut bank. But he wants visible proof of my credibility. So I plead with you to come with me to Paris and meet him. God love you if you do." On the advice of the little group of surrounding agents, Yul, Trevor, Romy and I agreed to go. It worked! We got the necessary funds to finish, and a grateful Terry, celebrating the good news as extravagantly as ever, threw us a lavish dinner back in Monte Carlo at the Hotel de Paris. He also took us all to see Nureyev and Fonteyn dance a magical *Gisele* outdoors under the stars—Annie Orr-Lewis, my date. Other parties followed, one on Stavros Niarcho's huge galleon with its black hull and deep red sails—surely the most beautiful private sailing vessel on any ocean. He had also rented the *Sea Huntress,* the Earl of Dudley's yacht, for a night of dining and dancing. The lights on the water made everything glitter in the night air and always the generous Terence at the center of it all, teetering dangerously on the edge of ruin!

It was time for Yul Brynner's death scene. As the Nazi general, he was to die shot on the tarmac as he was getting out of his Mercedes to board his plane. Yul had it all worked out painstakingly and described it to me with great glee the night before as we killed a bottle of vodka at the château. The next morning he met with Terence and the distin-

TERENCE YOUNG

guished French lighting cameraman Henri Alekan and told them how he would like his death filmed: "You just hear the shots—you don't see me at all—the camera focuses on the ground—you see my boots, then my monocle falls and smashes, and then the cigarette holder—and though you don't see me, everyone will know who it is!" It was a nice theatrical touch, I thought, and typical of Yul. I whispered to Terry, "Are you sure the *real* von Grunen is dead?" Terry looked down at me askance and in his most patronizing tones (he could be very pompous when he chose to be), said, "Of course, you silly fool, it's all been researched." Sharply corrected I slunk away embarrassed. Two days after Yul had shot the scene, we were all having lunch at the Victorine Studios under the awning when the film's publicity agent came over to our table leading by the hand a very feeble, doddering old man with thinning grey hair in a frayed suit shaking with early Parkinson's, and said, "This gentleman learned we were making a movie here in which he is portrayed and would like very much to watch the filming. May I introduce General von Grunen."

Terry's and Yul's faces were a picture—I need not tell you! But no one bothered to delete his death scene from the movie. No one would be the wiser, they said. There'll be no lawsuit—he's too far gone to know anyway. Callous as it seemed, they were probably correct. He was a pathetic figure, fading fast with one foot already in the grave. One of the few survivors from his unit at Stalingrad, that most horrific of World War II battles, he had been captured and tortured by the Russians. His sagging face and frightened eyes told the story. I don't think he even knew where he was. The poor old soldier was a wandering ghost from a war he was still haunting.

Even that shocking day couldn't put a damper on the enjoyment I had derived from this whirlwind engagement. Both the setting and life on the Cote d'Azur was not to be surpassed, particularly back then. The glamour that was still present everywhere in that beautiful and tempting part of the Mediterranean has now greatly diminished. My time there in the mid- to late sixties now seems a history ago—a different time— a different space. Quel temps! Comme c'etaient un rêve.

Romy Schneider

However, a little sadness can't help but creep in. If Romy Schneider had not been married to dear Harry Meyen, I would have boldly taken up the gauntlet for her. Before the film's end I noticed back at the Petit château her fresh, unsullied beauty had undergone a change—her face was becoming decidedly puffy and she had started to put on weight. The château's fridge was always stocked full of German sausages, bratwurst, salamis, with her name written on each package. What was happening? I was never to know, for some years after the picture was finished, Harry Meyen, back in Germany took his own life. Romy all of a sudden disappeared from a promising career that could have taken her to the top and only distinguished herself one last time as the Empress Elizabeth in Visconti's film about Mad King Ludwig of Bavaria. Next, her fourteen-year-old son died in a tragic accident. It was not long before she too committed suicide. Beauty, radiance, talent—she should have had everything to live for.

Just before the Eddie Chapman schedule came to an end, Terry threw a party at Victorine Studios for all the brass in order to show them a roughly edited version of the film. Lots of important "above the title" names came. The backers from Beirut, a few of the local "toffs," I think even the Rainiers were there (Terry had known them through David Niven). David came, as did Sean Connery, Annie Orr-Lewis, Dosia Young, most of the cast, and of course beaucoup des jeune filles malgardés. Good ol' Trevor Howard sat in the front row pissed as a newt as they say in love and war. Some of the film had Terry's slickness about it and looked fairly promising, but on the whole it was pretty rough and not too well written. When it was over there was a deadly silence while everyone sat motionless in the dark. Then out of the pitch-black came the only comment. It was Trevor's whiskey-coated voice sounding slightly irritated calling out to no one in particular—"Where are my fucking shoes?"

WHEN I GOT BACK HOME to 70 Park Street, Mayfair, Trish and I broke up for good. It was sad but inevitable. I had found it almost impossible to fully grasp the extent of the damage this bright and generous lady had suffered, but her heavy drinking continued. She paid heed neither to her doctors nor to me. One thing was certain; the accident had loomed over our marriage like the sword of Damocles. The life-threatening urgency and horror of it had inflated our romance to such an extreme it had robbed us of all passion, and everything that followed seemed dry and anticlimactic. An inexplicable resentment grew between us and our fights became dangerously more and more frequent. It had been only five years or so but for us—too long. Divorce proceedings were swift and painless. She got the Queen Anne house, the furniture, everything, as she deserved to, with the exception of two paintings, my favourite Corot and a rare Renoir. She sold the house immediately and moved into an attractive flat in Regent's Park where her many genuine friends gathered around her along with the usual freeloaders from Fleet Street. I moved into the Connaught Hotel to be greeted by the saturnine Mister Gustave, the general manager-cum-host, always impeccably attired in frock coat and stripes, and the two men in charge of that superb dining room, Mister Rose and his Man Friday, Monsieur Chevalier. I quickly set a beachhead at the bar with my familiar old friend Barry (the bartender) who made me laugh so much and whose martinis no one could match. His partner, Jimmy, was his greatest foil and together they could cheer up a walrus.

The Honorable Elizabeth Rees-Williams, an exceptionally attractive Welsh lass, who had just parted from her husband, that mad Irishman, actor Richard Harris, became my new friend. Liz and I, sharing divorce in common, had found comfort in each other's company. Her brother Morgan, a deliciously funny young man with a dark, self-deprecating humour, tagged along to cheer us up. He became my staunch friend and ally. Elizabeth was incredibly generous, knew a great many people in London and never stopped partying. We went everywhere together, even to Richard's premiere of *Camelot* in which he played King Arthur. At the private party afterwards at the Duke of St. Albans's house on Ennismore Gardens, Liz, giggling in her musical way, whispered, "You won't believe this. Both you and Richard are seated on either side of Princess Margaret at her request. Ironic, wouldn't you say? I'll see you later." Margaret's escort that night was Andrew Cavendish, Duke of Devonshire, of whom she was fond, so we found her in good form and great humour. When she chose, the princess could be quite witty. We had all consumed an enormous amount of hooch and everything started to sound hysterically amusing, even the most mundane remark. Suddenly, into the room came a tall, aesthetic-looking young man attired in head to foot velvet with a Bunthorne tie—a Restoration dandy with an enormous shock of wavy blond hair, très bouffant, indeed the very picture of effeminacy. I whispered under my breath to the princess, "Who's the raving puffter?" In an instant she assumed her royal put-down manner and, glaring at me with enough Arctic froideur to freeze me to my chair, hissed, "That's my cousin Patrick Lichfield." I banged my head with the palm of my hand. Of course, the famous international photographer who was also a belted earl was notoriously fond of women and a great ladies' man. I couldn't have been more wrong and dashed down my blunder with a glass of bubbling Krug.

MY NEXT ASSIGNMENT I learned was to be in Athens. I had always dreamed of going to Greece, so I ran down the Connaught staircase straight to the bar to share the news with Barry over a celebratory drink. "Guess what?" he said before I could get a word in. "The Harrisons are staying in the hotel—and there's *Mrs.* Harrison over there on the couch with *Mrs.* Harris." I joined the two Welsh ladies who turned out to be the greatest of friends and after several martinis we were feeling very little pain. Morgan rolled in happily primed and in top form. "Let's have dinner here in the dining room," I offered. "Rachel, go upstairs and get Rex." Rachel, who had a head start on all of us, left the room and Liz, Morgan and I waited and waited for an unconscionably long time. Rex finally called down, "Look, I'd love to come, but Rachel is pissed out of her mind—I think we'd better not." "Oh come on," I insisted. "We're having such a good time and it's been so long." The three of us went in and sat at the big table in the corner banquette— Table 10. I was in the midst of telling the well-known story of how Mrs. "Kitty" Gilbert Miller had choked to death at this very table (no Heimlich maneuver being offered) when the Harrisons at last made their appearance. Rachel immediately ordered another martini, which Rex snatched from her and put on a side table. "No, Rachel, I told you no more." Rex, Liz, Morgan and I carried the conversation while Rachel sulked in gloomy silence. She didn't look in the least inebriated, though God only knew just how much she'd already consumed. We were all so famished we literally attacked our dinner except Rachel who wouldn't touch any of her food. The evening was proceeding most pleasantly in its rose-coloured way when in an extremely loud voice which ricocheted off the dining room walls, Rachel shouted at Morgan, "You see, boyo, Sexy Rexy here believes he's the illegitimate son of George the Fifth when actually he's only the son of a dreary fucking Baptist minister."

It was a particularly "old" night, that night at the Connaught— veddy old, veddy British and veddy stuffy. The room fell silent. All one could hear was the rattling of expensive cutlery. Mr. Rose came over and in his quiet, charming way asked her if she wanted anything. "I want another bloody martini—for the love of Christ, boyo." It was at that moment that Rachel began a series of wolf howls. We had some-how expected this might happen and were prepared for it. Others in the restaurant were not. Some got up and left. As each person glared at our table on their way out, Mrs. Harrison would give another ear-piercing howl in their direction. It was quite hysterical to see Rex trying to make himself invisible. Morgan by this time had totally lost it and I thought he was going to burst he was laughing so hard.

That wildly macabre evening had strangely signaled a change in all our lives. It would not be long before the warmhearted, loving and tal-ented Rachel had remarried successfully and happily and my good friend Elizabeth was to become the umpteenth Mrs. Rex Harrison.

CHAPTER TWENTY-NINE

GREECE

The isles of Greece, the isles of Greece
Where burning Sappho loved and sung

— LORD BYRON

On April 21, 1967, came the infamous "Colonels' Coup" in which the military seized all power in Greece. The army held the opinion that a democratic government and a constitutional monarchy could not together or separately take effective or dramatic measures. The blundering misjudgments of Prime Minister Papandreou, which had led to this coup, subjected the country to seven years of military dictatorship. By so doing he had effectively removed Greece, the birthplace of democracy, from the community of civilized nations. The long history of instability, which had plagued this beautiful country for centuries, once more brought chaos to its people. It seemed they were never to be allowed to rest. All leading Communist agitators were sent to the islands. All artists, journalists and painters were considered Communist and were on the hit list. Although no blood was shed, something was only too clear—Athens was under fire. All shops were shut. There was no telephone service; no telegrams could be sent; there were no buses or taxis. The streets were filled with tanks—all Greece was in mourning for itself.

It was into this tension and gloom that I first set foot in the City of Truth. I was to play the role of Oedipus Rex on film in a brand-new English version of the old classic by the celebrated poet, Paul Roche. This might be viewed as an absurd contrast to the serious goings-on around one and yet the timing of it could not have been more ironic. Here on the one hand was the blinded King Oedipus forsaking his throne and fleeing to the wilderness and there, on the other, was the present King Constantine, also throneless, fleeing to Rome.

After spending one heavy ouzo-drinking night with Donald Sutherland (who was to play the Chorus Leader) at the old Hotel Grande Bretagne, I shook the dust of occupied Athens from my heels and was driven the six or seven hours' journey to Ioannina at the far end of the country where Greece borders on Albania. We were to shoot the entire film at nearby Dodoni in one of the very oldest and smallest amphitheatres in existence. It nestled itself against a hill of wild grass and a kind of rough gorse, its stone seats in ruins and at all angles as if earthquakes over the centuries had dislodged them. Unlike its tourist-ridden counterparts, it was neglected, sad and alone, an occasional olive tree bravely growing out from the seats and wildflowers everywhere. It was achingly beautiful and my very favourite theatre in the world. When it wasn't raining in Dodoni, which was rare, there was always an ominous little black cloud hanging above it—a presentiment of Fate. It wore its little cloud proudly like a cap. There is a wide belief that when the Oracle first arrived in Greece, it went straight to Dodoni, but realizing it did nothing but piss with rain there, it picked up its skirts and moved on to Delphi.

Oedipus the King, presented by Universal Pictures, was the ambitious brainchild of producer Michael Luke, the brother of Peter Luke, who had so successfully produced my "Hamlet at Elsinore." Michael was an extremely bright, knowledgeable and comfortable sort of Englishman with a deep mellifluous voice who couldn't quite conceal a number of interesting complexities which simmered just below the surface of his normally cool demeanour. A slight example of this was that he and his attractive family all lived in a house on the Dashwood estate in West Wycombe, just outside London. The estate sits on a steep rolling hill and gives the impression of great rural peacefulness as if Constable had painted it. Yet who would believe that in the nineteenth century Sir Francis Dashwood, England's premier baronet and Satan worshipper performed Black Mass rituals of every known variety, supposedly including human sacrifice right there on the grounds in the family chapel? I'm not suggesting for a moment that dear Michael Luke ever even contemplated devil worship, but his choice of residence, one must admit, is oddly intriguing. More evidence of the quirkier side of his imagination lay in the extraordinary group of genuine eccentrics he had gathered together for the fray—one Duncan Grant, the famed painter and a last survivor of the Bloomsbury Set; the great Greek designer Madame Vaglioti (who made me a wonderful snake belt); my old acquaintance Count Friedrich Ledebur to train the Greek horses which

My third Oedipus, this one in Greece

were as tiny as ponies; the country's premiere tragedienne, Irene Pap-pas, who was to play my mother, Jocasta, but couldn't because as a fierce protestor of the new regime, it was imperative that she leave the country before she was thrown in jail. Add to this a host of Greek poets, composers, painters, famous or infamous, whom Michael had hired as extras. He had spirited them away from Athens so they could hide behind their cowls lest overzealous military police might recognize them. The local farmers allowed them to sleep in their fields at night, where they drank wine and ate goat cheese, grateful and happy to be free. If you lifted a cowl or two, by God, if it wasn't Argirakis or Theodorakis or others of their ilk, a considerable collection of celebri-ties disguised as suppliants. So when I spoke my opening lines to the kneeling multitudes, "Children of Cadmus," etc. I was in reality addressing the crème de la crème of Greek intellectual society.

Also on board were the actors of Greece's National Theatre to play the Chorus, with Donald, as I mentioned, as their leader. Quel coup!! An irritating habit of dear Donald's, which drove us round the bend as well as kept us amused, was his constant low-key mumbling—effective in certain screen roles, but in *Hamlet* and *Oedipus* hardly suit-able. Fortinbras speaks the noble lines, "Bear Hamlet like a soldier to the stage," etc. As this is the very last speech in the play, it is rather important it be heard. In *Oedipus* the job of the Chorus Leader is to

explain the plot and then tell us what is to come, *desperately* important
to be heard, I would say—but in both cases, all one got from Donald
was a distant rumble. Of course, he fixed it in the looping room later
and all was fine, he was wonderful, but on the set he had caused a few
palpitations of the heart. That wondrous player from Ireland Cyril
Cusack was the Messenger and the old Shepherd who brings the final
truth to poor Oedipus was enacted by the endearing Roger Livesey (*The
Life and Death of Colonel Blimp, I Know Where I'm Going*), he of the
whiskey voice who could charm the pizzle off a Thessalian bull! The
urbane Richard Johnson from the Royal Shakespeare made a splendid
Creon, Lilli Palmer replaced Pappas as my mother and lastly Orson
Welles played the blind seer Tiresias as if he were Othello, Macbeth and
Charles Foster Kane rolled into one. How spoiled could a young Oedipus get?

My friend Philip Saville, who had been such a help with my Hamlet,
was once again my director. He arrived as dashing as ever on the arm of
young Diana Rigg, then the star of *The Avengers*. They looked like a
pretty serious item. To further pamper me, the "powers that be" had
given me an assistant to be at my beck and call. She was twenty or
thereabouts and her name was Bambi. Apart from being generous,
tremendous fun and immensely smart (she spoke Greek fluently),
Bambi was pretty easy on the eyes. She had a very sexy face and her long
thin legs seemed never to end—that illusion further enhanced by the
shortest of miniskirts. When she would stand over me at breakfast
awaiting instructions for the day, it left next to nothing to the imagination. Philip got quite stroppy with her and told her to wear something
less revealing as she was distracting the entire crew. Bambi just smiled
that innocent smile of hers and fortunately for us didn't trouble to
make the change. I thought Philip had spoken rather out of turn as he
and Diana never stopped spooning whenever they got the chance.

Something had happened that perhaps was far from helpful to the
production. Whether the magic of the location had softened us and
made us lazy or perhaps our hearts weren't in it, I don't know which, but
our playing was far from cohesive. There was no unity, no feeling of
ensemble. As a result, we all gave our own performances—some very
intimate and filmic, others, mine particularly, excessively theatrical, a
stage rather than a film performance. Also Philip was determined to
keep it all very simple and stark—quite rightly—but for some reason
he didn't cover the scenes adequately and his cameraman, a very gifted
fellow indeed, Walter Lassally (who had shot *Never on Sunday*), had his

own opinions as to how it should all look, so they never really got along at all, which was disastrous. However, there were many adventures to undertake offscreen, away from the work, many towns to explore and the exquisite surrounding country just waiting to remind us of its history.

As we had some time off, I took the ferry with Bambi across the Aegean to a very special island that is still floating around in my head all these many years later. We had come upon a temporary paradise— we had discovered Corfu.

Kerkyra, the proper name for Corfu, is Italianate in appearance, hardly Greek at all. It is abundantly verdant, a sea of greenery between tall cypresses, more restful to the eye, for there the sun beats down less ruthlessly than on the other islands. The town of Kerkyra nestles at the foot of a huge hill which makes up the island and the countryside beyond the town casts a sad and haunting spell that is quite indescribable. Well, perhaps not quite. Lawrence Durrell in his *Prospero's Cell* describes it all quite magically. I knew I would visit there, so I read it beforehand and was convinced that Corfu could never live up to Durrell's description of it. I was wrong. The steep hills that dizzily drop to the Aegean are covered in olive groves—the trees leaning at an almost 45-degree angle grow out of the cliffs bending over like Sirens, waving you down to the waters below. It is spellbinding. Yes, one could easily envision Austria's beautiful empress taking her daily exercise, running at high speed as was her custom through the olive trees, her nuns following her at a distance—a group of frantic blackbirds trying desperately to keep up.

The deserted white chapels hugging the hills also gave a look of enchantment to the place. I wanted instantly to acquire one and convert its interior into a home—how simple and attractive that would be. We visited the Achillion Palace where the Empress Elizabeth had spent her Grecian summers. Both aesthetic and elegant, it sits, perched on a cliff looking down on Kerkyra below, flanked by tall conifers standing as straight as sentries. Prince Andrew of Greece's house Mon Repos was also on our agenda. But the other side of the island was my very favourite—Paleokastritsa. At the topmost point of the hill, the little town of Paleokastritsa crowns its summit, its houses painted a variety of joyously vivid colours. There are barely any trees way up there and this jewel of a town is open to the skies—the air is so clear and vibrant, the tiled streets so clean you can eat off them, and the long walk from the hilltop down those thousands of steps yielded views that could catch one's breath.

At the foot of the steps lies a little bay sheltered from the sea by two cliffs of rock which we nicknamed "Charybdis" and "Scylla." Inside these hollow cliffs the seawater is very deep and the stalagmites and stalactites are awesome to behold. Here is some of the best snorkeling in the world. Bambi and I rented a small cottage on the beach from a retired crusty old English army major. We had the whole beach to ourselves—no one was about. We simply indulged our days, mostly nude, swimming and guzzling the crayfish that only Greece seems to produce—the sweetest, pinkest and most succulent ever. It was just the two of us—Robinson Crusoe and his Girl Friday.

But the time had now come for Oedipus to find the "way where three roads meet" and learn that he had killed his dad and married his mum, poor confused child. So Bambi and I, snobbishly spurning the ferry as being for tourists only, hired a motorboat for the long journey back to the mainland in order to get there in half the time. It turned out to be the most ominous few hours I've spent on the water. A huge wind got up at once—the Aegean can be a very treacherous body of water. Not only did we start bobbing up and down in our little craft; the stupid ferry passed us very early on, thumbed its nose at us and left us behind. As we kept lurching back and forth in the boat, the ferry became a little dot on the horizon. It was getting perilously dark when we finally docked beside the "stupid" ferry, which looked so complacent and pleased with itself, we could have kicked a hole in it.

THE LOCAL PEASANTS ride their donkeys too close to the neck. In fact they even sit on the neck—the same with their horses—so that the neck muscles of these unfortunate beasts are weakened dreadfully. Totally untrained, they were always skittish and nervous. When we got back, I saw that Friedrich was having a devil of a time trying to placate and train these miniature beasts which for the most part were neglected, useless nags that had suffered nothing but cruelty all their lives. I had never seen Friedrich so disappointed and frustrated. As usual, he blamed himself, not the horses. But *everyone* seemed a little on edge. Walter Lassally, our D.P., was becoming more irascible every day. Philip was exhibiting his customarily amazing gift of patience, but his mouth was starting to form a hard line. Everywhere there was a certain unease; a sense of high tension hung over Dodoni. And then I knew why—someone told me, "Orson arrives tomorrow." There are many lasting memories, mostly sweet, of the places and the people involved in our little project, but I don't exaggerate when I say that the memory which had the strongest and most lasting impact on me was of that mammothly talented, cherub-faced magician.

I had never met Orson nor seen him in the flesh, except from afar when he played Lear in New York, but a few years back he had offered me the role of Prince Hal in his Shakespeare film *Chimes at Midnight*. Incredibly, I had never been told about it until long after the film had opened. Kurt Frings, my then agent, whose sole interest was making me rich, had turned it down without consulting me, on the grounds that there was too little money in it. "But Kurt," I said, "I would have done it in a shot. How could you? What must he think of me?!" I told Orson's daughter Beatrice many years later, "I would have paid to work with your father." So as the time of his arrival approached, I knew that to vindicate myself, I must tell him the whole story. Orson had already mailed us his version of our script, along with his cuts. Philip and I read them over and they were absolutely succinct, necessary, economical and, in his scenes with me, vastly more playable. That incredible eye and ear of his never failed him.

On the propitious day I sat at the back of the amphitheatre conjuring up Wellesian reminiscences—the youth of nineteen riding through the streets of Dublin on a donkey in full view of Hilton Edwards and Michael MacLiammoir, who together ran the Dublin Gate Theatre. "What an interesting young man," they said. "We must hire him." Little did they know—Cagliostro had come to Ireland. I was remembering the story Peter Finch had told me when he played Iago to Orson's Othello at London's St. James's Theatre. "Every time I came on, mate, in the Cyprus scene, Orson would turn up the sound of seagulls so no one ever knew what I was saying." Also on the dress rehearsal of said play for which he directed, designed and wrote the music, Orson stood in the center of the stage and yelled out in his rumbling bass, *"Jesus Christ on his Cross has never suffered as I'm suffering now."* And way up in the "flys" above his head one stagehand called out to another, "Hey, Charlie, ya gotta couple o' nails?" Here was the man who reinvented radio and motion pictures with his astounding production of *The War of the Worlds* and his triumph—considered by many the greatest film ever made—*Citizen Kane*. Here was the man who mocked the establishment, who crucified the Philistines, an American who brought an edge, a wit, a sophistication to a country suffering from gullibility and naïveté. He had found its Achilles' heel and was determined to puncture it without malice.

I was aroused from my reverie by a sound like distant thunder coming from the stage. Orson had made his entrance. You could hardly miss him—he had become gargantuan—he was Ahab *and* the whale. I crossed my fingers and ran down to meet him. He looked through me with those eyes of fire, and then, a huge beaming smile spread itself across that moon-face of his, and he said in a deep rumble, "Hello, you son of a bitch."

No need for explanations, Orson had forgiven me and he became, for the duration of the film at least, my dearest friend. His overwhelming warmth was as surprising to me as was his quick Mozartean wit. He kept us mesmerized with his brilliant mimicry—another surprise. His voice which normally boomed away in the lower registers had an unexpected range that could travel up and down the scale at will. I realized that in spite of his size, he could have been most proficient as a light comedian. His appetite for life was, of course, legendary, and, my God, those breakfasts in the makeup room! Flown in from Athens, they included huge platters of pastrami, mortadella and salamis of all nationalities as well as large plates of jambon de Parme—enough for an army. While we were filming the noise of military helicopters flying much too low over the location played havoc with the sound. This would go on all morning. The reason for it was soon made clear. Orson's very attractive wife, a lovely dark-haired Italian contessa (Beatrice's mum), took to sunbathing in the briefest of bikinis on the hilltop above the theatre. The military, with nothing better to do, had decided to take a closer look. Orson shouted to anyone who would listen, "Someone tell her to come down off that goddamn hill or we'll never finish the picture."

Between takes we sat under huge parasols to avoid the heat. These parasols were held aloft by young Greeks on the payroll. Orson the raconteur would regale us with the most wonderful stories. As he spoke, the parasóls became palanquins borne by slaves and the stories—tales from Sheherazade. One morning, he invited me to coproduce with him a film version of *Julius Caesar* in Mussolini dress uniforms which would be shot in Rome. This would be reminiscent of the early Blackshirt version he so famously produced at the Mercury Theatre in New York. I became much excited at the idea and egged him on. Apart from my producer status I would also play Mark Antony as admiral of the fleet and he would cast Trevor Howard as Cassius. "And for Brutus," he began to say, but I cut him off at once knowing that if he undertook such a substantial role it would jeopardize him as director. I jumped

Orson Welles telling me outrageous stories

in—"What about Paul Scofield?" His eyes narrowed to slits for a second. "Of course. What an ideal choice." I could almost hear his teeth
grind. Then, quick as a flash—"Then I will play the small role of Caesar. But I will have huge blowups of myself as the Emperor on bill-
boards plastered over the walls of Rome so no one will forget me after
I'm gone." A great guffaw exploded deep inside his chest and his rich
diabolical laughter echoed off the ancient stones around us.

Orson Welles was never one person; he was, quite simply, a crowd.
He was not only a Renaissance man caught in the twentieth century; he
was comfortable in any period. He belonged to all ages except, perhaps,
the Age of Reason. Maybe it isn't such a bad thing after all that they
don't make critters like him no more. At least we mere mortals can
breathe what little oxygen he has left us.

GREEK COOKING though occasionally delicious when expertly done
(their lamb, moussakas and those mouth-watering langoustines) is far
from versatile and can, if one stays too long in the country, become
monotonous. Orson the gourmet gourmand was getting particularly
fed up; in fact, to put it mildly, he'd had it! The day finally arrived
when they would film Tiresias's famous psychic warning to Oedipus. It
was to be Orson's last day. But the shooting had progressed very slowly
that sluggish morning and by late afternoon they had still not shot
Orson's long speech. He was becoming understandably impatient and
restless. I could sense his temper beginning to boil. "I have a plane to

catch," he announced loudly. "I'm not staying here one more day, you know." The sun would soon disappear behind the hill. They began dismantling the camera. The assistant yelled, "I'm afraid we'll have to wrap—we've lost the light." "No, you haven't!" boomed Orson. "Put that camera back on its feet at once and shoot down at me from above. I'll be looking straight into the sun; there's still enough of it left and it will accentuate my blindness." As speedily as they could they tried to comply. But Orson wasn't going to wait. He launched straight into his speech. I've never seen a camera get ready so fast. They began to roll—he went on without a pause and did the whole speech to me staring straight into the sun. His eyes looked like sockets. It was absolutely uncanny. He spoke it quietly and with a great nobility, but it wasn't all Paul Roche. I distinctly recognized bits of Lear or Ahab and for a moment I was sure I'd caught a portion of a Clarence Darrow summation as well, but it didn't matter. It was riveting; he was quite magnificent. Joshua had halted the sun in the sky; it had waited for him and the moment he finished, it disappeared. Two of the Greek boys led him up the hill. As he passed, he winked at me—"See you in Rome, kiddo." Mr. Welles had made his plane.

FROM THEN ON everything was an anticlimax. The film began to rapidly wind down. I enjoyed one good scene I had with my mum Lilli Palmer whom I accused of giving everyone she came in contact with an Oedipus complex. I was being complimentary, of course. Donald Sutherland, who stayed up nights even later than me, would arrive on set hungover in the extreme, his mumbling now reduced to a whisper. God love him—he kept up the mirth. We shot the flashback scene where I see my father at the place where the roads meet and then proceed to kill him. Poor Oedipus had made all the wrong choices. Count Friedrich looked magnificent as old King Priam standing proud and tall in his chariot—his shock of white hair making him appear even taller.

Diana Rigg had gone back to London so Philip, Bambi and I had a few final farewell dinners together and then I left. It was sad saying good-bye to Bambi, who had been so good to me and such a joyous relief from the tension of the set. I privately took my leave of the old amphitheatre. It looked so beautiful with no one in it all by itself, except for Duncan Grant sitting on a rock still furiously sketching away wearing his great floppy hat—shades of Gordon Craig. I beat

Count Friedrich as King Priam

myself regularly once a year for being so stupid as not to get one of his drawings. He even drew *me* several times and like an idiot I never thought to ask him for one. Aside from their historic significance, think what they could be worth today. As I drove away I caught sight of Friedrich far off on the slopes. I rolled down the window and waved at him, but he didn't see me. He had two horses on either side of him which he was leading down the hillside and in the afternoon light, playing tricks as is its wont, it looked very much as if he were carrying them under his arms. The little horses, now so spruce and groomed, had found their new god. Friedrich had finally won!

I ARRIVED IN LONDON and checked into my favourite hotel, the Connaught. Since my separation from Trish, I had actually been living there, pampering myself rotten. Well, if the movie companies paid for it—why not?! This time it would only be for one night as I was to fly to Canada the next day where, believe it or not, I would be playing yet another Mark Antony, this one in Shakespeare's *Antony and Cleopatra*. I had just had a long rich and sumptuous dinner in the hotel's Grill Room—English cooking at its best when administered by French chefs. Filled to the brim with wine and brandy I staggered off to bed. About 3:00 a.m., the phone rang. There was a lot of mumbling at the other end and because I couldn't understand a word of what was being said, I knew at once it was Donald Sutherland. As far as I could make out, he was trying to tell me that he had an important audition in LA at the end of the week—so important, in fact, it could change his life. But he didn't have the money to get there, could I lend it to him? Still half asleep I murmured back rather grandly, "See my accountants in the morning, my good fellow," or something to that effect and hung up. I called them the next morning and he went to see them. It was the best investment I ever made. It *did* change his life. I got my money back and he got *M*A*S*H*!

CHAPTER THIRTY

A TASMANIAN DEVIL ON THE LOOSE

> *I dreamt there was an Emperor Antony.*
> *O, such another sleep, that I might see*
> *But such another man!*

Cleopatra is the greatest of Shakespeare's women and certainly one of the finest roles (male or female) ever written. Most actresses dare not touch it and the occasional few brave enough to try generally reach no more than halfway up that massive climb to the summit.

Some famous ladies from the past soon found that out. Katharine Cornell's "Serpent of the Nile" was far too prim and proper, much too polite, and she was about as regal as a rich Long Island matron. Tallulah Bankhead probably achieved the requisite naughtiness, but her every utterance would have become an obscene double entendre in the Mae West manner and John Mason Brown's caustic review simply stated: "Last night Miss Bankhead barged down the Nile and sank." Edith

Evans must have spoken it beautifully and brought out the inherent sarcasm brilliantly but, knowing her as I did, she could never have become that untamed, wild Macedonian gypsy queen. The beauteous Vivien Leigh played it opposite her husband Olivier as Antony, but her voice was too thin.

There is so much variety in the role, so many personalities bubbling beneath the surface, so many colours to capture, so much abandon to exhibit and sudden fire to ignite that one can only imagine a Cleopatra of one's dreams. Little did I know as I walked into the theatre halfway through rehearsals and caught sight of Zoe Caldwell letting fly for the first time that I had walked straight into that dream.

From the inception it was evident that Zoe and her "Eastern Star" had instinctively bonded. They had even managed to climb into each other's skin. The unnerving mood swings, the remnants of the sex kitten were all present and accounted for as was the towering magisterial temper. There was no question Zoe had the voice for it—a voice whose four-octave range could summon up an incredible variety of tones, from the deep cello notes to the violin's high-pitched whines. Her movements were liquid, sinuous as a snake and in her grief she swayed like a palm tree in a hurricane. Most Anglo-Saxons have built-in restrictions where emotion is concerned, but being native Aussie, Miss Caldwell's lack of inhibitions served her admirably. Her vulgarity was outrageously shocking and screamingly funny, and when in anger, her voice was as "rattling thunder." It was clarion clear to me that this performance was to reach greatness and that Zoe, who seemed blissfully unaware of her own powers, had suddenly joined the gods! O Day of the World! Was I going to have to work my butt off as Mark Antony!

The tragedy itself is Shakespeare at his most sophisticated—a risk commercially in any century because of its preoccupation with failure, the decline of power and success, the terrible price of fame and the disintegration of two fading stars whose fatal attraction becomes the instrument of their destruction. There is something uncomfortably familiar about political icons brought down by scandal, dysfunctional royal families or great heroes toppling from their pedestals only to reveal themselves as fragile and pitifully human.

People will always derive macabre pleasure from seeing the mighty fall. But failure is different. They are not too fond of watching failure take its course—it's not attractive—it worries them. And the very fact that it causes this uneasiness and hits too close to home is what makes *Antony and Cleopatra* such a tellingly modern play.

I loved taking a stab at Antony—what a glorious ruin he is. Olivier once described him to me as a movie star whose career had hit the skids, a slight oversimplification, I would say, but that's the part I got on the nose. The libertine, with his wenching, drinking, gourmandizing was fairly familiar territory for me and not too tough an assignment. What I didn't get at all were the flashes of the once great conqueror, legendary leader of men who "with my sword / Quartered the world, and o'er green Neptune's back / With ships made cities." Bob Jiras (the Powder Puff) had arrived to help line my face and age my hair, but my body was far too young—I was too young, only thirty-seven. Let's face it—I was Antony, Jr., still wet behind the ears.

Tanya Moiseiwitsch, with her usual brilliance, had designed the costumes, or rather clothes that looked as if they'd been worn for ages. My mentor Langham had given the piece a beautifully mounted production, most cinematic in its rhythmic lighting, which made those swift, sharp, geographical scene changes dissolve into each other with unobtrusive smoothness, and I was perfectly content to stand around, just as the real Antony might have done, and watch this whirling dervish circle all about me, play with me, taunt me, make me laugh. What gave Zoe so much added energy and spark was the fact that she was in love. She and her beau, my old friend Ratty Whitehead, last of the gentlemen producers, were on the brink of marriage, and Ratty commuted back and forth from New York every weekend to be with her. It was an exciting and joyous time altogether. The World's Fair (Expo '67) and Separatism had both hit Montreal, the queen was about to visit, tout le monde had come to Canada and, though chaotic, all seemed very right with the world.

Someone high up in government circles invited me to officially greet Her Majesty on her arrival and make some welcoming remarks, but it meant a plane trip to Parliament Hill on the very day I was playing Antony. Declining, I put it to them that if they wanted someone from the arts, Robert Whitehead, top Broadway producer and a Canadian to boot, was in the country and might appear in my stead. Of course, they were delighted at the possibility of such a distinguished replacement. I remember we were standing by the bar at a rather stuffy reception in the theatre's VIP lounge. "But I can't do it," said Ratty. "I didn't bring a dark suit." I happened to be wearing one freshly minted from Savile Row. "Here, try this on for size," and amidst many a jaw-drop and raised eyebrow, we stripped in front of everyone and exchanged clothes. My Sunday best fit Ratty like a glove! So off he went.

Zoe Caldwell, a firebrand as Cleopatra

Where have you been so spruce and clean? Kissing ass and bussing the Queen!

Alan Bates had come over from England to give us his Richard III, and William Hutt was superbly funny in Langham's other production that season of Gogol's *The Government Inspector*. Apart from the New York and London press, a lot of friends from all over the globe came to see us. Natalie Wood looking ravishingly beautiful visited with her about-to-be husband, my pal Richard Gregson. Appearing in a reveal-ing bathing suit at the Quarry for a swim, she nearly started a forest fire! Arthur Miller (a great friend of Ratty's) and his photographer wife from Austria, Inge Morath, came up to stay—Inge taking some sensational production photos. Enter Julian Bream, world-famous guitarist, to give concerts and master classes, but he was having such fun hanging around with us hams, he wouldn't leave. James Kennaway, author of that splendid film *Tunes of Glory* and a close drinking buddy, came over for a weekend, fell for a French girl predictably called Francine and got so drunk going to parties, he stayed for most of the summer, some of it recovering in a local hospital.

The hosts most responsible for those entertaining soirees were Jean Gascon and his lady Marilyn, who had taken an apartment for the season. He was directing as well as playing the lead in the French version of *Dance of Death* and giving us in English a superbly whimsical Dr. Caius in *The Merry Wives of Windsor.* More important than that, every other night, he and Marilyn cooked delectable feasts for us, which we washed down with stinging eau de vies and beefy wines. When the French and the Anglos are thus joined, that's what Canada is all about. My good friend Jean would one day in the future take over the Festival as artistic director. He had gone as far as anyone could go in the arts of our country—he was head of the National Arts Centre in Ottawa and had run Canada's two principal theatres, both French and English. He continued to blend our two cultures while ever burning the midnight oil. Then one day, his gigantic heart, much too big for one human, burst. The only cruel thing he ever did was to leave us all behind for the longest time, lost without him.

THE 1967 SEASON was Michael Langham's swan song as Stratford's figurehead. It seemed inconceivable that we were actually saying goodbye to the man who had been head of our "family" for twelve long years and who, more than anyone, had brought such enormous distinction to the Festival with his consummate style and taste. His *Government Inspector* and "A and C," were visible proof that he was leaving on a crest. As a last duty, he brought both to Montreal in the fall to represent Canada at Expo '67.

My city looked more impressive than ever with its new skyline and the magnificent panorama of architectural inventiveness created for the Fair by countries from all over the world. They spread across man-made islands in the St. Lawrence River like giant-sized lace, glistening silver and gold in the afternoon sun: Habitat, a new igloo-influenced cluster of modern condominiums designed by the brilliant Moshe Safdie; a most dignified French pavilion from Paris; Buckminster Fuller's imaginative American pavilion; the Swiss and Czechoslovakian pavilions—the Czech edifice winning all the prizes.

Perhaps the simplest and most original of all was the pavilion from Ireland. It was simply nothing but a pub—Guinness on tap and every trimming known to the Emerald Isle. Sean Kenny, sure enough, its designer and innovator, was ever present night and day, presiding with glass or mug in hand. Besides the pub, he had designed and built Gyroton, a massive funicular railway with silver train tracks high above the buildings running the entire length of the exhibition from which you could get a bird's-eye view of the whole experience from your seat in the sky. A prize student of Frank Lloyd Wright, Sean, Ireland's mad, baby-faced maniac, made up of blarney and genuine magic, was in his element as Mine Host of the Garter. Every conceivable nationality convened at his pub. It became a kind of headquarters to the World's Fair.

My old school chum, John Lynch-Staunton (John V), now a VIP and city councillor and pro-mayor, reintroduced me to Montreal. It was a revelation—truly our belle epoque! Mayor Jean Drapeau's expensive dream had given my hometown an international status and glamour that would attract tourism for years to come, but its proud citizens are still paying for it to this very day. Early rumblings from the Separatist movement were providing a contrapuntal rhythm to this atmosphere of jubilation. Not unlike the clash between Egyptians and Romans in our play, the long-suppressed differences between les Français et Anglais were beating at the door to be let out. This had already brought to light a splurge of new writing—poetry, music and song in the quasi-revolutionary mode of both languages—a highly tense but exciting background to a World's Fair. These local poets voiced their beefs, some discordantly, some eloquently in small clubs, cellars or boîtes from the bowels of the city. Sean, John V, myself and anyone who cared to come along would pay them a visit and then invade the many strip joints which were enjoying a thriving renaissance as they jostled with each other for supremacy.

Polly and her usual contingent led by her son Toby and his wife, Alice, came to see the play. She was aging, of course, but her vitality had not diminished in the slightest. I returned the compliment by paying a lone, nostalgic visit to my old family haunts at Senneville on the Lake of Two Mountains—a last bastion of gentility. I could sense with

Polly in old age

an ache that it was slowly giving in to time. I could almost hear it, like a long wistful sigh in a quiet room. But the city, on the other hand, was gathering strength—the strength of resolve. It had a drive to it now—an angry one perhaps, but one that was to signal the arrival of a dramatic change waiting just around the corner for Quebec and for the country.

Well, the time had come to leave. The play from which I had learned so much was over. Zoe Caldwell's unforgettable performance was never seen beyond the border. If there is any tragedy attached to the play, that was it. Of course, everyone knows she has gone on to win most of the honours her profession can bestow. Her amazing stage career has made its considerable impact on three continents. She has excelled as Medea, Lady Hamilton, Miss Jean Brodie, Tennessee Williams's Gnadiges Fraulein, Lillian Hellman, Maria Callas, Sarah Bernhardt, and a rich collection of portraits both classic and modern. She has won four Tony Awards and a fifth which she shares with her husband, and she has been honoured by Elizabeth II. But, to me, her most beguiling and inspired gift to the theatre was Egypt's Queen. It is sad that the rest of the world has been deprived of that glory, but the heavens surely witnessed it and

Antony and Cleopatra

so did I. As I flew down to New York, I could not keep from my ears, as I still can't to this day, the keening wail that came from somewhere deep within her as she held my dead body in her arms and rocked me back and forth:

> *The crown o' the earth doth melt. My lord!*
> *O wither'd is the garland of the war,*
> *The soldier's pole is fall'n: young boys and girls*
> *Are level now with men; the odds is gone,*
> *And there is nothing left remarkable*
> *Beneath the visiting moon.*

I would have gladly died many times over each night just to let those words and this great artist who spoke them wring my heart.

WITH ONE FOOT in Manhattan, I joined the old gang Ed Flanders, George C. Scott, et al., especially Le Robards! As Antony would have said, "Call to me all my sad Captains. Let's have one other gaudy night!" I also had to arrange a meeting between my new film agent from CMA (Creative Management Associates) and the guide and custodian of my life, dear Jane Broder. Jane was clearly upset. She didn't object to someone taking over my movie future. After all, she had become fond of Kurt Frings, who had always treated her with respect, but she liked not at all the smooth-talking, shiny-suited David Begelman who in the midst of his power plunge slyly inferred he intended taking over completely. He was coldly civil to Jane, but it was evident he could not have cared less for her revered place in theatrical history. Most people tended to forget that Miss Broder was a highly trained lawyer who, when faced with any sort of altercation or debate, could usually win hands down. She waited for some time in silence and then, unable any longer to countenance Mr. Begelman's lofty diatribe and his grandiose plans for my future, lit into him with full artillery blazing. He at once became Uriah Heap, wringing his hands apologetically, with an unctuous attempt at servility. She made it abundantly clear that the theatre was her domain and no one must cross it. So, for the moment, a truce was declared, and the three of us shook hands. After he left, Jane had a little weep; "I don't trust that man, honey—watch your back!" Her instincts were to prove correct, for some years later he was found guilty of using clients' money to pay his gambling debts. While he was my agent he had always been most courteous but soon brushed me off and put me in the care of his partner, Sue Mengers—une histoire unto herself—but that's another book.

Bidding Jane farewell that day, I joined my favourite posse to do the rounds once more—from the East to the West Side. One night at Frankie and Johnny's in the bar at the back manned by that most generous of drink pourers, Cappie, Jason's and my date was the young Faye Dunaway. To show off, I brought my sword cane along with me, made of shining black ebony, sleek and sinister. The blade, slim and elegant, was subtly decorated with encrusted swirls and scriptures embedded in Toledo steel—a thing of true beauty. So, I remember, was Miss Dunaway. The tiny bar sat only six in a very tight pinch. We were all merrily into the evening when an obnoxious little man seated alone at the far end began making abusive remarks about Jason's and my long hair (I had grown mine for Antony). "Must I sit here and listen to this garbage," he slurred, "especially coming from two useless faggots with long hair?" He burbled on, accusing actors in general of being homosexual vermin and gutless as well. In heroic defense of my fellow artists and with the noblest of swashbuckling gestures, I unsheathed the narrow sword in a flash. With that single movement, I accidentally pierced him in the neck. It was a perfect draw. D'Artagnan himself would have envied my skill and accuracy—no question, but no one could have been more surprised than I. The nick was minuscule, had drawn some blood but was hardly serious. The miserable creature, however, made much melodrama of it—demanding towels to stop the bleeding and a host of napkins with which to measure the wound. "Call the police!" he screamed at Cappie, and turning to me the varmint yelled, "I'll get you for this, I'll put you away, you son of a bitch! Have you ever heard of the Sullivan law? I'll put you inside, you miserable faggot freak!" After an assassination attempt on the mayor of New York in 1911, the Sullivan Law was passed which made it an imprisonable offense to carry a concealed weapon without a permit. Cappie took me aside. "He could do it, you know. This guy's a shyster lawyer in the city. He's always causing trouble. But he's so drunk, the bastard, he'll forget about it. Don't worry. I'm not serving him anymore. By the way, we love what you did!" The others at the bar and some of the waiters who'd witnessed the incident gave me a round of applause. Feeling on top of the world again, we kissed Cappie good night and I and my two musketeers—one tall beauty in her hunting mode and one scowling fugitive from the dark world of O'Neill—swept from the door, free once more to sniff out Philistines and rid the world of bigotry.

Well, Faye the Huntress soon became Faye the Screen Goddess and dear Jason, whose passion for the night remained unaltered but whose life was to take on an awesome transformation, kept on being wonderful in a host of plays and films. All over the map, the scenery was beginning to shift; the seeds of change had begun to sprout. People were now markedly different—the baby boomers were preparing to invade society in swarms; money now belonged to everyone and anyone, especially the untutored; sophistication in everything was getting rarer and rarer—subtleties and nuance were no longer recognized; in the theatre the straight play was more than ever being outmaneuvered by the musical, the extravaganza—stuff that was easier to take. In fact, it became more than evident as we stared across the footlights that English was no longer the first language.

Back home in London, then the center of the cultural revolution, things were slowly winding down. At one party, crowded with pop stars, actors, aristocracy and a considerable amount of nudity, screaming became the main theme of the evening, cruelly illustrating the desperation of a creative era now turned dysfunctional and crumbling. The hostess's living room was decorated, walls and ceiling, in a startling William Morris print depicting a jungle of thick interweaving vines. Sean Kenny had somehow managed to climb up the wall and with a lot of frantic nail scratching was trying to fight through the vines in order to get into the wallpaper—a crude enactment of Saki's famous short story. That was my last image of that crazy, gifted young genius. He must have got through, though, for soon after he left this world. I wager he is safely ensconced on the other side of the wallpaper, peeping through the vines, laughing at the rest of us.

For myself—I just went along with it all. I didn't harbour much self-respect. My family's correctness and high standards had made me want to be the *bad* boy always, convinced it made me more interesting and would bring me more attention. I was sadly deluded. Oh, I was proud that in the theatre I had at least learned the power to command, but once offstage my real existence had little in it to write home about. I suddenly saw there was nothing particularly original about me. I lived off the foibles of others—a resigned chameleon, if you will. Nothing much to recommend, I was in serious trouble. Barry the Bartender was kept busy watering my drinks. I was disappearing in a cloud of self-incrimination.

And so were the vanishing sixties, the last symbol of carefree life in the twentieth century. I was just about to go down with the ship when, to the rescue came, out of thin air and in the nick of time, a graceful angel, an angel of mercy with a soft beauty, a caring soul and the wisdom of Solomon, who pulled at my heartstrings and without my knowing it, at once took charge. Her appearance instantly broke a recurring dream that had plagued me most of my life but which now made complete sense. In it, I am the incubus fighting my way through bile and slime; something incredibly heavy is pushing down upon my face. I can breathe no longer, I'm suffocating, life is slipping away. Then far above a light begins to shine through and with one terrifying heave I am released. Some kind nocturnal monster has retched and spewed what's left of me out into the brilliant sunlight and like some beached flounder I land with a joyous slap onto the warm and welcoming white sands. Another temporary reprieve? No! This time I had been truly spared.

BOOK FOUR

BOOK FOUR

CHAPTER THIRTY-ONE

A LIGHT IN THE WILDERNESS

As I write this from my house in Connecticut, I look across the room at the lady who has been, for the past forty years or thereabouts, my partner and my life. Heavily engrossed in her reading, she does not look up. She is as beautiful now as she ever was. How can I begin to write about her—about us, even? We are too close. She has seen through me from the beginning, for pity's sake—as Hamlet might say—she has plucked out the heart of my mystery. After all our time together will I never be able to impress her as I would wish?

"Help me," I plead. "Take me back, in your own words, to the time we met." She looks up. "There must have been something about you. And oh yes, we tumbled into bed and all that, but I didn't like you very much. I thought you were the most conceited prig—the way you ponced about in that big convertible of yours. And you drank far too much—but there was something, I suppose . . ." she trailed off, couldn't think what it was and went back to her book.

We met in County Kilkenny, Ireland, on a film called *Lock Up Your Daughters,* a Restoration romp which was trying to match or even surpass the successful *Tom Jones.* It didn't! My friend Peter Coe directed. It was his first feature and it had an impressive British cast, ranging from Hugh Griffith, Glynis Johns, Georgia Brown and Susannah York to Ian Bannen, Tom Bell, Pat Rutledge and the two Roys—Dotrice and Kinnear—all very much in demand at the time. The script was a hodge-podge—a mess with too many characters and too many subplots. It desperately needed a central figure like Tom Jones, an anchor whom audiences might care about and root for.

I played Lord Foppington, a character taken directly from *The Relapse,* John Vanbrugh's famous play—surely the campiest popinjay in the rich gallery of Restoration buffoons. He changes wigs as he

Elaine Taylor, my future partner and my life

changes clothes in every scene—the wigs becoming higher and higher as the film progresses—the last one so high it is impossible to pass through doorways. I helped embellish my role by lifting dialogue straight from the play and had the most enormous fun with all this foppery, but it had little or nothing to do with the film. One day before I check out, I'd love to play that absurd ageless pantaloon on the stage.

My lady, Elaine Regina Taylor, or "la belle Elaine" (the first of a long list of nicknames) played Susannah York's maid with the required poitrine showing most daringly from her décolletage. Elaine was not only a beautiful young English actress, she was a damn good one. Half Irish from County Wexford and the other half from the borough of Westminster, she had red hair, freckles, a pert nose and looked just as delectable in miniskirts or hot pants. She also had a brain, was well read and startlingly astute for her twenty-two years; in fact, she was miles ahead of me on all counts—I should have been quite humbled and I was. To say I was also hopelessly smitten would be the understatement of my life.

As a teenager in the Welsh National Theatre, she had begun acting onstage and on both the big and small screens. Over the years, she found herself playing opposite such impressive luminaries as Bette Davis, Marcello Mastroianni, Sir Ralph Richardson, Donald Sinden, to name a few. She had a delightful singing voice and appeared in several musicals, one with the British star Dora Bryan, and on screen with Tommy Steele in *Half a Sixpence.* Ballet had also managed to fill her dance card. She was knee-high to a grasshopper when she danced opposite the great Anton Dolin in *Swan Lake* and others, as well as Roger Quilter's musical play *Where the Rainbow Ends* at London's Festival Hall in which she played Will-o'-the-wisp. Dolin was St. George and the Wicked Dragon was the eccentrically theatrical Michael MacLiammoir. I had always been fascinated by this English imposter who posed as the most Irish of the Irish. "And what about Michael?" I asked, dying to know. "Oh, he was so over the top, camp, funny, witty—an utter diva! The Wicked Dragon took more time getting into his street makeup than his stage makeup. He was no spring chicken, but he finally would emerge looking twenty years younger with long flowing hair and an opera cloak swirled about him—the reincarnation of Lord Byron who, of course, he was convinced he was."

Along with the bleeding toes and the grueling workouts, ballet was beginning to disenchant her. So to amuse herself and the rest of the cygnets in *Swan Lake* while they obeyed the required choreography by pirouetting offstage in one direction, she would grand-jeté off in another. Dolin, who was fond of her, turned a blind eye, but she didn't stay too long.

LOCK UP YOUR DAUGHTERS was produced by Columbia Pictures and David Deutsch. David, his wife, Claire, and her sister, Tita Wilson, were to become lifelong friends of ours. Claire was a serene beauty, Tita was glowingly attractive and enormous fun. With Glynis Johns in tow, darling whimsical Glynis, we did everything together.

We all stayed in one big rambling house called Kilkenny Lodge where we threw supper parties almost every other night. We would often pile into my dreaded green Mercedes with the top down and tour the countryside—Waterford, Galway, Kerry. We even drove as far as Connemara, with its red chalk hills, and then back in Dublin we would devour splendid dinners at the old, now long-gone Russell Hotel. Elaine and I would go pub-crawling with Tita—a hopeless and unconvincing chaperone. There was a small but enchanting castle just outside Dublin, which had belonged to King John in the eleventh century (one of his many stopovers, no doubt). Part of its land boasted a famous salmon fishing river. I learned that the whole package was for sale, at

I had more fun playing bits of Lord Foppington
from The Relapse

the unbelievably low price of eleven thousand pounds. I wanted to buy it without hesitation but "Mademoiselle E" put the kibosh on it by simply saying, "What about central heating?"

The mad Welshman Hugh Griffith had arrived with his long-suffering wife. They had taken a house just outside Kilkenny. Hugh had already waited a week without having been called to work—a very dangerous situation indeed. I warned Peter Coe and told him the story of how Hugh had travelled all the way from Wales to Tahiti to begin work on *Mutiny on the Bounty* with Brando and Trevor Howard. The production committed a huge boo-boo by not using him right away. It was a full two weeks before he was finally scheduled to work. He had been sent his call sheet the night before and everyone was there on set the next morning waiting for him to appear.

The whole morning went by—no Hugh. A posse of assistants were sent to search for him, starting with his hotel—no Hugh. They scoured the island—no Hugh. They looked in every bar—no Hugh. At last, at about three in the afternoon, they found him in a tacky little hut on the beach boasting only one room with a bed in it. There was Hugh, bollocks naked, dead drunk, his arms around two grizzly old Tahitian prostitutes, also starkers. "Mr. Griffith, you've got to come with us now—you're on! We've wasted a whole morning waiting for you!" "But I can't possibly work today, lads," he slurred indignantly. "Why not?" they demanded lamely. Hugh buried his face between four huge heaving breasts and mumbled, "It's the time change, the time change."

The same sort of thing occurred in *Tom Jones*—the film company kept him hanging around. When he did report for work, he kept falling off his horse in every take. At least they kept that in the movie as part of a very funny opening montage. "You can't make the same mistake," I kept saying to Coe. "The rule is, if you hire Hugh, put him to work even before he gets off the plane."

Elaine, Tita and I and, of course, the Welsh pixie Glynis, went over to welcome the Griffiths. Here was Hugh, beaming, larger than life, generously presenting me with a bottle of poteen he'd found some-where in Ireland. It was so ancient, so fermented, so overmatured, there were actual reptiles swimming around in it. "It's just about ready to drink now, boyo," he assured me. Of course, I merely had to smell it and I was paralytic.

A few more days went by before Hugh was put in front of the cam-eras. He was playing a periwigged Justice conducting a trial. He was absolutely marvellous in the role except he kept tumbling off his podium every time the cameras rolled. His legs simply buckled under him and they had to let him go—a shame because the film might have been received a tad more favourably had he remained in it. A fantastic actor was Hugh Griffith, of great imagination and talent, who much preferred his very own inebriated world to any other.

Elaine had now completed her role in the movie and was on her way back to London for yet another engagement—a busy and popular lady. I felt absolutely empty and as despondent as anyone could be. As she was leaving, I told her I was going to miss her dreadfully and hoped she would let me see her in London. "All right, but on one condition," she warned, "that you cut down on the booze. Take a look at yourself—you're falling apart." I searched for every flattering mirror I could find, but it didn't matter; true or false, they all told the same story. Here was

I, on my way to forty, already with bags under the eyes the size of trunks, puffy, starting a pot and my first set of love handles were developing nicely, thank you. I thought for a moment, picked up my bottle of Jameson's, crossed myself and poured it down the loo.

DIVESTING MYSELF of Lord Foppington's elegant coattails and hose, I hurried back to London. Once there, I found myself alternating between two homes—the Connaught Hotel and Elaine's charming little mews house in Knightsbridge, no. 15 Donne Place. To reinstate myself in her favour, I had faithfully chucked the hard stuff—think of it—the giant martinis, stingers, old-fashioneds, boilermakers, rum scorpions, moscow mules, all that nectar that had been my sustenance, all gone! Wine was different—I still drank gallons of that, but then so did she!

While Elaine and I were still at the Connaught, we would take Glynis out to dinner frequently so we could laugh a lot. One night, just down the street at the attractive Trattoria Terrazza, she brought along as her date Deborah Kerr. The restaurant was agog! These two beauties of advancing years—Glynis, so rapturously adorable, and Deborah, the silver screen's most poignantly exquisite siren—once primed with a few champagne cocktails, bombarded us with one personal saga after another, naughty enough to make your hair curl. As I looked across the table at these two minxes, both of them flushed with the innocence of English roses, I realized that between them they'd had more lovers than Napoleon's army. We were all having such a good time, including several neighbouring tables which had stopped talking to listen, that no one wanted the evening to end. When it was over, we literally poured the gorgeous Deborah into a cab and Glynis, her sexy voice huskier than ever and by now speaking an English which closely resembled Swabian, came back to the Connaught with us. Between gulps of fiery Calvados, the only words that emerged clearly from her lips were, "It's my pancreas, darlings—my pancreas—I must lie down." The suite had an extra bed; we lowered her onto it and she stayed for a week!

To help take my mind off our guest, the Rolls-Royce Sam Spiegel had promised me was delivered to the hotel's front door. It had been at least a year, and knowing Sam, it had probably fallen off a truck. But it was shining and beautiful to behold—a two-toned deep garnet and black four-door Silver Shadow, very sleek indeed, and my rating instantly soared with the hotel staff. I hired an ex-marine called Frank to be my chauffeur. A marvellous driver who had driven some high-level VIPs in his time, he was impeccable, smartly groomed and one hell of a nice guy. In those days employing a chauffeur was cheaper than paying for London cabbies and being able to enjoy the nightlife without getting nicked for driving under the influence. I, of course, loved swanning about in it, but Elaine was slightly embarrassed whenever it drew up in front of her mews house, for the car was almost as wide as the street. All her socialist leanings came boiling to the surface.

Feeling quite heady about everything, I also bought a house on Hyde Park Gate, the street where Churchill had lived. It was a handsome four-story Victorian mansion in need of conversion, which I was determined would be our future home. The next thing was to find an architect, and here Tita Wilson was invaluable, for she rustled up a charming and talented young Australian called Dougie Norwood whose reputation for taste and daring preceded him. Dougie had some stunning ideas and I felt we should throw all caution to the winds and go for it! Apart from the need to gut the place completely, staircases had to be built, marble floors laid, and I told him I wanted to add one more story to the top of the house, which would combine a garden terrace with a glassed-in solarium.

He designed a most unusual floor for the terrace—tiny tiles made of glass framed with wide squares of green marble—a magical sight particularly at night, lit from beneath; it made the entire floor seem transparent. To reach this upper level Dougie had constructed a long tall dome, cupolalike in appearance, which towered above the roof and from which hung a long circular staircase made of silver aluminum supported at the top. The roof of the dome had a hexagonal diamond shape to it made of tinted bevelled glass, and if you stood on the stairs below and looked up, you could see the stars at night—a miniature observatory. Douglas had some trouble with the LCC who insisted that aluminum was neither strong enough nor safe enough for a staircase. Dougie stood firm. "What do you think they make airplanes with?" he countered. It got built.

Our bedroom was directly below this new roof garden. We gutted the three rooms which had been there and opened it all up into one huge space. It was to have a classical futuristic look about it, so we took out an entire wall, replacing it with a floor-to-ceiling window at least twenty-five feet across. To complement the cubelike dome and to somehow support the huge window, he constructed a circular stainless-steel cone in the center of the window and the same height, with room in it for only one person. This was the loo. The steel cube miraculously had no visible join in it. If you had to go in a hurry, you merely touched it gently and the whole thing opened. The interior of the cone was covered in a carpet of deep burgundy—the cone of course was ventilated. Whenever I sat on the john, I felt that I was in a time machine or space capsule and every time I flushed it, I was convinced I was going to take off through the roof with the toilet seat stuck to my bum.

The pièce de résistance, which was to become a really serious bête noire, was the bath cum shower. At one corner of the room in the open for all to see was this completely circular tub, which could easily accommodate four people quite comfortably. Fixed into the ceiling was a giant spray funnel, which supplied the shower. For privacy, the tub and shower would be closed off by circular sliding doors fashioned out of thick opaque amber glass or Perspex, either one just an expensive as the other. The wide rim which surrounded the tub was to be made of pure white marble. All of this would be romantically lit from above.

I confess it was most exciting and it all looked ravishing, but I was rapidly going broke and Dougie, thinking I was either some rich kid from the movies or Ludwig of Bavaria, was on a sort of power rush and beginning to lose all control. He could hardly be blamed as I kept okaying more and more such extravagances. Well, he started on the bath. The wooden frame was erected, the huge tub from Godfrey Bonzac with its gold dolphin taps was lowered into place, the lights, the shower spray, everything was working—all we were waiting for now was the Perspex doors and the marble rim.

I had relinquished my rooms at the Connaught and was now fully ensconced at Elaine's house at no. 15 Donne Place and every so often we stayed in the guest room at the virgin no. 9 Hyde Park Gate, just to keep tabs with what was going on. Each new development brought me that much nearer to bankruptcy and raised eyebrows from Elaine, who, I discovered, had a wonderful talent for decoration—her knowledge of colour combinations and fabrics was most impressive, and when she subtly suggested things like, "Wouldn't it be simpler, less expensive and just as attractive if—" she was invariably right. However, progress at no. 9 was slowly coming to a halt, and Dougie hardly graced us with his presence. (I suspected he'd taken on too many assignments.) Both Elaine and I were beginning to go ballistic, so it was with enormous relief that I was able to busy myself with two film projects, *The Battle of Britain* and *The Royal Hunt of the Sun*.

The former was one of the last big epics to come out of England, and was produced by the Canadian impresario Harry Saltzman, who with Alfred "Cubby" Broccoli had created the Bond films. His online producing partner on *Battle* was the much loved Bennie Fisz, a Polish war hero and flying ace. The film, of course, dealt with the history and bravery of the RAF in their defense of Great Britain during the Second World War. It was written by my drinking friend James Kennaway and the musical score was by Sir William Walton. It starred just about everybody on the English stage and screen from Laurence Olivier (who played Air Chief Marshall Lord Dowding) to Trevor Howard, Michael Redgrave, Ralph Richardson and Michael Caine, and was inundated with technical advisors, each of whom had been a top air-ace in the war. Ginger Lacey was the principal tech expert—with a staggering record of dog-fight victories. He naturally was the most modest of them all and was absolutely loathe to tolerate any mention of his own heroism. Tom Gleave was another invaluable advisor, and always present, hanging about like a loyal groupie was Group Captain Peter Townsend (Princess Margaret's love for many years). Then there was the famously multidecorated Douglas Bader who had had both his legs amputated and who managed to get around at great speed with the help of two steel crutches. He shouted at the top of his voice all the time—a conversation with him was entirely one-sided and conducted at an ear-splitting level as if he were barking out his battle orders for the day. Rumour had it that he was not altogether popular with his men.

One morning, I got Frank to drive me to the set, which was a deserted airfield, in the green Mercedes. We were just leaving at the end of the day when I heard a lot of yelling directly behind us. I turned round—it was Douglas Bader lumbering towards us in the most threatening manner. "Get that filthy Kraut car out of here," he yelled. I could see he wasn't joking. "Are you speaking to me, sir?" I asked. "You know bloody well I am," he fumed. "Now get that filthy thing out of here—Now!" And with that he swung his two steel crutches with such force they made two great gaping dents in the Merc's beautiful rear end. I felt an enormous wave of sympathy for any Luftwaffe pilot who might have had the misfortune to come up against Air Commodore Douglas Bader.

My role in the film was that of a Canadian Squadron Leader (fictional). I'd asked that I be Canadian as so many of my countrymen had done valiant RAF and RCAF service. My fellow pilots were Robert Shaw, that gruff Cornishman, and Michael Caine, who was developing daily into what we now know as the Cockney raconteur. I was the only

She's obviously having second thoughts

fellow in the flick with a love interest. My WAF girlfriend was played by the exceptionally pretty Susannah York—she of the big baleful eyes. There were so many characters in this vast film that we were each allotted only the briefest of time to establish ourselves in the audience's mind. In the one short scene I had in bed with Susannah, we had only minutes to suggest that we were desperate and passionate war-lovers who at any moment might be separated forever. Not easy to do.

It was meant to be a rather hot, sexy scene and we were supposed to be naked under the sheets. I had stripped down to just a pair of briefs, but Susannah, whom I found surprisingly overmodest for such a free spirit, insisted on clasping the sheets tightly above her breasts, covering them completely so all one could see was just her neck, head and arms. Lovely as they were, they were hardly enough to indicate, let alone inspire, a torrid relationship. At one point in the scene we both hear an enormous explosion, jump out of bed without a stitch and run to the window to watch the bombs fall. We then turn to each other and play a tender scene of farewell—this we do in close-up. Her close-up, with me giving the off-camera lines, was tight enough to be above the line of her breasts, but still she stubbornly kept holding on tight to the sheet, which she'd brought along with her—have sheet will travel! When it came to my close-up, however, with her off camera, something utterly bizarre occurred. Now she had ample time, while they were preparing the shot, to put on a robe or a rain coat—*anything*—it wouldn't have mattered. Instead, the minute the director, Guy Hamilton, called "Action," she dropped her sheet halfway and I was treated to most of her natural beauty! Darling Susannah was always at odds with herself—regularly getting things the wrong way round, backwards or inside out—wacky and adorable, but her wistful pathos as an actress and a person were priceless and that otherworldly vagueness of hers was very much part of her allure.

There were so many servicemen, airmen, actors, actual war heroes— so many planes, old Spitfires, Mitchells, Lancasters, even Focke-Wolfe on the ground and in the air, it seemed to match the numbers in the real battle. There were even some casualties—flying accidents, as several dog-fights had to be reenacted with both stunt-flyers and war veterans. The film's cameraman, the brilliant Freddie Young (*Lawrence of Arabia, Doctor Zhivago,* etc.) had invented a process called front-projection, which enables spectators to see dozens of planes on the screen chasing the main plane in the foreground and all of them in frame.

The call sheets we received were totally different from any normal movie. We actors got our press calls before we got our scene calls. Each day there were so many journalists from all over the world on the set waiting for interviews one could barely move. Harry Saltzman was a master marketeer and I've never been in a film that received such coverage—right up to the Royal Premiere in Leicester Square, when not one or two, but the entire Royal Family turned up to salute not just us actors, but the hordes of decorated airmen from Air Vice Marshalls, Air Chief Marshalls, all the way down the ranks. Everyone had squeezed themselves into their old uniforms weighed down by dozens of medals in order to sit back and watch a pretty authentic, well-researched and enormously ambitious reenactment of their very own glory days—the best days of their lives.

ONE OF LONDON'S most enticing restaurants, l'Etoile on Charlotte Street, with its mahogany and glass screens discreetly surrounding the main tables, was Elaine's and my favourite. Edward VII, when he was Prince of Wales, had entertained many a shady lady in the once private quarters above the dining room. The wine list was superb and more important, the wines themselves were impeccably cared for. One evening, soon after *The Battle of B* had wrapped, enjoying yet another delectable supper there, I was just coming out of the boys' room when I felt a stabbing pain in my right foot. Robert Shaw had stamped firmly on my shoe, pinioning me to the floor. "We're doing *The Royal Hunt* in Spain one month from now as a film," he announced between his teeth. "You're going to play Atahuallpa and I'm going to play your old part Pizarro! Say yes *now* and I'll take my foot off ya!" An original sort of job offer, I thought. But I was smarting with pain—I had no choice but to say Yes. "Right!" the Cornish rooster crowed. "You're free to go."

Not such a bad idea, I thought as I limped back to the table. I loved the Shaffer play and how exciting it would be to play the "other" role, the young Inca ruler, particularly on screen. Atahuallpa rarely speaks—his thoughts and expressions, which tell his story are much more suited to film, whereas my old part Pizarro never draws breath, much more suited to the stage. It also hit me that Atahuallpa glides about in nothing but the briefest of loincloths, so there was *no* getting out of it—I had to go into serious training pronto. I sought out Ed Bolton, a brilliant but somewhat deranged phys. ed. instructor who had trained Robert Stephens, the creator of my role, into a stunning physical specimen. He had also done the same for Larry Olivier's Othello. I use the word "deranged" because Mr. Bolton occasionally suffered from deep angry depressions and took to hurling huge weights and dumbbells about the room even when trainees were present; happily I never saw his violent side. Moody though he was, his training programme was unusually inventive and before long I was in the best shape of my life.

It was a small-budget film directed by Irving Lerner, a well-respected documentary filmmaker (the definitive film on Toscanini), and rather interestingly shot by a cameraman called Roger Barlow who had once apprenticed under the great Robert Flaherty. There was no script per se, so we used an edited version of the play with Shaffer's blessing—he never showed up and left us totally on our own. Robert Stephens, whom I had seen give an inspired performance of my role at the National Theatre, made little birdlike noises whenever he spoke or reacted, making of Atahuallpa a fantastical creature, utterly removed from this world. I decided to do the same only more so by learning some Quechuan, a dead forgotten language, which could sound very much like wild bird cries. It was almost impossible to learn, but what I did manage to apprehend I added to the English dialogue.

Anthony Powell, the costume and set designer (who later designed *Indiana Jones and the Temple of Doom, Dragon Slayer,* and *Travels with My Aunt,* etc., winning countless awards) sat in a little room at Madrid's

As Atahuallpa in the film of The Royal Hunt of the Sun

Sevilla Studios sewing hundreds of birds' feathers together to make Atahuallpa's cloak—probably one of the most beautiful costumes I've ever worn. I was nervously pacing up and down the corridor outside, memorizing my Quechuan dialogue out loud, which I was just about to put on camera. Each time I passed the little room, I could see Anthony calmly sewing away, every now and then shaking his head and raising an eyebrow. Obviously he could take my Quechuan ramblings no longer for he called out, "You're wasting your time, dear. You do realize what all that means in English?" "No," I answered, "what?" "The *cat sat* on the *mat!*"

I had now run the gamut of nicknames for Elaine Regina Jane Taylor from Regina Jane, Reggie, Lainey, Bobby, Fuffenstein to Fuff. Don't ask me what Fuff means—I suppose a Fuff is a small cuddly creature. Anyway, Fuff stuck. We settled down in a most attractive casa just outside Madrid with a clear view of the mountains. Naturally, I took her to every bullfight I could all over northern Spain—Aranjuez, Toledo, Sevilla, Escorial, etc. The smaller rings were the most exciting because of the intimacy and the danger. The barriers were so low one could easily step over them and in some towns there were no barriers at all—an angry bull could jump into the audience at will. This happened twice while we were present; once an irate bull jumped over and gave an innocent spectator a serious goring. Back in Madrid we saved every Sunday afternoon for the big ring where afterwards at a little boîte nearby we would devour delicious venison cooked in whiskey washed down with a full rich marques de Murrieta.

Fuff had become almost as much of a bullfight fan as I and together we sought out every matador we could. There were the usual suspects—the clumsy El Caracol, the great Miguelin, the ever reliable and popular Paco Camino, and the promising nineteen-year-old Linares who insisted on fighting barefoot—so dangerous on a windy day. At Escorial we watched the great star El Cordobés, whose smile lit up the arena, turn down toro after toro for being too frisky, heavy or bad-tempered, finally picking a rather small docile bull, weighing in at five hundred pounds as opposed to seven hundred. The great man was getting lazy. The audience loved to boo him and he had made millions because of it. That day he was followed by the old master El Viti. What a difference! Perfection! The old classic style—standing so close to the bull we were not aware of any technique—just a lovely liquid rhythm, a ballet—giving back to the corrida all the artistry there is in it.

One breezy Madrid afternoon, a young novilleros in his teens had been given the chance of his lifetime. What he didn't have in technique he made up for in reckless courage. From the start, the crowd was aware that the boy was dealing with one oversized angry beast who had a nasty habit of hooking with his left horn very much like the famous bull who once took the life of the immortal Manolete. Nonetheless, the boy insisted on working so perilously close to the bull, our hearts were in our mouths. The crowd fell in love—they went wild. His last set of veronicas was staggering and he sauntered proudly away, his back to the snorting bull, dragging his red cape behind him through the sand. The crowd rose to its feet. I looked away for a second to see how Fuff was reacting to all this, but when I looked back, the boy had turned into nothing but a piece of paper, tossed about, flying through the air as if blown by the wind. Not a sound was heard in the arena. When he landed one could see that the whole area around his belly and groin was drenched in blood—his splendid new suit of lights covered in a deep scarlet.

He staggered around for a while, not quite knowing what to do. The horroniadors rushed out to distract the bull but the lad would have none of it—he fought them off and ran towards the beast. In his moment of pride and glory he hadn't noticed his state nor his pain. He drew his sword from the cape and fell backward on the sand. As they carried him off in silence, no one dared move, but the bull was still standing and had to be dealt with. There was one person near the barriers who had been watching the tragedy. It was Paco Camino, dressed in an ordinary business suit. He leapt into the ring, grabbed a sword and with one clean strike dispatched the bull and ran off to attend to the boy. I had never seen those cynical old Madrid afficionados quite so shaken. To this day I do not know if the lad lived, but I have strong doubts.

Most days off, Fuff and I spent largely at the Prada. Of course, there was never enough time to take it all in. We would follow this by lunching at Horchers, the Jockey Club or 21. Then we would sneak off to Philip the Second's great monastery fortress, Escorial, outside the city, its endless galleries filled with Tintorettos, Titians, Canalettos and da Vincis. There was always something brooding and sad about that immense palace and one could easily conjure up an image of the solitary Philip, supported by his cane, moving slowly through the long corridors, torn between his pious devotions and the daunting task of running the world.

The Royal Hunt as a movie didn't quite come off as it should. It was neither a play nor a film. There also was not enough in the kitty to photograph the whole story in the real Andes, but there were the occasional moments of suspenseful beauty (the snow scenes, particularly) and a general atmosphere that suggested something out of the ordinary due in large part to the Shaffer dialogue, what was left of it. However, for me it was an absolute boon because Atahuallpa took me out of myself, made me dare, forced me to invent and welcomed me into the world of character-acting.

To help with their social and professional life, Robert S. and Mary had hired a young Australian called John Kirby to help them out. As fate would have it, the Shaws no longer required him when the film was over and before I could say anything, Robert stomped straight into "mi casa" without knocking and announced with his usual brusqueness, "You're getting Kirby!—Good boy—damn efficient—poofy as they come, but harmless. Take care of him—you'll be grateful." Our lives decided for us, I obediently hired John. He was both popular and charming. He spoke Spanish, Portuguese, Italian, French and, having lived in South Africa, Swahili, which of course Fuff and I were desperately in need of. He was witty, single and enthusiastically gay. Every time the Spaniards teased him, "Ah bonito! Como esta, hombre?" quick as a flash, he would lisp back, "Gracias por lo hombre!"

For a holiday, we went straight to Majorca from Madrid. That lovely island has to this day remained relatively unspoiled, unlike so many others, and is very beautiful, the colour of the water a rich turquoise. We took Kirby with us and he proved invaluable, negotiating in Spanish with the owners of a luscious villa outside Formentor that I was angling to buy. It was snugly hidden away from everything and had its own inlet, which led to the sea beyond. I must have been mad to think my meagre fortune was a bottomless pit, and Fuff immediately put her foot down and saved my bacon. We stayed a month in the Formentor Hotel and explored the island. Kirby went everywhere with us, we'd become extremely fond of him. He took a load off our plates and became our trusted man Friday all over Europe. But down the road, all too soon, and quite unintentionally, I was to make a fatal boo-boo, causing the sensitive Aussie much anxiety and unhappiness. The severest way to test a friendship is to invite that friend to join you in Brezhnev's forbidding Russia of the seventies; and then set him down in a grisly little town near the western Ukrainian border called Uzgorod, the City of Snakes, which sits on a stinking bog, brown with sewage—a miniature hell on earth.

CHAPTER THIRTY-TWO

THE TWO GLOBES

Once upon a time, many centuries past, there was a playhouse. It was round—round as the world was round. Of all the jewels in the Crown, it was the most precious, the most vibrant, the most alive. A very great poet called it his "cockpit" where "once sat expectation in the air." It wasn't his alone, for his fellow writers who shared it with him were formidable indeed. He was in glorious company and so it followed that from that little playhouse came some of the noblest language ever conceived by man. It shone like gold in a Golden Age and then, one day, it turned to ashes. It was just a memory—time had swept it away.

ONE RAINY LONDON DAY, there was a loud knocking at the door of no. 15 Donne Place. "Who's there in the name of Beelzebub?" I yelled, as the Porter in *Macbeth*. The guilty party responsible for this blustering racket was none other than blustering George Murcell. Though as English as Falstaff in his bawdy good humour, his Italian blood gave him that extra passion which most Englishmen, when they have it, try to hide. Not our George! "Sit down, Tig," he commanded. Elaine's nickname for me had obviously stuck. In fact, we four, George, his wife Elvie, Elaine and I had become respectively Pooh, Piglet, Roo and Tigger. "I've got some sensational news!" He was breathless with excitement. "That old church in Islington—St. George's, you know the one—that circular edifice as round as an amphitheatre—the one they copied from an ancient house of worship in Salonica? Well, they are about to tear it down, the bastards, demolish it, but I'm going to save it and you're going to stop pretending you're some big movie star and you're going to help me. We'll turn it into an Elizabethan theatre, the shape is dead perfect, just like a globe, and we'll form a company of players. Don't forget, Islington is Burbage/Shakespeare country and St. George's is only a stone's throw from where they worked together, where it all began. Then when we've done that, we're going to resurrect the real old Globe Theatre on the South Bank as well as the Anchor Pub *and* The Swan—and you're going to be my partner. Come on, Tig, get off your bum. Let's go!"

When George 'Pooh' Murcell got hold of an idea, he was as tenacious as a terrier who won't let go of his bone. He was demonic, charismatic. Before I had time to think, I heard myself saying "Yes!" Well, the upshot was that he *did* save the fascinating old structure from demolition. To form an arsenal, we managed to persuade such actors as Peter Sellers, Paul Scofield, Dorothy Tutin, Vanessa Redgrave, Richard Johnson, and others to come on board. Also Sir Roy Strong, the new wunderkind custodian of the Tate Gallery. With names like these, the press got behind it and had a field day, and George, bless his chutzpah, had also commandeered Sir John Betjeman, poet laureate and head of the Historical Society of London, to come to our aid. He even button-holed

Plans for interior of St. Georges, Islington

the Bishop of Southwark. How George, with hardly a penny to his name and less collateral, was able to bend the ear and hold the attention of these men of influence is quite simple. His vision never once wavered. His enthusiasm and charm never flagged. His manner was totally persuasive, convincing. He told a wonderful story and believed every last word of it.

Now that one dream had been realized—the small dream—the large one was next, looming over us in all its magnitude—the total restoration of the Globe Theatre itself and with it London's South waterfront. So Pooh, Piglet, Roo and Tig took a trip to County Monaghan in Ireland to pay a visit to Christopher Robin in the person of the great man himself, Sir Tyrone Guthrie, and his wife Judy. Our mission—to beg him to be our Chairman of the Board. They gave us lunch in their massive old house on a huge overgrown estate called Ana-ma-Kerrig, which rambled down to the water—high ceilings from which hung wildly theatrical chandeliers and long refectory tables strewn with a bizarre collection of bric-a-brac, mostly props from bygone productions. The rooms reminded one of Miss Haversham's living quarters without the cobwebs, perhaps, but certainly a plentiful amount of age-old dust caught in the shafts of light filtering through the tall windows. Tony Guthrie very kindly agreed to our proposal and we went away as happy as clams, knowing that we could now boast as our figurehead such a precious catch. With his name attached, everything began to slowly fall into place. Our new Board consisted of the same actors mentioned as well as Sir Roy Strong and Sir John Betjeman. Even Jennie Lee, the Minister of Culture, promised her help. Gradually more influential figures, seduced by the venture, began to join forces. We now had the full blessing of the Bishop of Southwark and, thank our lucky stars, our architect was in place. One of the McAlpines agreed to join the Board—the McAlpine family owned just about the largest building/contracting firm in the UK and "Pooh" was heavily occupied in persuading him to take on the construction job for a song and for the honour of "jolly ol'" and all that. The green light was on.

It was then that people started dying off—Tyrone Guthrie was the first to go. The great bird of prey. The last spirit of sweeping panoply, the High Priest of Drama died of heart failure, leaving a gaping empty hole the size of a crater in theatre all over the world. Donald Wolfit, the famed touring Shakespearean scenery chewer, conqueror of the Provinces, knighted at last, to his great relief, stepped into Tony's shoes as Board Chair. Meanwhile, Pooh, who was immersed in nightmarish meetings with the GLC (Greater London Council) nevertheless seemed to be making headway. One of the most powerful men in England, solicitor in general to the prime minister and the government and who sat on all the major corporate boards in the country, Lord Goodman, agreed to be our chief advisor. Things were really looking pretty good, when suddenly Wolfit up and died—the position of chairman had begun to look fairly ominous.

Nonetheless, our august little Board could boast a good number of heavy hitters. The next step in raising funds was to get ourselves a patron—preferably a Royal one. Pooh spoke up: "That frustrated young actor, Charlie, is crackers about the theatre. Let's go after him." So Lord Goodman and Sir David Lewellyn put pen to paper and were just about to send off a formal request to Prince Charles when the news broke—the news about the *other* project. It appears there were two Globe Theatre projects—*ours* and Sam Wanamaker's. Without our knowing a thing about it, except for the odd rumour perhaps, Sam had been going about his business all along, steadily, painstakingly. While we were getting all sorts of media attention, he had been quietly soldiering on, unheeding, with one vision on his mind.

Sam Wanamaker was an American who years ago had left the United States, then very much under the cloud of McCarthyism—in other words, the witch-hunt. An exciting young actor, writer and director, he had been suspected of leftist leanings, so to save his name and reputa-

My gregarious good friend, George, or "Pooh"

tion and disillusioned by his country, he emigrated to England where he soon became recognized and highly respected. Sam, like Pooh, was a dreamer—a dreamer from afar albeit, but unfortunately a dreamer with the same dream. Now, suddenly, he was headline news. He had raised a considerable amount of money, much from America, he had his architect and Prince Philip had agreed to be his patron! What the hell were we going to do? We had been gazzumped!

Sam called Pooh and arranged a meeting—I came along. Pooh was devastated—so was I. "That bastard—I'll sue him. He's stolen our idea. We were there first! He just wants our board." Trying to placate Pooh was like trying to calm an enraged rhinoceros. "Anyone can have an idea," I said, "and besides, I suspect he was there first." At any rate, we all met. Sam was apologetic, charming and generous. Pooh circled him like a wild beast, sniffing at him at intervals. "There's only one thing we can do," Sam offered. "Let's join forces. We could really make this work if your team hooked up with mine." But Pooh wasn't having any of it. "And you'll be head man?" he demanded of Sam. The answer was yes. "No way," said Pooh and left. I hurried after him. "It's not a bad idea, you know." "It's a lousy idea and I'm finished with the whole thing," muttered Pooh as we walked to his car. "But you don't own the rights to the Globe. Nobody does—it's anybody's. Four hundred years old kind of makes it public domain. Come on, let's all get together with both our strengths and we'll see it happen." But stubborn old Pooh had had it. He would never admit defeat. I felt so sad for him—he'd worked so hard—he'd slept, dreamed, lived and suffered for the scheme. He was out of pocket because of it, but he didn't care because he was that kind of man, a man imbued with that Elizabethan energy that sparked his heart and his mind and his ambitions. Sam had seen it in him, because Sam was the same and he understood loners—he was one himself.

Well, try as I might, I could not get Pooh into Sam's camp. It was nonsense of him, of course, but he felt betrayed, his whole project shattered like broken glass. Also, our board was dispersing, some already joining the so-called opposition. Pooh threw himself with all guns blazing into the St. George's Islington venture, forming an acting company and tirelessly raising funds to transform the old church into a proper theatre. He had done a glorious thing rescuing it from certain ruin—he should have been happy, proud, content; but Pooh had history on his mind. He had seen the one restoration as a necessary stepping stone to the other, a neat compact package in which North and South London together could once more resurrect their shining past; that Glorianna would in our century again fly its splendid flag over the rooftops and gables. We saw quite a bit of him and Piglet over the next few years. His bubbling, gregarious nature never deserted him, but I think the whole Globe experience had a profound effect upon him that not only altered his life, but shortened it. He could never find anything to match that dream.

The newly restored Globe Theatre has been with us now for many years. We almost take it for granted. How easy it is in our complacency to forget the long hard struggle that finally brought it about, how one man continued on single-handedly, circling the planet to raise the necessary funds. How ironic that most of it was to come from the very country he had turned his back on so many years ago. Sam never once stopped, not for a moment. At last his jewel, our jewel, was being mounted and it was almost complete when, suddenly, he died—never to look his triumph in the face. He would have been so proud to see it now, so proud of young Marc Ryland, its first leader, who took charge with the same dynamic energy that burned in him—who had the taste, the intellect and the talent to make it work and to keep it pure, simple and true.

Sam had asked me to come onto the Board in both Canada and the

United States and I was honoured to do so, but after his death I noticed how many people began taking credit for its resurrection—magnifying their contributions out of all proportion, mostly for reasons of social prestige. So whenever I was asked to speak, I reminded all those present just who was truly responsible. That it was Sam's vision, Sam's playhouse—he had given his life to it. That the playhouse he dreamed of was never meant to be a mausoleum, dry and arid, a pretentious monument to Kultur with a capital K. What Sam wanted was what Pooh had wanted, the wooden O with a capital O—the little "wooden O" that Shakespeare, Burbage and Will Kemp knew, an honest-to-God hardworking space where a young, vital resident company of players would keep the place alive. He also saw it as a center for a romantic education—an inspiration to students the world over of all ages and creeds. A tall order, perhaps, but then Sam was a tall man. It sometimes takes the New Hemisphere to revive the Old, and by Jove he was living proof of it! In one short lifetime he managed to link the centuries together with his outrageous persistence. He has given us back one of the wonders of the world.

Sam, the man who shared the dream and saw it through

But he was not always alone—from the beginning there had been two of them, Pooh and Sam. Pooh came so close; Sam was blessed. How could two such crusaders of equal fervour ever have known that the Jewel on the Thames would claim both their lives?

CHAPTER THIRTY-THREE

THE BATTLE OF "BATTY-POO"

I think that being "made up" in a spacious, private makeup room in Rome's Cinecittà Studios is not the worst thing that can happen to you. In most film studios around the world, being made up in the early hours of the morning is an ordeal, a necessary evil that we learn to grin and bear. In Italy, it is a way of life. Like everything else they do, the Italians do it with great professional charm and style. All is immaculately laid out, the grease-sticks, powder, powder puffs, little espresso and cappuccino machines, the jars of biscotti and chocolates—it is no longer a makeup room, it's a café.

This particular morning, I was being transformed into looking as much like the Duke of Wellington as was possible. The man in charge was no less than that mega-star of maquillage Alberto di Rossi himself—the favourite of Sophia Loren, Elizabeth Taylor, Audrey Hepburn and Sylvano Mangano, an artist to his fingertips. A handsome man in his early sixties, permanently tanned with wavy white hair, Alberto's scathing wit was a mixture of rapier and high camp, typical of the sophisticated Roman. "What about Wellington's famous beaked nose?" I asked him as he was finishing the final touch-ups. "You don' need eet," he rejoined disdainfully. "Yours ees beeg enough as eet ees!"

The year was 1969. The film was, of course, *Waterloo,* an epic to end all epics. I mean that literally, for the next one of comparable size wasn't made till over thirty years later and that one, *Gladiator,* though spectacular, was considerably helped digitally. In *Waterloo,* I was about to play the Iron Duke to Rod Steiger's Napoleon and at this moment di

Rossi and I were waiting for the film's celebrated Russian director, Sergei Bondarchuk, to inspect the look we'd achieved. He was a long time coming—an early indication that nothing in the Russia of Leonid Brezhnev was ever hurried. Eventually, he marched in surrounded by a phalanx of Soviets who could have been colonels in charge of Intourist or KGB. A huge bear of a man with a chin that jutted pugnaciously forward, Bondarchuk nodded perfunctorily in my direction, grunted something unintelligible and proceeded to intensely scrutinize me from every angle, so close to my face I could smell his heavy pungent breath. While he circled me thus, the KGB (or whatever they were) stood at attention. Finally, he came to a standstill. I was grateful for that; I was becoming quite dizzy. He pointed to my mouth and shouted something in Russian—he spoke no English. The interpreter in the group stepped forward and addressed di Rossi, "Comrade Bondarchuk says the mouth is too normal." "Ees not supposed to be?" asked di Rossi. "Nyet! There was something wrong with Balleengton's mouth." I looked at Alberto, mystified—he gave an enormous shrug. A steady stream of Russian ensued which was eventually translated as, "Comrade Bondarchuk insists there was something abnormal about the lips—the upper lip in particular." With a wicked gleam in his eye, di Rossi asked, "Eet vas stiff? Ees dat vat you mean?" After much consultation they all nodded in unison, "Da! Da! Da! Da!" Alberto and I looked at each other open-mouthed. Bondarchuk had taken literally the famous expression describing Englishmen and their "stiff upper lips" and had narrowed it down to poor Wellington as the single offender. When di Rossi gently explained that it was a mere colloquialism and only meant to be taken in the spirit of mockery, Bondarchuk, still unconvinced, turned on his heel and without a word or a smile, marched from the room, his little army close behind him.

WATERLOO IN RUSSIAN is spelled BATTY-POO, hence our nickname for it, "Batty-Poo." A mammoth tripartite coproduction (Charlie Bluthorn's Gulf + Western in New York, Dino De Laurentiis's production company in Rome, and Mosfilm in Moscow), Batty-Poo had begun shooting in Italy where the locations and the sets were stupendous! The Royal Palace at Casserta became the residence of Louis XVIII (played by Orson Welles) and the vast ballroom set on the Cinecittà lot was where the Duchess of Richmond's famous ball on the eve of battle with Wellington as guest of honour would take place. Due to some slight

contretemps over my contract between CMA and Dino, I was instructed
by the agency not to report to work until it had been settled. Filming
was postponed at once. Even though Elaine and I were sharing the
Royal Suite at the Excelsior in the lap of luxury, it was still an unpleasant position to be in, an embarrassment. At last the dispute was settled
and I reported to work. Though it had been no fault of mine, I apologized profusely to everyone—the actors, Sergei Bondarchuk himself
and one of the most gracious of all Italian cameramen, that supremely
sensitive artist Armando Nannuzzi. At last the myriad chandeliers and
candelabra were lit, Viennese waltzes erupted in a rich confusion of
sound, the cameras were placed on carpets and pulled in a circle around
the room in the opposite direction to the dancers and the famous ball
exploded onto the screen.

This was the last scene to be shot in Rome and now, in stark contrast,
with the emphasis on *stark,* the film suddenly became a totally Russian
venture and we were on our way to Ukraine's rough terrain and the
siege of Waterloo itself. John Kirby had arrived from Madrid to be my
minder, helper and morale builder. Elaine was filming in London and
would join me later. Kirby and I flew to Budapest where we took the
Trans-Siberian Railway to the local military border town of Chop.
Kirby, so articulate in many languages, spoke no Russian! "You're supposed to bolster my confidence," I teased him. "What the hell use are
you to me, you linguistic dunce?" Kirby, who could be wickedly funny,
was basically a gentle soul, and at this moment in no mood for a retort.
As we boarded the filthy run-down wreck of a railway carriage, the foreboding darkness descended. He grabbed my arm. "I don't think I'm
going to last," he said, his voice trembling. Though I remained silent, I
didn't think I would either.

The so-called private first-class compartment my contract stipulated
was a damp, smelly cabin with only two makeshift wooden benches at
either end. These were already occupied by several inebriated Russian
soldiers, all asleep in the fetal position. Their boots, which they had
removed, were lined up in a row on the floor. The stench was unbearable. There was barely room for Kirby or me. There were no conductors
or brakemen in sight. The air was stifling so I tried to open a window.
It was locked—they were all locked. So too were the doors. The "loo"
at the end of the car was a mere opening in the wall—no door—no toilet—no basin—just a hole in the middle of the floor. If you had to crap
you'd be standing or squatting in full view.

Kirby and I, back in our seats, huddled together by the window

Trying to look like the young Iron Duke

straining to see through the filthy glass as the countryside jolted by. Every time the train stopped, which was constant, the Soviet police boarded, questioned us and demanded to see our papers. An eternity would pass before our journey was allowed to resume. Five or six hours later we were still chugging along without a clue as to where we were or when to get off. "We probably passed it long ago," whimpered Kirby. I thought he was going to cry. One of the soldiers had woken up and was staring at us as if we were overdressed Martians. I tried a little French—nothing. Then English—"When do we get to Chop?!" I shouted; still that vacant stare. Kirby and I began wildly pantomiming anything that might resemble the word "Chop," hitting our left wrists with the side of our right hands or madly wielding imaginary axes into invisible tree trunks. By now all the soldiers were wide awake, convinced, I am sure, that not only were we overdressed Martians, but *insane* overdressed Martians.

By some miracle we reached Chop. We had traveled across the entire Soviet-dominated Hungary and were now in Ukraine. It took forever to get through immigration. Poor Jack Hawkins, who played General Picton, one of Wellington's staff, had made the mistake of bringing *Playboy, Penthouse* and all the racy London sex mags with him, and was forced to wait almost an entire day while the border guards (who had never seen anything like it in their lives) studiously perused them from cover to cover. Once through, we were driven to our "headquarters" in the aforementioned town of Uzhgorod. Our hotel, the colour of Bolshevik grey, made Motel 6 look like the Winter Palace. As one entered the restaurant, the smell of urine was overpowering. Starving, we sat down, only to be told that everything was off—no meat, no eggs—only chicken, some meager tomatoes and tired cucumbers. Most of the English actors were holed up in minute cubicles, but Napoleon in the person of Rod Steiger, who had departed the day before, very generously had left me his "suite," the only one in the hotel. I use the word "suite" loosely as it consisted of two tiny rooms, one to sleep in and one to breathe in.

At the end of each floor at a desk with a clear view of the stairs sat a kind of concierge (a combination policewoman/gauleiter) checking on everyone who came and went. These huge ladies, akin to women wrestlers, had hairy armpits and hairy legs, long and full. The scent of good old BO permeated each corridor. One could imagine that a discreet assignation in one's room would result in nothing less than a death sentence. Rod, not so generously and quite diabolically, had left me a collection of pornography so brazenly graphic that if discovered I could be arrested on sight. I was about to light a match to the whole lot of them but reversed my decision. "Better have a quick look at them first, to be fair," I said to myself. I locked myself in, sat down to enjoy a detailed perusal, when suddenly there was a loud knocking at the door. "My God," I thought, "I've been caught." I quickly hid everything under the mattress and ran to the door. I opened it a crack—it was someone from Mosfilm. "Velcome to film Vaterloo." Comrade Bondarchuk sends you dis." He was holding a large tin of fresh Malossol caviar. Good ol' "Bondars," I thought, he's forgotten the stiff upper lip incident—bless him, he's come around. "Please tell Comrade Bondarchuk how kind of him to think of me. Thank him very much." I reached out to take the caviar, but he held on tight. "Dat vil be 250 American dollars, please!"

Impossible as it was from "Snake City" to reach anyone (telephone service simply didn't exist) I managed through the film office to wire Elaine in London not to come by train, whatever she did! I would arrange a car and driver to take her from Budapest to Chop as it would be far more comfortable. Mosfilm had decided to fly out the Irish actor Donal Donnelly at the same time so they could share the ride. It was estimated the journey would take no more than six or seven hours. Boy, were they wrong. All night I waited up—no Elaine. All next day—still no Elaine. I asked anyone in sight, through interpreters, if they could find out what was happening—no response. On the third day I became frantic. I made an ultimatum with the company that I would not shoot a single foot of film until she was found. They instructed Intourist to instigate a search at once. I became more frustrated and angry by the moment. Even dear Kirby couldn't cheer me up.

On the fourth day they found her. "Well, where the hell is she then?" I yelled. "She's on the other side of the bridge about a hundred yards from here. She and the Irishman were not permitted to cross over—no papers!" I threw another tantrum. Finally, Mosfilm gave them their papers; they crossed the bridge and I was with my lady at last!

It appears they had been detained at every village border crossing and whistle-stop, sometimes at gunpoint. If it hadn't been for the heroic Hungarian driver, they might all have ended up in some festering prison. Though he possessed the true Magyar hatred for the Russians, he spoke their language fluently and somehow persuaded them he was an employee of Mosfilm and was transporting actors to the Ukraine. One night they stayed at a farmhouse, the owners of which the driver had known. The next morning, they would start off again only to be stopped every few miles by more overly aggressive police. By this time, Donnelly had killed the two bottles of Jameson's he had brought from Dublin and began talking to himself. "Mother o' God—I shall never set foot on Irish soil, I shall never again see the Liffey or me darlin' wife and children!" "But you haven't got a wife *or* children," Elaine offered. "You may be right," he admitted. "I'd forgotten." Clearly he was not going to improve. At each stop the guards would roughly hurl the luggage about, search them and then take something for themselves. (Elaine's luggage was getting as light as a feather—there was hardly anything left in it.) By the time they reached the bridge, Elaine had her revenge. The officer threw open her suitcase and began rummaging in it and in the process broke a bottle of her Badedas cream. His hands and his uniform were so covered in oozing, dripping green slime he resembled some distant relative of Dracula just down from the Borgo Pass.

IT WAS SEVERAL MILES by van to the undulating countryside of Ukraine where filming was taking place. With nothing to do back in depressing Uzhgorod, my valiant lady along with faithful old Kirby would accompany me each morning, shaken and jostled over indescribably bumpy ground (trying hard not to be seasick) till, with great relief, I was able to mount my horse, which even at seventeen hands high and nervous as a kitten was infinitely more comfortable than either the van or my hotel bed.

I have to say the panorama which greeted us was impressive indeed. With great care and accuracy, our Russian set decorator had transformed the surrounding fields into an absolute replica of the famous Belgian battleground, at the same time re-creating to perfection La Belle Alliance—a scenic triumph. Mosfilm had employed the Russian cavalry (which I couldn't believe still existed) to represent both the English Tommys and the French cuirassiers. There were literally thousands of men and just as many horses. Each young soldier was paid $1 a day to be in the film (more than they had ever seen) and were made to sleep in their costumes with their horses on the hills at night so that they would be ready for the next morning's shooting. It was calculated that our film army was about one-third the size of the actual battle itself.

This little "army" was supervised by three five-star Russian generals, veterans of many a campaign, one of whom had served in the Crimean War. These dignified figures in their khaki uniforms buttoned to the neck (a fashion which hadn't changed since World War I) were military historians well versed on strategic maneuvers and formations, especially those at Waterloo. The generals, along with an ex-army major Chemedurov, Bondarchuk's assistant director and stager of all battle scenes, made up the production's technical advisors. There was one other who, incongruous though he must have appeared in that Soviet gallére, wearing kilts and sporting a monocle, was the ultimate authority on the English side—a man of great style and dash—one Colonel Willoughby Grey. "Willow," as we called him, whose great-great-grandfather had fought at Waterloo with the famous Scots Greys and knew the duke personally, could tell you most every moment of Wellington's daily routine—even what times he went to the bathroom.

The first morning I arrived on the set I was informed that the head stuntman, an Italian, had been thrown by his horse and had broken his back—not encouraging news! I watched in horror as the rest of the stunt riders vainly tried to calm their rearing nags, understandably terrified by the constant explosions, some of which reached to a height of fifty or sixty feet. If these crackerjack horsemen were having trouble, what the hell was I going to do? Every day the special effects department set off these explosives before each shot from a distance of two or three miles. The cameras would roll and we would have to wait after the word "Action"—sometimes four or five minutes until the horizon was blackened with clouds of the filthy stuff—before beginning to play a scene.

We were all terribly concerned about poor Jack Hawkins who recently had undergone a cancer operation where they performed a tracheotomy. Here he was sitting on his horse, sword at his side, wearing a top hat, carrying an umbrella, as was Picton's habit, while stuffing a protective handkerchief into the hole in his neck. Characteristically, he never once complained—but I did. I also complained about my quadruped, who was much too skittish and had knocked Kirby over several times. With nothing for him to do, I had given Kirby the privilege of holding my horse's reins when we stood still—a lackey's job. Fortunately, my contract called for nag approval, and as luck would have it they found me a wonderfully docile old police horse from Moscow with the stolid reliable name of "Stok." Stok was superb! While the rest of my army were being tossed about all over the place, I, as Wellington, sat absolutely "stok" still in the saddle, cool as a cucumber. I couldn't believe my luck until his groom whispered in my ear that dear ol' Stok, who was about thirty, had been in so many gun-battles in Moscow, his ears had been damaged and he was as deaf as a post.

The Russian special effects man in charge of all explosives had already worked six years on Bondarchuk's massive *War and Peace*. It had taken so long to film that some of the older members of the cast had died and had to be replaced. This meant they had to begin shooting all over again. No wonder he walked about in a punch-drunk daze. One day we shot a scene where the English were to ride much too close to a French contingent who would take shots at us as we passed. I noticed our man had planted red flags to indicate where the explosions were to take place at intervals over a radius of some three or four hundred yards. "When do they go off?" I asked through my interpreter, an old lady called Melita. "After your horse has crossed each of them," I was told. "You're sure?" I tremulously asked. There were lots of "Da Da's" and "Horrochos" and much effusive nodding of heads, so I felt temporarily reassured. Then someone yelled something that loosely resembled "Action" and off we went straight out of the frying pan into the you-know-what! Our crazed special effects friend with his strange sense of timing had set off each burst directly under my horse's belly. Dear deaf old Stok, whose highest speed in ten years was probably no more than a

Stok, my docile friend

trot, suddenly took off. My fiery-footed steed at full gallop had only one thing on his mind—the Grand National. There was no way to rein him in—he didn't want to know. He had taken the lead and my little army were right behind barrelling after us. I gave up the reins and held onto his mane for dear life. We must have covered three miles at least through the smoke before old Stok decided to slow down. When we finally came to a halt and the smoke had cleared, I looked about. There was no sign of a film unit anywhere in sight—just endless rolling fields. Terence Alexander who played Lord Uxbridge, trying to calm his sputtering beast, called out, "We must be in fucking Transylvania by now!" When we finally did get back to the set, after much snorting and puffing from our exhausted four-legged friends, all we could see were a lot of empty chairs and old Melita and Kirby standing in a cloud of dust. The rest of the bastards had broken for lunch.

LUNCH WAS THE ONE COMFORT we managed to look forward to. Dino had seen to that. Fresh pasta and vino were flown in from Rome every other day. The Russian crew and actors couldn't wait to demolish it as soon as it arrived. Poor things, they had never tasted anything like that in their lives; not only were they profoundly grateful, they were the happiest crew from the Urals to the Volga.

The other comfort awaited us at the end of each day when the sun went down. Because the food at the dreaded inn was inedible and the dining room so disgusting, the main English contingent would repair to our suite where Elaine cooked us all dinner. This became a nightly routine. With next to no equipment and very makeshift utensils, she managed superbly on the smallest two-ring burner imaginable. When not on the battlefield with me, she would set her alarm for 5:00 a.m., go into town and take her place in the long queues of Russian peasant women waiting to fight over the last bit of meat or what was left of very anaemic-looking chicken. There were never any vegetables. Rich farm country though it was outside Uzhgorod, by law everything fresh had to be shipped straight to Moscow. The unfortunate local farmers who had worked so hard on their crops were left only mere scraps to live on. As there was sometimes no meat or chicken for weeks on end, Elaine would make us curried eggs, having successfully smuggled in some curry powder—how I'll never know. She became known as St. Joan of the Bunsen Burner. Our dinner regulars included Jack Hawkins (Picton), Michael Wilding (Ponsonby), plus Rupert Davies, Geoffrey Wickham, Ian Ogilvy (William De Lancey), Terence Alexander (Uxbridge), Donal Donnelly (captain of the Inniskillins), John Kirby, of course, and Willoughby "Willow" Grey, still resplendent in kilts and monocle. Most of them had turned into lonely bachelors whose wives or loved ones had refused to accompany them. Lucky me! It seemed I had the only girl in the world.

One day Willow, Elaine and I went to see some assembled footage that the thoughtful American editor had put together. It all looked pretty impressive. Nannuzzi, who had been Visconti's favourite cameraman, was photographing it brilliantly. The look was stupendous—like a series of Old Masters. But the battle scenes and the acting in general had a chaotic hysteria about them, and quite understandably. Rod Steiger, with no help coming from Bondarchuk, had decided to make Bonaparte's well-known suffering from piles the main thrust of his character. It seemed it was piles that had motivated both his irascibility and his decline. Rod was a marvellous actor, but he could sometimes go too far and needed a strong director to rein him in. Because the script was so sparse, he would improvise constantly in front of the camera and as Bondarchuk never called "cut," the cameras would roll on long after the scene was over. So suddenly, there was the Emperor Napoleon barking away in his treble tenor, "Where are my maps? And where's the table?! How do you expect me to play the scene without my fucking table?!!"

There were a couple of shots of us English on the hill and although we all looked fairly authentic, our dialogue was commonplace, unin-spired and stilted. There was not the slightest suggestion that Welling-ton had his own special way of phrasing things, a uniquely oblique way of framing a command or a bon mot. There was also no indication of his depth as a man. I wanted him to be seen as he was—the austere patri-cian who kept his feelings in check, and the deeply emotional and humane creature who spent hours in his tent at night weeping over his losses on the field. I had tried to get them to suggest some of this on film, but it was useless, of course. After all, the driving force of an epic is spectacle and action, and very little else, I'm afraid. "Help me, Wil-low," I said. "You know practically every recorded statement the Duke ever made. Let's put them in the script, even if they are out of context. The writers have all gone; let's give him back some of his wit and style." Willow enthusiastically agreed and, to our amazement, "Bon-dars" accepted all the insertions we had proposed with a good grace—I don't think he'd ever had much time for the original script anyway. But we reached a serious misunderstanding when it came to filming the well-known exchange between the wounded Uxbridge and the Duke on horseback:

UXBRIDGE: *By Gad sir, I've lost my leg.*
WELLINGTON: [looking down] *By Gad sir, so you have.*
[They ride on.]

The bravado of that understated conversation was so utterly British it understandably escaped the utterly Russian Mister Bondarchuk. Appalled at what he took to be bare-faced callousness, he called out in exasperation, "Nyet! Nyet! Nyet!" and proceeded to mime what he thought we must do: I would dismount, examine the leg, look into Uxbridge's eyes with deep compassion, cradle him in my arms, lift him up ever so gingerly and, with head bowed carrying him thus, march slowly through the ranks. Filmically, it could certainly be visually telling but totally out of character and painfully melodramatic. And what time would there be in the heat of battle for such a charade? Terry, Willow and I spent the entire morning explaining that for the upper-crust Englishman to show emotion or sentiment at such a moment was simply not done and in order to rise above the situation, he must make light of it. Well, we won in the end, but I'm sure from the expression on Bondars's face he had thoroughly washed his hands of the entire Anglo-Saxon race.

THE RUSSIAN *War and Peace* as directed by Sergei Bondarchuk, though endlessly long like the book, was in my humble opinion a masterpiece. No other film version had come close to capturing the immense canvas of Tolstoy's narrative. Sergei's own very human performance of Pierre was itself worth the price of admission. Then again, the profound sensitivity Sergei had shown in his brilliantly poignant *Ballad of a Soldier* stays in the mind forever. But in *Waterloo,* he seemed distracted; there were too many languages involved—the script was in English, to him a foreign tongue—and there were so many cooks to spoil the broth that he began to mistrust anyone not in his camp. So it followed that an altercation took place which shook the very ranks and somehow cleared the air.

Willow had spent days organizing the famous "five squares" placing the army in the exact formations which Wellington, in one of his most strategic maneuvers, had executed: his men, bayonets drawn, facing outward in a line towards the enemy, in four different directions with a large space in the middle. There were five such squares on the battlefield. When Willow with Chemedurov's assistance had accomplished this, the men assembled thus on the hills made a startling sight with their red uniforms and their silver bayonets shining in the sun. All was ready when Bondarchuk suddenly went into a snit and refused to shoot it. "It may be authentic, but it's not cinema," he screamed through an interpreter. I remember Willow patiently explaining that it would indeed be cinematic if the aerial shots they had planned were put to good use. Bondars, however, his supreme authority threatened by someone who had actually done his homework, dug in his heels and refused to continue unless everything was changed. "But this is correct," Willow persisted. "This is how it happened. I can't change it. I won't change it." Bondars glowered, slumped in his chair looking like an oversized baby bear. There was an awful silence until finally, with the utmost calm, Willow spoke up, "There is really no point in my being here at all if you won't listen to anything I say!" With that, he walked off the set. The reflection of the sun bouncing off his monocle and his kilts blowing in the wind, he presented quite a figure as he marched with great military dignity past the camera crew, past the stuntmen on their horses, past the entire cavalry waiting silently, past all the foot soldiers, and in a gallant gesture of respect and support the three five-star Russian generals, having taken his side, fell in behind him.

Willow, back at the hotel later that afternoon, still moved by the events of the day, told us that the generals had invited him to their tent

A quiet day on the battlefield

where Chemedurov had joined them as interpreter. With great animation, they all began to discuss their own particular versions of Waterloo
whilst toasting Willow with so much vodka that in a few hours no one
was able to stand. Of course the "five squares" as originally arranged
appear in all their glory on the screen and remain one of the film's few
memorable moments.

IT WAS NEAR the end of September now and the threat of the dreaded
Russian winter loomed over our little garrison. Returning from the set
one freezing afternoon, we were astounded to find our normally frigid
hotel with the heating full on and warm as toast. I peeked into the
unspeakable dining room. The tables were nicely set and there were
open bottles of wine at each setting and I was told that there was plenty
of meat, chicken, eggs, everything our hearts desired. Then someone
explained—the Georgians had arrived! The actor playing Prince
Blücher and his entourage had taken over the hotel. Sergo Zaqariadze
was Russia's greatest actor (People's Artist Number One) and being
Georgian and independent demanded first-class tip-top service. The
wines on the table were Georgian, of course, which he had brought

himself—rich, full, wonderful reds. Communism and its restrictions didn't interest the Georgians in the slightest. In fact, for them, it simply didn't exist. Nothing could stop the gregarious nature of their lifestyle. We took to them at once. Zaqariadze was the leading player at the famed Vakhtangov Theatre, had portrayed all the great roles in Shakespeare and Pushkin and was reputed to be one of the greatest, if not the greatest, King Lear in any language. He was immensely tall, trim with flowing white hair and though pushing eighty, he could still stand straight up in his stirrups at full gallop.

He of course played his part in Russian, which would be dubbed later into English. In his small but important scene at the end of the battle, sitting on his horse surveying the field, the great old actor showed us what mettle he was made of. Napoleon's hat has been left behind and Blücher's men bring it to him. In the script he is supposed to make one simple scathing remark. Instead, Zaqariadze, the cameras rolling, takes up the hat ceremoniously with the tip of his sword, holds it high in the air, then puts it on his head the wrong way around. Next he takes it off, turns it around several times, holds it upside down and shakes it to see if anything drops out. He then smells it, makes a face and takes a bite out of it. Chewing away at it thus, he finds the taste repellent, spits it out onto the ground and with one extravagant flourish flings it like a Frisbee into the ranks for his men to fight over. Sadly, this inspired comic improvisation, because it was so gloriously over the top and took far too long, was cut from the movie. Many believe historically that had it not been for the last-minute appearance of Prince Blücher and his Prussians, the English would not have won at Waterloo. That may or may not be true, but *this* Prince Blücher and his Georgians had certainly saved our English bacon at Uzhgorod by bringing us food, wine, comfort, warmth and a great deal of cheer. Just the sort of victory we thespians find so much easier to understand.

ONE OF THE GREAT BLUNDERS in the history of war was the infamous abortive charge of Marechal Ney: a desperate bit of strategic recklessness which, as everyone knows, ended in disaster for the French. Cinematically, it was a huge undertaking involving at least six cameras, some aerial shots and several cranes. The smoke would fill the sky as usual from a great distance, and the charge, led by Dan O'Herlihy as Ney, would begin more than half a mile from where the English foot soldiers were waiting on the hill. Wellington and his party were not involved in this particular shot, so we all headed for the set, mounting one of the camera scaffolds in order to get a bird's-eye view of the proceedings. Already one could see how hopelessly disorganized everything was and how potentially dangerous. To add to the confusion, there were only a handful of horses that were film-tough—most having been borrowed from the army for this specific shot, having had no time at all to properly train. The horses belonging to the American, English and German stuntmen knew how to fall by their riders' leg commands—not painful. But the rest—the Cossacks, the Tartars and the Yugoslavians, all fantastic daredevil riders—had to employ the use of outmoded trip wires attached to the legs of the poor unsuspecting army horses. Very painful indeed! Suddenly everyone was called to their places and the explosions began in the distance. The horses started rearing. All at once, the guns were fired and the charge was under way.

It began from so far away that through the heavy smoke they looked like ghosts flying across the field. In actuality, it was so much more frightening and real than it could ever be on the screen, for the naked eye could take in 180 degrees of live action, and we could literally smell the fear. As the riders neared the foot of the hill they came out of the smoke covering the ground at hellbent speed. Now the crack of the rifles was heard as the English started firing and when the French reached the summit they fell, rolling and tumbling over each other. Most of the horses miraculously made it through and got up relatively unscathed—all except one who was trying so hopelessly to get to its feet. When it finally succeeded all it could do was to stagger pathetically about, its neck broken, its head hanging at a strange angle. It was an army horse that belonged to one of the young soldiers, who was watching devastated from the sidelines. The youth could stand it no longer and burst through the barriers to get up the hill, but the assistants tried to stop him and force him back. "You're in the shot—get back—you're in the shot," they yelled at him in Russian. The cameras were still filming, and, as usual, no one had called "cut." Ignoring them, the soldier, who couldn't have been more than seventeen, fought his way clear and ran towards his horse, who looked at him with pleading eyes. The boy had no gun and knew he must act quickly, so he took out his knife, held the horse's head, and before our very eyes and the still rolling cameras, he slit its throat in one swift movement, and the grateful horse sank to the ground. Now, finally, everything stopped— all was still. The field was in shock. The only sound came from the inconsolable young soldier who, with heart-wrenching sobs, fell on the still warm carcass of his dead friend.

This extraordinary act of mercy brought a sober end to all the carelessness and recklessness of the day, and we walked away across the smoke-filled fields, stunned and speechless.

IT WAS TIME for dear Jack Hawkins to leave. His character, the eccentric General Picton with umbrella and top hat, had met his maker. We were all very sad to lose him, of course, but relieved for his sake. Though a strong man physically, he had not been looking at all well. His throat and lungs had to have been damaged from all the smoke pouring down them day after day. But he only joked about his crackle of a voice and the halting speech that came from the hole in his throat: "My t-t-timing has n-never been better."

John Kirby left the next day. He'd had such a miserable time. "I can't take it anymore, I'm sorry." I could see he was about to choke up. Elaine and I gave him a big hug and told him, "There's nothing for you to do anyway—get the hell out of here," and off he went back to Madrid. Ian Ogilvy, Rupert Davies and Donal Donnelly were the next to leave. Our little English contingent was looking very sparse indeed. In Russia, there was no commercial pressure as there is in the West. There was all the time in the world. Mosfilm seemed to have buckets of money—how ironic when the people were so poor. But it was now getting very late; we were way over our schedule and the winter was seriously about to set in—the dreaded Russian winter! Bondarchuk seemed to have lost all interest in the English end of the story. It was only too apparent that he had sided with the French. Being a Soviet, he could more easily identify with la République, and I was certain he was racking his brains to find some way for Rod Steiger to win the war. At any rate, he kept trundling off to Moscow to receive medals, orders, honorary doctorates as the "People's Number One Director." All filming was put on hold. We were at the end of our tether, Dino De Laurentiis even more irritated than we. All we did was just hang around, waiting—when were we ever going to get out of there?!

Elaine and I had finally been blessed with a most efficient driver who knew the countryside like the back of his hand. He was in his late twenties, an outrageous character with a categorically unpronounceable name. We decided simply to call him Fred. Fred was from Transylvania and was as camp as a row of tents. He was slight, built somewhat like a girl, but was hilariously funny and tough as they come. He had to be, for he brazenly swished all over Uzhgorod, a town which insisted that in Russia homosexuality did not exist. He hardly spoke a word of English, but he fell in love with his new name. "I am Fred," he would scream to all and sundry. "Fred come," he would mince in; "Fred go," he minced out. We called Fred our "little vampire"—when I told him about the legend of the male Albanian vampire who when he pays his victims a visit always wears high heels, I thought Fred was going to have hysterics. Our little vampire (who flirted with everyone in German, French and "Swinglish") had in a sense taken over from Kirby. He would help Elaine with her shopping, and on our days off organize trips to other villages to see the countryside—no easy feat. To visit a village only ten kilometers away we had to take our passports and a letter of permission from the KGB. Ordinary Russians were not allowed to visit the next town at all, even if they had family there, unless they applied months in advance. Incredibly, they never showed their disappointment in any way.

The Soviet crew and actors were always so eager to be welcoming, they regularly asked us to join them in town after work. But we were never allowed to fraternize. Intourist, the KGB, even Mosfilm saw to that. They also saw to it that their artists were housed in separate villages. The Russian kids and their interpreters were just as bewildered by these bigoted laws as we were. Curiosity was forbidden and if they became the slightest bit friendly or close to us, they were transferred somewhere else—we never saw them again.

Things on the set were beginning to run amok. One morning, we arrived to find there was no sign of the army anywhere. We were told they had been ordered to settle a minor skirmish that had taken place near the border. With no time to change, they had taken off in their Waterloo costumes. To the enemy, whoever they were, the sight of nineteenth-century British red and French blue must have freaked them out of their minds. But more disaster struck—horses were dying all over the place. They had run out of fake "dead horses" and had started using real ones, old worn-out beasts, to whom they gave injections, sometimes overdosing them so they would lie still. There was no such thing as the SPCA in Russia. Then the hotel began to deteriorate even further. With the Georgians no longer there, it reverted to its old obnoxious self.

We had barely got back to our "suite" one afternoon after a busy day in the stirrups when there was a knock on the door. It was a very sheepish Michael Wilding. "I've just had an epileptic fit." Now everything he said was usually meant to amuse so we didn't take him at all seriously. But he was shaking as he confided in us, "I'm prone to them, you know—please don't tell anyone—it's too humiliating. But I had to tell you because you're friends and I'm going to need a doctor." The only way to get a doctor was to check into the local hospital—as sure as hell a death warrant. But Fred the Vampire drove us over and we did just that. The hospital was a disgrace: filthy waiting room, filthy wards filled with dust and mice droppings on the floor and lots of worn-out army boots lying about. In the midst of all this stood Michael—elegant in a pair of white ducks, scarf around the neck, blazer and espadrilles. He looked as if he'd just come off a yacht. "I think I'm going to die here," he murmured, trying to make light of it. "I'll never get to see Maggie as Cleopatra. She opens next week at Chichester." Michael, once married to Elizabeth Taylor, was now happily united with Margaret Leighton, one of Britain's finest actresses. "You'll be all right," we said without much conviction in our voices. As we left him standing there with fear in his eyes, we wondered if he mightn't be right, the poor old thing.

In the meantime, Bondarchuk had come back strutting about like a proud rooster. Wellington and his little band were up next and for a second it looked as if we might be out of there. Michael as Ponsonby would have to wait a few days more to lead the Scots Greys' charge. Terry, Willow, Jeffrey Wickham and I got together and decided we *had* to let Michael go first. He was too ill to stay on any longer, so we went to Bondarchuk and told him the story. Bondars was really quite touched and agreed. We got Michael out of the hospital, put him on a wooden horse (for the close-ups), and the day after, he was back in Chichester with his Cleopatra.

Well, not everyone was done, but it was over for me—finally over! Farewell to Batty-Poo! Farewell to "Bondars the Bear," to Armando and his camera, to Chemedurov the Firebrand, farewell to the little vampire Fred. As a parting gift I made him take my silk shirts that for some incomprehensible reason I had brought from London. He cried very melodramatically, but I suspect he would have preferred some of Elaine's clothes instead.

No ropy car rides this time. No sir. We took the train to Budapest—the same damn train I took with Kirby, I swear—the same broken-down compartment, the same wooden benches. For a moment it seemed we even had the same soldiers, only this time there were six of them, much more agreeable, with four goats tied to the cabin door. It was a jolly group, all shouting bawdy Slavic songs at the tops of their voices. The joy was contagious and we tried to join them in song—a rather difficult feat without the words.

The sight of these six young- sters with their goats braying accompaniment made me real- ize how much I'd come to admire the Russian character beyond all expectations; these people who in their long history never once had it good, these talented, imaginative, passion- ate creatures who had given the world such greatness in music, literature and dance and who, no matter what regime had tram- pled them under foot, would rise up each time with fearless energy and an unquenchable appetite for life.

Sergei Bondarchuk

Elaine and I snuggled by the window to keep warm, and as we began to drift off, my memory brought me back to the battlefield, to Terry and Jeffrey, still there, no doubt busy controlling their nags; and Wil- low in kilts and monocle, drenched in vodka, sitting with his five-star generals happily dissecting famous battles from Poitier to Salamanca, from Waterloo to Crimea; to the terrible hotel, the filthy restaurant, Snake City itself; then those fateful hills and dear deaf old Stok, who carried me to safety each day, and the other long-suffering animals, the gallant little cavalry, the explosive fire-balls, the danger, the horror, the fear, and I knew I wouldn't have missed any of it for all the world.

> *Though Bondarchuk found it a bit of a wrench*
> *That the English had successfully conquered the French*
> *He couldn't change history, it was far too late*
> *So he honoured the truth and told it straight.*
>
> *Then hold high your lance for la Belle Alliance,*
> *Cry your last boo-hoo for ol' Batty-Poo,*
> *But remember in battle if e'er you get beaten*
> *That the Brits won this war on the playing fields of Eton.*

On our return to London, before we could even catch our breath, Elaine and I had yet another Russian experience—the absolute flip- side of the coin. Marina Bowater, a formidable lady with strong Russian connections, ran a small antiques shop on Kensington Church Street which contained bric-a-brac of all sorts from la vielle Russie—prerevolutionary objets d'arts such as priceless icons and original costume designs for the Ballets Russes by Bakst and Alexandre Benoit. Her shop was always filled with old emigrés who had escaped the Bolsheviks in 1917 and settled in London. Marina, whose conversation sparkled in three languages, took pity on them and insisted on serving them small crested shot glasses of vodka, Russian tea from ornate samovars and delicious little cakes "on the house." I was sipping away from my shot glass one morning, regaling Marina with the *Waterloo* saga, when she interrupted, "You know, ma chère, it's Russian Easter next week and I'm having a party for some rather extraordinary friends. Why don't you and Elaine come? C'est trés petite, mon apartment, mais, peut-être vous pourriez trouver la scène trés interessant."

The apartment was most certainly trés petite. When we arrived it was jam-packed to the rafters with bawdy, rowdy Russians, most of them drunk as skunks and having the time of their lives. But these were different Russians—White Russians—many of them exiled nobility who had come from Rome, Paris or Madrid to celebrate, not just their Easter but some other mysterious cause, the nature of which I could not fathom. It seemed like the gathering of a clan. There were Obolenskys, Moukhranskys and God knows who—all wonderful-looking people, tall and imposing, if a trifle shabbily dressed. The most boisterous of these were the ancient boyar princes led by the Golitzin family and their cousins, some of whom had travelled all the way from Brazil and Argentina. They were holding up the bar, joking, laughing and gawking at Elaine, who was wearing the briefest of hot pants—the then fashionable London attire. To avoid their gaze, she decided to retire to a nearby couch where she sat down beside a mercifully docile, handsome but unassuming man in his late sixties sporting a slightly frayed grey flannel suit. They seemed to be getting along nicely together, and I saw him give her a small silver trinket. It looked like something one might acquire at an airport giftshop.

The party was now at its loudest, the vodka and caviar disappearing rapidly. The atmosphere was electric—excitement high. I turned away for a second and caught a glimpse of the man in grey flannel. He was bowing very graciously to Elaine, kissing her hand, and then he got up from the sofa. Suddenly, as if on cue, everything stopped—the little apartment went deadly quiet—not even the clink of a glass. I looked about in astonishment—the entire room was standing rigidly at attention. As he moved slowly among them, nodding his gratitude and his good-byes, the man in the grey flannel suit, His Imperial Majesty, Tsar Vladimir Romanov, pretender to the Russian throne, quietly and modestly left the room.

"HE WAS VERY SWEET and he spoke the most impeccable English," Elaine said later when we got back to the house at Hyde Park Gate. We couldn't wait to examine the little trinket. It was a tiny cup sitting in its own silver tray. Yes, there were the Romanov eagles engraved on it and yes, it was real silver all right, and yes, we've kept it polished ever since. But we still wonder if perhaps he hadn't just picked it up at Heathrow Airport after all.

CHAPTER THIRTY-FOUR

PEER GYNT WITHOUT PORTFOLIO

After a long period of time in front of the camera there is nothing more satisfying to me than going straight back to the theatre. All my life I've been mixing things up that way, switching back and forth. It's a trifle risky, for if you are busy in one medium, the other is convinced you're dead. But it's my preferred risk because I believe that replenishing one's craft regularly is an absolute must and, of course, the stage is the one place where we actors can do that best.

For some time Peter Coe and I had discussed doing a production of *Peer Gynt* together—he directing, me in the title role. Now this massive Norse allegory was, in Henrik Ibsen's own words, a dramatic poem never meant to be performed, only read. It was a theatrical manager in Oslo who persuaded him to put it on the stage. Ibsen followed his advice and in the process wrote Edvard Grieg asking him to compose the incidental music. As it turned out, these two original geniuses created two separate masterpieces. But on its feet, in translation, even in

Tyrone Guthrie's famous Old Vic production with Ralph Richardson as Gynt and Olivier as the Button-Moulder, the play was always far too top-heavy to really do justice to Ibsen's haunting tone poem.

To properly perform *Peer Gynt* in its entirety would take untold hours. The dramatis personae is, in itself, a mob scene. There are so many characters that not only create a confusion of identity, they render any production virtually cost prohibitive. Only subsidized companies could come anywhere near being able to afford it, but, generally, as a live piece of theatre it sadly remains, even when edited considerably, a long and bumpy ride. Ibsen's first instinct was probably spot on, but there are too many golden moments in it to be ignored, so Peter Coe and I together came up with what we thought might be a solution to this problem.

Heavily influenced by Ingmar Bergman's film *Wild Strawberries,* we both saw Peer as an old man throughout looking back over his past. Even Peer as a youth or Peer in middle age would be played old. He and Mother Aase (two old crones together) would spend the lonely nights in the little hut on that mountaintop by the fjords getting tiddly (to keep warm if nothing else) and tell each other stories. So the well-known tale of the ptarmigan and the deer that opens the play becomes a tale that Peer has told over and over, and over and over Aase has to pretend she is hearing it for the first time. They also play the game of Death repeatedly. Peer riding his mother to Soria-Moria Castle in her bed (the carriage) is an all too familiar improvisation, until one night she really *does* die, and not noticing, he still keeps whipping the bedposts (the reindeer) until finally he realizes it all too late.

The whole play, therefore, is Peer's dream. Everything in that little room, all his toys come to life—the big steamer that takes him to Africa and explodes is the little toy boat that sits in a corner, the stallion he rides with Anitra is the old wooden hobby horse by the door. All the people he meets on his travels are the same people he has known from his village. His father-in-law becomes the Troll King; the bad girls become Anitra; the priest becomes the Button-Moulder, and so on. The only one who never changes is Solveig—she is constant and has never aged. So at the play's climax when Peer has peeled the onion down to its last truth, he finds that love and "self" have been at home waiting for him all along. In other words, he has lived his life's voyage in his mind; in reality he never left his village.

If done properly, it could work well, and what a money saver as far as casting was concerned. Really first-rate actors would now have much more incentive to appear in it as they would be playing several characters each. Coe took the idea to Sir John Clements who was then running the Chichester Festival and he "bought" it instantly. But who would adapt it? There were excellent translations in existence, most of which had already been performed, but they all tended at times to be somewhat literal. Then who best to create the new definitive English version and still make it his own? Christopher Fry, we chimed in unison. It was the obvious choice. Fry knew Norwegian, he was conveniently living near Chichester and he had the right poet's brush to lift the whole thing off its canvas. So a

In love with language

lunch was arranged at the Garrick Club for the four of us—Coe, Clements, Fry and me.

I had acted in three of Fry's plays in the fifties: *The Lady's Not for Burning* twice, *The Dark Is Light Enough* and *A Phoenix Too Frequent*. When I was a teenager in the midforties he was my very favourite writer. His gentle wit and his gift for language enthralled me, so what an added pleasure it was to find him a thoroughly charming and engaging gentleman. He seemed without ego and unlike a lot of academics was at once warm and human. He was what one would call a comfortable sort, with his pipe and his tweeds. Because I had some pretty strong ideas on how to play Peer, Coe and Clements suggested that Fry and I work together at least twice a week. What an honour! He listened with great courtesy and interest to all my ramblings and then we'd take a break or two and share stories. I had to pinch myself to remind me I was in the same room with one of my all-time heroes.

Fry took hardly any time to accomplish his task, but the result for Peter and myself was a huge disappointment. We were staggered! All the poetry we'd expected from him had been denied us; instead the story was told in the straightforward manner of an Arthur Miller— very economical, down to earth and domestic. Where were the flights of fancy? For two decades Fry had given back to a limping lightweight

English theatre all its missing profundity and beauty of language. But by the midsixties, his style had become outmoded and was considered too florid, gentle and obscure for a rapidly changing world. Reading his new *Peer Gynt,* we could see that Fry, all too aware of this, was determined to find an editorialized style that reflected the present and that might bring him a newfound popular acceptance. Understandable, of course, but everything *we'd* hoped for had been sacrificed. Skillful though his adaptation was, it was a "Fry-up" without the bacon, sausage and tomato!

Coe and I kept mum for the moment, wondering what on earth our next step would be. Rehearsals were just around the corner, and it looked very much as if we would have to go through with it, that we were really and truly stuck. And then something occurred that rescued me from falling down the deepest, blackest fjord that old Gynt had ever "peered" into. One morning, I found myself in a studio recording some scenes from *Much Ado About Nothing* with Dorothy Tutin. It was to be for an LP promoting our new "St. George's Islington and the Globe Theatre Restoration." I had always had a crush on Dot Tutin and was a regular slave to her particular magic whenever she was on the stage. So I was especially proud to be acting with her for the first time and having the greatest fun being Benedick to her Beatrice.

While happily emoting one of Benedick's famous tirades, something grabbed me with such force it knocked all the breath clean out of me. It was as if an enormous claw of steel was crushing my back and chest. I had great trouble breathing, but I was too humiliated not to continue so I managed to finish the scene, gasp out a few incoherent apologies to Dot who was staring at me openmouthed and left the studio doubled up and hardly able to walk. Thank God, Frank was there with the car and he drove me straight to my doctor's office in Hans Crescent. Dr. Janvrin called the London Clinic, got me a room, gave me a huge injection of something and sent me on my way. In the emergency room at the clinic, they had a devil of a time trying to X-ray me—I couldn't lie still—I was in such pain, the injection had long since worn off. Everyone—the interns and nurses—was convinced I was having a massive heart attack, which was not the case as they would one day discover. But in the meantime, it all seemed a mystery to them and I was taken to my room, heavily sedated and as usual when there was doubt instantly put on an IV.

Frank had called my good friend Tita Wilson, who was acting as my secretary, and she, in turn, called Elaine who was busy filming over at the BBC. For days, I lay there on the drip, drugged out of my skull, while they took innumerable tests, never once coming up with any kind of diagnosis. The London Clinic in those days was mostly known as a rich man's hospital and never taken very seriously. Its nursing staff left a lot to be desired. It was also vastly expensive, and the rules were generally rather lax when they shouldn't have been—there were a lot of wealthy Arabs and their extended families and entourages partying till all hours in their private "suites." However, for some reason, probably because I didn't tip anyone, I was allowed hardly a visitor and Elaine, who had been trying to see me for days, was denied entry as she was not "next of kin." My only real next of kin in London was my ex-wife Trish and had she been allowed in, we both might have had an instant relapse. Stoned as I was most of the time, I was never too aware of the goings-on around me, but one morning as the drugs momentarily waned, I noticed that my intravenous bag had fallen off its perch and was on the floor. I groped for my buzzer, pushed it and a nurse I had not seen before came into the room. ("New," I thought to myself. "Just off the boat, no doubt.") I looked again and to my horror she was scooping up the escaped liquid off the floor and back into the bag. She was just about to hang it on its hook when I realized I wasn't the only witness to this act of second-degree murder. For as luck would have it, at that very moment the head nurse was standing in the doorway. "What do you think you're doing?!" she demanded of the culprit. Incredibly, the girl began to defend herself, but the head nurse in clarion tones cut her off with a single command—"Out and don't come back!"—and the assassin scurried from the room blubbing audibly as she ran. Of course, the bag was immediately replaced and I was allowed to resume my trip into the depths of an abyss whose bottom I seemed destined to reach.

One day, from deep in my never-never land, I thought I saw a vision I knew and loved. It was Elaine wrapped in a sort of haze looking down at me. She was smiling and so, I gather, was I. Her voice, though it came from somewhere miles away and sounded as if it were under water, was the most reassuring sound I could have prayed for. I'd just managed to be able to hear her mumble the words "I'll be back." Whatever she'd done, it had worked! For the next day, I was awakened abruptly to find my bed surrounded by several interns and doctors, all in their whites, standing quite formally and reverently, obviously waiting for something very important to happen. Then a distinguished-looking man with graying hair and a deep tan wearing a suit came into the room. The doctors practically genuflected. "Good morning, Sir

Ronald," they all intoned together like a group of schoolboys addressing their headmaster. Sir Ronald spoke softly in a deep calming voice
full of authority, "Get those things out of him at once. He doesn't need
any of that rubbish." He was referring, I gathered, to all my tubes and
tentacles. He leaned over me and with great charm said, "Hello, I'm
Ronald Gibson. You're going to be fine, don't worry. You're coming to
my hospital. See you there." And he walked briskly from the room.

Everything now happened so fast it made me even dizzier than I'd
already been on drugs. Tubes were ripped from my arms and hands—
they lifted me out of my bed—threw me onto a wheelchair—down
the lift, into an ambulance—I was driven through London at ninety
miles an hour—then up the ramp and through the back door of the
Brompton Hospital—up another lift—wheeled into an operating
room, where someone strapped me onto a table. Two men with two
oversized hypodermic needles the right dimensions for a horse, advanced towards me and without explanation rammed both of them
deep into my chest. I couldn't believe my eyes—they were actually
drawing gallons of white liquid from my lungs. That done, they rolled
me over and performed the same horrendous stabbing act through my
back. The second the needles came out I was wheeled into intensive
care, lifted onto a bed which was immediately cordoned off by screens.
I was just catching my breath when a nice young man in white leaned
through the screens and said, "I'm Sir Ronald's deputy. He is at the
moment in the Canary Islands on holiday. He will be back in a day or
two. He asked me to look in on you. You've had an attack of pericardi-
tis, which means a great quantity of fluid had collected in your chest.
The pain you felt was the pressure of that fluid against your lungs and
heart. You're not out of the woods yet, but you're in good hands and
everything will be fine. Rest well tonight." Rest? Was he serious?

That night I didn't sleep a wink. I noticed in the dim light that there
were other patients in the room, also behind screens, obviously all on
the critical list. I also noticed what was keeping me awake—the inces-
sant pounding of a machine at the far end of the room. The noise was
tumultuous but no one else seemed in the least perturbed by it. I rang
a buzzer and a young nurse told me it was three in the morning, that
she could do nothing and I'd have to speak to the head nurse. I must
have been maddened by sedatives because I started screaming for attention. The matron was there in a second. She glided in soundlessly, an
impressive figure in crisp starch with a Polish accent. "Meestah
Plummah," she began in a silky tone of mock servility; "Vat can I do for

you? Vy are you so upset?" "Please turn off that hideous damn machine in the corner—it's driving me bloody well crazy. I can't get a moment's sleep!!" She fairly purred, "Of course, Meestah Plummah, I vill be glad to do zat eff you veesh. But unfortunately ze old lady who is connected to it vill die." As I buried my head in shame amongst the pillows, I saw her give me a wicked smile as she just as silently glided away.

I was allowed to see Elaine and Tita in the morning. Elaine told me she had laid the law down with Dr. Janvrin. "I told him it was quite clear you were gradually disappearing and that he was to get you out of that ghastly place into a proper hospital *or else.*" Tita joined in, "You are now in one of the major heart and lung hospitals in Europe." All this made me feel considerably stronger but not quite strong enough to blow them kisses of gratitude, so I pursed my lips in an exhausted effort as they were whisked out.

The two or three days that followed in intensive care were most humbling indeed. I quickly learned to worship those nurses who worked so tirelessly and such long hours. They were a different breed altogether from the everyday nurse one is accustomed to. These girls were on a mission—this was the final room before the great unknown and they, the soldiers who barred the gates. In this room life and death were just a breath away from each other. Here were the true angels of mercy and grossly underpaid angels at that. I watched one nurse every few hours shout through a tube into the ear of an old lady who appeared to be in a permanent coma—trying so hard to make some contact with her, to get her to react in some way, "Hello darlin'," she would shout. "It's a beautiful day outside today. Can you hear me? Let me tell you about it. Can you hear me?" And she would go on having these long one-way conversations with this inanimate object in the bed. And always so positive, always so cheery. On my last day in that room I woke up to see an empty space where the bed had been. They'd taken it away in the night. I saw the young nurse who was called Peggy being gently led out by the other nurses—she was crying, her whole body sagged with exhaustion and disappointment. "Oh Peggy'll be all right," I was told. "She just needs a little rest, that's all—she'll be back. You get very close to your patients here, you know."

I left intensive care with a great feeling of admiration and respect for these gallant souls and much chastened by the whole experience. I certainly would never be caught shouting at a life-support machine ever again. I thanked them all profusely as they wheeled me down the corridor and put me in a private room. The moment I was in my bed, a tanned face peeked through the door. "Well," said Sir Ronald, "we got you just in time."

He explained in his smooth urbane manner that full recovery for me would take approximately eight weeks, that he was putting me on prednisone but that I must get off it as soon as I could, that I was to do nothing but rest and certainly *no work* as yet. "Get some sun somewhere and take that young lady with you." He turned to go, then stopped at the door. "Do you smoke?" "I do," I said. "Quit! This is the perfect opportunity!" And then he was gone. Well, there would be no Chichester Festival for me, that was certain. In one way I'd been saved, I would put it all behind me but, ironically, the first visitor to my room was Christopher Fry. He brought me some chocolates and a book or two and told me how sorry he was that I would not be opening as Peer. I suddenly felt rather desolate about the whole thing; it had been a project so very close to my heart—besides, I'd grown exceptionally fond of Christopher. I began to have other visitors sporadically. Tita, who was always so caring and kept me laughing a lot. Peter Coe dropped in once or twice before *Gynt* rehearsals began, but it was that very special lady Elaine of "Astelot," "Shallot" and Knightsbridge who with unbelievable regularity would cook me all sorts of extra goodies and smuggle them in as care packages—a veritable Nightingale, only this time in Brompton Square. All my life I've had a craving for English jellies, which she also conjured up and brought along for dessert, happily jiggling away in their moulds. She would then read me to sleep every night before curfew—spoiled pampered couch potato that I'd become.

Occasionally Sir Ronald would look in and deliver another lecture on smoking. "You like food, don't you? Then no cigarettes! It'll all taste much better, you'll see." A few days before I was to leave the hospital, he came for the last time, wished me luck and told me I'd never need see him anymore. He said his good-byes and at the door he turned once more. "You enjoy sex, don't you?" "Yes," I answered sheepishly. "No smoking then! Right?" He shut the door behind him—I never saw him again. Two years later at a friend's wedding in Gloucestershire, an attractive young lady with a rather county manner came up to me. "Are you Christopher Plummer?" "Yes, I think so," I said. "I believe you knew my father, Ronald Gibson?" "Yes indeed," I replied. "What an extraordinary man and what a career! I'll never forget him. He saved my life. Please give him my regards. Is he well?" "No, he died a few months ago," she said. "Lung cancer. He was a chain-smoker, you know."

WELL, I DID GIVE UP the weed and he was right—my taste buds began to enjoy a renaissance and that first glass of red wine slipping down my spanking new smokeless zone was so potent I nearly passed out. Elaine and I went to see the *Peer Gynt* opening at Chichester. Roy Dotrice was splendid in my relinquished role, much more physically suited to it than I was and blessed with the right sort of quirkiness which came to him naturally and which I would have had to assume. But the whole evening was strangely unsatisfying. Peter's and my concept was only half realized (there had evidently been insufficient time to delve further), and I couldn't help thinking that had I been there with Peter working together to resolve it, it would have made all the difference.

I took the young lady, as advised, into the sun of our beloved Majorca. We did nothing but lie on the beach at Formentor gazing longingly at another spectacular villa perched on a cliff hundreds of feet above the sea—a most pleasant way to live another hopeless dream. The prednisone which I had started to wean myself off had given me a great deal of bulk so I looked like a junior version of Sly Stallone. It was just as well, for unbeknownst to me I was going to need that extra weight for the next venture which was just around the corner. Tita was waiting for us with some vodka at No. 9 when we got back to London. "Oh, by the by, Laurence Olivier called while you were away. He wants you to play Coriolanus at the National Theatre."

CHAPTER THIRTY-FIVE

DIRTY LINEN AT "THE NAT"

S everal years had gone by since I'd seen Olivier as Othello, but the memory of that outrageous and titanic performance was still as vivid in my mind as it always will be. As usual, when playing the supreme roles, his main plan of attack was to overwhelm. That diabolical mountebank Edmund Kean, more than a century before, was reputed to have done the same and had, by some sort of osmosis, passed it down to the next generation of stage giants. All great actors have it in them to overwhelm. They make dead sure that they are at odds with everything that is happening around them; that whatever they do is unexpected and unsettling; that they know the trick of the light in the eye, the delayed entrance, the sudden dazzling vocal speed, the unearthly voice from the past, the instinct for milking poetry, the temper of Zeus, the stillness that silences—and that unexplainable thing called pathos.

Well Larry Olivier had all these at his command and more—all, that is, except pathos. Oh, he manufactured pathos to the hilt—he acted it expertly, wonderfully. He knew all its ingredients, and yet none of them came naturally to him. To have pathos one must be born with it. Ralph Richardson had it in spades; so had Brando and Chaplin; so, I believe, had Chaliapin and the great Salvini. I was deeply moved by the powerful Czech actor Frederick Valk's Othello because of his utter simplicity and the pathos he owned down to his fingertips. You couldn't see the wheels going round because his art transcended technique. But Olivier moved me *because* of his technique. It was evident throughout, I couldn't take my eyes off it. I was transfixed by its massive design. He mesmerized us with his effects, his tricks; he pulled out all the stops and showed us every one of them. In other words, he overwhelmed us into being moved, and though we could see the whole process, it didn't matter a damn because it was still shamefully exciting. He had quite ruthlessly overwhelmed his Iago as well (which undeniably got him more attention) mostly by placing poor Frank Finlay in the dim shadows so that you never really saw him all at once. At his own admission, Olivier was determined that Iago, who generally wipes the floor with Othello, wasn't going to get away with it this time.

As Sir Laurence shaped his Othello, this was no Moor as depicted by Johnston Forbes-Robertson and John Philip Kemble, nor drawn from the ultraromantic illustrations of Eugène Delacroix. This was a real, honest-to-God black Negro, blacker than any Cameroonian—a half-naked warrior with curly matted hair, bare feet and anklets and large, voluptuous lips that folded back in a grimace, a smile or a snarl covering his whole face (he even painted the roof of his mouth and his tongue white, I remember), not to mention the strange wild animal sounds that erupted from deep inside him. In an age when black actors are expected to own the role, he presented a shocking and quite salacious image. Though he moved like a panther, there was intentionally a great

Sir Laurence as Othello with Maggie Smith as Desdemona

deal of Stepin Fetchit in his gait, and his accent was a weird mixture of Arab and Jamaican.

Yet with all this, there were so many unforgettable moments: his slow undulating shuffle as he made his startling first entrance—naked save for a loincloth, carrying a single red rose (a conceit borrowed from Kean, no doubt)—received audible gasps from the audience. His unexpected humour on reading the line "the Anthropophagi and men whose heads do grow beneath their shoulders" as if challenging the Senate to share his laughter at the impossibility of such fanciful things existing. The great resonant power of his voice (he had worked hard to drop it at least two octaves) and that staggering range of his as he shook the theatre with the speech:

> . . . *O, now for ever,*
> *Farewell the tranquil mind! Farewell content!*
> *Farewell the plumed troop and the big wars*
> *That make ambition virtue! O, farewell!*

And then the horrid little epileptic fit that follows on the ground (his own invention) at the feet of Iago. Finally, near the play's end, Olivier is not afraid to milk all the romance from his final speech as he stretches the poetry to infinity:

> *. . . One, whose hand,*
> *Like the base Judean, threw a pearl away,*
> *Richer than all his tribe.*

Was it a great performance? Even without the pathos? The answer is yes, I think so. It was not the Moor of Venice; it was closer to John Buchan's Laputa or Emperor Jones, perhaps, but whatever it was, it was overwhelming — and probably the very last we will see of that timeless, larger-than-life kind of performing that belonged to an unidentifiable golden age when the actor reigned supreme.

BACK IN THOSE prosperous days, I was living at the Connaught in London. I was going through my "single period" again — a bachelor between ladies. Having finished a boozy Saturday lunch all alone in the Grill Room with coffee and several Poire Williams and musing on my wasteful life (a rare sixties guilt rush), I suddenly decided to intrude upon Larry in his dressing room after the *Othello* matinée. Hoping to wear off lunch, I staggered down to the Old Vic on foot — an ambitiously long trek indeed — and arrived miraculously on time. The curtain had just come down. I went to the stage door and was announced. A dresser was busy removing Larry's black makeup, an ordeal that seemed to take forever. "You weren't out front today, I hope," Larry screeched. "Oh myyy Gawd! They booed me, dear! They booed me! They think I'm a fucking racist pig, darling, a racist pig!" When Larry was in an exuberant mood, he would often assume this pseudocamp performance, which was miles over the top. He told a few off-colour jokes and then we fell into silence. His dresser was having the deuce of a time trying to remove the makeup — it wasn't coming off at all easily. What could this mean? Black Equity's revenge? Larry looked at me, his eyes becoming slits. I was sure he was thinking, "Is this inebriated jerk ever going to leave?" The cat had completely got my tongue. "Well," said Larry, "what can I do for you, Kit?" His weary, long-suffering tone implied, "Spit it out, for Chrissakes. I want my dinner." Whether it was the booze that made me a bit teary or a sudden attack of nerves I'll never know, but I heard my voice tremble as I blurted out, "I want to come and work here — more than anything — if there's ever a space?" but I couldn't find the words to go on. He came over and gave me a big hug which left a lot of black goo all over my Savile Row suit and I was gently ushered out. But he'd remembered — after all these years, he'd remembered! And it was to be Coriolanus! Well, well! Not bad for a start!

I telephoned at once to John Dexter, who was now one of the National's principal directors. "Is this true?" I asked. His answer was in the affirmative. "Then please, John, I'd love it if you would direct." "I can't," he replied. "My dance card is full." My heart sank. "You'll probably get a call from Larry, who very much wants to do it, but might I suggest the two Germans from the Berliner Ensemble, Joachim Tenschert and Manfred Weckworth? They will give it a different look, new and fresh, and because they are foreign their presence will smarten up the company. They need smartening up—they've become rather lax."

Olivier did call. In his carefully chosen extravagant verbiage, he began, "My dear Kit, may I have the pleasure of humbly offering myself to you as your director?" (God, I thought, what a wonderful bullshit artist he is.) "Think about it, dear boy. Take all the time you want." Now I was in a most awkward position. Great actor he may be but no great shakes as a director—that was universal knowledge. Besides he had himself been the last to play Coriolanus and was perhaps the finest in theatrical history. His famous performance at Stratford in the late fifties had elicited critical love letters and had ended with his own spectacular bit of business—falling from the balcony backwards and hanging by his heels head down in the image of the slaughtered Mussolini. I couldn't possibly let him direct me. He was much too close to the part. He would give me *his* business, give me *his* line readings, in short, make me his carbon copy. I'm afraid I said no. Sir Laurence was not accustomed to being turned down. There was a long silence. "Very well, suit yourself, dear boy," he said rather sulkily, and then in dulcet wooing tones, "but I am going to miss you." God, how he could get to you! But I didn't let him. I went with the Germans instead.

Kate Fleming was a crackerjack voice coach, one of the very best. It was she who had given Larry such help with his Othello. I spent several weeks with her slugging away at lowering my voice and giving it more power. Kate smoked like a chimney and never stopped coughing her insides out (odd for someone so dedicated to the vocal chords), but she made me spout yards and yards of Marlowe's *Tamburlaine* in my lowest tones until I was able to rattle off most of those big speeches in one breath. After *Tamburlaine,* Coriolanus seemed almost a snap, so by the time the first reading was to take place, I was more than ready to go into battle.

The reading was conducted in the National Theatre's offices down on old Aquinas Street. They had not as yet transferred to their new home. It was a series of ramshackle Nissan huts strung together in the shape of a railway train with a long narrow corridor stretching from one end to the other. The cafeteria and the rehearsal room were, illogically, as far from each other as possible. The administrative offices were lined up claustrophobically on either side of the corridor and there were a couple of floorboards which were always wet and if you stepped too heavily on them your feet went straight through. It was the tackiest-looking jerry-built structure you ever saw and quite filthy—if one had called the health department, I'm sure they'd have come and closed it. I had to remind myself that some very glorious work had come out of that grimy old building.

It never occurred to me at the time, but turning up that first morning in the Rolls-Royce Corniche with Frank attired in his splendid chauffeur's grey and cap did not exactly endear me to the company. It was a stupid insensitive thing to do, but—damn it!—it was my only mode of transportation. I soon couldn't have cared less, for apart from three superb actors, Charles Kay, Ronald Pickup and Denis Quilley, most of the company were made up of a bunch of unwelcoming, humourless malcontents whose socialist leanings not only were far left of Lenin but made Harold Wilson look like King Farouk. Also, to my great disappointment, stroppiness had taken precedence over talent. Well, we all settled down for the reading in the usual straight line— the management facing us. Wouldn't you know it, Larry sat in a chair directly in front of me, John Dexter to his left. The very agreeable stage management Diana Boddington and co. on his right. In one corner sat the National's dramaturge, of all people, Kenneth Tynan, and in the other, modestly hugging the wall, the two German directors from Berlin.

The read-through began. The first three pages sped by inaudibly as read by the mumbling "plebs" and then Coriolanus makes his entrance. Directing my first speech to the assembled company, I began with more ferocity and fervour than I perhaps should have:

> *What's the matter you dissentious rogues,*
> *That rubbing the poor itch of your opinion,*
> *Make yourselves scabs? What would you have, you curs,*
> *That like not peace nor war? The one affrights you*
> *The other makes you proud. He that trusts to you*
> *Where he should find you lions, finds you hares*
> *Where foxes — geese!*

I was enjoying myself thoroughly! The reading rolled on. Much of the cast continued to simply mumble their words with no expression and little understanding—they obviously had done no homework—and out of the corner of my eye I would catch the small-part players talking and giggling amongst themselves. Every so often Larry would get out of his chair, walk over and whisper in someone's ear, but that didn't deter me in the least; I was having far too good a time. Besides, I knew I must be doing well because he picked most of Coriolanus's key moments to create these minor disturbances—canny old theatrical bitch that he was. I even found it quite amusing, my character's arrogance had clearly rubbed off on me and given me a much-needed protective armour. There was little or no reaction from anyone after the reading was over except from Larry, who privately complimented me, but otherwise it had been the most unprofessionally conducted first reading I have ever attended. People just shuffled about aimlessly, wondering what was to happen next. The poor depressed younger members of the company wandered in and out of the cafeteria with obviously one thought on their minds. Am I going to be used next season or kicked out? There was no spreading of confidence in this company and certainly no love lost. Did I detect in the fetid air a tiny scent of National Theatre decay?

All the following week as we began to rehearse on our feet, the same strained atmosphere prevailed. There was no direction of any kind coming from the Germans who still seemed to be hugging the back wall of the rehearsal room showing little or no interest in anything at all. Aided by the very capable stage management, we were "blocking" the play by ourselves. It seemed the only thing to do; there was no choice. Denis Quilley, who was playing Tullus Aufidius, would look at me at intervals and we would both shrug. Was nothing to be forthcoming?

On the last day of that week, the Germans suddenly came alive. Joachim, the one who spoke a little English, announced with a smile on his face, "It's all right now. Ve can begin. The new texts have arrived! You can srow all doze odder vuns avay!" New texts?! What did they mean *new*? I had clutched my trusty little Penguin Shakespeare edition to my bosom for weeks now and had marked, underlined and annotated it so heavily, it was practically illegible. New? Had the Bard been doing some recent rewrites that we knew nothing of? Clever bugger—always determined to keep abreast of the times. But no! The title page of my fresh new manuscript read simply, *Coriolanus* by Bertholt Brecht.

Well, I took it home with me that night only to find that my role in the play which Shakespeare had once called *The Tragedy of Coriolanus* had been violently slashed to ribbons, reduced to a one-dimensional cardboard cutout, and, as expected, the archsocialist Brecht's favourites, the citizens, the proletariat, the mob, "the plebs" were now eliciting sympathy as the main characters of the piece. I called Larry in Brighton first thing next morning—he was after all the artistic director. He couldn't quite digest what I was telling him. "You mean, you didn't know?" I asked. "No—I—didn't know. Ah—my dear Kit, I'm late for my train—call Ken—he's in the office. We'll talk later—ah—" and he trailed off!

"You mean you didn't know?" I repeated to Tynan across his desk. "No—n-no, I didn't," he asserted in astonishment. At once sympathetic and helpful, he looked up the availability of possible directors who could take over the project, but being the usual suspects (Blakemore, Dexter, Elliot, Gaskill, Dunlop, etc.) they were, of course, all busy. What to do? "A-A-I-I'll l-look into this r-right away," he stuttered. As I left his office and started down the corridor, the administrative staff scattered and as if sensing trouble, ran back into their offices and shut the doors behind them. Confrontation of any sort was not their strong point. Of course, the whole thing was a fait accompli—the Nat was stuck. They had made the deal. That little bureaucracy had got the Berliner Ensemble cheap. They'd made the deal for the same set, the same costumes, the same two directors, the same production in English that London had just recently seen in German, and they'd made it behind Larry's back.

I met with the brass and explained my concern. The Germans generously agreed to put back some of the cuts, but it would never be the same. "I came here to do 'Shakespeare's' *Coriolanus,*" I stated simply and reluctantly went back to rehearsal. The poor Germans, as much in the dark about these shenanigans as I had been, patiently tried to carry on, but it was no use. I wouldn't accept direction from them. How could I? I was in the wrong play. We'd arrived at an impasse. Rehearsal was cancelled. A company meeting was called and I, as a guest artist and not permitted to attend, went home to await the results.

By late afternoon, Larry came to No. 9 with his henchman Paddy Donnell. "The bulk of the company voted you down," he said. "I knew they would," I said. "But they'll be happy campers. They're the stars of the show now!" Larry's expression was that of the tragic muse. "It's all right, Larry. It's a great relief, really it is, and thank you." "You will come and do something else for us, won't you?" "We'll see," I said, and he and Paddy left. I felt for Larry. He, like myself, had been placed in an untenable situation and I believe he was genuinely upset. He had been all for firing the Germans and replacing them with Michael Blakemore, but in that regard, he was powerless. If only I'd gone with him from the start, I thought to myself, none of this nonsense would have taken place.

KEN TYNAN would, over time, turn the tables and change his story. In his published diaries he maintains that I was the difficult one, that it was I who caused dissension in the ranks. That is not true—we were all of us victims of a devious plot and he had conveniently forgotten that at the time he could not have been more sympathetic to my plight. Of course, he is no longer with us and so can't defend himself. We'll just have to fight it out entre nous quand nous serons ensemble en enfer. But Ken, playing a role he was not accustomed to, embroiled in the petty intrigues of theatre management, had completely changed.

I remember, years before, a party at Lillian Hellman's brownstone in New York. Everyone in our business who mattered was there. I noticed a distinguished-looking older man I'd not seen before help himself to food and disappear all by himself to the upper regions of the house. "Who is that?" I asked Lillian. "Oh, that's Brooks Atkinson; he makes it a rule not to mix with actors." And I understood it. Mr. Atkinson had principles. He didn't necessarily dislike us as a race; he saw it his duty as a critic to remain professionally impartial. But Tynan had "crossed over." He was dying to be on our side of the fence and once there had lost all his raison d'être. He became the elite version of a star-fucker, hobnobbing with the famous, buttering up Larry, his major meal ticket, or Marlene Dietrich, his escort service, rubbing shoulders with Mick Jagger or Roman Polanski and, against all his socialist convictions, currying favour with the royals only too visibly represented by Princess Margaret. He also enjoyed being a sort of star himself—a wag at parties, a contrived Oscar Levant; to use his own words, he defrocked himself publicly. He wanted a breathlessly waiting world to know he alone had invented the word "kink," that he'd personally discovered "spanking" and that mutual masturbation was his new religion. As the National's dramaturge, he no longer wrote reviews, so apart from some entertaining pastiches on bullfighting and haute cuisine, his only contribution to society was O! Calcutta! an inferior sexical performed by numerous unknowns in the altogether, exposing their shrivelled parts in frigid London theatres. A far cry from the man whose brilliant, witty and discerning pen had for two decades helped restore the highest standards of the English stage.

WELL, I DID go back to "The Nat" and I did work with Larry. For a time, we had the most wonderful fun together—endless stories, ribald jokes, many dinners, with or without the ladies, and much wine and song. He loved reminiscing about the old Hollywood days. I think he often missed the glamour of those times. There is no question Larry was great company and he seemed to bend over backwards to make up for everything. In fact, there was much more joy backstage than the piece we were rehearsing could ever offer. The play was Sam Behrman's *Amphitryon 38,* based on a gossamer bit of fluff by Giraudoux—a satirical take on the Jupiter, Leda and the Swan myth as a design for living triangle, which had once been a vehicle for the Lunts. The triangle consisted of Alcmene, her dazzling lover Jupiter and her boring husband, Amphitryon. Larry, as director, thought it would be a novel idea if I was to play the *two* parts, Jupiter and Amphitryon. I did! I was appalling in both! I was so heavy-handed, if they'd filled me with helium, I couldn't have got off the ground! And if *I* was heavy as lead, wow, so was Larry's production. It was surf-n-turf when it should have been spun sugar! Only Geraldine McEwan, that wizard of artificial comedy, as Alcmene, came anywhere near the mark. It was generally so literal and ponderous they even constructed a mechanical cloud upon which Jupiter and Mercury could commute between Earth and Heaven, which, of course, broke down in front of the first preview audience, leaving "Merc" and myself stuck up there, halfway between the stage and the flies. Having run out of text, we began to frantically ad-lib as stagehands in the wings struggled with the mechanism. We found we got more laughs ad-libbing than any of the lines from the actual play itself, but now the laughter from the fed-up audience was taking on a more derisive tone. Exhausted of invention, sick of egg on our faces, we decided in spite of our shared vertigo to get the hell off the damn thing once and for all. We were just about to climb out and possibly fall to our deaths when the curtain finally came down. Think of it! This was only act 2. More such embarrassment was yet to follow. When at last we were safely back in our dressing rooms at the play's end, Joseph Mankiewicz (who was to direct Larry in the movie *Marathon Man*) came back to see me. All he could say was, "One day, dear Chris, your cloud will come in!" I wonder what he meant by that.

Geraldine McEwan (Alcmene) being wooed by me (Jupiter disguised as Amphitryon)

The last performance came none too soon and to appease me further, they handed me on a silver platter the role of Edmond Danton in Büchner's *Danton's Death.* This is an overly long work filled with complications and in desperate need of an exceptional director who can sort things out and give it some theatrical life. We got one in Jonathan Miller. It gave my spirits a giant boost to renew my acquaintance with this extraordinary man whose knowledge of painting, literature, anthropology, religion and medicine was so rich it dwarfed many an intellectual competitor and whose devastating wit was already well known in concentric circles on both sides of the Atlantic.

Elaine and I had seen Jonathan's splendid production of *The Merchant of Venice* with the Oliviers, Joan and Larry, as Portia and Shylock, respectively, and Charles Kay whose performance of the Prince of Aragon is the funniest I've witnessed before or since. We had gone with Raymond and Dorothy Massey who brought along their old friend Gregory Peck. Peck had just flown over from California and promptly fell asleep on Elaine's shoulder ("Be still my heart," she quipped later). The rest of us, wide awake, sat entranced by what we all agreed was the clearest interpretation of that difficult piece ever. And the sets Miller had created with his talented designer Julia Trevelyan Oman—giant books whose pages opened onto each and every scene, rich in color like a series of Old Masters, a stunning effect of great beauty and ingenuity.

Now with his designers for *Danton,* he arrived at an equally imaginative concept, placing the principal characters Robespierre, St. Just, Danton, etc. in glass cases as in a museum—wax creatures à la Madame Tussauds. Gradually we came to life, opened our glass doors, stepped out of our cases and the story began. Of course, we all had to spend hours beforehand slapping green and off-white greasepaint all over our faces to appear long dead and, in my case, squeezing into vast padding as well to resemble the porculent Frenchman. I think I spent more time in my dressing room than onstage preparing for the damn part and I'm not certain all that work paid off, for Elaine informed me that on opening night one old lady sitting behind her said loudly to her companion— "My God! Look at Plummer. He's put on so much weight, poor thing. *And* he looks so ill!" You simply can't win.

Another management secret that had kept me in the dark was that Danton had originally been promised to Anthony Hopkins and now to add insult to injury they had lumbered him with Coriolanus in my place. Anthony of course would have made the most wonderful Danton, ideally suited to it chemically, much more so than I. I think Anthony knew that and was not at all thrilled with the change. Sorry Tony, it wasn't my fault, honest! After the opening night, filled with booze, he stormed into my dressing room shoving aside some posh visitors, including Lord Rayne, the Nat's board president, and the Oliviers, and berated me in his wondrously rich Welsh tones for calling the supporting company "a bunch of repertory assholes." "After that performance you gave tonight, boy-o," he hissed with biting sarcasm, "you've no right to say things like that!" My God! It was John Wilkes Booth, Edmund Kean and Dylan Thomas in white heat all rolled into one. As the guests scattered right and left, he stormed out. It had been by far the most theatrical moment of the night.

Nevertheless, the production was of great value, the first success the Nat had yet enjoyed that season, and working with Jonathan Miller was, to me, more than fascinating. He never dealt with the play literally or even directly, but came to it from many an oblique angle, telling witty stories, describing medical cases or great paintings, yet somehow it all related to what we were doing and clarified everything without ever boring as with textual analysis. Rehearsals therefore were the most interesting part of the process, but once we were in front of an audience and there was no Jonathan around to inspire us, cheer us on, our excitement waned.

One of the very few affectionate memories from that strange erratic season was an afternoon in London I shall never forget. It was the

A cartoonist's perception of my Danton

anniversary of the victory at Agincourt and the dean of Westminster arranged a celebration in the Abbey where, of course, famous young King Henry is interred. The dean collected all the best-known living "Henry the Fifths" and huddled us into the narrow choir stalls that form a direct path to the great altar. Filling both sides of the stalls, there we sat, all of us Henrys, staring at each other. Then the senior Henry of us all, Sir Laurence Olivier (who had just been made a peer) walked to the altar, turned and gave us the St. Crispin's Day speech to honour the occasion. He spoke it quite beautifully and, in deference to the location, very quietly with great dignity and simplicity. The silence was unbroken as those words echoed through the vastness of Westminster Abbey. High above our heads, the late-afternoon sun shone through the stained glass, casting long shafts of coloured light which spilled upon the ancient stones. It was a haunting moment—one could imagine that the shades of Garrick and Irving had stolen away from Poets' Corner and now stood in rapt attention among the dark shadows around us; and that even Henry of Monmouth himself, tiny Henry, had risen from his effigy in the next room and had come forward, his head pressed against the arches to listen in the stillness. It seemed that some six hundred years had slipped away and we were suddenly there, all of us, again at Agincourt—then the sun went behind a cloud and the moment vanished.

No matter what kind of success *Danton* enjoyed, the run was to be drastically short-lived, for already forces were at work, nefarious plans brewing behind the management doors on old Aquinas Street. O'Neill's *Long Day's Journey Into Night* was to be mounted next with Larry playing James Tyrone. No doubt spurred on by Tynan, the plan was that it should crown the end of a ropy season and save the day. But *Danton* stood in its way. Because of our success, I was under the impression that we had already carried the first reprieve, but clearly that did not suit the brass. There was only one course for them to take—delete *Danton* from the repertory. Jonathan Miller, not afraid to throw his mind about just as a bouncer throws his weight about, had made a lot of people with pretensions feel uneasy and inadequate—pseudointellectuals in particular. There was a great deal of envy and jealousy going on behind the scenes; to some, he was a threat. Extermination seemed the inevitable answer. So we slunked back into our cases wearing our green makeup for the last time, closed the glass doors behind us and died.

It is the strangest of paradoxes that the two major creative forces at the National, one of the foremost critics of the twentieth century and the world's most honoured actor, should together, each in his own way, be so indefinably insecure. It would take a few more years following that strange frustrating season, but Laurence Olivier's reign at the Nat was coming to an end. The rumours of Peter Hall's succession cast a long shadow of gathering power over those last days—and when the announcement of his appointment came, it was handled just as badly as everything else had been. Max, Lord Rayne (don't Rayne on my parade) and the National's board bungled it badly and, as usual, Larry was the last to find out. No one in those stifling little cubbyholes on Aquinas Street knew what the other was doing. The withholding of information, the backbiting, the bickering, the bitching, the intrigue continued right up to the end. I have this image of a giant Othello, like a great oak about to be felled, trying to remain upright while swarms of nasty little Iagos keep snapping at its trunk and gnawing away at its bark until at last, weakened at the base, it can stand no longer and comes crashing down to earth.

FUNNILY ENOUGH, Anthony Hopkins, who one day would win an Oscar and a knighthood in the same year, had the last laugh on all of us that season. Abominably treated as he had been, at last poetic justice had raised its righteous head. It came in the form of a small cassette, one of which I still have in my possession. Bored in his dressing room at the Nat, over several nights he brilliantly improvised into his recorder a satire on the state of the London theatre and the decline of its Old Guard. In it he portrays Alec Guinness and Laurence Olivier, their careers over, eking out a pitiful living as two camp old theatrical dressers. They constantly bitch to each other about the new wave of young talent that are taking over and being knighted in the process. A mimic of sheer genius, Hopkins manages to capture with uncanny accuracy the voices of all the leading lights of the London stage. Paul Scofield, Alan Badel, O'Toole, Burton, Finney, etc., and of course the senior group Guinness, Olivier, Richardson and Gielgud. On the cassette, Olivier eventually goes into hysterics as more young talent commands attention. He cannot bear, for instance, that his wife, Joan Plowright, has just been cast as Lear and even the National Theatre's doorman begins to present a threat. The last straw occurs when young Albert Finney drives up in his new Rolls and announces, "Allo lads! I've just bought the Old Vic and am turnin' it into a supermarket." Olivier, in a screeching falsetto, hurls himself off a parapet into the River Thames. There is a long silence—then Tony, in the famous doleful tones of Ralph Richardson, says quietly, "Ah, poor old Larry. Never could stand competition, you know."

CHAPTER THIRTY-SIX

A STORMY WEDDING AND
A TASTE OF PROVENCE

The Perspex doors and marble surround were still not in place at Hyde Park Gate, which meant anyone coming up the stairs into the master bedroom would be treated to full frontals of both of us taking a shower. Controlling my ire, I finally tracked down Doug Norwood and gave him a call. "Where's the marble, Dougie?" "Marble? What marble?" "You know what marble." "Oh, *that* marble." There was a slight pause. "It's not in the country yet." "Not in the country?" I repeated like an idiot. "No," said Dougie. "What country is it coming from then?" I hissed between clenched teeth. "Greece" was the casual reply. There was a shop in the lane right behind our house that sold and cut marble slabs to order. I had quite recently seen some very attractive pieces of white marble at reasonable prices just lying about waiting to be snapped up. I told him so. "Ah, but the Grecian variety is clean, unblemished, not a fleck in it," he assured me. I was about to explode when the lady of the house, Mademoiselle Elaine, came into the room. "Tita Wilson just received an official letter from your governor general. He can present you with your medals at a private ceremony in Quebec's Citadel this October." I hung up on Dougie.

Of course, I'd forgotten. Two years before, I had been awarded my country's highest civil honour, approved by Queen Elizabeth II—Companion of the Order of Canada—the honour that would have made my mother so proud. I had not been able to receive it in the public ceremony as I was out of the country. Ever since Canada had become a separate dominion, our then uptight dull little government issued an edict abolishing all titles previously conferred upon Canadians. How then were their achievements to be recognized? No one could any longer accept knighthoods or peerages. It was just another colourless gesture and a slap in the face to a country that could use some colour. A few enterprising individuals decided, therefore, that we create our own honours coupled with royal sanction. It worked. So my special order was in a sense an honorary knighthood, or as we irreverently dubbed it, "the consolation prize."

"What a great idea," I said to Elaine, "we'll sail over on the *France*. I'll show you New York. We'll take a first-class sleeper on the train up to Canada, then over to Quebec, pick up the prize, then on to Montreal, where we'll get married!" Neither of us was dying to marry. We were perfectly happy "living in sin," but certain countries and the occasional hotel were still rather old-fashioned about it, so we reluctantly agreed to relieve the pressure.

On the way over from Southampton, the *France* shuddered under one of the worst storms to hit the Atlantic in many a year. The first day, we rather enjoyed being blown all over the upper decks, but that night, things were getting really serious. Here was a liner equipped with the world's best stabilizers, bouncing about the ocean as if she were a dinghy. The fabulous dining room was closed for most of the trip; the ship keeled over on its side at what seemed a fixed angle of 45 degrees. At night, the vessel creaked ominously as it rolled about the angry sea. It was so noisy, the wind and rain joining in chorus, you could barely hear the dogs barking and howling on the top deck. Elaine spent most of the time in her bunk—I didn't realize how much she disliked being on the water. But brave mutt that she was, she never once complained. What had promised to be a soothing crossing replete with every luxury had turned into a replay of "The Wreck of the Hesperus."

The last day on board was noticeably calmer and we did manage to sample at least one sumptuous repast in the main dining room. "What time do we dock?" I asked a waiter. "Dans le région de sept heures au matin, monsieur." I tried to convince Elaine that the very best view of Manhattan was coming up the Hudson, going past the Statue of Liberty and meeting head-on the whole spectacular panorama of skyscrapers, their pinnacles reaching to the sky. We set our alarm clocks for 5:30 a.m. in order to arrive on deck early and time it right. We did. I held on to her hand tightly to prepare her for what was to come in case she fainted at first sighting—but alas! Neither *we*, nor *anyone* on deck that morning glimpsed even a hint of the Statue of Liberty, nor a smidgeon of the city. The Hudson River, the harbour, the entire metropolis, all were covered in the densest of pea-soup fogs—you couldn't see your hand in front of your face.

It was only when we disembarked at Pier 47 that the fog began to lift. While waiting for our luggage, Fuff was treated to her first encounter with New York humour. Two of the porters, tall, tough Irish denizens, were joking amongst themselves when a couple of gay male lovers came down the gangway with four Afghan hounds. One porter turned to the other and in his best longshoreman dialect shouted, "Heh! Get a load of dem faggot dawgs."

Jane Broder was there to meet us, God love her. Elaine fell for her at once and vice versa. We were taken to the hotel, a surprisingly seedy and run-down Algonquin, another disappointment, only to learn that most of my friends in town were away. Would you believe what I did? I took my bride-to-be to see my first wife, Tammy Grimes, who was starring with Brian Bedford in *Private Lives* on Broadway, simply because she was the only person I knew left in the city. I even took Fuff backstage afterwards to meet her. How about that for tact?! However, we were soon boarding the train for Montreal. It was an overnight trip and the moment we entered our stateroom, which looked most comfortable, we hit the sack. We woke hours later as dawn was breaking outside the window. It was absolutely freezing in the compartment. We peered out. "Are those the Rockies?" she asked, not too familiar with U.S. geography. "No, I think they're just tall telephone lines and highrises." But I didn't recognize anything I was seeing. The train was not moving. "Where are we?" I asked a passing porter. It appeared there had been a power failure. We had barely started and were stuck a mile or two outside New York City. Finally we got going, both of us clutching each other to keep warm. To add to the horror, the trip to the border took another whole day. We were consoled by the beauty of Quebec City and the fact that I was being privately presented with my honour by the governor general himself in the throne room of the old historic Citadel. I imagined for a brief moment a fantasy that I was Wolfe accepting the surrender of Montcalm as the shimmering reflection of the St. Lawrence River played upon its fortress walls. And then lunch would follow with Their Excellencies à quatre!

The next day, we left that most European of North American cities for Montreal and my old stomping ground, the Ritz-Carlton, where we hit the Maritime Bar with no uncertain vengeance. The next morning, I took my bride-to-be for a long walk up the steep streets so she could see all the old mansions that had once enjoyed a proud past; and then onto the higher slopes of Mount Royal—nostalgic for me, bewildering for her, but she patiently humoured me. Poor thing, I was dragging her

Alice and Toby Johnson, who bravely gave us away

all over my town hoping to God she'd like it. On our wanderings, we passed the great stone wall that surrounded the old estate Raven'scrag. I half wondered if I might catch a glimpse of that woman in tweeds and scarf hurrying along by the wall whom I had seen haunting the place several times before, but there was no one about, just the sound of falling leaves and the swirling winds. "What are you looking for?" I heard Elaine say. "Oh, nothing," I lied. I felt embarrassed and too much of a fool to tell her.

THE ONLY PEOPLE at our wedding service the next day were my old childhood friend Toby Johnson (Polly's son) and his wife, Alice, who acted as best man and bridesmaid, respectively. The minister, Reverend Phillip Moreton of the Unitarian Church on Sherbrooke Street, had just remarried Elizabeth Taylor and Richard Burton there, quietly, without any hoohah. He was tall and exceptionally handsome with a beautiful speaking voice, which made the verses sing and gave our service an unexpected romance. Afterwards, Toby, Alice, and Mr. and Mrs. Plummer enjoyed a giggly, pissy lunch at the Ritz. It was the smallest and best wedding ever.

Next day, Toby took us out to Senneville to see Polly in her new abode—a charming old stone cottage of early French Canadian style, which had been one of the gardener's cottages on the estate. Polly, of course, had been forced off her island by the building of the Trans-Canada Highway Bridge, which tore right through the center of it with its great pylons and towered above it. Most of the island had gone. Gone was the house, the stables, the tennis courts, the beautiful inlet with its herons and water lilies; just a few sad trees by the lake remained to remind one there had once been an island there. Progress had torn asunder this particular paradise, but as expected, Polly's stoic spirit and her humour bore her along splendidly. I had always looked for her approval in everything; it had become second nature to me, and after lunch was over she put her arm around my bride and gave me a huge assuring wink. The brief reunion had been a welcome tonic, but it saddened me that Elaine would never see the magic island about which I had regaled her so often.

Once back in London, a few weeks had passed before we learned that the Unitarian Church where we'd tied the knot had burned down—evidently torched by a mad lady organist, who had seriously suffered from unrequited love for the handsome reverend. Toby and Alice reported that only the church's basic structure remained standing, that the roof was no longer there and the smoke-filled gaping hole was open to the sky. Had all our vows flown through the open roof to be scattered on the winds? Or was it merely the collective smouldering of passions that had suddenly ignited those sacred walls?

TITA (Don't-Shoot-the-Messenger) WILSON and her cheery, breezy manner were both there at the front door of no. 9 to greet us on our return with the surprising news that the unmentionable marble sur-round from Greece had at last arrived. "It's in one piece, a perfect circle and it's flawless," she reported with a devilish wink. "But how are we going to get it up to the fourth floor?" we asked nervously. "Don't ask me. Let's just have a drink!" I called Dougie and repeated the question. "We'll hoist it up by crane from the street below." "How is it going to get through the windows?" "We'll have to cut it in half, but not to worry; you'll never see the join." The day arrived. The men took one look at the windows above and shrugged helplessly. Oh, they got it in all right, but they had to cut it up in four pieces to get it through. That was the day I fired Dougie.

Tita turned up again the next day with the news that during our absence the Invicta had docked! It had been most carefully packed and there was not a scratch on it. Good ol' Jane Broder had seen to that. We put it in a garage I rented just down the lane behind the house. A total rehauling was in order—the engine examined and authenticated, the floors rebuilt, a new hood put on, the weepers and side-flaps seen to—it needed a lot of TLC. Tita, in her marvellously offhand way, proved once again invaluable. "I think I have just the man for you—he can be the greatest help." "Who's that," I asked. She blushed. I don't think I'd ever seen "Teets" blush unless it was a blood-rush from too much champagne. "My new friend." She actually primped. Now our Teets was used to a lot of romantic liaisons and took them all in her stride, but this time it looked serious. He was a Scot, handsome, blond, very Nordic in appearance, with a bucolic charm. He tried to drink everyone under the table but only succeeded in getting himself there first. He wore the same old sports coat with elbow patches and the same corduroy trousers day in and day out and loved beyond anything a good Indian curry. He also loved Tita and his name was Angus Clydesdale.

The Marquess of Clydesdale (the famed horses were named after his family, not the other way around) would upon his father's death become the fifteenth Duke of Hamilton and Brandon, Scotland's premier dukedom and titular head of the church. Once one of the most powerful families in that country for centuries, they had owned a huge landmass as well as large tracts in Canada and generous chunks of Florida. They had many castles—Broddick, Linlithgow, amongst others—as well as the immense Hamilton Palace, which had been destroyed in the nineteen twenties. However, over the years, their power and their fortunes had diminished, and they were now hanging on as land-poor lairds. When the Nazi Rudolf Hess came to England on that abortive mission for Adolf Hitler, his plane landed by mistake in Scotland on Angus's father's estates. Two of the Duke's old retainers and some farmhands apprehended Hess—called the authorities and Herr Hess spent the rest of his life in an English prison.

Angus inherited his mother's passion for music and we would compare our collections of classical albums, which in both our cases was considerable—especially opera. His favourite tenor was diStephano, mine was Bjeurling, and we would fight over which of them was superior. Angus also raced cars quite competitively. Ferraris were his preference, though I could never see how he could afford such an expensive pastime. He was serious about it, however, and raced at the Grand Prix and at Brand's Hatch. I showed him my Invicta—his mouth watered.

"I have some mechanics in Lincolnshire," he told me, "who will rehaul the whole thing, paint it, reupholster it, everything, for very little money. It'll probably take a year, but it'll be worth it, you'll see."

Well, it did take a year, but what a job they made of it! My beautiful Invicta was now painted a traditional British Racing Green, all the chrome so highly polished I could see my ugly puss in it, silver spokes in the wheels instead of red, a light beige interior, and the engine completely restored and polished just as it was in 1931. The whole procedure cost me no more than fifteen hundred pounds, an outright steal. Angus, the hero of the hour, and I took turns spinning it around Hyde Park. It ran as smoothly as a new Rolls, and when I took it into the countryside it actually gathered speed going uphill in high gear—a miraculous machine altogether! The BBC came to the house and filmed it for a documentary on antique and vintage automobiles. They informed me that, according to their research, there remained only twenty of my vintage in the world.

Things were looking up. Even though we were still very much on full frontal view while taking showers, good old no. 9 had all the potential of a being a most elegant townhouse. But the indulgent era we were living in was just about over and taxwise the Labour government had crippled every professional who was earning a decent living wage. It was no joke—people were leaving Great Britain like lemmings and my accountants advised that we seek foreign residence and place both our houses, nos. 9 and 15 on the market. What a boring PM was Harold Wilson! So it was good-bye to the good life in London, alas, but my fantasies as a grand seigneur were by no means over. But where to exercise them? "Why not the south of France?" suggested my better half. "You've always loved it there. And I don't mean by the sea where all the cigar smoke is. I'm talking of Provence—in the hills, where it's *real* and a tenth of the price."

About a quarter of the way down the road to Marseille from Antibes you will come upon the Frégus exit. There you turn right and head straight up into the hills of Var. It took us about forty-five minutes before we found the village of Bargemon, typical of the region, nestled comfortably on a hillside—its inhabitants, mildly helpful, staunchly socialistic, carefully guarding its secrets. The real estate agent, a Monsieur Bertaito (of course we called him "Potato" behind his back) took us through the town and up a steep road to the top of a hill. We stopped for a moment at a broken-down gate which opened onto a long drive. The drive was wildly overgrown, weeds and grass profusely smothering the cobblestones. Flanking the drive on either side was a long row of

Elaine "Fuff" Plummer with young "Sam" in our spanking new Invicta

lime trees. They had bent over and were growing into each other, forming an arch. It was as if they were embracing and all you could see at the
end of the drive was a single shuttered doorway—nothing more. We
didn't have to say anything except, "We'll take it!" "But, madame et
monsieur, you have seen nothing yet." "Monsieur Potato or Bertaito, it
doesn't matter—we'll take it."

Le Pavillon de Favas, or so the house was called, was a nineteenth-
century manor in bad disrepair. Yet it was simple and attractive—
shuttered windows, a fireplace in every room, even in the master
bathroom. Next to the manor circling a cobbled courtyard was a large
garage, an old boulangerie, a laundry house, two charming old barns
and about four hundred yards up another hill, a smaller manor house
presumably for guests. "How marvellous! We can have our own private
village," we chimed. But above all, it was the surrounding land that
made it so seductive. On the north side of the main house were trees of
every variety—huge oaks and giant elms, most unusual in these parts,
but thriving nonetheless. If you looked through them far into the distance, you could see the snow-covered peaks of the Basse Alpes, summer and winter. On the south side were different levels descending a
long steep hill to a rushing stream at the foot of the valley. They must
have once been formal terraces which now were nothing but a jungle of
overgrown raspberry bushes, damson plums, fraises des bois, every
known variety of wild berries and fruit.

Also growing all over the open fields in abundance were black truffles upon which herds of wild boar continuously fed. On the other side of the stream, the land rose dramatically to become a mountainous slope covered by a dense pine forest, and if your eye focused to the east, you could glimpse the Mediterranean, shimmering in the sun far down the valley. Potato also pointed out the open slopes on both sides of the main road impatiently waiting to yield grapes. "You can make five thousand bottles of your own vin blanc et rosé every year and, if you join the commune, you can go into serious business!" He was all smiles—there was no question; it was a Provençal paradise, and there were six hundred acres of it.

The next step was to audition for the two old ladies who owned the property. I drove all the way to Marseille with Potato in tow to visit the old crones. It was like sitting between two Madames Defarge. When they spoke, which was rare, the mixture of Niçoise and Marseillaise was so thick I understood not a word. I also felt they didn't approve of me, so I left them alone for a moment with Potato. On our way back to Bargemon, I broke the silence. "Well? What do they want for it?" "In English money? Sixty thousand pounds," he replied. I couldn't believe my luck. "Pour tous?" I said, stunned. Potato looked at me and shrugged, "Pour tous!"

The three of us celebrated our triumph at a small auberge (four stars) in Bargemon which would become our local. A six-course meal that made every upscale eatery in the vicinity of the ocean pale in comparison cost a mere 250 francs. Over a delicious local Marc, which le patron liberally poured on the house, Potato persuaded us to hire an armed guardien to check the place every day—to pare down the number of wild boar and keep squatters out. We were beginning to realize just how wild it was up there with no one about. The next item on the agenda was to find a builder. Potato again came to the rescue. "There is, monsieur, an Englishman who lives close by avec beaucoup de talent— il connait tous les gens dans le région qui peux travailler avec lui."

It was then that Tom Wilson (no relation of Tita's), a tall, aesthetic young Brit, came into our lives. He had already designed a phenomenal swimming pool for the famous Villa Fiorentina at St. Jean Cap Ferrat, which has often been seen in all the major magazines. On a more modest scale he had done over small country estates and cottages with consummate taste. Tom had a great knowledge and affection for the Provençal countryside. Every morning, he would wander from café to café in the little towns, gathering his workers for the day. While they sat enjoying their morning coffee and chocolat, he would join them, buy them a Pernod or Ricard, talk money and then, with his tiny regiment in tow, head for the hills and *us*!

Tom and his Japanese wife lived on a fascinating piece of property in nearby Auribeau-sur-Siagne. It was called Clavary and was owned by his father, Sir Peter Wilson, then head of Sotheby's. We went to dinner there and much admired two surrounding houses Tom had designed and built, one for himself and one for his brother. They were classically modern, made from indigenous stone, and had huge floor-to-ceiling glass windows—no view was spared. The main house, which had been there forever, was a tall, narrow structure reminiscent of Vita Sackville-West's famous Sissinghurst tower in Kent. It also had a completely circular entrance hall. At one point Picasso had stayed at Clavary, and, to while away his time, he painted in the center of the white tiled floor a matador killing a bull from horseback—magnificent figures all in black. So anyone coming to visit through the front door would be actually walking over a Picasso masterpiece.

Thankfully, Tom was madly attracted to our Pavillon de Favas, and he and his battalion began to work wonders. He transformed the garage into a vast Provençal kitchen with enormous squares of local sandstone tile covering the entire length of the floor. He had the little shed opposite the manor gutted and turned it into an adorable apartment for us to live in while the rest of the place was being restored. Tom proved to be not overly expensive either, but this was merely a small dent in what looked to be a hugely ambitious lifetime project. Our excitement knew no bounds, and we were just becoming accustomed to our new seductive rhythm of life, when a message from our accountants in London to stop all work on Favas came like a stab through the heart.

The French government, as was their wont, suddenly and capriciously changed their laws so that all foreign residents were to be taxed on their *world* earnings—rather foolish, as every foreign resident would be forced to flee the country, leaving a considerable dent in France's economy. The Gauls, acknowledging their folly, attempted to change the law three or four years later, but it was all too late. Everyone had located somewhere else. The film industry in Europe was suffering, ditto in England, due to unions and the shortsightedness of the Wilson government, which was teetering on its last legs. It was time to go back to America where television and film were beginning to boom once again, and all was business as usual now that the Vietnam War was mercifully over. Everyone's life had changed, British parliament toppled, clothes had become more conservative, a dullness was creeping into the seventies and Sir Peter Wilson would be suspected of being the "Fifth Man, along with John Cairncross," in the Philby, Maclean, Burgess, Blunt Soviet spy ring!

So, bidding a teary farewell to Tom, Fuff and I flew back to London to await our fate. And sadly, Le Pavillon de Favas and all its promise became just another cloud-capped tower. I'm not much for yearning through life. I prefer to get on with things. But the one thing I do regret most terribly is the day when we learned that we must leave all that enchantment behind.

CHAPTER THIRTY-SEVEN

I PLAY THE PALACE

B ack in the swim of London, we saw a lot of Tita and her marquess, our rendezvous taking place mostly on Fulham Road, where we devoured Indian curries by the bushel. They were in good form, happy, a little squiffy, but still very much in love. We missed John Kirby in our lives, however. I think the horrors of *Waterloo* had got to him and he was avoiding me in case I took him through another such experience. Fuff had got herself a BBC television programme, playing Rose Trelawny in *Trelawny of the Wells,* with a distinguished cast, but we were really just hanging about on hold, as it were, waiting for a good enough reason to take us to the United States. We found one—in the guise of an old friend, Cyrano de Bergerac.

Richard Gregson, now separated from Natalie Wood, who had gone back to her old love Robert "R.J." Wagner, was one of London's top literary agents with clients such as screenwriters Robert Bolt and Frederic Raphael. He never handled actors as a rule but occasionally would lower himself to take care of the odd stray—like me. Today, however, he was happily playing the role of producer. The two of us were hosting a small lunch for three at Le Vendôme on Albemarle Street. Our esteemed and only guest was that mercurially mad maverick, that wizard of words, the distinguished author and Elizabethan scholar Anthony Burgess. Richard and I had just offered him a commission to write what we were positive would be the definitive English version of *Cyrano,* Rostand's chef d'oeuvre. Burgess expressed his love of the work and, egged on by our enthusiasm and the prospect of ready cash, which Richard and I had split (a meager five hundred pounds), he leapt at the idea.

Until then there had existed in a major way only Brian Hooker's old, familiar warhorse version, somewhat stiffly Victorian in its manner, with a trifle too much sentimentality creeping in. It had, over the years, served rather nobly a number of English Cyranos from Walter Hampden to Ralph Richardson to José Ferrer to yours truly. But it didn't echo the rich robust flow of the original French. Neither was it as funny or as free. Burgess pounded the table so that all the glasses jumped in the air. "One must restore the alexandrine rhythm—it's the only thing that gives it life!" "We'll drink to that," we chorused in a barbershop duet. "But," said Richard, "once you've completed that massive task, Chris and I want to do it as a musical. Will you consider writing the lyrics?" Burgess mumbled something indistinguishable into his vichyssoise that could have been a yes, but he was clearly fired up for having the chance to give back to the stage, which he did with much panache, creating a work that sang with all the muscle and true music of the English language and the closest thing to Rostand's child that has ever been. There is no need to elaborate further, for this man, who joins the tiny list of geniuses I have had the fortune to meet, succeeded not just brilliantly but, as expected, definitively.

The world premiere of this new work would take place at the Guthrie Theatre in Minneapolis where my old mentor Michael Langham, who was to stage it, was artistic director. I was to play the new Cyrano, but, cursed with my usual mistiming, I got stuck in some "Four Walls" flick in Britain and was forced to withdraw. Paul Hecht, a fine actor and a fellow Canadian, appeared in my stead and gave a superb performance—damn it! I would have been easily moved to incendiary jealousy were it not that Burgess had dedicated the play to me, for which I shall always be insufferably proud.

Next on the agenda was the musical. Burgess quite rightly felt he had already delivered the most important and significant part of the bargain but resigned himself with a great deal of grumbling to undertake the lyrics. The "book" of course was already there in the shape of the play and it would be interrupted by music where certain speeches would be transformed into song. The big problem was to find a composer of sufficient note who could attempt to match the music of the poetry. Alan Jay Lerner had been right, "Nobody's going to want to compete with that language—you can't fight City Hall." It seemed a futile search, but crazy Mr. Burgess, bless his eccentric heart, came up with one—a talented young Welshman named Michael J. Lewis, who, though not widely known, had made a decent living so far composing film scores. "We'll muck through it together," said Anthony. "Don't worry, I'm fast and he'll bloody well have to keep up!"

True to his word, Burgess turned up at no. 9, dragging a rather worn-out young Michael with him. "We've come to play you a number or two." I called Richard and told him to report pronto. Michael sat down at my beloved Grotrian-Steinway, and Burgess half spoke, half sang the lyrics. One song was Cyrano's and the other Roxanne's. My song supposedly came at the end of act 1, a paean of worship for Paris, the city of lovers, which turns into a rollicking rabble rouser to bring down the curtain, "From Now Till Forever." It was terrifically in the right spirit, but Roxanne's song, "You Have Made Me Love," was exceptional and highly emotional—it had the necessary musical sweep. Anthony's lyrics sounded amazingly in tune with the play; after all, it was *his* play now. Richard and I couldn't believe so much had been accomplished so soon. That afternoon gave us the assurance that "Cyrano, the Musical" might just bloody well work.

Now we were obliged to find the ideal backer/presenter with guts enough to get behind it and give it a shove. For months already, Richard had been in touch with Ray Stark, the Hollywood suit who ran Seven Arts Productions, a prestigious and highly touted film company. When we had visited him in LA in an office that Mussolini would have lusted after, he was both ingratiating and pretentious. He would buzz his assistant in some distant cubicle and loftily call out, "Bring me the *Cyrano* file" or some such stuff. Once in his suite at the Dorchester (soon after breaking his leg skiing for which he had all his wardrobe remade by a Savile Row tailor with zippers up the side to accommodate his cast) he said in his most patronizing manner, "Ah, Chris, I think you'll be very good in the part, but you've got to get into shape and prepare. I don't want you to accept any other work for at least a year while we market this and build up the suspense." It was as if I'd never attempted the role, in his view. True, Mr. Stark was a marketing expert, a seasoned promoter, but it was plain to see that everything to do with this was going to be all about *him*. Richard and I exchanged a look, which read,

"Can you believe this bullshit?" Ray Stark behaved as if Edmond Rostand and Burgess were just more hacks in his stable full of writers. Whether this project was too risky for him to touch or he never had any real intention to pursue it at all, his interest in the matter soon waned but not as rapidly as did ours in him.

At last Richard, after much rummaging, was rewarded. A truly genuine angel in the person of Herb Alpert, he of the Tijuana Brass and a staggeringly lucrative record company, agreed to take over the production and to raise the moolah. What I had dreamed of long before those *Sound of Music* days was actually about to happen. By God, it was on!

The phone rang at no. 9. "Honey, it's Jane." "Jane?" "Jane Broder, who do you think it is!" "Where are you?" "I'm in London, honey, at the Connaught Hotel—you know, the one you told me about. I've got some papers for you to sign." "You made the trip all alone?" I queried, astonished, for she was an old lady now. "Sure, honey, why not? So come on over already. I'll be in the lobby." Elaine and I obediently heeded the summons. As we came through the hotel's front door, I could see her sitting in the big armchair, under the grandfather clock—a great vantage point for checking on who was coming or going. She was attired in her usual black with the little jaunty hat covered with a veil, head tilted slightly forward. Mr. Gustave came to meet us. "This lady's been waiting here for you for quite some time. She hasn't moved from this chair. I don't think she's very well." We came closer. "Jane?" I began. She seemed to be asleep. I nudged her—she slowly looked up and half smiled. She tried to speak, but only a slurred sound came from her lips and there was some saliva running down her chin. The three of us looked down at her. Mr. Gustave, breaking the silence, said, "I think she may have had a little stroke, sir. I'll fetch the hotel doctor right away." I noticed there was an envelope clutched tightly in her hand. I pried it from her grasp, opened it and saw it was my contract. She had come all this way to deliver it in person. "I never trust anyone else with it, honey," she had always said. We helped her up to her room. The doctor came and confirmed the stroke. "She mustn't leave her bed for the next few days. Then she better fly back to America where her own doctors can look after her." It didn't take long for Jane to disobey instructions. "I'm dying to see your house. I'm coming over." "But Jane—" "Don't argue, honey. I'm all right; don't worry." She came over two days later bustling with energy. We were having such a good time—she seemed more her old self than ever. But her speech was affected somewhat and I found it difficult to banish from my mind the awful thought that perhaps she didn't have very long. But now it was time to honour that blessed contract and the lady who carried the torch, time to buckle myself into my sword belt and stick on the large nose once more. "Don't send me dwarves. Bring me giants."

At the Guthrie in Minneapolis, Michael Langham began staging it with the same high style he had done in the past, but the result was a trifle too static for a musical and it was clear that we needed a top choreographer to move it along. Gregson and Alpert pulled the best rabbit out of the hat that money could buy and in a run-through just before the dress rehearsal in walked that miracle man of dance whom Agnes de Mille had let loose upon the world, Michael Kidd. Kidd, best known for his *Guys and Dolls* (stage and screen) and *Seven Brides for Seven Brothers,* among many another gem, was the most original and dynamic of all pre-Fosse innovators. It would have been ideal had Langham been in charge of the text and Kidd the musical numbers, but both men were too individual in their fields, too talented and too proud to settle for that. Kidd laid down the law firmly but with his customary twinkle. "If I'm not in total control, I walk!" He was right, of course. At this stage, the show needed a musical autocrat, so Langham gracefully gave up the reins. The cast, who had loved Langham, now fell in love all over again for M. Kidd—a dynamo who began to move the piece with such energy, vitality and humour, it was very difficult to catch one's breath.

The cast was a treat. Leigh Beery, a lovely lady with a most beautiful soprano, played Roxanne. Handsome young Mark Lamos, who later became a well-known stage and opera director, was our Christian. As Cyrano's old chum Le Bret, a very fine actor from Canada bubbling with charm, James Blendick, exuded such warmth in the role I had to fight extra hard to wrest some of the audience's sympathy from him. Although I missed the great John Colicos as le Comte de Guiche (he was sadly unavailable), Louis Turenne, who had enormous style, filled his shoes admirably and brought all the required grandeur to the evening. Arnold Soboloff, who excelled in eccentric comedy, gave a rich performance as the baker Ragueneau and all the dancers and supers had the proper period look, not always easy to find on Broadway.

Michael Lewis, at Kidd's insistence, kept plying me with new numbers as if I hadn't enough to do just playing the huge role itself. There was "From Now Till Forever," of course; then to replace the famous "No Thank You" speech, a solo number called not surprisingly, "No Thank You." Then the "Nose Song" to be sung during that exhausting duel with Ken Campbell as de Valvert. There was also a duet with Rox-

The old *Cyrano*

anne called "Bergerac" and my favourite, "I Never Loved You," which I sang as the dying Cyrano. There is no question I was "oversonged," and my singing voice, never much to write home about anyway, was beginning to feel the strain.

There is a scene with de Guiche in the play where a masked Cyrano jumps out of a tree, frightens de Guiche and tells him he has just landed from the moon. In the play, the scene works admirably, but in a musical, it is far too long and talky. It is an important one, however, and can't really be cut—what was one to do? Kidd instinctively knew. "The whole thing should be turned into one insane madly funny song. It's the eleventh hour and the audience will need to be kept awake. Where's Anthony?" "Just flew in from Rome," I said. "You go tell him, he doesn't always listen to me." I found Anthony in one of the offices. "We need a song urgently—a short one that replaces the whole moon scene." There was a long silence. Burgess, who always thought of song lyrics as utterly banal, gave me an icy glare and said, "All right, get out of here—give me ten minutes." I thought he was kidding, but in approximately ten, he came out of the office and handed me the new number scribbled on a piece of paper. It was just a series of unfinished sentences and it was the wittiest, zaniest, maddest piece of magic in the whole piece. He called it "On the Thither, Thother, Thide of The . . ." and it stopped the show!

In Toronto at the Royal Alexandra, where we next took it, I expressed my desire to make my first entrance swinging from a chandelier. This would be fairly risky as I would have to jump from a balcony on the set, catch hold of the chandelier and swing down to the stage below. A crew member offstage would control the rope attached, keeping it at a fairly safe speed so I could land on my two feet as gracefully as possible. This worked pretty well for a few performances, but one night the man in charge had got himself nicely pickled (beware alcoholic stagehands) and let go of the rope at the wrong time. I hit the floor so fast and hard I saw stars for several seconds and kept bouncing up and down rather like the Marx Brothers emerging from the elevator crash. We scrubbed that entrance idea quickly enough and I decided instead to jump onto the stage from an adjacent box in the dress circle—not quite so effective but twice as safe.

The next city was Boston where we were an instant hit. "Good," said slave driver Kidd. "We can stay here a few extra weeks and keep working on the show." Gregson and Alpert kept firing one conductor after another, so whenever I came on to the stage I never knew who was wielding the baton. All of them worked with a different tempi—it was absolutely terrifying. The Palace Theatre, where we were to open in New York, was still fully occupied with another show and a few more weeks went by before it was ready. It was now going into May in New York—very late to open anything—but we finally moved into the famous old building. We had played eight long prosperous weeks in Boston. It had been hugely popular—we could have easily stayed for the whole summer.

The Palace, if it could talk, would tell tales of its history that could leave one staggering. Of the many great ones who had trodden its boards, it was the "Divine Sarah" (appearing there more than once as part of her many farewell tours), who made it her own. Her dressing room was not on stage level. It was in the basement. She'd picked it as it was the roomiest one in the theatre. But because of her amputation and the fact that she hobbled about on a wooden leg, she had demanded that a lift be installed so she could ascend to the stage with ease. It was still there when I moved in and still operating, believe it or not. I was not in the least intimidated by her ghostly aura. After all, the play was French; I was Cyrano himself, and La Bernhardt had once played Roxanne to my role's creator, Constant Coquelin. It all seemed perfectly natural and right—like an anniversary of sorts, a celebration of

Cyrano *poster and record cover*

nineteenth-century Theatre Français where the spirits of both those old superstars could come to my aid.

Enfin, everything was now in readiness. The orchestration was placed into the hands of Philip J. Lang, our final music arranger. We now had a permanent conductor who would be there every night and who knew how to deal with actors. Kidd, with his perpetual cheerful countenance and generous heart, rallied us one final time. Burgess and Lewis nervously mumbled their messages of luck and bundled off to the nearest bar. Richard and Alpert & Co. took up their places standing at the back of the stalls biting their nails. It was a Sunday night; the place was packed. I shared the elevator with the Divine Sarah on my way to the stage. Behind the curtain, I heard the rousing overture begin—yes, we'd opened! What a splendid first night. What a reception! Everyone I knew in New York was there. Vince Sardi was the most gracious host. It was a high—Cyrano's little standard fluttered triumphantly aloft. I was to win the Tony and all the attending prizes; everyone in it was praised. Kidd's direction, Leigh Beery's Roxanne, Desmond Heeley's gorgeous sets, Anthony's play was golden—but not, alas, the musical. Leigh's songs were touted—they all had the proper size. Everyone agreed Lewis's score was charming and elegant, but there was no main "hit" song to really lift it off the ground. There was no "Impossible Dream" as in *Man of La Mancha* or "This Nearly Was Mine" from *South*

Pacific, and even if there had been, I would not have had the vocal power to sing them. No matter how beautifully Michael Kidd had moved it, the Burgess/Rostand words simply overwhelmed and swept everything before them.

No, to do a Cyrano musical, one must throw the great Rostand, that scene-stealer, out the window, make a clean sweep and start from scratch. Go back to Cyrano's own story, *Voyages to the Moon and Sun,* and begin from there—the real Cyrano, da Vinci's disciple, who tried to invent the balloon and succeeded, in a way, but like Howard Hughes's wooden masterpiece, *The Spruce Goose,* it did not remain airborne for very long. Start the evening with Cyrano in his balloon, falling out of the sky and crashing to earth. As long as the stagehands stay sober, that would be some entrance for the Great Schnozz, I'll wager.

CHAPTER THIRTY-EIGHT

CHEKHOV AND SIMON, KIPLING AND HUSTON

Neil Simon is the consummate professional. From gag writer to playwright, he has structured with architectural precision, play after play, sketch after sketch, to achieve phenomenal success. His mathematical formula has hardly ever let him down. He is so successful in fact that as a fairly young playwright he owned his own theatre, the Eugene O'Neill on West Forty-ninth Street. I can think of only two other playwrights in history who boasted a theatre of their own—Richard Brinsley Sheridan in Restoration times, and Edgar Wallace in the early twentieth century—both in London. Now, as I write, there is yet another theatre on the famous West Side that proudly bears the name of Simon.

A modest unassuming man in life, he nevertheless radiates a confidence in knowing how to get laughs in his sleep and how to design for the stage his particular sort of comedy—very New York Jewish. He knows the "street" and the characters that live on it like the back of his

hand. He even talks to you in one-liners. A Neil Simon play on Broadway is almost certain to be a surefire hit.

However, the general verdict has always been that his work, though
not quite of the boulevard variety, is alas, a mite short on substance.
But then why must he be anything other than hilariously funny or
warmly human? What on earth is wrong with that? But "Doc" Simon
was not content to remain so and decided to raise the bar a moitier by
adapting several short stories by his hero Anton Chekhov and turning
them into a play called *The Good Doctor.* The leading character is
Chekhov himself who talks to the audience, introduces the stories and
then becomes a character in each of them. One is high comedy, one is a
warm human yarn and one or two are outright farce. For the actors, it is
a delightful exercise in versatility.

His habitual producer and friend Emanuel "Manny" Azenberg, to
my pleasant surprise, arranged a meeting with Simon and me at the
Russian Tea Room. As most of my theatre life had been spent in the
classics, this promised to be a welcome change. I was also highly flattered that the Azenberg-Simon entourage seemed to trust me with
their brand of comedy. I got to like them immediately. They were
relaxed and funny, and I found Doc so easy to deal with simply because
he took on the habit of a fellow worker with no time for personal griev-
ances or the flexing of egos. He loved his profession so totally he
allowed nothing to impede progress or stand in his way. "How's your
memory?" he asked me. "Because I change things all the time, and I'll
throw a lot of new stuff at you every night." "Fine with me," I swag-
gered. I could see there was no chance I would ever be bored.

He was as good as his word. While we rehearsed onstage, we could
hear him typing away in a dressing room just behind the flats. Before
the end of the day I generally ended up with a new script. During the
tryout later in New Haven in front of the audience, I could hear him
typing away furiously in the background. It was deafening. Even
falling madly in love with Marsha Mason, who was playing the young
ingenue roles, didn't deter him. In fact, it spurred him on. He was his
own severest critic. He would slash and delete wonderful material at a
second's notice and give me his rewrites—most of them far superior.
However, he sometimes got bored and changed his dialogue purely for
the sake of change, a weakness which he was reluctant to conquer. One
night, he handed me a long speech he'd just written. "It goes into the
second act," he whispered urgently. "Can you learn it during intermission?" This was becoming a sort of Russian roulette. All at once, he

(clockwise from left) Me, Marsha Mason, René Auberjonois,
Barnard Hughes, Frances Sternhagen

decided to use the small orchestra in the pit for more practical purposes than mere background atmosphere, deleting whole scenes in favour of a song or two. I remember I had to sing at least two numbers, one rather mawkish ditty about "Little Toby Dogs"—for the life of me I could not see what bearing it had on anything at all.

Neither Fuff nor I wanted to live in the city, so we rented an adorable cottage perched right on the Sound at Bell Island, Connecticut. It belonged to Barron Polan who once managed Judy Garland and my ex-wife Tammy. Of course, it was winter now and we needed a car for the daily commute to the theatre. A friend, Dale Sarjent, who had driven me during *Cyrano* but now had an important job to go to, suggested we employ his sister Deborah. I got myself a big new Cadillac and did just that. Debs was an extremely pretty if a trifle tomboyish girl of eighteen. She was aggressive, efficient, had a lot of anger, was outspoken, fought constantly with her parents, Joan and Alex, had a fierce pride in everything she did, and we liked her a lot. We actually came to love her and she has remained both a friend and an ally to us, the very best kind, over the years. She was a terrific driver—if you liked speed and danger— but she always got me wherever I had to be in one piece, if a few years older. If someone was in her way or holding her up, she'd roll down the window and a salvo of obscenities would escape her mouth. Once in the city, this Boadicea of the wheel could make a cab driver wish he'd never gotten off the boat!

She would sit at the back of the theatre during rehearsals and get very impatient with me if I muffed a line. She seemed to know the whole damn play by heart. I think she became more exhausted by the changes Neil threw at me than I did. When "Little Toby Dogs" was introduced she learned it before me and would sing it to me in the car, with gestures, going full speed. Terror stricken tho I was, she did make me laugh!

A. J. Antoon, who had been praised highly as a director of the moment (*That Championship Season*), had been put in charge. We slowly discovered he was not exactly suitable for the material. The production team also thought, I am positive, that as he was a serious student of the Drama, he would understand the whimsical side of Chekhov and take care of that department with ease. But A.J., a devout Jesuit, seemed devoid of any humour. Now I've known one or two Jesuits who had terrific senses of humour, but in his case, being one certainly didn't help. I remember at a run-through early on, René Auberjonois, that splendid player so adept at wistful and outrageous comedy, had brought on all of his own design a new, hilariously inventive interpretation of his role as an experiment. He, like everyone else in the cast (the incomparable trio, Barnard Hughes, Marsha Mason, Frances Sternhagen), had been getting no help whatsoever, not that that experienced threesome needed much. When he was giving his notes afterwards, A.J. insensitively remonstrated René in front of everybody, telling him in no uncertain terms that he wasn't in the least bit funny. This was strange as we had all fallen about watching him. Looking helpless, René shrugged, "Well, tell me what I should do then." A.J. stared at him through his rimless glasses and snapped, "Just be funny."

Actors are vulnerable creatures who need encouragement constantly, so René went into a blue funk for the next few days, as did we all. Realizing he had lost our respect and finding himself uncomfortably at odds with the Simon formula, A.J. became defensive and began to sulk. He would not address anyone in the cast directly—only through a stage manager. At the first dress rehearsal wearing the sumptuously made costumes that Tony Walton had designed, I stopped for a brief moment to ask a technical question about the lighting. From the darkened theatre came the voice of the stage manager: "Mr. Antoon asks you not to stop but to proceed without further interruption." I was dumbfounded.

Then I remembered my name was above the title and decided to take full advantage. I walked to the front of the stage and called very quietly in the dark to Azenberg. "Manny," I said, "could I speak to you for a moment?" In two seconds he'd climbed onto the stage and was whispering in my ear, "Don't worry, he'll be gone tomorrow."

There are any number of directors who would give their eyeteeth to work for "Doc" Simon, but he wanted one in particular—the most sought-after musical director on Broadway, that precocious whiz kid Michael Bennett. Bennett came to watch a performance in New Haven and agreed to take over the reins. We were all extremely relieved and excited, but "Oh, my God," I thought, "he's going to throw a satchel full of songs at me!" The whole thing had become more a musical than a play. Doc had got out onto another track—was it possible that this normally secure craftsman had begun to distrust his own writing? We all sat around on the stage anxiously waiting for the verdict. Michael B. made his entrance and announced straightaway that he was taking every bit of music out of the show. "It's trying to be something it isn't. It's a perfectly charming and entertaining play as written and has to remain so."

So out went all the music and I think Doc was both relieved and grateful for such assessment and faith. In no time we were into previews at the Eugene O'Neill. Michael had worked tirelessly to whip us into shape. He proved without a doubt in those three short weeks that he was every bit as talented for the legitimate theatre as he was for musical comedy. We opened confidently and smoothly. Everyone was praised to the skies. Most critics recognized that Doc was trying to stretch himself and gave him huge credit for his subtlety and versatility. We were all convinced that he was now ready to write his "great work"! But Doc didn't need to. He'd served up enough greatness in comedy already and, of course, he could never resist, God love him, getting just one more laugh. I enjoyed immensely being the Good Doctor not just for the superlatively skillful company of actors I was privileged to be with but because I loved my time, short as it was, with Doc—getting to know him, watching him at work, a kind, industrious man, one of the very finest comedic masters the theatre has ever known. We owe a lot of the joy in our lives to Neil Simon. And Michael "Whiz Kid" Bennett? That little tornado who died so tragically young leaving a gaping hole in the life of the stage that can never be filled with the same special quality and courage that was his alone. Yes, Michael B. had some greatness in him all right. Where is he now when we need him?!

HARDLY HAD WE CLOSED *The Good Doctor* when Fuff and I found ourselves on the road to Morocco. Leaving Casablanca by car heading due east on that rustic highway brought back familiar memories of my first trip there so many years before with the late, lamented Janet Munro. The same rough desert road that passed through little scattered villages along the way, made up of huts, filthy, poverty-wracked, collapsing hovels. People would emerge like insects to stare at the car as it passed through. Dogs, some dead, some crippled, most starving, just skin and bone, littered the road. It all seemed so unjust and unfair when we finally reached our destination—that exotic, lush, wealthy oasis known as Marrakesh.

Upon our arrival we were driven straight to Hotel La Mamounia— where else? Not much vestige remained of French influence except for the language, which many of the Moroccans still spoke. Otherwise, everything was now totally Arab; the hotel was Arab owned, serving Moroccan food, delicious, spicy, scented and much too much of it. We were housed in a lavish suite with a colossal bathtub, which when the water ran out through the pipes made the sound of a lion roaring. We played that game often after a bath, opening our mouths in lip-sync fashion, silently roaring as the tub emptied. Sadly, I've never found another bath that made quite the same noise though, God knows, I keep trying. The windows of our suite looked out toward the distant dark blue of the Atlas range and there in the town itself the tall tower from which the muezzin wakes the dawn.

In the morning I was to have a session with John Huston, whose film *The Man Who Would Be King* had brought us there. Richard Burton had for some reason withdrawn at the last minute, and Janet Roberts of William Morris had persuaded John Foreman, an old friend and the film's producer, that I should be cast in his stead. The part was Rudyard Kipling, who as the author of the story, appears now and then spurring on his famous protagonists—Dravot, played by Sean Connery, and Carnehan, played by Michael Caine. Some time ago, Huston and his loyal cowriter Gladys Hill had taken Kipling's short story and enlarged it for the screen. They had originally wanted Bogie and Gable, now too old, of course. Instead of India as a location, which would have been prohibitive politically and financially, Morocco was substituted, a most suitable choice as it turned out.

I was ushered into the presence of Mr. Huston, the Great White Hunter, with the long, angular head who stared at me for an eternity through those famous hooded eyes. Back in New York I had hired a stu-

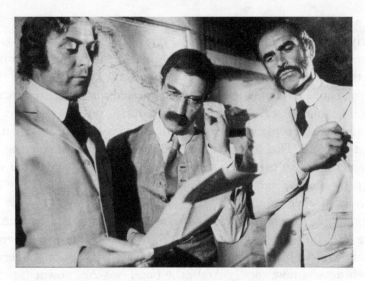

Michael Caine as Carnehan, me as Kipling and Sean Connery as Dravot

dent to do some quick research on the physical appearance of Rudyard Kipling as there was such little time to prepare. He had come up with a colour photo of the man which showed his hair as having a reddish tinge. I just as quickly got Paul Huntley, that superlative wig maker, to make me a "rug" resembling the photos as closely as possible. I now held it in my hand and showed it to Mr. Huston. "It's the wrong colour," he growled. "Kipling's hair was jet black, not a bit of red in it." I then showed him the photo. "It's been tinted," he snapped. "The Kipling Society insists it's black." I stammered lamely that I had paid someone four hundred dollars to research Kipling's appearance. "Then get your money back," he replied. "We shoot you in three days' time. You have three days to get another wig." He stalked out of the room followed by what looked like a retinue of beaters. With John Foreman's help, we got through to Paul Huntley who performed some miraculous sleight of hand and sent a fresh black wig and mustache through the Studio pouch to arrive just in time.

I didn't like Huston very much in the beginning and I don't think he liked me. I knew that he was capable of assuming a courtly old-world manner when the mood took him, but to me he was nothing but brusque, terse and downright rude. He clearly resented the fact that I wasn't Burton, whom he obviously wanted around for late-night drinking and good times. Fuff could sense, without my telling her, that I wasn't going to have much fun. But how wrong we both were. For a start, with Michael Caine around with his vast bag of jokes and his natural wit, Sean, Fuff and I did nothing but laugh most of the time. The four of us were for a spell inseparable. A beautiful dark girl from British Guiana appeared as Mike's new love. Her name, as everyone now knows, is Shakira and she of course turned out to be his future wife. Shakira and Fuff formed a companionship and they both entertained each other while we sahibs slaved away under the hot desert sun. I was now having a whale of a time playing Kipling and confident that I adequately resembled him, I did all I could to lose myself in the role. Unlike most film directors, Huston was very liberal with the dailies at the day's end and welcomed all and sundry to come and watch the results. In fact, if one didn't show up, he became quite hurt.

One day, I was doing a major scene outside in the streets. It involved a rather lengthy bit of dialogue, so concentration was in order. Huston, unbeknownst to me, had placed a camel directly behind me as part of the background who every few seconds would nudge me with its head, sending me quite off balance and completely out of the shot. "Let's do it again," grumbled Huston in that well-known slow drawl of his. "Could the camel be moved a couple of yards back?" I pleaded. "No, Chris—he deserves to be in the scene just as much as you do. Actors and animals should get used to each other. They are, after all, one and the same." If I hadn't been the butt of his joke and the camel's prodding, I would have enjoyed his dark humour a lot more. As it was, I laughed unconvincingly and valiantly made a few more attempts. The beast never stopped pushing me out of camera range as if he and Huston had from the start formed a conspiracy between them. Huston, obviously, found it immensely funny and he chortled away to himself from where he sat among huge comfortable cushions like some pasha. I swear it all was a kind of test to see if I had balls or not—everything in Huston's camp was macho to the nth degree. When finally the scene was in the can, he got up, came over and congratulated first the camel, then me, in that order. After that, John and I got on just fine.

As if he were some Arab sheik, a lot of his former wives would turn up out of the blue. I imagined he liked having them there just so he could mischievously sneak away in the night with his male tribe into the Atlas Mountains and camp out with the Berbers. His obsession was big game and once for days on end he was absent hunting elephants and tigers. While he was away, the irreplaceable Bert Batt, the very best assistant director ever, would take over the entire operation, still shouting the same affectionate insults at us actors, "All right, wind 'em up

John Huston

and bring 'em on." Bert was truly amazing, able to organize hundreds of horsemen and a hundred camels in a matter of seconds and still have time to see that the British caterers taught the Arab caterers how to make bangers and mash.

Then the Great White Hunter would return full of tales of conquest. He was an extraordinary personality, no question—a curious combination of latent cruelty and vulnerability—and when he was in action on the set I had to admit through somewhat clenched teeth that he was a great director. I could see something in him which he couldn't hide that had made his films so unique, so memorable (*The Treasure of the Sierra Madre, The Red Badge of Courage, The Maltese Falcon* and the last few moments of *Moulin Rouge*), and that something was an admiration and a passion for the rugged individual, the loner, cynical, disillusioned, who conceals beneath his bitterness a core of heroism that is pure, noble and utterly incorruptible. As a writer and filmmaker he understood satire, rare in an American (*Beat the Devil,* for example) and it crept into all his work as he continued to wink at the world. Like Hemingway, though never as beleaguered with problems, he possessed a goodly amount of sensitive genes which gave him his romance.

Huston surrounded himself with top professionals in every department, from Oswald "Ozzie" Morris, the British camera ace, on down. The atmosphere on the set was never tedious but rich and exciting. Each morning I felt I was going to some sort of ritual, an adventure or a search for hidden treasure. Like a fine chef he worked purely on instinct and never followed the recipe of others. John never appeared to be directing at all, actually; he would say that "once the damn thing's cast right, half the job is done—I can leave everyone alone." Only the occasional word or two would pass his lips—sparse, economical but which spoke volumes. I was having trouble saying a very important line which I longed to make touching. He finally came up to me, and as gently as his gravelly accent allowed, he said, "Ah—ah—Chris, just take the music out of your voice." And when at the end of the story Kipling stares in horror at the rotting severed head of his favourite character, Carnehan, what to do? There are no words, just the close-up camera. I tried everything from tears, to shock, to fear—what you will. Huston got out of his chair and whispered softly in my ear, "Don't think at all. Drain yourself of feeling. Empty your head—then look at him." By God, it worked. Those two bits of direction are the best I've ever received on any movie set.

One day, we went up into Berber country where on top of a small alp, Alexandre Trauner, the legendary set designer, had built Kipling's mythical kingdom of Kafiristan; Sean, as Dravot, was to be crowned there. Alexandre had designed many a European film classic, especially in France during the golden years of French cinema, including one of my very favourites, *Les Enfants du Paradis.* He almost outdid himself with the strange palace he had erected on the hill. It was an extraordinary feat and on a clear day could be seen for miles silhouetted against the mountains and the sky. Huston had gathered everyone there for a costume parade. He wanted to see them against the set before he approved them. They had been the work of Edith Head, that most famous of Hollywood designers. Edith was already there, pacing up and down, looking austere and in charge.

The parade began and the male models were all trouped out, decked out in their period gowns and cloaks. Bright, gorgeously rich colours flowed by in reds, golds, royal blues—magnificent but awfully Hollywood, I thought, for such a pagan scene. Fuff, John Foreman and I stood at a distance. I looked at John F. who was not reacting. He had put on his "producer" face, but I knew damn well what he was thinking. Standing behind us in a circle watching the proceedings bug-eyed were at least fifty of the local Berber peasants. Suddenly Huston called out, "Stop right there for a moment. Come here—ah—Edith, darling." With both hands on her shoulders he turned her around to face the Berber audience. "See those russet browns and torn cloaks? They've been wearing the same clothes since Biblical times—nothing's changed! Yours are very pretty, dear, but hardly native. These are the closest thing to what I want." I didn't see Edith's face, but she turned, walked off the set and soon went back to Hollywood. Smart lady! She'd made herself scarce, and so had her costumes. From a distance, most of the Berbers could have made quite convincing Indians; their apparel was similar. So in a matter of seconds many of them found themselves making speedy adjustments from audience to actors. Huston was fascinated by their dark, craggy, multilined faces. "Let's go for dinner up in the hills tonight," he would say. "I'm going to look at some old men. And we can smoke a hookah or two afterwards."

Now the Big Chief was one of those few directors who could demand "final cut" on a picture, but getting on in years, even he was losing his power and beginning to suffer from studio pressure—in this case from Columbia Pictures and Charles Bluhdorn's Gulf + Western. Though John Foreman was getting reports all the time from the United States which he tried to shield from Huston, some inadvertently slipped through. One thing Columbia was insisting upon was that the role of Kipling should be deleted from the film. Foreman, Connery and Caine simultaneously blew a fuse. "The fools! They've missed the point— they'd be cutting all its atmosphere. The presence of the author contributes to the story. Dravot and Carnehan are motivated by the appearance of Kipling and would be lost without his pen to guide them. If Kipling is cut, the movie will become just another ordinary action epic. What are they doing to Huston's script?"

The studio continued to complain that it slowed down the action. Where have we heard that before? Huston just threw up his hands in helpless dismay. He seemed too tired to fight, but dear Sean Connery, Michael Caine and John Foreman took up the banner and were ready to go to war to save Kipling's life—my life. The studio decided to fly its executives from la-la land to Marrakesh to sort us all out. Exhausted from their long journey, they finally arrived at the Mamounia early in the morning, only to find Sean and Foreman waiting for them in the lobby. "Hope you've had a pleasant flight," grinned James Bond with teeth clenched. "We'll go up in the lift wi-ye." As Foreman told me afterwards, as soon as the elevator doors closed, Sean grabbed one of them by the collar, lifted him off his feet, pinned him against the wall and hissed, his Edinburgh accent becoming a menacing Glaswegian, "If Kipling ish cut from the fillum, I'm going back t'London t'morrow morning an' ye'll nae see me agin!" Me and my mustache remained in the movie!

Another caveat the ever-interfering studio harboured was the choice of suitable background music. Bwana Huston had several times played us a tape of the music he had selected and approved. He had hired a British composer, a Mr. Joseph, to write the main theme of the movie, which would be simply performed on fife and drum. This would be the Dravot/Carnehan theme for the Brit side, which would be set against the wild haunting songs of India played on the sitar and many original native instruments—in fact, the famous Tagore poems set to music. The combination was irresistible, just another example of Huston's wisdom and taste. It commented so brilliantly on the romance and wit of the movie. Lightness of touch was all, and Huston owned it in spades. The studio, however, rejected it at once and against Huston's objections hired Maurice Jarre (the hottest film composer of the time) to write a huge epic score, just what the film did not need. Jarre had composed some fabulous sweeping music for many a famous movie, but *The Man Who Would Be King* was way out of his league—he attacked it like a bull in a china shop. Some people do not voice the same objections in this regard, but in my view Jarre's music worked seriously against the film's potential greatness.

Huston now spent most of his time, while directing, in and out of an oxygen tent they had installed on the set. The emphysema that would eventually kill him was growing worse. Typically, however, like a mischievous, disobedient child, he would take his beloved stogies into the tent with him, close the flaps and light up. By the time I had left African shores principal photography was over and he was no longer on the picture. The devoted Bert Batt, Ozzie Morris and John Foreman finished it for him.

I HAD GROWN UP on the works of the wondrous Rudyard Kipling and so had Huston. He could quote great chunks from *The Jungle Book*, the *Just So Stories* and of course Kipling's numerous poems. One of Huston's favourites and mine too was from "The Young British Soldier":

> When you're wounded and left on Afghanistan's plains
> And the women come out to cut up what remains
> Jest roll to your rifle and blow out your brains . . .

I think Kipling would have been so pleased with John Huston. No other film had ever captured his heart, his style and his essence as had *The Man Who Would Be King*. He also would have been most proud of Sean's rich performance of Dravot and Caine's marvellous Carnehan— one of his best performances ever. The Indian actor Saeed Jaffrey didn't just play Billy Fish, he *was* Billy Fish, and Morocco's major thespian, Doghmi Larbi, in the small role of Ootah the Terrible, gave a comic mime performance of sheer brilliance. Then there is the deeply atmospheric camera work of Ozzie Morris and its cleverly woven replication of India—its trains packed to the rooftops with natives and animals crushed together like ants—and Huston's insistence on keeping it all a magical story for children and their imaginings, just as Kipling himself would have wished. In spite of Maurice's jarring score, it really is a wonderful movie. And whenever I watch it I make sure I block out my ears so I can only hear in my mind the sound of the wailing sitar and the little fife and drum that the Great White Hunter had loved and wished for so much.

> *By the old Moulmein Pagoda*
> *Lookin' eastward to the sea,*
> *There's a Burma girl a-settin',*
> *An' I know she thinks o' me;*
> *For the wind is in the palm-trees,*
> *And the temple-bells they say*
> *'Come you back, you British soldier;*
> *Come you back to Mandalay!'*

CHAPTER THIRTY-NINE

THE RESTLESS SEVENTIES

Tita Wilson had lost her man. Angus's dad had just died. He was now the Duke of Hamilton and could not marry a divorcée. His new responsibilities were huge, he needed some sort of rehab and he was broke, so back he went to Scotland to tend to the crumbling castles. I remember some years later we were all watching Mountbatten's funeral on the BBC and there directly behind the royal family as they paraded into church was Angus in a black robe, his blond hair standing out in striking contrast; a tall Viking, all alone, bearing a rod that presumably represented the Scottish church. He looked absolutely splendid, but one could detect that his left foot was dragging just a little as it always did after a long rough night. We all stood up and cheered him. I missed Angus, I missed our tipsy musical sessions and, most of all, I missed the curry dinners.

Tita then had a brief romance with Freddy Forsyth whose novel *The Day of the Jackal* was being made into a movie produced by her brother-in-law, David Deutsch. Freddy was very nice indeed, extremely courteous if a trifle overserious, good-looking, with very small features and a rather long narrow head, which at certain angles made him appear as if he were wearing a stocking over it. After the romance was over, we would occasionally put stockings over our heads and pretend we were Freddy. This afforded much amusement for us—horrid creeps that we were!

One day outside Hyde Park Gate, a car drew up. Tita got out with a man who looked exactly like Forsyth. Uh-oh, I thought, the affair is on again. She was giggling away to herself, which I took to be giddy love. "Hello, Freddy," I called out as I walked down the street to meet them. "This is not Freddy," said Tita just about to double up. Then I saw that the man was wearing a stocking over his head. "This is Charlie—Charlie Carter," she said and collapsed against an iron railing. Charlie had a hell of a time removing the stocking, he was laughing so hard. He had a handsome young Guards officer look about him, a naughty crinkly smile and had as much penchant for giggling as Tita, which gave him a huge head start on charm. Fuff and I felt at once we'd known him always. Tita just stared at him with longing eyes. For her it was simply Charlie this and Charlie that and Charlie all the way. And it still is, almost forty years later. One of their children, Jamie, is my godson. Charlie's family name way back was Strapp-Carter, so of course, we immediately nicknamed him "Jockstrap Carter." Between them, there is indubitably no looking back now!

We had some frenzied soirees at nos. 9 and 15 to celebrate not just this new union but our hasty departure from the scene, for suddenly 9 and 15 were sold almost before we'd put them on the market. The Rolls Corniche convertible and the Jag were also disposed of and dear Frank, with no more cars to shine, went on to upgrade himself considerably by chauffeuring for the young Marquess of Bristol whose country house Ickworth was one of the grand stately homes of England. So it wasn't too tacky a change for Frank. We were not exactly sorry for him, but we missed his shining morning face.

Our move to America was accomplished in stages because of the flood of work that was taking place in the film industry. The unions which had slowly killed British films were making it impossible for

Charlie, Tita and a rather fumbling yours truly

foreign producers to invest any longer in Old Blighty. So in a panic they came up with the "Four Walls" scheme, which meant films could be shot on the cheap within the four walls of a studio on a movable set. There ensued, of course, a rush to make as many movies as possible before Britain's moviedom went under. I made one after another: *Conduct Unbecoming,* with Richard Attenborough and Trevor Howard; *Aces High,* a World War I RAF film; a ghastly remake of *The Spiral Staircase,* with lovely Jacqueline Bisset; and *Murder by Decree,* a rather gory and unusually sinister film about Sherlock Holmes uprooting the superbad killer Jack the Ripper, who turned out to be the Duke of Clarence, in which I had a very good time playing Holmes with James Mason, who turned in the best Watson I've ever seen. My own cousin Nigel Bruce was a famously entertaining Watson but too much of a buffoon to be the real McCoy. Mason had all the qualities demanded by Conan Doyle—a military bearing, the look of a believable MD, a witty companion and a steadfast friend. In a guest appearance was the attractive and talented French Canadian actress Geneviève Bujold for whom I had always carried a torch, and I now considered myself so fortunate to be able to work with her. Sir John Gielgud played the prime minister, Lord Salisbury, my old companion Anthony Quayle was on board, and Donald Sutherland graced us briefly as some sort of vagrant who mercifully didn't mumble. James Mason and I worked well together and we

Lucky to be sitting next to the best Watson I've ever seen!

had planned to make another Holmes story when he suddenly died of a heart seizure—a dreadful shock to everyone because he had always taken great care of himself and was up to this point in terrific shape. What a horrendous loss to motion pictures, what an artist of the celluloid, capable of such profundity and grace, and what an amusing and warmhearted friend—I felt wronged!

There were trips to Canada, which at last was forming an industry of its own. The government was shrewdly catching on that if it offered tax breaks to foreign filmmakers as long as they used a quota of Canadian talent in exchange, it would benefit the country in many ways. Early forays of mine included a film called *The Pyx,* made in Montreal in the early seventies, a groundbreaker for English Canada. Later I was to make *The Silent Partner* in Toronto with Elliot Gould and my old screen lover Susannah York. Included in the cast was the beloved John Candy in one of his first films. It was written by a young Curtis Hanson (now a top Hollywood writer/director) and I played a malevolently evil killer, a transvestite who beheads girls in fish bowls. He hates women simply because he wants to be one. It was a sneaky, well-made little movie directed by a talented Canadian, Daryl Duke, and produced by an ambitious young powerhouse known as Garth Drabinsky. My char-

Elaine and Sally at Fairlawne

acter was always robbing banks in different disguises—Santa Claus being one of many. But when he comes back in the end to seek further revenge on the bank manager (Elliot Gould), he is wearing ordinary men's street apparel—rather an anticlimax. Fuff suggested that he should come there for the final time as a woman. "After all, it's his favourite disguise. Why don't you wear a smart Chanel suit with sling backs, lipstick, wig, the lot, and when you're shot trying to escape climbing *up* the *down* escalator, your blouse opens and we see all the hair on your chest. What a shocking contrast!" I looked at my wife, astonished. "Why the hell aren't you directing this?" I said. All my life she has stunned me with her wildly inventive ideas. Fortunately, Daryl bought it; it's all there on the screen and I confess I felt rather suspiciously comfortable in my Chanel suit with high heels.

More work in films brought us back to England rather frequently, as if we'd never left, so whenever we hit London we took great delight in sponging shamelessly off our new best friends Sally and Geoffrey James, who offered us with their customary largesse ultracomfortable digs of various descriptions. Geoffrey had made his fortune as one of the few developers to have survived the property crash, a sort of erstwhile British Donald Trump. Sally, a most attractive blonde and terrific hostess, had a shrewd and cunning eye for decoration, so she and Fuff immediately struck a common bond. The Jameses owned a charming gabled house called Eastmanton in the Kentish countryside and later acquired the well-known classic Queen Anne mansion Fairlawne, which sat on two thousand acres of mouth-watering land, also in Kent. It had belonged to the Cazalet family and was reputed to be the Queen Mother's favourite country house for she visited there often when the Cazalets presided over it. The main guest room is still known as the Queen Mum's Room. There is also a lake near the wooded walk where it is believed that Lady Vane, the wife of a onetime Fairlawne owner, Sir Henry Vane, threw herself in. Reportedly, there have been several sightings of Lady Vane's ghost standing by the lake at dusk, presumably pondering her suicide. Sally and Geoffrey had also bought an attractive villa near the Mediterranean at St. Jean Cap Ferrat, which most conveniently serviced those of us who had our minds set for a short respite on the Riviera. But it was at their London house on Eaton Square with its lift conveniently going straight to our room at the top where we mostly alighted with full intentions to claim squatters' rights.

We happened to be staying there after our return from John Huston's Africa when sad news arrived from across the Atlantic. Jane Broder, the Mother Cabrini of my entire theatre life, had just passed away. We were too late for the funeral, but we flew to New York for her memorial where I gave the eulogy. There was an extraordinary number of people who came to pay tribute, old-time stars of the stage, famous character actors and actresses, producers, writers, directors, many ghosts from another age. I was simply overwhelmed by the fact that she had collected through her life so many friends and admirers who were still with us. Those who had already gone would have filled at least two cathedrals.

There is a line by Christopher Fry from *The Dark Is Light Enough* which describes Jane to a T: "She puts her own world down and takes yours up almost before you realize what made you need her." The few inadequate words I strung together that sad day were the closest I could find to express my feelings: "Because she was without greed and because she looked on us actors as her very own children, she was unique in her calling and every day she clung to it and never lost her faith in it. A mission had been assigned her and she followed her voices. She believed and taught us to believe that the theatre was an honourable profession. Nothing could shake her from that. And as long as she was around to serve it with quality and devotion, it fairly shone with honour." We all felt lost that day, and my one consolation was that not too long before, when she lay fading fast in her hospital bed and I was so afraid she would not recognize me, I'd felt her squeeze my hand.

A shining future cut off

NEWS BACK IN ENGLAND was also far from cheerful. My late-night partner, the hugely talented writer James Kennaway, had been killed on his way from London to his home in Lechlade, Gloucestershire. Jimmy had just received the glad tidings that Peter O'Toole had agreed to do the movie of his play *Country Dance*. He met with Peter in London, and, needless to say, they celebrated the occasion a trifle too enthusiastically. No longer having to worry about selling his delightful restaurant in the country, Pink's, named after the play's leading character, James was enjoying one of the happiest days of his life. Driving home, however, three sheets to the wind, he suffered a massive heart attack and totalled both himself and the car.

It was in a state of shock that we returned to England, heading straight for the funeral service in the tiny chapel down the street from his house in Lechlade. Memories of his gem of a film *Tunes of Glory* sang in my head as the bagpipers piped his coffin into the chapel. The front row of pews was reserved for immediate family, which included his long-suffering widow, Susan, and his cousin, who had made her debut in that film, dear Susannah York. Susannah entered dressed head to foot in solemn black, a black veil completely concealing her beauty. As she was about to take her seat in the pew, she somehow collided with the shelf containing all the prayer books, Bibles, etc., and succeeded in knocking them all down one by one in a concertina effect, a veritable landslide. The noise echoing off the chapel walls was deafening. Darling Sue—never could handle props! I glanced over at the coffin, which had been placed in front of the altar and I swear on a stack of fallen Bibles I could see it move ever so slightly up and down. I just knew it was Jimmy inside, shaking with laughter.

GIVING ME a creepy sense of déjà vu, my next engagement was once again in Africa—and once again in Marrakesh at Hotel La Mamounia. It was *The Return of the Pink Panther* with that diamond of comedians Peter Sellers. I was to play the Panther (a role David Niven had created). The usual suspects in the cast were once more assembled and the man in charge, as always, was the author and director Blake Edwards. Blake had only recently tied the knot with Julie Andrews, so in a sense it promised to be a sort of family reunion. This time my bride and I were given the Churchill Suite, second only in grandeur to the Royal Suite, which Blake had taken. The déjà vu of the situation was made all the cheerier when we found that our bathtub made the exact same roaring noise when the water ran out as had our former tub. Eureka!

One of the greatest cameramen in the world, Geoffrey Unsworth, that soft-spoken elderly Englishman, was also on board. He is the only DP I've ever worked with who, while lighting a massive set, he and his men in the flys, on the riggings, everywhere, never made one sound. They directed their lights by hand gestures from Geoffrey. It all worked as if by telepathy. Geoffrey's philosophy was that his department should never be seen to disturb the other artists. This method proved that one can be great at one's job and still have manners. What a superb artist he was and what a gentleman.

In *Return of the Pink Panther,* Peter Sellers had for the first time found his character Clouseau. It is, and my opinion is shared by many, his best and funniest performance of the role. Sellers's biggest weakness was that he never learned how to cope with success. Like a child, he had fallen in love with celluloid fame and had done all the things he believed movie stars were supposed to do, namely, acquiring the necessary pleasures—the villas, the yachts, the fast cars, the bimbettes and, of course, the obligatory choice of drugs. He had foolishly spent most of his quick fortune and had not worked for an astonishingly long time. Sir Lew Grade and Blake got together and decided to get him back with this latest script. He leaped at the chance and, realizing he really needed the work, knuckled under and put his whole being into it. Of

Clouseau, Sir Charles Litton and my accomplice, played by Catherine Schell

course, he was marvellous and *The Return* brought him back on top as a comedian and saved him financially. The outtakes that Blake collected of Sellers playing the final scene are priceless—Peter trying all sorts of accents from Indian to Polish, changing his lines, reversing dialogue on purpose, breaking himself up take after take, while the rest of us, including the crew, remained hysterically out of control.

I also loved working with Blake. He was easy and relaxed, at least on the surface. Plus he had this quirky, oblique, zany side to him I found most appealing. He improvised brilliantly with Peter, having a similar twisted sort of imagination, and his ideas, many over the top, never stopped flowing from that offbeat brain of his. Blake never saw anything straight in life—it had to be slightly crooked or off-kilter before he could accept it.

One mad morning at the Mamounia, Blake received a call from the hotel management. They reminded him that as he was occupying the Royal Suite, there were rules attendant to that privilege, namely, that should any royalty happen to show up in the vicinity, the guests in residence would be required to evacuate. "I know that," said Blake, sensing trouble. "Isn't it lucky there *is* no royalty around at present?" "But I'm afraid there is, Mr. Edwards. The king of the Cameroons is arriving shortly with his entourage and the honour guard." Blake was past all patience. "This is outrageous. I've moved my family into this suite. We've been here two months and we expect to stay at least another two.

It would be the greatest inconvenience. I'm not moving out—that's flat." "I'm afraid you'll have to, sir" was the terse reply, "or you will be ejected by force." "Well, goddamn it!" fumed Blake, "They must have given some decent notice. How the hell long do I have?" "About half an hour, sir."

Before the half hour was up, the long corridor outside his suite was totally commandeered by a small army of Cameroon soldiers in battle dress, armed with machine guns. He was soon moved into another suite, not quite so grand, temporarily. Down at the swimming pool I looked up and saw on the rooftops a row of snipers at the ready and just below them all the window shutters of the Royal Suite were tightly closed. The whole top floor had become its own occupied country. Then the king made his entrance. In the midst of all his surrounding battle force brandishing the most up-to-date war equipment moved His Majesty, the most beautiful shade of ebony, wearing wide white pantaloons resembling a loincloth, with bare legs and funny curled-up shoes of all colours, while his slaves held a parasol high over his sacred head, taking us back instantly to the nineteenth century. I used to sneak up by the back stairs and peek around the corner and the whole corridor was filled with many tables of every known viand, sweetmeats, spices, exotic dishes, enough for a small army. This was His Majesty's breakfast only. Most of it remained untouched, but the overpowering scent lingered down those corridors for days afterwards. By the end of their stay there was another smell, not so agreeably pungent, for the occupying force had clearly not bothered to use the amenities and had defecated quite liberally everywhere. After His Majesty's party had taken its leave, it took a whole month for the hotel staff to adequately clean the place. Blake, incidentally, did *not* move back.

In no time, it seemed, the film ended—and the brief friendships we had made began to dissipate almost as quickly. The gentleman cameraman Geoffrey Unsworth made many more films of note but sadly was to die while photographing the first *Superman;* the film quite rightly was dedicated to him. Blake and Julie would, of course, remain my friends forever, but I was never to see much of Sellers again. Peter, that strange, tortured soul, just a stone's throw from schizophrenia, could be delightful one moment and deeply sullen the next. The drugs, I am positive, were inviting him to self-destruct. But he was to make many more entertaining movies; one of my very favourites was *Being There* with the wonderful Shirley MacLaine. I am lost in admiration for Peter, that flaky genius—yes, I think genius is an appropriate description—

yet I would not have exchanged my life for his at any price. For like a great many comics, he suffered badly from the curse of Punchinello, the curse that relentlessly plagues them and makes them pay so dearly for their few moments of inspired magic.

AFTER A BRIEF STAY with the Jameses in England, Fuff stayed on to do a BBC television programme, and I ended up in Portugal to appear, incongruously, in a Swedish film in English which takes place in Mexico. I was at once fascinated by Portugal, the beauty of the Algarve, the elegant landscaping of Sintra, the music of fado at night in CasCais, and of course the unique galleon-like architecture of Lisbon, reminding one that this small country once ruled the seas. And then the unexpected splendour of its wines, comparable to the best French, for Portuguese wines generally do not travel well. It was at the old Aviz restaurant in Lisbon, once a hangout for exiled royalty, that I discovered my newfound favourite aperitif—white port—which entices the palate and gently glides down the throat as smooth as silk.

Annie Orr-Lewis had given me letters of introduction to two old ladies, the Wright sisters, who were well-known characters in Lisbon and knew every inch of the city. Their father was at one time British ambassador to the Chinese court, and the two little girls grew up playing games at the palace with the children of the last empress of China. He then became ambassador to Portugal where they remained for the rest of their lives. They were most kind to me and took me to lunch at Queluz, that most exquisitely unpretentious of royal residences; the kitchens of which had been turned into a restaurant, the center worktable being one single piece of thick travertine about forty feet long where sumptuous dishes were laid out in buffet style. The Misses Wright also took me to the carpet warehouses where only the designers are permitted to enter and began at once negotiating for me. "Choose any design you want. They'll make them especially for you." They put me in mind of a couple of Miss Marples joined at the hip, and wherever they made an appearance, doors were flung open. I'll never forget those two exceptional old biddies with their wonderful stories of a forgotten bygone China; the gorgeous carpets they had bargained for me for next to nothing did arrive as promised in mint condition at our new abode four months later.

WE HAD RELINQUISHED our little cottage on Bell Island to its master Barron Polan for we had just bought an old carriage house fif-

The Barn, enjoying the calm before the storm

teen feet from the water's edge in Noroton, Connecticut. Built in the late nineteenth century, it was part of an estate that had once belonged to Andrew Carnegie. This solid old building made of stone and wood was where they kept their carriages in one long room and their horses in another. It was quite large and had an upstairs which could easily serve as the living quarters. We began to renovate. The big carriage room over sixty feet long became the downstairs living room with four separate seating areas, and the horse stable next to it, almost the same length, would be the dining room. The big living room had wonderful wide floor planks, which we had bleached and then scattered over with the Portuguese rugs, but the dining room was a challenge. We gutted it completely, took out the horse stalls, opened it up to the sound by installing huge French windows all along the waterfront. What a view—we felt we were on a ship. It was all quite lovely, but it took the better part of two years to get rid of the smell of horseshit.

Nonetheless, it was a good house in which to entertain. A lot of chums came to stay. Sally and Geoffrey, of course, my brand-new agent, Lou Pitt, who, poor chap, has been stuck with me for all these years as my manager and friend. The beautiful Jill Melford, a very great chum, came for a Christmas weekend and stayed almost two months. She brought her son Alexander and left him behind after she'd gone, with instructions to find a local school where he could glean an American education. Some long weekend! Which prompts the age-old question—do the English, when they colonize, ever know when to leave?!

Sniffing around the house after she'd gone, we found several items that Melford had forgotten, including a sculptured head and shoulders of herself when young. A few days later, she sent a sweet note, which ended, "Thank you, darlings, I left my heart behind, but I also left my bust."

We lived at the "Barn" for a while longer, with and without the builders, until one day our fates were decided for us. First, we were maced in our beds and robbed (thievery from the water had become the mode); then not too long afterward, a tremendous nor'easter hit the coastline. Waves were huge, the winds almost hurricane force—it went on for two days. When the storm at last abated I decided to go down to the basement and assess the damage. We'd spent a considerable amount transforming it into comfortable quarters complete with shower and sauna, a bar area with stools and couches, and a game room next to this. Outside on the terrace behind a low seawall (our only buffer) we had planted a lovely garden which stretched the whole length of the house. The moment I descended to the basement floor, I was waist high in water. The garden was now inside where the bar had been, and the bar was now outside where the garden had been. I could see at least fifty yards from the shoreline all the bar and bathroom furniture floating farther and farther out to sea. It took just about the length of Melford's visit to clean everything up. We'd had enough—we were beaten thoroughly! We put the old Barn on the market and sold it in no time for a splendid amount. In fact, I think I've earned more in my lifetime from real estate than from showbiz, but I wish I'd waited a little longer, another thirty years, perhaps, because just recently it sold again—this time for ten million dollars.

What we really needed now was something permanent on the East Coast, near enough to Manhattan to make sense. We needed peace and privacy. And anyway, it was time we settled down. I was fifty and Fuff thirty-six and the game of buying and selling was on its way out. We found what we were looking for near the small inland Connecticut town of Weston, a rambling house of no architectural discipline which had been built around an old barn. It sat in a considerable amount of acreage, at least enough to ensure complete privacy and where no neighbours could be seen. It was also surrounded by a nature preserve, which meant no one could ever build near us. I knew we would have a massive landscape overhaul ahead of us and more building—a caretaker's house was essential. It was all pretty daunting, yet something was pulling me along, willing me to take it. When I got inside I knew why. My God, it was Raymond Massey's old house that I had visited so often in the fifties. I called Ray in Beverly Hills. "I think I've just bought your house, Pappy!" "No! It's not possible, Ignatius." (He'd remembered to call me Ignatius.) "But it's got the big barn as the living room and the loft is now a minstrel gallery just exactly like yours and it's got the same address on Honey Hill!" "No, Ignatius, you've bought the house right next door." "Who's got yours then?" "I sold it years ago to Theodore Bikel." Will coincidence never cease? Twenty years had passed and I end up not only next to my old mentor's house but the house that belongs now to the man who created Captain von Trapp on the stage! Can you imagine two von Trapps staring at each other across a picket fence? I can think of nothing worse.

CHAPTER FORTY

TWO PLUMS ON BROADWAY

My friend Peter Coe was on the phone. He was telling me he'd just taken over the much-maligned and neglected American Shakespeare Theatre at Stratford, Connecticut, the very place where, at its inception years ago, my Marc Antony had seriously jump-started my career. "Please come and do your Henry the Fifth again and then Iago. It's high time you played that one. I've got Jimmy Earl Jones to do Othello and some producers who want to take it to New York!" It didn't seem like an offer I could refuse and besides I only lived a stone's throw away. I said yes. But Peter wasn't finished. "I also want you to play the Chorus as well as Henry—because it has the best verse in the play and I can only hear you speaking it." Being an overindulgent maniac where verse is concerned and terribly susceptible to flattery, I said yes again!

What a workout it was! Though in good physical shape and at least slim enough to squeeze into fifteenth-century tights, I was fifty-one after all, and Henry was a mere twenty-six, or so history would have it.

Of course age mattered not where the Chorus is concerned as he could be young, old, anything—an ageless creature. I should have stuck to the Chorus only, but like a susceptible idiot, I was tempted by the trumpet-tongued rhetoric those two parts offered. Some moments in the production worked well—the night before the battle where it was sufficiently dark to hide my advancing years and whenever Roy Dotrice was on stage as Fluellen—but the combination of Henry/Chorus not only looked like an absurd ego trip, it was downright ludicrous. How can an actor play the storyteller who spouts nothing but iambic praise for the young King Hal and then come on immediately as the King himself?! I think one reviewer succinctly remarked that I never stopped bumping into myself. And it was John Simon of *New York Magazine* who mentioned that my eyes, as Henry, staring out at the battlefield were not the eyes of a youth discovering for the first time the hardships of responsibility but the eyes of an aging cynic who undoubtedly had seen it all before.

Also not particularly easy was sharing the stage with that old warhorse Dotrice. I had to fight tooth and nail to keep my head above water, for every scene we had together he quite mercilessly stole from under me. Each night during one or another of my long dissertations, he would sit beside me and slowly peel fresh leeks till the whole auditorium reeked from the stench. Roy made this important but relatively minor role seem as much a star part as Henry's. I told him that the play should be retitled "Fluellen the Fifth, Sixth, Seventh and Eighth." In spite of everything, the run did well, business was good, and I remember with pride Katharine Hepburn coming backstage to compliment me, which made me think I'd perhaps been better than I thought. Well, I said good-bye to Henry and the Chorus—at least my voice had had a superb workout and I was ready to tackle Iago.

What excitement this creature offers! With what Machiavellian wit and malevolent cruelty does his scheming mind take its revengeful course. After many an attempt at writing stage villains with breathtaking mastery, Shakespeare finally arrived at his greatest creation of all in that regard. Iago stands head and shoulders above all the other bad guys of literature—a truly major study of the dark embodiment of evil. The play is about jealousy. Iago, the most jealous of them all, preys upon Othello, who becomes jealous first of Desdemona, then of Cassio, until the whole piece is thoroughly infected by jealousy as if by a plague. Iago, like all major classic roles, gives the actor performing it a freedom of interpretation; it generously offers him many options. The most popular current view, it seems, is that he is a rough sergeant major of lower class, an ordinary man who becomes extraordinary when driven by his own deviltry, fiendishly jealous of the man he serves, a black man in a white man's world—and a very powerful one at that.

The Ernest Jones theory (referred to earlier) that he is a latent homosexual who lusts after Othello, partly to get closer to the seat of power that he may overthrow it the more swiftly, is also valid. However one may disagree, these two interpretations are not to be ignored. But I contend that though he is ranked several notches below the Moor, he is not in the least servant class but a seneschal of middle class who has bargained and blackmailed his way into Venetian aristocracy, cleating his way up the social ladder. He feels robbed of the post he's convinced he should have held. That a black man should be favoured above him is a true injustice and something he finds abhorrent beyond tolerance, archracist that he is. His mind is quicker than anyone else's in the play; he is sophisticated, cynical, well versed in the politics of Venice and how to play their game. He feels entitled: this is certainly not his first foray in the art of manipulation, but it is the very last chance he has in his quest for power.

I suppose my view is essentially a nineteenth-century one born from the idea that actors of that time, particularly star actors, looked upon the role as being equal in importance to Othello and they would be right—it is much lengthier and one of the longest roles in Shakespeare. This would not be applicable, perhaps, to the man who played opposite the great Salvini or the unfortunate fellow who had to share the stage with Kean, but it certainly applies to the end of the nineteenth century, when the American star Edwin Booth played Iago to Sir Henry Irving's Othello—they actually alternated roles. Reports of the time have it that Booth's villain did not die offstage as the author indicated. He came back in the end, straddled the body of the dead Moor and, shaking his fists at heaven, laughed a ghastly triumphant laugh as the curtain descended. How Irving, whose production it was, allowed this to happen boggles the mind. I wasn't quite as bold as Mr. Booth, but as I lay mortally wounded on the ground after the Moor's demise (James having ripped my testicles apart with his sword), I struggled to get up in vain and laughed a bitter laugh of both loss and victory. James Earl did not take to this at all, and, looking back, I don't in the least blame him. He claimed I was altering the author's intentions and of course in part he was right. He was also finding difficulty in comprehending why I was getting so many laughs throughout the evening. He

Othello *poster*

had already played the Moor more than once, before our production, and no Iago of his apparently had as much as forced a smile from the audience. So he became convinced that the laughter was of a mocking nature and directed at Othello's expense. But here he was wrong. The role of Iago is immensely witty (the opening scene alone offers eight legitimate laughs), all the more reason to charm the spectators so that when his evil side shows itself, it is so much more terrifying. Some of the critics, however, found my performance at Stratford overly melodramatic and said so. I will admit I was perhaps enjoying myself too much in the old cloak-and-dagger manner.

James Earl and Peter Coe did not exactly hit it off—they were constantly at loggerheads conceptually. One of them had to bend, and it was not going to be Peter. One night, after one of the *Henry* performances, a dark-haired lady came backstage to see me. My dresser, an overly protective young lass called Melinda Howard, full of spiky charm, shut the door in her face. "That was a bit rough, Howard," I said. "I think I should at least see her. She may be the producer they were talking about." Melinda gave me a look that read, "Okay, suck-ass," and grudgingly let her in. "Hello, I'm Fran Weissler. My husband, Barry, and I want very much to present *Othello* in New York. Both you and James have got to be seen in this play." Her voice was soft and intimate. She was most good-natured and didn't seem in the least perturbed by the noise Melinda was making as she cleaned the makeup table. She told me in soothing tones how much she loved Shakespeare (she made it sound as if she'd known him intimately) and how she and Barry had only done children's theatre up to that point and had never ventured forth into the big professional arena. She was cozy, comfortable to be with, and I fed off her enthusiasm. I listened to her story and politely suggested she call my agent. She had barely got up to leave when Melinda signaled that the audience was over by announcing loudly, "Here's your first of the evening," as she plunked down on the table an enormous snifter of red wine. Eventually, all was signed and sealed, and the Weisslers were to present us in New York.

Quarrels between Peter and James had now come to a crunch and Peter informed the Weisslers he was out. Zoe Caldwell was brought in and she took over like a whirlwind, helping everyone with their punctuation and breathing, essential to performing Shakespeare. She got on with James quite well and soon everything settled down and we were off on the road. The first stop was, incredibly, the Royal Poinciana Playhouse in Palm Beach and we opened in front of that bejewelled gathering, notorious for their minimum attention spans—even for simple fare, let alone Shakespeare. When Othello kissed Desdemona, an African black kissing an English rose, there was an audible intake of breath that sounded like a tidal wave receding. I had played the Poinciana once before and knew it was hard enough to keep them in their seats for the first act. But any second act, God help it, was a rude inconvenience, which cut straight into their dinner plans. Unbelievably, the magic of that strange language called Elizabethan somehow hypnotized or solipsized them sufficiently to keep most of them there to the end. The manager came running back foaming at the mouth and spluttering, "It's a hit! It's a hit! Only fourteen walkouts after the first act!"

The tour shuffled along back through the east. Zoe was very firm and worked us to the bone. It was in Baltimore that my rapier flew out of my sweaty hand during the duel with Cassio and embedded itself in the back of a front row seat just missing a poor woman's eye by a hair. I leaped off the stage, retrieved the sword and quickly whispered in her ear, "Are you all right?" "Yes, thank you, dear, I'm fine." She was smiling. I think she rather enjoyed being part of the action. It was in Boston on a cold winter's day in a barely heated suite at the Fairmont Copley Plaza that Natalie "Will we ever?" Wood called me. She was inviting me to play the Prince in *Anastasia* at LA's Ahmanson Theatre in which she was to play the title role. I had to tell her I wasn't free. Darling loyal Nat—always remembering friends. She and R.J. (Wagner) were together again. I missed their parties in Hollywood—there were always so many interesting relics present. For a young lady, it was most unusual to favour as she did the Old Guard.

It was not many weeks later when we hit Chicago that Roddy McDowall called me to say there was to be no *Anastasia*. Not only that—there was to be no Natalie, not anymore. She had somehow fallen from her yacht into the sea off Catalina Island. The roar of the motors prevented R.J. from hearing her screams and she perished. The little maenad who couldn't swim had given herself back to the waters she feared and hated so much. How ironic that they should claim her in the end. The world that loved her and had watched her grow up into the beauteous dark-haired creature who burned up celluloid with her eyes would mourn her forever. And so would I. The West Coast has never quite been the same for me without her there. Anyone who ever met her, as Orson Welles once said, was a little in love with Natalie.

With this sad fate hanging over our heads like a shroud, I added a lot more anger to Iago as we embarked on the final trip to Broadway and the Winter Garden Theatre. James was onto his third Desdemona. The first two had fallen into the usual trap of playing her as an ingenue. But this time, fortunately for us, it was Dianne Weist who came on as a real woman, mature beyond her years, sensual, proud and passionate. Her presence lifted the production to new heights—she was stunning. But after the New York opening, she departed and a brave young actress named Cecilia "CeeCee" Hart brilliantly replaced her and became in life the next Mrs. James Earl Jones. Also stunning was the Cassio given fresh life by an extremely adept young classical actor by the name of Kelsey Grammer, who would soon reach his destiny as a huge star of the small screen.

James Earl Jones was a wonderful Othello, particularly in his handling of prose. He made the voyage into jealousy and homicide crystal clear. He also had great authority. But somehow, for some reason, he had made the decision to restrain and underplay the great moments of surging poetry. Having played the role so often, he had begun to over-analyze it. James Earl owns all the equipment that can let him fly if he wants to, and he decided not to use it. Sadly, in my view, he denied the sweeping romance of the play. Zoe Caldwell had rapped my knuckles till they bled, so I opened with a new Iago, much more contained, less "hammy" and as good old John Simon confirmed—at last, terrifying. Walter Kerr, who had championed me in the past, did so once again as did Frank Rich in *The New York Times*. Perhaps starting out as the bad boy pays off!

Othello was a hit! Shakespeare on Broadway? Doing business? Unheard of! James Earl received marvellous press, deservedly, ditto all the actors. The play won the Tony for Best Revival, and the Weisslers could at last put children's theatre behind them—they were *on their way.* Neither James nor I ever dreamed that one day they would become richer than Croesus and just about the most successful producing team in New York, London, Berlin, Tokyo or wherever.

I THINK THAT Broadway season of '81–'82 was almost my favourite because the Plummer family was so well represented. My offspring, Amanda, had opened in a play not far from the Winter Garden called *Agnes of God* with a tornado of a performance that flattened everything in its path. But for a brief visit to London when she was eight, I had not set eyes on my daughter all those years in between. It was not intentional, of course; our separation was more than anything geographical. She had dropped out of many a fine school and college, had broken free of her mother and was now firmly established in our wacky profession. In *Agnes of God* she played a deranged young novitiate obsessed with the belief that the blood of Christ ran through her veins. Amanda attacked the role and filled it with such a frenzy of intensity, one marvelled how she could repeat such an exhibition night after night without inflicting serious damage upon herself. Elizabeth Ashley and Geraldine Page, wonderful artists in their own right, were her coplayers, but the evening was without question Amanda's.

Not too long before, Fuff and I had seen her memorable New York acting debut as Josephine in *A Taste of Honey*. She had proved in that piece alone that she possessed the rare and inexplicable gift known only as pathos. She was funny and touching and she received her first Tony nomination for that intriguing and charming performance. Watching her, I saw nothing of myself, except perhaps a facial similarity, poor thing. I didn't possess her kind of talent—nothing she did or suggested seemed familiar to me; none of it had come from my genes, nor from her mother's, except Tammy's croaked gravelly voice she made use

Amanda, preparing to unleash the furies

of so well. She was indeed unique. And now, at *Agnes of God,* sitting in an audience I didn't know was there, she succeeded in frightening me to death. It was not my daughter up there on that stage but a perfect stranger—nothing of me in her at all. There have been very few performances that have made me forget I was in a theatre. Ruth Draper's monologues, Ruth Gordon in *The Matchmaker,* Helene Weigel in the Berliner Ensemble's *Mutter Courage,* Bobby Morse as Truman Capote, Nigel Hawthorne as C. S. Lewis in *Shadowlands* and Amanda as Sister Agnes. She has occasionally been described as a mannered actress; she is not always easy to watch. She can make an audience uncomfortable because she has the guts to stick to her guns and never compromise, but there are more things in heaven and earth than are dreamt of in our philosophy. In *Agnes of God* she radiated such ecstasy one moment and such terror the next with no visible bridge between, I knew my "Manders" had greatness in her and I envied her like I'd never envied anyone.

WE SAT JUST A FEW SEATS from each other on the aisle waiting to receive our Tony Awards. When her name was called I held my breath. After all, you can't possibly have father and daughter win the same year—that would look ominously like nepotism. She got everything else as well—the Drama Desk, Outer Critics Circle Award and many others. They threw the book at her and so they should have. I have never been so thrilled.

CHAPTER FORTY-ONE

EAST WEST NEVER THE TWAIN SHALL MEET

I f you drive several blocks up from Sunset on Wetherly, you'll come
upon St. Ives Drive. It's a pretty street, and the house we were looking at, at the suggestion of Connie Wald, was set on several different
levels down to the pool and on to the gardens below—not a large place
but inviting. It had been built in the twenties so the trees were fully
grown and the undergrowth prodigious. It had at least four avocados,
some lemon and orange trees, and a mass of eucalyptus and bougainvil-
lea, which almost covered the house. I had first met Constance Wald
with Ray and Dorothy Massey. Connie was the sister of Barron Polan
(whose home we had rented in Connecticut) and she had married and
widowed the late Jerry Wald, a well-known Hollywood producer. She
lived in a New England–style house in the flats of Beverly Hills and,
since her husband's death, had thrown herself into her favourite hobby
of being an exceptionally warm and popular hostess. She, like my wife,
was a wonderful cook and entertained constantly.

It was there at her home that Fuff and I met a great many of Hollywood's Old Guard: Gloria and Jimmy Stewart, "Rocky" (Mrs. Gary
Cooper), Billy Wilder, Greg and Veronique Peck, Loretta Young, Irene
Dunne, the Jule Stynes, and when they weren't there, the Lew Wasser-
mans. It was there we met Alfred and Betsy Bloomingdale and renewed
our acquaintance with Dominick Dunne, his lovely wife, Lenny,
Audrey Hepburn, Mel Ferrer and Joseph Cotten. Connie had a talent
for collecting people and she went out of her way to be kind to us. She
had known the previous owners of the house on St. Ives who had gone
back East to their original home in Grosse Point. "The house is for sale.
Why don't you get it? You need to be here a lot, you know." Connie
could be most persuasive. Thus began our bicoastal life.

We spent the best part of five years commuting between LA and

House on St. Ives Drive

Connecticut, but our stay there, which at first had been most pleasant, was now becoming rather listless and a little odd, to say the least. In all that time, I hardly worked at all; there were some television programmes directed by one of my favourites, Boris Sagal, a TV adaptation of Michael Cristofer's *Shadow Box* with Joanne Woodward, directed by her husband, Paul Newman, and a popular miniseries, *The Thorn Birds*, with fellow Canadian Daryl Duke as director but very little else. Lou Pitt, my ever-diligent agent, simply shrugged his shoulders helplessly. LA, I was learning, was a place to visit only—do your work, have fun with your friends and get the hell out. Because if you stay permanently, and you're not flavour of the month, it begins to take you for granted. I got the impression that if one lived as far away as Siberia or Antarctica, it might prick up its ears and show some interest. Even so, I enjoyed having the gardens improved and installing redbrick walkways winding through them, and redoing the interior of the house, supervised by a very agreeable builder named John Kulhanek, of whom we became very fond. However, there was something uneasy hovering in the air— odd warnings and omens were subtly making themselves known. Then, on a balmy, peaceful Saturday morning, where nary was heard a discouraging word—it happened.

I was seated on the toilet in my bathroom reading, as was my wont, when I heard someone close by say something to me. It was a little voice, a girl's voice, very faint. I knew it couldn't be Fuff, for she was in the kitchen at the far end of the house, and it wasn't the wind whistling through the heating ducts because there was no wind. I froze and listened—there it was again—a small muffled voice crying, "Daddy." But it didn't sound quite human. There was a metallic ring to it as if it were coming down a long tunnel. I left the room and went up to the kitchen. "You didn't call me, did you?" I asked Fuff. "No, of course not." "But I just heard someone—" "Yes, I know," she broke in; "so did I." "All the way up here, it's not possible. All right, then, what did it say?" "It was a girl's voice saying 'Daddy.' It's happened before when you were away." "Why didn't you tell me?" I asked. "Because I wasn't sure and I didn't want to worry you."

From that moment on, more things began to happen, mostly on the staircase outside our bedroom and in the guest room at the bottom of the house, which was always clammy and cold, even on the hottest day. There were lots of little noises, sometimes tinkling mechanical laughter very near at one moment and far away the next, little feet scurrying across the roof above our heads at night. It's got to be some sort of animal, a squirrel, perhaps, I thought, but those footsteps were unmistakably human. "People are going to think we're mad if we tell anyone," said Fuff. "Nobody's going to believe us." Then one day a mason working on the brick paths heard the little voice too, so for the moment our sanity was not in question. However, we said nothing—we did not want to lose our Mexican help who were superstitious at the best of times. One of the men arrived one morning with his dog, an Alsatian, who all day long behaved most strangely, growling constantly, his hairs standing straight up on end. We never saw either of them again. There was also the morning when Fuff and I were having breakfast on the roofed-in balcony. I had my back to the house and she was facing it from the opposite side of the table. Suddenly she turned the colour of ash. "I just saw something float straight into the mirror." "What?" I whispered. "Oh, it was just some thick smoke, but it had a definite shape to it and it went right through that mirror behind you." It took a while for the colour to come back into her cheeks.

One weekend we decided to go to Catalina for a break. We'd carefully locked up the house, particularly making sure the glass doors opening onto the top balcony were properly secured. The masons would be working below in the garden on Saturday and we wanted to take precautions. When we got back on Monday morning, the foreman was already waiting on the front doorstep as jittery as they come. He told us they had barely begun work when doors in the house started to slam, especially the glass doors—making a terrible racket. The sound of slamming continued and he said he thought maybe we had not gone to Catalina after all and were having the most appalling family squabble. Embarrassed, he nevertheless decided to investigate and found to his utter amazement that every door in the house was tightly locked.

That was it! We called the previous owner in Grosse Point and told the whole story to him. "Ah," he said calmly, "that would be Phoebe, our daughter. She used to play on the stairs outside our bedroom. One day she had a bad fall, developed a blood clot that was so serious it eventually killed her. She was only six years old." His tone of voice suggested that there was nothing unusual about it, that it was inevitable. We also told John Kulhanek, and he suggested we have the house exorcized. He said he knew a cop who had contact with a lady psychic who occasionally worked with the police. We got the number and Fuff called her and told her we needed her help urgently, that we were being haunted, but she told her nothing else. The lady psychic agreed to come and the moment she stepped inside the house her eyes lit up. "Ah," she said with a long sigh. "It's a child. Oh, there's nothing to worry about. There is nothing malicious here. She's a happy child—she thinks you're her parents. She's trying to reach out to you so she shows off by playing her old games. But she is willful. Children can be difficult. You must be firm with her. Just keep saying, 'Phoebe, we're *not* your parents. Go away—you're free—go away now, don't be naughty.' " Fuff thanked her and asked her what it was like working with the LAPD. "You'd be surprised how these tough macho skeptics start to crumble and shake when they see books and objets d'art flying about the room of their own accord," she told us. "But don't worry, I've made a few converts!" And she was gone.

We must have looked silly—two grown people addressing the empty air in raised voices, "Now Phoebe, behave. We're not your Daddy and Mommy—go away." But it worked, temporarily; for the next few weeks the house was silent. We missed little Phoebe floating around in space, confused, puzzled, not knowing where to go. But we at least knew where we were going, and it was *out*. Phoebe would have to wait for the next occupants. We put the house on the market and went back East.

I'VE ALWAYS BEEN TEMPTED to call our house in Connecticut, which is on Wampum Hill, "Big Heap Wampum," but my dear wife talked me out of it. She's probably right. It was good to be back in the much more real world where not everyone talked showbiz talk and ratings, where there were actually other things in the world to discuss. Also the southern California weather was almost too perfect on a daily basis—sunny, dry. As the majority of starlets are groomed to look exactly alike, so is the climate. Everything in life there seems to use the same plastic surgeon. One can tire quite easily of too much lushness. What did Fred Allen once say about Hollywood? "It's a fine place to live—if you happen to be an orange!" Here in the East, there are rougher edges—you can dig deeper, get your feet wet. The four seasons were important to me—I'd been raised on them. My background music would be Sibelius rather than New Wave. I was a northerner through and through.

Our caretaker, Dick Garrity, a movie buff, and his family were now living in the little house I'd had built about fifty yards from ours. He'd just bought a puppy from the pound for five dollars. He instantly christened it Briggs. "But, Dick, didn't you notice?" I said. "It's a girl." "That's quite simple then," he responded. "We'll call her Briggie." So, like my wife, who had so many nicknames, Briggie would now answer to Brigitta, Brigadoon, Doonie, Doonbug, Dooners, Fluffy Puppy and Little Fox. She was a pretty dog, a cross between a collie and a shepherd which promises intelligence and loyalty and softens the look of both breeds. Fuff and I loved dogs with a devotion bordering on obsession, so she swiftly became our dog, much to Dick's relief. It didn't take long before we were surrounded by builders again. I'd bought the place for a relatively modest price, considering it was so private and only an hour from Manhattan—and with fourteen acres of attractive, slightly rolling countryside. But when I had the place properly surveyed, I noticed the surveyors were spending an inordinately long time doing their thing. They had told me it would take a couple of days, but at the end of the first week, I noticed their truck was still there, but there was no sign of them. "They're way into the woods somewhere down yonder," said Dick, who never stopped speaking in movie dialogue (would I ever escape it?). I shouted into the far distance, "What are you doing down there? That's a nature preserve!" "No it ain't, sir," the surveyor shouted back. "This is your property and we still have further to go." Out of breath, I caught up with them. How many acres did you buy this for?" "Fourteen," I said. "Oh no, sir, you're already closer to forty!"

Fuff, Briggie and I celebrated our windfall that night. At least back then it was a windfall—the property taxes were in no way as severe as they are now. We added on to the house, chopped off what had been the servants' quarters and turned it into a huge kitchen-cum-parlor. Here my bride came into her own. I knew she excelled in the culinary arts, but I had no idea just how fantastic a chef she was. As a youngster she had seriously taken a long Cordon Bleu course so she'd had a head start, but it was her instincts as a cook that made her so consistently good and so versatile. Every night there was a surprise on the table and that continues to this day. She can serve up authentic Italian, French, Greek, Mexican, Indian and the best of good ol' English—you name it; it's difficult to stump her, and she's always so eager to learn.

One springtime, I was standing by one of our stone walls at the top of the hill when a big beautiful blond golden retriever jumped up onto the wall and threw his arms around me. Every day he came to pay his respects. He had no visible owner, but we could sometimes hear him barking in the distance as he was doing his rounds at various people's houses. I'm sure he knew everyone in the neighbourhood and they him. They'd feed him hors d'oeuvres at drink time—God knows how many cocktails he'd consumed. He was a complete hobo—a bum! But oh so beautiful. The only thing wrong with this great baby with the wicked smile was a nervous flinch if anyone raised an arm too quickly. He was also wary of brooms and rakes. I learned later that the wife of his one-time owner used to severely beat him and abuse him early on in his checkered career. But he had taught himself to rise above his misfortunes and was generally a happy laughing dog and the biggest coward when it came to the smallest things, shirking even the bare rudiments of animal responsibility. But it was quite obvious he had fallen head over paws for Briggie. Briggs was now a full-grown lady with a gorgeous stripe down her forehead. The golden stayed all summer, sleeping outside the kitchen, rain or shine, waiting to catch a glimpse of her first thing each morning. When she was in heat and male canines would appear out of the woodwork for miles around—Dobermans, bulldogs, labs, dachshunds, even overambitious Chihuahuas, he would

With Rags, who taught me all about cowardice

gallantly see them off and in some cases fight them till they bled—he was one powerful Lothario. On sultry summer days we could see the two of them lying under a tree, just staring into each other's eyes.

We had to give him a name, and news from down the street at the local bar which he frequented confirmed that his name was Rags—so Rags it was. Fuff kept telling me not to let him inside the house on any account. "Once inside he'll never leave," she insisted. One freezing winter morning I got up about seven and went downstairs to turn on the heat—it was a blustery zero degrees Fahrenheit outside. There was Rags still asleep in a huge snowdrift outside the kitchen, his head on his paws with icicles hanging from his eyelids and his mouth. For a moment I thought he might be dead, but he moved slightly and seemed to be smiling. Briggie was awake and we both stared at him through the window. "That's it!" I said. "No one's claimed him. I'm letting him in!" I don't know who was more relieved, he or I. He was still shaking from the cold, but the first thing he did was to sit down and give me a paw. Rags was ours! And Briggie's too, of course. They romped together in the snow all winter long and then one day he must have taken her deep into the woods to some secret place he knew (he was a romantic soul) and ravaged her because pretty soon our Briggie, now thin as a rail, gave birth to eight puppies, one after the other, in front of our very eyes.

Adorable they were, of course, but God knows what kind of assortment—little bundles of black fur with occasional white spots—a predominance of sheltie in them, I'll wager. Though they were placed in a large baby crib, these eight little monsters never stopped pooping—on walls, floors, anywhere they chose. Life had become chaotic.

Into this morass came Janina Fialkowska to lend a much-needed hand. "Piggie," as we so rudely called her, came straight from my old family background in Senneville, Quebec. Her great-grandfather had bought that old pile Boisbriant from my own great-grandfather back in the dark ages. Not only were we distant cousins by marriage, but our association was very much en famille. Her mother, "Biddy" Todd Clouston, while a Red Cross ambulance driver in World War II, had fallen in love with and married a Polish officer, George Fialkowski. Biddy had studied piano under the legendary Nadia Boulanger in Paris, but her ambitions had exceeded her talent and she was determined her daughter would excel where she had failed. Her intense disciplinary methods, not without a certain sacrifice, paid off.

At the age of eighteen, Piggie had come in second in the Artur Rubinstein competitions in Israel. Her friend Emanuel Ax earned first prize. The chief judge was the great Rubinstein himself, and he and his wife, Nella, would soon take her under their wing. She lived with the Rubinsteins in Paris and in Marbella and learned a great deal from the master. In fact, Rubinstein had such confidence in her that he instructed his manager to arrange his contracts so that whatever engagements he undertook, Piggie would be given those same engagements the following year. This meant she would play major piano concertos with most of the top symphony orchestras—a daunting experience for a young girl, no matter how skilled. Now Rubinstein's reputation as a lady's man was universally known and musicians as well as conductors, believing she was just another of his conquests, treated her abominably in the beginning, without any justification. After all, Rubinstein was ninety-three. Once they heard her play, however, they changed their tune, but it was a little late, to say the least, and quite naturally the horrendous pressure on her did a certain amount of damage psychologically. However, Piggie rallied in the end after some hard knocks and was now travelling the world as one of its finest women pianists.

An important position at the Juilliard School assisting the maestro in residence, "Sascha" Gorenitzky, made it mandatory to hole up in New York for a time, so she would visit us on weekends and help with the dogs she loved. "You can't keep all these puppies," she reasoned. "It's ridiculous—you've got to give some away." We did. We gave

Janina "Piggie" Fialkowska, la grande pianiste

away six and kept a little beauty with an adorable white nose whom we called "Patches," and an ugly mutt, the runt of the litter, with a hugely funny personality and speckled spots of white all over her like a toad, whom we of course called "Toadie." Briggie, very Scottish indeed being part collie, was rather short with them and pretended not to show much interest, but Rags was a wonderful father, rolling with them in the grass and flower beds or cleaning them and washing their eyes. However, most everyone's attention was centered on the odd one, Toadie, obviously her father's favourite, and poor "Paddy," as we nicknamed her, who never stopped trying to please, was usually left out of things and became very jealous of her sister. We had our hands full training them, just as difficult a time as they must have had training *us*. To them we were members of their pack and privileged to be so. I'd been used to the canine world all my life but never a family like this, a family in which I was included—with all its loyalties and dysfunctions, who would fight to the death for each other.

OF COURSE, it was necessary to go on earning money in order to keep our pack in the style to which we were accustomed. As a consequence of

Toadie, drawn by dear friend Susan Hoquet

certain tax arrangements, in my country I had become what is known as Canadian content, which meant that any foreign film made in Canada as a coproduction would have to accept at least one or two Canadians in a principal or starring role. Canadian content sounded terribly cold and impersonal, like a prolonged prison sentence or a disease. "No I'm not an actor, I'm not even a person—I'm Canadian content—can't you tell?" But it certainly was a useful means of security, and I found myself appearing in many a picture and television production made in Toronto, Montreal, Vancouver, as well as in Europe, which fortunately still beckoned.

Two engagements stood out as a study in contrasts—*The Scarlet and the Black* made in Rome, and *The Day That Shook the World* (*Sarajevski atentat*) made in Prague and Yugoslavia. The former was the true story of an Irish priest who was secretly fighting the Nazi occupation of Rome through the underground. The Nazi commandant in charge of the occupation searches high and low for him. They strike up a strange sort of unspoken bond, even a mutual respect, as in honour amongst thieves. When the Nazis are finally defeated and the commandant is in prison, he sends for his enemy, the monsignor, and begs him to convert him to Catholicism. The monsignor does so with all his heart in a small modest ceremony in the jail itself. The Nazi dies soon after in his very cell, his only sanctuary, at peace with himself. Gregory Peck, with whom I renewed my acquaintance, played the priest, Sir John Gielgud was Pius X, the pope who famously sat on the fence, and I was the Nazi commandant. Jerry London directed, it was a cracking good story, and it was my great fortune to work with Gregory and John, two of the most generous actors in our profession.

The second project, *The Day That Shook the World,* was another story altogether—quite bizarre and utterly demented. It was a film about the murder of Archduke Franz Ferdinand and his wife, Sophie, by the young rebel Gavrilo Princip, the famous incident that ignited World War I. The film, an American, Czechoslovakian and Yugoslavian coproduction, starred me as the ill-fated archduke and as my wife, Florinda Bolkan, a beautiful, charming, immensely statuesque actress from Brazil. Besides ourselves, it was filled with actors from Czechoslovakia, Germany, Austria and Yugoslavia. We began shooting the Hapsburg section of the story in Prague, that most beautiful of cities with its multisconced candelabras on every street corner; the grand Charles Bridge that spans the river Moldau, blackened from the cheap petrol; the little house where Kafka lived; the enchanting old Jewish quarter; the fourteenth-century square in the center of town with its famous clock tower from which moving figures strike the hour; the vast cathedrals, St. Stephen on the lower level and St. Vitus cresting the hill— altogether an elegant jewel of a city waiting patiently for someone to come along and clean it up. Very soon Prague would become a festival once again and a favourite location for many filmmakers, its own Barrandov Studios being one of the most prestigious film schools in the world.

Of course, Prague had always been a major center for music in Europe, and though now restricted by the Communist takeover, its citizens were permitted the luxury of an odd concert. Fuff and I went one night to hear that most eccentric but brilliant pianist Arturo Benedetti Michelangeli give a solo recital of Schubert, Chopin and Ravel. The place was packed; the townspeople spent what little they had on things cultural. We were all crammed in like music-loving sardines when an extremely tardy Maestro Michelangeli made his entrance. He walked on, the portrait of melancholy, dressed entirely in black—a black frock coat, black gloves, long black hair—Franz Liszt playing Hamlet. He took his sweet time removing his gloves, adjusting his stool, smoothing his hair and examining the piano keys before he finally began to play. His Schubert was metallic, hard, furious, cold, much too fast—he obviously hated the piano he'd been given. Everyone went out into the lobby at intermission and lit up. The amount of cigarette smoking in occupied Communist countries was dangerously high. As they puffed away, they shuffled about the room in a circle—like prisoners in a barbed-wire pen.

A new piano had now been brought in (perhaps it was his and had arrived late) and Benedetti made the same sombre entrance and began testing the notes. As far as his melancholy nature would allow, a hint of a smile chased across his pale features and when he began the Chopin, he was another man—electrifying, mesmerizing. I have never heard Ravel's *Gaspard de la Nuit,* one of my favourites, played so magnificently—notes in the left hand were sounded that I never knew existed. It was as if Ravel had written it especially for him and this was its première performance. I don't know how long the audience stayed, but encore after encore was played until we left exhausted. That enraptured crowd of poor, deprived Czech citizens was so grateful and so moved, they simply wouldn't let him go.

I told this story years later to Terry MacEwan, the music world's hottest manager at that time (among his clients, Pavarotti and Domingo) on a plane trip we shared. He then told me his Michelangeli experience; he had also managed the pianist for a while. There was a concert scheduled with the New York Philharmonic, with Michelangeli to be the soloist. Terry picked him up at his hotel in a limousine. They are on their way. Michelangeli, in the backseat beside Terry, said, "E—Tayree fair ve goeen?" "To the concert." "Fair?" "The Philharmonic." "Vat ess playeen?" "Rachmaninov's third piano concerto." "Oh, oh—who plays dis?" "You, maestro." "Me? Oh no, Tayree, Tayree. Oh no, let's go cheenemah, Tayree. I vant go to cheenema." It took several rides around the block before Terry persuaded him he must play the concert.

The Czech government had allowed us to film in Franz Ferdinand's hunting lodge outside Prague called Konopiste. I have never seen so many animal heads mounted on so many walls as in this massive and most depressing mausoleum. We also shot in and around an exquisite castle that had belonged to the Cardinal von Fürstenberg, and yet another castle, the nineteenth-century Gothic pile Castle Schwarzenberg, deep in the woods. The Bohemian countryside that surrounded the city of Prague was very beautiful, soft and gently rolling. I was sad to leave it, for even in those stressful times it still reminded one of just how civilized a part of the world this once was.

Our esteemed director, Veljko Bulajic, a tall, proud Montenegren (is there any other kind?) behaved as if he had complete control over not just the film but all the Balkan states as well. A powerful high-ranking member of the Communist party and one of Tito's trusted right-hand men in the government, Veljko occasionally dropped little bon mots such as "My grandmother was queen of Montenegro, but I never use my title when I work." He had made some important films in Eastern

Veljko, thinking up some diabolical direction

Europe such as the gigantic epic *The Battle of Vareslava,* so he was some-one to be reckoned with. He had been most agreeably charming to Florinda and me while we were in Prague, but once the film unit moved to Sarajevo, more or less his home territory, he became a fiercely overbearing autocrat who trusted no one, especially, I am sorry to say, me. Even when I was speaking to my interpreter, George Petrarco, a multilingual American who lived in Rome, I could see in the distance Veljko, with daggers in his eyes, staring at me. I had one harsh dis-agreement with Veljko in which I felt he was trying to make the arch-duke merely a cardboard figure with no redeeming features. It was a mere discussion, only, but he never forgave me.

However, the film was being made impeccably authentic. The mas-sive Serbo-Croat army that Veljko had at his command seemed just as numerous as that of *Waterloo.* All military uniforms were magnificently reproduced and, through some miraculous arrangement with Vienna's Museum of Royal Collections, I was able to wear the actual sword and medals worn by the archduke himself. Florinda was dressed superbly; she appeared the very picture of supreme elegance — far more ravishing than the real Sophie. All the vehicles used on the film for the procession were the actual open-roofed Tantras, a rare Czech car, the very motors that had carried the royal couple. There was a great deal to admire

The Archduke (me) and Princess Sophie (Florinda Bolkan)
dreading Belko's next direction

about the production and I liked the Yugoslavs very much—they worked with such enthusiasm. It was just Veljko, riddled with this strange persecution complex, who made the atmosphere so tense and unpleasant, shouting orders, screaming at his excellent camera crew whom he continually accused of being incompetent. They all thought him quite mad, of course, but what could they do? The man had power.

Two nights were set aside to film a huge banquet scene. It was wonderfully arranged with a crowd of about one thousand. They had secured the actual speech Franz Ferdinand had spoken on that evening—I was to memorize it and deliver it in both English and German. We had started very early in the morning, but Veljko, for some pig-headed reason, refused to bring the camera round on me, his principal player. All day and night he shot reactions from the crowd—an unnecessary waste of film. The crew and the extras were utterly exhausted, and as there is nothing so tiring as hanging about waiting, so was I. It was 1:00 a.m. when he turned the cameras round on me. There seemed to be no rules or unions in this part of the world to set a time when to stop. I was so tired and angry my lips could hardly form words and by that time I'd forgotten everything I'd learned. I spoke up:

"Veljko, I'm the only one with dialogue in this entire scene. I've been waiting all day and night to do this, but now it's too late and I'm so tired I won't make any sense. As we have to be here tomorrow anyway and your cameras are pointing in the right direction, why not shoot it first thing when I'm fresh?" He whispered something to George Petrarco who came over to me white as a sheet. "He says you will do it now. If you refuse he will have you thrown in jail." That was the strongest and most direct note I've ever received from any director. He was deadly serious and I knew it. There was a long silence while I imagined Tito's soldiers coming in to arrest me and carry me off. I did my speech—I was very bad, I'm sure—but I did my speech.

Lucky Fuff managed to escape and fly back to Connecticut, and I would grab every opportunity to flee Sarajevo and drive the nearly five-hour trip through the hills to Mostar and then Dubrovnik so I could drink in the salty sea air and wake up on that spectacular coastline. But now the ordeal was just about over. Florinda and I were to shoot our last scene together—the assassination itself. We were to be filmed being driven through the whole town by two chauffeurs preceded *and* followed by several more cars and carriages of the period. We would stop momentarily at the town hall where we would be greeted by the mayor of Sarajevo, exactly as history recorded it. Then we would continue through the streets and turn a corner where the young assassin Gavrilo Princip would be waiting to put an end to us.

We began our slow procession. The whole town had turned out to watch and they mingled with the extras perfectly. Florinda and I sat, in all our splendour, in the backseat of our "Tantrum," as we nicknamed it, open to the skies. As we looked up to the rooftops where hundreds of people were leaning over staring down at us, I had the eerie feeling they had got the idea that it was really happening all over again—that the real Hapsburgs were returning to the scene of the crime. "Look at their faces," Florinda said to me under her breath. She was right—their expressions were sour, unfriendly, perhaps even hostile. When we got out of the car and had finished the scene on the red carpet with the mayor, the publicity man came up to me and said, "Mister Plummer, there is someone from the crowd I'd like you to meet and perhaps take a picture or two with her." He brought her over, an old peasant woman of ample girth with anger in her eyes. "This is Miss Princip—the sister of the real Gavrilo Princip." I gulped audibly. She stared at me with a look of perplexity and mistrust. Here was I, dressed in full regalia as the archduke, her sworn enemy, with real sword, plumed hat and authentic medals, and here was she, my assassin's sister! It was a swelteringly hot day anyway, and now my breath was coming short and fast. There was something sinister lurking in the air and Florinda and I could hardly wait to be shot dead around the next street corner—dead and free of it all at last!

The movie was seen by only a few people in the West, but in the Eastern Bloc, the satellite countries, it was most probably an unqualified success. Veljko had ruthlessly slashed the royals to ribbons and had turned what was left of us into cardboard figures, just as I felt he had intended from the start. The original script had interestingly given both factions a fair hearing, now it was all about the revolutionaries and their brand of heroism, nothing more. The film's Yugoslavian title was changed to *Assassination*, quite correctly. It was an assassination! The story that Florinda and I had both accepted one day long ago had been shot to pieces by the mad monster from Montenegro.

I was fascinated by that beautiful rugged country with its complexities, its bravery, its wild inbred history, but I don't think I've ever been so glad to get home to Wampum Hill and to see the rest of my little pack, their noses pressed against the window, and then the mad rush down the stairs to greet me with such an unabashed explosion of trust, I had to lie prone on the floor for my safety!

CHAPTER FORTY-TWO

THREE COMIC INTERLUDES

NUMBER 1

We must have got stuck somehow in Nancy Reagan's computer, for both Fuff and I kept getting invitations for small private dinners at the White House. The first was understandable enough as it was to honour Laurence Olivier, now a lord, and to show his film of *King Lear* in the little screening room. I must say it was quite flattering since I was the only other actor present. While waiting for the Oliviers to arrive, President Reagan came over to me and we started reminiscing about Hollywood days. It seems we had shared the same agents at one time and we exchanged Kurt Frings stories amidst hoots of laughter. It struck me as being more than a little bizarre, for here were two actors bitching about their agents and just a couple of yards behind us stood the man with the Nuclear Football.

At supper, I was placed next to Selwa "Lucky" Roosevelt, chief of protocol for the Reagans as well as two other presidencies before them. I remarked how simple and beautiful the White House was inside—and how young looking and without pomp. "It's all due to Nancy and Billy Baldwin. In my long experience here, the White House has never looked so attractive," Lucky told me. She had married Teddy Roosevelt's grandson Archibald and had emerged as a charming Washington hostess as well as a good friend. Fuff was seated next to Caspar Weinberger, secretary of defense, the most civilized of men—knowledgeable on so many subjects, especially painting, music and poetry. On her left sat George Shultz, flirty and amusing. But of all those present, it was Weinberger, with his beautiful speaking voice and elegant manners, who impressed her the most.

On the way to the screening room, I walked down the corridor with Larry and he said quietly, "Oh Kit, you don't want to see this. I'm not very good in it, you know. I was so bloody weak they had to lift me onto my horse." I congratulated him on his peerage. "You know my passion for kippered herrings?" he continued. "Well, I had them every morning on my commute to London on the Brighton Belle. When they were searching for my title, I suggested Lord Kipper of Brighton, but they wouldn't buy it." He stopped for a moment at the door, "You know, I've had too many honours—quite enough for several lifetimes—but there's one I still lust after, though of course I'll never get it." He paused dramatically, as if waiting for a cue. "And what is that, Larry?" I obliged. "An honorary American citizen."

We all sat down to a fascinating but overly long movie. Larry had been right. He was indeed very frail as Lear and his voice was pitched unusually high—he no longer owned those wondrous ringing tones. It was no surprise, considering the number of horrific diseases he had battled his way through. After it was over, the Reagans' court jesters, Bill Buckley and his wife, Pat, made their way up in the lift to the president's private apartments and the rest of us dispersed. While we were waiting for our car, Larry and Joan's drove up. He very slowly and gingerly climbed into the backseat, rolled down the window and gave me the most wonderful smile; he reached out, grabbed my hand and held on till I winced. That was the last time I was to see the greatest theatrical animal of the century.

THERE WERE OTHER OCCASIONS such as a state reception for Canada's premier Brian Mulroney when I sat next to George Bush père and renewed my old acquaintance with Prince Sadr Khan from Boston days. He was there with his brother the Aga Khan and at the same table was our country's gregarious ambassador Allan Gotlieb and his very amusing wife, Sondra, who served the best embassy food in Washington. But it was the smaller gatherings that perplexed me—it was either Lucky Roosevelt or Mrs. Reagan who invited us, mais pourquoi?

One Thanksgiving we were summoned to a supper for the prince and princess of Lichtenstein, who had lent their paintings to be shown in all the major cities of the United States. It is one of the world's most important private collections and includes the largest private collection of Rubens in the world. Everybody gathered in one of the anterooms; all the top brass in the cabinet were present at this one, and the after-dinner recital would be given by Burt Bacharach, playing his own compositions, rumoured to be the princess's favourite American music. We all formed a sort of line—Fuff again monopolizing Caspar W. while I stood beside my fellow Canuck, Bacharach, exchanging north of the border sentiments. Double doors were thrown open—the marines stood at attention and the Reagans entered, escorting Their Highnesses.

The prince looked stooped and old and much too feeble to shake hands, preferring to give everyone a perfunctory nod, but his wife, a tall buxom Valkyrie in a blue and silver reflecting dress, overcharged with aggressive energy and sparkling like a lit Christmas tree, greeted all about her with a resounding chortle. When I was introduced, she came forward to me, preceded by wafts of sickeningly sweet perfume which smelled like a mix of Joy and Old Spice. I bowed, but her eyes were centered somewhere above my head as if she'd expected me to be taller and I had failed her miserably by not being so. But when she saw Burt, she exploded with a loud shout of recognition, took two steps back, pointed a huge bejewelled finger at him and began to sing in a raucous Teutonic bellow, "Oho-ho, Oho-ho. Hrain drips kip fowling on mine hett, but chuss ven I'm sinking . . ." Just about bursting out of her dress, she performed it with such zest it looked as if she'd been rehearsing it in front of a mirror for weeks. I didn't dare look at Burt, though I'd have given anything to see his face.

At supper, the old prince sat on Mrs. Reagan's right and I was placed close to him on the other side. Ah, that's it, I thought, I'm here 'cause I can help out with the French. Every time Nancy Reagan tried to engage him in conversation, the slurping sound he made eating his soup rendered any response quite impossible. I thought I'd better begin to do my job and speak some French. I waited for the slurping to subside and started by apologizing for having never been to his country. He didn't seem to be listening to me at all and only stared at his soup. I tried flattery and said something idiotic about how beautiful I'd been told it was and how great it was for skiing. He was back slurping his soup again and it was at least a whole minute before he wiped his mouth, turned to me very slowly and said in a voice sounding like Mike Nichols mimicking Albert Schweitzer, "Ah, oui, ils y a beaucoup des collines a Lichtenstein." There was a sonorous profundity ringing through this staggering bit of information. I felt he had spoken to me in code and was giving me my secret bank account number. I gave up and, thankfully, Katharine Graham, as was her wont, instantly monopolized all further conversation.

The president rose and said a few charming words of thanks for the wonderful gesture the Lichtensteins had made toward America, and sat down again. There was a silence while we all waited. All eyes were on the prince. Someone—I think it was Nancy Reagan—nudged him and he rose as if in slow motion. It was many seconds before he found his glasses and his notes. Finally, he spoke. "Monsieur le President—et Madame—uh, uh—" There was an awful moment. Most present, especially the cabinet, were now on the edge of their seats. The prince looked around as if for help, then brought his notes right up to his face, "uh-uh—*Reagan*!" At last he'd remembered— Red Alert was cancelled, war postponed. There was an audible sigh that echoed off the dining room walls and the evening, which so far had been limping along, threw away its crutches and became a major four-minute miler.

NUMBER 2

A small break for Fuff from running with the pack was another visit to the Royal Poinciana Palm Beach, where I was in a comedy written and directed by Garson Kanin called *Peccadillo* as a tryout for Broadway. I was playing an eccentric orchestra leader in the mold of a middle-aged Toscanini who is leading a double life with his wife (Glynis Johns) and his mistress-cum-protégé (Kelly McGillis). I needed a comedy badly and this seemed to be the ticket. Garson's first two acts were skillfully written and funny indeed; after all, he was a comedic master (*Pat and Mike* and *Born Yesterday*). For my character, he had been inspired, or so he told me, by the famous true incident when Toscanini, during a rehearsal, started screaming at some poor violinist, calling him by every name under the Tuscan sun for his incompetence. As the story goes, the gutsy violinist walked out and, as he reached the edge of the stage, turned and yelled at the maestro, "And by the way, Fuuuuck you!" To which Toscanini shouted back, "Dere-ees-a-no-need to apologize!"

Although acts 1 and 2 worked a treat, the third was a disaster. Garson didn't seem the slightest bit interested in fixing it either. We worked ourselves to the bone hoping to make some sense of it, but it simply didn't have an ending. We tried new things every night, wildly improvising, ad-libbing to the point of breaking each other up, but there was nothing we could do—nothing seemed to work. I had a great time being with Kelly and darling Glynis, in spite of her old trick of never knowing her lines, so that we had to take turns cueing her continuously till the dress rehearsal when, with that apologetic pixie charm of hers, she would drop the book and launch into a word-perfect performance whilst the rest of us floundered about in a mild state of amnesia.

Gar had had a stroke in the middle of rehearsals, and he and his wife, Ruth Gordon, who stuck to him like glue, left the play for the hospital. I got Michael Langham to agree to take over and the moment Gar got wind of this, he instantly recovered and to my utter surprise and shock flew down to Palm Beach, walked straight into rehearsal and said in a loud voice, "I'm back." Langham had to withdraw, sadly, as he had been contributing some wonderful ideas. The whole venture, however, was a great success in Palm Beach. It was just their cup of tea—even the third act hodgepodge. "You ought to know better than anyone that Palm Beach ain't New York," I said rather frankly to Gar. He smiled that wide, captivating smile of his and assured me he had written a brand-new third act and that I would like it enormously. That night after the performance he handed it to me with much ceremony in Ruth's presence. With mounting excitement, I took it home and read it. I could not believe my eyes—nothing had been changed, not a word, not a comma. It was exactly the same, just written on cleaner manuscript, that was all. Was it the stroke? Or was it his way of saying, "If you think I'm changing a word of this play, you son of a bitch, you're insane"?

Written in my contract was a clause which stated I need not go to New York with the play if I felt it wasn't worth it. Well, without a third act, it wasn't. So I told the cast and I think they understood. The play closed and we went our separate ways. It was a long time before I saw Garson again. The great Ruth Gordon had died and he had married their good friend and mine, Marian Seldes. By now I think he'd forgiven me or else had banished it from his mind. But I'll take my oath he knew all along. He was too much of an expert at constructing comedy—too much of a pro—*not* to have known. I think he just loved playing the devil.

The adorable Glynis Johns

NUMBER 3

Fran and Barry Weissler, still reeling from the success of *Othello,* must have seen themselves as the fresh new harbingers of classical theatre on Broadway. They would be justified in feeling so, as no one for many a decade had had the chutzpah or insanity to push Shakespeare smack into the commercial lion's den. Drunk with power, they decided to follow it up with the Bard's most salable ticket, the Scottish play—*Macbeth.* So being loyal to the Old Boys' Club, they commandeered me once again. Having been burned in Birnam Wood once before, I had obviously learned nothing, and with a death wish of suicidal proportions, I said yes. There was a plus side, however, for Glenda Jackson, the two-time Oscar winner and so far, in my view, the definitive Elizabeth I, had agreed to do the Lady. At least we'll sell some tickets, I thought, as I comforted myself.

Miss Jackson, or "Gloriana," was not to arrive until the third week of rehearsal. But by that time, enough bad omens had hovered over that bubbling cauldron to give credence to the superstitions surrounding the play. The first Macduff left before rehearsals had barely begun. He was replaced with a fine young actor from Canada, Stephen Russell, who could stay only for the beginning of the out-of-town tryout as he had previous commitments. He, in turn, would be replaced by another fine actor, and another Stephen—Stephen Markle. The poor girl playing Lady Macduff simply waited with resigned good nature for husbands to come and go. This poor girl, incidentally, was enjoying her Broadway debut—a powerful, young actress of much promise with a fresh natural beauty whose face was an open book. She reminded me very much of a young Patricia Neal and her name was Cherry Jones.

Even before Miss Jackson was to set foot on American soil, I could tell that the director we had selected would not be with us long. He was terribly nice, terribly competent and suffered terribly from catarrh. It was clear after a few days that he was incapable of lifting this lofty piece much above the level of a first reading. Tony Walton, that brilliant designer whom I thought might bring us all luck, had designed a raised set representing a hill on the heath that was so perpendicularly steep and high I almost had a nosebleed every time I made an entrance. At last Gloriana arrived. She took one look at the set and, forgetting to say even a cursory good morning, barked a strident Elizabethan command, "Well, all that will have to go, for a fucking start!" Hello? St. Joan of the Stockyards had just walked in! All my insipid tact and controlled patience had gone for naught—truth and brutal candor now ruled supreme. I was struggling with that most difficult of soliloquies before the banquet scene. "To be thus is nothing; / But to be safely thus." My tendency was to underplay it because I was afraid it could be overly melodramatic. In front of the entire cast, Miss Gloriana said, "You're not going to play it like that, are you? For God's sake, Plummer, where are your balls?" She got me so angry that when I did it again, I kicked a chair violently across the room. "That's more like it," piped Lady Macbeth, who appeared to have become my unauthorized personal coach.

But hiring a new director was of the utmost urgency. Glenda, the Weisslers and I put our heads together. We had a list of potential young geniuses from England who were, as usual, in demand and unavailable. I suggested Ken Russell, that daredevil maverick who had directed Glenda on film in *Women in Love* and *The Music Lovers* as well as four of the most wonderful docudramas, on Isadora Duncan, Frederick Delius, Wordsworth and Coleridge; plus, he was a Scot. "He's maddeningly unpredictable," said Glenda, "but go ahead, you have my blessing." The Weisslers thought I should meet him alone. Because I had director approval in my contract, I had the interview set up and we met. He obviously had never seen any of my work, didn't know me from Adam, which was not a good start. He remained silent through most of the meeting—glaring at me—sizing me up. Who the hell was conducting this interview, anyway? "Can you wear kilts?" he suddenly blurted, breaking the interminable silence. "Yes, my legs are pretty good," I said proudly in self-defense. "Good," he said and that was it. He got up to leave. I quickly asked him what period he had in mind for the play. "Somewhere in the indefinite future," he said and slammed the door behind him.

Some weeks later on the road, we were still without a director. Now that we would have to extend the out-of-town dates, the costs were becoming prohibitive and the Weisslers were not as flush then as they are now. Fuff suggested we contact Garth Drabrinsky, my old *Silent Partner* producer friend, to be our new backer. Garth was now reveling in his huge cinemaplex company and had become an entrepreneur extraordinaire. The Weisslers approached him, he came on board and what's more, gave us our new director, Robin Phillips, someone of whose caliber we should have had from the start. Phillips, brilliant and adventurous, who revitalized Canada's Stratford Festival beyond recognition by bringing in such performers as Maggie Smith, Margaret Tyzack and the like, was an innovator who demanded full and final authority in everything he did. When he joined us, he brought in his own set design, weeded out a few stragglers but for the most part kept our company pretty well intact. He and Glenda got along right from the start. Suddenly she was more confident, if that could be possible; she trusted him completely. I don't think he particularly liked me and thought me miscast—something that should have occurred to me ages ago. It would have saved a great deal of trouble. More accidents started occurring—members of the crowd were always getting hurt. Tony's huge set was still with us while they were building the new one, looking very Wagnerian—as well as anticipating the story of the play. The floor was made of something similar to Astroturf and one night, during the duel, I turned quickly and my foot did not follow my leg. It was still pointing in the other direction.

Thus began the long treks early each morning to every hospital in every town for treatment of my knee, showing the first signs of permanent arthritis. At night, I would perform in a huge support all the way up my leg—the solid one athletes use. It must have looked unbelievably strange. Melinda Howard, my usual dresser, had wisely opted out of this engagement, being madly superstitious, and had recommended a friend of hers, an extremely sexy Texan lass who strapped me into this "contraption" each night—the only pleasant part of the whole ordeal. Robin, with a certain amount of sadistic humour, was enjoying my plight enormously. He had a habit of getting results by describing what he wanted physically. One morning, while I was steadying myself by holding on to two chairs, trying one of the early soliloquies, he grabbed my shoulders from behind, pulled them roughly back and said, "*Now* say the speech. You'll see the exertion will change everything and affect the way you speak it. That's how I want you to do it!" He pulled them back so hard he damaged a nerve in my neck, which caused the beginnings of a disintegrating disk from which I've never recovered. (Not too late to sue you, Robin.) Now I was coming to rehearsals on crutches wearing a huge neck brace made of steel. "Here comes the fucking cripple," he would gleefully shout, which delighted the cast who I'm sure were only too pleased to see their leading player brought down to size.

Playing on the Tony Walton set at night and rehearsing on the new one the next day was both confusing and exhausting. But Robin's contribution in such a short time was immense. At last we were in a production we might be proud of. Every now and then Robin would come up with an insanely spectacular idea right out of the blue—his brain moved in mysterious ways. We were now tackling the final moments of the play, the famous "Tomorrow, and tomorrow" speech. I would say a few lines and without breaking the rhythm of the poetry, a door would slam shut. Some soldier or servant would leave the stage, shutting a door behind him. Then other doors would slam farther and farther away in the castle. It was an extraordinary effect—the Thane's followers deserting their crazed leader one after the other. It was marvellously cinematic and I was lost in its spell for a moment, but pinching myself awake, I had to say, "Robin, that's great, *but* it is a soliloquy—you know that—and that means I have to be alone." "Oh bugger!" he said, and stomped off and that original and devastating invention was instantly banished.

When we reached Toronto, the production raked it in at the O'Keefe Centre. Garth Drabinsky was happy, for one, as the piece grossed over a million in a two-week stay. On the opening night, it didn't seem to matter nor did anyone really care that, making my entrance in the dark for the banquet scene, I bumped straight into a stagehand running at full speed into the wings. When the lights went on, my mouth was full of blood as I began to speak. It hadn't quite struck me that I'd lost two or three of my front teeth. Suddenly the Thane had a harelip. It was just another infliction from the witches' curse, which my voluptuous Texas cowgirl would be willing to look after. When the curtain finally descended that night, someone rushed up to me on stage and said, "Prime Minister Trudeau will be at the reception and we want to take some pictures." "He'll have to wait, I'm afraid, I'm still looking for my teeth."

As a matter of fact, our *Macbeth* sold out pretty well everywhere it went—partly because of the clever gossipy publicity our PR lady cooked up to make it look as if Glenda and I were constantly fighting. This gave an added soupçon of sensationalism that attracted the curious. If one of us forgot that we were supposedly feuding and smiled at each other during a curtain call, she would kick me and I her with my good foot just to remind us to glower. When we reached Boston, where we were to play for three weeks before hitting New Haven and then the Mark Hellinger on Broadway, Robin called us all together and announced he was leaving. "I never said I'd stay with it till New York. I have other things to do—sorry—you're on your own and good luck." It was the worst kind of coitus interruptus. Glenda was devastated—so were the Weisslers and the cast who had worshipped him. There would be no more warm-ups in the morning, no third-form shenanigans—they'd lost their headmaster.

Robin was extraordinarily talented but darkly perverse. Certain rich and original ideas of his, and there were many, he would suppress, cut off in midcreation and turn them back into himself, as if he hated anyone to see his vulnerable, creative side. What a wasted brilliance! Though, of course, he was highly regarded in theatre circles everywhere, had this perverse nature of his not been so powerful, I think he could have achieved real greatness. And yet perhaps that sort of self-flagellation was, after all, the very source of his brilliance. One thing was certain, his talent was his own worst enemy.

Zoe Caldwell, bless her Aussie heart, yet again came to the rescue at the Weisslers' invitation. She was quickly becoming the play doctor in residence. She noticed that my dresser was always present, helping me as I limped along. "Who's that great girl looking after you and all your wounds? She's tuh-rrific!" "She's my Texan nurse, Zoe—nothing more." "Well," said Zoe, "you better obey her and get well 'cause

Caricature for Macbeth, *me and Glenda*

you've got your work cut out for ya." Zoe began by taking all the neurotic tension out of my performance and made me relax in it. *She* was tuh-rrific! She and Gloriana, however, did not get along. One day, Zoe made the mistake of taking my head in her hands and showing her just how she wanted Lady Macbeth to kiss me. That was it. I heard Gloriana mumble under her breath, "I think she wants to play the part herself." She refused from that moment on to take any further direction and I don't think they spoke to each other ever again.

The *fourth* Macduff now made an appearance in the person of Alan Scarfe, a powerful leading stage actor who looked wonderful and spoke the verse beautifully. Cherry Jones was now giving us such a simple, touching Lady Macduff, you could have thrown a dozen more Macduffs at her—she wouldn't have turned a hair. Well, we opened, at last, at the big Mark Hellinger just west of Eighth Avenue. Glenda, in her own world, was splendid and her sleepwalking scene was particularly spinechilling, winning her a Tony nomination. Cherry Jones was simply magnificent; Alan Scarfe was tops—and that offbeat, eccentric Jeff

Weiss, very funny as the drunken Porter, took so long crossing the stage to answer the knocking at the gate, three productions of Macbeth could have been presented by the time he got there. But I was properly chastised for my poor Thane. Rather than Irving's famished wolf, I was much more in the mould of Road Runner's Wile E. Coyote. My press for the most part was gently reprimanding. Walter Kerr, in one of his last critiques, praised my verse-speaking, but John Simon discussed my Macbeth as being far too old to have ambitions of any kind—even accusing me of being out of shape and growing a middle-aged pot. Where the hell was that old witch Dame Olwyn when I needed her?!

GLENDA "GLORIANA" JACKSON, CBE, came to stay with us at Wampum Hill for a short spell. In contrast to her leftist angry young rebel image, she was the easiest and most perfect houseguest imaginable. She did everything the best-brought-up Victorian maiden was trained to do. In the absence of staff, in our case regularly absent, she made up her own bed every morning with hospital-required perfection. In order to stay out of our hair during the day, she would retire to her room and read or if she tired of that she would go out into the garden and weed. She left the flower beds immaculate. Fuff and I considered asking her if she'd remain permanently as our gardener. Even the dogs accepted her as part of the pack, but Toadie, the ugly mutt, fell in love. She followed her everywhere, lay down beside her at the table or by her chair. She would hit her with her paw to get her attention and then just stare lovingly into her eyes. When Gloriana left us, the place looked more stunning than ever.

It was clear that she was becoming disenchanted with the theatre and much more dedicated to politics, for when she returned to England she retired from acting and was voted into the House of Commons as the Labour MP for Hampstead and Highgate. For a while, she was a junior member of the Blair government as transport minister, which prompted me to say, "If you ever have trouble getting a cab, call Glenda." As a formidable backbencher, she also became a regular critic of Tony Blair, calling him to resign on several issues but principally for supporting the Iraq war. She was, for a moment, a probable dark-horse contender to replace him as prime minister, and I believe she could have made a most powerful one—as powerful as that famous role she owns. Can you imagine—a left-wing Elizabeth I?

CHAPTER FORTY-THREE

DRAMA AT HOME AND ABROAD

One afternoon, not too long after Glenda had left, I was relaxing in the large back room which opened out onto our orchard and pool. The dogs were having a wonderful time jumping around their favourite old apple tree, gnarled and wizened like an Arthur Rackham drawing. They were hunting squirrels which used the old tree as their condominium. I dozed off for a second and had quite forgotten where I was, when I was awakened by the most terrible scream—like that of a child in agony. I ran out to see from whence it came. It was no child—it was Toadie. The rest of the pack was standing around in shock, staring at her. I saw that both her upper and lower jaws were broken so badly that they pointed in opposite directions. She was also making weird little choking sounds. "Toadie! Toadie!" I cried and the poor mutt actually wagged her tail. My God, I thought, she's swallowed her tongue as well. I picked her up in my arms as gently as I could, but I couldn't find her tongue—what the hell was I going to do? Just then Fuff came around the corner like a whirlwind and took complete command. "Give her to me. Don't just stand there—call the vet—I'll get the car." As I turned to leave, I noticed Paddy was skulking behind the tree, looking more than guilty—a look no dog can ever conceal. So that was it. Her jealousy had gotten the better of her, and she'd finally snapped.

I drove ninety miles an hour with Toadie in the back, Fuff holding her and wiping away the blood with a towel. Once inside, the vet opened the door of the operating room, literally pushed some poor old heavily sedated German shepherd off the table and lay Toadie down in his place. "If you'd been ten minutes longer you'd have lost her. Don't worry, we'll fix her up. If you just look into her eyes so she knows you're here while I give her a shot—that's it." I'll never forget those sad little eyes looking up at us with such love and fear.

Twelve days later, the vet called. "You'd better come down now and take Toadie home. She's going to be okay. At the moment, she's got steel clamps holding each jaw in place, which she'll get used to, but she needs to see you both because she thinks you've all left her and she's losing her will to live." We tore down and the moment she saw us, that poor beaten face lit up. The rest of the pack was glad to see her, even the culprit Paddy seemed happy. They sniffed her a lot and were very interested in the steel jaw our bionic patient kept opening and closing with a resounding crack that resembled a bear trap going off. We took her for a walk with the pack and Rags was so gentle with her, licking her stitched-up face and generally being so attentive that Paddy, once more overcome with jealousy, attacked her again, opening her stitches. Blood started to pour and there we were, déjà vu, rushing her back to the vet.

Once the overwhelming desire to be a pack leader is satisfied and once blood has been tasted, there is no turning back. We should have known that. It was our fault. Poor Paddy didn't know what she'd done. She loved her sister more than anything and never stopped looking for her. In desperation, I called my friend Barbara Johnson, Polly's daughter-in-law, who lived in Senneville, Quebec, on a six-hundred-acre farm. Her husband, Louis, had just died — she was alone and I was hoping she might like some company. "I know this is a long shot, Barbara," I began, "but we have a dog, a lovely dog who, if someone doesn't take her, we might have to put down." I then told her the truth of what happened and I tried to describe Paddy as best I could. "Well, I think she sounds terrific," said Barbara. "You think so?" I said, my heart pounding away double time. "Let me send you some pictures of her and her papers and everything before you make up your mind." "No," said Barbara, "don't send me anything — just send me the dog!" I was so choked I could barely get the word "thank-you" out of my mouth. Well, it worked out. Paddy lived to a great old age, loving her life with her friend Barbara, as the "star" dog with no competition, ruling the roost.

"THERE IS THE AWFUL insinuating and overwhelming significance of money in the affairs of life. It is the string with which a sardonic destiny directs the motions of its puppets."

Mr. Somerset Maugham may well have hit the nail on the head, but every so often I bless that sardonic destiny. Lest we forget — prostitution is also an art! So I said yes to my first television series. It wasn't all that bad, actually. *Counterstrike,* in spite of its title, had a certain swashbuckling style to it and enough edge not to make it clawing. I played the part of a billionaire modern-day financier who sponsors his own private group of sleuths to rout out crime in the international corridors of power that the law's arm has failed to reach. I admit for a while I had good fun playing this character—a contemporary mix of Howard Hughes and the Scarlet Pimpernel. I got wonderfully paid for working no more than forty days a year, leaving me enough rope to hang myself in plays or movies.

The series shot in Toronto and Paris. The exterior of my office was in Paris, the interior in Toronto. For the most part, I never left my office. I just sat behind a gigantic desk and issued cryptic orders over a sophisticated hookup apparatus from which I could speak to anyone in the world. Ensuring that I was not required to do stunts, in fact nothing exerting—not even much walking—I insisted the character Mr. Addington always sport a cane as his leg had been shot up in the war. What war, I didn't care—just any war would do. My only real physical action each day was to get in and out of a very expensive well-cut wardrobe, made especially for me. As I was usually seen sitting at my desk, I didn't even have to learn my lines. They were all spread out before me, either mingling with the official papers or on the teleprompter, an actor's dream. My partners in hunting crime were the main private eye played by Simon MacCorkindale, an Englishman, and a couple of very attractive French girls—no complaints there. The "suits" behind the series were Alliance Films, run by Robert Lantos in Canada, some very smooth suits from Canal Plus in France, Kay Coplick of USA Network, in partnership with the most hands-on team of Sonny Grosso and Larry Jacobson—all of them "characters" in their own right, especially the last two.

Sonny Grosso was the real-life personage that Roy Scheider played in *The French Connection*. He had been heavily involved in enforcing the Marseille drug cartel back in the early seventies and gained fame as a hero cop, a supercop. Now he was retired. What was he to do? Become a producer, of course. So he invaded the portals of television and with his partner, Larry Jacobson, produced the smash-hit cop shows *Night Heat* and *Top Cops*. As the main technical advisor on *French Connection*, he had learned very quickly about the world of film. He also had a good eye for a story. Like all really tough guys, he had a kind and gentle side and loved taking us all to suppers in little trattorias that had the Mafia's blessing. Ironically, he seemed better known and more respected in underworld circles than in the so-called law-abiding world. He was a walking hero right out of a comic strip, and he always carried a gun. As he sat down at the dinner table, there it was, bulging in his belt. He kept a large launch, which he shared with Larry in the Norwalk docks in Connecticut. I went to supper one night on board and there, for the first time, I saw his vulnerable side. Sonny hated the water, so that big beautiful boat of his hardly ever left its moorings. He would wait for the other boats to return from their day's outing—then he would go on deck and swab it off with the hose to make it seem as if he'd just got back to shore.

The series, after three years, was still doing well and the ratings were improving, when suddenly Sonny closed it down. I'll never know why exactly, but one thing was sure, he was stubborn as a mule, and I remember him saying of Kay Coplick (a terrific lady, by the way), "I guess I just can't work wit broads!" What an enigma! And what fun! Our paths separated, and I miss him a lot.

It seemed destiny could be sardonic after all—I guess I was never meant to be a rich man. Comfortable, perhaps, but not rich. Instead I was doomed to go back to the meager scraps the theatre had to offer and remind myself that the higher the quality, the less one gets paid, for the telephone rang and my old friend Jason Robards was rasping in my ear, "Come on, doctor, come back to the stage and let's do Pinter's *No Man's Land* together." That sounded good enough for me.

SOME OF THE SCREEN ICONS of bygone days I have appeared opposite are: Bette Davis, Greer Garson, Gregory Peck, Kirk Douglas, Ray Milland, Buster Keaton, Sylvia Sidney, Henry Fonda, Sophia Loren—all superprofessionals. The camera loves them and the spell they cast manages to penetrate the lens with laserlike precision aimed at a vast illusionary public they can only imagine is out there, somewhere, beyond. And in the process, what they give their fellow workers such as myself, is as generous, genuine and truthful as they can offer, considering the chaos that surrounds them; the ever-present publicity machine, the hangers-on, the arc lights, sound booms, cranes, squeaking dolly tracks, clapboards, not to mention the cynical crew who has seen it all before. Impervious to these distractions, they remain resolute, determined to guard that special quality that has made them popular, without any audience reaction to reward them. They have been, for me, a fascination and a pleasure to watch and work with.

But nothing is as thrilling or satisfying as sharing the stage with a first-rate theatre actor and that other indispensable partner—the real-life groundlings who have paid through the nose for their seats and who work every bit as hard as we. For we are now in the marketplace, the arena where it all began, and once we set foot on those boards, there is no doubt that the circus has come to town. At each performance, as the climate changes in the house, we change with it. Even before the raising of the curtain, we know by sensing the waiting crowd just how much energy they are willing to expend. Sometimes, as one man, they refuse to react at all. All we can do is to win them over as best we can. It may be a bumpy ride—even a minor war can break out—but we must fight like hell to gain control; if they get the upper hand, we're done! And in the end when we've all come through the wars together, it is our duty to make certain that that bond between us is stronger than ever. That is a rule of the game.

The theatre is not for sissies. It separates the men from the boys. My actor-partner knows that. There is a gleam in his eyes—the promise of adventure, a challenge to invent. At every performance his eyes tell me a different story—I can see in them the events of his day. I can sense what he's feeling behind his character. This is not just a play we're in together; there is a life going on here on both sides of the footlights. The eyes of a truly fine actor are constantly negotiating—save me and I'll save you, they seem to say. That is the bargain we've made and that trust is all we can hang on to as we steady ourselves on the tightrope. My partner begins to sniff the air—he smells the scent of danger and excitement. He knows the jungle well. Such an animal was Jason Robards Jr.

Jason never failed to bring two lives onto the stage with him—his character's and his own. If he'd been telling me a story offstage and had not completed it because we both were to make our entrances, he'd finish it on. He did this by whispering out of the audience's earshot, interweaving it around the actual lines of the play. And I would do the same. In the middle of a scene we would plan our after-show pub crawls, in between the lines, sotto voce, without destroying the rhythm of the dialogue. It was a dangerous and daring exercise, but it certainly strengthened our control. When a golden passage came along, however, calling for passion and the storm took him, away he would fly, leaving me behind on the ground, openmouthed till he decided to come back down to earth and join me once again. More than anything, Jason truly loved the fireworks of the theatre—it was his lifeline.

Our paths had not crossed for the longest time. A near fatal car accident years before had shattered his whole frame, particularly his face, which suffered multiple fractures of so serious a nature that his entire jaw had to be reconstructed. It took an endless amount of time and patience to endure the various stages of surgery, the constant pain and spitting out of teeth. He and Betty Bacall had divorced and the lady he was courting at the time was Lois O'Connor whose administering strength and devotion helped save his life. It was not surprising then that soon after, a grateful and loving Jason made her his wife. The accident and her tender nursing combined were responsible for his finally slowing down. He would soon join Alcoholics Anonymous and dutifully mend his ways, even able to perform again on screen, winning two Academy Awards—one for his Ben Bradlee in *All the President's Men,* and the other for his Dashiell Hammett in *Julia,* a film about Lillian Hellman. With a vengeance, he went back to the theatre: *Long Day's Journey Into Night,* this time as the father; Grandpa in *You Can't Take It with You;* and a superb *Moon for the Misbegotten* opposite Colleen Dewhurst. The good news was that in spite of his tortuous recovery, his huge personality had remained unaltered. He had lost none of his spark nor his bubbling good humour. And now here we were, with so much water under so many bridges later, about to join forces once more.

Though I had only read *No Man's Land* and had never seen it, it was by far my favourite work of Harold Pinter—that master of the unfinished thought. It is one of the least obscure of his plays and offers two marvellous star roles for actors. It is a study in painful nostalgia, the story of two aging eccentrics, Hirst, an old Tory establishment figure (Robards) and a failed poet and scholar named Spooner (me), whose lives are fading away and who have absolutely nothing in common except loneliness. As a play it is both cleverly funny and wistfully touching. It all takes place in the living room of Hirst's suburban house where he never stops pouring drinks throughout as the two old souses relive their pasts, neither really listening to what the other is saying.

Harold himself was present at several of the early rehearsals. It was wonderful having him there, his bitter tongue highly amusing, but I'm not sure that he proved much help. There were those unexplained mysterious Pinter pauses throughout the play and some murky dialogue that to this day still passeth all understanding. When I asked Harold what he'd meant by a certain non sequiturial utterance, he fell silent for so long—at least twenty Pinter pauses strung together as one—then replied, "I haven't the foggiest." Now, he said and did everything in deadpan, hardly ever smiled, so he could easily have been pulling my

Jason and me

leg. But you never know with Harold and I still suspect that he was occasionally guilty of creating effects for the sake of effect only and that they just luckily happened to fall into place and miraculously worked in context.

Jason's and my roles had been originally played by Ralph Richardson and John Gielgud, but as I had not seen that production there was thankfully little chance of being influenced by those two great artists. Jason put on an old tweed sports coat and Jane Greenwood, the designer, made me a frayed grey suit, a little short in the trouser legs complemented by a pair of filthy sneakers, and we played it for sixteen weeks at the Roundabout to the strangest variety of audiences I can ever recall. There was Deaf Night, Gay Night, Lesbian Night, First-date

Night, any sort of combination that would hopefully increase attendance. Then, of course, there was the usual average American audience for whom Pinter was total anathema. Nevertheless, Jason and I had enormous fun soldiering on aided and abetted by David Jones—a most astute and excellent director, very much a Pinter specialist, and as the audience numbers grew, we found ourselves enjoying quite a success.

Todd Haimes, the young producer/impresario, had only recently begun to turn the Roundabout into a major artistic force in the city. With none of the accompanying ballyhoo that usually tries to propel such a new project, Todd simply went quietly and modestly about his business presenting plays of quality, new and old, with the odd musical thrown in for good measure. He also was able, because of the limited runs, to cast them with top-grade artists. Located as it was on Seventh Avenue between Forty-fourth and Forty-third Streets, right in the heart of "your money or your life" commercialdom, it reminded me of a brave little fortress of culture battling to defend itself against the surrounding honky-tonk of Times Square. If it worked there, it could work anywhere.

Jason and I admired Todd tremendously, both for his toughness under fire and his utter unpretentiousness. He asked us if we would consider joining his board of directors and we accepted at once. Liam Neeson and his now wife, Natasha Richardson, had just scored a huge success for the Roundabout in O'Neill's *Anna Christie* and they came onto the board as well. Todd was swiftly commandeering a substantial fighting force to back him up. There was another space for a stage in the

existing building and a generous lady patroness named Laura Pels had given an enormous sum towards its construction. In the hopes of obtaining sponsorship from various corporations, I began making fund-raising speeches. I even put on a one-man show I had devised to promote world literacy, and that also raised some much-needed cash. But the Roundabout continued to face untold problems including a restless landlord who wanted to close the theatre down, evict us all and sell the place.

Today, of course, Todd's insuperable ambitions have been more than realized. He can boast the beautifully restored Selwyn Theatre on West Forty-second Street as a prized possession, as well as Studio 54 and the completed Laura Pels Theatre. If the quality of his material and the high standard of performance is maintained, this prolific conclave of his could very well be the closest thing to a national theatre the United States has yet seen. But those exciting early days when the promise and the dream were about to come together are rich in my memory, and though I was never to act with Jason again, his last journey to Valhalla slowly approaching, the joy and comfort of playing *No Man's Land* with my old friend made that year of 1994 one of the happiest of my life.

AS I GROW GRAYER, everything—moments, incidents, friendships that have touched me and that I have carelessly brushed aside or taken too lightly—now begin to close in and narrow themselves down to the essentials. Not content any longer to let me get away with anything, they single out the most important things to which I must give my attention and the people around me that matter the most. My neglected daughter, for instance, whom I hardly knew except through her work, has become more of a friend now and I think we feel much closer than we have in the past. She has arrived at middle age, her most original personality intact—that of an immensely talented, strangely spiritual recluse. There is nothing in her eccentricities that is calculated or affected in any way; they are as natural, spontaneous and real as life is real. Unfortunately, they render her quite vulnerable and unprotected. How many of her romances has she subsidized? How many waifs and strays among her male lovers has she cared for so tenderly only to have them fly away without a nod of thanks once their wings have found their strength? The passionate, almost frenetic energy she burns onstage is the same energy she burns in life. Why she never seems to tire is inconceivable to me. Having had not much help from her parents, she long

Amanda and Diane Lane, the dangerous duo

The free spirit and her father

ago decided to be her own master, so she made herself a little world—a world that is not as comforting nor as gentle as it could be, perhaps, but one she has come to regard as the safest escape hatch she knows.

It is no exaggeration to say that her career has been unique—varied, temperamental, inconsistent, brilliant, but always unique. On and Off Broadway, in England, Canada, even Yugoslavia, her theatre work has embraced the writings of Shaw, Tennessee Williams, Sam Shepherd, Anouilh and a host of important moderns. Her film career began when she, aged twenty, and Diane Lane, aged fourteen, starred as two young desperados who lassoed a wild west town as well as the public in Lamont Johnson's *Cattle Annie and Little Britches.* She bounded onto the screen and made herself felt in Tarantino's *Pulp Fiction.* She showed a much different side as Robin Williams's girl in Terry Gilliam's *Fisher King,* ditto in *Needful Things* with Max von Sydow and Ed Harris and was mostly responsible for the wacky insanity of *So I Married an Axe Murderer,* not to mention the tons of smaller independent films in which she has shown her uncanny versatility—one called *Butterfly Kiss* which could hardly have been given a normal release (only in England was it shown), the subject being so violent and brutal.

She spends most of the picture stark naked as a mad serial killer who in graphic detail seduces her victims, then kills them for the sake of the one person she loves on earth. And all this, before our very eyes. If it wasn't so extraordinarily well acted and improvised, it would be classed as hard-core horror porn. She slipped me a tape and I watched it in a hotel room in Toronto. I just sat there dumbfounded. It was made in Liverpool with an all-Liverpool cast except for her. No one would have guessed she wasn't native born, her adenoidal accent was so perfect, so accurate. But I couldn't believe my eyes—it was like watching a little demon creating havoc wherever she chose with no one to stop her. Yet the motivating pain behind all this she made so moving and so true. I was deeply affected by this horrific movie and I felt suddenly terribly old-fashioned, conventional and cautious. I longed to have the same sort of freedom and daring that came so naturally to her. It upset me, not as a father but as an artist, and I couldn't help admiring her and her fearless courage more than ever.

AS T. S. ELIOT MEASURES HIS LIFE with coffee spoons, so I measure mine by the plays I've been in. I'm too vague to measure it any other way. So when someone asks, "When was it that they shaved your pubic hairs?" I think for a moment, then say, "Uh—wait a minute. Uh, yeah, that would be Henry V—1956—removal of kidney stone!" Then does everything else fall into place, more or less. The eighties ended with Vladimir Nabokov, one of my favourite authors, as a one-man docudrama for public television. A Professor Fleming at Princeton University had collected the material and written it all down. However, it needed orchestrating, so its director, Peter Medak, my Hungarian friend, and I helped by arranging the playing order. I carefully studied Nabokov's voice and accents and got them down pretty well—that extraordinary mélange of Mittel-European wood-notes wild. Though in my sixties, I still needed to apply prosthetics to my jowls, smooth my hair down, give him a balding appearance and put some padding behind the shoulders to resemble his slight stoop. We filmed it all at Cornell University in Ithaca where he had taught European literature and where, as a world-renowned lepidopterist, he kept his endless collection of butterfly specimens permanently pinned inside large glass cases in the library. "My pleasures are the most intense known to man: writing and butterfly hunting."

> *There, in a glade, a wild angel slumbers,*
> *a semi-pavonian creature.*
> *Poke at it curiously*
> *with your green umbrella,*
>
> . . . .
>
> *And there you stand, not yet believing*
> *your wordless woe.*
> *About that blue somnolent animal*
> *whom will you tell, whom?*
>
> *Where is the world and the labeled roses,*
> *the museum and the stuffed birds?*
> *And you look and look through your tears*
> *at those unnamable wings.*
>
> —V. N.

We chose Nabokov's lecture on Kafka and his *Metamorphosis* as the programme's content, using actual Cornell students to fill the lecture hall.

It turned out quite well, enough to be proud of, and, with all due deference to the great Vladimir, I had much joy invading his privacy. Forgive me, Master.

MOST OF THE NINETIES were spent globe-hopping again—sometimes with Fuff, sometimes without—it depended on how much patient dog sitting was required. There were several movies and television programmes made in England, allowing us to catch up with our friends there—now narrowed down to a precious few: Sally James, Jean Headley, the "Jockstrap" Carters, their son Jamie, Ruth and Ismond Rosen (the great psychoanalyst and sculptor), the Geires, Phil and Faith, and of course Jill Melford-Lyon and her precocious offspring, Alexander. Sally, Fuff and I took off for postperestroika Russia to the newly restored St. Petersburg, perhaps the most fantastic fairy-tale city in the world. The film was yet another take on the life of Catherine the Great with Vanessa Redgrave and the beautiful Julia Ormond. We shot it in and around most of the Romanov palaces (how they got permission beats me) which had been face-lifted by the Russian government to resemble some of their former glory. The one we used most was the immense summer palace Tsarskoe Selo, all in blue and gold and as big as a town, to which as late as 1916 Nicholas and Alexandra would travel to spend a few weeks, accompanied by two thousand five hundred servants. The whole experience was a feast for the eyes. Everything around us outdazzled the film we were making so completely that I don't remember what on earth it was all about.

Sally, Fuff and I, after all that splendour, would return to our meager lodgings in a very Spartan hotel and eat caviar, which we bought at Intourist with American dollars, and tinned pork and beans—this was our nightly diet. Prince George Golitzin, whose daughter Katya was dialogue coach for the Russian actors, had just been granted permission to return to Mother Russia and claim his estates. To earn some necessary cash, he had organized a series of expeditions to tour St. Petersburg privately with a select few and himself as guide. We all put our names down with the hope of revisiting the magical city in this special manner when sadly Golitzin fell ill and died and there was an end.

After depositing Sally in London, we made for New York and *Malcolm X*, with Denzel Washington. Spike Lee, the writer/director, was a tonic to work with and proved most loyal to me. As an actor, and a terrific one at that, he spoke our language and wasted no time on bullshit.

As Colonel Chang, my favorite Klingon

In fact, he was such a cool customer and so easy to be with I felt, at first meeting, I'd known him all my life.

Then, leaving Fuff with the dogs, I was off to California and *Star Trek VI: The Undiscovered Country,* bringing me together after so many years with Bill Shatner, my onetime coplayer back in Montreal during the forties. As directed and written by Nicholas Meyer, this was, I think, the most fun to watch of all the *Star Trek* movies, tongue-in-cheek from start to finish. I played my first and only Klingon ever, General Chang. I refused to wear all the phony makeup, the oversized brow and the long mane of hair, so after much argument with the traditionalist producers, gaining Nick's support by the moment, I won. That masterful makeup artist, the late Richard Snell, created a baldpate with the smallest pigtail in the back and a patch over one eye with a nail driven through it. I was the most soignée Klingon yet and closely resembled a Mongolian Moshe Dayan. They sent someone from Washington, D.C., to instruct us on the Klingon dialogue—why am I not surprised that Klingon is an actual registered language there? However, I insisted on grunting as little as possible and instead leaned on Shakespearean quotes since Chang never stopped spouting from the Bard: "Let us sit upon the ground / And tell sad stories of the death of Kings" or "Let slip the dogs of war" or dying in midphrase "To be or *not*—." The film's funniest line as spoken by David Warner, "You haven't heard anything till you've heard Shakespeare in the original Klingon!"

Then a return trip to New York for Mike Nichols's *Wolf,* with a spectacularly effective Jack Nicholson whose charm could melt an iceberg in one moment but in the next could exit Planet Earth swifter than an arrow from the Tartar's bow. He has my undying respect as a riveting screen presence almost unmatched and I would like to have been a friend, but his gregariousness was a particularly private one and he clearly preferred to keep "Narnia" as his permanent address. In *Wolf,* I played the gorgeous Michelle Pfeiffer's wealthy father and in one scene was required to lose my temper and slap her in the face. Gazing into those deep limpid eyes of hers, I was so hypnotized, my expertise at faking a slap utterly deserted me and I let her have it with full barrels— one of the worst days of my life.

After a couple of trips to Rome to shoot some diabolical sci-fi flick whose name thankfully escapes me, it was back to California for *12 Monkeys,* a Terry Gilliam film starring the excellent Bruce Willis and Brad Pitt. I was Brad's dad. God bless Terrence—that multitalented zany old whiz kid who was so nice to my daughter and who keeps asking me to work with him in films that never seem to be made. Don't stop asking, Terry; I'm available.

My director in *Dolores Claiborne,* an intriguing story which starred Kathy Bates and Jennifer Jason Leigh, was the quick-tempered but richly gifted Taylor Hackford, a jazz afficionado and superb filmmaker, whose particular expertise was conjuring atmosphere which gave each story he filmed its own potency and meaning. I got along with Taylor well, but I will always be jealous of him, for he married one of my favourite ladies, a woman for all seasons and certainly one of my most admired actresses, the invincible Helen Mirren.

However, for me, the most rewarding of all these activities was performing alone with symphony orchestras on both sides of the pond in a new concert version of Shakespeare's *Henry V* set to the music of Sir William Walton. This was the brainchild of the celebrated British conductor Sir Neville Marriner, and we presented it with the symphony orchestras of London, Minneapolis, Washington and Neville's own orchestra, the Academy of St. Martin in the Fields, with whom we recorded it for Chandos Records. Neville had started his career as a violinist and had actually played violin with the London Philharmonic under Muir Matheson's baton in the original Walton soundtrack for Laurence Olivier's great film. Neville is now probably the most recorded conductor in the world, full of mischief and fun, and he and his wife, Molly, who runs his life with the precision of a fine Swiss timepiece, are, I am thrilled to say, my cherished friends. I also performed this work with other conductors—among them Michael Lankester, an old cohort, for the Toronto Symphony and Leonard Slatkin with the Cleveland Orchestra and the New York Philharmonic. It is a feast! I get to speak all the best speeches in the play; I get to play all the best parts—Henry, Chorus, Duke of Burgundy, Exeter, Pistol, even a speech of Falstaff's taken from *Henry IV, Part 2.* The beauty of it all is that I don't have any changes. I do it all in black tie and smoking jacket. Perhaps one day I'll slip into drag and play the French Princess as well.

My appetite whetted for more of this new and attractive venue, I solicited Lankester's aid; we both put together concert versions of *A Midsummer Night's Dream,* with the music of Felix Mendelssohn, and Ibsen's *Peer Gynt,* with the music of Edvard Grieg. Michael arranged the scores, and I the words. We premiered both versions with the Toronto Symphony. *Peer Gynt* was exciting but still very much a work in progress. *The Dream,* however, was ready to go anywhere it chose. Years later, I would do *The Dream* playing Oberon, Puck and Bottom with Sir Neville at Tanglewood with the Boston Symphony and at Carnegie Hall, reunited with the boys and girls of St. Martin.

If all this makes the bulk of the decade look overcrowded, it most assuredly was. My career custodian, the ever-faithful Lou Pitt, my comrades at ICM, and Perry Zimel had done masterfully and deserved a much-needed break. Though the traffic of my work seemed to have piled up bumper to bumper, there was still time for my beloved canine pack "back at the ranch." For, naughty and bouncy as they were, their very presence, like a friendly hypodermic, never failed to blow all tensions to the winds.

MY POLISH COZ PIGGIE, who had been eating us out of house and home, had at last bought her own house down the street nearby and, during our occasional absences, gallantly continued her role as "la guardienne principale des chiens." This politically correct, somewhat dreary decade had been good to her as well. In 1990, she had the honour of performing with the Chicago Symphony Orchestra the world premiere of the recently discovered lost Piano Concerto no. 3 by Franz Liszt. The Abbé Liszt had most likely left the score lying about the house, and the cook had stolen it to wrap the fish in—who knows? The work was aptly called "Opus Posthumous," and although it didn't hold a candle to his other concerti, nos. 1 and 2, it was nevertheless a huge coup for the lucky pianist who would first play it in public.

For Piggie, justice had been served. Since she was something of a Liszt specialist herself, the honour had fallen into the right hands. But that wasn't all—she was on a roll and she found the time to come up with an inspired idea. Why couldn't a number of celebrated pianists get together and perform the classics (for expenses only) in the most obscure and distant hamlets to people who had never had the good fortune to hear or see a live concert? So she began in her native Canada. She approached five of the country's top internationally known pianists—Angela Hewitt, Angela Cheng, Marc-André Hamelin, André Laplante and Jon "Jackie" Kimura Parker—who all gave a resounding *yes!* So depending on availability and some private funds that Piggie helped raise, off they sped, each his or her separate way into the frozen north and such isolated places as Portage la Prairie, Squamish, BC; Wainright, Alberta; Iqaluit; Baffin Island and more and more, farther still to the tip of the compass it seemed, presumably to benefit musically starved penguins. There were five of them, and Piggie made six, so she christened the enterprise quite naturally Piano Six. The success of the venture grew each year and since then it has become Piano Plus, for it now includes famous singers and other instrumentalists as well. For founding this culture-spreading troupe and for her own role as a musical ambassador for Canada, Piggie was at last recognized and honoured by her grateful country.

Yes, in our immediate circle we were all doing nicely, thank you, but there was a sameness about my lot that was gnawing at the vitals. Financially, there were no complaints. I was regularly bringing home the bacon—enough to build a new pool house, erect stone walls, buy something in Florida and keep the dogs in steak tartare. But I had fallen into a dangerously comfortable rut—I really wasn't going anywhere at all when suddenly something yanked me from my quicksand onto more solid ground.

Rescue had come in the form of two familiar figures who had made a considerable impact on my youth, the notorious John Barrymore, one of the great Hamlets, a beau ideal of actors, and the feisty, pugnacious doyen of hard-core TV journalism, Mike Wallace; the former a dissipated but potent phantom, the latter still dangerously alive. Between the two, my career was elevated to another level entirely. I was promoted, rediscovered and winched onto the top deck, eager to hoist anchor and set sail at last, into the third and final act of my life.

CHAPTER FORTY-FOUR

MY ACT III

S eated at his favourite table in the old Sea Hag, a restaurant in
Depoe Bay, Oregon, the author and playwright William Luce had
managed to exile himself as obliquely far west as he dared so that
he'd become not only reclusive but exclusive. His choice of abode was
so remote, so tucked away, it was out of bounds for homing pigeons. In
fact, he might have easily disappeared off the face of the planet had not
e-mail been invented. Bill was an old hand at writing one-man shows.
He'd had terrific success with a graceful one called *The Belle of Amherst*
on the poet Emily Dickinson, and another, *Lucifer's Child,* on the writer
Isak Dinesen, both penned for Julie Harris. He also wrote *Lillian,* a fascinating take on the romantic and political side of Lillian Hellman for
Zoe Caldwell, whose performance came as uncannily close to that fiery
lady as anyone might choose to. I am one of the few people left alive
who knew Lillian Hellman and I can vouch for that.

Zoe's husband, Robert "Ratty" Whitehead, had produced it for her
in New York and Luce and he had gotten on well. So one day Bill
showed him an early draft of yet another one-person play on the great
John Barrymore. Ratty told him that if he took out all the usual well-
known Barrymore stories and started afresh, it could have a future. He
also told him I would be ideal to play the "Great Profile." I was sent the
new and latest version—I loved it. It was funny, extremely Barry-
moresque, a trifle lightweight, perhaps, and it needed work. Nonetheless, Bill Luce had caught the old soak right down to his booze-ridden
socks. I was dying to do it—this could be a nest egg.

For some reason, Bill had granted the rights to a couple of novice
producers (husband and wife) from the Midwest who weren't sure of me
at all, hoping for bigger fish (movie-star fish) to take the bait. So I was
put on hold while they shopped around. Stacy Keach, who had origi-

nally commissioned Bill to write the piece, now having found religion, had given up on it. O'Toole passed, stating he didn't want to play another drunk, and several most unlikely candidates from the film world were either too frightened to tackle the subject matter or too terrified of appearing on a stage for the first time in case they might fall off.

I was getting fed up, so I began to bully Bill: "Why did you go with these wets?" I said ungraciously. "Let's get someone else to produce it. If we wait any longer we'll all be too old." So Bill got on the phone and told them I was his choice and that they were going to need to raise a lot more money for an advertising budget if this thing was going to work. Naive to the end, they said they would hang up and think about this seriously and that they were very disappointed. Well, I wasn't going to wait, so I begged Garth Drabinsky and his company Livent to buy them out, produce and promote the show themselves. Garth, who had now established himself on Broadway as some sort of modern-day David Belasco, saw its potential and agreed. Finally, when Gene Saks, the perfect director for the piece, and Santo Loquasto, the set and costume designer, were signed on, our ship was ready to hoist anchor.

The play takes place on a stage where Barrymore in civilian clothes is trying to rehearse his Richard III, for which he was once famous. Now, at the end of his life, destitute and ravaged by time, he is dying to make his comeback. Though of course all this is fictional, it could very easily have occurred. He is constantly forgetting his lines and during these pauses shares with the prompter in the wings and the audience out front jokes old and new as well as reminiscences of his checkered, colourful and bawdy life. If his charm works on the audience, it certainly does not work on the prompter who severely reprimands him and tries to get him back on track. There is a bar onstage which Barrymore has wheeled on so that he can more than frequently pour himself drinks. There is also, of course, a fair amount of Shakespeare to recite, which I always look forward to, devout Bardaholic that I am. Having myself performed Richard III at Stratford, England, and listening carefully to J.B.'s recorded rendition, I took the two performances, mine and his, and shaking them together like a lethal martini, I found the result slipped down quite smoothly.

We opened in Stratford, Canada, took it to Florida (Palm Beach and Fort Lauderdale), had Christmas off and then seriously hit the road in freezing Detroit. All this time we worked like slaves to improve it — even the prompter, played beautifully offstage by Michael Mastro, was forever coming up with good ideas. Bill Luce proved incredibly flexi-

The closest I could get to "The Profile"

ble, throwing out whole chunks of his writing and putting in new stuff without so much as a moan. And Gene Saks was worth his weight in gold. He knew vaudeville and had a built-in comedy sense that was priceless. He not only was a fine comedic actor himself but had directed many an original Neil Simon hit onstage and on screen (*The Odd Couple*, for one). But Gene also knew how essential it was for the show to have some depth and substance, how vital it was to see the inside of Barrymore, what drove him to self-destruction, and what Brooks Atkinson had meant when he likened his downfall to "Icarus who flew too close to the sun." We eventually found a certain dark side which was invaluable in tracing a tragic line, particularly his pain when he ultimately realizes it's all too late and he's not going to make it.

The tour took us to Chicago, Boston, Pittsburgh, Delaware and Baltimore. Everywhere the play was received with great enthusiasm and laughter galore—except Baltimore. That town used to be such fun to play to—I had appeared in many a pre-Broadway tryout there—but now, whether it was the economic slump or God knows what, people went about their business looking particularly glum. There wasn't a smile in the streets and certainly nothing in the theatre. Lines that were surefire laughs were greeted with stony silence. To add to this misery, one night after the show, the stage manager said, "Your wife just telephoned. She's on the line—it's important—something about the dogs, I think." My heart sank as I heard her voice saying shakily, "Little Toadie died tonight. She came into the room where I was reading, looked at me with those sad eyes, staggered a little, then wagged her tail. 'What do you think you're doing, you silly thing?' I said. I didn't realize she'd come in looking for me. Then she fell into my arms and let out her last breath." I went back to my hotel room and howled all night long. In fact, I cried myself to sleep for weeks afterwards. I no longer had trouble bringing on tears when I broke down near the end of the play. I just had to think of Toadie, and they came in floods.

We opened in New York. What a feeling! It not only smelled of success—it was a success. For press and public alike, it went right across the board. No place like New York for success. After the audience had dispersed on the first night, I found myself alone on the empty stage of the Music Box, that most intimate of theatres, and the feeling was overwhelming. Suddenly, everyone who'd helped was beside me, somewhat out of focus. Bill Luce; dear Gene Saks; Santo; Natasha Katz (who did the lighting); Michael Mastro, the loyal prompter; the stage crew headed by Michael Farrell; Sue, the production stage manager;

Gene Saks — actor, director, friend and wit

and Robin, who took her place for the rest of the run; Garth, beaming, surrounded by henchmen. There they were, a staunch little family group, all standing about looking slightly drunk—a strange glow about them. Then Garth's party at "21" (he had taken over the whole building) where I was seated next to Douglas Fairbanks, Jr., that elegant, rakish fellow, who always managed to see every play I was in. He had known Jack Barrymore well, told some extremely wicked stories about him and happily endorsed my portrayal.

All through the run, stars and celebrities from LA, New York, London, Washington came backstage to pay their respects—prime ministers, ambassadors and I think just about everyone in Actors' Equity, Screen Actors Guild and Spotlight. Robin made a list of them each night and pinned it on the notice board. It looked like a glorified *Who's Who*. If I wasn't so conceited already, it might have gone to my head. One matinée, Robin informed me that Elaine Barrymore would be out front. Elaine had been Jack's ultimate spouse, the one whom the rest of his family had spurned as a social climber and gold digger who'd taken advantage of a man at the end of his rope. Well, whether true or false, she was the last lady to have known and loved him, after all. I was shaking with nerves so I made damn sure that the opening few lines would sound exactly like him. For the first ten minutes I put on my best Barrymore impersonation; then I relaxed for the remainder of the show. When she came backstage afterwards, she paid me the best compliment I could have wished for. She said simply, "My God, how Jack would have loved to have gone on the town with you!" She came to see it all over again a few days later and presented me with the handwritten love letters she and Barrymore had sent each other—I treasure them still. They are loving, passionate and funny. She was actually a very funny lady indeed, and I could see why he'd loved her and needed her so desperately. Apart from their obvious physical attraction for each other, she'd made the old ruin laugh.

What I'd thought was going to be a modest but distinguished run of twelve weeks or so turned out to be almost nine months! And that only because I'd decided to quit at the risk of my sanity. Garth yelled at me, "The winter months are already building. We could do this for another year!" And we could have at that, but I wasn't a machine and for the moment I'd had enough. When it closed, I couldn't stop thanking people over and over again, but it was the ghost of Jack Barrymore I needed to thank most. His was the image I'd fallen for when I was a youth of fourteen, which had propelled me toward the theatre I loved in the first place, and Diana, his daughter, who had worshipped him—dear, kind, sad, loving Diana who had been so good to me so long ago—it was for her in a way that I'd done it; how badly I needed her approval and how I wished she'd been there to see it. I hope she might have been proud.

THE SCREENPLAYS that now came my way were worlds apart from the "money pics" I'd been occasionally wallowing in. Funny what a hit play will do for one—this was a real shot in the arm. One that stood out above all the others was a story by Eric Roth about the man who blew the whistle on the cigarette companies, Professor Jeffrey Wigand. The film would eventually be called *The Insider*. Two industrious ladies—my new friend and agent Andrea Eastman, and an astute casting director—convinced that I portrayed historical figures with a certain accuracy (Kipling, Wellington, Roosevelt, Nabokov, Barrymore) had fought bravely for me to play Mike Wallace, who had figured so prominently in the exposé and eventual capitulation of the tobacco industry.

My first meeting with Michael Mann, the film's director, was confusingly nonproductive. Through most of it, he rather sullenly arranged

Russell Crowe as Wigand and me as Mike Wallace

the papers on his desk and hardly looked in my direction—he seemed to have the bedside manner of Nosferatu. I put it down to a very real and deep-rooted shyness and I may have been right. But my second meeting, with Al Pacino in tow, was entirely different. I felt very much that Mr. Mann had become my enthusiastic ally; he was full of interest and encouragement. By the end of it, I'd made the team—I was the new Mike Wallace. Both the real-life Wallace and Don Hewitt of 60 *Minutes* hated the project, not just because they felt the script was slanted and made them appear weak, indecisive and overcautious where possible lawsuits from Brown & Williamson were concerned, but mostly because they felt that 60 *Minutes* producer Lowell Bergman, played by Pacino and who was also the film's technical advisor, was a quisling and had somehow betrayed them.

However, nothing in our script could be proved untrue so the cameras rolled on without incident. Al Pacino was wonderful to work with as was Russell Crowe, who played Jeffrey Wigand. Crowe has the most extraordinary ear for characterization and for zoning in on the key frailties and strengths of the people he portrays. Wigand was there on the set with us continuously and after a while I couldn't honestly tell them apart. Crowe managed to emulate his speech impediments and his nervous demeanour with deadly accuracy. As a young leading man, there is hardly anyone on the screen today that can match his intensity and versatility. Both Russell and I had to play actual scenes in which Wallace was interviewing Wigand, already recorded on tape. So we were obliged to be completely accurate during these takes and do and sound exactly as they did. In scenes apart from actual footage of Wallace, however, I could steer myself away from impersonation and feel free to suggest rather than mimic. It was perhaps easier for me to sound like Mike than for Russell to sound like Jeffrey simply because my voice has the same timbre as Wallace's. All the more remarkable, then, that Russell was able to catch so uncannily the much-higher-pitched sounds made by Jeffrey Wigand. Since no one in the general public knows who Lowell Bergman is or what he looks like, Pacino just let fly, as he always does so marvellously, both onstage and on screen.

But the revelation for me was Michael Mann. What a superb filmmaker he is. I had heard of his ability to run a tight ship, to completely take command in the manner of the old European demagogues or C. B. DeMille and his ilk. Whenever he walked on the set—or stalked on, perhaps, is a better description—you could hear a pin drop. There was not a peep out of anyone. He certainly had earned his nickname of "Napoleon." He also, I quickly learned, had the rather exhausting, sometimes irritating custom of doing untold numbers of takes in every scene. Thirty or thirty-five would not necessarily be an exaggeration. I nudged Al and whispered, "You worked with him before, does he always do this?" Al raised his eyes to heaven. "Yeah," he said, "I'm afraid so, but hang in there, because it's all worth it!" Even though he probably chose takes one, two or three as his final preference, there was something different Mann was looking for in each one. He knew exactly what he wanted, but he wanted to see it all at the same moment. I had rarely witnessed such intensity of concentration in a director—Elia Kazan, perhaps, but in a different way.

I had felt that my character of Wallace was a little too cynical and harsh—a little too on the nose, perhaps a trifle expected. I asked for a scene to be written showing the vulnerable side of Wallace—his bruised Achilles' heel. After all, he did have a vulnerable side; I'd seen it in a most moving moment in an interview in which he talks about his son's fatal accident in Greece. He was clearly grief stricken yet determined to avoid any undue sentiment. It showed a side of him that certainly I'd never seen before. I told this to Michael Mann and Eric Roth and asked for a confrontation with Bergman (Al) where Wallace lets loose his feelings and confesses his fears. They both listened patiently and agreed to it. I couldn't believe my luck.

Just before it was to be released, one of the film's producers deserted and left the project, ultimately afraid of threats and repercussions from the tobacco industry. He had not followed through with the original courage it took him to promote the film in the first place. Only Michael Mann and Eric Roth were left holding the bag and only they took it all over the globe on a prerelease tour—only they had the guts to stay with the ship. It was a wonderful film, an important film, and I am proud to have been in it. Only recently I bumped into Mike Wallace at some film showing. We talked for several minutes; then he took me aside and, to my great surprise, told me how much he had admired what I had done for his character in the movie. As I had for some time been extremely nervous and wary of his reaction, I cannot describe the extent of my relief. The only resentment I harbour for the handsome Mr. Wallace, damn him, is that in his late eighties, he looks like my son.

MEANWHILE, POOR FUFF had been lumbered with the ever-increasing responsibility of taking care of our remaining two dogs, who were both slowly nearing their end. When Toadie died, the old golden retriever Rags, her dad, began to go crazy. His heart had broken. He had never stopped loving her, kissing her eyes, cuddling her in sleep, and now she wasn't there anymore so the night terrors began. He would sleep through the day, but at night he would prowl about the house, howling his lungs out and then would bark furiously at the shutters flanking the French windows as he tried in vain to climb into them. Fully awake through all this, Fuff would stay up with him trying valiantly to lull him to sleep. This sad ritual had been going on for the best part of two years. One day both of us had to travel somewhere together, so Piggie very generously took him in. At the end of three weeks, Rags decided he'd waited long enough for our return, so, rather noisily, I'm told, he gave up the ghost. What a remarkable old dog. He was seventeen, a great age for a goldie, and he must have been, for the most part, the happiest of dogs, for he never stopped singing.

Briggie followed soon after. She was the first dog we took in and the last to go. Dear staunch bossie Briggie, armed with that astonishing intelligence, had now become infirm. It didn't seem possible—she was the mother of us all. Briggs suffered from a kind of vertigo that dangerously disturbs the balance and made her wonder constantly if she was standing on a cliff's edge or on a flat surface. Her appetite had given up as well and she'd begun walking around in circles. On the day she was put down, coward that I am, I couldn't summon up the courage to go. I knew I couldn't handle it—that I would collapse completely. But Fuff and Piggie took her. The vet was very gentle with her and as he inserted the needle, he said to Fuff, "Now make her look at you—you're the last person she'll see that she loves." Afterwards, Fuff told me that when Briggie had looked at her, those consoling eyes of hers seemed to say, "Don't worry—it's all going to be all right." She was looking after us right up to the end.

Without the rest of the pack, we felt silly and more than a little empty as we gazed out the windows at our large rambling grounds, which now seemed quite superfluous. Of course, they are still with us really, for Toadie, Briggie and Rags are all buried together beside the old orchard wall at the top of our hill. The oddest thing was that come the spring after Briggie died, the little dogwood tree she had always sat under for so many years, her favourite tree, sprouted no leaves. There was no life left in it—it too had given up its ghost.

IT WAS A GODSEND that my next assignment came swiftly and took place in England—at least two thousand miles between us and sad memories of departed friends. I was to play Ralph Nickleby, the bad uncle in a film of Charles Dickens's masterpiece *Nicholas Nickleby,* along with a superlative British cast—Juliet Stevenson, Jim Broadbent, Timothy Spall, Tom Courtenay, the Aussie Barry Humphries, Edward Fox and two Americans, Nathan Lane and Anne Hathaway. Doug McGrath directed. I had seen his production of *Emma* for the screen and respected his work highly; he had captured so thoroughly the essence of Jane Austen. I was convinced that McGrath must be a young Irishman from the auld country, more at home with eighteenth- and nineteenth-century English literature than most of his contemporaries. Imagine my surprise when he turned out to be an honest-to-God Texan, complete with Southern drawl.

Doug McGrath directed us with the same stylish instinct he had demonstrated with *Emma.* The Dickens novel is impossible to film in its entirety; there are too many extraordinary characters, too many subplots and episodes—truly an embarrassment of glorious riches. Needing to edit it drastically, Doug chose to keep as the clearest and most essential story line the relationship between the two Nicklebys, Nicholas and Ralph. The film was a delight, won several prizes, includ-

Briggie under her favourite tree

ing a nomination for Best Ensemble. At the National Board of Revue, we all marched up to the podium to accept, and Nathan Lane, our spokesman, quipped, "Personally, I don't do ensemble. I believe in every man for himself."

While in London, we stayed at the Goring Hotel tucked behind Buckingham Palace. It is a private hotel run by the Goring family, a miniature Connaught, with superb cuisine and half the price. I did my usual damage at Turnbull & Asser (I have had more shirts made for me there than there are days of the year); Fuff hit the Burlington Arcade and Theo (ouch!) Fennell; we put on huge poundage at Mark's Club, Mossemon's, Harry's Bar, the Ivy, and our favourite Knightsbridge restaurant from early courting days—Le Poissonerie de l'Avenue.

I got to know my new and dynamic London agent, Pippa Markham of Markham & Froggatt (a Dickensian name if ever I heard one), who held court in rickety old office quarters on Windmill, off Charlotte Street, which also couldn't have been more Dickensian if they'd tried. Pippa and her delightful partner, Stephanie Randall, held the monopoly on the most talented young actors and directors in England, and Pippa, no matter what time of day or night, could be seen bicycling her way through London traffic, trouser clips, helmet and all. She even bicycled to film premieres in full evening dress, with helmet accessories—the terror of the red carpet!

One day I bumped into Jonathan Miller on Shaftsbury Avenue. We both expressed our desire to work together again—much time had passed since *Danton's Death* at the National. "I'd love to do one of the great comedies, such as *Volpone,* and you more than anyone know all about those wild Elizabethan romps," I said, buttering him up as forcefully as I could. "Let me think about it—I've thought about it—you're on," he promptly responded. I suggested we rehearse and open it at the Stratford Shakespeare Festival, then take it to New York. He agreed to that too. But now the London gourmandizing came to a halt; filming was completed on Doug McGrath's *Nickleby,* so Fuff and I carried our distended tummies onto British Airways and flew them back home where a message was waiting from a friend, an old friend I hadn't seen for the longest time.

"WE'RE GOING TO DO a tour of the east coast in a thing called *A Royal Christmas,*" said Julie Andrews when I called her back. "You and I will emcee it; Charlotte Church will do the singing. The Royal Ballet, the Royal Winnipeg Ballet and the Shumka Ukrainian dance company will do the dancing to the music of Tchaikovsky (who won't be coming with us) which will be played by London's Royal Philharmonic under the stylish baton of George Daugherty, who is very funny and very experienced at these things. We will travel in buses (ours will be v. posh indeed). The whole thing will take three weeks—we'll be home by Christmas and the money ain't nothing to sneeze at either!" I jumped at it!

It was great being with Julie again. What a pro that lady is! And what fun! Our bus was decked out with all the latest sound equipment, all the comforts of a first-class hotel—bar, kitchen, beds. Our driver had driven all the major pop icons, a couple of presidents—Clinton being one—as well as Queen Elizabeth II. He carried a sort of honorary sheriff's badge, which when flashed got us all out of trouble in an instant. Local police in each town practically curtsied to him when we drove by. "No doubt who's the star of this show," quipped Julie. With us on our bus were Francine Taylor; Julie's girl Friday; and her two pals, the hair and makeup team of John and Rick—John who ran London's famous hair salon, Michaeljohn. They kept all our spirits up to such an extent, we never had time to be serious. The Royal Philharmonic musicians, apart from making a gorgeous sound, proved an absolute hoot with their diabolical practical jokes and wisecracks during the performances, giving us loud raspberries from the bassoon and horn sections.

Once when I forgot my lines, the entire violin section prompted me from the pit loud and clear. It worked so well as a double act that we tried keeping it in.

George Dougherty, the conductor, besides being an excellent musician, was not in the least averse to spontaneous naughtiness and outrageous shenanigans. He gave me such confidence in the singing department, something I've always shied away from, that I began to think I actually had a future. Julie could no longer use the middle to high range of her voice due to an abortive attempt to operate on her vocal chords, which had failed miserably. The doctor responsible had also done the identical damage to Teresa Stratas, the famous opera diva and actress whose glorious tones were now forever in jeopardy. Still, Julie bravely carried on, singing most attractively in the lower registers, which gave a torch-song sensuality to each number she performed.

The tour itself was quite hysterical—we played in huge hockey rinks seating fifteen thousand to twenty thousand people at a time from Columbus to Boston, Long Island to Minneapolis, Washington to Ottawa, Toronto to Syracuse—and though there were no tears when it all came to an end, we'd had a hell of a good time, Julie and I, despite our frozen feet from walking over so much ice.

I WAS JUST ABOUT to open up my copy of Ben Jonson's *Volpone* and start committing it to memory when the telephone rang. It was Jonathan. "I don't want to do *Volpone* at all. I've looked at it and it's such an unwieldy bugger of a play with huge gaps when neither Volpone nor Mosca are accounted for. I think it's a waste of time for both of us. At this stage, you should be doing your Lear before it's too late—I'll direct it gladly, if you say yes." "But I wanted to do a great comedy—my heart was set on it," I pleaded. "Well, what's the matter with Lear?" he countered. "It's one of the funniest plays ever written." "But I've just turned down Peter Hall's offer to do it. What on earth am I going to say to him?" "Tell Pierre Foyer that you've changed your mind, that's all." He was unflappable. So I wrote a groveling letter to Peter Hall and took the plunge.

CHAPTER FORTY-FIVE

APRÈS LEAR—WHAT?

No, it is not Mount Everest! Perhaps the play is but not the role. Richard III is much more vocally and physically challenging. Hamlet is monstrously more daunting. Just to capture its great simplicity and its supreme eloquence is an art in itself. But Hamlet and Richard are true "stars"—they drive and carry all before them. The first hour or so of *King Lear* has a devastating emotional line to it, as the kingdom crumbles: "You think I'll weep? . . . I have full cause of weeping, but this heart / Shall break into a hundred thousand flaws / Or 'ere I'll weep. O fool! I shall go mad," and he makes his exit for the heath. Once on the heath, however, the problems begin. After a few of Lear's rantings against storms and the commencement of his long day's journey into madness, the author begins to ignore his protagonist by removing him from the play for an unconscionable length of time while he presents us with yet another—the tragedies of Gloucester, Edmund and Edgar. It is only toward the end, way past bedtime, when Lear is finally led back on by Cordelia—he has been absent so long that only the more astute members of the audience remember him at all.

Of course it is all written in divine fire and the actor who is willing to leap into those flames is fortunate indeed. He will learn the hopelessness of self-pity, the folly of self-importance; he will look in horror through the king's eyes at what the real world is like and when it's over, he may be just that much more prepared for his own old age. But Shakespeare was not kind to his "star." He forbade him to drive his own play. He barricaded his progress—coitus interruptus at its most flagrant. Perhaps when poor old Lear is sitting alone in his dressing room, waiting interminably to reenter, dying for a drink or a fix, anything to help provide the adrenaline that will carry him to the summit— perhaps that is the Everest to which everyone is alluding.

All this aside, I loved playing Lear's remarkable first half; I loved the odd heart-searing moment near the conclusion; I loved the impossible celestial beauty of the end itself and I remain defiantly loyal to Jonathan Miller's interpretation. Like all geniuses—and Jonathan's membership in that small exclusive club was unanimously approved long ago—whatever he touches, whether one violently disagrees with it or not, he makes as clear as the clearest diamond. For him the bourgeois idea of a cosmos surrounding the play does not exist nor ever did. The idea of an ancient druidlike king with flowing robes and beard resembling a pre-Raphaelite version of God he completely discards; even Blake's more stark vision of Lear he banishes to the coffee table. The tragedy, as he sees it, may begin with the changing winds of society, the disbanding of divine rights, but it quickly descends to a private family matter—the dysfunctional life of a family whose members are at their wits' end. The ultimate blame is attached to the father whose fate is to learn just that, and the timeless message that after all the baubles, bangles and beads, after all the titles and vestments of power have been stripped away—man is nothing more than "a poor, bare, forked animal." The play is tough, violent and ageless. It is more modern than most contemporary plays that have taken its theme in some form as their inspiration. It is just as modern, if not more so, than *Long Day's Journey Into Night* and far more universal.

It is believed that James VI of Scotland, 1st of England, was most probably part of the audience which saw *Lear* when it was first presented and that he also could have been the personage on whom Shakespeare based his old king. So Jonathan, with the aid of Clare Mitchell's gorgeous designs, had it performed in the period when Shakespeare wrote the play—in other words, contemporary. He was also right about its being funny. There are heaps of blackly ironical exchanges throughout: *Lear:* "Dost thou call me fool, boy?" *Fool:* "All thy other titles thou has given away; that thou wast born with." Or, *Fool:* "Can you make no use of nothing, uncle?" *Lear:* "Why no, boy, nothing can be made out of nothing." And after his daughters have refused to accommodate his attending knights, whittling them down from a hundred to five, and Lear has left the room to go out and face the storm, Regan after a long silence motivates her reasoning by simply stating, "This house is little." The audience collapses. One of Jonathan's many inventions was to have Lear forget the Duke of Burgundy's name every time he mentions it so that he has to be continuously prompted. It was not just because Lear might possibly have thought that all French aris-

*Jonathan Miller, surgeon, anthropologist, director,
author and wit.*

tocrats were an effete bunch of poofters but that he was also suffering from early signs of Alzheimer's. There were so many little human touches in this production that did not escape the brighter critics.

Jonathan, an anthropologist as well as surgeon, mapped Lear's downward course with the accuracy of a medical chart. After returning to the care of Lear's daughter Cordelia, I spoke the lines, "You do me wrong to take me out of the grave," with a slight slur as if Lear had just suffered a stroke, not an impossibility considering his age and the horrors he endured, half naked on the heath. "Pray do not mock me; / I am a very foolish, fond, old man . . . And, to deal plainly, / I fear I am not in my perfect mind." He is disappearing fast, his head hangs over his chest, his bent figure becomes smaller and smaller—all believable stages of his disintegration. Then, at last, that awesome burst of strength. The death of Cordelia has made him momentarily superhuman as he rails against the world:

> *. . . O! Are you men of stones?*
> *Had I your tongues and eyes I'd use them so*
> *That heaven's vault should crack. She's gone forever.*

We are now set firmly in Greek tragedy. The end is sublime. His going is swift. For a second, he hallucinates that she is still alive before him and his last breath comes as he cries out ecstatically:

> *Do you see this? Look on her, — look — her lips —*
> *Look there! — look there!*(He dies.)

BECAUSE OF SOME FABULOUS NOTICES, we brought it to New York and Lincoln Center. The run was exciting and more than satisfying, short enough that Perry Zimel in Canada; Pippa in London; Andrea, Carter Cohn, Lisa Gallant in LA; and the long-suffering Lou Pitt—tout mes agents provocateurs—had not forgotten me. Screenplays continued to arrive at the doorstep. *Syriana; The New World; Must Love Dogs,* with the lovely and talented Diane Lane; *Alexander,* with that

"Vex not his ghost. O, let him pass." The dying Lear.

Irish imp Colin Farrell; a charming bit of froth called *Man in the Chair;* and *Inside Man.* Faithful Russell Crowe continued to ask for me in his pictures (*Gladiator,* which I didn't do, and *Beautiful Mind,* which I did). I have recently worked with some wonderful directors—Ron Howard, Oliver Stone, Steve Gaghan, Terrence Malick, Lord Richard "Dicky" Attenborough, Michael Schroeder and an ever-loyal Spike Lee.

My daughter never stops working as well. She was a superb St. Joan in Anouilh's *The Lark,* born to play it, and just as marvellous though entirely different as the girl Alma in Tennessee Williams's *Summer and Smoke. The New York Times* stated: "Alma Winemiller is the old maid's old maid. And Amanda Plummer is all over her like a swarm of drugged Southern bees in this heartfelt and heart-wrenching new production." I watched her closely through *Summer and Smoke,* and I noticed something that only happens to the rarest of champions. Like Roger Federer on the tennis court, she too makes no sound as she moves; her feet never seem to touch "the boards."

And speaking of "the boards," what do I do after Lear? It really is a farewell of sorts. But life goes on, doesn't it? There are all those ageless comics hanging about, Volpone, for one, Falstaff perhaps, or Gogol's government inspector, Malvolio—and all those wonderfully rich Molière characters. Then there's the melancholy Jacques, not to mention old Prospero, and as a last resort, perhaps Methuselah or, God knows, even God. No matter what I do between, the stage always beckons and gets me every time. I suppose it's because there are no tedious retakes, no endless waiting, no cutting-room floor upon which I can end up. Once on the stage, we are thrown to the lions, no barrier comes between us and the mob; everything is exposed, dangerous and now. Since the burning of the Globe, Cromwell's locking of the doors, the Restoration riots, right up to the overwhelming invasion of twentieth-century technology, the theatre has always seemed in jeopardy. Everything now is made too literal, too easy—the power of suggestion is all too often forgotten. A painted moon can tell more stories than a real one and I swear that when all the effects and robots and holograms have been exhausted, and we poor thespians have been replaced by clones and digitized out of existence, there will still be an empty stage somewhere waiting for someone to make an entrance in order to satisfy human nature's insatiable need to work its imaginary forces. I take some comfort in that.

A WORD OR TWO, BEFORE YOU GO is a one-man pastiche I put together a good many years ago. It lasts about an hour and a half on the stage, there is no intermission and people go home afterwards hopefully wanting more. I've never earned any money from it because I mostly perform it for charities such as World Literacy or to help artistic endeavours in need of financial aid. It is simply about my own personal journey through literature—literature that I have loved and treasured since I was a mere boy. I perform selections from plays, poems and novels and link them with autobiographical anecdotes and interludes. The works I have chosen are silly and sad, sacred and profane. They range from *Winnie the Pooh* to the Bible, from Lewis Carroll to Rudyard Kipling, from Shaw, Wilde and Byron to Shakespeare, Jonson and Blake, from Swinburne, Melville, D. H. Lawrence to Leacock, S. J. Perelman and Ogden Nash, from Chesterton to W. H. Auden, Rostand to Nabokov—every writer who has stirred my imagination and marked my passage.

A Word or Two is something I can perform in my dotage—the only taxing thing being memory—but as long as I still have my voice I could even read the whole damn thing. If there must be a theme or purpose to the evening, it is twofold: to make parents aware that they must encourage their children to read in this nonliterate world, as I was once when in my swaddling clothes; and to salute and pay tribute to my calling—a profession that has treated me for the most part with kid gloves, allowed me to indulge and has been, let's face it, quite honestly, my education. It has taught me music, poetry, painting and dance; it has introduced me to the big bad world outside; it has made me face rejection; it has taught me humour in its blackest and gentlest forms; it has made me think; it has even taught me about love. It has shown me the majesty of language, the written word in all its glory, and it has taught me above all that there is no such thing as perfection—that in the arts, there are no rules, no restrictions, no limits—only infinity.

As the years pile up, it is strange how one's memories careen back further and further. I can see the old Airedale walking by my baby carriage more vividly now than ever before. I can see my mother's laughing face as she picks me up, holds me above her head and shakes me. The memory of the suffocating rubber mask over my nose and mouth when I was a tot in some hospital room and the sickly smell of ether has never deserted me, and I can hear still with awful clarity the ear-piercing cries of that poor child down the hall from me who was in such pain and the dreadful silence that followed when they rolled his bed away.

Even one's dreams become retroactive. Everything that occurs takes place in the settings of one's youth, all the participants disguised as people from one's early days, now long gone but temporarily granted life for the duration of the dream. Even your first dogs come back to talk to you, whisper advice, share gossip. When the last pylon of the huge Trans-Canada Highway bridge was driven mercilessly into what little remained of Polly's island on the Lake of Two Mountains where I grew up, and when Polly died not too long after, I began to have a recurring dream which haunts me still.

It begins with the sound of water lapping against the wooden frame of an old white scow by the docks. Across the water through the mists is the vague thin outline of a distant quay. The scow is now moving silently toward the quay. The mists part and there is the island at last. A great blue heron languidly rises from some hidden inlet and disdainfully passes overhead as I step down from the wharf and make my way up the path. A sculpted St. Giles cradling a fawn stands in stone by the rushes at the entrance to a small bridge. Now I am leaning over the little bridge, long a familiar habit, staring down at the giant lily pads that carpet the black waters below. Even at the height of day no light intrudes—it is always dark and peaceful here under the tall elms, still as a cathedral. I leave the bridge. My pace quickens and everything becomes brighter as I move up the hill towards the house. The wind gets up—the house flies by—once again there's the scent of cut grass and heliotrope—the trees are bending away from me, waving me on. I am gliding swiftly over the long sloping lawns down to the point and in the distance through the branches the light shimmers, and as lake and sky meet it is hard to tell which is which. My feet touch the ground. For the longest moment I stand transfixed by the wonder of it, just me and the island, my breath catches and all that can be heard is the soft exhalation of a sigh that comes like another wind from so far off that no matter how long I search, I am never to find the secret of its source.

SOMEONE ONCE SAID—it had to have been Nöel Coward in one of his withering putdowns—that "man consistently labours under the delusion that he really matters!" But it becomes necessary to have certain delusions if one is to compete in our overcrowded profession and more than overcrowded life. Orson Welles, the Marquis de Sade, Augustus John, Dylan Thomas and John Barrymore, each in his own way took life by the throat and forced it to its knees. I wish like hell I could have done that. I don't pretend to own a speck of their recklessness or daring—but, damn it, I think I gave it the old college try. The desire was always there, still is, so is the ambition.

How lucky I have been to have made the acquaintance of such an extraordinary collection of vagabonds from both halves of the twentieth century, a century that allowed me to know its Old and New Testaments—the vanished grace of an era that can never return and the new mechanized age of enlightenment where Science, changing its colours more swiftly than Earth hurtles through space, is, indisputably, king. And how fortunate that the same century sent such remarkable women to show me the way—my mother "Belle," who gave me a soul; Polly, who made me a romantic; Jane, who tried so hard to keep me in touch with quality; Amanda, who made me proud; and my last and final wife—Bob Taylor, Reggie, Roo, Erp or Little Fuff—she of a thousand names who has been, since I first set eyes on her, my true strength.

Faith, I confess, Your Honours, has been hard to come by—in higher things I mean, as in who created the animals and trees and the love that is "strong as death." No, I'm a bit of a lost soul in that regard, I'm afraid—a trifle shaky. I've never quite known what it was that I was supposed to hang on to. I so envy the ancient races their commitment to a faith that has made religion and family one and the same. Yet those same religions have spawned so many wars, so much horror—what price faith now, I say? Gloucester says in *King Lear*, "We have seen the best of our time," and he may be right, but I can truthfully confess with few regrets that I have immensely loved and relished my allotted span, and as I creep deeper into the twilight, it is not so much the fear of dying that disturbs me but the sudden awareness that I've just begun to live and how dreadfully I'm going to miss it all when I'm gone. If only I might linger on by painting myself into the landscape, so I could always see the beginning of the day. Or perhaps I could just sit forever with Little Fuff and a dog or two besides somewhere on a shore at Polly's Island and gaze across the dark northern lake till the light finally vanishes behind the distant hills. That would be a particle of faith, surely.

NOT SO LONG AGO, we went on one of our occasional visits to Montreal. It was mid-October, but some leaves were still on the trees in all their colourful glory. From our hotel nestled at the foot of the steep streets, Fuff and I took our usual walk up the "mountain," Mount Royal, going to the very top near the "lookout" just below the cross and working our way down the different levels. Only a few scattered people were left, but they were scurrying home—it was late afternoon, getting quite cold and the light was disappearing fast. About a hundred yards ahead the old stone wall surrounding the Raven'scrag estate came into view. Suddenly in the near distance, I caught sight of a woman coming up the path by the wall, the same woman I had seen there once or twice before during my lifetime. She was wearing an old tweed suit, a beret and brogues, much in the style of the thirties. She was walking briskly now as if she were late for something. I started running towards her. "You see that woman?" I called back as I ran. "Yes," came the reply. "I've got to find out where she goes," I said, still running. I was almost upon her, her face was turned away but when I stopped for a second, she was gone. "There's no door, no gate, just the wall—there's nowhere she can hide," I said, trying to catch my breath. Fuff was right behind me now. We both stared at the wall and she said in a very quiet voice, "It's your mother, isn't it?" I stopped breathing—I turned and looked at her.

It was cold and the streetlights below on Pine Avenue were slowly coming on one by one. Neither of us needed to say a word as we hurried back down the hill.